The Reserve Bank of India

The Reserve Bank of India

Volume 4
1981–1997

भारतीय रिज़र्व बैंक
RESERVE BANK OF INDIA
www.rbi.org.in

ACADEMIC FOUNDATION
NEW DELHI

www.academicfoundation.com

First published in 2013
by

ACADEMIC FOUNDATION
4772-73 / 23 Bharat Ram Road, (23 Ansari Road),
Darya Ganj, New Delhi - 110 002 (India).
Phones : 23245001 / 02 / 03 / 04.
Fax : +91-11-23245005.
E-mail : books@academicfoundation.com
www.academicfoundation.com

in association with:

Reserve Bank of India
Central Office Building,
Shahid Bhagat Singh Marg, Mumbai - 400 001.
Tel: 022 - 2260 1000
Fax: 022 - 2266 0358
E-mail: helpdoc@rbi.org.in
www.rbi.org.in

Cataloging in Publication Data--DK
   Courtesy: D.K. Agencies (P) Ltd. <docinfo@dkagencies.com>

The Reserve Bank of India.
   v. 4   cm.
   Includes bibliographical references and index.
   Contents: v. 4. 1981–1997.
   ISBN 9788171889860 (v. 4)
   ISBN 8171889867 (v. 4)

   1. Reserve Bank of India--History. 2. Banks and banking,
Central--India--History.   I. Reserve Bank of India.

DDC 332.110954   23

Typeset by Italics India, New Delhi.

Printed and bound by The Book Mint, New Delhi.
www.thebookmint.in

Contents

I. Consolidation and
Early Liberalisation: 1981 to 1989

II. Crisis and Reforms: 1989 to 1997 (*contd...*)

PART B

II. Crisis and Reforms: 1989 to 1997 (*concld.*)

III. Organisational Aspects

IV. Miscellany

V. References and Index

Part B

II

CRISIS AND REFORMS: 1989 TO 1997

15

Public Debt Management

INTRODUCTION

The size and method of financing the Government's budgetary deficit have an important bearing on prudential macroeconomic management, in general, and monetary management, in particular. This is because fiscal imbalances in the long run engender serious consequences for macroeconomic stability, which became strikingly evident in the events leading to the balance of payments (BoP) crisis in India in 1991. All along, the Reserve Bank, which has been entrusted under its statute[1] with the internal debt management of the Government, has been co-ordinating closely with the Ministry of Finance in formulating and implementing the latter's annual market borrowing programme, appraising the Central Government from time to time of its concerns over the building up of unsustainable fiscal imbalances and monetisation of budget deficits *via* the Reserve Bank accommodation and other related developments as well as issues impacting on internal public debt management. These features of the pre-crisis period have been brought out succinctly in the chapter, Monetary-Fiscal Interface, which covers the developments from 1981–82 to 1988–89.[2]

---

1. In terms of section 21 of the Reserve Bank of India (RBI) Act, 1934, the Reserve Bank is vested with the responsibility of the management of the public debt and issue of new loans of the central government and that of the state governments by virtue of agreements entered into with them under section 21A.

2. Reverting to the 1980s, the Reserve Bank's role was basically one of debt manager to the central government (as also to the state governments). Moreover, the internal debt management policy followed was a passive one due to various reasons. More important

contd...

PASSIVE TO ACTIVE DEBT MANAGEMENT

The financial system until the 1980s was devoid of market orientation and was subjected to tight regulations relating mainly to portfolio choices by institutions, instruments and their pricing. The policy was to offer low coupon rates on government securities in order to keep government borrowing costs down. More or less the same situation prevailed till the 1990s in respect of the bond market as well. In this restrictive environment, the fundamental debt management functions discharged by the Reserve Bank in the capacity of agent of the Government remained passive and monotonous, with the Government's demand for borrowed funds being met from a captive group of investors. The Reserve Bank was a participant in absorbing the marketed debt not subscribed by others and the supply was at non-market-related interest rates, which at times translated into negative real rates of return. Consequently, money and government securities markets hardly gained vibrancy. The Reserve Bank's monetary management was also constrained by the practice of automatic monetisation of government budget deficits at a fixed and below the market rate of 4.6 per cent in the form of placement of *ad hoc* 91-day Treasury Bills, which had been in vogue since the mid-1950s.

The adoption of an active internal debt management policy assumed significance from the early 1990s with the launch of the financial sector reforms that ushered in a market-oriented system. This new direction also opened more vistas for monetary management. However, the impetus for the reform had been provided much earlier by the report of the committee to review the working of the monetary system (Chairman: Prof Sukhamoy Chakravarty)[3] which strongly recommended that the borrowing requirements of the Government should be financed from the open market by evolving a market-clearing interest rate mechanism. This was expected to reduce the extent of debt monetisation. The actual thrust

---

concld.

> of these were, the absence of any definite limit on excessive automatic monetisation of the Central Government's fiscal deficit, low coupon rates offered on government securities and the gilt-edged market being dominated by institutional investors, who were required to mandatorily invest a portion of their resources in government and other approved securities. All these circumstances severely inhibited the development of a secondary market in the government securities and thereby the conduct of active open market operations by the Reserve Bank. More importantly, in such a milieu, the effectiveness of monetary and credit policy became attenuated. These, among others, form the subject matter of the previous link chapter 3: Monetary-Fiscal Interface.

3. Refer to Appendix 4.1.

for activating the government bond market in the reform era came from the report of the committee on the financial system (Chairman: Shri M. Narasimham). These developments have been covered subsequently in this chapter.

The debt management function was traditionally performed by the Secretary's Department in the Reserve Bank since its inception. With a view to strengthening internal debt management, evolving policy options and issuing guidelines for trading in government securities, the Reserve Bank set up an Internal Debt Management Cell (IDMC) within the Secretary's Department in April 1992. This was carved into a distinct entity in October 1992. Initiating the steps for the formation of the cell, the Governor, Shri S. Venkitaramanan, envisioned that it would attend exclusively to internal debt management and operations, consisting of open market operations (OMOs), market borrowings, state governments' ways and means advances (WMA) and related matters. It devoted attention to evolving an active role in internal debt management operations, devising new policy instruments and shoring up delivery capabilities to facilitate the development of a dynamic and efficient government securities market.[4]

The Reserve Bank, in co-ordination with the Central Government, initiated several reforms in quick succession in the government securities market from 1992 to 1997. The reform process comprised active policymaking, strengthening of the institutional infrastructure, setting-up of dedicated clearing and settlement systems, expansion of trading, diversification of market participants and instruments, consolidation of a transparent regulatory system, implementation of state-of-the-art technology and enactment of enabling market-related legislation, rules and procedures.[5] Special mention may be made of the introduction of auction-based sale of 91-day Treasury Bills and auctions for dated government securities. The market practically had to be groomed and nurtured during this period by having dialogues with treasury managers, periodic meetings and workshops. These paved the way for the development of government bond market that enabled the Reserve Bank to progressively move away from direct instruments, namely, cash reserve ratio (CRR) and refinancing facilities, to indirect market-based instruments like OMOs, interest rates and other liquidity management techniques, including the repos. In consonance with this path-breaking policy shift, reserve requirements

---

4. The IDMC was converted into a full-fledged department in May, 2003.

5. A reference may be made to Annex I to this chapter.

were scaled down in a calibrated manner. Greater reliance was placed on evolving an integrated and active internal debt management policy. In this regard, a far-reaching event was a gradual increase in the interest rates of government securities to a level closer to market-determined rates and also a lowering of their maturity profile.

The long-term objective was to facilitate the emergence of a market-based yield curve. Since the secondary market was slow to develop in the initial stages, the term structure of primary market yields through auctions served as the yield curve. State government loans were floated first during a financial year that set the 10-year benchmark and auction-based central government debt during the rest of the year set the primary yield curve. Later, with the secondary market yield gradually emerging, the primary yield curve was adjusted taking into account the secondary market trades, before the secondary market acquired the necessary depth and was able to eventually provide a genuine market-based yield curve.

Perhaps the most defining event in public debt management was the phasing out of automatic monetisation of the budget deficit (the first supplemental agreement of September 1994) and the discontinuation of *ad hoc* Treasury Bills (the second supplemental agreement of March 1997). This imparted an element of discipline in budgetary finances and strengthened the effectiveness of monetary policy. The manoeuvrability of the Reserve Bank in managing the public debt consistent with its monetary policy got a boost with these supplemental agreements with the Government. The overdraft regulation scheme in operation since the mid-1980s in the case of the state governments served, in a way, as a model for related practices for the Central Government, though stoppage of payments by the Reserve Bank for the Central Government was not envisaged for practical reasons.

CHAPTER OUTLINE

Under a long-standing arrangement, the Reserve Bank and the Ministry of Finance conduct an annual dialogue on the monetary projections and the overall market borrowing programme of the Central Government, state governments and government-guaranteed institutions as part of the exercise for preparation of the Union Budget for the ensuing financial year. Against this backdrop, the section that follows flags various policy matters that were suggested by the Reserve Bank in the correspondence exchanged from time to time. Besides, there were other important topics and events that occupied the centre stage during this period, which are narrated in the following order:

(i) Discontinuation of the issue of *ad hoc* Treasury Bills in a phased manner, which paved the way for the Central Government to meet its borrowings through market-based instruments.

(ii) Major developments in the Reserve Bank's internal debt management policy and operations with special reference to instruments and institutional growth.

(iii) Progress in fiscal consolidation and the Reserve Bank's interest in organising its debt management and monetary management functions in a co-ordinated and integrated manner.

(iv) Significant developments in the government securities market which strengthened and supported internal debt management policies and operations.

(v) An insight into policymaking aspects on select issues, *viz.*, consolidated sinking fund (CSF), sovereign bond issue, and foreign institutional investors' (FIIs) investments in government securities.

(vi) Special features of the borrowing programme of the state governments.

(vii) Concluding observations.

FORMULATION OF ANNUAL MARKET BORROWING PROGRAMME

Every year, either in December or at the beginning of January, the Reserve Bank and the Ministry of Finance engage in consultations (in the form of letters and personal discussions) on the monetary projections and the Government's market borrowing programme for the coming fiscal year to arrive at an acceptable level of budget deficit and determine the stance of fiscal and monetary policies to be pursued during the year. This process of co-ordination and exchange of views enables formulation of integrated and mutually supportive monetary and debt management policies. Besides, this dialogue helps the Reserve Bank firm up a number of macroeconomic projections for the following year on a consistent basis. More significantly, after the adoption of financial sector reforms in 1991–92, it provided the Reserve Bank with the opportunity to apprise the Government of its views and suggestions on a wide range of topics concerning internal debt management strategies, such as, strengthening the government securities market, coupon rates, maturity pattern of dated securities, introduction of long-dated Treasury Bills on auction basis, funding of Treasury Bills and automatic monetisation of budget deficit through the issue of *ad hoc* Treasury Bills. Policy issues relating to internal debt management closely linked with monetary and credit policy, also gained importance.

The keynote of each year's projected borrowing programme varied in both content and emphasis depending on the behaviour of the macroeconomic fundamentals and economic policy priorities, *viz.*, restraining pressure on prices and reducing the budget deficit (1990–91 and 1991–92); activating the internal debt management policy and modernising the financial sector (1992–93); reducing gross fiscal deficit (GFD) and controlling strong liquidity growth emanating from inflow of foreign capital (1993–94); phased elimination of automatic monetisation of budget deficit (1994–95); and follow-up measures consequent to the abolition of *ad hoc* Treasury Bills to bridge the budget deficit (1996–97).

Except for the years 1993–94, 1995–96 and 1996–97, the actual borrowings (net) were lower than the borrowings projected by the Reserve Bank (Table 15.1). However, this hypothesis is only of academic interest because soon after the Reserve Bank communicates its market borrowing projections to the Government for the ensuing year, the Governor of the Reserve Bank invariably follows this up with discussions with the officials of the finance ministry as part of the overall budget formulation exercise. At this meeting, the estimated budget deficit, RBI credit to the Government and the quantum of market borrowing by the Centre and states during the ensuing year are firmed up after discussions for inclusion in the Union Budget. In others words, in every probability, the preliminary figures forecasted by the Reserve Bank for market borrowing (in its letter) undergo revision as an outcome of the pre-budget confabulations.[6]

MARKET BORROWING PROGRAMME FOR 1989–90

Concerns Over Emerging Macroeconomic Trends

The letter dated January 7, 1989 from the Governor to the Finance Secretary conveyed the perceptions of the Reserve Bank stemming from the monetary exercise for the year 1989–90, which were symptomatic of a deepening crisis.

---

6. In terms of a long-established practice, after the regular Budget is presented in Parliament (by convention, in the last week of February), the Union Finance Minister addresses the meeting of the Directors of the Central Board of the Reserve Bank of India, which is mostly convened in New Delhi.

TABLE 15.1

Market Borrowings of the Central and State Governments:
Projections and Actuals

(₹ crore)

	1989–90	1990–91	1991–92	1992–93
Overall Market Borrowing Programme as projected by RBI	12,200	12,925	14,125	12,000
Market Borrowing (Gross)	10,599	11,558	12,284	17,690
Market Borrowing (Net)	9,654	10,570	10,865	11,932
Excess over projected estimate	−2,546	−2,355	−3,260	−68
	1993–94	1994–95	1995–96	1996–97
Overall Market Borrowing Programme as projected by RBI	7,500	33,030@	30,150#	31,300
Market Borrowing (Gross)	54,533	43,231	46,783	42,688
Market Borrowing (Net)	32,164	25,197	32,721	32,892
Excess over projected estimate	24,664	−7,833	2,571	1,592

Notes: @: The earlier RBI estimate was ₹ 9,650 crore in dated securities and ₹ 10,000 crore in 91/364-day Treasury Bills.

#: The earlier RBI recommendation was ₹ 23,700 crore.

Table 15.1 represents the market borrowings of the central and state governments, local authorities and institutions sponsored by central and state governments.

Source: Reserve Bank of India, *Annual Report; Report on Currency and Finance,* various issues.

The Reserve Bank had earlier agreed on a target of M_3 growth in 1988–89 of 16.3 per cent, taking into consideration the overhang of primary liquidity. But the M_3 increase in 1988–89 (up to December 16, 1988) had touched 11.8 per cent and the annual overall increase was expected to be at the targeted level. Meanwhile, the Reserve Bank was concerned that the net Bank credit to the Central Government had already increased by ₹ 9,065 crore as against ₹ 6,628 crore in the previous year and the indications were that even the budget document figure of ₹ 7,484 crore could well be breached. Additionally, policymakers in the Reserve Bank had to contend with the fact that the overhang of reserve money creation in the past had still to work itself out. The rate of growth in the economy in 1989–90 even under the most favourable circumstances was not expected to be higher than 5.0 per cent and it was recognised that measures would have to be initiated to moderate the rate of inflation. Given this bleak scenario, the Reserve Bank opted for M_3 expansion target of 15.0 per cent in 1989–90.

In order to contain the M_3 expansion at 15.0 per cent, the Reserve Bank posited that it would be desirable to limit the increase in net Bank credit to the Central Government in 1989–90 to ₹ 8,200 crore, of which the budgetary deficit was to be ₹ 7,000 crore (as compared with the budgeted amount of ₹ 7,484 crore in 1988–89) and the balance ₹ 1,200 crore was to be bridged by way of Reserve Bank support to the borrowing programme. Within these overall parameters, the Reserve Bank suggested that the total market borrowing programme should not exceed ₹ 12,200 crore, *i.e.*, ₹ 479 crore more than the limit for the previous year. The Bank indicated:

> ...would recommend that once the allocations are agreed to at the start of the year ad hoc increases should not be made during the course of the year. This policy has worked well so far in 1988–89 and ... would strongly advocate its continuation next year.

MARKET BORROWING PROGRAMME FOR 1990–91

Primacy for Inflation Control

Taking into account primarily the prevailing and emerging trends in national income growth and broad money/money supply (M_3) expansion in 1990–91, bank deposits and non-food credit, the Governor, Shri R.N. Malhotra, in his letter dated February 8, 1990 to the finance ministry, postulated that the overall market borrowing programme for the Central Government in 1990–91 could be ₹ 12,925 crore, of which the share of the Centre was ₹ 7,400 crore. Further, given the trends in money supply growth and inflationary pressures and the need to contain monetised deficit, the Reserve Bank advised that it did not propose to provide support to the market borrowing programme in 1990–91 and as such the entire 'permissible' increase in the Reserve Bank credit to the Government should be shown as budget deficit. The Governor added that the overall budget deficit could be progressively reduced to zero and the longer-term resource needs of the Government met through a mutually agreed WMA from the Reserve Bank and Treasury Bills raised from the market by 1993–94. Thus, the seeds for discontinuing the automatic monetisation of budget deficit were sown in the early 1990s, but it became a reality much later in 1997–98, after the financial markets became vibrant with the launching of the financial sector reforms.

The Centre's gross market borrowings of ₹ 8,989 crore comprised cash subscriptions of ₹ 8,531 crore and conversion of maturing loans

₹ 458 crore. In respect of the state governments, there were no maturing loans in 1990–91. The Reserve Bank's initial subscription to central government loans during 1990–91 formed 49.3 per cent of the total loans floated, as compared with its initial subscription of 60.4 per cent of the total in the previous year. During the year, the Central Government issued to the Reserve Bank special securities worth ₹ 30,220 crore, of which ₹ 30,000 crore were towards funding *ad hoc* Treasury Bills. The funding of *ad hoc* Treasury Bills was last undertaken in 1987–88 for ₹ 17,500 crore.

MARKET BORROWING PROGRAMME FOR 1991–92

Emphasis on Moderating the Central Government's Budget Deficit

Consistent with the expected growth in bank deposits and non-food credit, the Reserve Bank predicated that the increase in net RBI credit to the Central Government should not exceed ₹ 8,000 crore. On this analogy, the Centre's budget deficit in 1991–92 was placed at 1.4 per cent of gross domestic product (GDP) at current market prices. The overall market borrowing in 1991–92 was fixed at ₹ 14,125 crore. In his letter dated January 8, 1991, the Governor, Shri S. Venkitaramanan, stressed that statutory liquidity ratio (SLR) had been increasing sharply in 1990–91; with an unchanged SLR in 1991–92, there was 'no way' in which the overall market borrowing in 1991–92 could be higher than that in the previous year; the Reserve Bank would not provide any support to the market borrowing programme; and the entire increase in net RBI credit to the Central Government should be indicated as budget deficit in the documents.

The letter also conveyed the Reserve Bank's perceptions on major policy issues relating to public debt management and sought the Government's agreement for initiating measures to activate the government securities market as well as internal debt management. It was pointed out that in immediate past, the government borrowings other than under the market borrowing programme had been increasing rapidly and the effective cost of such borrowing, taking into account the fiscal concessions, worked out substantially higher than the costs incurred under the annual market borrowing programme. The Reserve Bank made a strong case for applying market-related interest rates on government securities, which would reduce the monetisation of the deficit and, ultimately, result in a decline in nominal interest rates, *viz.*:

Extremely high reserve requirements and below market rates of interest on the Government's marketable debt, far from improving the resource allocation, cause avoidable distortions. This also results in the monetisation of a large part of the Government borrowing. It is often argued that higher interest rates on Government securities could raise the cost of servicing the Government's internal debt. It needs to be recognised that market-related rates on Government securities would widen the demand for these securities thereby reducing the monetisation of the deficit. Eventually, as inflation comes under control there would be a reduction in the cost of borrowing as nominal interest rates would decline.

Further, a number of policy prescriptions were proffered, such as removing the cap on interest rate on 182-day Treasury Bills, the introduction of longer maturity Treasury Bills, increase in the discount rate on 91-day Treasury Bills and an increase in the rate of commission on state government flotations. What is important to note is that both the Reserve Bank and the Government acted in close understanding and rapport to activate internal debt management strategy as an adjunct to fiscal consolidation and more effective monetary management.

The net market borrowings by the Central Government were placed at ₹ 7,501 crore as against ₹ 8,001 crore in 1990–91; this reflected the results of the concerted efforts to reduce the reliance on market borrowing for financing government expenditure. The Reserve Bank's initial subscription to the 1991–92 central government loans, however, was 54.1 per cent of the gross market borrowings as against 49.3 per cent in the previous year. The Central Government issued special securities to the Reserve Bank against funding of *ad hoc* Treasury Bills to the tune of ₹ 5,000 crore during 1991–92.

MARKET BORROWING PROGRAMME FOR 1992–93

Focus on Implementation of Financial Sector Reforms

The strong inflationary potential in the economy and the on-going financial sector reforms called for major policy adjustments in directed credit and downward revision in the existing statutory reserve prescriptions, based on the recommendations of the Narasimham Committee.

The Reserve Bank's perceptions and suggestions relating to the market borrowing programme for 1992–93 were influenced by the recommendations of the above committee and the need to nip in the bud the strong inflationary potential. In his letter dated January 2, 1992 to the Secretary, Economic Affairs, Ministry of Finance, the Governor cited the following facts: the Centre's budget deficit in 1991–92 even by the third quarter of the year (*i.e.*, up to December 13,1991) was as high as ₹ 17,419 crore as against ₹ 7,719 crore (BE) for the full financial year 1991–92; adherence to the tentative numbers agreed to with the International Monetary Fund (IMF) for 1992–93 (*viz.*, net RBI credit to Central Government of ₹ 6,200 crore and M_3 expansion of 11.0–12.0 per cent); the budget deficit and the market borrowing programme to be in conformity with the Government's primary objective of reducing the GFD from 6.5 per cent of GDP in 1991–92 to 5.0 per cent in 1992–93; and the overall market borrowing programme for 1992–93 to take into account the recommendations of the Narasimham Committee for a decrease in SLR on incremental domestic deposit liabilities, from 38.5 per cent to 30.0 per cent. Moreover, the Reserve Bank recommended that M_3 growth in 1992–93 needed to be contained within 12.0 per cent and the budgetary deficit of the Centre (*i.e.*, net RBI credit to the Central Government), not to exceed ₹ 6,200 crore during that year. Accordingly, the overall market borrowing programme for 1992–93 was determined lower, at ₹ 12,000 crore, compared with the actual ₹ 14,726 crore for 1991–92; of this, the share of the Central Government was not to exceed ₹ 5,000 crore.

The debt management measures envisaged by the Reserve Bank included a reduction in SLR on incremental domestic liabilities from 38.5 per cent to 30.0 per cent during the year, a phased movement to market-related interest rates on government securities, institutional measures to activate a secondary market in government securities and funding of part of the existing stock of Treasury Bills.

Concerned about the less than satisfactory GFD position, the Central Government from 1991–92 consistently scaled down its market borrowing programme. Consequently, net market borrowings were placed lower at ₹ 3,670 crore during 1992–93 (₹ 7,501 crore in 1991–92), while gross market borrowings were ₹ 4,821 crore (₹ 8,919 crore in 1991–92). As a strategy to move towards market-related operations, the Reserve Bank, on behalf of the Centre, conducted for the first time auctions of dated securities. During 1992–93, according to the Reserve Bank's records, net market borrowings of the state governments amounted to ₹ 3,471 crore (₹ 3,364 crore in 1991–92).

MARKET BORROWING PROGRAMME FOR 1993–94

Reductions in Fiscal Deficit, Reserve Requirements and Development of Financial Markets, including the Government Securities Market

The letter from the Governor, Dr C. Rangarajan, to the Secretary, Economic Affairs, Ministry of Finance, dated January 7, 1993 advised that the market borrowing programme for 1993–94 was not to exceed ₹ 7,500 crore as against ₹ 12,000 crore in 1992–93. In consonance with the proposed reduction in the GFD of the Centre to 4.0 per cent of GDP in 1993–94, the projections made by the Reserve Bank were to contain the expansion in M_3 at 12.0 per cent and the budget deficit of the Centre at ₹ 4,000 crore. Other important measures contemplated for the year were reductions in the effective SLR and CRR by 2.0 and 1.5 percentage points, respectively, and funding of 364-day Treasury Bills into dated securities while continuing with their auctions. Based on the trends in inflation rate until the middle of December 1992, the Reserve Bank indicated that monetary policy in 1993–94 should curb inflationary expectations while promoting growth, reduce further the reserve prescriptions and progress towards market-related interest rates for government borrowing. The central bank anticipated that as a result of SLR and CRR reductions, a sizeable release of lendable resources to banks would take place, leading to bank credit expansion. The internal debt management policy issues identified were: increase in the amount of the auction 91-day Treasury Bills, reduction in the maximum maturity period of dated government securities, review of the structure of yield pattern of dated securities, issue of zero coupon bonds to minimise interest outgo in the future and development of market infrastructure.

A critical component of the financial sector reforms was the large reductions to be effected in the incremental reserve requirements of banks. Apprehending that a sharp reduction might carry serious implications for the Government's borrowing programme, the Governor in his letter dated February 3, 1993 conveyed to the Government his 'great anxiety' about an effective SLR reduction in 1993–94 that was larger than two percentage points, at the same time conceding that such a reduction of less than two percentage points would affect the 'credibility' of a strong financial sector reform. The Reserve Bank also mooted the idea to the Centre issuing its securities partly at controlled rates with an SLR requirement and partly at market-determined rates devoid of an SLR requirement, but hastened to admit that such a strategy was neither feasible nor conducive to the development of the government securities market, since it was not advisable to issue securities with the same risk and maturity at widely varying rates of interest. "The choice is to move to market entirely or to mimic the market by controlled but realistic rates," was the perceptive observation of the Governor, Dr Rangarajan. In view of the likely difficulties in adjusting to lower borrowing levels, the Reserve Bank discerned that the latter course (*i.e.*, controlled but realistic rates) was a more feasible proposition, at least for 1993–94. In conclusion, the Governor stated that whatever was decided on the rate and maturity should be made applicable to all government securities and the authorities should not 'artificially fracture' the market.

In this letter, the Reserve Bank suggested tapping mutual funds to finance the large gap of ₹ 4,800 crore in the budget. The entire funds mobilised by the mutual funds were completely free of any reserve requirements. From a prudential viewpoint and as a move towards a level playing field, the Reserve Bank was in favour of prescribing a liquidity requirement in government and other approved securities to the extent of 5.0 per cent of the monthly net asset value of all mutual funds (including that of the Unit Trust of India [UTI]) to be phased in four steps of 1.25 percentage points each during 1993–94. With the total asset value of all mutual funds at around ₹ 50,000 crore, ₹ 2,500 crore at the maximum was expected to be garnered. At the same time, the Reserve Bank clarified that the legal position about prescription of a liquidity requirement for mutual funds was somewhat 'hazy' and, as such, until the Reserve Bank of India (RBI) Act was amended to make the position explicit, it was best to set this requirement as a guideline from the Reserve Bank as part of overall monetary control. Securities and Exchange Board of India (SEBI) guidelines were also expected to reinforce this measure. The Reserve Bank admitted that although introducing a liquidity requirement at a time when there was a back-off from SLR for banks might appear somewhat embarrassing, this could be projected as part of an expeditious move towards a 'level playing ground'. The letter concluded:

> I must stress that in the absence of this measure, the borrowing programme for 1993–94 envisaged by the Government cannot be successfully implemented. We need to take an early decision on this matter to ensure that the liquidity requirements for mutual funds are in place early in the financial year 1993–94.

The Reserve Bank, after analysing the monetary and banking data available until the middle of March 1993, conjectured that the estimate of the resources available for the overall market borrowing programme in 1993–94 remained unchanged at ₹ 7,500 crore, but in the light of the BE for 1993–94 it would be necessary to raise from non-captive resources a large amount of ₹ 6,800 crore at market-related rates. In its letter to the Finance Secretary dated March 27, 1993, the Reserve Bank emphasised the need to explore other avenues for raising such a large amount, including re-examination of the earlier suggestion of imposition of a small reserve requirement of 5.0 per cent of the net asset value on mutual funds (including the UTI). In a subsequent letter dated April 20, 1993 to the Additional Secretary (Budget), Department of Economic Affairs, specific suggestions were made, namely, issuing in the middle of May 1993 the first tranche of state governments' borrowing programme for ₹ 1,200 crore of 10-year duration, limiting the programme of central guaranteed institutions to ₹ 1,270 crore [inclusive of any allocation to the City and Industrial Development Corporation of Maharashtra Ltd (CIDCO)] and continuing the 91-day Treasury Bill auctions throughout the year 1993–94 within a ceiling of ₹ 5,000 crore (outstanding).

In August 1993, the Government enquired of the Reserve Bank about the possibility of increasing the market borrowing allocations in 1993–94. The latter, in its letter dated September 8, 1993, conceded that the deposit growth in the full financial year could be higher than the estimated growth of 13.0 per cent (namely, about 15.5 per cent), but expected the Government to take strong measures to reduce the budget deficit and the automatic monetisation. It was pointed out that despite the higher deposit growth in future, banks might not be inclined to invest further in government securities as they had already large excess investment over and above SLR stipulation. The 'considered' advice of the Reserve Bank was that the borrowing should not be raised merely because monetary expansion was higher than that earlier envisaged; since the basic reason for such larger expansion was the large budget deficit, the Government would soon be required to undertake in the current year a large funding operation for 91-day auction Treasury Bills and, until this was put through, the Reserve Bank was not in favour of sizeable enhancement in the borrowing programme. "While the overall borrowing programme for 1993–94, as approved, is well ahead of schedule, it would be best not to load the programme with large borrowing till existing commitments are successfully completed," the Governor indicated. The Reserve Bank also suggested that this matter could be reviewed by the end of October 1993 after the funding operations.

The BE for 1993–94 placed the gross and net market borrowings of the Central Government at ₹ 4,848 crore and ₹ 3,700 crore, respectively, which were marginally higher than the RE for 1992–93. A significant aspect of the domestic borrowing strategy of the Central Government was the increased reliance on the market through the issue of dated securities, zero coupon bonds, 91-day auction Treasury Bills, 364-day Treasury Bills and funding of Treasury Bills. The Reserve Bank's initial support declined to about 9.0 per cent of the gross market borrowings in 1993–94, as against 45.9 per cent during 1992–93. Moreover, the initial subscription by the Reserve Bank was fully sold off in the secondary market during the year. This indicated the increased market absorption of government securities following the move towards market-related interest rates.

MARKET BORROWING PROGRAMME FOR 1994–95

Impact of Strong Accretion to Foreign Exchange Reserves and the Decision to Phase Out Automatic Monetisation of Budget Deficit

The Governor, Dr C. Rangarajan, in his letter dated December 27, 1993 to the Finance Secretary proposed the market borrowing programme (dated securities) for 1994–95 at a reduced level of ₹ 9,650 crore, of which the Centre's share was ₹ 3,700 crore (excluding funding of Treasury Bills), while a further ₹ 10,000 crore could be raised by the issue of 91-day and 364-day Treasury Bills. This estimate was considered consistent with a GFD of 4.5 per cent of GDP in 1994–95. Perhaps the most important determinant was the decision to curtail during the year the automatic monetisation through the creation of *ad hoc* Treasury Bills so that auctioned Treasury Bills formed two-third of the short-term financing of the Government (*i.e.*, up to 91 days); at any point during the year, net RBI credit to the Centre was not to exceed twice the end-year figure set out as the budgetary estimate and any deviation would trigger an increase in the amount of auctioned 91-day Treasury Bills.

The other measures contemplated during the year in accordance with the overall monetary projections and borrowing programme were: (i) reducing the effective SLR from 33.0 per cent to 30.5 per cent in conjunction with other monetary policy measures; (ii) in view of the prevailing high level of liquidity, CRR was not to be reduced except as a component of any rationalisation without adding to the primary money creation; (iii) lengthening the maturity structure of government dated securities, continuation of the auction procedure and attempts towards freer interest rates on state government flotations; (iv) funding of Treasury Bills; and (v) development of market infrastructure.

While arriving at the figures for market borrowing for 1994–95, the Reserve Bank provided for a further build-up of liquidity to the extent of ₹ 10,000 crore, over and above the large excess liquidity in 1993–94. This perception, along with the contemplated further reduction in SLR in 1994–95, made the authorities apprehend that sooner or later the smooth floatation of the borrowing programme of the state governments could be seriously disrupted in 1995–96, if not in 1994–95. Under the circumstances, the Reserve Bank advised that it would be extremely 'hazardous' to plan on the basis of a continuing and increasingly large excess liquidity, since, when it became necessary to quickly turn to non-inflationary level of financing of market borrowing, the entire market borrowing programme could be in disarray.

The major source of the large expansion in reserve money (up to November 26, 1993) was net RBI credit to the Central Government, which increased by ₹ 11,989 crore as against an increase of ₹ 9,549 crore in the corresponding period of 1992–93. The sizeable accretion of ₹ 6,111 crore to the foreign exchange assets of the Reserve Bank also contributed to the bulge in the growth of reserve money during the financial year. This would have been substantial but for a decline of ₹ 3,353 crore in scheduled commercial banks' (SCBs) borrowings from the Reserve Bank in the financial year up to November 26, 1993 as against an increase of ₹ 345 crore in the comparable period in the previous year. The Reserve Bank's understanding was that the strong increase in primary liquidity in 1993–94 and the substantial unutilised refinance limits of banks could trigger an explosive increase in the overall liquidity in the economy at very short notice and, as such, the overall monetary situation was very 'vulnerable'.

The price trends also pointed to inflationary pressures touching double digits. For the Reserve Bank, the most disquieting aspect was the exceptionally large monetisation of the deficit of the Central Government. The budget deficit of the Central Government, after recording a high of ₹ 21,755 crore on August 13, 1993, weakened in the following weeks and stood at ₹ 16,529 crore on December 17, 1993, as against the BE of ₹ 4,314 crore for the year. Both the budget deficit and the net RBI credit to the Centre would have been even higher but for the extremely good response to the market auctions of Treasury Bills and dated securities.

Quite apart from the large increase in net RBI credit to the Centre, the borrowings of the Centre from the market in 1994–95 were estimated at an unprecedented ₹ 26,250 crore (BE of ₹ 9,700 crore). The Reserve Bank was, therefore, constrained to point out (in the aforesaid letter): "Drastic measures would have to be taken early to restore fiscal stability; otherwise, the credibility of the financial sector reform measures would be jeopardised and the manoeuvrability of monetary policy responses would be severely impaired."

The Reserve Bank concluded that within the overall financial policy framework, the opening up of the external sector underscored the need for mutual consistency between monetary policy and exchange rate policy and, accordingly, the objective of monetary policy during 1994–95 should be to bring about a perceptible reduction in the excessive primary money creation and thereby a reduction in the inflation rate. Monetary policy was also expected to provide an enabling framework for implementing the overall financial sector reforms. The Governor reiterated that appropriate fiscal measures were required to be taken to contain net RBI credit to Central Government so that monetary policy had enough 'head room' to support growth of output and that, consistent with the projected growth of M_3 and reserve money in 1994–95, the increase in net RBI credit to the Centre was to be contained within ₹ 5,000 crore.

Internal debt management was progressively becoming a vital element for transmitting monetary policy signals and these instruments needed to be further strengthened in 1994–95, the Reserve Bank stated in its letter to the Government. In particular, attention was to be focused on reducing the automatic monetisation of budget deficit if the programme of reduction of SLR to an average of 25.0 per cent by 1995–96 was to be meaningful and also for the development of a healthy secondary market in government securities.

MARKET BORROWING PROGRAMME FOR 1995–96

Onwards to a Cohesive Monetary and Fiscal Policy

In his letter dated December 20, 1994 to the Finance Secretary, the Governor envisioned that the total market borrowing programme for the Centre, states and others for 1995–96 could be reduced to ₹ 30,150 crore compared to ₹ 33,030 crore in 1994–95, of which the share of the Centre under all heads was to be ₹ 23,700 crore. A further amount of ₹ 14,700 crore could be raised through medium and long-term loans and ₹ 5,300 crore by means of short-term loans (*i.e.*, 364-day Treasury Bills). The creation of *ad hoc* Treasury Bills was not to exceed ₹ 4,000 crore, in accordance with the agreement signed between the Reserve Bank and the Central Government on September 9, 1994 on phasing out the issue of *ad hocs* over a three-year period. The increase in *ad hocs* was not to exceed ₹ 6,000 crore for more than 10 continuous working days at any time during 1995–96 and, if this limit was breached, the Reserve Bank would automatically sell fresh Treasury Bills or dated securities in the market.

The Reserve Bank pointed out that the Centre's total market borrowings in 1993–94 at ₹ 27,151 crore and in 1994–95 at ₹ 26,700 crore were 'phenomenally' high compared with the level of ₹ 8,461 crore in 1992–93, and that this quantum jump was made possible due to very special features, which resulted in banks and other institutions holding very large excess liquidity. Due to the large liquidity overhang in the economy, there arose a compulsion to contain M_3 growth in 1995–96 at 15.5 per cent, and it was felt that it would not be possible to sustain the Centre's borrowing in 1995–96 at the high level of the previous years. On this analogy, the Reserve Bank recommended a diminution in the Centre's total market borrowing from ₹ 26,700 crore in 1994–95 to ₹ 23,700 crore in 1995–96. The other important measures contemplated — consistent with the overall monetary projections and market borrowing programme — were that CRR would not be reduced, the average effective SLR would be lowered from 29.5 per cent at the end of March 1995 to 27.5 per cent at the end of March 1996, and Treasury Bills would continue to be funded as a matter of policy with the objective of elongating the maturity structure. The Reserve Bank decided that against the background of large capital inflows during 1994–95 and the resultant explosive growth in net foreign assets (NFA), the objective of monetary policy in 1995–96 would be to contain reserve money growth and to bring about a significant reduction in inflationary pressures. The thrust of the policy was to persevere with financial sector reforms.

SLR holdings of securities by SCBs in excess of the prescribed level were estimated at ₹ 41,000 crore at the end of March 1996. But the Reserve Bank was not oblivious of the fact that the continued dependence of market borrowing on such excess investment made by a few financial institutions (FIs) could sooner or later pose a serious problem to the authorities since banks and other investors might increasingly explore other outlets for lending and investments, in which case it would no longer be possible to sustain the level of borrowing achieved in 1993–94 and 1994–95. Based on this assessment, the Reserve Bank advised the Government that any attempt to keep the Centre's borrowing programme at a high level could lead to an explosive increase in interest rates and that this was one reason for scaling down the Centre's total borrowing programme in 1995–96 to ₹ 23,700 crore as against ₹ 26,700 crore in the previous year.

The Reserve Bank stressed (in the letter to the Government) that fiscal and monetary developments in the recent past underscored the need for a cohesive fiscal and monetary policy strategy. The basic objective of fiscal policy (supported by financial sector reforms and monetary policy) was to effect a gradual reduction in the GFD as also in the monetisation of the budget deficit, so as to achieve a sustainable rate of economic growth with reasonable price stability. The objective of monetary policy in 1995–96 was to offset the impact of the persistent large inflow of foreign exchange on monetary expansion. The Reserve Bank averred that the success of monetary policy instruments in containing monetary expansion and inflation would largely depend on the fiscal responses, which had a bearing on the internal debt management strategy. A number of policy measures were suggested to achieve this objective.

First, whereas the CRR limit would not be reduced, it might be necessary to increase the CRR rate over certain segments of banks' liabilities to prevent the attenuation of monetary control because of the shift in liabilities among the various non-resident deposit schemes. However, if the primary monetary expansion turned out to be explosive, the Reserve Bank would have to raise CRR across the board. Second, the overall market borrowing programme was becoming increasingly distanced from the SLR prescription and, therefore, an even faster reduction in the prescribed SLR was considered feasible if the borrowing programme for 1995–96 took off well in the first half of the year. Third, the outstanding 364-day Treasury Bills at the end of March 1995 could be large and maturing of this debt might pose problems for the Government. Therefore, the Reserve Bank considered it prudent to fund a substantial part of these bills into dated securities. Similarly, it was felt that suitable opportunities should be availed of to fund 91-day Treasury Bills into dated securities. Fourth, OMOs impacted on the profits of the Reserve Bank and also raised the interest rates, but these costs were reckoned to be unavoidable. In this connection, the conversion of non-marketable 4.6 per cent securities into marketable high-yielding securities — which the Government had recently approved — was expected to facilitate effective OMOs for overall liquidity management.

Gross market borrowings (consisting of normal market borrowings, other medium and long-term borrowings and borrowings through 364-day Treasury Bills) stood at a high of ₹ 40,509 crore in 1995–96. Despite a substantial increase in interest rates on government paper, there was a devolvement on the Reserve Bank to the tune of 32.8 per cent of gross issues. The lower absorption of government securities by the market was attributable to a number of reasons, *viz.*, the excess liquidity that was present in the banking system in 1994–95 being unavailable in 1995–96, lower growth in bank deposits during 1995–96 than in the preceding year, a tapering off of commercial banks' investments owing to larger demand for credit in response to buoyant economic activity and large stocks of government securities in their investment portfolios in excess of the required SLR stipulations.

In this connection, the Reserve Bank's Annual Report for 1995–96 conjectured that the large market borrowing would necessarily keep nominal interest rates at a level that would result in very high real rates of interest due to the distinctly lower inflation rate. In 1995–96, the Reserve Bank absorbed a sizeable proportion of the new issues, thus preventing a further rise in interest rates although this caused primary liquidity creation. Up to August 2, 1996, the increase in net RBI credit to the Centre in 1996–97 was significantly lower than that in the corresponding period of the previous year, largely because of very transient investments in 91-day tap Treasury Bills.

Government borrowing operations encountered a relatively difficult phase during 1995–96, following a large increase in demand for commercial credit and perceptibly lower growth in bank deposits. With hardening of interest rates, the absorption of government securities by the market was weak. There was large devolvement on the Reserve Bank. The intra-year cap on the issue of *ad hoc* Treasury Bills was exceeded on three occasions for extended periods, and the end-of-the-year limit was also surpassed. Due to relatively tight conditions in the money market, the gross amount raised under 364-day Treasury Bills was distinctly smaller in 1995–96 compared with 1994–95, and net repayments under these bills were substantial.

In 1995–96, concerned over the fact that extremely high real interest rates would affect the economy adversely, the Reserve Bank decided to strike a balance and allowed interest rates on government paper to rise, while absorbing sizeable amounts of government securities in its portfolio by way of devolvement. Such devolvement was to the extent of 32.8 per cent of the gross central government borrowing. In addition, the Reserve Bank absorbed sizeable amount of 91-day auction Treasury Bills.[7]

MARKET BORROWING PROGRAMME FOR 1996–97

Discontinuation of Automatic Monetisation of Budget Deficit

The total market borrowing programme of the Centre, states and other bodies was determined at ₹ 31,300 crore for 1996–97, of which the Centre's component was ₹ 24,000 crore, as per the Governor's letter dated January 2, 1996 to the Finance Secretary. These figures implied the Reserve Bank's support of ₹ 10,000 crore. A suggestion was made to the Government for consolidation of the Centre's market borrowing under one head rather than three heads, *i.e.*, conventional, medium, long and short-term (364-day Treasury Bills). The repayments of the Centre during 1996–97 were estimated at ₹ 10,500 crore and, consistent with net market borrowing of ₹ 24,000 crore, the Centre's gross borrowing worked out to ₹ 34,500 crore. These estimates for 1996–97 were based on two tenets. First, CRR would not be altered other than for any restructuring and provided such a change did not have an overall impact on monetary aggregates. Second, SLR would not be changed; but as a result of the 25.0 per cent prescription on incremental domestic net demand and time liabilities (NDTL) and zero SLR on certain specific liabilities, the overall effective SLR would continue to decline from an estimated 28.2 per cent in March 1996 to 27.2 per cent in March 1997.

For 1996–97, the year-end figure for the increase in *ad hoc* Treasury Bills was set at ₹ 5,000 crore and the within-the-year ceiling for 10 consecutive working days was ₹ 9,000 crore. The year 1996–97 being the final year of the adjustment programme for phasing out the instrument of *ad hoc* Treasury Bills, the outstanding *ad hocs* as on March 31, 1997 were proposed to be funded into 4.6 per cent non-marketable undated securities. From April 1, 1997, the mechanism of *ad hoc* Treasury Bills was to be replaced by a ways and means limit at the Bank Rate, which had to be cleared before the end of the financial year.

While framing the policy, the Reserve Bank factored in that during 1995–96 there would be considerable difficulty in meeting the Central Government's market borrowing programme and it would have to extend

---

7. Review of Internal Debt Management Policy and Operations for the period from November 1, 1994 to March 31, 1996: Memorandum to the Central Board of Directors of the Reserve Bank of India dated April 26, 1996.

support to the market on several occasions. By the end of December 1995, the Central Government could raise only ₹ 17,180 crore against the net borrowing of ₹ 27,087 crore and the balance was raised in the last quarter of the fiscal year. The letter advised the Government that the support which the Reserve Bank could provide in meeting the balance to be raised would depend on future trends in money supply and prices. In retrospect, the Reserve Bank was in a position to provide considerable support to the Government in 1995–96, largely on account of a decline in the NFA, but such a situation was not expected to recur in 1996–97. With rising demand for credit, banks might not be willing to augment their holdings of securities above the existing level. Any attempt to raise the Centre's net market borrowing above the figure set out would have a cascading effect on other interest rates in the system. With large repayments due in 1996–97, it was no longer meaningful from policy and operational viewpoints to focus on the net market borrowing programme, as investors could not be expected to automatically reinvest maturities in government paper. Given this uncertain prospect, the Reserve Bank stressed that the Centre should plan for a net market borrowing of ₹ 24,000 crore (gross ₹ 34,500 crore) in 1996–97, which might turn out to be a difficult target to achieve.

The substantial improvement in liquidity, on one hand, and sluggish credit off-take, on the other, led to improved market absorption of government securities, which facilitated early completion of the Government's borrowing programme during 1996–97. The aggregate net market borrowing (including the 364-day Treasury Bills) of the Central Government during fiscal 1996–97 at ₹ 26,356 crore exceeded the budgeted amount of ₹ 25,498 crore (as per Reserve Bank's records). In order to raise this amount, the Central Government accessed the market on 12 occasions, with lower devolvement on the Reserve Bank and primary dealers (PDs), as also with less pressure on the interest rate.

'MARKET-RELATED' BORROWINGS AND GROWTH OF
PUBLIC DEBT: AN ANALYSIS

The decade of the 1990s (up to 1996–97) was an era of fiscal consolidation and financial sector reforms that were interlinked in operation. The continuous enlargement in the overall market borrowing of the Centre and state governments inexorably resulted in a large accumulation of domestic debt. There was an increased reliance on the market through the sale of dated securities, 91-day auction Treasury Bills, 364-day Treasury Bills, zero coupon bonds and, last but not the least, the funding of Treasury Bills. A welcome feature was the increased absorption of government securities following the move towards market-related interest rates accompanied by an active internal debt management policy. In addition, there was a sizeable demand for government paper by institutional investors, principally the commercial banks, which preferred safer means of investment.

Over the six-year period from 1991 to 1997 (end-March), the domestic liabilities of the Government grew two-fold. Of this, market loans expanded nearly two-and-a-half times; the other major component accounting for the rise was the 91-day auctioned Treasury Bills. Also, 91-day Treasury Bills funded into special securities (in 1991–92) at ₹ 71,000 crore was a large item. In 1991 (end-March), it was nearly the size of the market loans, but by 1997 its comparative share came down because of the relatively more rapid growth in market loans and 91-day Treasury Bills (Statement 15.1). Since the borrowings took place at market-determined rates, the burden of interest payments also concurrently escalated.

Growing Burden of Repayment and Amortisation

Perhaps a not so apparent incidence of market borrowing was the accumulated burden of repayments in future due to the steep humps in the repayment schedule, both of the Centre and the state governments. This aspect was not lost on the Reserve Bank.[8]

The total outstanding domestic liabilities of the Government (Centre and states combined) were equivalent to about 54.0 per cent of GDP in 1994–95 as against 56.0 per cent in 1993–94 and 51.0 per cent in 1985–86 (Statement 15.2). It was much higher in 1990–91 (i.e., 59.6 per cent). However, in 1995–96 and 1996–97, this domestic debt-GDP ratio started coming down, albeit slowly. Overall, this trend was symptomatic of a turnaround from the unsustainable debt scenario of the 1980s. The Reserve Bank voiced its concern that accumulation of debt at this pace would have serious implications for the coming Union Budget and the state budgets in terms of higher interest payments as well as larger amortisation.[9]

In 1995–96, interest payments accounted for about 47.0 per cent of the revenue receipts of the Central Government, 15.0 per cent of state governments and 18.0 per cent to 28.0 per cent for the Centre and states together (after adjusting for inter-governmental transactions). Moreover,

---

8. A specific proposal for placing a ceiling on public debt was suggested in a technical paper on the subject published in the Reserve Bank monthly bulletin, December 1997. This was intended to elicit informed and wider debate on the subject.

9. Reserve Bank of India, *Annual Report, 1994–95.*

this repayment burden was expected to be more severe in the years ahead. Another disturbing phenomenon was a shift in the debt pattern of government securities towards relatively shorter maturities ever since the Government moved to a system of market-oriented borrowing. The proportion of marketable debt in the total domestic debt of the Government increased rather sharply. It only deferred the repayment problem to the future. The rising interest burden on domestic debt (*i.e.*, the ratio of interest payments to revenue receipts) made the Reserve Bank comment:[10]

> It is, therefore, imperative that the growth in interest payments should be arrested over the medium-term through further reduction in GFD-GDP ratio so as to achieve a perceptible decline in the debt-GDP ratio. This, in turn, would satisfy the necessary but not the sufficient condition, for a sustainable fiscal policy. What is crucial is, however, to generate adequate primary surplus which could meet the entire debt service obligation.

Shifts in Composition of the Debt and Maturity Pattern

Following the move towards market-related interest rates for central government borrowing from June 1992, there was a shift not only in the composition but also the maturity pattern of the Centre's debt from the long end to the short end. The proportion of marketable debt in the total debt of the Government strengthened from 24.6 per cent in 1991–92 to 28.6 per cent in 1995–96. Similarly, the short-term loans (maturity below 5 years) in the total market loans raised by the Central Government escalated from 20.7 per cent in 1992–93 to 64.9 per cent in 1995–96. This movement in favour of short-term debt signified more frequent repayment obligations and the accentuation of amortisation problems for the Government.

The share of dated securities in total domestic liabilities of the Centre increased from 24.6 per cent at the end of March 1992 to 29.9 per cent at the end of March 1997. The larger recourse to borrowing from the market exerted pressure on interest rates and triggered concomitant policy response to minimise the cost of borrowing by placing a large part of borrowings at the shorter end of the market. This compressed the average maturity and gave rise to problems of debt roll-overs. As a consequence, the share of shorter maturities (*i.e.*, under 5 years) in total outstanding

---

10. Reserve Bank of India, *Annual Report, 1995–96.*

market loans, rose sharply from 7.4 per cent as at the end of March 1992 to 38.4 per cent at end-March 1996.

In its dual capacity as monetary authority and manager of public debt, the responsibility of the central bank became onerous and unenviable. The Reserve Bank posited that even though there were indications of a steady decline in the domestic debt-GDP ratio, there were nagging concerns regarding the high level of public debt and its long-term implications for fiscal stability, which continued to pose challenges for the fiscal system.[11] Looking ahead, the Reserve Bank tried to highlight certain critical issues, namely, the long-term macroeconomic consequences of public debt, the stability of the debt-GDP ratio, interest burden and monetisation of debt, viz.:[12]

> The long-term macroeconomic consequences of public debt depend on how quickly the volume of public debt grows in relation to the growth in nominal GDP, the extent of increase in private savings in absorbing the additional public debt, and the impact of public debt on monetary situation. The condition for the stability of the debt-GDP ratio implies that the real interest rate must be lower than the growth rate of output which ensures its convergence to a stable value in the long-run. However, the immediate concerns of a high level of debt-GDP ratio relate to its impact in the form of interest burden, the 'crowding out' of productive outlays, the higher proportion of private saving being absorbed by the Government, the pressures on the interest rate and the monetisation of debt.

Reserve Bank's Initial Support to Central Government Borrowings

Statement 15.3 titled: Reserve Bank of India's Initial Support to Borrowings of the Central Government throws up some interesting facts. The 91-day *ad hoc* Treasury Bills, which were issued exclusively in favour of the Reserve Bank and held by the latter as a proxy for financing the budget deficit, went into oblivion consequent to the phased elimination of monetisation of budget deficit (namely, the first supplemental agreement with the Government of India, dated September 9, 1994 and abolition of *ad hocs* from April 1, 1997 in terms of the second supplemental agreement

---

11. Reserve Bank of India, *Annual Report, 1996–97.*

12. Rangarajan, C. (1997). "Activating Debt Markets in India". *Reserve Bank of India Bulletin.* October.

dated March 26, 1997). The subscriptions to 91-day auction Treasury Bills and dated securities, unlike in the past, did not burden the Reserve Bank, because commercial banks had an appetite for these types of investments (despite large reductions in SLR) due to their security and liquidity features. Moreover, coupon rates came to be related to market trends. The net result was that banks invested in them by choice and not by compulsion.

WITHDRAWAL OF THE 91-DAY *AD HOC* TREASURY BILLS

An epochal event in the long-standing monetary-fiscal inter-relationship was the accord in September 1994 to delink the budget deficit from automatic and unlimited monetisation, thereby vesting the Reserve Bank with greater flexibility in monetary management. Historically, the net Reserve Bank credit to the Central Government had been the predominant factor that propelled primary liquidity expansion. For the Central Government, this development had far-reaching significance by strengthening fiscal discipline and transforming the method of financing the budget deficit.

The Reserve Bank accorded great importance to tackling the debilitating phenomenon of monetisation of fiscal deficit against the backdrop of inflationary pressures gaining strength from excess liquidity in the system. The Central Board of Directors of the Reserve Bank in their Annual Report for the year 1988–89 expressed serious concerns over the emerging situation and its impact on monetary management.

Further, in his Presidential Address at the Annual Conference of the Indian Economic Association held at Calcutta (now Kolkata) in December 1988, the Deputy Governor, Dr C. Rangarajan, articulated the views of the Reserve Bank as follows:

> The essence of co-ordination between fiscal policy and monetary policy lies in reaching an agreement on the extent of expansion in Reserve Bank credit to Government. This will set a limit on the extent of fiscal deficit and its monetization and thereby provide greater manoeuvrability to the monetary authorities to regulate the volume of money. It is in this context the introduction of a system of monetary targeting mutually agreed upon between the Government and central bank assumes significance.

On behalf of the Reserve Bank, the Governor, Shri R.N. Malhotra, pursued the issue with the Finance Minister, Prof Madhu Dandavate, in his letter dated December 18, 1989 and urged the Government to launch corrective measures. These initiatives during the 1980s (and even earlier) have been covered in the chapter titled Monetary-Fiscal Interface.

The Governor, Dr C. Rangarajan, in his letter dated December 27, 1993 to the Finance Secretary, (regarding the Reserve Bank's projections about the market borrowing programme for the financial year 1994–95), charted a strategy for phasing out *ad hoc* Treasury Bills, which ultimately formed the framework for the first supplemental agreement signed about nine months later.

The Reserve Bank postulated that a phased programme of reduction of SLR to an average of 25.0 per cent by 1995–96 would be 'meaningful' only if it was dovetailed into a programme to phase out the automatic monetisation of the budget deficit over a period. The proportion of auctioned Treasury Bills in the total increase in 91-day Treasury Bills (including the 91-day Treasury Bill conversion into a funded security) in 1993–94 up to December 17, 1993 was about 30.0 per cent; this proportion was to be increased to two-third in 1994–95, three-fourth in 1995–96 and from 1996–97 onwards the system of issue of *ad hoc* Treasury Bills was to be completely discontinued (as envisaged then). The Central Government would then be provided a WMA limit from the Reserve Bank to meet its temporary requirements, with the limit liquidated by the end of the financial year. The interest rate on this limit was to be linked to the Bank Rate, as in the case of state governments.

As part of its OMOs, the Reserve Bank would decide on the extent of government paper it wanted to hold. Once the figures of net RBI credit to the Centre and the budget deficit for the full financial year were incorporated in the budget document of the Central Government, net RBI credit to Central Government at any point of time in 1994–95 should not exceed more than twice the budgeted figure; beyond this level, the Central Government would not be provided additional accommodation from the Reserve Bank and it would have to raise additional resources from the market. To operationalise this for 1994–95, the peak permissible increase in net RBI credit to the Centre was envisaged at ₹ 10,000 crore (on the assumption that net RBI credit to the Centre and the budget deficit being set out in the BE was ₹ 5,000 crore). If net RBI credit to the Centre remained above ₹ 10,000 crore for 10 working days, no further increase in net RBI credit to the Centre was to be permitted and the Centre would immediately issue auctioned Treasury Bills or dated securities to set right the position. This scheme was also highlighted in the Reserve Bank's Annual Report for 1992–93.

AUTONOMY OF THE CENTRAL BANK AND FISCAL DISCIPLINE

Besides corresponding with the Government to phase out monetisation of budget deficit, the Reserve Bank expressed its views on strengthening fiscal discipline in public forums also. The Tenth M.G. Kutty Memorial Lecture delivered by the Governor, Dr C. Rangarajan, at Calcutta on September 17, 1993 was a seminal contribution to this topic. The gist of his speech as it relates to fiscal policy and monetary management is given in the following paragraphs.

On the independence of the central bank *vis-à-vis* funding of the Government by the Reserve Bank, the Governor at the outset stated that since in actual practice central banks could acquire government securities as part of their OMOs, there could not be a ban on the central bank acquiring government debt. While statutory limits on credit to the Government could be got around, quite clearly direct funding of the Government without limit by the central bank might come in the way of an efficient conduct of monetary policy. Nevertheless, the freedom of the central bank to pursue monetary policy according to its judgment required that direct funding of the Central Government be restricted and the limits made explicit.

In the past few years, there had been conscious attempts to contain fiscal deficit and budget deficit, which had strengthened the Reserve Bank's efforts to moderate M_3 growth. However, the system was far from perfect. The Governor pointed out: "So long as the practice of issue of *ad hoc* Treasury Bills continues, there is no immediate check on the expansion of RBI credit to Government." Even in the past few years, when year-end deficits had moderated, deficits 'within the year' had been large. The speech advocated the necessity to move away from the system of issue of *ad hoc* Treasury Bills and the consequent monetisation of the budget deficit. While the ultimate objective was for the Central Government to meet its needs from outside the Reserve Bank, it did not necessarily imply that the central bank would not hold any government paper. "It may and will," the Governor affirmed. As part of its OMOs, the Reserve Bank would decide on the extent of the government paper it wanted to hold. More importantly, with the shift away from automatic monetisation of deficit, monetary policy was expected to come into its own. The regulation of money and credit would be determined by the overall perception of the monetary authority on what the appropriate level of expansion of money and credit should be, which, in turn, was dependent on the behaviour of the macroeconomic fundamentals.

As the system of automatic monetisation of deficit got phased out and pre-emption of funds in the form of SLR came down, the Government would be obliged to place nearly all its borrowings in the market at market-determined rates and, in fact, this situation was being approached. Interest rates on government securities were then in the realm of 'substitutability' — the maximum rate on government securities was 13.5 per cent, while the weighted average lending rate of banks was around 15.0 per cent. The banks' choice of asset holdings would be increasingly determined not by statutory prescriptions, but by the 'risk-reward' perception on securities and bank lending. With market-determined rates, an active secondary market would develop and acquire depth, making it possible for the Reserve Bank to undertake OMOs effectively at its discretion.

In the concluding part of his speech, Dr Rangarajan emphasised that, in the Indian context, the first step should be to move away from a system in which the deficits incurred by the Central Government automatically got financed by the Reserve Bank through the issue of *ad hoc* Treasury Bills, which was distinct from the question of setting limits on government borrowing. To elaborate:

> In the context of increasing interest payments, as a proportion of revenue and the consequent preemption of resources for non-development expenditure, there exists a compelling need to see that the Government, either on its own or statutorily limits its borrowing. However, when the borrowing gets monetized, there is an additional impact on money supply growth with all the attendant consequences. Thus, the situation towards which we should move, if not today but at least within a year time frame, is where the central government should borrow whatever amount it wants from the market and not rely on direct credit from the Reserve Bank which is what the issue of *ad hoc* treasury bills does. Then, the onus of responsibility for conduct of monetary policy will be squarely on the shoulders of the Reserve Bank, where it should logically rest.

THE BUDGET ANNOUNCEMENT

The Finance Minister, in the course of presenting the Union Budget for 1994–95, announced in Parliament that there would be a limit on resort to the Reserve Bank for *ad hoc* Treasury Bills by the Central Government. This arrangement was formalised by an agreement between the Government of

India and the Reserve Bank, which was signed on September 9, 1994.[13] Consequently, automatic monetisation of the budget deficit through the issue of *ad hoc* Treasury Bills was to be phased out over three years and from 1997–98 this instrument was set to be abolished. The Union Budget placed a cap on the net issue of *ad hocs* during the course of fiscal year 1994–95, namely, while the net issue of *ad hocs* in 1994–95 should not normally exceed the estimated budget deficit of ₹ 6,000 crore for the year as a whole, at any point of time during the year the *ad hocs* were not to exceed ₹ 9,000 crore for more than 10 continuous working days. If this limit was breached, the Reserve Bank was authorised to sell fresh government paper to bring down the level of *ad hocs* to the stipulated within-the-year ceiling. After three years (*i.e.*, from April 1, 1997) when recourse to *ad hocs* was to be completely phased out, the Central Government would cease to avail of direct credit from the Reserve Bank for financing the deficit, and meet its entire financing needs through borrowings from the market. For each of the two succeeding years when the agreement was in force, the two ceilings underwent revisions with the mutual consent of both the parties.

The Reserve Bank in its Annual Report for 1994–95 termed this a 'landmark development'; the Government's decision to move to market-related rates of interest and to curb the monetisation of budget deficit by limiting the access to *ad hoc* Treasury Bills was intended to impart an element of financial discipline, and delinking the fiscal deficit from automatic monetisation was essential if the impact of monetary policy was not to be whittled down. However, the Economic Survey for the year 1994–95 was more effusive. It stated that the decisions taken during the year resulted in the link between the fiscal deficit and monetary growth through the budget deficit would be completely broken in the next two years, and that this would make monetary policy independent of the Government and thus devolve much greater responsibility on the Reserve Bank. Further, the interaction between the finance ministry and the central bank would focus on the target growth of M_3 to balance the twin objectives of inflation control and output growth, as was the practice in developed countries.

---

13. The first supplemental agreement dated September 9, 1994 and the second supplemental agreement dated March 26, 1997 have been reproduced in the 'Documents' section of this history volume.

PHASING OUT *AD HOCS* IN THE PERIOD OF TRANSITION

During the base year 1994–95, within-the-year ceiling under the framework of the supplemental agreement of September 1994 was adhered to and at the end of the year recourse to *ad hoc* Treasury Bills (outstanding) was a modest ₹ 1,750 crore (Table 15.2). The Government's financial position in 1995–96 experienced considerable strain. The within-the-year limit of ₹ 9,000 crore for net issue of *ad hoc* Treasury Bills was exceeded on three occasions for extended periods and the end-of-the-year ceiling was breached to a small extent. At the end of fiscal year 1996–97, the net issue of *ad hoc* Treasury Bills could be contained well within the agreed limits, but the position was different for within-the-year performance. The net issue of *ad hoc* Treasury Bills was high during the first two quarters of the year, but declined rapidly in the third and fourth quarters, largely because of a shift to tap Treasury Bills for financing the budgetary gap. This figure

TABLE 15.2

Net Issues of Ad hoc Treasury Bills
Annual Ceilings Agreed upon for 1994–95, 1995–96 and 1996–97@

Fiscal Year	Within-the-year	End-of-the-year (end-March)
1994–95	(i) Ceiling: ₹ 9,000 crore (BE)	(i) Ceiling: ₹ 6,000 crore (BE)
	(ii) Actual: Within the ceiling (Full-year fortnightly average decline was ₹ 3,249 crore)#	(ii) Actual: ₹ 1,750 crore
1995–96	(i) Ceiling: ₹ 9,000 crore (BE)	(i) Ceiling: ₹ 5,000 crore (BE)
	(ii) Actual: Exceeded the ceiling for extended period on three occasions (Full-year fortnightly average increase was ₹ 10,280 crore)#	(ii) Actual: ₹ 5,965 crore
1996–97	(i) Ceiling: ₹ 9,000 crore (BE)	(i) Ceiling: ₹ 5,000 crore (BE)
	(ii) Actual: Exceeded the ceiling for an extended period during the first half of the financial year (Full-year fortnightly average increase was ₹ 7,612 crore)#	(ii) Actual: ₹ 4,685 crore

Notes: @: as per RBI records.

BE: Budget Estimate.

#: The average of all fortnightly reporting Friday figures for net issue of *ad hoc* Treasury Bills and the end-March figures after the closure of government accounts.

Source: Reserve Bank of India, *Annual Report*, various issues.

even turned negative on a few occasions in the second half of the year; this was the outcome of an improvement in the absorptive capacity of institutions other than the Reserve Bank for the 91-day Treasury Bills, which was facilitated by substantial cuts in CRR during the year.

WITHDRAWAL OF *AD HOC* TREASURY BILLS AND INTRODUCTION OF WAYS AND MEANS ADVANCES

The Finance Minister's budget speech for 1996–97 in Parliament on July 22, 1996 evaluated that the experience so far to phase out the system of *ad hoc* Treasury Bills by 1997–98 had shown the difficulty of staying below the within-the-year limit. Nevertheless, the Government was not deterred from its resolve to phase out the system of *ad hoc* Treasury Bills:

> However, before this could happen, we need to put in place a better expenditure control mechanism. We also need a more transparent method of defining and reporting the true budget deficit, including all forms of monetization. I shall present concrete proposals in this regard at the time of presentation of next year's budget so that the RBI can have greater autonomy in formulating and implementing monetary policy.

Accordingly, in July 1996 the Government requested the Reserve Bank to prepare concrete proposals setting out the modalities to phase out *ad hoc* Treasury Bills from 1997–98. In response, the Reserve Bank forwarded a self-contained note setting out proposals for phasing out *ad hoc* Treasury Bills from April 1, 1997 and also recommended a transparent method of defining and reporting the budget deficit and the monetised deficit. The scheme provided for granting WMA to the Government to meet its temporary mismatches between receipts and payments. The Reserve Bank also took the opportunity to convey its views on a number of related policy issues, namely:

(i)   From the point of view of credible fiscal operations on a day-to-day basis and of having a mechanism to take care of the problem of lags in receipts, especially in the face of leads in expenditure, the Government would need to borrow from the central bank for temporary periods under transparent terms and conditions.

(ii) A system of providing WMA to the Government of India under section 17(5) of the RBI Act, 1934, could be considered as a possible means of accommodating temporary mismatches in government receipts and payments from April 1, 1997 onwards after the practice of issuing *ad hoc* Treasury Bills was discontinued. In this regard, it would be useful to draw appropriately from the experience of the system of WMA to the state governments which had been in vogue since 1937.

(iii) The underlying principle of the WMA arrangement was that it should not become a supplementary source for the Government to finance its budgetary deficits, but would cover only day-to-day mismatches in receipts and disbursements of the Government. There would, therefore, be no WMA in an *ex ante* sense and it could not be a part of the capital receipts or of financing GFD. The temporary accommodation to be viewed as credible by the public should be subject to certain limits.

(iv) It was possible that temporary cash surpluses might accrue in government accounts on some occasions after vacating WMA. When the cash surpluses went consistently beyond, say, ₹ 100 crore, they could be utilised for premature repayment of maturing 91-day auction Treasury Bills held by the Reserve Bank.

After detailed discussions between the officials of the Reserve Bank and the Ministry of Finance, the second supplemental agreement was signed on March 26, 1997. In terms of the agreement, the practice of issuing *ad hoc* Treasury Bills to replenish the cash balances of the Central Government to the agreed minimum level was discontinued from April 1, 1997. The outstanding *ad hoc* Treasury Bills as on March 31, 1997 were funded into special securities without any specific maturity, at an interest rate of 4.6 per cent per annum, on April 1, 1997. The outstanding tap Treasury Bills at the end of March 1997 were paid off on maturity with an equivalent creation of special securities without any specific maturity, at an interest rate of 4.6 per cent per annum.

From April 1, 1997 the Reserve Bank extended WMA to the Central Government at rates of interest that were mutually agreed upon from time to time and up to the agreed maximum limit. The advances were to be fully paid off within a period not exceeding three months from the date of making such an advance. Interest was calculated on daily balances and debited to the government account with the Reserve Bank at such intervals. In the event of the Government's account at the close of business on any working day emerging and remaining overdrawn beyond the agreed limit for WMA, the Reserve Bank could charge interest on the daily balances overdrawn at rates mutually agreed upon from time to time.[14] As and when the WMA was drawn upon to the extent of 75.0 per cent, the Reserve Bank would automatically trigger flotations of government securities. On the other hand, if the Government happened to run surplus cash balances beyond the agreed level, the Reserve Bank would make investments as mutually agreed upon.

Thus, the Union Budget for 1997–98 formalised the 'dismantling' of the system of *ad hoc* Treasury Bills as announced in the 1994–95 budget. The Reserve Bank expressed the hope (in its Annual Report for 1996–97) that the new system of accommodating temporary mismatches in cash flows of the Central Government by WMA, apart from encouraging fiscal discipline, would contribute to strengthening fiscal and monetary policy co-ordination in several directions. First, the new arrangement would prevent unplanned creation of money through 'unbridled' expansion of *ad hoc* Treasury Bills and improve the degree of monetary control in the economy. The explicit and exhaustive nature of the WMA limit during the year would put in place an effective ceiling on the automatic monetisation of the fiscal deficit and create a favourable macroeconomic environment for setting a 'monetary target'. Second, since the elimination of *ad hoc* Treasury Bills would mean a certain degree of compositional shift in the funding of the fiscal deficit towards market borrowing, it would in due course reflect the true level of the Government's credit requirement from the market and strengthen the interest rate mechanism. Third, the new system would improve the credibility of macroeconomic policies and dampen the adverse inflationary expectations that arose from the uncertainty inherent in the automatic monetisation of the fiscal deficit. The attainment of this objective, however, required a concomitant discretionary fiscal policy in place that aimed at long-run sustainability of public debt and deficit.

The Reserve Bank also conceptualised certain long-term advantages to flow from this new set up. From the operational point of view, the WMA would necessitate improvement in cash management by the Central Government as well as debt management by the Reserve Bank, so as to keep the cash deficit within the WMA limits for the year. The monthly pattern of the flow of receipts and expenditures of the Central Government over the past three years (April 1994 to March 1997) indicated that, on average, during the first quarter and the fourth quarter, the cash flow mismatches

---

14. However, the Reserve Bank, in its note (September 1996) outlining the modalities of phasing out *ad hoc* Treasury Bills had suggested that while the WMA would be provided at the Bank Rate, overdrafts would be charged at the Bank Rate plus 2.0 percentage points.

tended to be larger than in the other quarters of the fiscal year. Moreover, there was a high concentration or bulge in both receipts and expenditures in the last month of the financial year. This skewed distribution of monthly flows in receipts and expenditures was particularly glaring in the revenue account. Although the volatility in monthly cash flow of aggregate receipts and expenditures had declined sharply in the recent past, this process would have to be carried substantially further through improved efficiency in cash management. This would be of utmost importance during the next few years — the period of 'transition' as per the arrangement — so as to switch over fully to the new system in a smooth manner and to avoid the problems of overdrawing of accounts with the Reserve Bank. The Economic Survey for 1997–98 observed that the discontinuation of the system of *ad hoc* Treasury Bills as a means of financing the budget deficit was a significant step that would further strengthen fiscal discipline, while affording greater autonomy to the Reserve Bank in its conduct of monetary policy.

INTERNAL DEBT MANAGEMENT:
POLICY AND OPERATIONS

Management of domestic debt forms an integral and dynamic part of monetary macroeconomic management. The need for an active internal debt management policy in India came into prominence in the wake of the fiscal consolidation process launched in 1991–92. Over the period beginning in the early 1990s, the Reserve Bank fine-tuned the policy framework and operating procedures of debt management.

Whereas the size of market borrowings was determined by fiscal policy, the composition of public debt was determined by debt management operations conducted by the Reserve Bank. The latter denoted the timing, instruments of borrowing, method of issue, maturity pattern of a specific loan and coupon rates. A large part of the Centre's borrowing programme had perforce to be completed in the first half of the financial year, given the seasonality of demand for credit on private account. The skill of debt management was to insulate, to the extent possible, internal debt from the short-term effects of monetary policy, as also to optimise the maturity and cost of government borrowing from the market. It is also true that much depended on the perception of the future course of interest rates.

The Government's borrowing programme was budgeted each year and appeared on the receipts side of the Union Budget. The net investible resources was estimated largely on the basis of surplus funds likely to be available with the banking system (allowing for SLR prescriptions), insurance corporations owned by the Government and provident funds (PFs). While deciding to float a loan, the Reserve Bank took into account the cash needs of the Government, liquidity conditions in the economy, market preference for maturity *vis-à-vis* the repayment schedule of the Government, maturing loans during the year, expectations of the market and the primary and secondary yield curves. There was also an element of judgment by the Reserve Bank in this process. If the system was flush with liquidity and prevailing interest rates were low, it was advisable to float a long-term loan. In conditions of tighter liquidity, while deciding on the maturity, the leeway available to the Reserve Bank was to accept a possible devolvement, which depended on the monetary situation, became an important consideration. On some occasions, *e.g.,* the estimated net RBI credit to the Central Government being well within the acceptable/ agreed limits, the Reserve Bank took up a private placement instead of going to the market, especially if it did not want to disrupt the yield curve. A private placement could also be used to beef up the stock of securities for OMOs. Thus, a variety of considerations went into making the borrowing programme successful and transparent. The Reserve Bank attempted to complete the borrowing programme for each year with the objective of ensuring a smooth flow of funds to each of the floatations, while pursuing its interest rate objectives and without jeopardising the external balance.

The Reserve Bank was also responsible for the smooth conduct of overall borrowing programme of the state governments. Generally, state loans were for a single issue and the longest maturity of the central government security issued during that particular year. The coupon rate was also pre-determined. The conduct of the borrowing programme posed several problems, such as the prevalence of large inter-state economic disparities, meeting the preferences indicated by state governments and the unwillingness of banks and other institutional investors to subscribe to state loans in a liberalised environment, unless compelled to do so. While several reforms in debt management policy were introduced in the 1990s in respect of sale of central government securities, the sale of state government loans continued to be on the old pattern and procedures, at least until 1996–97.

ENVIRONMENT PRIOR TO 1991–92

The government bond market before the 1990s was characterised by administered interest rates, high reserve requirements that led to the presence of captive investors and the absence of a liquid and transparent secondary market for government securities. During the 1980s, the volume of government debt expanded considerably — particularly the short-term debt — due to the automatic and unlimited accommodation that the Reserve Bank was compelled to provide to the Central Government under a long-standing arrangement. The mechanism was through the issue of *ad hoc* Treasury Bills of 91 day duration on behalf of the Central Government. With a captive investor base and low interest rates, the secondary market for government securities remained dormant. The artificial yield on government securities was kept below the market yields, which had an overwhelming impact on the entire structure of financial assets in the system. The distorted yield structure of the financial assets led to an overall high interest rate environment in the rest of the market. Driven by these compulsions, the Reserve Bank's monetary management was distinguished by a regime of administered interest rates, rising CRR and SLR prescriptions, which left little room for monetary manoeuvring.[15] As a corollary, direct instruments of control proved ineffective and there was little scope for deployment of market-based tools like OMOs and Bank Rate.

The Reserve Bank had little operational control over some of the essential facets of debt management. These included the volume and maturity structure of securities to be marketed and the term structure of interest rates or the yield curve, which were not market-related. The maturity structure of market loans remained highly skewed towards the longer term of more than 15 years. The situation was aptly summed up by Dr C. Rangarajan: "Monetary and internal debt management policy in India was undermined by excessive monetization of Central Government fiscal deficit by the central bank."[16]

Early Reform Initiatives

The Reserve Bank had taken quite a few important policy measures even before the reform period. The maximum coupon rate on central

---

15. Mohan, Rakesh (2006). "Recent Trends in the Indian Debt Market and Current Initiatives," Based on the lectures at the *Fourth India Debt Market Conference* (organised by Citi Group and Fitch Rating India, on January 31, 2006) and at the *Annual Conference of FIMMDA* (jointly organised by the Fixed Income Money Market Dealers' Association of India and Primary Dealers' Association of India), March 14, Mumbai.

16. Rangarajan, C. (1994). "Developing the Money and Securities Markets in India". Paper presented at the *Sixth Seminar on Central Banking*. International Monetary Fund. Washington, D.C., March 9.

government loans, which was as low as 6.5 per cent in 1977–78, was raised in stages to 11.5 per cent by 1985–86 and the maximum maturity period was reduced from 30 years to 20 years. The coupon rates for 5-year and 10-year loans were stepped up in 1986–87 by one percentage point each to 10.0 per cent and 10.5 per cent, respectively. In November 1986, 182-day Treasury Bills were introduced as a new instrument to serve as an alternative avenue for short-term investment, thereby aiding the development of a secondary market. These bills were sold in competitive auctions held monthly up to June 1988, and fortnightly from July 1988 until April 1992, when they were replaced by 364-day Treasury Bills.

Acting swiftly on the report of the Chakravarty Committee,[17] the Reserve Bank initiated steps to evolve a market-clearing interest rate mechanism for sale of government dated securities. The objective was that the Government should increasingly finance its borrowing needs from the open market and thereby reduce the extent of debt monetisation. Measures were introduced to restructure the maturity pattern and also telescope the interest rate structure on government debt instruments. With a view to develop Treasury Bills as an active monetary instrument, the Reserve Bank revised upwards the yield on these bills, and this led to institutional investors, banks as also other corporate bodies, local government agencies, trusts and individuals, constituting a sizeable market for Treasury Bills and dated securities. In the process, the Reserve Bank's holdings of these instruments would be lowered to a substantial extent, resulting in a corresponding reduction in the Reserve Bank's credit to the Government and hence, in reserve money. In the long run, this was expected to give a fillip to the development of money and capital markets and improve the overall efficiency of the financial system.

The Discount and Finance House of India Ltd (DFHI) was set up by the Reserve Bank as a money market institution. It initially aimed at affording liquidity to 182-day Treasury Bills and short-term commercial bills, which imparted greater flexibility to banks in their fund management operations. To perform its functions effectively, DFHI was provided with refinance from the Reserve Bank. By varying the quantum and the rate of interest on refinance to the DFHI, the Reserve Bank was able to transmit signals to the short-term money market.

The Narasimham Committee had recommended that interest rates on government borrowing should progressively be made market-related

---

17. Refer to Appendix 4.1 for details.

in order to facilitate the reduction in SLR. Over the years, a regime of moderation of the GFD and an active internal debt management policy assisted in the integration of debt management policy with monetary policy.

EVOLUTION OF POLICY

The Reserve Bank recognised as early as in 1992 that the development of a vibrant, deep and broad government securities market should be an essential piece of financial sector reforms for various reasons. First, in order to conduct sizeable OMOs without undue adjustment to interest rates, sufficient market depth was necessary. Second, a broad and deep market to absorb new issues of government securities without residual reliance on the Reserve Bank facilitated macroeconomic stabilisation. Third, an efficient securities market, which established a market-based curve, could act as a benchmark for other rates of return and thereby transmitted quickly the monetary policy impulses to the rest of the economy. Fourth, a well-developed government securities market would be supportive of exchange rate policy. Fifth, a liquid secondary market reduced the cost to the Government of raising long-term debt and elongated the term maturity of outstanding debt.[18] To sum up, the healthy development of the market for government securities not only strengthened monetary policy, but also helped fiscal policy and developed financial markets in general.

For the first time, in 1991–92 the Reserve Bank declared its intention to activate the internal debt management strategy. The letter from the Governor, Shri S. Venkitaramanan, dated January 2, 1992 to the finance ministry (in regard to the market borrowing programme and monetary projections for 1991–92), *inter alia*, enunciated, "As part of the development of the financial system, it would be necessary to activate internal debt management policy, reduce the pre-empted resources under the SLR, move towards marked related rates for government securities and develop a secondary market in securities." This letter also contained far-reaching suggestions for reducing SLR, increasing the coupon rates on government dated securities, developing an active secondary market in dated securities, dispensing with the interest rate cap on 182-day Treasury Bills, introducing Treasury Bills with a maturity of 273 days and 364 days on auction basis

---

18. Note on *Issues in Developing the Government Securities Market and Open Market Operations in Support of Financial Sector Reforms*, prepared by the IMF Advisory Mission to Study the Government Securities Market in India, headed by Mr Sergio Pereira Leite. July 1992. Annex II to this chapter gives the main recommendations of the Leite Report.

and enhancing the discount rate on 91-day Treasury Bills. The monetary policy announcement in April 1992 (circular to commercial banks dated April 21, 1992) marked a new approach to internal debt management by introducing market-orientation with regard to absorption of Government of India (GoI) rupee dated securities and longer-term Treasury Bills. In furtherance of developing dated government securities as a monetary instrument with flexible yields to suit investor expectations, the Central Government started to sell these securities of different maturities through auction from June 3, 1992. Earlier, auctions for sale of Treasury Bills of 364-day duration were introduced in April 1992. With the proposed reduction in the effective incremental reserve requirement from 63.5 per cent to 45.0 per cent, the Reserve Bank re-organised the gilt-edged market. Keeping this in view, a number of innovations were introduced to move towards a market-related internal debt management policy.

The Reserve Bank in its Annual Report for 1991–92 articulated that with a view to promoting an active market for government securities, the gilt-edged market was being re-organised in such a way that the Government reduced its dependence on credit from the Reserve Bank and the banks. The Reserve Bank was adopting an internal debt management policy that would serve as a tool of monetary control with flexibility in interest rates, introduction of new instruments and liquidity expansion/ contraction through OMOs. In another context, the report expressed the view that the move towards market-related interest rates on government dated securities and Treasury Bills was a prerequisite for successful reform of the financial system as also the pursuit of an effective monetary policy.

Additional measures were taken in October 1992 to develop the government securities market and, in the process, alleviate to some extent the problems that arose from a dormant secondary market. A new refinance arrangement, called the government securities refinance facility, was introduced from October 31, 1992 at a rate of interest of 14.0 per cent, repos auctions in central government securities commenced with a view to even out the liquidity within the fortnightly make-up period and IDMC was set up (in the Reserve Bank) as a policymaking unit from April 1, 1992.

In fact, serious discussions had been in progress much earlier between the monetary and fiscal authorities for evolving an active internal debt management policy, and the Reserve Bank was eager to start active internal debt operations in the April–June 1992 quarter as evidenced by its letter dated April 20, 1992 to the Finance Secretary. The Reserve Bank in the letter urged the ministry to take early decisions on four issues, namely: (i) removal of the discount rate cap of 11.5 per cent on 182-day Treasury Bills as well as on 273-day and 364-day Treasury Bills (proposed to be issued shortly on auction basis) and leave the choice of maturity at each auction to the Reserve Bank, depending on its perceptions of the conditions in the short-term money market; (ii) the existing 91-day Treasury Bills auctions not to be subject to an interest rate cap; (iii) periodic funding of these bills into dated securities; and (iv) auctioning of the 5-year dated securities without an interest rate cap but with a reserve price and Reserve Bank intervention. A year later, the Reserve Bank reaffirmed its commitment to activating the internal debt management system in its letter to the Government dated January 7, 1993 (relating to projections for the market borrowing programme for 1993–94) thus:

> During 1992–93, a number of measures have been taken to evolve an active debt management policy and the measures include the introduction of 364-day Treasury Bills on an auction basis, auction of Central Government dated securities, Repos auctions, the recently announced auction of 91-day Treasury Bills and the raising of the maximum interest rate on Government dated securities. We admittedly have a considerable amount to traverse before open market operations become the principal instrument of Reserve Bank's intervention. Hence, we need to reinforce the measures taken in 1992–93 by further measures in 1993–94 and in particular, we need to give attention to the institutional structure necessary for developing the secondary market in securities.

The Annual Report of the Reserve Bank for 1992–93 (as also the report for the following year 1993–94) devoted a separate section to Internal Debt Operations in its thematic chapter on Monetary and Price Trends, which signified its growing importance in monetary policymaking. The report for 1993–94 averred that internal debt management assumed added importance in the face of the large monetary expansion engendered by capital inflows and the consequent inflationary pressures, and that in the context of easy liquidity conditions in the economy it was possible to contain the cost of government borrowing despite the borrowing requirement being high.

OVERVIEW OF DEBT MANAGEMENT POLICIES AND PROCEDURES

As far back as January 1991, the Reserve Bank gave serious thought to developing an active market for government securities by re-organising the gilt-edged market in such a way that the Government reduced its dependence on credit from the Reserve Bank and banks. With this objective, the Reserve Bank suggested to the Government in January 1991 and January 1992 to introduce various internal debt management measures. However, it was only after April 1992 that these measures could be initiated, after obtaining the concurrence of the Government.[19]

In furtherance of the financial sector reforms, the most important initiatives taken by the Government and the Reserve Bank were: resort to market-related government borrowing; a shift from direct to indirect tools of monetary regulation, most notably activating OMOs; innovations in money market and government securities market instruments; development of secondary market in government securities; and phased elimination of automatic monetisation of central government budget deficits. The principal objectives were to smoothen the maturity structure of debt, enable debt to be raised at close to market rates and improve the liquidity of government securities by developing an active secondary market. Shri S.S. Tarapore, Deputy Governor, who at that time was entrusted with the responsibility of re-orienting internal debt management, observed: "When the definitive history of the post-July 1991 economic reform process is written up, the activisation of internal debt management policy will perhaps stand out as the single most important element in the reform process."[20]

While the various policy measures taken during the period from 1991–92 to 1996–97 in different segments, such as the government securities market, coupon rates on government dated securities and Treasury Bills, have been described elsewhere, the gist of policy formulation during this period, both by the Reserve Bank and the Central Government, is given below.

In 1992–93, the second year of reform, the main features of the re-oriented debt management were, to reduce the statutory pre-emption of the resources of commercial banks to achieve a more efficient use of their resources on one hand and to make government dated securities attractive to investors (other than those in the captive category) on the other. This

---

19. A detailed account of the developments may be found in the article, "A Review of Internal Management Policy and Operations for the Period ended March 1995", *Reserve Bank of India Bulletin*, November 1996.

20. Tarapore, S.S. (1994). *The Role of an Active Debt Management Policy in the Economic Reform Process.* Speech delivered at the Department of Economics, Mangalore University. Mangalore. September 19.

objective was to be achieved by issue of securities at market-related rates, primarily through a system of auctions (introduced on June 3, 1992). The 364-day Treasury Bill auction started from April 28, 1992. Since these auctions were conducted every fortnight, it was expected that at any point in time the market would have bills of varied maturities up to 364 days. Therefore, auctions of 182-day Treasury Bills (issued on a limited scale since November, 1986) were discontinued.

From January 8, 1993, 91-day Treasury Bill auctions commenced. Moreover, interest rates were allowed to respond to the market situation within an overall ceiling. For the first time, in 1992–93, the Central Government raised its entire gross market borrowing of ₹ 4,821 crore through the auction system. While the Reserve Bank initially subscribed ₹ 2,214 crore, the bulk of these securities were later sold in the market. Following the introduction of an auction system, coupon rates for central government loans emerged through cut-off yields at which competitive bids were accepted in auctions. The Reserve Bank conducted periodic auctions of repurchase agreements (repos) for central government dated securities to even out short-term liquidity in the banking system within the fortnightly make-up period. This was another step towards activating OMOs. The first auction was held on December 10, 1992. Initially, the repo auctions were for very short periods of one or two days. The cut-off repo rate generally tended to move in tandem with other short-term rates and also took into account the 91-day Treasury Bill rate. After an initial period of experimentation, the repo period stabilised at 14 days from August 1993, consistent with the reserve make-up period for banks. The Reserve Bank envisioned a multi-pronged role for an active debt management policy in its Annual Report for 1992–93 as follows:

> ...it is here [attempt to reduce the use of instruments of direct monetary control and to give greater attention to the development of indirect instruments of monetary control over the money and securities markets] that there is a need to co-ordinate monetary and internal public debt management policies so that the two segments are mutually supportive. The Government securities operations are a key element in the evolution of a well-developed system of monetary control. For open market operations to be really effective, it is necessary to have an active secondary market for Government securities. If such a secondary market is to develop, it is essential that there should be investors other than

captive investors. It is only when non-captive investors become predominant that the secondary market can develop depth and it is only under these conditions that it is possible to develop a system of primary dealers who would underwrite the entire issue at the auctions and thereafter access these securities to final investors. An important feature of a well developed securities market is that the Reserve Bank should not take up any part of a primary issue of a Government security but it should buy and sell securities as part of its open market operations, depending on its assessment of the liquidity of the system. An active secondary market in securities requires that there must be institutions dedicated to foster the secondary market.

The Government placed its market borrowing through auctions during 1993–94, and funding was undertaken to lengthen the maturity pattern of rapid accumulation of short-term debt by way of Treasury Bills. SLR on incremental deposits was fixed at 25.0 per cent from September 17, 1993. Interest rates on government dated securities over the period were lowered from a maximum of 15.0 per cent to 13.0 per cent and the maximum maturity was shortened from 20 years to 15 years. The Government floated in January 1994 zero coupon bonds of 5-year maturity on auction basis for the first time to test the market for such an instrument. One salient aspect of debt management in 1994–95 was the emphasis on development of an institutional infrastructure for a secondary market in government securities. The Reserve Bank issued guidelines for enlisting PDs in the government securities market on March 29, 1995. In order to develop a vibrant secondary market in government securities, the Securities Trading Corporation of India Ltd (STCI) was set up and it commenced operations on June 27, 1994. Its objective was to make available improved liquidity to government paper and to stimulate market-making activity by other parties. To provide greater transparency as also information on secondary market transactions in government securities and Treasury Bills, the data on daily transactions in subsidiary general ledger (SGL) accounts reported at the Public Debt Office (PDO) and the Public Accounts Department (PAD) at Mumbai were released regularly from September 1, 1994.

A system of delivery *versus* payment (D*v*P) was started in Mumbai from July 17, 1995 for transactions in government securities to reduce counter-party risk and the risk of diversion of funds through securities transactions. The system operated through the SGL accounts maintained with the PDO of the Reserve Bank. A new line of reverse repo facility was opened up for the DFHI and the STCI by way of liquidity support. The mechanism of reverse repos enabled the Reserve Bank to indirectly intervene in the market to correct undue upward pressure on call money rates. In its credit policy circular dated April 17, 1995 the Reserve Bank enunciated that while the link between monetary policy and budget deficit had 'weakened' due to the historic accord between the Government and the Reserve Bank limiting the Government's unilateral access to borrowing through *ad hoc* Treasury Bills, there were several aspects that had a bearing on controlling the overall growth of money and credit. It added that the continuance of large fiscal deficits necessitated the Government's large recourse to market borrowing and this posed a problem for monetary management, as under such circumstances it became difficult to undertake OMOs to the desired extent without pushing up interest rates to unduly high levels.

Following the move towards market-related rates of interest for central government securities, there was a shift not only in composition but also the maturity pattern of the Centre's debt from the long end of the market to the short end. The large market borrowing had the potential to keep nominal interest rates at a level that would result in very high real rates of interest due to the distinctly lower inflation rate. In 1995–96, the Reserve Bank absorbed a sizeable proportion of the new issues, which prevented a further rise in interest rates although this resulted in primary liquidity creation. The mounting interest obligations budgeted at ₹ 60,000 crore for 1996–97 (₹ 52,000 crore in 1995–96) and the accumulation in government debt pointed to emergence of debt management problems, which were aggravated by marked shortening of the maturity structure of fresh issues of government securities together with generally high interest rates being paid on government paper. The Reserve Bank expressed the view that large and persistent deficits would militate against the objective of pursuing growth along with non-accelerating inflation.[21] The new arrangement of WMA to the Central Government in force from April 1, 1997 — in lieu of the accommodation by issue of *ad hoc* Treasury Bills — was expected to improve debt management practices by the Reserve Bank. In 1996–97, the Reserve Bank continued to be concerned that the growing size of debt had led to bunching of repayments, besides increasing concentration of borrowings at the shorter end of the maturity spectrum.

---

21. Reserve Bank of India, *Annual Report, 1995–96*.

INTRODUCTION OF AUCTIONS: A CHEQUERED PATH

The introduction of the auction method for issuing government dated securities, including Treasury Bills, was by far the single key innovation in active debt management policy pursued since the early 1990s. The essence of auctioning was to ensure that the price discovery of government securities was competitive and market-based. This was not an easy task because within the Reserve Bank and also outside among the major participants, such as commercial banks, insurance companies and PFs, it meant embarking into an entirely new realm. Further, the non-market practices and methods in vogue could not be dispensed with by following a 'big bang' approach, as this would have caused serious dislocation. The early period of public debt management reform until about 1997 was, therefore, characterised by non-market practices receding and the market-based methods getting entrenched, but in a slow and a gradual manner. As a result, the market had to be nurtured in the initial period with detailed meetings with treasury managers before practically every auction to explain the procedures, method of bidding and the likely range in which the bids could be expected to fall, depending on past trends and liquidity conditions. By around 1996, the system got established and market participants became comfortable with the procedures evolved by the Reserve Bank. Several institutional reforms, including the modernisation in settlement practices, helped this process.

EARLY IMPEDIMENTS

Any new system faces teething troubles, and the introduction of the auction method was no exception. A few major impediments, which the Reserve Bank had to overcome, are illustrated here.

One major impediment in using the auction process was the prevalence of issue of *ad hoc* Treasury Bills of 91-day maturity at a fixed and below-market discount rate of 4.6 per cent. Added to this was the regular issue of 91-day tap Treasury Bills, available on tap from the Reserve Bank with unlimited rediscount facility. Market participants could acquire these bills at will and rediscount them with the Reserve Bank as and when needed. At any point of time, banks and state governments with cash surpluses were the major holders of tap Treasury Bills. In this environment, the Government not only got used to making a substantial part of their borrowing through this 'cheap' instrument, but also did not bestow any thought on efficient handling of its cash management. The monetisation through these bills, therefore, tended to remain high.

Second, thanks to the Reserve Bank's open window for 91-day Treasury Bills, the Central Government showed a lack of interest even in raising the fixed coupon rates of loan flotations.[22] In fact, due to this legacy, the Government in the initial stages of auctioning dated securities and Treasury Bills was indicating the yield or specifying a ceiling on yield that was to be fixed in an auction. Though this contravened the fundamental principle of fixation of yield on a competitive basis in an auction, the Bank was able to take this in its stride, since it was a passive participant in having to take up any unsubscribed portion of notified issuance amounts in auctions. This was gradually overcome by progressively avoiding devolvement on its own account and encouraging participants to bid, using moral suasion as needed and evolving the procedure of under-writing by the PDs by 1996.

Third, the weak knowledge base of market participants had to be tackled by practically educating treasury managers of banks and others in the auction method and procedures. It needs to be mentioned that there were instances of wrong bidding that, to maintain the integrity of auctions, had to be accepted by the Reserve Bank's auction committee, occasionally resulting in substantial loss to certain participants. This, nevertheless, did not come in the way of the auction system taking deeper roots over time.

Fourth, while the elimination of *ad hoc* Treasury Bills and tap Treasury Bills had to wait until early 1997, the Reserve Bank had to manoeuvre strategically around the prevailing distorted system. The auction system initially started with the introduction of 182-day Treasury Bills in 1986, following the recommendations of the Chakravarty Committee and as part of the efforts to develop new money market instruments. The Government advised that the ceiling rates be fixed in these auctions. Despite the setting-up of the DFHI in 1988, both primary and secondary market volumes in 182-day Treasury Bills remained subdued. With the launch of financial sector reforms and activation of debt management beginning in April 1992, efforts were made to develop Treasury Bills of longer and varied maturities. The auctioning of 364-day Treasury Bills was introduced in April 1992, which became instantly popular with market participants. The auction mechanism was extended to repo auctions (introduced in December 1992), with the main objective of absorbing excess liquidity from the system and steering the net RBI credit to the Government target under the IMF loan programme in effect at that time.

---

22. Refer chapter 3: Monetary-Fiscal Interface.

An early step away from the system of *ad hoc* Treasury Bills was to introduce auction sales of 91-day Treasury Bills. This initially met with resistance, because of the low interest rate on *ad hoc* and tap Treasury Bills and the likely higher yield on auction bills. The Governor, Shri S. Venkitaramanan, ultimately succeeded in introducing 91-day Treasury Bill auctions by convincing the Government that the cost on account of interest rate differential would be compensated through transfer of profits from the Reserve Bank.

Fifth, beginning in 1993, the auction method was extended to the sale of dated government securities. But in the early stages, with a view to building a market and making the securities attractive, the maturities were kept below 10 years, which also took into account that the state governments continued to borrow at 10-year maturity and the coupon rate was to be fixed for state flotations. State government securities were treated on par with those of Central Government and the Reserve Bank was not inclined to make any discrimination on state securities' yields as an SLR instrument. Thus, in the first stage in each financial year, the Reserve Bank fixed the coupon rates of state government securities for 10-year maturity administratively. At the lower end, 364-day Treasury Bills offered the auction-based yield for one-year maturity. The dated securities of the Central Government were issued in the range of 2 years and 9 years, and gradually the primary market yields provided some kind of a market-based yield curve. During the year, the yield structure was actually influenced by the Reserve Bank through moral suasion and the bidding process to offer the yield of a security along the primary market benchmark already set through previous auctions.

Sixth, as a result of shortening of the debt maturity, redemption turned out to be a problem in the middle of the 1990s, with maturities bunching in the case of shorter maturities including 364-day Treasury Bills. This was mitigated by introducing the conversion of existing shorter maturities with issuance of longer-maturity securities. This method started with the conversion of 364-day Treasury Bills, and was extended to other shorter-maturity dated securities (more on this later in the chapter). Here, both the redemption price of the security being converted as also the issue price of the new security were determined through the auction process. Participation in such auctions was voluntary. This method proved to be very effective in overcoming the refinancing problem in the early stages before the auction system took root.

Seventh, several innovative instruments such as zero coupon bonds, partly paid stock and floating rate bonds were issued through the auction method. This provided market participants with an opportunity to diversify maturity, undertake refinancing and manage liquidity risks while participating in auctions. Most of these instruments proved to be a success and treasury managers showed great enthusiasm in subscribing to these new issues.

Last, but not the least, both the Reserve Bank and market participants were on the learning curve and progressed with higher levels of skills and knowledge through mutual consultations and discussions. These processes led ultimately to the evolution of guidelines for PDs and the formation of the Fixed Income Money Market and Derivatives Association of India (FIMMDA). These initial interactions also served subsequently as a prelude for the Reserve Bank to form a technical advisory committee on money and government securities markets.

AUCTION METHOD

When a choice had to be made between two types of auction methods, namely, the multiple price auction and uniform price auction (popularly known as the European and Dutch auctions, respectively), the multiple price auction was preferred, though the Reserve Bank later experimented with the uniform price auction. The advantage with the multiple price auction was that bidders were required to pay the price/yield that they quoted. It was felt that the Government could maximise its revenues in that process; in the case of uniform price auctions, every bidder was allocated securities at the cut-off yield/price uniformly. While the uniform price auction satisfied the economists' popular concept of a single price, the multiple price auction was also associated with the problem of the 'winners' curse', which roughly meant that successful bidders at lower yields than the cut-off who won the auction would find it difficult to sell securities in the secondary market without incurring losses in their books. International experience of these two methods was mixed.

Another choice to be made was between yield-based and price-based auctions. Since market participants were familiar with 'coupon rates' and 'yields', initially the auctions were yield-based and price equivalent formed the purchase value of the security. Hence, when the cut-off yields were fixed at odd fractional values, these securities carried odd coupon rates that were set equivalent to the cut-off yield. This process was rationalised over time, when price-based auctions were introduced.

Yet another issue related to communication of auction results. The knowledge base was not uniform across all participant groups. While foreign banks and some public sector banks (PSBs) with active treasury departments were quick to pick up experience in bidding and trading, other banks, including state co-operative banks, lagged behind. This raised the question of the type of information to be disclosed about auction results. Initially, only the cut-off price/yield, the amount accepted at the cut-off, partial allocation amount and the balance unsubscribed amount, if any, taken up by the Reserve Bank were announced to the public. The implicit reason was that if weighted average price/yield was also made known, it would give an idea of the bid distribution in the auction, which would be taken advantage of by only a group of participants who were relatively more adept at treasury operations. It was in early 1996 that for the first time the weighted average price/yield was also announced along with the cut-off.

One more problem encountered was the timing and manner of announcing the auction results. In the initial stages, pending the issue of a press release, the IDMC of the Reserve Bank responded to phone calls and announced the cut-off price/yield. Following complaints from some participants, this practice was discontinued. There was also a complaint that all media persons were not getting access to press communications at the same time. This was resolved by the results being announced simultaneously to a group of media persons at an appointed time of day. This responsibility was entrusted to the press relations division (PRD), which organised information dissemination and fine-tuned this process over time by announcing the results at a fixed time of the day.

DICHOTOMY BETWEEN AUCTION YIELDS AND SECONDARY MARKET YIELDS

In the absence of an active secondary market for government securities, the auction-based yields of different maturities initially provided the basis for the 'primary market yield curve'. In fact, this curve showed kinks across maturities, since it was a combination of yields that emerged at different points in time. Nevertheless, this was used after some smoothening was done internally and served the purpose of announcing sale/purchase of securities in OMOs. The secondary market development was also affected in the early 1990s by the adverse impact of the securities market scam and the removal of brokers from the government securities market who had played a major role in the secondary market. Though in parallel the limited use of brokers with regulatory safeguards was in vogue especially for non-bank participants, inter-bank trades were to be mostly done directly. The introduction of the DvP system also took some time. In the meanwhile, the Reserve Bank evolved the practice of announcing prices and yields of all securities that were settled in SGL accounts at the end of the day. This provided some information base for secondary market trades.

An outcome of this development was that the primary market and secondary market yields did not converge that soon. Since primary yields were still distorted by participation from non-competitive bidders and the Reserve Bank itself, the price discovery through auctions was not in alignment with secondary market yields. This wedge between the secondary market and the primary market yields at any point of time created the problem of proper pricing of securities for OMOs. The Reserve Bank at this stage evolved a complex procedure of constructing after every new auction of dated government securities a 'primary market yield curve adjusted for secondary market yields'. This was a unique practice, but a compromise that was necessary. Since this curve was used for announcing indicative yields to banks for valuation of government securities in their portfolio at the end of the financial year. At the end of March 1994, when securities yields touched a peak, banks were required to provide considerable depreciation in their tradeable portfolio because of the significantly high yields. In fact, to reset the yield curve for the purpose of valuation, the Bank offered to conduct an open market auction, but unfortunately the auction was not a success and failed to serve the intended purpose. In any case, the Reserve Bank was absolved of its role in fixing a high yield for valuation for that year-end. Ultimately, when the FIMMDA was formed, it was given the responsibility of announcing indicative yields for valuation of securities by banks.

CENTRAL AND STATE SECURITIES

In the above process, it was observed that the market was pricing state government securities at a higher yield than central government securities. Therefore, the Reserve Bank discontinued the practice of applying the same yield curve for central and state government securities. But all state government securities were issued at a fixed coupon rate and flotation was combined for many states. It was possible that some states that deserved a better treatment due to their relatively better fiscal parameters had to grudgingly accept the situation. The eventual introduction of the auction method for state government securities much later corrected this, but discussion on that aspect is beyond the scope of this history.

CERTAIN OPERATIONAL ASPECTS OF INTERNAL DEBT MANAGEMENT

In its secular objective to activate internal debt management policy in an environment of economic liberalisation, the Reserve Bank took a number of initiatives to broaden the government securities market as well as to develop the secondary market in such securities. This was primarily directed towards re-invigorating the Treasury Bills market, which was critical for meeting the short-term financial needs for the Government as well as being a critical component of OMOs. The Government's broad concurrence with these measures enabled the Reserve Bank to quickly introduce changes in the internal debt management system, which ultimately increased the efficacy of monetary management and also helped meet the challenges posed later by the huge inflow of foreign funds.

Government of India Dated Securities
Auction Sales of 5-Year Dated Security

Towards the close of the year 1991–92, high level discussions took place with the Ministry of Finance to draw an active internal debt management policy and to start active operations in the quarter of April–June 1992. The Governor, in his letter to the Finance Secretary dated April 20, 1992, strongly recommended introducing an auction system for sale of government securities without an interest rate cap but with a reserve price and Reserve Bank intervention. "You will appreciate that interest rate cap and open market operations would be a contradiction in terms," reasoned the Governor. In elaborating this aspect, the letter stated that since the Reserve Bank would be in a position to set a reserve price and intervene at its discretion, an element of 'proactive' market operations would emerge in place of the prevalent restrictive operations under which the Reserve Bank absorbed securities passively and, more importantly, the reserve price mechanism would moderate a very large increase in interest rates.

Increase in Coupon Rates

The Reserve Bank discerned in early 1989 that, given the relatively low interest rates on government securities *vis-à-vis* other instruments floated by the Central Government, there was a strong case for enhancing the coupon rates on the former. Notwithstanding this perception, at that time the Reserve Bank preferred to keep the rates unchanged with a view to providing some 'stability' for the rates (letter dated January 7, 1989 to the Government).

Later, in May 1990 the Reserve Bank recommended to the Government the need to increase the coupon rates on government securities, as the subscriptions to these securities were predominantly at the maximum maturity of 20 years. In terms of the prevailing structure of coupon rates, the rate varied from 10.0 per cent in the case of securities having a maturity period of 5 years to 11.5 per cent for those with a maturity period of 20 years, or an increase of one-half of one percentage point for every 5 years' elongation of maturity. The Deputy Governor's letter dated May 3, 1990 to the Finance Secretary proposed that in the interests of flexible use of different maturities in the Centre's market borrowings without raising the interest burden on the Government, the structure of coupon rates and maturities could be narrowed by keeping the rate for 20 years' maturity unchanged at 11.5 per cent. Moreover, since the 6-month Treasury Bill rate was close to 10.0 per cent, it was considered apt that the coupon rate for securities of 5 years' maturity should be at least 10.75 per cent to attract some funds at lower maturities and thus activate the secondary market.

In its annual policy letter (dated January 8, 1991) to the Government on projections for the market borrowing programme for 1991–92, the Reserve Bank placed this issue in its macroeconomic context, i.e., the measures being taken by the Reserve Bank to minimise the distortions that arose from low administered interest rates, on one hand, and various steps taken by the Government to ensure that the resources were priced correctly, on the other. In the immediate preceding years, the government borrowings other than under the market borrowing programme had been increasing rapidly and the effective cost of such borrowing, taking into account the fiscal concessions, was substantially higher than the rates paid under the market borrowing programme. The Reserve Bank emphasised that extremely high reserve requirements and below the market rates of interest on the Government's marketable debt, far from improving resource allocation, caused avoidable distortions and, more importantly, the monetisation of a large part of the government borrowing. Allaying the fears of the Government that higher interest rates on government securities might raise the cost of servicing internal debt, the central bank countered that instead the market-related rates on government securities would widen the demand for these securities, thereby reducing monetisation of the deficit and, eventually as inflation was brought under control, the cost of borrowing would come down as nominal interest rates declined.

This subject was again pursued in the Reserve Bank's letter dated May 11, 1991 on the grounds that the maximum coupon rate had remained unchanged over the past five years, whereas interest rates in general had moved up recently. While taking note of the Government's concern about the large interest burden, the central bank stressed that it was a good policy to ensure that the rate on government securities was not too far out of alignment with other rates prevailing in the system. The suggestion to the Government was to move up the prevalent rate structure by at least 0.50 percentage points as a recognition of overall financial stringency, but if the decision required some more time, the proposal was to compress the rate structure and float an 11.5 per cent security for 15 years. In other words, as an interim measure, the maximum coupon rate was to be left unchanged, while the maturity was to be telescoped. The Government was requested to convey its decision early, as the first tranche of borrowing for 1991–92 was scheduled to be announced during May 1991. However, the Government was not favourably disposed towards the proposal. In a letter dated June 6, 1991, the Additional Secretary (Budget) countered that any change in the interest rate structure would impact both the central and the state governments and that in any case it was not the appropriate time to consider these changes.

Consequently, the Governor, Shri S. Venkitaramanan, took up the matter with the Finance Secretary in his letter dated June 4, 1991, when market interest rates had started to firm up. The other reasons were that the interest rates on loans of over ₹ 2 lakh by commercial banks were raised from April 13, 1991 by one percentage point, from 16.0 per cent (minimum) to 17.0 per cent (maximum); imposition of an interest surcharge of 25.0 per cent on import financing; a sharp increase on post-shipment export credit interest rates for periods over 90 days and 180 days; two increases in the maximum term deposit rates in October 1990 and April 1991; and the moves by FIs to remove the ceilings on interest rates on lending and the ceiling on debenture rates. The Reserve Bank advised that in this milieu keeping the coupon rates on central government dated securities unchanged was clearly not 'appropriate'. Further, since 1985 when coupon rates were fixed, the cost of funds to the banking system had considerably increased and reserve requirements had been raised; in such a situation, keeping coupon rates unaltered on these securities would further erode the profitability of banks. The Governor reasoned in a persuasive manner that an upward revision in the coupon rates was 'unavoidable', and the country might be vulnerable in negotiations with international financial agencies, if the rates were kept unaltered, *viz.*:

It would be best not to have to do a sharp change after we go to the Fund and finalise the settlement. I would, therefore, suggest that tactically it would be desirable before we undertake any further negotiations with international agencies to at least implement the suggestion in Dr. Rangarajan's letter (dated May 11, 1991) to raise the maximum rate by 0.5 per cent. If a decision on Alternative I which involves a rise in the maximum rate by 0.5 per cent would need a few weeks, we could go ahead with Alternative II which does not involve a change in the maximum rate for the Centre's first tranche of borrowing which is to be issued in the next few days.

The Finance Secretary in his letter dated June 12, 1991 responded that the changes suggested by the Reserve Bank would be considered and decisions taken in due course; meanwhile, the Reserve Bank could go ahead with floating the first instalment of central and state government loans for the year, because several state governments were likely to run into ways and means problems very soon. After a long delay, the Government accorded its approval in September 1991 for an increase of 0.25 percentage points for maturities of 5, 10 and 15 years (as against the 0.50 percentage points proposed by the Reserve Bank) and a rise of 0.50 percentage points for 20 years' maturity.

This topic again came to the fore in the context of the recommendations contained in the report of the Narasimham Committee. The Reserve Bank, in its letter dated January 2, 1992 (market borrowing programme exercise for 1992–93), addressed to the Secretary, Economic Affairs, reiterated that as part of the reform of the financial system there should be a phased movement to market-related interest rates on government securities, and that in the long run government dated securities would need an active market that presaged market-related interest rates. "While there are certain apprehensions that a sudden freeing of these interest rates would be disruptive, a phased programme could be considered under which interest rates on Government securities could be raised in stages and the rates could be telescoped to different maturities," the Bank emphasised.

In early 1992, the dated securities market was gripped with uncertainties. As a result, banks and other traditional subscribers to the bonds of state governments and state government bodies were staying out of the market in anticipation of changes in the interest rates of dated securities, about which speculation had been rife ever since the submission of the report of the Narasimham Committee. The Governor in his letter dated February 21, 1992 to the Finance Secretary stated that there was no way in which the Reserve Bank could ensure that these flotations were subscribed, and that despite holding down the amount to be accepted under the 182-day Treasury Bill auctions, banks and other FIs were not subscribing to state government issues. Moreover, the Reserve Bank substantially reduced the offers of 182-day Treasury Bills to a token sum in the next few auctions. The Reserve Bank, in its capacity as the manager of public debt, suggested that the Government might review the interest rates and put in place a new structure from March 1, 1992, implying that the last tranche of the central flotation of ₹ 1,208 crore would also have to be floated at the revised rates. A related recommendation was that to avoid the authorities getting locked into high interest rates for the long term, medium-term maturities should be issued at a higher rate.

The Government's response was prompt as well as positive. After discussions between the Finance Minister, Governor, Finance Secretary, Secretary (Economic Affairs) and Deputy Governor, the Government, in its letter dated March 6, 1992, conveyed its agreement to raise with immediate effect the coupon rate on 15-year securities from 11.50 per cent to 12.50 per cent per annum. Subsequently, the coupon rates for 5-year and 10-year securities were raised in April 1992 from 10.75 per cent and 11.00 per cent to 12.00 per cent and 12.25 per cent, respectively. The Finance Minister also consented to the Reserve Bank's proposal for introducing Treasury Bills with a maturity of 273 days and 364 days on auction basis, at a discount rate cap of 11.50 per cent. Incidentally, the 182-day Treasury Bills, which were being sold on auction basis, had no interest rate cap.

For quite a long time, the Government did not relent on its stand against the removal of the cap on coupon rates, compelled by considerations of the interest rate burden. In connection with the market borrowing programme for 1994–95, the Government in its letter dated May 16, 1994 conveyed the approval of the Finance Minister for the first auction of 10-year bonds for an aggregate amount of ₹ 1,200 crore, with a rider that the cap on interest was to be maintained at 12.00 per cent per annum. The Governor, Dr Rangarajan, spoke to the Chief Economic Adviser to the Government of India about the problems of such a cap, especially as there was a pre-determined amount to be raised by the auction and the 10-year security issued at the end of March (conversion of 364-day Treasury Bills) was at 12.50 per cent and the same rate was fixed for the state governments' 10-year security in April 1994. The Reserve Bank's perception was that while the Centre should be able to raise loans at a rate somewhat lower than the states, the tightening of monetary policy (announced on May 14, 1994) would have an upward impact on interest rates in the auctions. The problem of a rigid cap of 12.0 per cent was explained to the Finance Secretary, that is, the Centre had a heavy borrowing programme in 1994–95 and a poor market response could send the 'wrong' signal. Finally, the Government acceded to a 12.35 per cent cap, which was applied as the cut-off for the auction held on May 23, 1994.

TREASURY BILLS

The resolution of the issues that surfaced during the formulation of the policy on Treasury Bills was more complex than in the case of government dated securities, mainly because the Government was extremely wary about the interest burden in servicing the debt.

Improving the Yield on 182-day Treasury Bills

For the year 1990–91, the yields on short dated 5-year government securities went up from 10.0 per cent to 10.5 per cent, which were expected to induce investors to retain a large part of the outstanding 182-day Treasury Bills until the end of March 1991. The Reserve Bank suggested (in letter dated October 22, 1990) to the Government that to provide some manoeuvrability in managing the auctions, the cap on the cut-off yield on this instrument might be raised from 10.0 per cent to 10.5 per cent. Surprisingly, the Government took the stand (in letter dated November 9, 1990) that the existing cap of 10.0 per cent on 182-day Treasury Bills was adequate and seemed 'reasonable' considering that the yield on 5-year government securities was 10.5 per cent. After the Governor discussed the matter with the Finance Secretary, the Government agreed that the yield in 1990–91 could be raised to 10.5 per cent, which would help to get a reasonable proportion of the maturing Treasury Bills reinvested.

The Reserve Bank was not very comfortable with the approach to the cap on interest rates. The Governor, in his letter dated January 8, 1991 (which pertained mainly to the projections for the Government's borrowing programme for 1991–92) to the Finance Secretary suggested that in the context of the overall stance of financial liberalisation, the cap on the interest rate on 182-day Treasury Bills should be completely dispensed with in 1991–92 and the Reserve Bank given the freedom to mobilise resources for the Government by altering Treasury Bill rate from time to time. "The Reserve Bank should use this flexibility bearing in mind the overall administered interest rates on dated securities," indicated the Governor. Incidentally, the Reserve Bank proposed that state governments and PFs should be allowed to participate in the 182-day Treasury Bill auctions on the basis of non-competitive bids, namely, at the weighted average of accepted bids. The Chief Economic Adviser to the Government of India in his letter dated April 10, 1991 replied that, keeping in view the cost on account of this form of borrowing, the lower cap of 10.0 per cent might be reverted to. This stand of the Government was not acceptable to the Reserve Bank and the Governor made a remark on the letter: "I do not agree to this, considering our overall approach to liberalisation. Please put up a letter to F.M." However, the Deputy Governor, Dr Rangarajan, discussed this with the Chief Economic Adviser and followed it up with a detailed letter dated August 20, 1991, elaborating the rationale for the Reserve Bank's point of view. The main argument was that in the auctions held during the year (up to August 21, 1991), it had been able to mobilise substantial amounts, reduce marginally the yield and yet collect sizeable amounts. Moreover, it was expected that by raising the yield, the Reserve Bank's hand in monetary management would be strengthened, *viz.*:

> I hardly need to stress the beneficial effects of reducing the extent of reserve money particularly in the context of short-term management at the present time. You will appreciate that we would be well advised to use all the available tools in the armoury to attain the objectives of short-term management and given the present inflationary context and the upward increase in certain interest rates in the present period, it would not be apposite to lower the cap on 182-day Treasury Bills from 10.5 per cent to 10.0 per cent. We would, of course, use the cap with due discretion to the advantage of overall monetary control as also garner resource for the Government and thereby reduce the Government's dependence on the Reserve Bank.

The 182-day Treasury Bills evoked a favourable response from investors. The outstanding bills as on November 1, 1991 stood at ₹ 3,376 crore, and the cut-off yield ranged between 9.95 per cent and 10.08 per cent. The Reserve Bank, in January 1992, apprised the Government that its endeavour had been to garner the maximum resources for the Government in the 182-day Treasury Bill auctions at a reasonable cost. It enquired whether the cap of 10.5 per cent could be completely dispensed with in 1992–93 and if it could be given the freedom to mobilise resources for the Government by auctioning 182-day Treasury Bills at 'appropriate' rates, since this would provide the Reserve Bank with the flexibility to raise and lower the rate in accordance with the Government's short-term needs and in due course develop this as an adjunct to monetary control. The Governor assured the Ministry that the Reserve Bank would use this flexibility with caution, bearing in mind the overall structure of interest rates on dated securities.

In February 1992, the Reserve Bank became concerned when it came to know that the Ministry of Finance was seriously considering suspending 182-day Treasury Bill auctions. The Governor, Shri S. Venkitaramanan, in his letter dated February 5, 1992 to the Secretary, Economic Affairs, remonstrated that this would be a most 'unfortunate' step and suggested that the matter be discussed in detail before such a drastic decision was taken. The Reserve Bank enumerated various benefits of this instrument. It was a means to garner additional resources and served as an important short-term money market instrument. If the Government was concerned about the GFD, the Governor postulated that the increase in 182-day Treasury Bills did not *ipso facto* alter the GFD, as this was determined more by the Government's receipts and payments position; on the contrary, this deficit financed by net RBI Credit to Government could be reduced by mobilising the 182-day Treasury Bills.

The Reserve Bank reasoned that it was not valid to compare the cost of raising 91-day Treasury Bills at a discount rate of 4.6 per cent with the cost of 182-day Treasury Bills at around 10.0 per cent, since the former, which was really the inflationary burden of created money, was being kept artificially low. In the interests of the Government's commitment on net RBI credit to the Government, the need to curb created money, the consequent inflationary pressures and finally the development of the financial system, the Governor urged that the auctions of 182-day Treasury Bills should not only be continued but also the maximum amount be raised. The Government seemed to have veered round to the Reserve Bank's views, because 182-day Treasury Bill auctions continued without interruption for some time.

Longer-maturity Treasury Bills

The sales of 182-day Treasury Bills followed a seasonal pattern, rising in the first half of the financial year and tapering-off in the second half of the year. This meant that the support to the Government at the end of the year was limited. Therefore, the Reserve Bank in its letter dated January 8, 1991 mooted having auctions for 273-day and 364-day Treasury Bills. It was envisaged that with the development of an active secondary market by the DFHI, these long-dated Treasury Bills could become popular and provide greater support to the government budget in the second half of the year. By April 1992, the Government had agreed to introduce Treasury Bills of these maturities, but with a discount rate cap of 11.5 per cent. The Reserve Bank's letter dated April 20, 1992 apprised the Government of certain modalities in implementation. First, since the Reserve Bank did not hold any 182-day Treasury Bills, it would not hold any 273-day and 364-day Treasury Bills either. The DFHI would, however, provide liquidity to these longer-term Treasury Bills. Second, the broad strategy was to issue initially only single maturity at each fortnightly auction, although this procedure was to be reviewed as the market developed. Third, the Reserve Bank indicated that the choice of maturity at each auction should best be left to the Reserve Bank, since it would depend on its perceptions of the conditions in the short-term money market. "The endeavour would be to ensure that the Government was not faced with large net repayments of Treasury Bills, particularly in the latter part of 1992–93," the Bank emphasised. Fourth, and most important, the Reserve Bank again emphasised that there was a pressing need to remove the discount rate cap of 11.5 per cent as it intended to vary the discount rates to reflect market conditions. In actual practice, the discount rates varied from auction to auction and the cap put a constraint on the efforts of the Reserve Bank to raise the maximum amount possible at an optimal rate.

With a view to providing financial instruments with varying short-term maturities to cater to the needs of different classes of investors and thereby developing the Treasury Bill market, Treasury Bills of 364-day duration were introduced in April 1992.[23]

---

23. In the investment committee meeting of the Secretary's Department, which took place in April 1992, the proposal to issue Treasury Bills for all the three maturities (*i.e.*, for 182, 273 and 364 days) either in one auction or in different auctions initially found favour. But after some discussion, the case for 273-day Treasury Bills lost ground for three reasons. First, if all the three maturities were offered at a time, as in the case of dated securities, the investors' preference would be for the longest maturity, *i.e.*, 364 days. Second, the 364-day Treasury Bills after running for 3 months would automatically be of 273 days' duration. Third, if three types of maturities were floated, it would be necessary for the Reserve Bank to decide upon different yield spreads in consultation with the Government, *viz.*, the minimum and maximum yields for each type of maturity, to avoid overlaps and distortions in the yield structure.

Sale by Auction of 91-day Treasury Bills

A decisive step towards activating the debt management operations and a gradual move away from the system of *ad hoc* Treasury Bills was the introduction in April 1993 of sale by auction of 91-day Treasury Bills for a predetermined amount, but with Reserve Bank participation in each auction as necessary. The system of *ad hoc* Treasury Bills was continued.

The Reserve Bank's letter dated April 20, 1992 conveyed its views to the Government on the functioning of the scheme. The amount to be raised at each auction was to be predetermined and there would be a reserve price with Reserve Bank intervention. While the Reserve Bank would not provide automatic rediscounting facilities at a predetermined price, it would retain the option to subscribe to these bills under the reserve price and buy and sell these Treasury Bills depending on its perception of market conditions. The DFHI would extend strong backing to this instrument by offering an element of liquidity at a price. Particular emphasis was laid on the fact that the 91-day Treasury Bills auctions should not be subject to an interest rate cap and that in all these operations, the Government should look at the average effective cost of borrowing over a period of say, a year, and not restrict these operations by imposing discount rate caps for each auction.[24] The Government was advised to periodically have recourse to funding of these securities into dated securities, the maturity period to be dependent on the absorption capacity of the market. Taking a long-term view, the Reserve Bank proposed taking up periodic funding of these Treasury Bills, *viz.*:

> Furthermore, market operations in Treasury Bills will be smooth only if we undertake a periodic funding of these bills into dated securities of say 5–15 years which would need to be absorbed by the market. A large overhang of Treasury Bills built over a number

---

24. In the office note, a number of objectives and advantages were seen in introducing 91-day Treasury Bills. The important among these were: (i) to absorb excess short-term liquidity in the market; (ii) to even out interest rates in the call/notice money market and reduce the volatility in call money rates; (iii) to popularise 91-day Treasury Bills as a money market instrument with discount rates closer to market-related rates; (iv) reduction in net RBI credit to Government by encouraging holdings of Treasury Bills for 91-day by non-RBI investors; and (v) development of an active secondary market in government securities through repos or otherwise, as there would be no rediscount facility from the Reserve Bank.

of years would jeopardise the effective functioning of the Treasury Bill market and absorption of dated securities by the Reserve Bank cannot be construed as a genuine funding operation as it merely would result in created money.

Nearly six months later, the Reserve Bank again took the initiative to request the Government (letter dated October 19, 1992) to approve the pending proposal, pointing out that in accordance with the objective of improved short-term monetary management, the authorities had a commitment to issue short-term securities at market-related rates to the extent of ₹ 2,500 crore. To allay the fears of the Government, the Reserve Bank clarified that while the auctions would imply a higher cost to the Government, the additional burden (estimated at ₹ 30 crore) was unavoidable, and to keep such a burden within manageable limits, the amount was being restricted to ₹ 2,500 crore in 1992–93. The Governor clarified that the gain had to be measured in terms of avoiding monetisation and inflation and reassured the Government by stating: "I had argued earlier on behalf of the Reserve Bank that the excess income of RBI could be returned to GoI as additional profits. In principle, this agreement continues to hold. We can discuss modalities for doing this." The Government seemingly took the latter averment rather too seriously, as is evident from what followed.

The Government's letter dated November 4, 1992 informed the Reserve Bank that the Finance Minister had approved the scheme of auction of 91-day Treasury Bills and noted that the Governor's proposal indicated a discount rate of 9.5 per cent per annum. Further, the letter made a specific mention: "We have also taken note that the extra cost to Government in 1992–93 will be compensated by the Bank through transfer of additional profits in 1993–94." The Reserve Bank hastened to clear the Government's perceptions on these two vital aspects, in its letter dated December 3, 1992:

> ...the calculation of the additional interest burden during 1992–93 of the order of ₹ 30 crore was based on an illustrative average effective rate of 9.5 per cent as against 4.6 per cent discount rate at present. As already discussed with you, the illustrative rate of 9.5 per cent is not intended to be used as a ceiling rate. We would, however, keep in mind the fact that the Government has made a provision of additional ₹ 30 crore for these Treasury Bills.

The excess income from this instrument would accrue to the RBI only to the extent the RBI holds these Treasury Bills.[25]

In the first auction held in April 1993, the implicit cut-off yield for 91-day Treasury Bills at 11.0997 per cent was significantly higher than the fixed discount rate of 4.6 per cent per annum. Thereafter, apart from certain fluctuations, the rate generally drifted downwards until early June 1994. On the few occasions that the Reserve Bank participated in the auctions, it was a passive participant, with the market determining the rate. To sum up, the 91-day auction Treasury Bill served as a powerful instrument for financial market participants and heralded a significant move towards market-related rates of interest on government securities.

Interest Rate Cap on 182-day Treasury Bills

The Reserve Bank and the Government had an understanding since June 1987 that while the cut-off yield on 182-day Treasury Bills could fluctuate, the former would ensure that the yield did not exceed 10.0 per cent per annum. Since then, the yields rose gradually from 9.01 per cent in June 1987 to 9.07 per cent in the auctions held in October 1990. The quantum of outstanding 182-day Treasury Bills showed a nearly six-fold jump during this period and, from the auctions of April 18, 1990 onwards, the cut-off yield remained static at 9.97 per cent or just near the 10.0 per cent cap fixed by the Government. This instrument turned out to be useful not only for investment of short-term surplus funds, but was also attractive in view of the liquidity it provided. However, the Reserve Bank noticed that while the outstandings tended to come down at the end of March, the Government secured support from this source year after year as was evident from the steady rising trend in the outstanding level at the end of March each year. Another interesting feature was that investments in Treasury Bills tended to rise during the early part of the year, thereby providing the much-needed assistance to the Government when its receipts were at a low level.

Funding of Treasury Bills

In the 1970s, the Reserve Bank had been funding Treasury Bills in small quantities, mainly to correct the uneven distribution of maturities of

---

25. Incidentally, the surplus profits of RBI transferred to the Central Government had jumped from ₹ 350 crore for 1990–91 (July-June) to ₹ 1,500 crore for 1991–92 and were maintained at that level for each of the years 1992–93 and 1993–94. This item increased more than two-fold for 1994–95, viz., ₹ 3,558 crore.

outstanding central loans in various financial years and partly to replenish the Reserve Bank's holdings of particular loans and meet the requirements of banks and other investors during the Bank's OMOs. Another objective was to provide high-yielding long-dated securities to various PFs. Internally, the need for funding Treasury Bills was felt acutely to get over the problem faced by the Reserve Bank in finding eligible assets for transfer to the Issue Department as statutory backing for note issue. Between 1958 and 1982, the Reserve Bank had funded *ad hoc* Treasury Bills for an aggregate amount of ₹ 3,795 crore.

During the 1980s, the funding of *ad hoc* Treasury Bills took place on three occasions, *viz.*, March 31, 1982 (₹ 3,500 crore), March 31, 1987 (₹ 15,000 crore) and March 31, 1988 (₹ 17, 500 crore). No funding of *ad hocs* was resorted to between 1983 and 1986, or in 1989 and 1990. This was followed by funding on March 31, 1991 (₹ 30,000 crore) and March 31, 1992 (₹ 5,000 crore). The funding took the form of issue of special securities that carried the coupon rate of interest applicable on Government of India Treasury Bills of 91-day maturity, *i.e.*, 4.6 per cent per annum.

Funding of 91-day Ad Hoc Treasury Bills (March 1991)

In 1991, the Reserve Bank decided that a large portion of 91-day *ad hoc* Treasury Bills needed to be funded for several reasons. The volume of Treasury Bills in January 1991 was nearly ₹ 40,000 crore and would be soon due for a large volume of discharge after their tenure. The discount rate on 91-day Treasury Bills at 4.6 per cent per annum had remained unaltered for over 16 years. The Reserve Bank, in its letter to the finance ministry dated January 8, 1991, suggested that these 'purposeless exercises' could be dispensed with and a major funding into undated securities undertaken at an interest rate of 4.6 per cent at a slightly lower cost to the Government compared with the discount rate of 4.6 per cent.

A year later, in its letter dated January 2, 1992 (in connection with the annual projections for the Central Government's market borrowing programme for 1992–93), the Reserve Bank apprised the Government that the state governments investing in this instrument had pleaded 'not without force' that the yield on 91-day Treasury Bills was 'unrealistically low' relative to other rates in the system and that there was a case for increasing the discount rate to 9.0 per cent per annum. The Governor, in his letter, made the proposal attractive for the Government by suggesting that: (i) the bulk of the existing 91-day Treasury Bills could be funded into undated securities at 4.6 per cent at the end of March 1992; (ii) the discount could be raised initially to 9.0 per cent and later the rate could be determined at auctions; and (iii) increase in earnings of the Reserve Bank as a result of this measure could be transferred to the Government.

Funding of 91-day Auction Treasury Bills

With the ongoing tempo of issue of 91-day auction Treasury Bills, its outstanding level crossed the ceiling of ₹ 5,000 crore by the 39th auction on October 1, 1993. At the same pace, by the 40th auction on October 8, 1993, the outstanding level of 91-day auction Treasury Bills was expected to touch ₹ 5,450 crore. The IDMC, in its letter dated September 18, 1993, informed the Ministry of Finance that the market response to these bills was overwhelming, with no devolvement on the Reserve Bank in the weekly auctions (August–September 1993) and, with the discount rate coming down, funding would have an 'enduring' effect on monetised fiscal deficit. Therefore, the Reserve Bank in its letter dated October 5, 1993 proposed that the funding operation be undertaken on October 15, 1993 by issuing two-year government stock at a pre-announced fixed coupon rate. Based on its experience in funding 364-day Treasury Bills in April 1993, the Reserve Bank felt that pricing the bills on the basis of the holding period yield applied on the maximum weighted average price would be attractive and beneficial to investors opting for conversion.

The advantages adduced to the proposal were three. First, the funding operation would help to obviate the cash flow problem for the Government arising during the latter part of the fiscal year when liquidity conditions might turn out to be tight. Second, as the bills had almost been absorbed by the market, funding would secure a longer-term reduction in the monetised portion of fiscal deficit and, moreover, the conventional deficit would be smaller. Third, in the absence of funding, the manoeuvrability of the Reserve Bank in keeping up the tempo of fresh issues of these bills would be constrained, because turning over a large volume of bills every three months was a very difficult task, especially as the volume of such bills increased.

Ad hoc Treasury Bills amounting to ₹ 34,130 crore were converted into special securities without any specific maturity at an interest rate of 4.6 per cent per annum, effective April 1, 1997. Similarly, 91-day tap bills amounting to ₹ 16,688 crore were converted to special securities on similar terms as they matured during the period April–June 1997.

Funding of 91-day Treasury Bills (March 1994)

Before the start of the borrowing programme for 1994–95, the Reserve Bank wanted to get through the funding of 91-day Treasury Bills outstanding at the end of March 1994 for the same reasons cited earlier in the case of 91-day auction Treasury Bills, namely, to alleviate the cash flow problem for the Government and to enable the Reserve Bank to keep up the tempo of fresh issue of bills in the following year. The Reserve Bank, in its letter to the Government dated March 29, 1994, suggested extending the inter-bank repos facility to the 5-year government stock to be issued in conversion of Treasury Bills, provided the transactions were carried out at Mumbai and through SGL accounts.

Funding of 364-day Treasury Bills (March 1993)

The 364-day Treasury Bill auctions were introduced in April 1992. At the end of March 1993, the outstanding 364-day Treasury Bills were expected to be over ₹ 8,500 crore; this was much in excess of the modest budgeted figure of ₹ 500 crore for the year 1992–93. There was a strong demand for these Treasury Bills due to special reasons, such as the portfolio adjustments made by investors, this being a new type of security; the setback to the secondary securities market in the aftermath of the irregularities in securities transactions; and the attractive rate offered on these bills — especially before the maximum rate on dated securities was raised to 13.0 per cent. The Reserve Bank, in its letter dated January 7, 1993 to the Government, conjectured that retiring these bills (expected to take place in the financial year 1993–94) could be a large drain on the resources of the Government unless an equivalent amount was raised in the auctions to be held in 1993–94 and, therefore, recommended floating a 3-year funding security at an attractive rate before these bills matured towards the end of April 1993. This was open only to holders of 364-day Treasury Bills. Of the 364-day bills eligible for conversion, amounting to ₹ 8,777 crore (face value), into 12.75 per cent central government stock, 1996, ₹ 7,123 crore (face value) was offered by holders for conversion, representing about 80.0 per cent of the eligible bills.

Again in March 1993, the Government was approached to fund 364-day Treasury Bills maturing in 1993–94 into dated securities on the grounds that the bills issued during 1992–93 would mature for payment in 1993–94, leading to high net discharge of bills and cause an imbalance in funds flow to the Government. The letter dated March 17, 1993 favoured making the terms of funding sufficiently attractive to smoothen the flow of funds and, since these bills did not need be held by investors until maturity, the Government was not required to pay prematurely 100.0 per cent maturity value. The Reserve Bank's Annual Report for 1993–94 propounded that the funding operations of 364-day and 91-day Treasury Bills were an important aspect of internal debt management, because each of these funding operations was large and the back-up of liquidity through repos provided a benchmark for other operations and more important, just as the 12.75 per cent three-year stock at the time of the April 1993 funding of 364-day Treasury Bills acted as a signal for a sharp up-trend in coupon rates, the March 1994 funding of 364-day Treasury Bills could serve as an indicator for lowering coupon rates. Further:

> Thus, an array of market-related interest rates are emerging through auctions of conventional market loans, new instruments like Zero Coupon Bonds and funding operations. In a market-related system it is not always necessary for the coupon rate to be determined at the auctions. It is equally legitimate as part of a debt management strategy to test the market by an offer at a certain coupon rate; the fixed coupon rate on the funding of securities is particularly suited as the holder of a Treasury Bill has the option to convert Treasury Bill into a dated security or to opt to remain in Treasury Bills. Conjectural variation between investors and borrowers is a legitimate market play.

In March 1994, the Reserve Bank discerned that with the prevailing easy liquidity conditions, there was a large demand for 364-day Treasury Bills in 1993–94, and the outstandings of these bills touched ₹ 19,263 crore on March 4, 1994. With one more auction to be held on March 16, 1994, the total outstandings at the end of the financial year might be over ₹ 20,000 crore. The strong demand for 364-day Treasury Bills was partly a reflection of the shortage of dated securities in the market, as was evident from the fact that large sales from the Reserve Bank's portfolio of dated securities had taken place in the past three months. The Reserve Bank, in its letter dated March 7, 1994, strongly recommended to the Government a funding operation of 364-day Treasury Bills towards the end of March 1993 as this would ease the cash flow problem of the Government in 1994–95 and, in the absence of funding, the manoeuvrability of the Reserve Bank to maintain the tempo of fresh issues of these bills would be constrained, as turning over a large volume of bills could be difficult, especially as the volume of such bills increased.

The Reserve Bank, in its letter dated December 12, 1994, proposed that a part of the remaining target of net borrowing could be achieved by funding 364-day Treasury Bills maturing between January and March 1995 to be undertaken on December 29, 1994. It was reasoned that if all eligible bills were converted, the funding would cost the Government ₹ 3.73 crore; even if 50.0 per cent of the eligible bills were converted, this would be satisfactory, as it would reduce the remaining borrowing to be undertaken. In another letter dated December 20, 1994, the Reserve Bank expressed the view that since the maturing of large volume of outstanding 364-day Treasury Bills at the end of March 1995 could pose problems for the Government, it would be prudent to fund a substantial part of these bills into dated securities.

Conversion of Special Securities into Marketable Securities

The conversion of ₹ 7,000 crore of special securities (4.6 per cent) into marketable securities was mooted by the Reserve Bank in its letter dated October 31, 1994. But the Government — in its letter dated December 2, 1994 from the Chief Economic Adviser — was not in favour, because it would entail hidden transfer/subsidy and given the move towards greater transparency (evidenced by the supplementary agreement between the Reserve Bank and the Ministry of Finance to phase out *ad hoc* Treasury Bills), similar transparency was required in the profits and losses arising from the open market and sterilisation operations of the Reserve Bank. More important, any change in the Reserve Bank's profits/losses would impact the government budget through variation in dividends.

The Government responded that instead 4.6 per cent special securities up to ₹ 7,000 crore could be exchanged for an equal value of dated securities of appropriate maturity at a coupon rate equal to the corresponding market interest rate. The Reserve Bank was to pay in perpetuity the difference between this coupon rate and the 4.6 per cent interest rate on special securities. This implied that immediately after this exchange, the annual cost to the Central Government and the annual income from the Reserve Bank would remain unchanged. The use of this security for sterilisation was expected to entail a cost to the Reserve Bank as in the case of earlier OMOs. In principle approval from the Finance Minister had been obtained for the proposal, the letter advised.

PROGRESS IN FISCAL CONSOLIDATION

Fiscal consolidation was the centre-piece of the comprehensive economic reforms launched in 1991–92 by the Government to restore the macroeconomic imbalance that had been severely disturbed.[26] Both the stabilisation of the BoP and control of rising inflation warranted an immediate and drastic reduction in the fiscal deficit. The regular Union Budget for 1991–92 (presented to Parliament on July 24, 1991) represented a major and conscious effort towards restoring fiscal balance, mainly by reducing the fiscal deficit by nearly two percentage points of GDP, i.e., from 8.4 per cent in 1990–91 (RE) to 6.5 per cent in 1991–92 (BE and based on GDP projections at that time). However, it is worth noting that the Economic Survey for 1996–97 postulated that although it was relatively easy to say whether the trend in fiscal deficit was up or down, it was much more difficult to define the 'appropriate' level for each country at any given time in its stage of economic development.[27]

The topic of fiscal adjustment was of critical concern and interest for the Reserve Bank in monetary management since unrestrained budget deficits would culminate in burgeoning public debt. In retrospect, fiscal consolidation and the accompanying financial sector reforms substantially scaled down the Centre's dependence on net bank credit from the Reserve Bank and also the draft on the resources of the banking sector. The Governor, Dr C. Rangarajan, stressed that sustained fiscal adjustment must underpin further reforms and that, in the absence of credible fiscal control and price stability, there was some risk that interest rate deregulation could result in overshooting and, thus, disrupt the reform process.[28]

The Reserve Bank, in its Annual Report for 1995–96, suggested that with the impending termination of the system of ad hoc Treasury Bills, the concept of the conventional budget deficit would have to be abandoned and the GFD formally used as the benchmark for assessing fiscal performance. While the components of the GFD would be along familiar lines, e.g.,

---

26. The topic of fiscal consolidation continues to be in the limelight even today.

27. Incidentally, the Economic Survey, 1993–94 commented that a large fiscal deficit might have provided a useful expansionary counterpoise to the contractionary effects of financial sector reforms.

28. Rangarajan, C. (1994). "Developing the Money and Securities Markets in India". Paper presented at the Sixth Seminar on Central Banking. International Monetary Fund. Washington, D.C., March 9.

indicating external and internal financing and within internal financing, market loans and non-marketable debt, a clear mechanism would have to be drawn up to indicate the sources of financing the GFD as between non-banks, banks and the Reserve Bank. The budget would then indicate the total recourse to the Reserve Bank by way of dated securities, Treasury Bills and other temporary accommodation. "The budget would need to present a figure on monetisation of fiscal deficit consistent with the objectives of overall monetary control," emphasised the report.

Steady progress was made in reducing the GFD up to 1996–97, except for a setback in 1993–94, as can be seen from Table 15.3.

TABLE 15.3

Gross Fiscal Deficit, Primary Deficit, Budgetary Deficit and Monetised Deficit of the Central Government

(As percentage of GDP at market prices)

Year	Gross Fiscal Deficit	Net Primary Deficit	Budgetary Deficit	Monetised Deficit
(1)	(2)	(3)	(4)	(5)
1990–91	8.33	3.35	2.12	2.75
1991–92	5.89	1.45	1.11	0.89
1992–93	5.69	1.65	1.74	0.60
1993–94	6.87	2.77	1.25	0.03
1994–95	5.56	1.16	0.09	0.21
1995–96	4.95	0.89	0.81	1.63
1996–97	4.73	0.64	0.94	0.14

Notes: 1. Ratios for the period 1993–94 onwards are based on new GDP series (1993–94 =100).

2. With the discontinuation of *ad hoc* Treasury Bills and 91-day tap Treasury Bills from April 1997, the concept of conventional budget deficit lost its relevance.

3. GFD is the excess of total expenditure including loans net of recovery over revenue receipts (including external grants) and non-debt capital receipts.

4. Primary Deficit means GFD minus net interest payments.

5. The conventional deficit (Budgetary Deficit) is the difference between all receipts and expenditure, both revenue and capital.

6. Monetised Deficit is the increase in net RBI credit to the Government, which is the sum of increases in Reserve Bank's holding of central government dated securities, Treasury Bills, rupee coins and loans and advances from the Reserve Bank to the Centre since April 1, 1997, adjusted for changes in the Centre's cash balances with Reserve Bank in the case of the Centre.

Source: Reserve Bank of India, *Annual Report,* various issues; *Handbook of Statistics on the Indian Economy, 1999.*

CHANGES IN FINANCING PATTERN

During the period from 1991–92 to 1996–97, fiscal consolidation was responsible for a compositional shift in the financing pattern of the GFD (Table 15.4), *i.e.*, the manner in which the Government financed its deficit. There was a perceptible shift away from captive sources of borrowing at below market rates towards market-related borrowings. The market borrowings were budgeted to finance 30.0 per cent of the deficit in 1996–97 (BE) as against 20.7 per cent in 1991–92. The budget deficit (conventional) displayed a mixed trend varying from a high of 30.6 per cent (1992-93) to 1.7 per cent (1994–95). The proportion of external finance in the financing of GFD was budgeted at 4.5 per cent in 1996–97 (BE), much lower than 14.9 per cent in 1991–92, but this was unrelated to the process of fiscal consolidation. The correlation between GFD and net RBI credit to the Central Government came down markedly in the 1990s, except for a sharp reversal in 1995–96 (Table 15.5).

TABLE 15.4

Financing of Central Government's Gross Fiscal Deficit

(Percentage)

Year	Internal Finance			Total (2+3+4)	External Finance	Grand Total (5+6)
	Market Borrowings	Other Liabilities@	Conventional Deficit*			
(1)	(2)	(3)	(4)	(5)	(6)	(7)
1989–90	20.8	42.2	29.7	92.7	7.3	100.0
1990–91	18.0	49.5	25.4	92.9	7.1	100.0
1991–92	20.7	45.5	18.9	85.1	14.9	100.0
1992–93	9.2	47.0	30.6	86.8	13.2	100.0
1993–94	47.4#	26.0	18.2	91.6	8.4	100.0
1994–95	34.8#	54.6	1.7	91.1	8.9	100.0
1995–96	54.9#	28.3	16.3	99.5	0.5	100.0
1996–97	30.0#	45.8	19.7	95.5	4.5	100.0

Notes: # : Includes normal market borrowings, other medium and long-term borrowings and short-term borrowings (364-day Treasury Bills), from 1993–94 onwards.

@ : Other Liabilities comprise small savings, provident funds, special deposits and reserve funds.

* : Defined as variations in 91-day Treasury Bills issued net of changes in cash balances with the RBI. Up to March 31, 1997 this included *ad hoc* Treasury Bills support as well.

Source: Reserve Bank of India, *Annual Report*, various issues; Government of India, budget documents.

TABLE 15.5

Trends in Budgetary Deficits and Net RBI Credit to the Government

(₹ crore)

Year	Budgetary Deficit	Gross Fiscal Deficit (GFD)	Net RBI Credit to Government (NRBICG)	NRBICG as percentage of GFD
1989–90	10,592	35,632	14,068	39.5
1990–91	11,347	44,632	15,166	34.0
1991–92	6,855	36,325	5,168	14.2
1992–93	12,312	40,173	4,433	11.0
1993–94	10,960	60,257	851	0.1
1994–95	961	57,703	2,178	3.8
1995–96	9,807	60,243	19,871	33.0
1996–97	13,184	66,733	2,832*	4.2

Note: *: As per the RBI records after closure of government accounts.

Source: Reserve Bank of India, *Report on Currency and Finance; Handbook of Statistics on the Indian Economy*, various issues.

RESERVE BANK'S KEEN INTEREST IN FISCAL CONSOLIDATION

The Reserve Bank followed closely the Central Government's efforts towards fiscal consolidation and their results since they impacted both the efficacy of monetary management as well as the conduct of debt management operations. The central bank made known its views and perceptions on this subject through its Annual Report on several occasions.

In the initial stages of reform, the Reserve Bank expressed the view that fiscal correction at the Centre and in the states was long overdue if debt was to be kept within reasonable levels; as long as revenue deficits continued at the Centre and were financed by borrowing, the vicious cycle of increased borrowing and attempts to force banks to lend at below market rates would continue; and that the correction of the balance should focus on the basic flaw of the governments not balancing their consumption outlays with revenues, which was the root cause of disequilibrium.[29] The impact on market borrowing under the new system was expounded as follows:

> The Government's medium-term objective of substantially reducing the Central Government's gross fiscal deficit has to be perceived in the context of ensuring that the level of domestic debt is kept within a sustainable limit. This is all the more necessary in view of the fact that the need to move towards market-related

---

29. Reserve Bank of India, *Annual Report, 1991–92*.

interest rates on Government dated securities and Treasury Bills is a pre-requisite for successful reform of the financial system as also to enable the pursuit of an effective monetary policy. While the Government's reliance on market borrowings has rightly been sought to be reduced, a word of caution is necessary in that the pace of reduction in market borrowing has to be consistent with the downward adjustment of the gross fiscal deficit. While reducing the market borrowing, care needs to be taken to ensure that the monetised deficit does not increase because of high cost of borrowing from other sources as this would be counterproductive to an early fiscal correction. At the same time, it is necessary to ensure that the system of financing the Government budget deficit is altered by an early date.

As far back as in 1991–92, the Reserve Bank had visualised that its accommodation should take the form of only WMAs to the Central Government up to an agreed level to be cleared at the end of each year, since excessive reliance on net RBI credit to the Centre resulted in considerable monetary instability. It even went to the extent of advocating a law restricting the extent to which the Centre could run a deficit and a legal ban on the government borrowing from all sources beyond a certain ceiling, with a sub-ceiling on borrowing from the Reserve Bank and the re-introduction of a CSF to redeem the public debt. The dilemma (as a result of the pressure on the overall borrowing programme in 1992–93 in the context of the policy decision for a phased reduction in SLR) was that the increase in coupon rates on government securities — a direct consequence of inflationary trends and the need to maintain a real interest rate — led to a problem for all borrowing entities, in particular, the states.

The sudden upsurge in the fiscal deficit during 1993–94 prompted the Reserve Bank to remark that containing fiscal deficit, and more particularly the revenue deficit, within moderate levels was essential in order to ensure that interest payments did not pre-empt a greater part of the revenue receipts.[30] More importantly:

The experience in relation to the market borrowing programme towards the end of the fiscal year 1994–95 and in the current year so far, highlights the problems faced in placing increasingly large amount of Government debt in the market. What the

---

30.   Reserve Bank of India, *Annual Report, 1994–95.*

recent experience indicates is that there are limits to Government borrowing and there is a need to contain expenditures within what can be raised from the market at reasonable rates of interest. The need for pruning fiscal deficit becomes even more compelling in this context.

Finally, the Reserve Bank indicated that the problems of increasing debt and interest payments should be resolved on an urgent basis by having a more credible fiscal reform programme and placing a statutory ceiling on public debt. This should include the total liabilities of the Government; whereas the existing provisions of the Constitution of India placed a limit on public debt secured under the Consolidated Fund of India and precluded other liabilities. The Reserve Bank's Annual Report for 1996–97 contemplated that it was time to evolve a strong and qualitatively improved fiscal correction strategy, with the accent on achieving further compression in fiscal deficit along with a shift in the composition of expenditure in favour of crucial social and infrastructure sectors.

Even five years after the economic and financial sector reforms became an integral component of the monetary and credit policy framework as well as of the internal debt management policy, the Reserve Bank subscribed to the view that reduction of fiscal deficits was *sine qua non* for attaining the objective of fiscal and monetary stability. The Governor of the Reserve Bank reiterated that fiscal and monetary stability should be an important aim of any macroeconomic policy framework. Almost all the economic adjustment programmes involved, at the first instance, reduction of fiscal deficits and credit-induced expenditures, besides exchange rate shift to market levels. The idea of stability became relevant after addressing the immediate problems of the economic crisis. Even while undertaking drastic measures to overcome the crisis situation, countries sought to build on these to consolidate macroeconomic gains and to move to a position of stability.[31]

MARKET DEVELOPMENT STRATEGY

Debt markets were essential for financing economic activity. In India, debt markets basically comprised: (i) the government securities market, which was the oldest and most dominant; (ii) the public sector undertakings

---

31. Rangarajan, C. (1997). Address at the conference organised by the Wharton Economic Forum. Philadelphia. March 21.

(PSU) bonds market which developed since the late 1980s; and (iii) the corporate securities market.

The government securities market, the principal segment of the debt market, performed several crucial functions other than merely providing a means of financing government expenditure and that was why the governments issued securities even when they were in a comfortable surplus![32] A deep and liquid gilt-edged market emitted timely signals to the monetary authorities of the perceptions of the market regarding their expectations about economic activity and yields. Thus, it was pivotal in bringing about an effective and reliable transmission channel for the deployment of indirect instruments of credit control. More significantly, the government securities market provided the Reserve Bank with the instrumentality of conducting monetary policy through OMOs, which was the most flexible of the instruments of monetary policy. Finally, as a market for sovereign paper, the yield curve relating to the gilt-edged market served as a benchmark in the financial markets as a whole.

Apart from the Treasury Bills, government securities in a broad sense included term or dated securities of different maturities issued by the central and state governments and institutions guaranteed by these entities. They had an initial maturity in excess of one year and interest was usually payable by coupon. The size, maturity and coupon rates of these issues were being managed by the Reserve Bank. Government securities might not carry several of the typical risks attendant with corporate securities, but they did carry a risk that had to be managed well purely from the portfolio point of view.

The policy objectives relating to government securities market operations had been to smoothen the maturity structure of debt, enable debt to be raised at close to market rates and improve liquidity by developing an active secondary market. The first stage of reforms included the selling of government securities through auctions in a move to market-related interest rates on government paper, introducing new instruments such as zero coupon bonds, floating rate bonds and capital index bonds, introducing Treasury Bills of varying maturities, the conversion of Treasury Bills into dated securities, establishing specialised financing institutions, building a viable institutional framework centred on the PD

---

32. Rangarajan, C. (1996). Inaugural Address at the *Conference on the Government Securities Market*. STCI: Mumbai. April 6.

system and operationalising the DvP system of settlement to instil greater transparency in operations.

STAGES OF MARKET DEVELOPMENT

In the pre-Independence period (*i.e.*, prior to 1947), the government securities market had a relatively wide base with active secondary trading. However, in the 1950s, 1960s and 1970s, with the expansion of the market borrowing programme on a massive scale to finance the Five Year Plans, banks, insurance companies and PFs were statutorily required to invest in these securities. The average maturity of government securities remained fairly long — above 20 years — reflecting the preference of issuers rather than those of investors. The combination of a tightly controlled interest rate structure and statutory requirements to hold these securities deprived the secondary market of any vibrancy.

From the 1960s and just before 1990, the government securities market remained dormant, since the Government borrowed at pre-announced coupon rates from primarily a captive group of investors, namely, banks and insurance companies. They also happened to be the final investors in government securities, driven by considerations of statutory requirements. *Ipso facto,* this led to the conduct of a passive internal debt management policy. This, coupled with the system of automatic monetisation of the budget deficit, impeded the development of a deep and vibrant government securities market. Nevertheless, even within the framework of administered interest rates, the Reserve Bank made efforts during the second half of the 1980s to impart some flexibility to the money and government securities markets, based mainly on the recommendations of the Chakravarty Committee.

To encourage secondary market activity, the maximum coupon rate was raised in stages from 6.5 per cent to 11.5 per cent in 1985–86. Concurrently, the maximum maturity period was reduced from 20 years to 10 years. To develop breadth and depth in the market, the placement of 182-day Treasury Bills by auction, not rediscountable with the Reserve Bank, was introduced in 1986. The DFHI was set up in 1988 as a Reserve Bank subsidiary with participation from other money market institutions to help smooth short-term liquidity imbalances and to impart greater flexibility to the money market.

With internal debt management transforming itself into a potent instrument of economic and financial sector reform, the Reserve Bank, in co-ordination with the Ministry of Finance, set in motion a series of policy initiatives towards instrument development, institutional development and improving market transparency and efficiency with special reference to the secondary market.

TREASURY BILLS OF DIFFERENT MATURITIES INTRODUCED

Since 1992, the central government borrowings had been undertaken at market-related rates, primarily through auctions of government securities of different maturities. A new instrument of 364-day Treasury Bills through auctions was introduced in April 1992 that, along with 91-day Treasury Bills, widened the Treasury Bill market. This instrument became extremely popular and despite three large funding operations, the volume of outstanding bills remained high and was acclaimed as under:[33]

> The lesson from this experience was that if an instrument took into account the maturity preference of the market and there was a reasonable degree of liquidity for this instrument, the Government would be able to raise funds at reasonable rates of interest. Furthermore, there had been a basic degree of stability in interest rates on this instrument; while there were changes in interest rates on this instrument the changes had been extremely gradual. As the instrument did not suffer from volatility, it became very popular and was soon emerging as a reference rate in the system. The experience of the two and a half years was that the 364-day Treasury Bill had truly earned its place as a reference rate in the market for determining other rates in the system.

The method of auction for sale of government dated securities came into operation in June 1992 and for the sale of 91-day Treasury Bills in January 1993. Consequent to the primary market acquiring depth with market-related rates, some innovative instruments were introduced, *viz.*, conversion of auction Treasury Bills into term security, zero coupon bonds, tap stocks and partly paid stocks. With the discontinuation of *ad hoc* 91-day Treasury Bills from 1997–98, 14-day Intermediate Treasury Bills were initiated to enable state governments, foreign central banks and other specified bodies with whom the Reserve Bank had an arrangement to invest their temporary surplus funds. Funding of auction Treasury Bills into term securities at the option of holders turned out to be a successful

---

33. Tarapore, S.S. (1992). "Towards an Active Internal Debt Management Policy". Speech delivered at the *Seminar on Management of Government Securities*. Mumbai: UTI Institute of Capital Markets. October 10.

technique of debt management and gave a boost to activity in the secondary market.

INSTITUTIONAL DEVELOPMENT

With the primary market acquiring depth, the emphasis turned to building the institutional infrastructure. To activate the secondary market in government securities and PSU bonds, the STCI was set up in May 1994, which commenced operations in June 1994. It provided immediate liquidity to government paper and stimulated market-making activity by parties other than captive investors. Further, in order to strengthen the infrastructure of the securities market, improve secondary market trading, liquidity and turnover and encourage voluntary holding of government securities among a wider investor base, a system of PDs started operating from March 1996, with PDs offering two-way quotes with bidding commitments in the auction of dated securities and 91-day and 364-day Treasury Bills. In addition, to broaden the market with a second-tier dealer system and impart greater momentum in terms of increased liquidity and turnover, guidelines for satellite dealers (SDs) were issued in December 1996. Guidelines were issued on April 20, 1996 for the scheme of liquidity support to mutual funds dedicated exclusively to investments in government securities, either through outright purchases or reverse repos in central government securities outstanding at the end of the previous calendar month.[34]

The impact of competitive pricing of securities was evident in shifts in the yield curve that reflected changing liquidity conditions and market expectations about interest, inflation and exchange rates. In a highly liquid market, the yields in the secondary market should anticipate the yields in primary issues. However, depending on the demand-supply balance in different maturities and the liquidity conditions in the system, the divergences between the two yields should be reasonably limited and credible. The trends in the preceding years showed that because of high liquidity in the secondary market for government securities of varied maturities, there had been a convergence between the secondary market yields and market expectations about the primary yield. This had also brought about a more efficient price discovery process.[35]

---

34. This topic also finds a place in chapter 14: Monetary Management.

35. Rangarajan, C. (1997). "Activating Debt Markets in India". Keynote Address delivered at the *SBICAP Debt Market Seminar*. Mumbai. September 5.

IMPROVING MARKET TRANSPARENCY AND EFFICIENCY

The measures taken to strengthen market transparency and impart efficiency included: (i) introduction of the D*v*P System to ensure settlement by synchronising transfer of securities with cash payment — from July 1995 in dated securities and from February 1996 in Treasury Bills — and its extension to all PDOs by May 1996; (ii) publication from September 1994 of transactions in government securities recorded by the Reserve Bank under SGL accounts; (iii) changes in strategies of OMOs and repo auctions; and (iv) a larger percentage of mark-to-market valuation of investment portfolio of banks, namely, banks having to mark-to-market all their investments in a phased manner from 40.0 per cent to 50.0 per cent for the year ended March 1997.

STIMULATING SECONDARY MARKET DEVELOPMENT

A highly liquid and vibrant secondary market was a *sine qua non* for strengthening the primary issues market in government securities and also for the Reserve Bank to conduct active OMOs. There were close links between the development of the primary and secondary markets. Trading in liquid secondary markets helped to establish a market yield curve and to support a network of specialist traders in government paper, who could be engaged for the distribution of fresh issues.

Towards the close of the 1980s, the institutional structure of the secondary market was weak, because the predominant players belonged to the captive category and, therefore, had the same perceptions. Again, all the major players had more or less identical profiles and, hence, at any point of time were either all buyers or all sellers.

As mentioned earlier, the Reserve Bank made major efforts towards institutional development so that a two-way market with players with different perceptions emerged. The primary objective of setting-up a system of PDs and SDs was to enhance the distribution channels and encourage voluntary holding of government securities among a wider investor base, *i.e.*, increased depth and liquidity in the market. Further, in order to facilitate PDs and SDs in their objectives of trading and distribution of government securities, a scheme for availing of liquidity was made available to them. Second, the establishment of the STCI provided immediate liquidity to government paper and promoted market-making activity by other interested parties. Third, the Reserve Bank announced liquidity support for special dedicated gilt funds in April 1996. Fourth, banks were allowed to freely buy and sell government securities on an outright basis and retail government securities to non-bank clients without any restrictions on the period between sale and purchase to promote retail market segment and to provide greater liquidity to retail investors. Fifth, deregulation of interest rates on government securities promoted an active secondary market. Sixth, the move to market-related rates of interest enabled the primary and secondary markets to send effective signals to each other. Seventh, to afford greater transparency in operations, the Reserve Bank: (i) began publishing from September 1994 details of transactions in government securities recorded by the Reserve Bank under its SGL accounts; and (ii) introduced an efficient electronic clearing settlement and depository system for transactions in government securities as also a system of DvP to reduce counter-party risk and risk of unauthorised diversion of funds through securities transactions. The commencement of operations by the National Stock Exchange (NSE) in June 1994 gave a fillip to trading in the secondary market. As a result of the initiatives taken by the Reserve Bank to activate the secondary market, an institutional structure with market participants of different interests and perceptions emerged, as also a transparent system of trading and a secured mechanism of payment and settlements.

The Reserve Bank discerned that while several measures had been taken to develop a secondary market, the liquidity in government securities continued to remain a 'vexatious' issue. Since the major players in the market also had the same perception, a two-way market could develop only if the investor base was diversified to include non-traditional segments, such as individuals, firms, trusts and corporate entities. The Reserve Bank resolved to take further steps in this direction.[36]

'SWITCH QUOTAS'

There were two other changes in the securities operations. The first related to 'Switch Quotas'. A system of allotting annual 'Switch Quotas' had been prevalent since 1973, mainly to enable banks/institutions to improve the yields on their investments in government securities. Under the system,

---

36. These included liquidity support to gilt-edged funds, introduction of retailing scheme by banks, tap sales through the PDOs of the Reserve Bank, State Bank of India (SBI) and its associates and creation of a second layer of SDs. The Review of Internal Debt Management Policy and Operations for the period from November 1, 1994 to March 31, 1996: Memorandum to the Central Board of Directors, dated April 26, 1996.

an annual quota to each bank/institution was fixed for purchase of one loan against sale of another. After a review, the system was dispensed with from April 1, 1992, as it did not have any impact on monetary aggregates and was not consistent with the objective of developing OMOs as a tool of monetary policy. The Reserve Bank effected a change by offering for sale only a select number of securities that it wished to sell instead of including in its offer list all dated securities in its portfolio. Moreover, the Reserve Bank put on its purchase list certain securities for cash with a view to providing total liquidity to at least a few securities.

DEDICATED GILT MUTUAL FUNDS: TAX CONCESSIONS

With the objective of encouraging schemes of mutual funds dedicated exclusively to investments in government securities, the Reserve Bank decided to provide liquidity support. The guidelines for availing of such liquidity support were issued in June 1996. The Governor, in his letter dated June 18, 1996 to the Finance Secretary, requested the Government to provide tax incentives as well to unit holders in gilt mutual funds, reasoning:

> I am fully aware that Government is generally of the view that it would be preferable to have a system of lower rates of income tax without concessions rather than higher rates of income tax with large concessions. In fact, the Government has slightly moved away from this approach when the concession of deduction from income under Section 80-L of the Income Tax Act was raised to ₹ 13,000. We face a difficult problem in relation to Government borrowing. Widening the investor base is very essential in this context and gilt Mutuals provide one means to reach individuals. This will also eliminate the problems of dealing in Government securities in scrip form by small retail holders. While raising the coupon rate is a straightforward way of making such paper attractive, it may not be appropriate at this stage because the Government bond rate serves as a bench mark rate in the market.

The specific proposal of the Reserve Bank was that income to unit holders arising out of investments in mutual funds exclusively dedicated to government securities up to ₹ 7,000 could be exempted from Income Tax; this exemption was to be in addition to the exemptions granted under section 80-L of the Income Tax Act. The letter added that it was preferable to provide the concession under section 80-L than under section 88, as the amount invested in gilt mutual funds could be withdrawn after 46 days and there could be frequent in-and-out movements.

In early 1997, the Government opined that there was need to reduce the coupon rates on government securities, and conveyed this perception to the Governor during discussions on March 13, 1997. The Reserve Bank, however, dissented and postulated that a reduction in coupon rates on government securities would be possible only if the investor base was expanded by reaching individuals through retail.[37]

TAX INCENTIVES TO INDIVIDUALS ON INCOME FROM GOVERNMENT SECURITIES

The Finance Minister, in his budget speech for 1997–98, proposed including gilts for the higher deduction limit of ₹ 15,000 under section 80-L of the Income Tax Act. In the memorandum on the Finance Bill, 1997, it was indicated that the Bill proposed to provide that any income by way of interest on any security of the Central Government or a state government would also be eligible for the additional deduction of ₹ 3,000 (section 80-L already provided for a deduction of ₹ 12,000 in the normal course and a further deduction of ₹ 3,000 on dividends from any Indian company and income received from units of UTI or approved mutual funds). The Reserve Bank reasoned that this proposal would not confer any additional benefit to savers to invest in government securities, particularly when a reduction in the coupon rate on government securities was being contemplated. Therefore, the letter strongly advocated that 'having regard to the spirit' of the Finance Minister's speech and with a view to encouraging investment in government securities by individual investors, of the deduction limit of ₹ 15,000 under section 80-L of the Income Tax Act a deduction of ₹ 3,000 might be earmarked towards income on government securities and units of mutual funds exclusively dedicated to gilts.

BENEFITS OF GOVERNMENT SECURITIES MARKET REFORMS

In the initial stages the major focus of the reform was on the primary market, namely, a move to market-related rates of interest on government paper, introducing new instruments and strengthening the institutional framework. Perhaps the two most far-reaching steps were: (i) bringing

---

37. Letter from the Deputy Governor, Dr Y.V. Reddy, dated March 18, 1997, to the Finance Secretary, Shri Montek Singh Ahluwalia.

down the maximum maturity of government securities from 30 years in the early 1980s to 10 years and enhancing coupon rates; and (ii) placing limits on the use of the instrument of *ad hoc* Treasury Bills at artificially low rate of interest. The functioning of the government securities markets showed good improvement, which enthused the Reserve Bank to re-orient its monetary policy tools and bring down the level of government securities that banks were mandated to hold (*i.e.*, SLR). Also, the measures went a long way in deregulating interest rates and stimulating the development of the primary and secondary markets. Yet by 1996–97, the investor base was still not fully diversified to include non-traditional investor groups like individuals, firms, trusts and corporate entities.

The diversification of the investor base was important because only then could there be an active market in which the intent of investors to buy and sell was not in the same direction at various points of time. High expectations were placed on the role of the government securities market, *viz.*: "As one moves away from the present situation and envisages the architecture of the financial markets a few years down the line it is clear that the Government securities market will be the fulcrum for the monetary policy of the Reserve Bank of India."[38]

The 364-day Treasury Bill auction found ready acceptance in the market. Similarly, the 91-day auction Treasury Bill proved popular among market participants. The auctioned bills (91-day) were being absorbed almost entirely by the market and the rates emerging through competitive bids had become money market reference rates. In an encouraging development, some FIs introduced floating rate contracts linked to Treasury Bill rates. The 364-day and 91-day auction Treasury Bills were funded (1993–94) into dated securities of three-year and two-year maturity, respectively. These funded securities formed the basis of an active secondary market.

Turning to the government securities market, since the entire central government borrowing programme was conducted through auctions, it fostered an elastic band of interest responsiveness from investors for a range of maturities up to 10 years. This was an important step in the process of 'price discovery'. There took place a major correction in interest rate disparities. To elaborate, revisions in coupon rates as also

---

38. Tarapore, S.S. (1996). "The Government Securities Market: The Next Stage of Reform". Valedictory Address at the *Conference on the Government Securities Market*. Mumbai: STCI. April 6.

in the maturity structure of dated securities over a period brought these rates into better alignment with market terms, especially the prevailing lending rates of commercial banks. Despite relaxations in SLR, the market absorbed all primary issues without any significant devolvement on the Reserve Bank. A new treasury culture developed among banks and institutions. In an environment where new investors existed side by side with sophisticated institutions, the auction system within an administered framework enabled improved bidding skills among all market agents. Non-captive investors like FIs and the private corporate sector started showing greater keenness to acquire government securities. "Indeed, the accusation sometimes now made is that government securities yields are too attractive, and are responsible for keeping up the entire level of interest rates. In short, this experience provides an example of how market grooming combined with yield curve flexibility can take place even within an administered structure."[39]

In contrast to the past practice, the Reserve Bank showed its willingness to purchase certain securities for cash. It responded to market yields more quickly, using bidding patterns at its auctions as a guide. Depending on the term preferences of the market and the coupon rates, the Reserve Bank made selective offers to the market at competitive prices. This provided an instrument of yield-curve management even in the absence of a primary dealer network. It would be apt to conclude this narration with the following appraisal:[40]

> The groundwork has been laid to expand investor base gradually towards the non-traditional investors. Auctions have contributed to a new treasury culture and a progressive development of bidding and portfolio management skills among market agents. The yield curve has become flexible showing shifts according to market conditions and expectations. The increase in the secondary market activity combined with the improvements in payment and settlement system has brought about greater integration between money and capital markets and a better alignment of interest rates. The market aligned interest rates have enabled the Reserve Bank to

---

39. Rangarajan, C. (1994). "Developing the Money and Securities Markets in India", Paper presented at the *Sixth Seminar on Central Banking*. Washington, D.C.: International Monetary Fund. March 9.

40. Rangarajan, C. (1996). Inaugural Address at the *Conference on the Government Securities Market*. Mumbai: STCI. April 6.

use active open market operations to partly sterilise the liquidity impact of foreign exchange inflows in 1993–94 and 1994–95.

SELECT POLICY ISSUES

Since the Reserve Bank acts as an agent for managing public debt, close consultations with the Ministry of Finance become necessary at almost every stage of planning and formulating policy and procedures (including the flotation of loans and Treasury Bills). This largely explains the time taken to streamline the procedures and implement reform measures. A few interesting issues that came up are sketched below.

CONSOLIDATED SINKING FUND

The tenth finance commission had recommended creation of a sinking fund to ease the burden of repayments. The Ministry of Finance desired to know the views of the Reserve Bank in July 1996. The Reserve Bank in a detailed letter dated July 31, 1996 saw merit in the proposal, but explained various difficulties in implementing the same.

At the outset, the Reserve Bank reminded the Government that all along it had been in favour of setting-up a CSF, having brought this to the notice of the Government some time earlier. While conceding that at a time when the Centre and the states were already facing a resource constraint, setting-up a CSF imposed a further burden and there was a general reluctance to take on any such additional burden at that time. The Reserve Bank submitted that the problem of repayment of debt had become 'unsurmountable' and unless early action was taken to address these problems, the fisc could progressively face serious difficulties. The Reserve Bank pointed out that giving up a CSF for states in the seventies did appear, in retrospect, to be unfortunate, since the existing system provided no arrangement for repayment of debt other than throwing it forward by larger borrowing. Moreover:[41]

> Fiscal prudence, however, would require that the burden of repayment should be transparently reflected in the budget even if the Government is faced with a budget deficit. In the absence of a CSF, the present approach of gross borrowings to cover repayments would require gross borrowings to rise year after year

---

41. Letter from the Reserve Bank to the Ministry of Finance dated July 31, 1996.

and the interest burden would mount and sooner or later create a budgetary *impasse* which would then require drastic adjustment.

The Reserve Bank further stated that initially the CSF should be started on a relatively modest scale and there would need to be a sufficient gestation period before the CSF took on the repayment burden. According to the debt profile, the prevalent practice of gross borrowings meeting repayments would pose a more serious 'bind' on the Centre and the states. Therefore, there was merit in implementing the CSF concept for both these entities. "Postponing the introduction of a CSF till the fisc is in better balance would not be in the best interests of fiscal stability as the servicing of the public debt is itself a major factor accounting for the fiscal imbalance," propounded the Reserve Bank. The Reserve Bank strongly recommended that a CSF be started from 1997–98 for both the states and the Centre. It was clarified that the CSF resources should be operated by the Reserve Bank and, hence, the CSF would purchase securities only from the Reserve Bank's stock. If this procedure was followed, the Reserve Bank would ensure that the securities held by the CSF provided total liquidity as and when required for meeting the repayments and this would maximise the return on the corpus of the CSF, the letter averred.

SOVEREIGN BOND ISSUE

The Government sought the comments of the Reserve Bank on its going in for sovereign bond issues. Two main reasons were adduced. First, the sovereign bonds would establish a benchmark for sovereign country risk, enabling more successful bond issues by Indian corporate entities abroad as their bonds, with a sovereign benchmark, could be priced more objectively in international capital markets. Second, it would broaden the investment base and possibly supplement domestic borrowing requirement, given that there was going to be continuing requirement of long-term funds to finance infrastructure projects, on a substantially non-recourse basis. The Reserve Bank, after examining the suggestion, advised that taking into account the prevailing macroeconomic situation, the government should not go in for a sovereign bond issue and instead consider opening the government rupee debt market to FIIs (letter dated August 9, 1996). The reasons given were as follows:

(i)   The establishment of a benchmark for pricing Indian issues need not necessarily be through a sovereign bond. All issues by the corporate, including quasi-government agencies, were then being cleared by the Government of India and the Government had a certain amount of manoeuvrability in the pricing of issues. A sovereign issue would jeopardise the prospects of borrowing by other Indian entities at fine rates.

(ii)   A single sovereign issue could not establish a benchmark. This would need to be repeated at periodic intervals and in different markets. Such large volumes of issues had to be weighed against critical considerations of debt management, such as cost effectiveness and exchange risk exposure.

(iii) The cost of Government's domestic borrowing for a 10-year maturity was around 14.0 per cent. For an international bond issue of similar maturity, the coupon rate could be around 200 basis points over the US treasuries, i.e., around 9.0 per cent. This implied that to be cost-effective the exchange risk should not exceed 5.0 per cent and this might not be realistic.

(iv)   Although there was a large demand for funds for infrastructure, the current policy favoured inflows through foreign direct investment (FDI) rather than debt creating flows.

(v)   The experience of project financing even with government guarantees was that foreign investors preferred project-tied lending with specified amortisation schedules and special arrangements, such as escrow accounts. Therefore, it would be better for the Government to guarantee such project-specific bond issues by sectors like infrastructure rather than directly issuing government debt denominated in foreign currency.

(vi)   From the angle of properly sequencing the debt management policy measures, even the rupee debt of the Government was not open to foreigners including the FIIs. It would be prudent in the initial stages if the rupee debt market was opened up to the FIIs before embarking upon sovereign debt issues abroad. This had been the sequencing followed by the East European countries, Thailand and South Africa.

(vii) Institutional investors (pension funds, mutual funds and insurance funds) allocated a certain proportion of their portfolio exposure to a particular country, irrespective of whether the issuers were private bodies or the governments. Considering this investor profile abroad, there was not much scope for immediately enlarging the share of Indian issues in the international market.

FIIs INVESTMENTS IN GOVERNMENT SECURITIES

The Government decided on January 30, 1997 to permit FIIs in the category of 100.0 per cent debt funds to invest in government (central and state) dated securities in both the primary and secondary markets. The objective was to encourage further flow of foreign capital into the Indian capital market and help bridge the gap between domestic savings and investment in a more cost effective manner as also to provide greater depth and liquidity to the government securities market. The Reserve Bank issued guidelines on March 8, 1997 prescribing the manner of FII investment in government securities.

For the purpose of FII investment, government dated securities included dated securities of both the Government of India and state governments of all maturities, but not Treasury Bills. Investments by FIIs could be undertaken only through designated banks. Secondary market transactions by FIIs would be permitted through recognised Indian Stock Exchanges or over-the-counter with SGL account holders and would be covered by the DvP system of the Reserve Bank.

This liberalisation was the result of a drawn-out correspondence with the Government, which, in the main, pertained to the broader canvas of encouraging investment in government securities by non-residents. In November 1995, the Reserve Bank took the initiative by broaching the subject of permitting FIIs in dated government securities. The Governor, Dr C. Rangarajan, in his letter dated November 4, 1995 to the Finance Secretary recalled that the question of allowing FII investment in government securities had been discussed in the high level capital market committee meeting, but a decision was deferred. He opined that the time was appropriate for a decision in the matter. "Given the high level of requirement of the Central Government in the current year and the difficulties faced in raising funds, my view is that we should permit FIIs to invest in the Government dated securities market subject to the condition that the FIIs will not be allowed to sell these securities in the secondary market for a minimum period of six months after acquisition. The earlier concern that such an opening will lead to a large inflow of funds appears unlikely under the present market conditions," the Governor elaborated.

In the same letter, the Reserve Bank pointed out an anomaly that whereas non-resident Indians (NRIs) were allowed to invest in government securities, they were not permitted to participate in auctions for primary issues of government securities. It was considered desirable to allow NRIs also to participate in government dated securities' auctions, as this would obviate the criticism that NRIs were placed in a less-favoured position than FIIs. The Reserve Bank further suggested to the Government to consider separately whether FIIs could be allowed also to have 100.0 per cent debt funds rather than be subject to the existing 30.0 per cent ceiling on investments in debt instruments.

While on this topic, it may be mentioned that in September 1993 the Government had requested the Reserve Bank (in a letter dated May 11, 1993 from the Chief Economic Adviser) to work out 'schematic' details regarding the broadening of the government securities market by allowing non-residents to participate in primary and secondary market investments in government securities. Within the Reserve Bank, after examination of the issue and discussion among the officials, it was decided that certain relaxations could be suggested to the Government. First, in addition to the investment opportunities available to NRIs (including bodies predominantly owned by NRIs) and FIIs, non-resident foreigners might be permitted to invest in government securities including Treasury Bills on a repatriation basis through authorised dealers (ADs)/FIIs. There would be no exchange rate guarantee. Second, investment in government securities including Treasury Bills by non-residents and FIIs would be subject to an overall ceiling of 30.0 per cent on investment in debt instruments including debentures. Third, investment by non-residents and FIIs in central government securities including Treasury Bill auctions would be on a 'non-competitive' basis. Investments in state government securities and tap Treasury Bills would be on application.

SALIENT ASPECTS OF STATE FINANCES

The quality of fiscal adjustment also depended on the fiscal initiatives at the state level. The rising level of state revenue deficits and a high order of implicit subsidy offered little scope for improving the states' financial health and enlarging their development role in the economy. The resources of the states were under severe strain in 1996–97 as revealed by the frequent resort to overdrafts with the Reserve Bank by several of them. The strain on the states' resources had adverse implications for social allocations and development outlays. The revenue deficit of the states increased from an average of 0.3 per cent of GDP during 1985–1990 and 0.7 per cent during 1991–1996 to 1.2 per cent in 1996–97; however, it was expected to be restricted to 0.9 per cent in 1997–98. As a result, capital expenditure (comprising direct capital outlays and loans) of the states suffered a sharp cut, with its ratio to GDP declining from 3.2 per cent during 1985–1990 to

2.5 per cent during 1991–1997. Much of this cut took place in the critical social and infrastructure sectors, which had a bearing on the long-term growth prospects of the economy.

A general characteristic of the state budgets was their structural weakness in the form of large revenue deficits, rising interest burden, increased distortions in expenditure pattern and small growth in non-tax revenues. One fundamental weakness in their finances was the quantum jump in non-development expenditure, particularly in its revenue component, and interest payments as a proportion of revenue receipts.

The consolidated position of the state government budgets showed large budgetary gaps, particularly on the revenue account, and increased reliance on market borrowings as well as on loans from the Centre (Table 15.6). Consequently, the large repayment obligations to the Centre were expected to absorb a substantial and growing proportion of fresh loans, while the continued recourse to market borrowings at higher coupon rates and shortened maturity pattern might result in increased interest burden and the bunching of repayment obligations in the medium-term.

TABLE 15.6

Gross Fiscal Deficit, Revenue Deficit and Market Borrowings of State Governments (Consolidated)

(₹ crore)

Fiscal Year	Gross Fiscal Deficit	Revenue Deficit	Market Borrowings (net)
(1)	(2)	(3)	(4)
1989–90	15,433	3,682	2,298 (14.9)
1990–91	18,787	5,309	2,556 (13.6)
1991–92	18,900	5,651	3,305 (17.5)
1992–93	20,892	5,114	3,500 (16.8)
1993–94	20,596	3,813	3,620 (17.6)
1994–95	27,697	6,156	4,075 (14.7)
1995–96	31,426	8,201	5,888 (18.7)
1996–97	36,167	15,555	6,350 (17.6)

Notes: 1. Figures in brackets are percentages to GFD.

2. Revenue Deficit denotes the difference between revenue receipts and revenue expenditure.

Source: Reserve Bank of India, *Handbook of Statistics on the Indian Economy, 1999; Annual Report, 1996–97.*

The Reserve Bank in its capacity as banker to state governments, offered its perceptions about the condition of their budgetary finances in its Annual Reports, the gist of which is presented here. A view was expressed that the existing mechanism of market borrowings from the viewpoint of conformity with the on-going financial sector reform needed a review. A system had to be evolved under which it might be possible for financially sound states to access funds at market rates, while ensuring a stipulated level of borrowings in the case of less developed states. In its Annual Report for 1993–94, the Reserve Bank observed that the structural aspects of state government finances underscored the need for fiscal reforms primarily aimed at phasing out their revenue deficit and it was advisable for the state governments as a group to initiate budgetary reforms to improve the efficiency of resources, *viz.*, by reducing the size of non-Plan non-development expenditure and augmenting the revenue base. Again in the 1996–97 Annual Report, the Reserve Bank averred that the quality of fiscal adjustment would improve considerably if there were enough fiscal initiatives at the state level as well, and reiterated that balancing the revenue accounts of states in a medium-term horizon through tax reforms as well as re-orientation and reduction of subsidies should constitute an essential element of overall fiscal reform.

WAYS AND MEANS ADVANCES AND OVERDRAFTS FROM THE RESERVE BANK OF INDIA

The aggregate sum of WMA provided by the Reserve Bank to 23 states to tide over temporary gaps in their cash flows remained unchanged at ₹ 744.8 crore in 1990–91, 1991–92 and 1992–93. Likewise, the special WMA given to these states against the pledge of central government securities remained at ₹ 266 crore during these three years. During 1990–91 and 1991–92, all the state governments complied with the overdraft regulation scheme, 1985, under which any overdraft had to be cleared within the stipulated period of seven working days. However, in 1992–93, a few states could not comply with the above stipulation and the Reserve Bank had, therefore, to stop payments on behalf of these state governments until the overdrafts were cleared. Similar action was taken during 1993–94 when one state government could not clear its overdraft within the specified time frame.

Despite the enhancement of the WMA limits from November 1, 1993 (to 84 times and 32 times of their minimum balances in the case of normal and special advances, respectively) as well as the extension of the time limit to clear overdrafts (to 10 consecutive working days), some state governments frequently resorted to overdrafts during 1994–95, probably due to their unsatisfactory liquidity management. Certain state governments were unable to clear their overdrafts within the specified time limit on eight different occasions and, therefore, the Reserve Bank stopped payments on their behalf until the overdrafts were cleared. It was the same case with a few state governments in 1995–96.

To alleviate the problems faced by state governments, the Reserve Bank doubled the existing normal limits for WMA to ₹ 2,234 crore and of the special WMA to ₹ 851 crore from August 1, 1996. State governments were not expected to treat the WMA as a liquidity management device or as a perpetual financing item. There was a marked deterioration in the liquidity management of the state governments during 1996–97 emanating from the aggravation of structural imbalances in their finances, as reflected in the downturn in the major deficit indicators. Eight state governments frequently resorted to overdrafts; one of them could not clear its overdrawn account with the Reserve Bank within the stipulated limit of 10 consecutive working days and payment had to be stopped on behalf of that state government. What perturbed the Reserve Bank (as brought out in its Annual Report for 1996–97) was that the sharp deterioration in the liquidity position of the state governments came about despite the enhancement in the WMA limits from August 1, 1996. Simultaneously, the interest rate structure in respect of the Reserve Bank's advances was rationalised, with the Bank Rate being made applicable to the shortfall in the minimum balance and availment of WMA and a rate of 2.0 per cent above the Bank Rate for overdrafts. This rationalisation was expected to have a moderating effect on the interest payment obligations of the states.

CONCLUDING OBSERVATIONS

In the long run, the macroeconomic consequences of public debt are dependent on the volume of its growth in relation to nominal GDP growth, the extent of increase in private savings in absorbing the additional public debt and the impact of public debt on the monetary situation. The condition for stability of the debt-GDP ratio implies that the real interest rate must be lower than the growth rate of output, which ensures its convergence to a stable value in the long run. However, the more immediate concerns for policymakers in respect of a high level of debt-GDP ratio are its interest burden, the 'crowding out' of productive outlays, the higher proportion of private savings being absorbed by the Government, the pressures on the interest rate and more importantly the monetisation of debt.

From 1992, a number of structural and institutional changes were brought about. These included the reform in the government debt markets, which ultimately facilitated the introduction of the WMA scheme to the Central Government in April 1997. For the Reserve Bank, in its conventional role as debt manager to the Government, the annual exercise of monetary projections for the market borrowing programme became a cardinal means of communicating to the Ministry of Finance at the highest level its own assessment of the balance of forces operating within the economy as the latter decided on the design and thrust of fiscal policy in the budget formulation. There evolved a general recognition among the monetary and fiscal authorities that a qualitative fiscal adjustment would, in the long run, enhance the scope for greater flexibility in the conduct of monetary policy and increase the confidence in proceeding with the financial sector reforms.

As a pre-requisite to developing an active government securities market, the Reserve Bank took measures to fashion market clearing rates of interest on government securities. This provided a strong benchmark for other interest rates and ensured that debt was priced correctly in the entire financial system. More importantly, market orientation to issues of government securities paved the way for the Reserve Bank to activate OMOs as a tool of market intervention. For the government securities market to remain active and possess depth, trading in securities should be highly liquid, which again called for an active secondary market. The establishment of the DFHI fostered an active secondary market, first in Treasury Bills and subsequently in government dated securities. The main task of the STCI, which was set up in 1993, was to develop a secondary market in government dated securities and public sector bonds.

Ever since the late 1980s, Treasury Bills, which were a short-term financing instrument of the Central Government, played a proactive and catalytic role in public debt management. The 91-day Treasury Bills were in the main held by the Reserve Bank at a very low discount rate of 4.6 per cent. With a large overhang of these bills, the authorities were reluctant to move up the rate for this instrument to a more realistic level. More disturbingly, under the administered structure of interest rates, the Treasury Bill rate was the lowest in the system. In a major policy departure, 182-day Treasury Bills were introduced on auction basis and the rate of interest was close to market trends. With the objective of reducing monetisation of public debt and developing the government securities market, the auction system was adopted for 91-day and 364-day Treasury Bills (in April 1992) as in the case of dated securities.

The auctioning of government securities obviated the need for recourse to borrowing from the Reserve Bank. From the perspective of macro monetary management, the evolution of a truly active system of internal debt management served as a strong impetus for a shift in monetary policy strategy from the use of direct instruments of monetary control (*i.e.*, reserve requirements, administered interest rates and selective credit controls) to indirect instruments (*i.e.*, OMOs, repo transactions and interest rates). Special mention should be made of the introduction of repo auctions in government securities and a fresh approach to pricing of these securities for secondary market operations. Relations between the Reserve Bank and the Government were bolstered consequent to the phased elimination of automatic monetisation of the budget deficit through the issue of *ad hoc* Treasury Bills. There took place timely and systematic exchange of information on macroeconomic developments and assessments thereon between the central bank and the Ministry of Finance in framing and operating in conjunction monetary policy and debt management policy.

Nevertheless, the Government's increased recourse to borrowing from the market exerted pressure on interest rates, and triggered concomitant policy responses to minimise the cost of borrowing by placing a large part of borrowings at the shorter end of the market. This compressed the average maturity and gave rise to the problem of debt roll-overs. As a consequence, the share of shorter maturities (*i.e.*, under 5 years) in total outstanding market loans rose five-fold, from 7.4 per cent as at the end of March 1992 to 38.4 per cent at end-March 1996. The shorter maturity loans constituted almost 50.0 per cent of the total market loans raised by the Central Government during 1996–97.

The series of policy measures taken to strengthen public debt management by the Reserve Bank in co-ordination with the Government keeping the structural aspects in view during the eventful years from 1991–92 to 1996–97 had beneficial effects on the system in terms of greater market absorption of government securities, lower devolvement on the Reserve Bank, competitive pricing of securities, emergence of a market-responsive yield curve and increased attention accorded to treasury management and interest rate risk management by bankers and investors. On the part of the Reserve Bank, the main challenge was in the pursuit of a strategy for elongating the maturity pattern of outstanding government debt to reduce the refinancing risk by lessening uncertainties in financial markets and widening the range of maturities.

ANNEX I

Progress in Strengthening the Government Securities Market
(1992–93 to 1996–97)

I. GOVERNMENT SECURITIES

(i) The entire central government borrowing programme in dated securities conducted through auctions from April 1992.

(ii) Government securities refinance facility introduced at 14.0 per cent.

(iii) 5-year, 6-year, 7-year and 10-year securities sold through auctions.

(iv) Maturity period of new issues of central government securities reduced from 20 to 10 years. Maturity of state government securities shortened from 15 to 10 years.

(v) Ceiling interest rate on dated securities raised from 11.5 per cent (20-year) to 13.0 per cent (15-year).

(vi) Five new instruments introduced, namely, zero coupon bonds on January 18, 1994, tap-stock on July 29, 1994, partly paid government stock on November 15, 1994, another instrument, combining the features of the tap-stock and partly paid stock on September 11, 1995 and floating rate bonds on September 29, 1995.

(vii) Guidelines for PDs in the government securities market issued in March 1995.

(viii) Dedicated mutual funds for gilt-edged securities.

II. TREASURY BILLS

(i) 364-day Treasury Bills sold by fortnightly auctions from April 1992. Sale of 182-day Treasury Bills discontinued.

(ii) Auction of 91-day Treasury Bills commenced in January 1993.

(iii) Funding of auction Treasury Bills into fixed coupon dated security at the option of holders introduced from April 19, 1993.

(iv) State governments and eligible PFs allowed to participate in 91-day Treasury Bill auctions on a 'non-competitive' basis from August 1994.

(v) Funding of Treasury Bills into dated securities introduced through auction mechanism in April 1995.

III. OPEN MARKET OPERATIONS/REPOS

(i) Introduction of repurchase obligations (repos) auctions collateralised by central government securities (December 1992) — a precursor to active OMOs.

(ii) The system of 'Switch Quota' for banks and FIs discontinued from April 1992 as they did not have any effect on monetary aggregates.

(iii)   A scheme for auction of government securities from Reserve Bank's own portfolio as part of its OMOs announced in March 1995.

(iv)   Reserve Bank offered a select list of securities, depending on supply and demand conditions, instead of offering for sale most of the securities in its portfolio.

(v)   Reverse repo facility with the Reserve Bank in government dated securities extended to DFHI and STCI. The earlier refinance facility to these institutions for such securities was withdrawn. Refinance facility against Treasury Bills, however, continued.

IV. GREATER TRANSPARENCY IN SECURITIES TRANSACTIONS

(i)   Details of transactions in government securities put through SGL accounts with the Reserve Bank being published from September 1994.

(ii)   A system of DvP in SGL transactions introduced in Mumbai in July 1995.

(iii)   Changes in accounting and valuation norms for banks' investments in government securities, *i.e.*, increase in the level of marking to market from the year ended March 1997.

V. INSTITUTIONAL INFRASTRUCTURE

(i)   IDMC set up in the Reserve Bank in April 1992 to initiate active debt management operations.

(ii)   STCI set up in June 1994.

(iii)   A system of PDs (March 1996).

(iv)   Guidelines issued for SDs system in government securities market.

(v)   DFHI strengthened its presence in the government securities market.

ANNEX II

IMF Monetary and Exchange Affairs Department
India: Development of the Government Securities Market
Mr Sergio Pereira Leite and Others[42]

At the invitation of the Reserve Bank of India, an advisory mission from the Monetary and Exchange Affairs Department of the IMF visited India in 1992 to propose measures to foster government securities market in India and allow the Reserve Bank to use OMOs as a major instrument of monetary policy. This mission was headed by Mr Sergio Pereira Leite and submitted its report in July 1992.

The mission suggested various measures aimed at providing the Reserve Bank with the instruments and internal structure needed to conduct OMOs; establishing a market structure for government securities which would be conducive to liquidity and efficient pricing in that market, and improving public debt management practices. The mission indicated its preference for a swift liberalisation of all interest rates, along with an accelerated move towards elimination of market distortions. At the same time, the mission recognised that budgetary considerations required the liberalisation process to be undertaken in the context of the adjustment programme.

As a minimum, the mission recommended five important measures, as follows:

(i)   The placement of Treasury Bills should be carried out on a competitive auction basis. The Reserve Bank should not participate at the auctions, but instead purchase securities from the secondary markets. Detailed results of every auction should be made public.

(ii)   The Reserve Bank and the Government should allow the interest rates on Treasury Bills to rise to levels consistent with competing instruments in the money market.

(iii)   The 364-day Treasury Bill should be used as the main instrument for monetary policy purposes, as well as a key funding instrument for the Government. In particular, the mission was not in favour of the issue of new 91-day Bills at the moment, but rather market attention should be focused on a single instrument.

(iv)   Repurchase agreements could be a major financial instrument that, contrary to popular belief in India, could reduce risks in the banking system, rather than increase them. Therefore, repurchase agreements between banks and other government securities dealers should be

---

42. Note on *Issues in Developing the Government Securities Market and Open Market Operations in Support of Financial Sector Reforms.* Prepared by the IMF Advisory Mission to Study the Government Securities Market in India. Headed by Mr Sergio Pereira Leite. July 1992.

encouraged rather than condemned. Repurchase agreements with all interested parties, banks and non-banks should also be permitted as soon as the PDO book-entry system is improved, the RBI sets clear prudential rules for authorised dealers and puts in place mechanism to enforce these rules.

(v)   The SLR and CRR should be reduced as fast as conditions permit, and they should be based on banks' average positions over some period.

Open Market Operations

The mission averred that OMOs were a flexible instrument of monetary policy. As such, they were gradually becoming the monetary instrument of choice in industrialised and developing countries alike. However, in order to derive the full advantages of the use of open market policies, a few key conditions were needed to be in place. These included interest rates to be market-determined, the financial market should be relatively competitive and free of excessive market segmentation and the central bank should have the means to undertake open market policies and necessary internal structure that would allow it to intervene in the market purposefully and efficiently.

In order to effect OMOs on a day-to-day basis, the Reserve Bank would need three elements: (i) a market instrument that could be used for intervention; (ii) up to date information on market developments and good forecasting capabilities on money market developments and liquidity; and (iii) an adequate institutional set up at the Reserve Bank. The following recommendations applied to Reserve Bank's operations relating to open market policies:

(i)   The Reserve Bank should use repurchase and reverse repurchase agreements with securities dealers as its main open market policy instrument. Outright sales and purchases of Treasury Bills could also be used in cases where a reversal of the arrangement was not expected in the near future. The 364-day Treasury Bill would be the main security used in these transactions.

(ii)   In order to separate monetary policy from 'on demand' government financing, the mission recommended that the Reserve Bank should stop accepting *ad hoc* Treasury Bills. Temporary financing of the Government could be achieved through repo auctions, using Treasury Bills placed on a SGL account by the Government, but managed directly by the Reserve Bank. Until the Reserve Bank was ready to implement this recommendation, the issuance of Treasury Bills on an *ad hoc* basis should be limited and the yield on these bills should be raised to market levels. No additional 'special securities' should be created as these assets were arbitrarily priced and entirely non-marketable.

(iii)   The Reserve Bank should develop its capacity to monitor market conditions, and to forecast liquidity over the short term, if it was to intervene in a purposeful manner.

(iv)   The Reserve Bank should consider establishing an open market committee that would meet, say, once every two weeks to review monetary conditions and decide on the detailed direction of open market policy. Policy would then be carried out by a dealing room, supported by a back office, by requesting quotes from dealers and carrying out transactions.

Thus, emphasis was laid on a market instrument that could be used for intervention, up to date information on market developments and good forecasting capabilities on money market developments and liquidity and an adequate institutional set up at the Reserve Bank (*i.e.*, money market desk, and open market committee). The report observed:

The RBI seems to be experienced in financial forecasting over longer horizons. Forecasting liquidity from week to week or day to day is conceptually similar. Inputs from many sources need to be assembled to predict the major sources of variations in bank reserves. The Government itself, as the largest agent in the economy, can often disturb markets through its large transactions, be they regularly timed, such as salary payments or exceptional, such as payments for "big ticket" capital goods. Under these circumstances, the need for short-term government cash flow forecasts should be clear. The foreign exchange market can often provide at least a day's warning on major transactions because settlement takes at least two days. Indeed, day-to-day forecasting is normally easier than forecasting over somewhat longer horizons.

Institutional Structure of the Government Securities Market

The development of a vibrant, deep and broad government securities market is an important objective of the Reserve Bank reforms: to carry out monetary management through OMOs and debt management through an auction programme. Attainment of this objective would be facilitated by a transparent market structure that had well-specified roles for each participant and operated in a well-supervised and regulated environment. In structuring the market, the micro-objectives were to (i) formalise the role of various market participants; (ii) establish an underwriting capability to support primary auctions of government securities and OMOs; (iii) centralise market information on prices, quantities and trading in money market and dated securities market operations; (iv) standardise market trading practices in money market instruments, debentures and government securities; (v) create a competitive framework for dealers in government securities; and (vi) establish a regulatory and supervisory framework for the government securities market.

The preferred structure of the government securities market was to be three layered, namely, government securities dealers, PDs and inter-dealer brokers. End-investors would purchase government securities through dealers. This structure was expected to achieve the best balance between competition and the need to concentrate demand and information.

Improvement in Public Debt Management

The mission believed that improvements in the practices of public debt management would not only encourage the securities market but also contribute to minimising the cost of government funding. Moreover, the long-term development of the securities market was considered an essential part of the reforms, especially because the traditional securities market investment was diverted into non-marketable debt. In this regard, certain recommendations were made on public debt management, namely, the Government should not lock itself into high debt servicing costs by issuing very long-dated securities, auctions should be the normal funding mechanism, new issues should be concentrated in a smaller number of securities that could act as benchmarks at various representative maturities and the procedures of the PDOs should be improved and its operations computerised immediately.

In the aftermath of the securities market scam, the mission noted that the PDO (the existing system in the Reserve Bank for clearing securities transactions) suffered from a number of problems. Although ordinarily transactions were cleared in a day, in some periods such as around banks' 'make-up' day, clearing could take up to 10 days and many orders were rejected because the seller lacked the securities. Credit advices were sent with a 10-day delay and statements were sent only half-yearly. The system for settling transactions in other securities also needed improvement. Improvements in the functioning of the PDO would contribute to the information flow in the market and to the safety of the system. The mission fully supported the recommendation in the interim report of the Janakiraman Committee that reporting by the PDO needed to be improved and its work computerised immediately.

The report admitted that the Government was implementing a challenging programme of fiscal consolidation and therefore the extra costs relating to higher, market-determined interest rates came at a difficult time. But the mission was of the opinion that this was a worthwhile investment in the efficiency of the economy as a whole, and in the effectiveness of monetary policy.

STRATEGY FOR ACTIVE DOMESTIC PUBLIC DEBT MANAGEMENT

According to the report, the Government faced a major task of public debt management in meeting both its gross funding needs (including the refinancing of treasury bills and other maturing securities) and in ensuring that it would be in a position to secure funding at reasonable cost in the future. It was, therefore, necessary to develop a strategy for active public debt management in India. The mission considered that the essential element of such a strategy was the improvement in the depth and liquidity of the market in government securities. To this end, it would be necessary to offer competitive market-related yields on government securities, thereby inducing into that market a wider spectrum of players. The strategy envisaged was:

Harnessing these divergent sources for government funding in an orderly and efficient manner will require not only competitive yields, but also drastic improvements in the management, functioning and efficiency of the primary and secondary markets in government securities. In this context, particular regard must be paid to the optimal duration of the Government's stock of securities, the issuance procedure, and avoiding a proliferation of new issues; extension of the auction system and development of the secondary market...[43]

SECOND IMF MISSION (APRIL 1993)

As a follow-up to the Leite mission, a second mission from the IMF visited India in March 1993, led by Mr William E. Alexander. Its task was more specific, namely, to make recommendations for the establishment of an appropriate market infrastructure, especially in the areas of clearance and settlement systems for government securities, and regulation and supervision of the government securities markets. At the same time, the mission was asked to consider measures that might be implemented in the near term to resuscitate activity in the public sector undertakings (PSU) bond market. However, the mission was unable to complete its assignment due to bombings that occurred at the end of the first week of its stay in Mumbai. The mission therefore submitted an incomplete report in April 1993 that 'at best could be regarded as being in the nature of a progress report whose conclusions and recommendations must be regarded as tentative'. The proposals to resuscitate the PSU bond market are not covered here.

Adverting to the earlier report of the Monetary and Exchange Affairs Department (July 1992) for adoption of a PD system as the market form for trade in government securities, the Alexander Committee considered alternative market forms. These were auction markets, dealer markets, and combination and hybrid markets. It came round to the view that when the conditions for an auction market were not met, including natural liquidity, a dealer market was likely to be the most appropriate choice. In such a system, dealers played an active role in the secondary market by generating secondary market trading, appropriately pricing the security, absorbing the order flow, distributing the security and educating the investor base. Further, it strongly suggested that the microstructure of a dealer market was superior to that of the auction market for government securities, because, in the case of India, it was likely to take a number of years to develop sufficient distribution of government securities to provide the degree of natural

---

43. The Reserve Bank apprised the Ministry of Finance in November 1992 of the main recommendations of the IMF Mission Report. The latter, in turn, proposed in February 1993 setting-up a Co-ordination Committee with participation from the Ministry of Finance and the Reserve Bank to co-ordinate debt management and monetary policy issues, which, however, did not find favour with the Reserve Bank. More details on this issue are given in chapter 14: Monetary Management.

liquidity that was needed to drive an auction market. Of the two practical options for the choice of the primary dealer market form, namely, the PDM and the Over-the-counter Exchange of India (OTCEI), the mission felt that an active role by the Reserve Bank in the development of a competitive PDM[44] in government securities would lead to an efficient market for government securities in a shorter time than envisaged under the parallel development of the OTCEI and the NSE. Two additional reasons were adduced to favour the development of PDMs. First, because the number of banks and FIs that invested in government securities was small and individuals did not normally invest in government securities, all current investors would wish to become PDs and would likely qualify. Thus, PDs and final investors would likely to be the same, reflecting the captive nature of the market. However, looking to the future when government securities would be more widely held and provide the foundation for the capital market in India, it could be assumed that individuals and non-bank FIs (notably mutual funds) would become investors in government paper without, at the same time, wishing to become market-makers. Others might wish to deal in government securities by distributing them to retail investors, again without wishing to develop the expertise or employ the capital necessary to become a market-maker. The result was that a distinct role for a PD would emerge. Second, it was important for the central bank to encourage the development of a market form that would be conducive to the future conduct of active OMOs. The PDM offered clear advantages, which was evident from the almost exclusive reliance by industrialised countries' central banks on this particular market form. Finally, the mission strongly recommended the inter-dealer market (rather than OTCEI, where inter-dealer direct trading took place) as it could promote price discovery, act as an information intermediary by reducing search costs to determine the best price for a security and promote liquidity in the market. The mission believed that developing the PDM to include inter-dealer brokers would add significantly to the dynamic efficiency of the market and reduce systemic risk.

---

44. PDM: Primary Dealers' Market.

ANNEX III

STATEMENT 15.1

Domestic Liabilities of the Government of India (As at End-March)

(₹ crore)

Item	1991	1992	1993	1994
(1)	(2)	(3)	(4)	(5)
Internal Debt (i to viii)	1,54,004	1,72,750	1,99,100	2,45,712
(i) Market Loans	70,520	78,023	81,693	1,10,611
(ii) Market Loans in course of repayment	46	52	59	70
(iii) Special Bearer Bonds	951	277	43	15
(iv) Compensation and other bonds	788	1,111	1,200	1,249
(v) Treasury Bills				
(a) 91 Days	6,953	8,840	20,613	32,595
(b) 91 Days funded into Special Securities	66,000	71,000	71,000	71,000
(c) 182 Days	1,078	3,986	-	-
(d) 364 Days	-	-	8,777	8,386
(vi) Special Securities issued to RBI	1,102	1,046	1,046	1,046
(vii) Special Securities issued to International Financial Institutions +	6,566	8,415	14,669	20,365
(viii) Gold Bonds, 1998	-	-	-	375

contd...

concld.

Item	1995	1996	1997(RE)
(1)	(6)	(7)	(8)
Internal Debt (i to viii)	2,66,467	3,07,869	3,34,914
(i) Market Loans	1,30,908	1,63,986	1,83,976
(ii) Market Loans in course of repayment	99	108	108
(iii) Special Bearer Bonds	3	-	-
(iv) Compensation and other bonds	1,079	1,757	2,274
(v) Treasury Bills			
(a) 91 Days	32,327	43,790	43,790
(b) 91 Days funded into Special Securities	71,000	71,000	71,000
(c) 182 Days	-	-	-
(d) 364 Days	8,165	1,875	7,383
(vi) Special Securities issued to RBI	1,046	1,046	1,046
(vii) Special Securities issued to International Financial Institutions +	20,635	22,771	19,681
(viii) Gold Bonds, 1998	1,475	1,534	1,534

Note: + : These represent non-negotiable non-interest bearing securities issued to International Financial Institutions.

Source: Reserve Bank of India, *Report on Currency and Finance, 1996–97.*

STATEMENT 15.2

Debt Indicators of the Central and State Governments

(As percentage of GDP)

Year	Domestic Liabilities of Centre	External Liabilities of Centre[+]	Total Liabilities of Centre (2+3)	Aggregate Liabilities of States
(1)	(2)	(3)	(4)	(5)
1989–90	52.5	6.2	58.7	20.6
1990–91	52.9	5.9	58.7	20.6
1991–92	51.5	6.0	57.5	20.5
1992–93	50.9	6.0	56.9	20.1
1993–94	49.1	5.4	54.5	18.3
1994–95	47.0	4.9	51.9	17.8
1995–96	45.6	4.2	49.8	17.4
1996–97	44.1	3.8	47.9	17.3

contd...

concld.

Year	Combined Domestic Liabilities of Centre and States	Combined Total Liabilities of Centre and States (3+6)
(1)	(6)	(7)
1989–90	59.1	65.3
1990–91	59.6	65.5
1991–92	58.5	64.5
1992–93	58.2	64.2
1993–94	55.8	61.2
1994–95	53.7	58.6
1995–96	52.4	56.6
1996–97	51.0	54.9

Note: + : at historical exchange rate.

Source: Reserve Bank of India, *Handbook of Statistics on Indian Economy*, various issues.

STATEMENT 15.3

Reserve Bank of India's Initial Support to Borrowings of Central Government +

(₹ crore)

Fiscal Year	Ad hocs	Subscription to 91 Day Auction Treasury Bills	Subscription to Dated Securities in Auctions
(1)	(2)	(3)	(4)
1991–92	5,750	--	4,822
1992–93	11,445	1,147	2,214
1993–94	6,300	839	435
1994–95	1,750	2,405	157
1995–96	5,965	7,789	12,655
1996–97	4,685	3,316	3,698
1997–98 (BE)	#	--	--

contd...

concld.

Fiscal Year	Total Initial RBI Support to Borrowings of Central Government@ (2+3+4)	Net RBI Credit to Central Government (Book Value)
(1)	(5)	(6)
1991–92	10,572	5,508
1992–93	14,806	4,257
1993–94	7,573	260
1994–95	4,311	2,130
1995–96	26,409	19,855
1996–97	11,699	1,934
1997–98 (BE)	16,000*	16,000*

Notes: +: The difference between the initial support to Centre's market borrowing (which included *ad hocs* till 1996–97) and net RBI credit to the Central Government could be explained by net outright sales and repo transactions of the RBI in Government securities, receipts from repayment of dated securities and 91-day auction Treasury Bills from the portfolio of the RBI during the year, rediscounting of 91-day tap Treasury Bills by banks and others with the Reserve Bank, change in Central Government deposits, Government's currency liability, and valuation differences (book value for net RBI credit and face value for initial support data).

@ : Reserve Bank's holdings of rupee coin are excluded.

: In pursuance of the Supplemental agreements between the Government of India and the Reserve Bank the system of *ad hoc* Treasury Bills was abolished with effect from April 1, 1997 and was substituted by a system of WMA from the Reserve Bank.

* : Expected level of Reserve Bank's support to central government borrowing as per the BE for the fiscal year 1997–98.

-- : Nil.

Source: Reserve Bank of India, *Annual Report, 1996–97.*

16

Financial Markets

INTRODUCTION

Financial markets play a key role in transmitting monetary policy signals by the central bank in a market-oriented policy environment. Until about the 1990s, functioning of most of the financial markets was subject to several constraints, such as controls over pricing of financial assets, restrictions on the flow of transactions, barriers to entry, low liquidity and high transaction costs. Monetary policy was also not attuned to the use of market-based indirect instruments. The financial markets in India in the pre-reform period functioned in an environment of financial restrictions, driven dominantly by fiscal compulsions. Dealings in the money market were confined to overnight call money and notice money. Financial intermediaries in the money market were practically non-existent. Rates of interest on instruments in this market were tightly controlled, with ceilings prescribed on almost all the rates. The government securities market was narrow and dealings in this market were on a limited scale. Thus, the money and government securities markets could not provide the needed basis for the conduct of credit policy through indirect instruments of control. A regime of tight exchange and trade controls prevalent in the 1980s precluded the growth of an active foreign exchange market. The Reserve Bank made attempts in the second half of the 1980s to impart some measure of flexibility to the money and government securities markets. However, on account of lack of financial market integration, there were no dynamic linkages between the money market and the conduct of monetary and credit policy.

Financial sector reforms since the early 1990s sought to remove the constraints through liberalisation and deregulation of the financial sector.

The Reserve Bank embarked on a programme of developing the financial markets, such as money, government securities and foreign exchange markets, in a smooth and seamless way. Repos (repurchase agreements) were introduced as an operating instrument for liquidity management and coincidentally served as a money market instrument.[1] The Government participated in this endeavour by guiding the policy direction of the Reserve Bank.

As the securities market regulator, the Securities and Exchange Board of India (SEBI), is entrusted with the responsibility of developing the capital market comprising the debt and equities markets. Since some of the money market instruments and government securities are also traded in the stock exchanges, there evolved a regulatory co-ordination between the Reserve Bank and SEBI. This chapter covers related developments in institutions, instruments and market infrastructure, mainly during the period from 1989–90 to 1996–97, linking some earlier developments as necessary. Annex 16.1 presents a consolidated view of developments in the financial markets.

THE SETTING: RECOMMENDATIONS OF VARIOUS COMMITTEES

The initiation of the financial sector reforms by the Reserve Bank was aided by the recommendations of three committees. The committee to review the working of the monetary system (Chairman: Prof Sukhamoy Chakravarty) laid the foundations, *inter alia*, for the reform and development of the money market, contemporaneously with the strengthening of the government securities market. It made a strong case for an active money market. First, the development of an efficient money market required developing institutions, instruments and operating procedures to widen and deepen the market and allocating short-term resources with minimum transaction costs and minimal delays. In India, this task should be performed by the Reserve Bank, the report declared. Second, the central bank as an important constituent in the money market on account of its role as lender of last resort to banks formed a sizeable segment of the money market. The committee also envisaged the development of an active secondary market for Treasury Bills by providing necessary support to brokers and dealers and permitting banks to avail of their services.

---

1. Repo and reverse repo meant absorption and injection of liquidity, respectively. The nomenclature of repo and reverse repo were interchanged with effect from October 29, 2004 aligning with international usage.

The report of the working group on the money market (Chairman: Shri N. Vaghul) framed its main recommendations on three tenets. First, the money market should evolve as an equilibrating mechanism for evening out short-term surpluses and deficits; second, this market should serve as a focal point for central bank intervention for influencing the liquidity in the system; and, third, it should afford reasonable access to users of short-term money to meet their requirements at a realistic price. These objectives were to be realised by a four-pronged strategy, *viz.*:

(i) Widen and deepen the money market by selectively increasing the number of participants. This would broaden the base of money market operations by ensuring adequate supply of funds.

(ii) Activate the existing operational instruments and develop new market instruments so as to have a well-diversified mix of instruments suited to different requirements of borrowers and lenders.

(iii) Make an orderly move away from a structure of administered interest rates to market-determined interest rates.

(iv) Create an active secondary market by establishing new sets of institutions that would impart sufficient liquidity to the system.

The working group recognised that while continued supervision of the money market was necessary and the phased deregulation of the market needed to be approached with caution, there should be transparency of rules rather than a predominance of discretion. It observed, "The objective should be to move towards a more efficiently operating money market which would generate a ripple effect through the monetary and banking system."

The committee on the financial system (Chairman: Shri M. Narasimham) identified the main building blocks for reform of the working of the commercial banking sector and development financial institutions (DFIs). It noted that inter-bank call money transactions still formed the major part of money market activity, and even though instruments such as the 182-day Treasury Bills, certificates of deposit (CDs) and commercial paper (CP) had been introduced, there was still a high degree of volatility in this market. The report observed that efforts had been made to broaden activity in the money market and to create a secondary money market, and hoped that broadening the money market by inducting more participants, especially of market-makers, and enlarging the variety of instruments would help develop and activate the secondary market. It added that market activity would expand if more scope was given for the bills discounting business, and wanted the Reserve Bank to use its bills rediscounting function in larger measure as a method of refinancing in order to popularise the bill as an instrument of finance.

In addition to these three committees, the Reserve Bank followed a consultative approach to the development of financial markets by forming various internal working groups and committees with participation from outside institutions and market players from time to time.

ORGANISATIONAL STRUCTURE OF THE FINANCIAL MARKETS

MONEY MARKET

Money markets perform the pivotal role of acting as a conduit for equilibrating short-term demand for and supply of funds, thereby facilitating the conduct of monetary policy. A freely operating money market is a sensitive barometer of the prevailing and evolving conditions in the financial markets and, ideally, this market provides a mechanism for clearing short-term surpluses and deficits. In India, the strengthening of the money market and its structure was an integral component of the overall deregulation process of financial sector reform. The instruments in use were money at call (overnight) and at short notice (up to 14 days), CDs, CP and bill rediscounting of commercial banks. Activities in most segments other than the call money market and, to some extent, CDs, were few and far between.

Until about the year 1987, the money market suffered from paucity of instruments, and both the interest rates and participants were tightly regulated. Thus, the market was practically moribund. However, a series of policy measures taken from 1987 paved the way for significant changes in the structure of the money market in the next few years.

The progress made towards strengthening the money market was highlighted by the Governor, Shri R.N. Malhotra, in the H.S. Kamath Memorial Lecture delivered at the Academy of Administration, Bhopal, on September 1, 1989. He termed the changes that had been ushered in as a "metamorphosis", the major being: (i) the introduction of 182-day Treasury Bills on auction basis; (ii) setting-up the Discount and Finance House of India Ltd (DFHI) to develop an active secondary market in money market instruments; (iii) launching two types of inter-bank participation — one with risk and the other without risk; (iv) removal of interest rate ceilings on call and notice money, inter-bank term money, rediscounting of commercial bills and on inter-bank participations without risk; and (v) the induction of two money market instruments — CDs, which provided a market-determined rate of return on bulk deposits, and CP, which enabled prime borrowers to raise short-term funds from the market.

The Reserve Bank promoted the development of the money market in diverse ways. First, interest rate ceilings on inter-bank call/notice money (as mentioned above) were withdrawn from May 1, 1989. Second, there were several innovations in money market instruments, *e.g.,* Treasury Bills auctions (commencing from the auction of 182-day bills in November 1986), CDs (June 1989), CP (announced in March 1989 and introduced in January 1990) and repos (December 1992). Third, the barriers to entry were gradually reduced, thereby increasing the number of market players, beginning with the establishment of the DFHI in April 1988, followed by primary dealers (PDs) and satellite dealers (SDs) (announced in December 1996) and money market mutual funds (MMMFs); relaxing both issuance and subscription norms for money market instruments and allowing the yields to be determined by demand and supply of such paper; and enabling market evaluation of associated risks by withdrawing regulatory restrictions, such as, bank guarantees for CP. Fourth, the market for short-term funds at market-determined rates got a boost with the gradual switch from a cash credit system to a loan-based system, shifting the onus of cash management from banks to borrowers, as well as the phasing out of the 91-day Treasury Bills on tap at 4.6 per cent interest rate, which had served as an outlet for investing short-term surplus funds. Finally, measures were taken to strengthen inter-linkages between the money market and the foreign exchange market; this gained impetus after a market-based exchange rate system was put in place in March 1993. The DFHI, through its manifold activities, played an active role in this reform process.

Thus, the money market got a shot in the arm with the repositioning from a regime of administered interest rates to market-determined pricing of assets and liabilities. Other developments that hastened the process included limiting and then discontinuing the automatic monetisation of fiscal deficit, thus necessitating raising of funds through the gilt-edged market and relying less on statutory liquidity ratio (SLR) as a policy instrument for debt management; a shift towards indirect instruments of monetary control; and emergence of an institutional framework in the form of PDs, SDs and MMMFs.

CALL/NOTICE MONEY MARKET

The overnight inter-bank call money market, in which banks traded positions and maintained reserves, had been a key component of the money market in India. It was basically an 'over-the-counter' market without the intermediation of brokers. Since the 1980s, participation was progressively widened [i.e., originally banks, Life Insurance Corporation of India (LIC) and Unit Trust of India (UTI)] to include other financial institutions (FIs), mutual funds PDs/SDs, participants in the bills rediscounting market and the corporate (through PDs). The banks and PDs that were part of the payments system were allowed two-way operations, namely, lending and borrowing, while other participants with surplus short-term funds were permitted as lenders, to provide them with short-term investment opportunities in the absence of other avenues and ease the strain on the inter-bank market caused by pressures on short-term liquidity.

The movements in the call money rates were influenced mainly by the liquidity position of banks and other FIs, and these were dependent on a variety of considerations. On the supply side, the main factors were changes in the reserve requirements of banks, impounding and release of incremental cash reserve ratio balances, flow of funds from abroad and their outflow and trends in deposit mobilisation. On the demand side, the government borrowing programme, tax outflows, off-take of food credit and seasonal fluctuations in demand for funds impacted the money market rates. For a considerable period, the call money market suffered from two asymmetries, namely, few lenders compared with a large number of borrowers, which resulted in less than optimal management of funds and, second, a chronic reliance by some banks on money market funds to comply with statutory reserve requirements. However, over time, the Reserve Bank widened the money market by increasing the number of participants, namely, LIC, General Insurance Corporation of India (GIC), Industrial Development Bank of India (IDBI) and National Bank for Agriculture and Rural Development (NABARD), on the supply channel. All participants in the bills rediscounting market who were not operating in the call/notice money market were allowed entry as lenders from October 20, 1990. Select all-India FIs were permitted to operate as borrowers in the term money market from October 1993. For a long time, only mutual funds set up by public sector banks (PSBs) operated as lenders in the call/notice money/rediscounting market. In April 1995, the Reserve Bank provided access to mutual funds set up in the private sector and approved by the SEBI as lenders in this market with a view to facilitating a level playing field among participants.

COMMERCIAL BILLS MARKET

Traditionally, the commercial bills market was very small and the volume of commercial bills rediscounted by commercial banks with FIs not large. Moreover, operations in the commercial bills market were constricted by the cash credit system, where the onus of cash management was borne by commercial banks. The success of the bills market depended heavily on the financial discipline exercised by borrowers. The Reserve Bank tried to improve the working of the market in several ways, but with little effect. With this objective, the interest rate ceiling of 12.5 per cent on rediscounting of commercial bills was withdrawn from May 1, 1989. The Reserve Bank enhanced refinance limits to the DFHI against the collateral commercial bills/derivative usance promissory notes in 1990–91 to augment the flow of funds to the bills rediscounting market. Later, in July 1992 the Reserve Bank restricted financing of bills by banks to the extent of the working capital needs based on credit norms. To encourage a bill culture, the Reserve Bank advised banks in October 1997 that at least 25.0 per cent of inland credit purchases of borrowers should be through bills.

GOVERNMENT SECURITIES MARKET

The government securities market[2] in India in the past had been narrow principally due to low coupon rates. Moreover, the captive market was dominated by institutional investors who had to compulsorily invest in government and other approved securities to comply with statutory requirements. No doubt, during the 1980s coupon rates on dated securities were raised, but still they were not attractive enough to potential investors outside the captive market. Furthermore, the growth of the gilt-edged market was severely constrained by unlimited and automatic monetisation of the budget deficit of the Central Government and the low coupon rates offered on government securities in order to reduce the Government's burden of interest payments. The abnormally low yields on government securities (especially for the 91-day *ad hoc* as well as tap Treasury Bills) resulted in the yield pattern of financial assets in the system becoming artificial and far removed from the 'real' rate of interest.

---

2. The topic of government securities market has also been covered in chapter 15: Public Debt Management.

The Reserve Bank realised that a strong and vibrant government securities market was a *sine qua non* for discharging its responsibilities as debt manager and regulator, as also for effective monetary and public debt management. After the launch of wide-ranging economic reforms in 1991, the Government also subscribed to this view. This was because the size of the Central Government's annual borrowing programme was substantial and it not only overreached the viability of the debt market but also affected adversely the fundamental monetary, fiscal and other related macroeconomic variables, if not managed properly. In the event of the Government having to borrow more than what the market could absorb, interest rates would have to be set at higher than normal or real levels. Ultimately, the non-governmental sector would be 'crowded out'.

The implementation of the recommendations of the Chakravarty Committee had already provided an impetus to the development of the government securities market. However, it was only since 1992–93 that this market underwent remarkable transformation and gained in strength and importance. In the credit policy circular to banks (dated April 21, 1992) the Reserve Bank declared that the development of government securities market was an important step towards the evolution of tools of monetary control other than those provided by reserve requirements and credit controls. Further, the Reserve Bank affirmed therein that the policy was intended to ensure that the Government's credit needs were increasingly met directly from the market instead of through pre-emption of deposit resources. This also marked adoption of an active internal debt management policy in place of a passive one.

The sale of dated government securities and Treasury Bills by the method of auction (from June 1992) was a milestone event because it affirmed the move to market-related rates on government securities and improved the 'price discovery' of these instruments. The most preferred selling technique was 'multiple price auction'. However, the practice of entertaining non-competitive bids in Treasury Bills to state governments, non-government provident funds (PFs) and foreign central banks at the weighted average price determined in auctions continued. The Reserve Bank participated in primary auctions and, on occasions, took up some part of the issues in cases of under-subscription at the accepted yield/price.

FOREIGN EXCHANGE MARKET

The foreign exchange market in India became an active one by the mid-1990s, as it emerged from a regime of exchange control to fulfil its principal function of price determination in its various segments, particularly after current account convertibility was introduced in 1994. Quantitative controls and barriers to entry were progressively dismantled to allow greater volumes in trading and diversity in transactions to be cleared in the market.

The Indian foreign exchange market had a three-tier structure. These included: (i) the Reserve Bank of India at the apex level; (ii) authorised dealers (ADs) licensed by the Reserve Bank to undertake foreign exchange business under the Foreign Exchange Regulation Act, 1973 (FERA)[3]; and (iii) customers, such as importers and exporters, corporate entities and other foreign exchange earners. In addition, there were foreign exchange brokers, who brought buyers and sellers together, but were not permitted to deal in foreign exchange on their own account.

ADs were governed by the guidelines framed by the Foreign Exchange Dealers' Association of India (FEDAI). Dealings in the foreign exchange market covered transactions between ADs and exporters/importers and other customers, inter-bank transactions among ADs themselves, transactions with overseas banks and transactions between ADs and the Reserve Bank.

With the introduction of the unified exchange rate management system[4] in March 1993, the Reserve Bank was not required to sell foreign exchange in the market. All commercial transactions were put through at market-determined exchange rates. The Reserve Bank quoted its buying and selling rates, which were generally in accord with the market rates and could move within a 5.0 per cent band of the prevailing market rates. The Reserve Bank also, at its discretion, intervened in the market to ensure that orderly conditions prevail.

The Indian foreign exchange market had a thin but growing forward market. With the exchange rate being market-related, the need for protection against adverse currency movements grew and banks increasingly made use of hedging instruments to cover their foreign currency exposures. Prior to 1994, the only hedge instrument was forward cover for foreign currency exposures, which was available to corporate entities. In January 1994, banks were permitted to offer cross-currency options on a fully covered basis.

---

3. FERA, 1973, was subsequently replaced by the Foreign Exchange Management Act (FEMA, 1999).

4. The Liberalised Exchange Rate Management System (LERMS) was instituted in March 1992 and the dual exchange rates were merged in March 1993.

Risk Management in the Forex Market

In a regime of exchange control, risk management subserved the interests of exchange and payments restrictions. Moreover, the law of 'one price' could not operate in a milieu where interest rates were regulated and capital controls were in vogue. Therefore, the risk management by banks was limited to the decision whether or not to hedge.

Up to 1994–95, the exchange risk arising out of foreign exchange transactions was regulated by adhering to certain limits on the open positions of banks. These limits included daylight limits for dealing room operators by the managements of individual banks, overnight limits for open position in each currency as well as for all currencies put together and cut-loss limits that limited the loss if the rate continuously moved against the bank.

The Reserve Bank had stipulated much earlier in 1978, that ADs should maintain a square or near-square position at the end of the day. In October 1992, the authorities imposed a cap of US$ 1.0 million oversold against rupees to prevent excessive speculation; this limit was raised to ₹ 16 crore overbought or oversold in May 1994. Exchange risk that arose due to a mismatch in the forward maturities for which the market was shallow, thin and volatile was controlled by adhering to individual gap limits placed on mismatches in various currencies bought and sold for a particular month and the aggregate gap limit (AGL) that was fixed for all the gaps irrespective of their being positive or negative for all currencies put together. The Reserve Bank guidelines issued in 1994–95 stipulated that the total AGL should not exceed US$ 100.0 million or six times the owned funds of the bank, whichever was less. This ensured control over uneven inflows and outflows due to mismatches.

Measures to Deepen the Foreign Exchange Market

Prior to February 1992, ADs could cover the exchange risk of their customers only for trade transactions and customers had to directly take cover in the currency in which they were exposed against the rupee. From March 1992, ADs were allowed to offer forward cover not merely for trade transactions, but for all other genuine transactions as long as the amounts and maturity dates were identifiable. To allow customers greater flexibility in their hedging decisions, the Reserve Bank permitted covering of exposure in currencies other than the US dollar by splitting it into two components (both against the US dollar). The customer was given the freedom to cover each component separately or to cover only part of the risk, leaving the other exposed. Banks could offer long-term forward cover using structured rates on a case-by-case basis. Forward contracts could also be entered into for remittances of dividend and capital for foreign direct equity investment. To impart liquidity to the foreign exchange market and provide market participants with operational freedom and manoeuvrability, corporate entities were permitted to cancel and re-book forward contracts. Earners of foreign exchange were allowed to retain 16.0 per cent of their foreign currency earnings (enhanced to 25.0 per cent in March 1994) with ADs, which could be used for certain approved purposes. At the same time, the limit on 100.0 per cent export oriented units (EOUs) in export processing zones (EPZs), software technology parks (STPs) and electronic hardware technology parks (EHTPs) was raised to 160.0 per cent. In November 1993, the Reserve Bank introduced a scheme of pre-shipment credit in foreign currency (PCFC) to enable Indian exporters to avail of credit at competitive international rates; however, this scheme was withdrawn in February 1996.

ADs were empowered to negotiate bankers' acceptance facility (BAF) with either overseas banks or discounting agencies or a similar arrangement with any other agency without the prior approval of the Reserve Bank for the purpose of rediscounting bills abroad. The rate of interest on BAF or similar arrangement was not to exceed 1.0 per cent over the six months' London interbank offered rate (LIBOR) in the case of rediscounting with recourse and 1.5 per cent over the six months' LIBOR in the case of rediscounting without recourse. In addition, ADs could on-lend in foreign currency as well as invest abroad in certain specified instruments.

The Reserve Bank set up in November 1994 an expert group on foreign exchange market in India to recommend measures for the growth of an active, efficient and orderly foreign exchange market and for the introduction of new derivative products. The expert group made several recommendations concerning removal of market constraints, the development of derivative products, with suggestions for short and long-term measures, and risk management accounting and disclosure standards. It also dealt with aspects such as information systems and clearing mechanisms relating to the forex market.

IMPORTANT DEVELOPMENTS IN THE FINANCIAL MARKETS AND THE RESERVE BANK'S RESPONSES

In view of the close relationship and inter-linkages among the financial markets that have a bearing on the conduct of monetary and exchange rate policies, it is useful to focus on certain important developments in each of the markets and the responses of the Reserve Bank to the same.

MONEY MARKET

Money markets broadened and diversified with the operationalisation of CDs and CP and the introduction of 182-day Treasury Bills, and deepened with the increase in the number of participants and abolition of stamp duty on bills. However, with the deregulation of interest rates on money market instruments, the money market was subjected to occasional bouts of interest rate volatility and banks found it unremunerative to have chronic dependence on this market. Consequently, banks accorded high priority to improved funds management. Even though the Reserve Bank provided the DFHI with as much as ₹ 1,000 crore in March 1990 as temporary support to ease the extreme stringency in the market, continued support was not possible from the point of view of conducting effective monetary policy. The Reserve Bank also cautioned banks that a well-functioning money market could only smoothen short-term imbalances, but could not be a good source for financing their structural disequilibria.[5]

Spells of Volatility

The call money rates remained stable until the middle of October 1990, but immediately thereafter, they escalated to high levels as reflected in the call money rate of the DFHI touching a high of 61.0 per cent on October 19, 1990. To moderate the volatility, the Reserve Bank increased the access to its discretionary refinance facility, softened the loss of interest on cash reserve ratio (CRR) defaults and enhanced the limits for issue of CDs by banks. The call money rates softened from the fortnight ended November 2, 1990 and the maximum call rate came down to 16.25 per cent during the fortnight ended December 28, 1990; they remained range-bound between 16.0–17.0 per cent until February 22, 1991. There was a temporary hardening of rates during the months of March and April 1991 and the DFHI's call rate rose to a peak of 46.0 per cent in the fortnight ended April 5, 1991. The scene was repeated in the months of April and May 1991, with rise in call money rates to very high levels and the average for the fortnight ended May 17, 1991 was 43.0 per cent as against 23.0 per cent for the comparable fortnight in the previous year. The demand for funds came down, because such high call rates were not viable for borrowers.

---

5. Reserve Bank of India, *Annual Report, 1989–90.*

However, by the end of May 1991, the call money market turned easy and remained so until the end of March 1992.

The Reserve Bank discerned that high call rates distorted the pattern of investment in favour of short-term lending rather than more productive purposes, and if reasonable rates were to prevail, banks should not over-extend themselves in terms of provision of credit in the expectation that the call market would meet the gap.

The comfortable conditions in the money market between December 1991 and the end of March 1992 were mainly due to excess short-term liquidity in the financial system on account of foreign inward remittances, counterpart funds of the India Development Bonds (IDBs) and sluggish demand for non-food credit.

The reasons for the instability in call money rates in 1990–91 were traced to factors, both systemic and regulatory, governing the maintenance of reserve requirements by banks. The Reserve Bank came round to the view that the existing system of maintenance of CRR on the basis of a daily average for a fortnight had contributed to the volatility. Though this system provided flexibility to banks both on the borrowing and lending sides; this flexibility turned out to be the cause of volatility. Since any change in the method of maintenance of reserve requirement needed a fundamental change in the legislative framework, the Reserve Bank was reconciled to the fact that since some banks were structurally dependent on the money market, call money rates would remain erratic, and the resolution of high volatility in call money rates rested more in the method of reserve requirement system than in the over-extended position of these banks.

Although the Reserve Bank was working towards greater integration of various sectors of the money market, it was realistic enough to concede that this was a long-term objective, namely:[6]

A prerequisite for a well-developed financial system is close integration of various segments of the money market leading to greater stability in and narrowing of differentials among the relative interest rates. Convergence in interest rates on different money market instruments will have to wait till the rates in other segments of the financial markets are freed. A precondition for this to be achieved is that the phenomenon of large monetisation of the Government debt would need to come down drastically.

---

6. Reserve Bank of India, *Annual Report, 1991–92.*

Reflecting the relatively comfortable liquidity conditions in the banking system, call money rates ruled generally easy during 1992–93, except for a brief period in April and May 1992 when rates flared up to a high of 100.0 per cent on April 28, 1992. This extreme volatility was caused by increased borrowing by some banks to cover their enhanced CRR requirements on year-end increase in deposits within a short period due to a number of bank holidays in April and May 1992, inadequate supply of call funds and uncertainty in the market caused by irregularities in fund management by some commercial banks and FIs, particularly in their operations in government securities.

The DFHI commenced its operations in central government dated securities in April 1992, but the overwhelming proportion of these transactions during 1992–93 pertained to repos with the Reserve Bank. The activity in commercial bills was at a low ebb consequent to reduced recourse to the bill system following the Reserve Bank's stringent action in July 1992 to curb irregular use of the bill discounting/rediscounting facility.

During 1993–94, the money market witnessed easy availability of short-term funds, particularly call money, at comparatively low and stable rates of interest for most part of the year. Banks and FIs began to park their surplus funds in Treasury Bills (both at primary auctions and in the secondary market), and, as a result, the cut-off yields at Treasury Bills auctions drifted downwards.

The call/notice money market enjoyed comfortable liquidity conditions during the greater part of 1994–95. In September 1994, however, the markets turned somewhat stringent following, *inter alia*, a pick-up in non-food credit. The peak lending rate of the DFHI touched 53.0 per cent on September 23, 1994 (as against the normal range of 5.0–10.0%). The Reserve Bank, in order to facilitate a return to orderly conditions in the call/money market as also to improve the effectiveness of monetary management, advised banks to minimise day-to-day swings in their CRR balances. The rates returned to normal by early December 1994, but this proved to be short-lived. Immediately thereafter, banks faced a liquidity crunch due to moderation in capital inflows and continued high demand for non-food credit. The call money market once again became tight in December 1994, accentuated by transient causes such as advance tax payments and public sector undertakings' (PSU) equity sales. To ease the situation, the Reserve Bank injected liquidity into the system through additional money market support to the DFHI and the Securities Trading Corporation of India Ltd (STCI), as well as through some limited open market purchases of government dated securities. A new line of reverse repo facility was opened to the DFHI and the STCI as liquidity support. The conduct of reverse repos enabled the Reserve Bank to indirectly intervene in the market, arresting any upward pressure on the call money rates.

The rates in the call money market ruled steady from April to October 1995. However, from the end of October 1995, the call money rates of banks rose sharply, touching a peak of 85.0 per cent on November 3, 1995 that mirrored the turbulence in the foreign exchange market and the Reserve Bank's intervention in that market to prevent unusual depreciation of the Indian rupee. Moreover, the massive borrowing programme of the Central Government contributed to the volatility in call rates. After the spot foreign exchange market stabilised, the Reserve Bank provided money market support, which rose to an unprecedented level of ₹ 5,555 crore on November 8, 1995. This intervention, coupled with other policy measures, such as a reduction in reserve requirements and enhancement of limits for banks under the government securities refinance facility, helped moderate call money rates by December 1995, notwithstanding the underlying pressure on the call money rates of banks caused by asset-liability mismatches amidst high demand for non-food credit in the face of sluggish deposit growth.

The call money rates once again firmed up between the middle of February 1996 and the middle of March 1996. The Reserve Bank's money market support during this period was, however, minimal. This was deliberate since a large injection of liquidity would have jeopardised the efforts to maintain exchange rate stability. The call money rates ruled easy once again after the middle of March 1996, following the inflow of funds into the banking system, aided partly by spot foreign exchange market purchases by the Reserve Bank. Subsequently, the phased reduction in the average CRR (spread over April–July 1996) as well as the relaxation in CRR and SLR on non-resident (external) rupee (NR(E)R) deposits further helped to ease the call money rates.

During 1996–97, there was a substantial pick up in liquidity — particularly in the last quarter of the year — emanating from policy-induced cuts in CRR and the revival of capital inflows from abroad. This led to significant softening of interest rates at the short end of the money market. However, the interest rate spread across varying maturities was high, as evident from the steep yield curve, the continued presence of market segmentation and high inflationary expectations. The market absorption of government securities was comparatively high, while the off-take of commercial credit was sluggish. The call money rates in general exhibited moderate fluctuations during the year in contrast to the volatility during the previous year.

With a view to provide a reasonable floor to call money rates as also a short-term avenue for banks to park their surplus funds, the Reserve Bank resumed its repo auctions in November 1996. Another objective was to ensure that money market rates did not dip to unreasonably low levels. Accordingly, repo auctions were conducted on a regular basis during January–March 1997. During the year, a conscious attempt was made to broad base the call/notice money market by increasing the number of participants. Four PDs were additionally permitted to participate in the call/notice money market as both borrowers and lenders, and seven mutual funds were allowed to participate as lenders. Consequently, the turnover in the market improved.

GOVERNMENT SECURITIES MARKET

The price movements in the government securities market[7] were considerably influenced by various factors, such as, the Central Government's actual borrowing *vis-à-vis* the budgeted amounts, the maturity structure of debt issued or proposed to be issued, the absorptive capacity of the market and the policies on domestic debt management. The Reserve Bank, in its Report on Currency and Finance for 1995–96, postulated that for the growth of a market with adequate depth and liquidity and to avoid unidirectional movements in the market, players with different perceptions and liquidity requirements needed to emerge. A well-developed government securities market, it was felt, would in turn enable other segments of the debt market to develop.

The market for government securities was activated by the Government reducing its dependence on credit from the Reserve Bank of India and commercial banks. The Reserve Bank, on its part, recast its debt management strategy to serve as a tool of monetary control with flexible interest rates, devised new market instruments and modulated liquidity expansion/contraction through open market operations (OMOs). Also, existing financial instruments were made available with varying short-term maturities to cater to the needs of different classes of investors.

---

7. Also refer to chapter 15: Public Debt Management.

During the 1990s, as already referred to, a system of auctions was introduced to develop government securities as a potent monetary instrument and to bring about flexibility in the market rates of interest. For example, the auctioning of 364-day Treasury Bills was undertaken in 1991–92 and auctioning of 5-year and 10-year bonds was done for the first time in 1992–93. The DFHI started dealing in dated government securities on a limited scale from April 2, 1992 and this marked the first step in the direction of developing a secondary market in government securities.

However, during the early part of this period, the irregularities unearthed in government securities transactions temporarily affected the standing of the Reserve Bank as debt manager. The manipulations that took place in ready-forward transactions by banks and other entities turned out to be at the root of large-scale irregularities in the securities market transactions. This prompted the Reserve Bank to impose a ban on ready-forward transactions in government securities provisionally. The perceptions of the Reserve Bank on this episode were reflected in its Annual Report for 1991–92:

> In the recent period there had been a phenomenal increase in the amount of churning in the dated securities market largely in the form of ready-forward transactions; such activity, ostensibly to adjust reserve requirements, *inter alia,* facilitated the recent irregularities in the securities market. It was for this reason that the Reserve Bank felt it necessary to put a temporary ban on ready-forward transactions in dated securities…There are a number of reasons for not immediately resuming ready-forwards in dated securities. First, the present reserve requirements and the interest rate regulations could provide scope for predatory activity to circumvent the regulatory framework. Secondly, the unwinding of transactions prior to the ban needs to be completed in view of the serious problems faced by the system. Thirdly, the market borrowing programme and auctions for longer-dated Treasury Bills have been proceeding very smoothly despite the disruption of the secondary market. In view of all these factors, it is prudent to continue the ban on ready-forward transactions in government securities at least for some time.

The monetary and credit policy of April 1992 was a landmark in terms of a new approach to internal debt management by introducing a market orientation to the absorption of dated government rupee securities and longer-term Treasury Bills. A system of regular auctions was started for central government securities, including issue of Treasury Bills of varying maturities. Another notable aspect of the re-oriented internal debt management policy was to make dated government securities attractive to investors in terms of coupon rates.[8]

Interest rates were allowed within an overall ceiling to respond to market conditions. In 1991–92, the maximum coupon rate was raised in two stages from 11.50 per cent to 12.50 per cent, while the maximum maturity was reduced from 20 years to 16 years. The maximum coupon rate in 1992–1993 increased to 13.0 per cent for 16 years' maturity. The central government securities were auctioned for shorter maturities up to 10 years at cut-off yields/coupon rates ranging from 12.0 per cent for a 5-year maturity to 12.75 per cent for a 10-year maturity. In 1993–94, the maximum coupon rate was raised to 13.5 per cent, with a further reduction of maximum maturity to 10 years. Auctions of 364-day Treasury Bills were conducted on a fortnightly basis and later such auctions became a regular feature. These auctions evoked good response, partly because of the relative attractiveness of the instrument and to some extent because it provided a safe avenue to investors in the face of uncertainties prevailing in the government securities market consequent to the irregularities in the securities transactions.

Another important step in the direction of active debt management operations was the introduction of an auction scheme for 91-day Treasury Bills for a pre-determined amount, and with Reserve Bank participation. The cut-off yields were significantly larger than the fixed discount rate of 4.6 per cent per annum on such bills sold on tap. The absorption of 91-day Treasury Bills by the market picked up fast. For the first time, in 1992–93 the Central Government raised its entire gross market borrowing through the auction system. While the Reserve Bank initially subscribed ₹ 2,214 crore (out of the total issue of ₹ 4,821 crore), the bulk of these securities were later sold by the Reserve Bank in the secondary market. With the introduction of the auction system, the coupon rates for central government loans emerged through cut-off yields at which competitive bids were accepted in auctions. The coupon rates so brought about were

---

8. The maximum coupon rate on central loans was as low as 6.50 per cent in 1977–78. It was raised in stages to 11.50 per cent by 1985–86. Subsequently, the maximum maturity period was reduced from 30 years to 20 years. These developments, to some extent, augmented the profitability of banks and the attractiveness to other categories of investors.

more attractive than the pre-determined coupon rates for comparable maturities. The improvement in the coupon rate was on top of the shortening of maturity profile. The Annual Report of the Reserve Bank for 1992–93 conjectured that coupon rates that had emerged on securities (both central and state governments) over the past three years were an indication that the yield curve was sloping upward gently as years-to-maturity expanded.

The Reserve Bank conducted auctions of repos for dated central government securities from time to time to even out short-term liquidity in the banking system within a fortnightly make-up period. The first auction was held on December 10, 1992. This was another definitive step towards developing OMOs. Initially, repo auctions were for very short periods of one or two days, but later repos up to 14 days followed.

'Switch quotas' that had been in vogue since July 1973 were abolished. By this process, annual quotas of government securities bought by banks and insurance companies could be switched over to the Reserve Bank to improve their yield on investments. The Reserve Bank decided to offer for sale only a select number of securities as its option instead of including in the offer list all dated securities in its portfolio.

During 1993–94, the Government continued to place its market borrowing through auctions, and funding was actively undertaken to lengthen the maturity pattern of short-term debt. The policy of placing state government securities and government guaranteed bonds at fixed coupon rate was, however, continued. To provide better liquidity to government paper and stimulate market-making activity by other parties, the Reserve Bank established the STCI to play the role of market-maker by offering two-way quotes for government securities. The new institution, which commenced operations from June 27, 1994, actively bought and sold securities at market prices, thereby ensuring liquidity and facilitating turnover for various maturities. The system of delivery *versus* payments (DvP) was instituted to reduce counter-party risk and diversion of funds through securities transactions. There was good buyer response for Treasury Bills, both at the primary auctions and in the secondary market. Banks and other FIs found it convenient to park their surplus funds in these instruments with the result that the cut-off yields in Treasury Bill auctions tended downwards.

Steps were taken to further widen and deepen the government securities market in 1994–95. Repo auctions had to be suspended after February 3,

1995 in the context of the stringent liquidity conditions prevailing in the market. The Reserve Bank later extended the reverse repo facility in dated government securities to the STCI and the DFHI to inject liquidity into the system. The reverse repos enabled the Reserve Bank to arrest undue upward pressure on call money rates. There was a resurgence of demand for commercial bank credit in 1995–96, which led to a hardening of interest rates and a concurrent slowdown in market absorption of government securities by banks. Consequently, there was substantial devolvement of government securities on the Reserve Bank. During 1995–96, the OMOs of the Reserve Bank were subdued, due to large and frequent primary issues of central government securities and increased demand for commercial credit in the face of moderation in foreign capital inflows.

Yield Curve

There were frequent shifts in the yield curve during 1994–95 due to varying liquidity conditions in the money and credit markets. The yield curve for different maturities, which had shifted downward in the early part of 1994–95, moved up particularly sharply in the middle of September 1994. The yield, which was 11.55 per cent for 8-year stock issued on November 16, 1994, shot up to 12.71 per cent with the issue of the 5-year zero coupon bonds in February 1995, evidencing an uptrend in the interest rates of government securities. The spells of tight liquidity conditions witnessed since September 1994 caused larger trading in shorter maturities and pushed up yields on long-term securities, thus resulting in an inverted yield curve. This could be explained by the differences in the long-term and short-term inflationary expectations and temporary imbalances in the short-term money markets and foreign exchange markets. It further suggested that the secondary market had a substantial influence on the activities in the primary issues market.

The substantial improvement in liquidity on one hand and the sluggish credit off-take on the other led to larger market absorption of government securities, facilitating early completion of the Government's market borrowing programme for 1996–97. There was also lower devolvement on the Reserve Bank and PDs and less strain on the interest rate. OMOs, including repos, came into sharper focus during the year, given the imperative need to neutralise the excess liquidity generated from the build-up of foreign exchange reserves as well as the rates of interest and exchange rates to rule at reasonable levels. A system of announcing a calendar of repo auctions on a monthly basis was started in January 1997 so that participants could plan their treasury management operations in an optimal manner.

The Reserve Bank took a series of major policy decisions during 1995–96 and 1996–97, which had a bearing on the level of activity in the money and financial markets. The more important among these were reduction in CRR, exemption/reduction of reserve requirements on certain categories of external deposits, liberalisation of interest rate on domestic term deposits with a maturity of over one year, rationalisation of lending norms, liberalisation of the guidelines for setting-up MMMFs and aligning the operations of financial companies closer with the organised financial system. As a result, the relative rates of return on various instruments moved within a narrow range, suggestive of a move towards greater integration of financial markets than before.

Easy liquidity conditions in 1996–97 were reflected in the softening of the interest rates on securities across the maturity spectrum, especially at the shorter end. The maximum coupon rate on 10-year maturity bonds declined from 14.0 per cent to 13.65 per cent in February 1997, while that for a 3-year security came down from 13.70 per cent in June 1996 to 13.40 per cent in December 1996. The fall in interest rates for short-term paper was more pronounced, as the implicit yield at cut-off prices for 91-day Treasury Bills lost ground substantially from 12.97 per cent as at end-March 1996 to 7.96 per cent as at end-March 1997. The rate for 364-day Treasury Bills also eased considerably from 13.12 per cent to 10.10 per cent over this period, and declined further to 8.42 per cent by end-July 1997. Thus, while improved liquidity impacted more strongly at the shorter end of the market, its impact on the longer end of the market was distinctly weaker, resulting in steepening of the yield curve. The yield spread (based on primary yield rates) between 91-day Treasury Bills and 364-day Treasury Bills, which stood at only 16 basis points at end-March 1996, widened to 214 basis points at end-March 1997, while the yield spread between 91-day Treasury Bills and 10-year government paper shot up from 103 basis points to 569 basis points over the same period.

Data in Table 16.1 show that the weighted average interest rates on dated securities of the Centre progressively rose during the period 1980–81 to 1996–97, which, *inter alia,* imposed a larger interest burden on the Government.

TABLE 16.1

Coupon Rates on Government Dated Securities

(Per cent per annum)

Fiscal Year	Weighted Average Rate	Range
(1)	(2)	(3)
1980–81	7.03	6.00 – 7.50
1985–86	11.08	9.00 – 11.50
1989–90	11.49	10.50 – 11.50
1990–91	11.41	10.50 – 11.50
1991–92	11.78	10.50 – 12.50
1992–93	12.46	12.00 – 12.75
1993–94	12.63	12.00 – 13.40
1994–95	11.90	11.00 – 12.71
1995–96	13.75	13.25 – 14.00
1996–97	13.69	13.40 – 13.85

Source: Reserve Bank of India, *Annual Report, 1996–97.*

The comparative movements in the rates of return on various financial assets in the 1990s give an idea of the liquidity conditions in the domestic financial markets as well as the degree of integration among different markets. Table 16.2 shows that despite a sharp decline in the inflation rate as at end-March 1996, interest rates tended to increase across the board, reflecting probably the higher demand for funds emanating from the revival in real sector activities.

FOREIGN EXCHANGE MARKET

The sharp narrowing of the current account deficit (CAD) and substantial inflows of foreign capital in the form of foreign investments and deposits in non-resident accounts in 1992–93 resulted in excess supply of foreign exchange in the inter-bank market. As against weak market absorption, the excess supply augmented the foreign exchange reserves in the form of purchases of foreign currencies by the Reserve Bank.

The exchange rate of the Indian rupee was market-driven effective March 1, 1993. As a result, the market distortions caused by the system of dual exchange rates came to an end. This development, along with attractive rates of return on investments in India and limited absorption by way of imports, was responsible for excess supply in the foreign exchange market. This situation provided an opportunity to the authorities to liquidate the

TABLE 16.2

Relative Rates of Return in Major Financial Markets

(Per cent per annum)

Item	1991	1992	1993	1994	1995	1996	1997
			(last week/fortnight of March)				
Call money rate (Mumbai) (DFHI average lending rate)	21.50	30.63	17.38	6.38	16.10	16.28	3.66
91-day Treasury Bills auction/cut-off yield	--	--	10.97	7.46	11.90	12.97	7.96
182/364-day Treasury Bills (cut-off yield)	10.08	9.27	11.10	9.97	11.94	13.12	10.10
Certificates of Deposit (middle rate)	12.44	14.50	14.50	9.60	12.50	17.13	11.38
Commercial Paper (middle rate)	15.10	16.50	15.88	11.50	14.50	20.16	11.88
Deposit rate* (3-year)	10.00	12.00	11.00	10.00	11.00	free	free
Prime lending rate (PLR)#	16.00	19.00	17.00	14.00	15.00	16.50	14.50–16.00
Coupon rate of 10-year	10.75	11.00	12.75	12.50	12.35	14.00$	13.65
GoI securities (issued during the fiscal year)							
Memorandum item							
Inflation rate (WPI: point-to-point basis)	12.10	13.56	7.02	10.81	10.41	5.00	6.90

Notes: * : Deposit rate for March 1995 was the ceiling rate for term deposits of 46 days to 3 years and above. The rate for March 1996 was for maturity of 46 days and up to 2 years. From October 1, 1995 banks were free to determine deposit rates for maturity above 2 years. From July 2, 1996 the ceiling on term deposits of 30 days and up to one year was 11.00 per cent, and banks were free to determine deposit rates for maturity above one year.

: Relate to five major scheduled commercial banks (SCBs). For 1995, the rate pertains to prime lending rate of the SBI.

$: Pre-announced. For 1994, the figure relates to the fixed coupon rate offered in conversion of Treasury Bills.

-- : Not applicable.

Figures on gross yield calculated on the basis of annual average for the respective financial years.

Source: Reserve Bank of India, *Annual Report*, various issues.

costly and volatile liabilities that were a feature of the country's foreign exchange reserves and to re-organise the reserves in terms of durable components that carried no obligation to repay. With this objective, the Reserve Bank absorbed foreign currency offered to it at its buying rate. Foreign currency assets (FCA) increased from US$ 6,434.0 million at the end of March 1993 to US$ 16,068.0 million at the end of March 1994. The Reserve Bank's gross purchases of foreign currencies amounted to

US$ 13,940.0 million during 1993–94. Consequent to the accretions to the FCA through purchases from the market, liabilities amounting to US$ 1,243.0 million in the form of swaps that had been incurred during 1991–1993 could be completely eliminated.

The Reserve Bank effected three major changes in 1994–95 to deepen the foreign exchange market. As already mentioned, the limit of US$ 1.0 million or its equivalent prescribed on banks' oversold positions in the rupee against foreign currencies was raised in May 1994 to ₹ 16 crore, with an identified cap on overbought position. In December 1994, corporate bodies were authorised to book forward contracts in any permitted currency irrespective of the currency of invoice, subject to certain credit enhancements in the form of obtaining suitable margin deposits or earmarking against counterparty/default risk. The Reserve Bank banned from January 16, 1995 the roll-over of forward contracts at historical rates in order to achieve transparency in the financial statements of corporate entities/banks.

Episode of Volatility (October 1995)

The year 1995–96 was notable for considerable volatility in the foreign exchange market, particularly in the second half of the year, despite strong macroeconomic fundamentals. Since the rupee was overvalued as evident from the continuing inflation differentials, a correction was overdue. The exchange rate of the rupee exhibited sudden volatility in October 1995, triggering expectations and causing a bandwagon effect. The rupee came under considerable pressure. The Reserve Bank intervened in the spot foreign exchange market, which stabilised the market and the rupee remained at the level of US$ 1 = ₹ 35.00 until the end of December 1995. Further depreciations in the rupee towards the end of January and early February 1996 were due to speculative dealings by market entities.

The Reserve Bank responded in February 1996 by terminating the PCFC scheme, freeing the interest rate on post-shipment rupee export credit for over 90 days and enhancing the interest rate surcharge on import finance. These measures helped to restore some semblance of stability in the foreign exchange market by reversing the strong 'leads and lags' in external payments and receipts. While the Reserve Bank did resort to large interventions in the foreign exchange market in October 1995, subsequent interventions in the swap market restored domestic rupee liquidity. For the year 1995–96 as a whole, the overall impact of foreign exchange intervention on domestic liquidity was minimal.

The theoretical underpinnings of exchange rate stability in the Indian context *vis-à-vis* monetary management were propounded in the credit policy circular to banks dated April 3, 1996 as follows:

> While it is not feasible to have a specific nominal exchange rate target, the real effective exchange rate provides a measure of competitiveness and this can be used as a reference for assessing sustainability of the exchange rate in relation to an earlier period, say, March 1993 when the exchange rate could be deemed to be in equilibrium. In the ultimate analysis, exchange rate stability can be achieved only if Indian inflation rates are not seriously out of alignment with inflation rates in major industrial countries and this, once again, underscores the need for a cautious monetary policy.

Measures were taken to fine-tune the policy responses to evolving market conditions during 1995–96, even while carrying forward the progressive liberalisation of the trade and payments regime. The first set of measures was directed at easing excess demand conditions in the foreign exchange market and reversing the build-up of speculative expectations. Besides encouraging the inflow of foreign exchange through non-resident deposits, Euro-issues and external commercial borrowings (ECBs), the Reserve Bank took steps to even out 'leads and lags' in receipts and payments by inducing repatriation of export proceeds and terminating the PCFC scheme. The second set of measures was aimed at improving the functioning of the foreign exchange market and stemmed from the recommendations of the expert group on foreign exchange market in India. Banks were allowed to set their own aggregate overnight positions and AGL subject to certain conditions.

The average monthly turnover in the foreign exchange market rose moderately during 1996–97 in comparison with the high growth phase of 1993–94 to 1995–96, when significant increases in current and capital account transactions led to a robust rise in the monthly turnover of merchant transactions. There was moderation in the average monthly turnover during the year. However, the share of inter-bank transactions in the total turnover remained well over 80.0 per cent. An encouraging development was the progressive integration of the forex market with the money market as evidenced by softening of the forward premia from the second half of 1996–97 in the wake of a significant moderation in short-term interest rates and sustained stability in the exchange rates.

*Growing Inter-linkages between the Foreign Exchange Market
and Financial Market*

By 1994–95, the foreign exchange market was increasingly viewed as a continuum stretching from debt markets at the long end to markets for call and notice funds at the short end.[9] The forward market provided conditions for integration of the foreign exchange market with the financial markets. Forward transactions served as the mechanism whereby the foreign exchange market coalesced with the money market. While the linkage between the money market and the foreign exchange market was weak in the pre-LERMS period (*i.e.*, before March, 1992), introduction of market-determined exchange rates and growing importance of the forward market for foreign exchange strengthened the conduits for transmission of impulses between the short-end of the money market and the foreign exchange market. The changes brought about in the reserve requirements from time to time resulted in the increasing use of swaps by commercial banks to bolster their local currency reserves. Tight liquidity conditions in the money market and the resultant rise in call money rates induced demand for swaps, whereby banks acquired spot rupees to be swapped for forward dollars. This exerted an upward pressure on the swap premia which had, in general, been on the rise since November 1994 in tandem with the movements in the call money rates.

In October 1995, the downward pressure on the rupee intensified due to speculative forces, and the nominal exchange rate fell to ₹ 35.65 per US dollar. A panic demand for cover by importers and cancellations of forward contracts by exporters created persistent mismatches between supply and demand in both spot and forward segments of the market. Forward premia surged sharply in October 1995, particularly for shorter maturities, with the highest rise recorded in the cash spot range. The premia were far out of alignment with the interest rate differentials. The prohibitive cost of foreign exchange cover acted as a deterrent to banks from mobilising foreign currency deposits and employing them to fund domestic assets. In the circumstances, large dollar balances were held in their *nostro* accounts.

The exchange market intervention (net sales) by the Reserve Bank in the spot market led to withdrawal of liquidity in October 1995 to the extent of ₹ 2,780 crore from the money market. There was a sharp hike in call rates, touching a peak of 85.0 per cent on November 3, 1995, largely mirroring the turbulence in the foreign exchange market and the Reserve

---

9.   Reserve Bank of India, *Annual Report, 1994–95.*

Bank's intervention in that market. Given the buoyant demand for credit to support real sector activities, there was a need for liquidity injection, which was resorted to by the authorities. Besides, reverse repo arrangements with the DFHI and the STCI, the relaxation of banks' reserve requirements augmented liquidity in the market. Intervention, in turn, was supported by measures such as a surcharge on import finance (effective October 1995) and tightening the concessionality element in export credit for longer periods.

The cumulative net liquidity impact of the Reserve Bank's domestic monetary and exchange rate management after November 1995 turned out to be positive. The rupee was generally maintained at the level of ₹ 35 per US dollar in the spot segment until the middle of January 1996. A bout of sharp depreciation, however, was witnessed between the end of January 1996 and the first week of February 1996, when the rupee plunged to a record low of ₹ 37.95 per US dollar in the spot market, while premia rose to around 20.0 per cent in the forward segment.

In counter-response, the Reserve Bank took several measures in early February 1996 to accelerate the receipt of export proceeds and to prevent deceleration in import payments. The PCFC scheme was discontinued from February 8, 1996 as the negative rate of interest charged under the scheme created serious disruptions in the foreign exchange market. Exporters were asked to discharge their statutory obligation to realise export proceeds within six months from the date of export of goods, failing which punitive action was envisaged under the relevant statute.

The progress made in forging increased financial market inter-linkages during the 1990s was reviewed by the Reserve Bank in its Annual Report for 1996–97, besides providing its perspectives about future trends. The Indian financial market in the past had been characterised by marked segmentation among its various constituents due to a variety of regulations, including barriers to entry. This impaired the free flow of resources and impinged on efficient utilisation of scarce resources. Since the introduction of reform measures in the early 1990s, broad segments of the market, *viz.*, the money market, government securities market and foreign exchange market had responded 'favourably' with growing inter-linkages among them, thus facilitating faster liquidity pass-through. This was borne out by the fact that improvements in liquidity in 1996–97 got translated into significant softening of various money market rates, interest rates on government paper, particularly those at the shorter end, and forward premia in the foreign exchange market. Further:

The increasing complementarity between credit market and capital market on one hand, and credit market and external sources of financing on the other, has become evident in giving the corporates a wider choice among alternate sources of funds. The integration between yield rates on Government paper and those of other debt market instruments is, however, currently at a formative stage on account of, *inter alia,* narrow investor base and the lack of depth in secondary markets. While these changes are symptomatic of a greater interplay of market forces, the thrust of the Reserve Bank's policy is on elimination of the factors constraining these segments and to facilitate opportunities for larger arbitrage.

Deepening of the Forex Market

In April 1997, the Reserve Bank announced two decisions to deepen and widen the forex market. Under the forward cover based on business projections, exporters and importers were allowed to take forward cover without having to produce documentary evidence of a firm order or opening a letter of credit (LC) through a bank. The ADs could, without any limitation on the period of such contracts, book contracts based on a declaration of exposure supported by past performance and business projections but subject to certain conditions. This measure was expected to provide flexibility to corporate entities and improve liquidity in the forward markets for periods even beyond six months.

The second pertained to development of the rupee forex swap market. Several corporate entities that had foreign exchange exposures arising out of external borrowings were unable to procure long-term forward cover for such exposures. They, therefore, tended to go in for six-month roll-over forward cover. There were corporate entities in the system that were willing to convert some or whole of their rupee liabilities into forex liability. The Reserve Bank decided to allow ADs to run a swap book within their open positions/gap limits to enable them to arrange such swaps without its prior approval.

Exchange Rate Movements of the Rupee and Interventions by the Reserve Bank

With the institution of the market-based exchange rate regime in March 1993, the exchange rate of the rupee strengthened rapidly from its level in February 1993, when speculative attacks in the period leading up to an announcement of the Union Budget for 1993–94 had weakened the rupee to a low of ₹ 33.14 per dollar. Subsequently, however, a remarkable degree of stability in the movement of the exchange rate prevailed and the rupee remained anchored at a level of ₹ 31.37 against the US dollar. A sharp improvement in the current account balance and large capital inflows resulted in the foreign exchange market being flush with excess supply of funds, the demand being dampened by low import growth. The consequent upward pressure on the rupee was staved off by the Reserve Bank's intervention in the market in the form of large spot purchases. There was a clustering of the inter-bank rates around the Reserve Bank buying rate. The Reserve Bank's passive intervention was motivated by the need to protect export competitiveness by preventing an appreciation of the rupee, which, in any case, would have been against the fundamentals. The Reserve Bank's Annual Report for 1993–94 conceded that while the intervention to hold the nominal value of the rupee in the face of large capital inflows implied generation of primary liquidity, it also underscored the need to maintain the role of the exchange rate as a nominal anchor for the economy.

The remarkable stability of the rupee *vis-a-vis* the US dollar continued during 1994–95. The surge in imports and the deceleration in the inflow of foreign capital impacted the surplus conditions that existed during 1993–94 and the first half of 1994–95 in the foreign exchange market. The buying rate of the Reserve Bank was unchanged at ₹ 31.37 per US dollar. The rupee, however, came briefly under pressure in March 1995, touching a low of ₹ 31.97 per US dollar, when the supply of foreign exchange was affected by the temporary drying up of foreign remittances due to the closure of the markets in the Gulf region and pre-budget expectations, as also by a rise in demand due to seasonal spurt in imports. The rupee, however, recovered its stability soon after and generally remained steady against the US dollar, but depreciated sharply against other major currencies and the SDR. This weakness mirrored the behaviour of the US dollar, the intervention currency.

Reflecting the weakness in the US dollar, the rupee depreciated in terms of the index of nominal effective exchange rate (NEER) based on a 36-country export-weighted index. By March 1995, this index depreciated by 7.8 per cent over its level in March 1994. The nominal depreciation in the rupee was strong enough to offset the adverse inflation differential between India and the rest of the world. As a result, the rupee also depreciated marginally in 1995 in real terms, as indicated by the index of real effective exchange rate (REER) over its level in March 1994.

In the market for forward foreign exchange, with the deregulation of lending rates in October 1994, a loose relationship seemed to emerge between the swap premia and the prime lending rate. While this link was not manifest when considering nominal interest rates, an examination of the real interest rates, *i.e.*, interest rates adjusted for inflation differentials, tracked reasonably well the movements in the swap premia. Another factor affecting the swap premia was call money rate movements, which assumed importance with the increased recourse to swaps by commercial banks to augment their rupee resources to meet their reserve requirements. The Reserve Bank declared that the growing importance of the forward foreign exchange market in an environment of economic liberalisation underscored the need to have a well-developed market for foreign exchange derivatives.[10] In India, the main instruments of hedging at that time were forward contracts, swaps and cross-currency options. In the absence of international quotes for the rupee, it was not possible to introduce rupee-based options.

The prolonged stability in the exchange rate of the rupee from March 1993 came under stress in the second half of 1995–96. The widening of the CAD in the face of a rising trade deficit, the ebbing of capital flows and pronounced appreciation of the US dollar against major international currencies triggered market expectations that resulted in the depreciation of the rupee in the second half of 1995–96. The exchange rate began, thereby, to increasingly reflect the interplay of market forces.[11] The Reserve Bank closely monitored the market to ensure that exchange rate movements were in alignment with macroeconomic fundamentals. It stood ready to take action to curb any speculative activity in the market.

In August 1995, the rupee weakened to ₹ 31.94 per US dollar essentially because of the strengthening of the US dollar, as also the increase in demand for foreign exchange (to meet burgeoning import payments) that far exceeded the supply in the market. Further, the spread between buying and selling rates widened, reflecting uncertain conditions in the foreign exchange market. The downward pressure on the rupee intensified in October 1995, when the nominal exchange rate fell to ₹ 35.65 per US

---

10. Reserve Bank of India, *Annual Report, 1994–95.*

11. Reserve Bank of India, *Annual Report, 1995–96.*

dollar in terms of FEDAI indicative rates, amplified by speculative factors. Unidirectional expectations of a 'free fall' of the rupee reinforced the normal 'leads and lags' in external receipts and payments, vitiating orderly market activity. Panic demand for cover by importers and cancellations of forward contracts by exporters created persistent mismatches of supply and demand in both the spot and forward segments of the market. The forward premia rose sharply in October 1995 and banks held large balances in their *nostro* accounts as the high cost of foreign cover dissuaded them from mobilising foreign currency deposits. The Reserve Bank intervened in the market in response to these upheavals to signal that the fundamentals were in place and to ensure that the market correction of the overvalued exchange rate was orderly and calibrated. Exchange market intervention by the Reserve Bank was initially supported by withdrawal of liquidity from the money market to prevent speculative attacks on the exchange rate. As call money rates soared in the face of stringent liquidity conditions, the policy stance of intervention in the exchange market was tempered by restoration of money market support, an easing of reserve requirements on domestic as well as non-resident deposits and an increase in the interest rates on NRE deposits. As a result of the Reserve Bank's exchange market operations the six-month forward premia, which rose to over 23.0 per cent in March 1996, declined to less than 13.0 per cent in June 1996. While the Reserve Bank's operations culminated in net sales between October 1995 and February 1996, it turned into much larger net purchases during March–June 1996.

The decisive and timely policy responses restored stability to the market and the rupee traded within the range of ₹ 34.28–₹ 35.79 per US dollar in the spot segment until mid-January 1996. In the first week of February the rupee touched a record low of ₹ 37.95 per US dollar in terms of FEDAI indicative rates in the spot market, while the three-month premia rose to around 20.0 per cent. The range of forward premia moved broadly in tandem with the fluctuations triggered at the very short end of the spectrum, *i.e.*, the cash-spot segment. The forward premia for the relatively longer maturities of three months and six months during the period did not reflect the prevailing interest rate differentials.

The Reserve Bank intervened actively in the spot, forward and swap markets from October 1995, which had the desired impact on the exchange market and the domestic liquidity (Table 16.3). In this regard two significant developments stood out. First, the net sales in the foreign exchange market between October 1995 and June 1996 broadly evened out and the intervention smoothened the volatility rather than propping up the exchange rate. In fact, the exchange market intervention in October 1995 was carried on until the rupee appreciated to a point considered consistent with a real exchange rate. A steep fall in the rupee value at that time could have undermined confidence in the currency. The intervention was done in the spot market first, followed by intervention in the forward market. According to, Dr C. Rangarajan,[12] one important lesson learnt from the experience was the need for integration between the domestic money market and the foreign exchange market since the latter could not be controlled without controlling the former. Second, while the intervention initially impinged quite sharply on domestic liquidity, the overall impact had been broadly balanced with a net injection of liquidity.

TABLE 16.3

Reserve Bank's Foreign Exchange Market Operations

(US$ million)

Period	Purchases*	Sales*	Net Purchases (+)/Sales (–)
(1)	(2)	(3)	(4)
1995			
October	7	792	–785
November	290	401	–111
December	272	328	–56
1996			
January	1,368	1,770	–402
February	140	468	–328
March	1,135	175	+960
April	577	209	+368
May	336	235	+101
June	1,150	365	+785
Total	5,275	4,743	+532

Notes: * : Include spot, forward and swap transactions effected during the month.

– : net sales from FCA.

+ : net accretion to FCA.

Source: Reserve Bank of India, *Annual Report, 1995–96.*

The external sector during 1996–97, displayed welcome signs of stability in contrast with the turbulence in the foreign exchange market in

---

12. Transcript of the interview with Dr C. Rangarajan, former Governor, Reserve Bank of India, December 2006.

the second half of 1995–96. A surge in net invisible receipts and a strong resumption of capital flows after a brief interruption during October 1995 to February 1966 caused a large overall surplus in the balance of payments (BoP). Reflecting these developments, easy conditions prevailed in the foreign exchange market throughout the year. While the spot market was awash with supplies of foreign exchange, premia in the forward market declined significantly due to the easing of downside expectations of the future exchange rate of the rupee as well as a narrowing of short-term interest rate differentials *vis-a-vis* the rest of the world.

The nominal exchange rate was subjected to considerable upward pressures that were mitigated by continuous passive interventions by the Reserve Bank. Consequently, there was a build-up in foreign exchange reserves to a peak of US$ 26,423.0 million at the end of March 1997 — the equivalent of seven months of imports. Despite the interventions, the appreciation of the US dollar *vis-a-vis* other foreign currencies as well as continued inflation differential culminated in a strong appreciation of the REER of the rupee. A related and far-reaching development was the gradual integration of the foreign exchange market with the money market as signified by the softening of forward premia from the second half of 1996–97 in the wake of significant moderation in short-term interest rates and sustained stability in exchange rates.

In 1996–97, exchange rate management policy was guided mainly by the underlying market conditions, namely, contraction in the CAD and resurgence of capital inflows. Subsequent to the market-driven downward correction in the exchange rate of the rupee in the second half of 1995–96, the stability of the rupee was restored by the beginning of 1996–97 and prevailed throughout the year. Following large scale capital inflows and to prevent the appreciation of the rupee, the Reserve Bank undertook large purchases of the US dollar from the market during the year essentially to protect international competitiveness. Nevertheless, the trade-based REER appreciated by 9.6 per cent by March 1997 over its level in March 1993.

The Reserve Bank perceived that attaining the stable exchange rate objective in the context of large capital inflows necessitated maintenance of a delicate balance between the required rate of growth in exports and price stability. Thus, the interventions by the Reserve Bank during 1996–97 ensured that the nominal exchange rate was bound in a narrow range of ₹ 35 to ₹ 36 per US dollar between May 1996 and June 1997, and this insulated the economy from imported inflation and anchored expectations[13] (Table 16.4).

TABLE 16.4

Rupee Exchange Rates
(FEDAI Indicative Rates)

(₹ per unit of SDR/US dollar)

	SDR*	US dollar*
Annual Exchange Rate (April – March)		
1993–94	43.8863	31.3655
1994–95	45.7908	31.3986
	(– 4.2)	(– 0.1)
1995–96	50.4768	33.4498
	(– 9.3)	(– 6.5)
1996–97	50.8858	35.4999
	(– 0.8)	(– 5.8)
Exchange Rate as on		
March 31, 1994	44.3133	31.3725
March 31, 1995	49.1558	31.4950
	(-10.9)	(-0.4)
March 29, 1996	50.1633	34.3500
	(– 2.0)	(– 9.1)
March 31, 1997	49.8032	35.9150
	(+ 0.7)	(– 4.4)

Notes: 1. FEDAI : Foreign Exchange Dealers' Association of India.

2. * : Rupees per SDR arrived at by crossing the US dollar rate with the RBI reference rate.

3. Figures in brackets indicate percentage appreciation (+)/depreciation (–) of the rupee over the previous period.

Source: Reserve Bank of India, *Annual Report*, various issues.

INSTITUTIONS AND INSTRUMENTS

Financial markets operated through institutions and instruments, evolved to suit the requirements of the respective markets. The effective functioning of the markets and, as a corollary, the two-way transmission mechanism for the monetary policy of the Reserve Bank depended on the efficiency and dynamism they exhibited.

---

13.   Reserve Bank of India, *Annual Report, 1996–97.*

The main institutions functioning in the financial markets besides banks and FIs were the DFHI, STCI and PDs. The Reserve Bank established the DFHI in 1988 to develop an active secondary market for money market instruments and integrate various segments of the market to facilitate the smoothening of short-run imbalances. As a first step in developing a secondary market in central government dated securities, the DFHI started dealing in such securities from April 2, 1992, but its efforts received a temporary setback in the aftermath of the irregularities in securities transactions when new inter-bank ready-forward deals in dated government and other approved securities were prohibited (June 1992). In October 1992, the Reserve Bank introduced a new refinance facility against dated government and other approved securities to provide liquidity to banks affected by the above development. Since its inception, the DFHI made successful efforts to develop the short-term money market and the secondary market for money market assets and, more importantly, served as the fulcrum of activities in the money market. It also functioned as a PD. The DFHI was eligible to obtain refinance from the Reserve Bank.

In the pivotal gilt-edged market, a need was felt to develop an institutional infrastructure that would serve as a base for an active secondary market in these securities. This matter assumed urgency in the context of the Central Government's decision to meet its budgetary credit needs through the government securities market rather than from the Reserve Bank or commercial banks. Therefore, the Reserve Bank set up in 1993 a specialised institution entrusted with the task of fostering the development of a vibrant market in government securities, including Treasury Bills. The new institution, the STCI, commenced operations in June 1994. While the development of a secondary market in dated government securities and public sector bonds was its main responsibility, it could also hold short-term money market assets like Treasury Bills as part of its liquidity management operations. The STCI acted as a PD and market-maker in government securities.

To further strengthen the secondary market, the Reserve Bank granted in principle approval in November 1995 to six entities to be accredited as PDs to undertake transactions in government securities. Subsidiaries of scheduled commercial banks (SCBs), all-India FIs and companies that had net owned funds of the prescribed minimum amount were eligible to apply to become PDs. PDs underwrote the auctions of government securities, operated as market-maker by offering two-way quotes and provided access to securities to a wider base of investors. Besides improving secondary market trading, liquidity and turn-over in government securities, PDs extended further support to the active deployment of indirect instruments of monetary control.

The Reserve Bank announced on December 31, 1996 the guidelines for setting-up SDs for strengthening the infrastructure in the government securities market, enhancing liquidity and turnover, providing a retail outlet and encouraging voluntary holding of government securities among a wider investor base.

The instruments inducted for the first time in the financial markets during the period covered by this volume were CDs, CP, units/deposits in MMMFs, Treasury Bills of different maturities and repo transactions. They helped improve banks' assessment of their daily cash flow position and strengthened the Reserve Bank's own liquidity management.

CERTIFICATES OF DEPOSIT

CDs were introduced in June 1989 in pursuance of a recommendation of the Vaghul Committee. Their principal objective was to widen the range of money market instruments and give corporate investors as well as non-bank financial intermediaries greater flexibility in the deployment of their short-term surplus funds at competitive rates of interest. This instrument also aided banks contain the process of disintermediation of deposits. CDs could be issued only by SCBs (excluding the regional rural banks [RRBs]); had to conform to the prescribed minimum limits; and the maturity had to be between 91 days and one year. CDs were issued at a discount to face value and the discount rate could be freely determined. They were freely transferable by endorsement and delivery but only 45 days after the date of issue. Banks were not allowed to grant loans against CDs or buy back their own CDs.

An internal review in March 1990 (in the Credit Planning Cell [CPC]) concluded that, by and large, banks had successfully handled the new instrument and the scheme had evoked good response from individuals and corporate investors due to higher rate of interest that it offered as compared with fixed deposits, short-term maturity and free transferability. However, certain features inhibited the development of a secondary market in this instrument, such as, the reluctance of holders of CDs to disinvest them owing to their attractive rate of return, banks' disinclination to invest in them since they carried no fiscal advantage and the limited size of the primary market. To boost its growth in the primary market, from April 1990 the Reserve Bank enhanced the limit for issue of CDs by individual banks from 1.0 per cent to 2.0 per cent of their average outstanding deposits.

At the same time, the denomination of issue was fixed at multiples of ₹ 10 lakh instead of ₹ 25 lakh. The perception of the Reserve Bank was that banks should be encouraged to place relatively large amounts in the primary market at somewhat lower rates if CDs were to become a viable instrument. The bank-wise limits for issue of CDs underwent upward revisions in December 1990, April 1992, October 1992 and April 1993 before they were withdrawn; this gave banks greater flexibility in mobilising deposits at competitive rates of interest and was also a step towards deregulation of the interest rate structure. Banks were given the freedom to issue CDs depending on their requirements. The minimum size of issue of CDs to a single investor was also progressively reduced to ₹ 5 lakh in multiples of ₹ 1 lakh by October 1997.

A tendency was noticed whereby banks mobilised more resources through CDs whenever stringent conditions prevailed in the money market, and in times of easy conditions in the money market, they showed less reliance on high-cost CDs, or the interest rate on mobilised CDs came down.

COMMERCIAL PAPER

To enable highly-rated corporate borrowers to diversify their sources of short-term borrowing and to provide an additional outlet to investors, the Reserve Bank, on the recommendations of the Vaghul Committee, permitted CPs to be introduced from January 1990. The features of CPs were: unsecured promissory notes not tied to specific transactions; could be privately placed with investors (excluding non-residents) through banks or other FIs; only companies that had a net worth of at least ₹ 10 crore, a maximum permissible finance limit of at least ₹ 25 crore and listed at the stock exchanges were permitted to enter the CP market; the issuing company to obtain every six months an excellent rating from an agency approved by the Reserve Bank; the maturity period of CP ranged from 91 days to 6 months; the instrument to be issued in multiples of ₹ 25 lakh subject to a minimum size of ₹ 1 crore; CP to be issued at a discount to face value and the discount rate could be freely determined; the maximum amount of CP issue by a company limited to 20.0 per cent of the maximum permissible bank finance; and CP to be freely transferable by endorsement and delivery.

The Reserve Bank had been periodically relaxing the guidelines for the issue of CP to broad base the primary market; the relaxations covered various aspects, *e.g.,* tangible net worth of the company issuing the CP, minimum rating from Credit Rating and Information Services of India Ltd (CRISIL), denomination of issue, working capital (fund-based limit) of the issuing company and the maximum maturity period for issue of CP. Finally, the requirement for banks to obtain the prior approval of the Reserve Bank was dispensed with.

MONEY MARKET MUTUAL FUNDS

The MMMFs, a special genre of mutual funds, invested only in high-quality money market instruments that were short term. They undertook the process of disintermediation to bring a wide range of short-term money market instruments within the reach of individual investors. Commercial banks and FIs or their existing mutual funds/subsidiaries engaged in fund management were permitted to set up MMMFs.

The Reserve Bank issued guidelines for the MMMF scheme on April 29, 1992. As MMMFs were primarily intended to be a vehicle for individual investors to participate in the money market, their units/shares could be issued only to individuals. Non-resident individuals could subscribe to these units, subject to the condition that both the capital and the dividend would be non-repatriable. MMMFs were free to determine the minimum size of investment by a single investor. The resources mobilised by MMMFs should be invested exclusively in money market instruments, such as Treasury Bills and dated government securities that had an unexpired maturity up to one year, call/notice money, CP, CDs, and commercial bills arising out of genuine trade/commercial transactions and acceptable or co-accepted by banks. The minimum lock-in period for investments in MMMFs was 46 days and they could offer buy-back facilities to investors. MMMFs were required to calculate the net asset value (NAV) of each scheme and disclose NAVs periodically for the benefit of their investors.

Setting-up an MMMF required the prior authorisation of the Reserve Bank, which was empowered to issue directions, call for any information and inspect their books and accounts. In December 1995, to make the scheme more flexible and to impart greater liquidity and depth to the money market, institutions in the private sector were allowed to set up MMMFs, the ceiling on the size of MMMFs was removed and the prescription of minimum and maximum limits on their investments in individual instruments were withdrawn. The restriction that the units could be issued only to individuals was withdrawn effective April 9, 1996 and, consequently, MMMF units became available to corporates and others on par with other mutual funds as regards their eligibility to invest in such a scheme. The scheme was made more attractive to investors by reducing the minimum lock-in period from 46 days to 30 days from July 1, 1996.

TREASURY BILLS

The Chakravarty Committee had recommended that Treasury Bills should be developed as a monetary instrument with flexible rates, which would enable banks to better manage their short-term liquidity. The objective was to provide an alternative avenue for short-term investments for which an active secondary market would develop over time. Accordingly, the Reserve Bank introduced in November 1986 182-day Treasury Bills, initially on a monthly auction basis, without any rediscounting facilities. State governments and PFs were not allowed to participate in these auctions. The discount rate was flexible and varied with the outcome of the auctions. To impart flexibility, the amount for each auction was not fixed in advance. With the liquidity provided by the DFHI, these 182-day Treasury Bills were established by 1991–92 as a useful monetary instrument.

The Reserve Bank made a significant pronouncement in its credit policy circular to banks dated April 21, 1992, that the gilt-edged market would be reorganised in such a way that the Government would decrease its dependence on credit from the Reserve Bank and banks. This circular also announced that the Government proposed to float Treasury Bills of varying maturities up to 364 days on auction basis.[14]

Consequent to discontinuation of the 91-day Treasury Bills on tap and *ad hoc* Treasury Bills from April 1997, the Reserve Bank decided to issue Treasury Bills of different maturities to facilitate the cash management requirements of various sectors of the economy. To assist in the formation of a more comprehensive yield curve, sale of a new category of 14-day Treasury Bills on auction basis was announced on May 20, 1997 at a discount rate equivalent to the interest rate charged on ways and means advances (WMA) to the Central Government. This was different from the 14-day Intermediate Treasury Bills introduced earlier on April 1, 1997 to cater to the needs of investing the surplus funds of state governments,

---

14. For details, see chapter 15: Public Debt Management.

foreign central banks and other specified bodies with whom the Reserve Bank had entered into special arrangements.

REPOS (REPURCHASE AGREEMENTS)

Repo transactions play an active and positive role in increasing the turnover in government securities and Treasury Bills in the secondary market. Repos enable collateralised short-term borrowing through selling of debt instruments. Under repo transaction, the security was sold with an agreement to repurchase it at a pre-determined date and rate. Reverse repo was a mirror image of repo and represented the acquisition of a security with a simultaneous commitment to resell. In other words, the repo was a form of sale of dated securities by the Reserve Bank for very short periods with a confirmed buy-back provision. The Reserve Bank often used this in conjunction with the refinance arrangement to ease stringent conditions marked by very high call rates. The reverse repo operations were generally conducted through PDs.

Repo transactions with the Reserve Bank served as a handy instrument for banks to optimise returns on short-term surplus liquid funds. Repos were introduced in December 1992, but gained prominence a few years later as part of the open market strategy to neutralise the impact of liquidity on the domestic economy due to inflow of foreign funds. The Reserve Bank extended the reverse repo facility in dated government securities to the DFHI and the STCI to inject liquidity into the market. In particular, the conduct of reverse repos enabled the Reserve Bank to arrest undue upward pressure on call money rates during 1994–95. However, repo operations were suspended after February 3, 1995 due to the stringent liquidity position in the money market, but resumed about a year later.

In April 1997, the Reserve Bank activated the repo market, since it functioned as an equilibrating force between the money market and the securities market. First, the instruments eligible for repo/reverse repo transactions were expanded to include all central government dated securities besides Treasury Bills of all maturities. Earlier, the transactions could take place only in Treasury Bills of all maturities and dated government securities that were approved by the Reserve Bank in consultation with the Government. Second, non-bank entities that held a subsidiary general ledger (SGL) account with the Reserve Bank were allowed to enter into reverse repo transactions with banks/PDs in Treasury Bills of all maturities and all dated central government securities. However, the first leg of the transaction by non-bank entities was to be by way of purchase of securities eligible for repos from banks/PDs and the second leg was to be by selling back securities to banks/PDs. The transactions had to be effected in Mumbai.

INSIGHTS INTO POLICYMAKING

For the Reserve Bank, the strategies for development of the financial markets had been drawn up in an elaborate manner by the Chakravarty Committee in the case of the market for government securities, and by the Vaghul Committee in the case of the money market, its institutions and instruments. The Reserve Bank started implementing the suggestions soon after the respective reports were submitted. The process gained momentum when the Narasimham Committee came out with recommendations relating to policy and institutional issues that would have a bearing on the efficiency and functioning of financial markets and the institutions. In respect of the government securities market, there was a further thrust with the signing of the agreement between the Reserve Bank and the Government to phase out automatic monetisation of budget deficit (September 1994), which necessitated the Central Government to have recourse to the market to meet its short-term needs for budgetary finance. Evolving a strong financial market structure required the Reserve Bank to initiate measures at different points of time to widen market participation, to relax guidelines for issuance of different market instruments and to frame a 'reference rate' for the money markets. These initiatives were responsible for the entry of more participants in the call money market and flagged the need for the development of a 'reference rate' that was fully market determined.

ENTRY OF MORE PARTICIPANTS IN THE CALL MONEY MARKET

With the freeing of the call money rates from May 1, 1989, at times the money market experienced bouts of extreme volatility in interest rates. The rates in call money markets ruled high on certain fortnights, subsequently declined when borrowers found it unremunerative to operate at such high rates and alternative sources of funds became available at lower rates. The DFHI quoted moderate rates, but with the limited resources at its disposal found it difficult to calm the market. After call money rates were freed, many banks alternated between lending and borrowing, which reduced the lopsidedness of the call money market. The Reserve Bank was concerned that the credit operations of some banks were not backed by their own resources and, in the process, they were indulging in over-extension of credit. In other words, these banks considered the call money market as a means for meeting structural disequilibrium in their sources and uses of funds. Despite financial support from the Reserve Bank, the DFHI was unable to impart stability to the market by reducing its volatility.

The need for the entry of more participants in the call/notice money market was internally reviewed in the Reserve Bank (CPC) in March 1990. It was recognised that the periodic flaring up of the call money rates would persist as long as banks had a structural dependence on the call money market, and that widening and deepening the call and notice money market would help integrate the call and rediscount markets. Moreover, banks that had a structural dependence on the call market had to be weaned away from this disproportionate reliance on this market. If these banks were to be provided any assistance, they first had to build-up a large portfolio of Treasury Bills to protect their CRR position during any period of tight liquidity, and gyrations in the call money rates would continue as long as the CRR was based on an average of fortnightly balances.

In principle, the Reserve Bank was not averse to opening up the call market to a larger number of participants, but at the same time it did not rule out the possibility that such a move inevitably exerted increased pressure on the administered structure of deposit rates. On balance, it was felt that eventually a smooth transition had to be made by freeing deposit rates.

The Reserve Bank decided that it was preferable to selectively increase the number of participants as lenders in the call and notice money markets. The institutions selected for this purpose were the GIC, the IDBI and NABARD, and the facility was to be offered subject to their complying with certain conditions. The policy note suggested that banks that were chronic borrowers could be excluded from the market and taken care of through long-term measures that would bring down the extreme volatile conditions in the market, but this perception did not find favour. The authorities realised that as long as deposit rates remained below market rates, efforts would be made to get round the regulations and the stage had not been reached where a drastic change in deposit rates could be ventured. The Vaghul Committee had recommended that the bills rediscounting market might be completely opened up to companies and trusts. The Reserve Bank, however, considered it advisable that first the call and rediscount markets should be integrated.

During this period, the concept of starting MMMFs took shape. The Executive Director, in his note dated March 29, 1990, postulated that with the increasing number of participants in the call market, the pressure from other institutions for access to this market would increase and there would be pressure to move away from the administered deposit rate structure. For this purpose, a scheme for introducing MMMFs was mooted with regulation over their activities.

RELAXATION IN GUIDELINES FOR ISSUE OF COMMERCIAL PAPER

The Reserve Bank in January 1990 had circulated to banks the guidelines for issue of CP. In some quarters, certain features of the scheme were seen to be restrictive, *e.g.*, the limit on tangible net worth, working capital limit, credit rating and the period of issue. Accordingly, the Reserve Bank made a few relaxations. The net worth criterion of a company was reduced from ₹ 10 crore to ₹ 5 crore, thereby enabling more companies to become eligible to issue CP; the limit for minimum working capital (fund-based) was reduced from ₹ 25 crore to ₹ 16 crore so that the more efficiently run companies satisfying the eligibility criteria in all other aspects could avail of the CP facility; the minimum CRISIL credit rating was relaxed from P1+ to P1, which would allow investors to differentiate between companies; and the denomination of issue was reduced from ₹ 25 lakh to ₹ 10 lakh while keeping the minimum issue in the primary market unchanged at ₹ 1 crore, which was expected to bring in a large number of transactions at the primary stage and result in more active trading in the secondary market. The Deputy Governor expressed the hope that after the relaxations, both the primary and secondary markets would become more active and that increased activity would take place with the onset of the slack season.

CERTAIN ISSUES RELATING TO CDs CONSIDERED

In its internal review in December 1990, the Reserve Bank came to know that certain banks had offered unusually high rates to mobilise CDs despite its advice that the freedom to determine rates should be used judiciously and that there was considerable variation in the rates offered for similar maturities. The interest rates offered on CDs tended to be high because reserve requirements had to be maintained on CDs. Another finding was that certain banks had issued CDs at high rates of interest during periods when conditions in the call money market were relatively easy and, hence, there was scope for further improvement in fund management by banks.

Although the growth of the primary market in CDs was not insignificant, the secondary market for this instrument had not developed. It was feared that if this situation continued, CDs might turn out to be as illiquid as fixed deposits. The lack of activity in the secondary market was attributed to the high interest rates paid on CDs, which served as an incentive to investors to hold CDs up to maturity. Since, in the long run, the growth of primary market was dependent on the growth of the secondary market, it was considered necessary for banks to offer rational rates on CDs and evolve suitable procedures for making CDs more liquid in the secondary market. These inputs were expected to facilitate the authorities in framing the policies in future.

PARTICIPATION OF PRIVATE MUTUAL FUNDS IN THE CALL/NOTICE MONEY MARKET AND BILLS REDISCOUNTING MARKET

Towards the middle of 1994, seven mutual funds set up by PSBs and public sector FIs were allowed to participate in the call/notice money market as lenders. Several private sector institutions were granted permission in 1994 to set up mutual funds and some of them approached the Reserve Bank for permission to deploy their short-term surplus funds in the call/notice money market and bills rediscounting market as lenders in order to earn income.

The CPC saw merit in the proposal since the increased flow of funds could provide more resources to the banking system and denying the request might tantamount to 'discrimination'. However, the Deputy Governor, Shri S.S. Tarapore, did not agree with the discrimination argument on the grounds that the new entrants had other avenues for deployment of their surplus funds and that the request had to be viewed in a broader perspective:

> We are in a difficult situation on the co-ordination of various segments of the reform. CPC is right when it talks of "discrimination". But I do not know which course of action would be more hazardous—continuing the discrimination till the basic conditions are met for a general freeing of the call and notice money market or facing the situation of our having to open up the money market without conditions for a free money market or not. The basic issue is deposit rate control. My own preference is to live with the discrimination for the time being; then potential candidates can use their short-term funds in 91-day Treasury Bills, CPs and CDs. We should not open up the call and notice money

and bill rediscount market to these mutual funds at this stage. We can review the situation after a few months. Meanwhile, the mutual funds can use other avenues.

The Governor concurred with this appraisal.

A 'REFERENCE RATE' FOR MONEY MARKETS

In 1994 the Reserve Bank contemplated the feasibility of introducing a 'reference rate' for money markets. The need for a 'reference rate' was felt because the Treasury Bill rate and the interest rates on CDs and CP were not considered suitable for evolving a 'reference rate'; the former was determined in the auctions as cut-off yields and the market for the latter instruments was narrow. However, different views emerged out of extant circumstances. During March–June 1994, a study in the CPC examined the possibility of introducing a 'reference rate' akin to the LIBOR, which would serve as a benchmark for other interest rates in the financial system. In the absence of any 'reference rate', the institutions operating in the capital and money markets were facing a problem of pricing market-related instruments. The 'reference rate' in consideration was to be market-determined and had to serve as an anchor for other short-term and long-term rates. It was conjectured that all the administered controls on interest rates would be either removed or reduced considerably. This new rate, to be termed the Bombay interbank offered rate (BIBOR), was comparable to LIBOR.

It was, however, felt that the immediate objective was to establish a link between the Bank Rate and the other short-term interest rates (such as the Treasury Bills rates, call money rate, deposit rates, lending rates and the interest rate on dated government securities). The Bank Rate would be the anchor rate and the other short-term interest rates would move in tandem with changes in the Bank Rate. In the process, interest rates were expected to emerge as an effective instrument of monetary control and the Reserve Bank could regulate interest rates in the short-term money market. Moreover, the practice of daily forecasting of liquidity conditions and management of liquidity through market interventions using the policy rate would become important. Succinctly put, the internal review (1994) conceptualised the process as:

> It is desirable to develop the Bank Rate into an ideal reference rate by the RBI, standing ready to provide supplementary resources to banks through the bridging of temporary reserve shortages

through discounting some eligible collateral. The Reserve Bank can influence the BIBOR through this mechanism. The yields on Treasury Bill and long-term government securities could be truly market determined if a system of primary dealers is developed for these instruments and the Reserve Bank provides a line of credit to these dealers at the Bank Rate [the reference rate].

However, another view was that the Treasury Bill auction rates, the repos rate and dated securities OMO rates were better placed to develop into 'reference rate/s' in the system. Moreover, for a 'reference rate' signal from the Reserve Bank, the refinance rate (linked to the Bank Rate) could not be a 'reference rate' unless sector-specific refinance became relatively small and the bulk was in the category of general refinance facility. While the Bank Rate could be an appropriate candidate for the 'reference rate', "ultimately, a reference rate has to earn its position in the market and cannot become an effective reference rate merely by RBI calling it so," noted the review. The Governor finally reasoned that the emergence of a 'reference rate' would have to wait until the lending rate structure had been deregulated and that stage had not been reached.

CONCLUDING OBSERVATIONS

The Indian financial system grew rapidly during the 1980s and 1990s and comprised an impressive network of institutions, instruments and markets. The deepening and widening of the financial structure was most impressive in the case of banking and term lending institutions.

When the comprehensive financial sector reforms were launched, macroeconomic policies and operational measures were directed towards improving the allocational and functional efficiency of the economic system in general. The reform of the financial sector was a critical component. The financial sector reforms and supervision under the *aegis* of the Reserve Bank strengthened the inter-play of market forces and fostered the process of integration among various segments of the financial markets; this was manifest in relative rates of return on various instruments moving within a comparatively narrow range. The development of a liquid and deep market for government securities instilled dynamism into the financial system and imparted flexibility in the conduct of monetary policy.

By the year 1996–97, the role of the financial markets had become crucial for economic development in several ways, namely, in mobilising and allocating savings in the economy, in transmitting signals for monetary policy formulation and in facilitating liquidity management consistent with the overall short and medium-term policy objectives. While the long-term goal of achieving integration among different segments of the financial markets was very much in the picture, the main thrust of the Reserve Bank's policy was on removing factors that inhibited the free flow of resources within these segments and improving opportunities for arbitrage across segments and maturities so that pricing and allocation of resources became more efficient. However, the growing inter-linkages gave another dimension to the conduct of monetary policy in view of the necessity to assess, on a continuous basis, the liquidity conditions in the system and to initiate appropriate measures for minimising volatility in the financial markets. It must be conceded that not much progress could be made in developing a smooth short-term yield curve in the absence of term money market and an active secondary market for Treasury Bills, CP and CDs, an aspect that required more policy initiatives to facilitate the evolution of an appropriate benchmark for pricing short-term instruments.

ANNEX 16.1

A Survey of Developments in Financial Markets in India

A. Markets and Institutions

Year	Markets *(Money Markets, Government Securities Market, and Foreign Exchange Market)*	Institutions *(DFHI, STCI and PDs)*
1986–87	The working group on money market (Chairman: N. Vaghul) submitted its report on January 13, 1987. The central theme of the report was that there should be an activisation of the money market.	
1987–88	The main recommendations of the report of the Vaghul Committee were implemented. The ceilings on interest rates were abolished over a period in respect of call and notice money, inter-bank term money, rediscounting of commercial bills and inter-bank participation certificates without risk. New instruments, such as, CDs and CP were introduced without interest rate stipulation in June 1989 and January 1990, respectively.	
1988–89		The DFHI was set up in April, 1988 to develop an active secondary market in money market instruments. DFHI was exempted from the ceiling on bill rediscounting rate (April 1988) and allowed to participate in call and notice money market both as lender and borrower (July 1988). Its operations were exempted from interest rate ceiling prescribed by IBA in the call/notice money market (October 1988).
1989–90		To augment the resources of DFHI, RBI sanctioned separate peak refinance limits against the collateral of 182-day Treasury Bills and eligible commercial bills of exchange (March 1990).

contd...

contd...

Year	Markets *(Money Markets, Government Securities Market, and Foreign Exchange Market)*	Institutions *(DFHI, STCI and PDs)*
1990–91	Access to the call/notice money market was widened. IDBI, NABARD and GIC were permitted to participate in the market as lenders only (May 2, 1990). Until then, only SCBs, co-operative banks and DFHI were allowed to act as both lenders and borrowers in this market. Subsequently, (*i.e.*, on October 20, 1990), all the participants in the bills rediscounting market were granted entry as lenders in the call/notice money market.	
1991–92	Access as lenders in the call/notice money market and bill rediscounting market was extended to those entities which were able to submit evidence to the Reserve Bank of bulk lendable resources (April 1991).	
1992–93	RBI repos introduced (December 1992). The Reserve Bank initiated several measures to develop and activate the government securities market (October 1992 onwards). These included, introduction of government securities refinance facility to provide liquidity to banks holding these securities; repos auction for government dated securities for better short-term management of excess liquidity and to even out interest rates in the call/notice money market (December 10, 1992) and setting-up of an Internal Debt Management Cell in the Reserve Bank of India (October 1, 1992). From April 1992, the entire borrowing programme of the Central Government (*i.e.*, dated securities) was conducted through auctions. Under the LERMS forex market became active. Banks were permitted to offer forward exchange cover for trade and all other genuine trade transactions (March 1992).	

contd...

contd...

Year	Markets *(Money Markets, Government Securities Market, and Foreign Exchange Market)*	Institutions *(DFHI, STCI and PDs)*
1993–94	Some FIs (which were allowed to lend but not borrow in the call/notice money market) were permitted from October 1993 to borrow from the term money market for maturity periods in the range of three to six months within the limits stipulated for each institution. These institutions were IDBI, ICICI, IFCI, SIDBI, Exim Bank and NABARD. Banks were allowed to offer cross-currency options on a fully covered basis (January 1994).	The STCI was set up in 1993 as a specialised institution entrusted with the task of fostering the development of an efficient secondary securities market in government dated securities and public sector bonds. It commenced operations from June 1994.
1994–95	An expert group was set up in November 1994 to recommend measures for growth of an active, efficient and orderly foreign exchange market. Large scale intervention had to be done by the Reserve Bank since the foreign exchange market experienced volatile conditions during October 1995 – February 1996.	
1995–96	In order that the facility of rediscounting of commercial bills and derivative usance promissory notes was availed of in accord with its intended purpose, such rediscounting had to be made for a minimum period of 15 days (April 21, 1995). The mutual funds set up in the private sector and approved by SEBI were permitted to operate as lenders only in the call/notice money/bills rediscounting market (June 27, 1995). Until then only mutual funds set up by PSBs were allowed to operate as lenders in this market. Repos (ready forward transactions) in Treasury Bills of all maturities and some dated central government securities had been introduced to provide liquidity to banks holding these securities. A minimum holding period of three days was laid down (September 30, 1995) since some banks were found to be using repos for as short a period as one day merely as a change in nomenclature from call money.	

contd...

contd...

Year	Markets *(Money Markets, Government Securities Market, and Foreign Exchange Market)*	Institutions *(DFHI, STCI and PDs)*
1996–97	The Reserve Bank began providing liquidity support to dedicated mutual funds (floated with the approval of SEBI) in the form of purchases of central government dated securities up to certain prescribed limit (April 3, 1996). Guidelines for SDs were issued to further strengthen the infrastructure in the gilt-edged market (December 1996). The Government decided to permit foreign institutional investors (FIIs) in the category of 100.0 per cent debt funds to invest in central government and state government dated securities in both the primary and secondary markets (January 30, 1997). The Reserve Bank issued guidelines on March 8, 1997.	Prior to April 1996, banks authorised to deal in foreign exchange were not permitted to initiate cross currency trading positions in overseas forex markets. They could transact overseas only to square a position acquired in the local foreign exchange market. This restriction was withdrawn (April 3, 1996) taking into account the gradual deepening of the forex market and setting-up of sophisticated dealing rooms by many banks. Initially, only a few selected banks were permitted to avail of this facility. A foreign exchange market technical advisory committee was set up by the Reserve Bank to prepare policy papers on specific market-related topics (April 1996).
1997–98	A standing committee on money market was set up to advise the Reserve Bank to further develop the money market and make it more efficient (April 1997). Measures were announced for deepening and widening of the forex market, *viz.*, forward cover based on business projections and development of rupee forex swap market (April 1997). Till April 1997, only two entities were permitted to operate in the call/notice money market as lenders by routing their transactions through DFHI. This facility was extended to all PDs and also the minimum size of transaction was reduced (April 26, 1997). Two decisions were taken in April 1997 to activate the repos market so that it served as an equilibrating mechanism between the money and securities markets. First, repos/reverse repos were permitted among select institutions in Treasury Bills of all maturities and central government dated securities which were approved by the Reserve Bank. Secondly, non-bank entities which were holding SGL accounts with the Reserve Bank were allowed to enter into reverse repos transactions with banks/PDs in Treasury Bills of all maturities and dated central government securities subject to certain conditions.	

contd...

contd...

Year	Markets (Money Markets, Government Securities Market, and Foreign Exchange Market)	Institutions (DFHI, STCI and PDs)
	The minimum size of transactions for entities reduced from ₹ 10 crore to ₹ 5 crore (October 1997).	
	The Reserve Bank took a number of initiatives during October 1997. The more important were, a move towards price auction, fixing of an issue amount for all auctions, making non-competitive bids outside the notified amount, allowing FIIs with 30.0 per cent ceiling on debt to participate in the government securities market and relaxing regulations applicable to banks in regard to retailing of government securities.	

contd...

contd...

B. Instruments

Year	Instruments *(Treasury Bills, CDs, CP and MMMFs)*
1986-87	The 182-day Treasury Bill was introduced in November 1986 on auction basis with the objective to develop Treasury Bills as a monetary instrument with flexible rates and to serve as a financial instrument with an intermediate maturity between dated securities and the existing 91-day Treasury Bills. Reserve Bank introduced 182-day Treasury Bill refinance facility (April 1987).
1989-90	CDs were introduced in June 1989 to widen the range of money market instruments and to give investors greater flexibility in deployment of their short-term surplus funds. CDs provided for a market-determined rate of return on bulk deposits. CP was introduced in January 1990. Thereby, highly rated corporate borrowers could diversify their sources of short-term borrowing and also it provided an additional outlet to investors.
1990-91	The limits for issue of CDs by commercial banks were enhanced and the denomination of issue reduced (April 1990). In December 1990 the minimum size of issue and the denomination of individual CD were lowered. Also, bank-wise limits for issue of CDs were raised from 2.0 per cent to 3.0 per cent of average aggregate deposits in 1989–90. Guidelines for issue of CP were relaxed (April 24, 1990) to broad base the primary market and widen the scope for secondary market.
1991-92	Further relaxation made in the guidelines for issue of CP (April 1991) to facilitate wider participation and greater flexibility in operation.
1992-93	In April 1992, 364-day Treasury Bills were introduced on auction basis, without support from RBI and without pre-determined amount. In January 1993, 91-day Treasury Bills were introduced on auction basis with pre-determined amount and with RBI support at the cut-off yield. Issue of zero coupon bonds. Total permissible limits for issue of CDs by the banking system were enhanced (April 1992 and October 1992), which provided greater freedom to banks in determining interest rates on deposits. Guidelines for issue of CP were relaxed (April 1992) to widen the scope for its issue in the primary market.

contd...

contd...

Year	Instruments *(Treasury Bills, CDs, CP and MMMFs)*
	MMMFs were allowed to be set up by commercial banks and their subsidiaries. The objective was to provide additional short-term avenue for investors and to bring money market instruments within the reach of individuals and small bodies. The scheme was introduced in April 1992.
1993-94	The total permissible limits for issue of CDs by banks were enhanced in April 1993. Later, with a view to give banks greater flexibility in mobilisation of deposits at competitive rates of interest, the Reserve Bank withdrew the bank-wise limits. Banks were granted freedom to issue CDs depending on their requirements.
	The maximum maturity period of 6 months for issue of CP by companies was raised to between 3 months and less than one year. To be eligible to issue CP, the requirements of a minimum net worth of a company and its minimum working capital limit (fund-based) were reduced (October 18, 1993).
1994-95	The facility of stand-by arrangement with cash credit limits was abolished (October 1994). As a result, whenever CP was issued, the bank effected *pro tanto* reduction in the cash credit limit of the company. The objective was to delink the repayment out of cash credit limits of the issuer and thus impart a measure of independence to CP as a money market instrument.
1995-96	Changes were made in the scheme of MMMFs (December 11, 1995) to make it more flexible and attractive to banks and financial institutions and at the same time to impart greater liquidity and depth to the money market. Important changes were, allowing entry of private sector, removal of the ceiling on the size of MMMFs and withdrawal of the prescription of minimum and maximum limits on investments in individual instrument.

contd...

concld.

Year	*Instruments* *(Treasury Bills, CDs, CP and MMMFs)*
1997-98	Treasury Bills of different maturities were issued to facilitate cash management needs of different segments of the economy and also to activate the Treasury Bills market. (This was in the context of the issues of 91-day Treasury Bills on tap and *ad hoc* Treasury Bills having been discontinued from April 1, 1997).
	The minimum size of issue of CDs to a single investor was reduced twice (April and October 1997).
	The minimum period of issue of CP was reduced (April 15, 1997).
	Investments by MMMFs relaxed to include corporate bonds to improve their earnings and liquidity (October 1997).

Notes: 1. This brief survey covers the money market, government securities market and the foreign exchange market, the operations over which the Reserve Bank exercised direct control. The developments in the other two segments of the financial market, namely, the organised market, dominated by commercial banks and hire-purchase and leasing finance companies in which the NBFCs played a leading role, are dealt with in chapter 6: Banking and Finance and chapter 17: Reforms in Banking and Financial Institutions.

2. The developments in the other important markets in the financial system, namely, the equity market, capital market and debt market comprising PSU bonds and corporate debentures and housing finance are excluded as they come within the purview of different regulatory authorities.

17

Reforms in Banking and Financial Institutions

INTRODUCTION

The banking and financial policy during the 1970s aimed at aligning the financial sector, in particular, banking operations, with the Plan priorities and social goals. This policy thrust continued during the early 1980s with the pursuit of target-oriented lending and a plethora of interest rate and credit controls. In the process, especially among public sector banks (PSBs), commercial considerations became secondary, which resulted in weakening the soundness and operational efficiency in banking. To reverse this tendency, efforts towards consolidation began in the mid-1980s through various regulatory and supervisory interventions by the Reserve Bank. These initiatives continued till the late 1980s and the Reserve Bank provided the necessary conducive environment in the 1990s, in tune with the spirit of liberalisation and deregulation in developed and developing economies. These initiatives aimed at moderating branch expansion, while continuing to cover spatial gaps in rural areas, improving the financial viability of banks, introducing mechanisation and inculcating a better professional management and work culture. The social objectives of banking were re-oriented without jeopardising the need to sustain viability, profitability and professionalism in banking.

WAVE OF DEREGULATION: GLOBAL INFLUENCE

When India embarked upon financial sector reforms in the early 1990s, the Reserve Bank was conscious of the need to eliminate structural impediments to adjustment and growth. The aim was to allow the price mechanism to operate as freely as possible, in the real and in the financial sector.

The conditions in which financial activities were conducted were liberalised, while subsidised loans were cut back sharply. During the 1990s, Indian banks operated in a far more competitive climate than ever before. Quantitative and qualitative credit controls were progressively replaced by a more flexible monetary policy framework. The range of financial instruments and services was broadened. Restrictions on international financial transactions were reduced. Transactions became more transparent, paving the way for allocation of resources to become more optimal.[1]

Increased emphasis was placed on three pre-requisites for the efficient functioning of the financial sector, viz., a well-designed infrastructure, effective market discipline, and a strong regulatory and supervisory framework. A well-designed infrastructure comprised a proper legal and judicial framework, good corporate governance, comprehensive accounting standards, a system of independent audits and an efficient payments and settlement system. Effective market discipline required a sound credit culture and well-developed equity and debt markets with a wide variety of instruments for risk diversification. The Basel Committee came out with the guidelines for capital adequacy and risk weights of book assets. Based on international consensus on what constituted sound practices in many areas of banking supervision and securities regulation, the Basel Committee released the core principles for effective banking supervision and the International Organisation of Securities Commission (IOSCO) proposed the necessary guidelines for the securities industry.[2]

The financial sector reforms of the 1990s offer interesting insights into the overall policy framework evolved by the country's policymakers. First, the financial sector reforms were undertaken early in the reform cycle. Second, the reform process was not driven by any banking crisis and it was essentially home-grown, the initial trigger been provided by the structural adjustment packages supported by the International Monetary Fund (IMF) and the World Bank. Third, the design of the reforms took on board, international best practices. Fourth, the reforms were carefully sequenced with respect to instruments and objectives. Thus, the prudential

1. Larosiиre, Jacques De (1992). "The Worldwide Adjustment Process in the 1980s", *C.D. Deshmukh Memorial Lecture*. Mumbai: Reserve Bank of India. March 24.

2. Jalan, Bimal (2002). "International Financial Architecture: Developing Countries Perspective", in *India's Economy in the New Millennium: Selected Essays*. UBS Publishers. pp.76-77.

norms and supervisory strengthening measures were introduced initially in the reform cycle, followed by interest rate deregulation and a gradual lowering of statutory pre-emptions. The more complex aspects of legal and accounting measures were addressed subsequently, when the basic tenets of reforms were already in place.[3]

LEARNING FROM INTERNATIONAL BEST PRACTICES

The Indian thinking on financial reforms was greatly influenced by global developments and practices. The Reserve Bank kept a close watch, attempted to learn, imbibe and internalise new policies and practices, adapting them to Indian conditions. Several constraints *viz.*, government ownership of major financial institutions (FIs) and banks, directed lending with substantial allocation for the priority sector, regulated interest rate structure, pre-emption of bank resources under reserve requirements at very low rates of return and exchange controls limited the scope and speed of deregulation. The Reserve Bank in close co-ordination with the Government provided momentum to enhance the efficiency of the financial system with the objective of reducing rigidities and delays, improving flexibility and speed of operations, allowing for functional and institutional diversification and generally bringing about a more competitive environment in the system.

The Reserve Bank's success as a central bank at this time can be attributed to its ability to understand the approaches followed by central banks the world over in their regulatory and supervisory systems and attempt to customise these to the domestic financial system, particularly the banking system. Knowledge-sharing through lectures by eminent international bankers in the late 1980s and early 1990s was a notable feature in the Reserve Bank. The benefits of such information dissemination had a positive reflection in the working of the Indian banking system. In furtherance of the initiatives, the Reserve Bank became a shareholding member of the Bank for International Settlements (BIS) on November 1, 1996.

The period 1989–1992 proved to be a turnaround because of the severe impact of the balance of payments (BoP) crisis. Policymaking at this point was caught between two mindsets. One was the urgently felt need to switch

---

3. Reddy, Y.V. (2009). *India and Global Financial Crisis, Managing Money and Finance.* New Delhi: Orient BlackSwan. p.125.

to the process of liberalisation in tune with the international trend and give up the restrictive practices prevalent in the financial system. The second was the fear that adjustments could create imbalances in the economy, and the achievements in terms of social and economic priorities as well as equitable distribution could be thwarted. However, the successful experience of other developing economies, particularly in the rest of Asia, prompted the authorities to go ahead with the liberalisation, albeit in a gradual manner.

The period 1992–1997 witnessed a sea-change in the financial system in general and in the banking system in particular. There was a transformation in the outlook, and the need to foster a sound and healthy banking structure took root, especially in the Government's philosophy and the Reserve Bank's approach. The market-oriented approach in line with the international trends and adoption of best global practices helped the banking system become resilient to shocks emanating both from the domestic and international financial markets.

The first wave of financial liberalisation during this period took the form of interest rate deregulation. This represented a shift from a prolonged period of administered system of interest rates that was influenced by budgetary concerns and characterised by a high degree of concessional directed loans. Under the administered system, interest rate margins were kept sufficiently large by keeping deposit rates low in relation to the non-concessional lending rates along with an element of cross-subsidisation. The yields on government securities also reflected the demand and supply conditions in the market. Based on the recommendations of the Chakravarty Committee, the coupon rates on government bonds were gradually increased.

The process of bank consolidation that had begun in the late 1980s continued in the 1990s. It meant moderation in the pace of branch expansion, filling the spatial gaps in rural areas, improvement in the financial viability of banks and introduction of mechanisation and computerisation to inculcate a more effective management culture. The target orientation for the priority sector was, however, retained but in a more pragmatic manner, avoiding indiscriminate lending and without loss of viability and sustainability of banking operations. Overall, the Reserve Bank's policy initiatives from 1992 were directed at building strength and ensuring safety and stability of the financial system. Compared with the experience of many developing countries embarking on financial sector reforms, India tread cautiously to minimise the adjustment costs involved in the process. In other words, the frictions of transition were tackled by both a gradualist and a balanced approach, rather than by a 'big bang' approach.

Following the report of the Narasimham Committee, more comprehensive reforms were pursued. The reforms consisted of: (i) a shift of banking sector supervision from intrusive micro-level intervention over credit decisions towards prudential regulations and supervision; (ii) reduction in cash reserve ratio (CRR) and statutory liquidity ratio (SLR); (iii) interest rate deregulation and entry relaxation; and (iv) adoption of prudential norms. Further, in 1992, the Reserve Bank issued guidelines for income recognition, asset classification and provisioning, and also adopted the Basel Accord of capital adequacy standards. The Government established the Board for Financial Supervision (BFS) in the Reserve Bank and recapitalised PSBs in order to give banks sufficient financial strength and enable them to gain access to the capital markets. In 1993, the Reserve Bank permitted private sector to enter the banking sector, provided that new banks were well capitalised and technologically advanced, and at the same time prohibited cross-holding practices with industrial groups. The Reserve Bank also imposed some restrictions on new banks with respect to the opening of branches, with a view to maintaining the franchise value of existing banks.[4]

As a result of the reforms, the number of banks increased rapidly. In 1991, there were 27 PSBs and 26 domestic private banks with 60,000 branches, 24 foreign banks with 140 branches, and 20 foreign banks with a representative office each. Between January 1993 and March 1998, 24 new private banks (9 domestic and 15 foreign) entered the market; the total number of scheduled commercial banks (SCBs), excluding specialised banks, such as regional rural banks (RRBs), rose from 75 in 1991–92 to 99 in 1997–98. Entry deregulation was accompanied by progressive deregulation of interest rates on deposits and advances. From October 1994, interest rates were deregulated in a phased manner and, by October 1997, banks were allowed to set interest rates on all term deposits of maturity of more than 30 days and on all advances exceeding ₹ 2 lakh. CRR and SLR, interest rate policy and prudential norms were applied uniformly to all commercial

---

4. Shirai, Sayuri (2001). "Assessment of India's Banking Sector Reforms from the Perspective of the Governance of the Banking System", Paper presented at the ESCAP-ADB Joint Workshop on *Mobilizing Domestic Finance for Development: Reassessment of Bank Finance and Debt Markets in Asia and the Pacific.* Bangkok, November 22-23.

banks. The Reserve Bank, however, treated foreign banks differently with respect to regulation that required a portion of credit to be allocated to the priority sector. In 1993, foreign banks — which were earlier exempt from this requirement — while all other commercial banks were required to earmark 40.0 per cent of credit — were made to allocate 32.0 per cent of credit to the priority sector.

The Governor, Shri R.N. Malhotra, speaking on the occasion of silver jubilee of the Reserve Bank Staff College (RBSC) in 1989, indicated that there were three challenges confronting the banking industry that required appropriate policies. The first challenge was posed by the rapid changes taking place in the international financial markets. Although the Indian banking industry had generally remained immune to these changes, the linkages between domestic banking and international markets was gradually increasing. Most of the changes related to computerisation and the communication technology. The second challenge that had a bearing on the work of a training institution was that the traditional roles of commercial banking were undergoing transformation abroad and with the result that the distinction between the operations of banking and non-banking entities was getting blurred. In India also, banks had started the business of merchant banking, venture capital, leasing and other activities. The interface of commercial banks with the financial market had, therefore, broadened. The third challenge was how to handle the transition from conventional banking to the evolving situation. While certain traditional practices and principles were no doubt valuable, the new developments could not be ignored and had to be assimilated.

CHAPTER OUTLINE

This chapter covers four related aspects. First, the road map set for financial sector reforms, including that for the banking system, based on the recommendations of the high level committee appointed by the Government to review the financial system under the chairmanship of Shri M. Narasimham (also known as the committee on the financial system, i.e., the CFS), which submitted its report in November 1991. The nature and dimensions of these recommendations and the action taken form a significant part of the narrative that follows. Second, the financial system in the early 1992 was afflicted by irregularities in government securities market transactions that threatened systemic stability. An immediate scrutiny by a Deputy Governor of the Reserve Bank and later by the Joint Parliamentary Committee (JPC) on the nature of the irregularities resulted in several safeguards being placed in the functioning of government securities markets and in particular, in the operation and settlement system of securities transactions. The major steps taken in this regard are discussed next. Third, several aspects of financial sector regulation and supervision were examined either internally or by working groups and committees appointed for specific purposes, and fresh guidelines and directions were issued by the Reserve Bank over the period. Such guidelines largely followed international best practices and aimed at placing the system on a stable and sound footing, while making the operations more flexible and market-oriented. The details of such developments appear thereafter. Subsequent to this, developments relating to the urban co-operative banking sector are covered. During the 1990s, there were parallel changes in the process of financial intermediation and the role of FIs including non-bank financial companies (NBFCs), in the inter-institutional linkages, and the Reserve Bank's role in the regulation and supervision of such institutions. While the general aspects of reform and policy developments are covered with reference to FIs and NBFCs, some specific developments in policy and the operations of these two categories are narrated before making the concluding observations.

FINANCIAL/BANKING SECTOR REFORMS: THE NARASIMHAM COMMITTEE, 1991

BACKDROP

It was increasingly felt that developments in the financial sector, in particular the banking sector would have to be supportive of the metamorphic changes being undertaken in response to the challenges posed by the twin deficits, namely, fiscal deficit and the current account deficit (CAD). The financial sector reforms were expected to generate greater competition between banks, FIs and NBFCs, with a move towards establishing a level playing field between different types of institutions and between public and private sector institutions. The reforms were aimed at further development and integration of the money and capital markets. A concomitant of these changes was the need for structured prudential norms and discipline that was to be applied universally. Increased competition was seen as a means to provide an efficient system of financial intermediation, with diversified FIs and instruments catering to the varied needs of savings and investment classes. In order to ensure that the institutions did not lag behind in facing a more competitive environment, they were supposed to revamp in terms of organisational systems and procedures, and modernise and improvise.

Easier access and exit and rigorous prudential norms for risk management, as also transparency in operations, needed to be induced expeditiously. Inefficiencies in the financial system tended to make the cost of intermediation unduly high. The changing environment of competition amongst various segments of the financial system called for work and management ethos that were professionally oriented and goal and performance-driven. The tasks before the banks and FIs in this respect were onerous and, as the financial sector reforms had to be consistent with the overall economic reforms, banks and FIs were required to undertake major changes in their operations.

These issues were examined by the Narasimham Committee. The committee made wide-ranging recommendations, which formed the basis of financial sector reforms relating to banks, development financial institutions (DFIs) and the capital market in the years following the BoP crisis. The committee's recommendations included, *inter alia*: (i) phased reduction in SLR to 25.0 per cent over a period of five years; (ii) progressive reduction in CRR from its high level; (iii) phasing out directed credit programmes and redefining the priority sector; (iv) deregulating interest rates so as to reflect emerging market conditions; (v) achieving a minimum 4.0 per cent capital adequacy ratio in relation to risk-weighted assets by March 1993; (vi) adopting uniform accounting practices, particularly with regard to income recognition and provisioning against doubtful debts; (vii) imparting transparency to bank balance sheets and ensuring full disclosures; (viii) setting-up special tribunals to speed up the process of recovery of loans; (ix) establishing an asset reconstruction fund (ARF) to take over from banks and FIs a portion of their bad and doubtful debts at a discount; (x) restructuring of the banking system so as to have 3 or 4 large banks, which could become international in character, 8 to 10 national banks with a network of branches throughout the country engaged in universal banking, local banks whose operations were generally confined to a specific region, and rural banks (including RRBs) whose operations were confined to rural areas and whose business was predominantly to engage in financing agriculture and allied activities; (xi) setting-up one or more rural banking subsidiaries by each of the PSBs to take over all its branches; (xii) permitting RRBs to engage in all types of banking business; (xiii) abolishing branch licensing and leaving the matter of opening or closing of branches to the commercial judgment of the individual banks; (xiv) liberalising policy with regard to allowing foreign banks to open offices in India as branches or as subsidiaries; (xv) rationalising the foreign operations of Indian banks; (xvi) permitting individual banks the freedom to recruit officers; (xvii) inspection by supervisory authorities being based on the internal audit and internal inspection reports; (xviii) ending duality of control over the banking system between the Reserve Bank and the Banking Division of the Ministry of Finance and making the Reserve Bank the primary agency for regulating the banking system; (xix) hiving-off the supervision over banks and other FIs to a separate authority to operate as a quasi-autonomous body under the aegis of the Reserve Bank, separate from other central banking operations of the Reserve Bank; (xx) making recommendations on the appointment of chief executives of banks and directors on the boards of PSBs and institutions; (xxi) transferring the direct lending function of the Industrial Development Bank of India (IDBI) to a separate institution, while retaining only its apex and refinancing role; (xxii) obtaining resources from the market on competitive terms by the DFIs and phasing out their privileged access to concessive finance through SLR and other arrangements; (xxiii) enabling substantial and speedy liberalisation of the capital market and dispensing with the prior approval of any agency for any issue in the market; (xxiv) providing supervision over institutions such as merchant banks, mutual funds, leasing companies, venture capital companies and factoring companies by a new agency to be set up under the aegis of the Reserve Bank; (xxv) enacting new legislation along the lines existing in several countries to provide an appropriate legal framework for the constitution and functioning of mutual funds; (xxvi) laying prudential norms and guidelines governing the functioning of such institutions as in the case of banks and FIs; and (xxvii) properly sequencing reforms in the financial system.

The recommendations of the Narasimham Committee were extensive in their scope and had far-reaching implications for the working of the banking and financial system. The feasibility of implementing the recommendations, the sequencing of measures and the infrastructure necessary in a reformed financial system were examined by the Government and the Reserve Bank in the second half of 1992. Accordingly, financial sector reforms were initiated as part of the overall structural reforms to impart efficiency and dynamism to the financial sector. The country's approach to reforms in the banking and financial sector was guided by five principles: (i) reform measures were to be cautious and sequenced; (ii) introduction of norms that were mutually reinforcing; (iii) introduction of complementary reforms across sectors (monetary, fiscal, external and financial sectors); (iv) development of FIs; and (v) development and integration of financial markets.

IMPLEMENTATION OF THE RECOMMENDATIONS
OF THE NARASIMHAM COMMITTEE

Many of the recommendations of the CFS were accepted and implemented,[5] with some implemented in a manner that was somewhat different from what was intended.[6] The actions taken by the Reserve Bank with regard to commercial banks and the FIs are the main areas reviewed in the following paragraphs.

DIRECTED CREDIT

The committee recommended that directed credit programmes should be phased out. It recognised that it was necessary for a measure of special credit support through direction to a redefined priority sector for which the suggested target could be fixed at 10.0 per cent of aggregate credit. As regards credit to the target group, which was not included in the new definition, the Reserve Bank and other refinance agencies could institute a preferential refinance scheme to cover incremental credit to these sectors.

According to the assessment of the Reserve Bank, the priority sector as redefined by the committee accounted for a little less than 30.0 per cent of net bank credit. It was, therefore, decided to maintain the existing targets for priority sector lending. Concessional finance was, however, limited to small loans below ₹ 2 lakh and for differential rate of interest (DRI) advances. For advances above ₹ 2 lakh, banks were free to charge an interest rate linked to the prime lending rate (PLR). The scope of priority sector lending was enlarged to include finance to the state industrial development corporations (SIDCs)/state financial corporations (SFCs), refinance to RRBs by sponsor banks and investments in bonds issued by specified institutions. Overall, the target orientation of lending was considerably diluted over the years by relaxing the norms of coverage of the priority sector.

---

5. Implementation of recommendations pertaining to monetary instruments and operations is covered in chapter 14: Monetary Management.

6. Those relating to SLR, CRR, payment of interest on CRR balances, interest rate structure and interest rate on government securities have been dealt with in detail in chapter 14: Monetary Management.

CAPITAL ADEQUACY

Identifying the causes for the deterioration in the financial health of the banking system over time, the committee recommended measures that included, *inter alia*, capital adequacy norms, prudential norms for income recognition, asset classification and provisioning for bad debts. The committee proposed that the BIS norms on capital adequacy should be achieved over a period of three years ending March 1996, the period being accelerated for banks that had sufficient international presence. Profitable banks could immediately approach the capital market to enhance their capital, and for the other banks the Government could meet the shortfall either by direct subscription to equity or by providing a loan that could be treated as subordinated debt.

In 1988, the Basel Committee decided to introduce a capital measurement system, the Basel Capital Accord, popularly known as Basel I. This system provided for the implementation of a credit risk measurement framework with a minimum capital standard of 8.0 per cent to be attained by end-1992. Since 1988, this framework has been progressively introduced not only in member countries but across all countries with an international banking presence.

In April 1992, the Reserve Bank announced detailed guidelines on the phased introduction of norms on capital adequacy, income recognition, asset classification, and provisioning in pursuance of Basel I norms. Banks with an international presence were directed to achieve the capital adequacy norms by March 1995 and other banks in two stages by March 1996. Eight banks could not achieve the prescribed norms as on March 31, 1996. As on March 31, 1997 only two banks had not achieved the 8.0 per cent norm. Five nationalised banks, the State Bank of India (SBI) and two subsidiaries of the SBI successfully raised capital from the market from 1993 for a total of ₹ 6035 crore (including the premium on the issue prices). The Government also directly subscribed to the capital of nationalised banks to the extent of ₹ 20,046 crore up to February 28, 1998.

The committee defined the term non-performing asset (NPA) and recommended that no interest should accrue in respect of NPAs. Income recognition norms were to be introduced in a phased manner over a period of three years. It recommended a four-way classification of assets and provisions against each category of sub-standard assets. A four-year period was suggested for banks to conform to these provisioning norms.

Banks were directed that income from NPAs should not be taken to the profit and loss account unless income was realised. NPA was defined as a credit facility in respect of which interest had remained 'past due' for a period of four/three/two quarters as on March 31, 1993, March 31, 1994, and March 31, 1995, respectively. A credit facility was 'past due' when the instalment had not been paid within 30 days from the due date. Similarly, banks were required to classify assets as NPAs, based on their status, into sub-standard, doubtful and loss assets, and make appropriate provisions. These norms were applied to DFIs, except that in the case of DFIs an advance became an NPA if interest remained overdue for more than 180 days and/or the instalment of principal remained overdue for more than 365 days.

TRANSPARENCY IN FINANCIAL STATEMENTS

The committee recommended that transparency and disclosure standards as proposed in the international accounting standards (IAS) be implemented in a phased manner. The Reserve Bank modified the format of balance sheets of banks in 1992 with a view to introducing greater transparency and disclosures. In their 1996 accounts, banks were required to disclose the capital adequacy ratios and in the 1997 accounts, further disclosure requirements were introduced, the more significant being the break-up of provisions made during the year, percentage of net NPAs to net advances and investments on gross and net basis. For the year 1998, banks were directed to disclose seven critical ratios relating to productivity and profitability.

FOREIGN BANKS

The committee recommended a liberal approach in permitting foreign banks to open their branches or subsidiaries, as the Reserve Bank considered appropriate, subject to minimum assigned capital and reciprocity. Joint ventures (JVs) between foreign banks and local banks would also be permitted. Foreign banks/finance companies were permitted to invest up to 20.0 per cent as a technical collaborator (within the overall 40.0 per cent ceiling) in a new private sector bank, subject to the government approval, provided the foreign bank did not have a presence in India. Foreign equity in new Indian private banks was also permitted. JVs between foreign and local banks in non-bank financial services were allowed in accordance with the foreign investment policy of the Government. In January 1992, 19 new foreign banks with a total of 47 branches were allowed to operate in India. The committee had recommended that foreign banks should be subject to the regulation as domestic banks and, in case of constraints, if foreign banks were unable to fulfil requirements such as targeted credit, the Reserve Bank could work out alternative methods.

It was accordingly made mandatory in April 1993 for foreign banks to achieve the minimum target of 32.0 per cent of net bank credit for priority sector lending by March 1994. Within the target of 32.0 per cent, two sub-targets in respect of advances: (i) to the small scale sector (minimum of 10.0 per cent); and (ii) exports (minimum of 12.0 per cent) was fixed. Foreign banks were exempted from targeted credit for agricultural advances because they did not have branches in rural areas.

TAX TREATMENT OF PROVISIONS

The committee recommended that income recognition norms be implemented by the Reserve Bank. The specific provision made by banks and DFIs in line with its recommendations should be tax deductible. As regards general provisions, the tax deductibility should be restricted to 0.5 per cent of the aggregate average non-agricultural advances and 2.0 per cent of the aggregate average advances by rural branches to all banks including those with overseas operations. While income recognition norms were implemented as proposed in respect of the specific provisions made by banks against classified assets, these were not considered tax-deductible unless the amount was written-off. The Reserve Bank took up the matter with the Government. As regards general provisions, the limit of admissible deductions was enhanced to 5.0 per cent of the income and 10.0 per cent of average aggregate advances of rural branches.

DEBT RECOVERY TRIBUNALS

The committee's recommendation for setting-up special tribunals to speed up the process of recovery by specific legislation was implemented in August 1993 with the passage of the Recovery of Debts Due to Banks and Financial Institutions Act, 1993. Eight debt recovery tribunals were established to cover 20 states and 4 union territories (UTs). An appellate tribunal was established in Mumbai.

ASSET RECONSTRUCTION FUND

The committee recommended setting-up an ARF to take bad and doubtful assets off the balance sheets of banks and FIs, so that banks could recycle the funds realised through this process into more productive assets. The

ARF, funded by the Government, the Reserve Bank, PSBs and FIs, was to be provided with broader powers for recovery as an entity. The committee also suggested the manner in which assets could be transferred.

However, the Reserve Bank felt that there were several critical issues that needed attention, and, before implementing such a scheme, it was necessary to be clear about the sources of funding and the impact of the scheme on the recovery climate. Although special recovery tribunals would enable the speedy enforcement of banks' claims, an ARF combined with the prudential requirements would require large amounts of funds. If these large capital requirements were to be met by the Government or the Reserve Bank, it implied large-scale monetisation with obvious deleterious effects on the economy. Thus, the strategy for raising fresh capital by banks needed to be carefully worked out. An ARF also posed the problem of moral hazard of lenders being distanced from the recovery process and this was seen as not providing the most efficient procedure for recovery. Further, such a fund could erode accountability by perpetuating a climate of expectations of such waivers in the future. A limited ARF could, however, be considered for weak banks, provided the alternative of a merger was ruled out and the modalities of avoiding further repetition of the bad lending scenario were worked out. These banks could be provided the facility of bad debts being taken over at face value, but this would have to be conditional on major adjustments being made by banks in terms of drastic changes in their management, sacrifices by the staff, control on the growth of assets and, above all, increase in productivity. These were required to be clearly spelt out through memoranda of understanding (MoU). Issues remaining to be solved were the management of such ARFs and their ability to recover more efficiently than the parent banks, among others. Once such aspects were resolved, a limited approach to ARFs could be considered. The ARF route was supposed to be the option available only to banks that could not undertake the adjustments through other options and that could also be restructured to come under effective management.

ENTRY OF PRIVATE SECTOR BANKS

The Reserve Bank Central Board considered the recommendation of the committee regarding entry of private sector banks in its meetings held on September 11, 1992 and January 21, 1993 and agreed to grant permission for establishing such banks, subject to certain terms and conditions. In accordance with this stipulation, the Reserve Bank issued guidelines on January 22, 1993 for the entry of new private sector banks. The Narasimham Committee had envisaged a larger role for private sector banks in the system. While at that time, there was no legal restriction on the entry of private sector banks, no new private bank was licensed in practice. However, it was considered that time was apposite to allow entry to a few new private sector banks, so as to generate competition in banking.

In the case of new private sector banks, it was desirable to set a sufficiently high minimum start-up capital to ensure that banks had inherent strength and a comfortable capital risk assets ratio. The prudential norms were to be observed from their inception. The minimum paid-up capital for a new private sector bank was set at ₹ 100 crore and it was required to observe prudential norms and a capital adequacy ratio of 8.0 per cent at inception. The question of a level playing field in areas such as rural branches and priority sector credit needed to be addressed, along with issues relating to limits on the concentration of shareholding by individuals/groups and limits on voting power. The issue of whether financial companies should be allowed to set up banks also came up; in such cases the question of cross-share holdings and cross-directorships needed to be given attention. Important aspects that deserved consideration included controlling groups lending money through banks to projects owned or managed by them and commingling of industrial groups and banks leading to the concentration of economic power, which was best avoided.

The committee's recommendation to allow the entry to new private banks was implemented and, as on March 1996, nine private sector banks had commenced business, with a network of 76 branches spread over semi-urban, urban and metropolitan centres. None of the banks opened branches in rural areas.

STRUCTURE OF THE BANKING SYSTEM

The committee had indicated a broad structure for the banking system, consisting of 3 or 4 large banks, which could become international in character, 8 to 10 national banks with a network of branches throughout the country engaged in universal banking, local banks whose operations were generally confined to a specific region and rural banks that operated in rural areas.

The Reserve Bank took the view that the move towards this structure should be market-driven, based on considerations of operational efficiency and brought about through mergers and acquisitions. Except for the merger of one weak PSB, namely, New Bank of India, with another PSB, namely, Punjab National Bank (PNB), on September 4, 1993, there was no restructuring of banks. Six[7] weak private sector banks were closed/merged during this period.

REGIONAL RURAL BANKS

The committee's recommendations that each PSB should set up one or more rural banking subsidiaries to take over all its rural branches and, where appropriate, swap its rural branches with those of other banks was not accepted. The approach instead was to strengthen and restructure RRBs on a 'stand-alone' basis.

BRANCH LICENSING

The committee recommended that branch licensing be abolished and the matter of opening or closing of branches (other than rural branches, at that point of time) be left to the commercial judgement of individual banks.

Branch licensing policy was not abolished, but banks were given greater operational freedom to open specialised branches, offsite automated teller machines (ATMs) and other non-branch offices. Banks were free to close branches in urban, semi-urban and metropolitan centres and to convert rural branches into satellite offices. In 1994, it was decided to allow banks that fulfilled specified criteria to open branches, *viz.*, net owned funds (NOFs) of ₹ 100 crore, three-year track record of net profits, 8.0 per cent capital adequacy ratio and percentage of gross NPAs to total advances not exceeding 15.0 per cent.

FOREIGN OPERATIONS OF INDIAN BANKS

The committee recommended rationalising the foreign operations of Indian banks. While the SBI's international operations continued and were strengthened, other Indian banks with the significant presence overseas could jointly set up one or more subsidiaries to take over their existing branches abroad. It was also suggested that larger Indian banks could be permitted to acquire smaller banks abroad to intensify their presence. This recommendation was, however, not implemented.

---

7. Bank of Tamil Nadu Ltd, Bank of Thanjavur Ltd, Parur Central Bank Ltd, Purbanchal Bank Ltd, Kashinathseth Bank Ltd and Baridoab Bank Ltd.

AUTONOMY MEASURES

The committee recommended that individual banks should be free to make their own recruitment of officers and, wherever appropriate, banks could voluntarily come together for a joint recruitment system for officers. As regards clerical cadres, the system of banking services recruitment boards (BSRBs) in vogue could continue. It was also recommended that guidelines relating to matters of internal administration, such as creation and categorisation of posts, promotion procedures and similar matters, be rescinded.

The Government announced in 1997 a package of measures for PSBs that fulfilled certain criteria, *viz.*, capital adequacy of more than 8.0 per cent, net profit during the past three years, net NPA level below 9.0 per cent and minimum owned funds of ₹ 100 crore. Banks that fulfilled these criteria were allowed to recruit specialised officers and undertake campus recruitment for partly meeting their requirements for probationary officers. The boards of banks were given powers to decide their own policy for creation, abolition, upgrading/modification of posts up to the level of deputy general managers (DGMs).

SUPERVISORY AUTHORITY

The committee recommended that duality of control over the banking system between the Reserve Bank and the Banking Division of the Ministry of Finance should end, and that the Reserve Bank should be the primary agency for regulation. The supervisory control over banks and FIs be hived-off and entrusted to a separate authority to operate as a quasi-autonomous body under the aegis of the Reserve Bank, but separated from other central banking functions of the Reserve Bank. This recommendation was implemented, but in a somewhat different manner. The BFS under the aegis of the Reserve Bank with four members drawn from the Reserve Bank Central Board and serviced by a separate Department of Supervision (DoS) was constituted on November 16, 1994. An expert advisory council was set up to advise the BFS on various policy matters. A clarification on the issue of instituting the BFS revealed that if the BFS were to be constituted outside the Reserve Bank, the process would have entailed a separate legislation providing statutory powers to the former for exercising supervision over banks. After detailed deliberations, the BFS was constituted under the aegis of the Reserve Bank, a position somewhat similar to that in the Bank of England (BoE).[8] On the issue of banking regulation and supervision remaining within the purview of central banks, Shri S.S. Tarapore[9] noted in the year 2000:

> While in some countries regulation/supervision has been separated from the central bank there are some disadvantages in doing so. In a crisis, it is the central bank which has to act and a central bank without hands on experience of banking organisations faces a tremendous handicap. Hence at this stage of our financial development, there is much merit in keeping regulation/supervision within the RBI.

> While on the issue of regulation and supervision it is necessary to recognise that the days when more administrative controls would restrict activity are clearly over. Thus regulators and supervisors have to learn to work with, rather than against, market forces.

APPOINTMENT OF CHIEF EXECUTIVE OFFICERS/BOARD MEMBERS

Laying stress on the de-politicisation of appointments for the post of the chief executive offices (CEOs) and board membership of PSBs and FIs, the committee recommended that such appointments could be based on a convention of the Government accepting the recommendations of a group of eminent persons invited by the Governor of the Reserve Bank.

The Government set up an appointments board for board-level appointments in PSBs. The board, which was chaired by the Governor, Reserve Bank made recommendations to the Government for the appointment of chief executives and executive directors in nationalised banks and the chief executives of FIs. The selection by the board was based on professional experience and expertise in the relevant fields. The other members of the board were the Finance Secretary; the Deputy Governor, Reserve Bank; a management expert and a banking expert. The Special Secretary (Banking)/Additional Secretary (Banking) functioned as the member secretary of the board.

---

8. Minutes of the first meeting of the Board for Financial Supervision (BFS), December 7, 1994, Reserve Bank of India, Bombay.

9. Tarapore, S.S. (2000). "Financial Economics". *Special Lecture: T.S. Santhanam Chair.* Chennai. June 23.

SECURITIES SCAM: IRREGULARITIES IN
SECURITIES TRANSACTIONS (1992)

THE BREAK-OUT

In 1992, the Reserve Bank came to face an unprecedented situation when banks and the brokers colluded in irregular securities transactions. The scam, which broke through a news report in April 1992, involved the siphoning-off of about ₹ 5,000 crore from the financial system through a nexus between stockbrokers and senior executives of the nationalised banking industry. The scam exposed weaknesses in market regulation and securities settlement practices, along with highlighting serious technological gaps.

It was noticed that some banks had been engaged in large-scale transactions in government securities through brokers, in the course of which they violated the Reserve Bank's guidelines issued in July 1991 to refrain from undertaking certain transactions in securities, which were considered irregular. They had also been advised to frame and implement a suitable investment policy to ensure that operations in securities were conducted in accordance with sound and acceptable business practices. While evolving policies, with the approval of the respective boards, banks were required to adhere to the prescribed guidelines. For the purpose of diversification of their portfolio business, the Reserve Bank issued instructions to banks and their subsidiaries to offer portfolio management services to their clients in the form of investment consultancy/ management for a fee for long-term investible funds and provided entirely at the customers' risk. Banks/their subsidiaries were prohibited to accept funds for portfolio management for a period of less than one year. The funds accepted for portfolio management were to be deployed in capital market instruments and were not to be used for lending in the call money/bill market and lending to/placement with corporate bodies. One foreign bank, viz., ANZ Grindlays Bank, was permitted to make portfolio investments in a leasing company up to 30.0 per cent of the paid-up capital of the companies.

It was a different world then in that it posed potential market failures in the absence of appropriate safeguards. At this point SEBI existed, but without any statutory powers; there were no demat accounts and no computers. Bank managers and chief dealers used calculators, while bond traders in the banks checked manuals that looked like logarithmic tables to match the price and yield of a security. According to a former chairman of the SBI, the bank that was badly hit in the scam, one broker had precipitated the problem as most dealers in government banks did not know the difference between current yield and yield to maturity, or the basics of bond mathematics. They were taken for a ride by smarter multinational banks. Money was scarce and a few big brokers could cut favourable deals with banks that financed them.[10]

At this point, the broker responsible for the irregularities thought that he could make it big. Traders followed him blindly, while bankers looked the other way. Companies with IPO issues backed him, and the Reserve Bank, which made single-entry records of banks' bond deals in a ledger, was clueless about what was happening. The brokers used the government bond market to access finance and used the money to buy stocks. The stock buying fuelled the 1992 boom and took share prices to hitherto unseen high levels. As interest rates surged in the inter-bank market, call money rates touched 100.0 per cent. Bond prices fell as a result, and the brokers could buy back bonds at a cheaper price to cover up. Often, borrowing banks, which were not in a position to give securities, issued bankers' receipts (BRs).

The original intention behind issuing the BRs was to enable institutions to sell bonds against a letter of allotment. The practice was misused and irregular deals multiplied with some banks issuing BRs with no proper underlying assets or securities. They thus sold fake securities. There were parallel deals by another set of operators who shorted bonds as well as stocks. Instead of buying stocks with bond market money, they lent the money against shares in *badla* trades to those who wanted to roll over positions. Almost simultaneously, they sold these shares, building a short position to buy back shares at a cheaper price. Both groups with opposite views on the stock market misused the bond market to raise money. The web of transactions in the securities scam involved public sector undertakings (PSUs), banks, scores of operators, foreign lenders, FIs, co-operatives and small banks. This reflected the failure of markets to perform their designated roles, which led to a perverse kind of market integration.[11]

As one bank borrowed money from another against bonds in a transaction where brokers were involved, the cheque was not credited to the borrowing bank's account. Instead, money went to brokers' current

---

10. Ghosh, Sugata (2011). "Spook on the Bond Market", *The Economic Times*, Golden Jubilee Special Edition. March 24.

11. Ibid.

accounts. In a way, the brokers were shorting the bond market and going long on stocks. This reflected weaknesses in the internal governance practices in the banks.

THE JANAKIRAMAN COMMITTEE AND FOLLOW-UP

At the instance of the Government, the Reserve Bank set up a committee with the Deputy Governor, Shri R. Janakiraman as chairman on April 30, 1992 to investigate the irregularities in funds management by commercial banks and FIs, particularly in their dealings in government securities, public sector bonds, Unit Trust of India (UTI) units and similar instruments.

The committee submitted three reports dated May 31, July 5 and August 23, 1992 that were immediately released to the public. The committee detected serious deficiencies in the functioning of banks and FIs involved and the absence of necessary internal control in various functions — raising money without the backing of genuine securities, diverting call money funds to the current accounts of chosen brokers, and massive collusion between the concerned officials and brokers in dealings in government securities, public sector bonds and units. The committee listed the devices adopted for diverting funds from the banking system to the individual accounts of the brokers that prima facie constituted evidence of fraudulent misrepresentation. Fund management operations were conducted in gross violation of and with utter disregard to instructions and guidelines issued by the Reserve Bank. The report detailed the breakdown of essential discipline regarding the issue and recording of the BRs, the receipt and delivery of securities, and the receipt and payment for settlement of the transactions. The committee also came across instances where brokers were financed by banks through discounting of bills that were not supported by genuine transactions.

The committee made a series of suggestions for remedial action, which included the introduction of proper control systems, strengthening of monitoring and removing lacunae in the existing systems and procedures so as to avoid the recurrence of such irregularities. In this regard, the Reserve Bank and the Government moved with the single objective of restoring confidence in the country's financial system, both in India and in international markets. It was envisaged that the financial system would become stronger and more efficient by undertaking appropriate follow-up measures in light of this episode.

The Reserve Bank and the Government took several steps to unearth the ramifications of the irregularities, recover the bank dues, punish the guilty and set in motion enduring measures of a preventive nature. They also took follow-up action on several recommendations of the committee. The measures included examining the securities transactions of banks and FIs undertaken in the immediate past, placing the Bank of Karad Ltd under liquidation, placing Bank of Madura Ltd under a Reserve Bank observer, initiating wind-up proceedings against Metropolitan Co-operative Bank Ltd, de-listing three brokers from the Reserve Bank's list of approved brokers, entrusting the entire investigation to the Central Bureau of Investigation (CBI), attaching the properties of those involved, establishing a 'special court' to attend to the cases relating to the securities transactions of banks and FIs, appointing reputed firms of chartered accountants to conduct a special audit of the treasury operations of major players in the market under the provisions of section 30 (1B) of the Banking Regulation (BR) Act, 1949 and issuing special guidelines, including prohibiting inter-bank ready-forward deals in dated securities and approved/trustee securities other than Treasury Bills of all maturities and forbidding double ready-forward deals in government securities including Treasury Bills.

There were other important guidelines issued along the following lines: (i) the prohibition on buy-back deals between banks in other securities, such as PSU bonds and units, was continued; (ii) banks were to ensure that subsidiary general ledger (SGL) transfer forms covering their sale transactions in government/approved securities were issued only if they had sufficient balance in their respective SGL accounts in the Public Debt Offices (PDOs) of the Reserve Bank and in the event SGL transfer forms bounced, banks were liable for penal action; and (iii) banks were not to issue BRs under any circumstances on transactions in government securities for which the SGL facility was available. BRs could be issued in the case of other securities issued for covering transactions relating to either portfolio management scheme clients or other constituents, including brokers.

In its third report submitted on August 23, 1992, the Janakiraman Committee gave the statistics for the securities transaction undertaken by banks and FIs from April 1, 1991. Data were presented as the total value of the transactions — both sales and purchases — put through by banks during the period. Also, the report provided the findings of the scrutiny in respect of 16 banks/FIs, including two co-operative banks. The amount aggregated to ₹ 3,543 crore, after taking into account the value of securities seized by a bank from a broker for the amount of ₹ 350 crore. Though it represented only around 5.0 per cent of the total investment of SCBs in government securities amounting to

₹ 75,945 crore in 1992–93, what was critical was the systemic nature of the risk that would have undermined confidence in the banking system. The government ownership of most of the banks saved the banking system from any serious run on that occasion.

Another aspect brought out by the committee related to transactions that had resulted in problem exposures and the links between banks and the brokers in this regard. The committee also commented extensively on the features observed in operating the portfolio management scheme (PMS) and similar schemes, under which banks and FIs mobilised large sums of money, mainly from PSUs, and pointed out that in handling PMS clients' funds, there were large-scale violations by banks of the Reserve Bank's prohibition on ready-forward deals in PSU bonds and units, which were undertaken primarily to yield guaranteed return to those clients and that these funds seemed to have played a significant role in financing brokers. In this context, the committee highlighted the substantial volume of PSU bonds held by banks either in their own account or on PMS account and the significant erosion in their value due to the fall in market value of the relative bonds. Funds were diverted to brokers involved in these irregular transactions and their associate concerns in several such transactions put through particularly by the National Housing Bank (NHB), State Bank of Saurashtra, SBI and SBICAPS.

In many transactions, the counterparties mentioned in the contracts provided by the concerned broker existed only in name. Further, the facility of netting the contracts afforded by the SBI and SBICAPS to the brokers, the collection and credit of bankers' cheques issued in favour of SBI in the broker's accounts and the issue of bankers' cheques of SBI as per the instructions of the concerned broker had resulted in irregular operations. The irregularities observed by the committee with regard to SBI's transactions with the broker indicated that the investment account in the SBI's books and accounts with the PDO of the Reserve Bank were manipulated to accommodate the broker's transactions. The committee found that the functioning of the PDO of the Reserve Bank required considerable tuning and computerisation to handle the large number of transactions and to provide relevant information to banks for reconciliation at regular intervals to detect fraudulent/irregular transactions.

The committee made the following recommendations in its first interim report: (i) The practice of banks entering into ready-forward and double ready-forward deals with other banks should be restricted to government securities and should be prohibited in other securities, including PSU bonds, units and shares. (ii) Ready-forward and double ready-forward deals should be prohibited under PMS. (iii) The Reserve Bank's prohibition regarding banks entering into buy-back deals with non-bank clients should be strictly enforced. (iv) Banks should be required to formulate internal exposure limits for transactions including limits concerning brokers. (v) Brokers' contract notes should indicate the counterparty and brokerage charged. (vi) When banks act as custodians of brokers' or other parties' securities, the documentation for all transactions effected for such customers should indicate the banks' status. (vii) The prohibition on banks issuing cheques drawn on their account with the Reserve Bank for third-party transactions should be strictly enforced. (viii) Banks' transactions on behalf of their merchant banking subsidiaries should be transparent, giving full details to the subsidiaries. (ix) Banks were required to conduct all their transactions in PSU bonds, units and similar securities through a separate institution like the Stock Holding Corporation of India Ltd (SHCIL), which could be established to obviate the need to issue BRs. (x) Work in the SGL section of the PDO and furnishing information to banks should be speeded up. (xi) The scope of Reserve Bank inspections should be widened, with greater emphasis on treasury transactions, and the on-site inspection should be supplemented by reporting the compliance by banks duly certified by statutory auditors, with prudential and other guidelines. (xii) The Reserve Bank should review the adequacy of the internal audit department of banks. (xiii) There should be a separate audit by the bank's statutory auditors for the portfolio management operations of banks. (xiv) The Reserve Bank's organisational arrangement responsible for market intelligence should be strengthened. (xv) Institutional arrangements for inspection of the NHB should be made.

Apart from accepting these recommendations and initiating follow-up action with utmost speed and urgency, the Reserve Bank took several other steps to avoid a repeat of such irregularities. The scrutiny of the securities transactions of banks/institutions was continued with a view to tracing the flow of funds involving various cheques drawn by banks and the brokers. The Government and the Reserve Bank took serious note of the gross violation of the Reserve Bank guidelines and the failure of internal control systems, as also the flouting of banking norms regarding account payee cheques. The process for fixing responsibility for lapses and fraud was initiated and a CBI enquiry was instituted. The Government initiated steps to ensure that action was taken to recover dues of banking system.

The Governor held a special meeting with the chairmen, managing directors and chief executives of banks and FIs on June 9, 1992 for a detailed discussion on the findings and recommendations of the Janakiraman Committee's first interim report. The meeting took note of the public concern at the revelations in the securities transactions of banks and FIs and emphasised the need to restore public confidence in the functioning of the financial system as quickly as possible. The chief executives informed the Governor that remedial actions had already been initiated to introduce proper internal control systems, strengthen monitoring and remove lacunae in the existing systems and procedures so as to prevent the recurrence of similar lapses. The executives expressed their commitment to implementing guidelines as and when issued by the Reserve Bank based on the Janakiraman Committee report.

The Reserve Bank and the Government took the following steps to unearth the ramifications of the episode and enable appropriate remedial measures: (i) The complete record of securities transactions of all banks and institutions for the past few years were to be examined by the inspecting officers of the Reserve Bank. (ii) Actions were taken to facilitate the investigations by the committee, as also the CBI, which was asked by the Government to investigate the matter. (iii) The chairman and two directors of the Bank of Karad Ltd, which was involved in the case, were served with show-cause notices by the Reserve Bank, asking them to step down; subsequently, to protect the interests of the bank's depositors, the Bank of Karad Ltd was put under liquidation, and a liquidator was appointed to take care of the assets of the bank. The Bank of Karad Ltd, a private bank with an asset base of ₹ 80 crore, had an exposure of ₹ 753 crore on account of issuing BRs without any backing or against non-existent securities. Any option other than liquidation (*i.e.*, amalgamation/merger or moratorium) was not considered feasible in the circumstances. The decision to place the bank in liquidation was also in the best interests of small depositors. An amalgamation/merger with some other bank would have meant that the acquiring bank would have to take on a liability of ₹ 794 crore. A moratorium would have made it possible for institutional creditors to move their preference claim against the banks' assets to the detriment of the interests of a large number of small depositors even to get their deposit insurance money released to the extent of ₹ 30,000 each. On the recommendations of the Reserve Bank, the Deposit Insurance and Credit Guarantee Corporation (DICGC) was directed to release necessary funds against their insurance liabilities. (iv) The operations of the Bank of

Madura Ltd were investigated and an observer from the Reserve Bank was appointed. (v) The Reserve Bank had recommended to the Government of Maharashtra to direct the Registrar of Co-operative Societies in the state to proceed with winding-up of the Metropolitan Co-operative Bank, which was involved in the securities malpractices. (vi) To safeguard the interests of the banks/institutions and speed up the process of recovery of their dues, the Government promulgated an ordinance to attach the properties of all those involved in the malpractices and place them with the custodian appointed by the Government. (vii) The Reserve Bank de-listed four brokers from the Bank's list of approved brokers. (viii) The Reserve Bank directed SBI and ANZ Grindlays Bank Ltd, to make provisions for squaring up their obligations to the NHB. Both the SBI and ANZ Grindlays accordingly settled the claims. (ix) The Government set up a 'special court' to attend to the cases relating to the securities transactions of banks/institutions.

The Reserve Bank took up the work of computerising the SGL section of PDO on a priority basis. Computerisation of SGL transactions was operationalised in 1992–93 and SGL transactions including interest calculation for both central and the state government loans were undertaken at Bombay (now Mumbai), Madras (now Chennai), Calcutta (now Kolkata), New Delhi, Ahmedabad, Bangalore (now Bengaluru), Hyderabad and Kanpur. Software packages were developed and made operational for processing the auction of 91-day Treasury Bills and open market operations (OMOs) by the Internal Debt Management Cell (IDMC). The system provided for prompt and immediate processing of SGL transfer forms and the despatch of certain essential statements to the individual SGL account holders.

A committee under the chairmanship of Shri S.S. Nadkarni, chairman of IDBI was appointed by the Reserve Bank to suggest modalities for setting-up a depository along the lines of the SHCIL for banks and institutions to trade in units and PSU bonds and the committee's report received on August 8, 1992 was considered. The Reserve Bank also appointed experienced firms of chartered accountants to verify the securities transactions of several banks/institutions, including subsidiaries of banks, mutual funds and four foreign banks.

The inspection procedure of the Reserve Bank's Department of Banking Operations and Development (DBOD) was modified to allow detailed annual inspection of all banks with a focus on financial evaluation. The treasury operations of banks were specifically looked into and at more regular intervals. The role of the audits was enlarged in the Reserve Bank's supervisory process with immediate effect.

The committee presented its fourth report in March 1993 and the fifth and the sixth (final) reports in April 1993. While the fourth and fifth reports covered specific banks and FIs, the final report set out the overall findings. The reports contained detailed findings for 32 banks and institutions, where the irregularities were serious. The findings reiterated the nexus between brokers/FIs and banks and the fact that banks and their subsidiaries covered in the reports consciously sought to circumvent the Reserve Bank's guidelines on PMS to facilitate brokers/financial companies access large funds for use in the stock market for huge profits.

The reports identified four key factors in the perpetration of irregularities: (i) improper and indiscriminate use of BRs; (ii) brokers increasingly dealing on their own accounts and taking positions; (iii) banks' failure to periodically reconcile investments; and (iv) complete breakdown of internal control system in several banks. The committee observed that as a consequence of these irregularities, the investment portfolios of banks had become fragile and weak. The committee's final estimate of the gross problem exposure of banks was of the order of ₹ 4,024 crore in 1992–93, which was 31.6 per cent of the total assets as on March 19, 1993 of all scheduled banks.

In addition to the existence of weak internal control systems in banks, and lacunae in the supervisory mechanism, the committee pointed to the lack of specialised knowledge of the sophisticated electronic data processing systems used by foreign banks, the absence of sound market intelligence system, the overstretched resources of the supervisory system due to stipulation about coverage of a large number of branches during the inspections, and the insufficient importance given to treasury functions during inspections as some of the main reasons for the delay in detecting the widespread irregularities. Commenting on the role of external auditors, the committee, *inter alia*, observed that the auditors did not examine all the transactions and did not perceive this as part of their duty to examine the violations of the Reserve Bank's guidelines. The committee further observed that the irregularities could possibly have been detected earlier, if there had been greater co-ordination among the different controlling agencies.

Banks were asked to undertake an immediate review of the adequacy of their internal audit department. Modifications were also made in the inspection system of the Reserve Bank, providing for more detailed annual financial inspection of banks and the appointment of experienced firms of chartered accountants to verify the securities transactions of some banks; a ceiling of 5.0 per cent of total transactions put through the brokers was placed on the transactions through each approved broker in a year. Banks were advised to place adequate systems in place for undertaking security transactions so that irregularities of the nature pointed out by the committee did not recur. Other measures included setting-up an electronics clearance settlement and depository (ECSD) system. A group set up in the Reserve Bank was entrusted to guide and co-ordinate the work of establishing an electronic system for clearance and settlement of trading in public sector bonds and units by the SHCIL and the UTI.

A central depository for all securities in which banks normally dealt needed to be set up. This was in line with the recommendation of the Nadkarni Committee on trading in public sector bonds and units of mutual funds. Regional offices of the Reserve Bank were asked to look into the compliance aspect *vis-a-vis* major and important instructions/directives of the Reserve Bank during the course of inspection and were also entrusted to scrutinise compliance certificates submitted by banks at prescribed intervals.

The SGL operation in the PDO at Bombay, Calcutta, New Delhi, Madras, Hyderabad and Bangalore were computerised. The expertise of retired senior government officials was drawn on by appointing them as special officers to fix responsibility for the irregularities in some banks; a detailed circular was issued by the Reserve Bank to all commercial banks for suitably regulating their investment transactions. While exhorting the FIs to strictly follow the spirit of the instructions issued to commercial banks, they were also advised to place before their respective boards of directors, a comprehensive note regarding the policies and practices followed in their respective institutions for ensuring that the transactions were handled and accounted for in a transparent and accurate manner.

At the instance of the Reserve Bank, banks in which serious irregularities had occurred lodged criminal complaints with the CBI and simultaneously initiated departmental proceedings against the errant officials. By the end of June 1994, the reports submitted by four retired senior officials of the seven appointed as special officers in six subsidiaries of five banks were examined and were sent to the Government with the recommendations of the Reserve Bank. The progress with regard to the action taken by banks and FIs against erring officials was monitored by the Reserve Bank on a quarterly basis and communicated to the Government periodically.

The Reserve Bank carried out a special audit of 10 banks with irregular securities transactions. The audit firms, against whom adverse comments appeared in the report of the Janakiraman Committee, continued to be denied bank audit assignments for the second year, *i.e.,* 1993–94. Following the submission of further reports by the committee, 17 more firms were denied bank audit assignments for the year 1993–94. Besides, the Institute of Chartered Accountants of India (ICAI) was requested to take suitable disciplinary action against the erring auditors. In the case of foreign banks, the irregularities in securities transactions were kept in view while permitting them to open branches in India and before they remitted profits.

In order to trace the end-use of funds raised by brokers during the securities irregularities and to recover the assets created from these funds, the Reserve Bank, in consultation with the Government, constituted an inter-disciplinary group (IDG) under the chairmanship of the custodian with representatives from the Reserve Bank, the CBI, the Income Tax Department and the Enforcement Directorate. The IDG prepared a draft interim report, which was submitted on June 28, 1994 to the Government and the Reserve Bank.

After the Joint Parliamentary Committee (JPC) was set up in August 1992, the committee called the Deputy Governor of the Reserve Bank for a briefing in the matter. The Reserve Bank emphasised the issues involved and stated that while such irregularities could not be condoned, these irregularities occurred in the context of very large pre-emptions of banks' resources through CRR and SLR and regulations on interest rates. There were, however, undoubtedly certain lacunae in the monitoring system and market information collection mechanism. Subsequently, when the issue of imposing penalties for these irregularities came up, notwithstanding the fears about prolonged litigation, the Reserve Bank commissioned detailed work on the extent of the irregularities and undertook to oversee the entire process to ensure that there was no slackness on its own part in the exercise. Further, the Bank went ahead with imposing penalties, which all banks paid-up without demur and there was no recourse to any litigation.[12]

---

12. Tarapore, S.S. (2011). "Episodes from Monetary and Other Financial Policies (1982–1997): An Anecdotal Presentation", in Sameer Kochhar (ed.), *Growth and Finance: Essays in Honour of C. Rangarajan.* New Delhi: Academic Foundation.

PENALTIES FOR SECURITIES IRREGULARITIES

After considering the issues and taking into account the gravity of the irregularities committed by banks in respect of PMS/ready-forward transactions, the Reserve Bank issued a show-cause notice on July 25,1994 to banks about why the funds accepted by them under PMS and deployed in violation of the Reserve Bank's instructions should not be treated as deposits for the purpose of determining their net demand and time liabilities (NDTL) for arriving at the minimum average daily cash balances to be maintained by them with the Reserve Bank under section 42 of the Reserve Bank of India (RBI) Act, 1934. Similarly, in the case of banks that had undertaken ready-forward deals in PSU bonds and units of the UTI and also ready-forward deals in government and other approved securities with non-bank clients, the Reserve Bank asked the banks why the funds so obtained should not be treated as 'borrowings' for the purpose of determining NDTL. On September 26, 1994, the Bank issued a show-cause notice to one more PSB for violation of ready-forward deals. The aggregate amount of interest recovered as well as the penal interest levied, for which show-cause notices were issued, amounted to around ₹ 146 crore. All the 21 banks paid the penalties.

In the case of 35 SCBs, the Reserve Bank decided to withdraw with effect from August 6, 1994, and in respect of two more banks with effect from October 1, 1994, the exemption given in April 1992 under section 42(7) of the RBI Act, 1934 from maintenance of 10.0 per cent incremental cash reserve ratio.

THE JOINT PARLIAMENTARY COMMITTEE

A 30-member JPC comprising members from both Houses of Parliament was constituted in August 1992 with the following terms of reference: (i) to go into the irregularities and fraudulent manipulations in all its aspects and ramifications in transactions relating to securities, shares, bonds and other financial instruments and the role of banks, stock exchanges, FIs and PSUs in transactions relating thereto, which had or might come to light; (ii) to fix the responsibilities of the persons, institutions or authorities in respect of such transactions; (iii) to identify the misuse, if any, of and the failures/inadequacies in the control mechanism and the supervisory mechanism; (iv) to make recommendations for safeguards and improvement in the system to eliminate such failures and occurrences in future; and (v) to make appropriate recommendations regarding policies and regulations to be followed.

The JPC, in its report submitted in December 1993, identified non-observance of the prescribed rules and procedures as the major factor for the irregularities, with critical comments on the mode of functioning of banks, both Indian and foreign, the brokers, PSUs and ministries and the failure of the supervisory authorities. The committee heavily drew upon the findings of the Janakiraman Committee.

GOVERNOR'S DEPOSITION BEFORE THE JPC

The Reserve Bank Governor deposed before the JPC on November 26 and 27, 1992. The deposition began with a *suo moto* statement by the Governor giving his assessment of the irregularities in the securities transactions and the role played by the Reserve Bank in unearthing it. He enunciated his views on the supervisory role of the Reserve Bank and suggested an agenda for strengthening the Bank's supervisory functions in view of the experiences. In recognition of the need for a self-review, the Governor placed on record the Reserve Bank's ongoing efforts and clarified that restructuring required legislative changes and had to meet parliamentary requirements before implementation.

The Governor submitted that it was the supervisory operations undertaken by the Reserve Bank that broke the chain of fraudulent transactions in the banking system; the Bank took quick action to unravel the irregularities in the securities market and found out the *modus operandi* in respect of the concerned bank and its subsidiaries. It was the Reserve Bank inspecting officials who alerted the system to the abuse of BRs and issued instructions in July 1991 that pointed out the absence of reconciliation of the SBI investment accounts with the PDO and sought for the reconciled accounts as on March 31, 1992. The Reserve Bank supervisors alerted the chairman of the SBI on March 13, 1992 to the possibility of irregularities in the account of a broker Harshad Mehta and the need to monitor the account.

A word of caution was passed on to banks and institutions regarding the impact of the stock market boom. The irregularities committed by M/s Fairgrowth Financial Services Ltd (FFSL) were also unearthed by the Reserve Bank officials who zeroed in on the forgery of documents by the FFSL. The Reserve Bank speeded up the inter-bank reconciliation of bank receipts, which helped to bring out the large irregularities at the Standard Chartered Bank and the Canbank Financial Services Ltd (Canfina). It was emphasised that a strong supervisory system must be accompanied by continual improvement in bank management, internal controls and audit.

Further, the quality and efficiency of bank managers must be constantly upgraded. Failure to observe the professional, prudential and supervisory guidelines, it was felt, needed to be dealt with firmly.

Submitting on weaknesses in the system, the Governor emphasised that the Reserve Bank did not and in fact should not continually monitor the internal management and operations of bank branches and FIs. This responsibility primarily was vested with the top-level executives of these institutions. While external inspection and audit did expose violations of regulations and policies, it was beyond even the most efficient supervisory organisation for continuous policing of the follow-up to policy instructions. Changes in terms of the supervisory skills and techniques were not fully commensurate with the increased complexity of the markets. The disclosure that top management of any of the affected banks was not aware of the activities of the funds management division under their charge was a pointer to the laxity in approach in this vital area. The source of profits arising from funds management was not being scrutinised carefully by the managements of the banks. The Reserve Bank's instructions were also being flouted.

Referring to the question whether the Reserve Bank was alert to the movements in the stock market, the Governor said that the Reserve Bank was closely monitoring the stock market indices and modulating its actions accordingly to restrict speculative market activities that could have adverse consequences for unsuspecting investors. Securities and Exchange Board of India (SEBI), which was the primary agency for the regulation and control of the stock market, was empowered to exercise fuller control and the Reserve Bank, as the monetary authority, had always acted in close concert with SEBI.

Dwelling on the policy reforms, the Governor emphasised transparency with no concealing or window dressing. The inspection and audit systems of banks and FIs were expected to be made thorough and more systematic. A focus was required on systems becoming sensitive to potential fraud and taking immediate action. Supervision was anticipated to be highly professional and guided by a group of people with experience and skill. The Governor explained the Reserve Bank's supervisory methods and the steps required to improve supervisory skills and institutional reforms at the Reserve Bank. Enumerating the details of the important committees set up as a follow-up, the Governor stated that a committee under the chairmanship of Shri S. Padmanabhan to review the system of inspection at the Reserve Bank and to identify its defects and inadequacies had been constituted. A committee was also appointed under the Deputy Governor, Shri A. Ghosh to suggest a system of preventing fraud in banks. Matters relating to urban co-operative banks were comprehensively reviewed by Shri S.S. Marathe.

In conclusion, the Governor stated that the Reserve Bank was a strong pillar of the financial system of the country. He explained the significant role played by the officials of the Reserve Bank during the BoP crisis of 1991. During the period of irregularities in securities transactions, the Bank was able to avert panic in the banking system. He felt that it was his duty to appreciate the arduous work done by the officers and staff, but also recognised that, like all human institutions, the Reserve Bank needed critical evaluation and re-organisation.

INVOLVEMENT OF NBFCs

While dealing with irregularities in the securities transactions of NBFCs, the JPC had observed that certain non-bank subsidiaries of major PSBs had accepted sizeable deposits as inter-corporate placements from private and public sector companies at various rates of interest and for varying periods by entering into 'ready-forward sale' deals with these corporate bodies purporting to cover the sale of long-term investments. These non-bank subsidiaries also indulged in irregular transactions through imprudent investment of funds in the securities market under the PMS on the stock exchanges through brokers. The major observations of the committee were:[13]

> Scrutiny of various transactions in various banks has revealed that the non-banking subsidiaries of major public sector banks such as SBI Capital Markets Limited, Canbank Financial Services Ltd., Allbank Finance Ltd., Andhra Bank Financial Services Ltd. etc. indulged in irregular transactions and in imprudent investment of funds into the security market under the portfolio management scheme and in unauthorised investments on the stock exchanges through brokers even though these companies were incorporated essentially for undertaking Merchant Banking and such other activities. In a large measure they adopted portfolio management of temporary surplus funds of PSUs and other larger corporate clients of their parent banks. These subsidiary companies

---

13. At serial no. 15 of the chapter titled: Observation/conclusion/recommendations of the report.

violated PMS guidelines of the Reserve Bank in various ways and almost as of routine. The funds so deployed became one of the principal sources for fuelling the stock market. Large volumes of unauthorised investment transactions were undertaken by these NBFCs through repos, BRs, *etc.* All these investment operations of public funds were not supervised adequately and there was absence of suitable policies for investments. The transactions also revealed nexus with select brokers through whom sizeable transactions were put through. In many cases brokerage was not also being paid as the deals were at the instance of brokers and for their benefit. These NBFCs had the advantage of the names of their parent banks to attract deposit funds and at the same time offered high returns. Each company devised its own scheme to attract funds. Competitive and wholly unverifiable claims about returns were advertised to attract investments. This gross irresponsibility was not checked either by the parent bank, who in fact encouraged it, or by the government, who in the ultimate are the trustees of this public asset.

The committee's observations on certain non-bank subsidiaries of banks were: SBICAPS violated all established norms and that it was with the knowledge of the parent bank that the company parted with substantial funds in favour of the broker Harshad Mehta and it did so without any security. Canfina took the role of 'market maker' and handled 75.0 per cent of the total PSU bonds issued. It also shifted its activities to 'portfolio management' and 'corporate investment advisory services'. Canfina had been violating the Reserve Bank guidelines on PMS for a long time. There was practically no internal control machinery to check irregularities. It was observed that the parent bank had not conducted any inspection or periodic scrutiny of the affairs of Canfina.

The bulk of funds collected by Andhra Bank Financial Services Ltd (ABFSL) were from PSUs. Thus, as on March 31, 1992, of the total deposits collected by way of 'inter-corporate' and 'security transactions' at over ₹ 500 crore, an amount of ₹ 350 crore was from PSU clients. A substantial portion of these funds raised was passed on to three parties, *viz.*, FFSL, H. P. Dalal and Standard Chartered Bank, ostensibly under ready-forward transactions and without complying with the Reserve Bank guidelines in this respect. Thus, the company had merely acted as a conduit for the diversion of funds from public sector enterprises to private sector companies and foreign banks, thus circumventing the investment guidelines for PSUs that prohibited their investing/depositing money with private sector finance companies. Allbank Finance Ltd had functioned mostly for the benefit of M/s V.B. Desai and, in contravention of all principles of safety of funds, passed on its customers' deposits to the broker for investment and speculative deals in the share market.

With a view to affix the responsibility of the top management, including the chairmen of the subsidiaries, for irregularities in securities transactions, special officers were appointed by the Reserve Bank. The reports of the special officers in respect of SBICAPS, ABFSL, Canfina, Allbank Finance Ltd and BoI Finance Ltd, which brought out the lapses on the part of the top management of the subsidiaries, were sent by the Government to the CBI for consideration.

TABLE 17.1

Officials Against Whom Action Taken by Banks

Subsidiary	No. of Officials
SBICAPS	11
ABFSL	7
Canfina/Canbank Mutual Fund (CBMF)	15
BoI Finance Ltd/BoI Mutual Fund	11

Source: Reserve Bank of India, internal documents and notes.

Departmental action was also initiated or taken by the respective parent banks against the officials involved in the irregularities (Table 17.1). The departmental action involved dismissal, compulsory retirement or termination. In the case of Allbank Finance Ltd, the case was referred to the CBI for investigation.

The committee concluded that the control mechanism in the parent banks to monitor the activities of the subsidiaries was inadequate. Several measures were introduced for effective control over the activities of the subsidiaries as discussed below.

From December 1992, SEBI was empowered to inspect banking subsidiaries that undertook merchant banking activities. The Reserve Bank also conducted inspection of the subsidiaries of banks. The Bank took steps to ensure adequate supervision of these institutions by the banks themselves through a regular review by the board of the working of the subsidiaries and their periodic inspection by the parent bank/outside agencies, if necessary.

The lacunae highlighted by the scam regarding non-adherence to the guidelines issued by the Reserve Bank were rectified and comprehensive guidelines were issued to commercial banks relating to securities transactions that covered prudential investment policy, prohibition of buy-back deals, use of SGLs/BRs, internal control systems, accounting standards, submission of reports to the Reserve Bank regarding monthly concurrent audit of treasury transactions, half-yearly review of investments and half-yearly certificate of compliance with Reserve Bank instructions. Statutory auditors' certificates about compliance in key areas were made applicable, *mutatis mutandis* to subsidiaries/mutual funds established by banks.

Banks were also advised that when they exercised custodial functions on behalf of their merchant banking subsidiaries, such functions were subject to the same procedures and safeguards as other constituents.

FFSL and its associate companies were issued directives[14] that prohibited them from undertaking deposit acceptance, borrowing and investments, and practically froze their functions till further orders. The company was directed to report compliance on a daily basis.

FURTHER FOLLOW-UP MEASURES

Pursuant to the recommendations of both the Janakiraman Committee and the JPC, the Reserve Bank initiated several measures to prevent the recurrence of such irregularities. Detailed instructions that covered several areas, including norms for the proper conduct of investment transactions, were issued that comprised: (i) framing of investment policy; (ii) restrictions on the use of BRs; (iii) use of SGL transfer forms, including penalty provisions if they bounced; (iv) restricting ready-forward deals to Treasury Bills and certain specified government securities among banks; (v) conduct of business through brokers, including prescribing a ceiling of 5.0 per cent per broker on the business routed through them annually; (vi) internal control measures such as concurrent audit of investment transactions; (vii) separate audit of PMS transactions; (viii) capital adequacy norms and accounting standards for FIs as well as NBFCs; and (ix) exercising precautions in the sphere of bills discounting and rediscounting. In particular, during the year 1993–94, banks were advised

---

14. Reserve Bank of India, letter no DFC (COC) No. 17/169-91/92 dated July 1, 1992.

not to restart or introduce any new PMS or similar schemes without obtaining specific prior approval from the Reserve Bank. Further, banks were advised to introduce a system of concurrent audit covering at least 50.0 per cent of the business operations during the year 1993–94. For this purpose, a note broadly defining the concepts of concurrent audit, scope, coverage of business/branches for the audit and reporting system was circulated to banks for their reference.

Considering the lapses in the observance of the regulatory framework, on July 25, 1994 the Reserve Bank withdrew the exemption from maintenance of 10.0 per cent incremental CRR for 35 SCBs and for two more banks on September 26, 1994. The Bank simultaneously issued show-cause notices for levy of penalty on 20 such banks and on one more bank on September 26, 1994 for irregularities in PMS/ready-forward transactions and also for shortfalls in maintaining minimum average daily cash balances with the Reserve Bank.

The manner in which irregularities committed by banks should be dealt with came up for discussion at the meetings of Central Board of the Reserve Bank. The BR Act, 1949 provided for levying only nominal penalties by the Reserve Bank for violation of its directives. The Act had to be amended to penalise the errant banks and the Reserve Bank took recourse to the provisions relating to the maintenance of CRR in the RBI Act, 1934 to impose penalties, as major irregularities committed by banks related to these areas. These were the issues commented upon by the Janakiraman Committee and also the JPC. These banks were, therefore, asked in July 1994 to show why the funds accepted and deployed by them under PMS should not be treated as 'deposits' and the amount received by them as sales proceeds under ready-forward deals as 'borrowings' and included in the demand and time liabilities on reporting Fridays for calculating the minimum average daily balance for the minimum balance commencing from August 9, 1991 to June 26, 1992. Show-cause notices were issued to 21 banks for payment of penalty for an aggregate amount of ₹ 146 crore.

In addition to the above penal action, the exemption given to SCBs for maintenance of 10.0 per cent incremental CRR was withdrawn in respect of 37 banks for lapses in observing the regulatory framework.

Several measures, such as reduction in the validity period of BRs from 30 days to 15 days, specifying penalties for misuse of the BR facility, introduction of D*v*P system and appointment of audit committee of boards in banks were introduced by the Reserve Bank to strengthen the supervisory mechanism in banks and improve their overall functioning.

Administrative action was initiated based on a preliminary investigation against officials directly or indirectly responsible for the irregularities that were committed. The chairman of the NHB resigned; the chairmen of UCO Bank and SBI were asked to proceed on leave as also the deputy managing director of the SBI and the managing director of Canbank Financial Services Ltd. The chairman, Bank of Karad and two directors on its board were removed, while the board of Metropolitan Co-operative Bank was superseded; subsequently, these two banks were taken into liquidation. The services of the chairman of UCO Bank were terminated.

The Reserve Bank issued fresh instructions to regulate transactions in securities by banks. Treasury transactions were now subject to a concurrent audit by internal auditors and the findings were to be put up to the chairman and managing director (CMD) once every month. It was decided that a special cell in the Reserve Bank would also scrutinise these reports.

The Reserve Bank modified its inspection procedures to provide for detailed annual inspection of all banks with a focus on financial evaluation. The absence of computerisation and reliance on manual processing in the PDO was one factor that made it difficult for banks to set up effective internal control systems to supervise trading in government securities. A process of computerisation of the PDO was initiated. Certain officials in the PDO were suspended.

RELATED QUESTIONS

Questions were raised about whether the Reserve Bank, which was responsible for supervision of banks, could have been more vigilant. There were references in the media to a circular issued by the Reserve Bank in July 1991 that laid down norms for banks dealing in securities transactions. The press reports emphasised that the Reserve Bank should have been more cautious in pursuing compliance. The fact was that the Reserve Bank had directed banks to submit compliance reports, and also received compliance reports from most banks indicating that their procedures were in line with the July circular. Subsequent developments, however, showed that this was not the case.

The Reserve Bank could not undertake micro-management in all the cases, and it was only in identified problem cases that detailed scrutiny, with onsite inspection, was undertaken. The Reserve Bank, after the detection of fraudulent deals, undertook inspection of Bank of Karad,

Andhra Bank and Bank of Madura, and these investigations indicated evidence of continuing irregularities. Action against these banks was being contemplated when the wider dimensions of the scam became apparent. However, it was true that even these enquiries did not reveal the full extent of the problems in Bank of Karad, which surfaced only later when the Reserve Bank carried out inter-bank reconciliation.

The irregularities and fraud that came to light were, contrary to the general perception, not attributable to financial liberalisation. They had surfaced under a regime of well regulated banking activity. Over-regulation of interest rates and excessive pre-emption of bank resources into low interest assets had contributed to some extent to the bank managements looking at non-traditional activities to bolster profits. Measures, therefore, were initiated by the Reserve Bank in consultation with the Government to allow flexibility in determining interest rates and reducing the statutory pre-emptions of banks' resources.

STRENGTHENING MARKET INTELLIGENCE IN THE AFTERMATH OF THE SECURITIES SCAM

As a sequel to the unearthing of irregularities and fraudulent transactions in the banking system in the early 1990s, the Government conveyed to the Reserve Bank its concerns about the need to strengthen the system in three areas to ensure that such events did not recur. Shri Montek Singh Ahluwalia, Secretary, Department of Economic Affairs, in a letter to the Governor dated July 14, 1992 identified these areas, namely, market intelligence, the mechanism of bills discounting and manipulation in foreign exchange transactions.

The Government stressed that apart from overall supervision through a system of rules and guidelines with periodic inspections, a more systematic method of gathering market intelligence was needed. It was expected to serve as an early warning system, alerting authorities to the possibility of misuse within the system. The Government suggested setting-up the banking intelligence cell in the Reserve Bank.

The Government's perception was that even though the guidelines issued by the Reserve Bank were clear that bills should be discounted only against genuine trade transactions, industrial companies were misusing this mechanism to raise fictitious bills in order to obtain short-term liquidity from the banking system. These accommodation bills were particularly easy to draw between companies within the same group and represented no substantive trade transactions. The Government strongly felt that the credibility of the banking system would be considerably shaken if companies defaulted when payments of bills to banks became due and if it was subsequently found that the bills were not genuine trade bills. The imposition of deterrent penalties on banks that failed to identify the underlying trade transactions before agreeing to discount bills was mooted. Spot checks were also envisaged on banks that liberally provided such rediscounting facilities. While conceding that there was a danger that banks might become more risk-averse in discounting of bills, the ministry felt that this was all for the good, as it would lead to disappearance of fraudulent transactions in the bills market.

Next, the area of foreign exchange transactions was accorded special attention. According to informal reports received by the Government, extensive manipulation took place in the foreign exchange dealing rooms of banks. This occurred because arbitrage possibilities opened up due to exchange rate fluctuations in a day's trading, which enabled banks to take the most favourable exchange rate from their point of view in converting funds across currencies. The Government was of the view that the solution lay in ensuring complete automation of dealing rooms with a mandatory stipulation that a continuous record was kept of transactions and exchange rates through the day, with information recorded on a magnetic tape or a disc that the Reserve Bank could access. "Unless such tough signals are sent to banks, it is likely that the existing permissiveness in their attitudes would continue and dubious transactions may easily be accommodated", was the prognosis of the finance ministry. The letter added that these comments and suggestions were submitted by way of communicating perceptions that had surfaced in their internal discussions. Further, the Finance Minister was kept informed that the Reserve Bank would be advised on these issues.

The Reserve Bank acted with alacrity. The Governor, in his letter dated July 28, 1992, conveyed his concurrence with the contents of the letter and outlined the actions taken. A decision was taken to set up a market intelligence cell (MIC) to go beyond the developments in banking and extend its reach to stock exchanges. Even though the Reserve Bank had impressed upon banks the need to ensure that there was an underlying trade transaction behind the bills rediscounted, to put the issue beyond doubt, instructions were issued prohibiting the discounting of accommodation bills in a circular to commercial banks dated July 27, 1992. The Reserve Bank shared the Government's apprehensions in foreign exchange transactions, and hastened to assure that while detailed guidelines existed for dealing room operations, the Bank was examining the issue of mandatory prescriptions relating to maintenance of a continuous record of transactions and exchange rates during the day, and was also contemplating imposition of severe penalties on those found engaged in dubious transactions.

MAJOR DEVELOPMENTS IN BANKING POLICY AND OPERATIONS: 1990–1997

The reforms process for the banking sector included, *inter alia* — monetary and credit policy issues (dealt with elsewhere in this volume) as well as institutional matters, such as introducing competition through entry of new banks, mergers, improvising supervisory and surveillance mechanisms and in house strengthening of banks. The measures initiated touched upon several areas, such as, strengthening and consolidating banks, prescribing prudential norms relating to assets classification and income recognition, adequate provisioning for bad and doubtful assets, introducing a system of capital to risk-weighted assets ratio for banks and establishing a strong supervisory system. The reforms were necessitated by the fact that over time Indian banks had developed many stresses and strains and had to be revitalised. There was, however, opposition to the reforms and, in particular, to the privatisation of nationalised banks.

The implementation of prudential norms and guidelines constituted a significant step towards introducing transparency in accounting practices and bringing the norms up to international standards. This was expected to help build confidence in the efficiency of the Indian financial system, improve the competitive position of the banking industry and enhance public accountability. All these were, in turn, expected to significantly improve the functioning of the banking system.

Prior to initiation of the reforms process, several external and internal factors impinged on the functioning of the banking system. External factors broadly related to the high levels of CRR, SLR and the administered structure of interest rates. Reduction in the CRR and SLR requirements and simplification of the administered structure of interest rates were some of the measures successfully implemented to address the external issues. Among internal factors, the introduction of prudential norms relating to income recognition, asset classification and capital adequacy worked to assure the viability of the banking system. These norms not only ensured that the balance sheets and income and expenditure statements provided a true reflection of the health of banks, but also acted as a tool of financial discipline and compelled banks to look more carefully at the quality of loan assets as well as the risks attached to lending. The policies also ensured that banks conformed to international accounting standards and got their due place and recognition in the global financial market. Despite severe budgetary constraints, the Government extended capital support to banks to enable them to conform to the capital adequacy requirements.

The major task before the banks was to improve their financial performance and bring about a change in the mindset. The banks in the early 1990s were classified into three categories based on their performance, viz., banks that had positive operating profits and positive net profits after provisioning, banks that had positive operating profits but negative net profits after provisioning, and banks that had negative operating profits and negative net profits. Improving the profitability was a major issue and it required special emphasis. The major drag on the profitability of Indian banks was the presence of a high level of non-performing loans (NPLs). The situation warranted that banks should cut costs, improve productivity and ensure better recovery of loans, which was possible only if they became competitive, notwithstanding the fact that they had to drastically bring down the large amount of NPAs. Against this backdrop, a need was felt to set up debt recovery tribunals and special recovery branches to concentrate on bad loans and their recoveries.

As part of the additional capital made available to PSBs, banks had to draw a memorandum of understanding with the Reserve Bank indicating their performance criteria and commitment to achieve the business targets. This imposed a greater sense of discipline among banks. Since then, banks made significant progress year after year in the areas of computerisation, achievement of priority sector targets, reduction in NPAs, and improvement in operating results. It also ensured that banks complied with the requirement of full provisioning against NPAs and did not allow accumulation of NPAs in their over-enthusiasm to improve net margins by taking risky decisions or even becoming prone to concentrating loan portfolios among a few borrowers in certain sectors. Steps were initiated for progressive deregulation of interest rates to evolve a diversified competitive market place, move towards market-determined exchange rate mechanism and introduce technological changes in line with the advances in information technology.

The approach to lending was also liberalised, although the directed credit and interest rate administration remained largely untouched. Industrial sector credit, where the banks could make some margin of profit, was under the discipline of the credit authorisation scheme (CAS), which was replaced later by a credit monitoring arrangement (CMA); it got a boost in the later part of the 1980s. This led to some indiscriminate lending by banks. The initial liberalisation extended by the Reserve Bank and the Government was not without some adverse impact on the lending portfolio, but these measures paved the way for rapid expansion of the industrial sector.

Banks were required to equip themselves to operate in a more deregulated interest rate environment. This implied that they had to fix the rate on deposits and loans depending on overall liquidity conditions and demand factors. Banks were given the freedom to fix the rates on deposits, subject to a maximum. This forced banks to determine, on their own, the rate of interest on deposits of different maturities below three years, which enabled some market leaders to emerge. Similarly, on the lending side, there was only the prescription of a minimum lending rate. Over the years, banks developed appropriate criteria for determining the rate to be charged to individual borrowers. They also learnt in the process, the limitations of this freedom in a competitive market and the demand for and pressures on the available resources.

BRANCH LICENSING POLICY

After the branch licensing policy of 1985–1990 came to an end in March 1990, the Reserve Bank did not frame a new policy. Instead it issued policy guidelines to enable banks to take up need-based expansion of branches. The validity period of the licenses issued under the earlier policy in rural/ semi-urban areas, which could not be utilised before March 31, 1990 was extended by a year to March 31, 1991 and further to March 31, 1992 to enable banks to fully utilise their pending licenses. Considering that the objective of providing adequate infrastructure throughout the country, particularly in rural areas, was broadly achieved with the completion of the branch expansion policy for the period 1985–1990, the Reserve Bank decided to confer greater freedom on banks to rationalise their branch network by relocating branches, opening specialised branches, spinning-off business at their locations, setting-up controlling offices/administrative units and establishing extension counters. Banks were permitted to close down branches other than those in rural areas, as well as swap branches that were not remunerative or those in remote areas, with a view to protecting the financial viability of banks.

As per the new guidelines: (i) no fresh branches in rural areas were to be considered in cases where the service area allocated to a particular branch was unmanageable and where there was a large spatial gap or if the increased volume of business warranted opening an additional branch; (ii) in semi-urban centres, branch expansion was to be considered on the basis of well-established need, depending upon growth in trade and industry, increase in other economic activities and the viability of the proposed branch; (iii) the criteria for industrial/project areas were clearly spelt out, wherein the new branches were to be considered with reference to the immediate need and outlay on projects; and (iv) in urban and metropolitan/port town centres, the identification of unbanked/under-banked localities was entrusted to small working groups, consisting of, *inter alia*, representatives of major commercial banks and under the overall supervision of the Reserve Bank's concerned regional office.

MOVE TO BRING PUBLIC SECTOR BANKS/FIs UNDER THE AUDIT PURVIEW OF THE COMPTROLLER AND AUDITOR GENERAL

The Reserve Bank had all along enjoyed autonomy over regulation and supervision of banks and FIs. The Comptroller and Auditor General (CAG) wrote to the Finance Minister in 1989 about bringing banks and FIs within the purview of CAG audit. The issue was examined in detail by the Reserve Bank and the Government was advised that the Bank had sufficient means to judge the efficiency, economy and performance of commercial banks and, therefore, the need for adding another element of supervision by way of CAG audit was not clear. The Governor's views are best captured in the following:[15]

> The main business of commercial banks was lending the resources which were provided by depositors. By comparison, the involvement of government funds as bank capital was very small. Bank credit was essentially a matter of discretion and there was necessarily an element of risk involved in the business. This was also the position of financial institutions which were in the lending/investment business. Bank inspections had, therefore to be approached in a manner which was very different from expenditure audit. The Reserve Bank provided the requisite specialised supervision under the Banking Regulations Act and the

---

15. Letter from the Governor, Shri R.N. Malhotra to Finance Secretary, Dr Bimal Jalan, dated July 18, 1990.

Reserve Bank of India Act. The Reserve Bank had also the powers to call for information from and conduct inspections of financial institutions other than banks under Section 45 L and Section 45 N of the RBI Act. The Reserve Bank's oversight on financial institutions was exercised in an informal manner through periodic meetings and the nomination of senior Reserve Bank officers on their boards. However, considering large amounts of money which passed through the financial institutions it was decided by the Reserve Bank after discussions with Chairman, IDBI and several other heads of financial institutions to structure our supervision mainly with a view to ensuring financial health and sound quality of their assets and greater co-ordination between commercial banks and financial institutions. To that end, in consultation with the institutions, an annual financial review was introduced. These institutions were also subject to external audit. In this background the Government was advised that introduction of yet another supervisory agency was likely to cause confusion and conflict of opinion entailing a lot of extra work and correspondence.

The BR Act, 1949 contained provisions for maintaining the confidentiality of a bank's business with its clients. It also provided protection to banks against disclosure of some elements of their financial operations. While the latter protection was gradually relaxed, a crucial concern continued to be the maintenance of public confidence in the viability of commercial banks. Further, under the existing provisions of the law, the Government kept Parliament informed about the accounts and performance of banks. Besides, the parliamentary committees reviewed the functioning of banks/FIs from time to time. A larger number of questions pertaining to banks/FIs were also answered by the Government in successive sessions of Parliament. This enabled Parliament to exercise sufficient oversight over the working of banks and FIs. The Governor, Shri Malhotra concluded in his letter that he was of the firm view that the present supervisory regime should continue.

FINANCIAL HEALTH OF THE BANKING SYSTEM

In the early 1990s the concern for banks' health attracted wide attention, leading to frequent correspondence between the Reserve Bank and the Government on the subject. The Reserve Bank's responses to individual complaints can be illustrated by a few instances during that period.

The chairman of the Institute of Public Affairs (India) addressed a letter in February 1990 to the Finance Minister, with a copy to the Governor, expressing serious apprehensions about the financial health of nationalised banks and the Reserve Bank's supervisory control over banks, citing a specific case involving UCO bank. Enclosing a press report on the state of affairs at UCO bank, he wrote that it was a disturbing situation, which must have arisen over the years and not just in one year.

The Reserve Bank sent a detailed reply, clarifying and explaining the extensive powers of regulation, supervision and control that the Reserve Bank had over the commercial banks under the BR Act, 1949 and the RBI Act, 1934 with a view to: (i) ensure solvency of the banking system, quality of assets, adequate liquidity and profitability; (ii) watch adherence to statutory and regulatory requirements; and (iii) oversee implementation of national socio-economic policies and development objectives. After referring to the internal control and governance mechanisms in place, the Bank added that the general public had access to information in the audited annual accounts of banks that contained the auditors' observations. Wide publicity about the operations of banks was given in various publications of the Reserve Bank. Under the circumstances, there was no reason for the depositor community to think that their interests were not being protected. The continued confidence in the banking system was corroborated by the fact that the deposits of SCBs were increasing steadily every year. There had been no commercial bank failures since the early 1960s.

In another instance, in April 1990 the Government of Maharashtra sent a note to the Reserve Bank indicating the problems faced by Indian banking and suggesting line of action to improve their position. The difficulties that were highlighted included a continuous decline in bank profitability, the increasing number of loss-making branches because of the breakneck speed of branch expansion, the expansion of manpower without a corresponding increase in productivity, the high overhead costs of banks, managerial deficiencies in running the banks, the imposition of social objectives without ensuring the efficiency of the existing schemes, a lack of market-orientation, deficiency in customer service, problems due to overstaffing and intense unionisation, recovery issues involving the Board for Industrial and Financial Reconstruction (BIFR) and lack of infrastructure for efficient functioning of RRBs.

The Governor in his reply, while highlighting the steps already taken by the Reserve Bank to improve the functioning of banks in almost all the areas, added that the major aim of the Reserve Bank was to ensure the strength and stability of the financial system through higher capital provisions, diversification of business, recognition of bad debts, strict enforcement of health classification of all loan accounts and introduction of innovative instruments to meet the growing and diverse demands of market participants.

PRIORITY SECTOR TARGETS FOR FOREIGN BANKS

An issue relating to the treatment of foreign bank branches in India needed to be dealt with. For a considerable period, foreign banks were not subject to priority sector targets on par with other commercial banks. For many, this seemed to be banking without social responsibility. Foreign banks countered the argument and opined that they not only had a limited deposit base, but also lacked extensive branch network akin to the domestic banks. They were also not allowed to set up separate merchant banking entities, nor could they offer insurance or mutual funds or provide stock broking services. Consortium lending was also difficult.

Nevertheless, there were pressures to bring foreign banks under the discipline of lending to the social and priority sectors. The Reserve Bank started laying down targets for the priority sector for foreign banks beginning with 10.0 per cent to 12.0 per cent in 1990 and further to 15.0 per cent of total advances in 1991. However, despite all the difficulties and some major disinvestments by international corporations, foreign banks continued to find good business. New entrants were limited to the major centres; the Reserve Bank had put a freeze on the increase of foreign bank branches since 1969. However, the Reserve Bank did not relax this ruling, although it relented on the question of allowing entry to new banks.

CONCERNS ABOUT CUSTOMER SERVICE: THE GOIPORIA COMMITTEE

In the annual budget for the year 1990–91, the Finance Minister indicated:

> Our bank managers and employees are, as a group, the most qualified, dedicated and hard working. But it is also a fact that the level of public satisfaction with the banking services is not as high as it should be. Over the years, perhaps some structural rigidities have crept in. These need to be removed. There is need for greater competition and greater operational flexibility in respect of banking services. The banking culture has to be made

more responsive to the needs of the public. I am requesting the Reserve Bank of India to set up a Committee of Bankers, bank employees, depositors and borrowers to consider these aspects and make recommendations to the Government.

The Reserve Bank in a notification dated September 15, 1990 appointed a committee on customer service in banks under the chairmanship of Shri M.N. Goiporia. The terms of reference of the committee were: (i) identifying causes for the persistence of below-par customer service in banks; (ii) ascertaining areas in which deficiencies in customer service were prevalent and how these could be remedied; (iii) improving work culture and inculcating greater customer orientation among bank employees; (iv) identifying structural and operational rigidities and inadequacies in the existing systems and procedures that adversely affected the working of banks and suggesting remedial measures for greater flexibility and faster transaction of business; and (v) upgrading technology for improving customer care on one hand and achieving better housekeeping, faster flow of information, effective supervision, managerial control and greater competitive strength on the other. The committee submitted its report in December 1991 with notes of dissent by two members.

After examining the recommendations of the committee, the Reserve Bank initiated speedy action and issued guidelines to banks relating to advancing working hours, extending business hours, introducing bank orders on various denominations, accepting small denomination notes, exchanging mutilated and soiled notes, publishing the full text of interest rate directives and their amendments in newspapers, immediate credit of local cheques up to ₹ 5,000, and paying interest at an enhanced rate on delayed collection of outstation instruments and at minimum lending rate when the proceeds of instruments were to be credited to cash credit, overdraft or loan account with a view to compensating such customers equitably. The implementation of the recommendations was closely monitored and revised guidelines were issued after taking into consideration representations received from members of the public and banks, which included: (i) not to insist on photographs of customers for opening new savings bank accounts without cheque facility, and for term deposits up to ₹ 10,000; and (ii) reducing the time frame for collection of local as well as outstation cheques. The Reserve Bank asked chief executives of all commercial banks to constitute a committee under a general manager to identify the areas and factors responsible for the delays in collection of outstation instruments and put in place new systems, procedures and necessary infrastructure for faster collection.

ACTION PLANS 1990–1992

The action plans for 1990–1992 placed a heavy emphasis on augmenting banks' profitability and strengthening their financial base. The Reserve Bank advised banks to observe prudent accounting standards and guidelines for classification of advances under the prescribed health codes, as also to stop application of interest on advances classified under the health code 5, besides those under codes 6 and 8. Banks were advised to improve their volume of business, concentrate on effecting quicker recoveries of their dues, ensure efficient management of funds by exploring new avenues of income, control expenditure effectively and reduce the incidence of bad debts. Banks were also asked to reduce the quantum of sticky advances and NPAs in a time-bound manner (Table 17.2). Smaller banks were advised to consider reverting to a 3-tier organisational structure from their 4-tier structure to save costs as well as to improve the speed and efficacy of decision-making. More importantly, banks were advised to devote continued attention to improving branch-level performance.

TABLE 17.2

Non-Performing Advances of Public Sector Banks as on March 31, 1992

(₹ *crore*)

Health Code	
Sick, non-viable (4)	4,955
Debts recalled (5)	1,757
Suit-filed Accounts (6)	3,479
Decreed Debts (7)	814
Bad & Doubtful Debts (8)	6,385
Total	17,389

Source: Reserve Bank of India, *Report on Trend and Progress of Banking in India, 1992–93.*

In terms of the recommendations of the Ghosh Committee to consider full disclosure in published accounts, SCBs (excluding RRBs) were advised to give details of accounting policies in key areas of operations at one place along with notes on accounts in their financial statements for the accounting year ended March 31, 1991 and onwards on a regular basis. Working results of SCBs for 1991–92 are captured in Table 17.3.

To obviate the major shortcomings in the annual financial review (AFR), a modified scheme of bank inspection for all PSBs was introduced on an experimental basis from January 1, 1991. To make the AFR more purposive and its findings more pointed, the regional offices of the Reserve Bank were advised to take up inspections of as many larger branches as possible with the intention of covering all branches with advances of more than ₹ 5 crore each. The principal inspecting officers were instructed to factor in and update/supplement their findings with observations from the branch notes.

COMMITMENT CHARGES

With a view to bring in discipline in availing the bank finance among borrowing units and facilitating better management of funds by banks, the Reserve Bank advised banks to levy effective January 1, 1991 a minimum commitment charge of 1.0 per cent per annum on the unutilised portion of quarterly operative limits, subject to a tolerance level of 15.0 per cent of such limits. The measure was applicable to borrowing units with working capital limits of ₹ one crore and above.

BILL CULTURE

On the recommendations of the Reserve Bank, the Government exempted certain categories of bills from stamp duty. Borrowing units availing of discretionary inland bill limits were exempt from the additional interest of one per cent over the normal rate of interest. To ensure better compliance with bill discipline, effective January 1, 1991 interest at 2.0 percentage points above the relevant rate of interest charged for cash credit limits was levied by banks on the portion of the book-debt finance that was in excess of the prescribed norm of 75.0 per cent of limits sanctioned to borrowing units under the CMA for financing inland credit sales.

SICK INDUSTRIAL UNDERTAKINGS

The Reserve Bank issued fresh guidelines to banks in August 1991 on industrial sickness, including measures to strengthen banks' organisational machinery for detection of incipient sickness, taking corrective measures like augmentation of capacity by promoters, better co-ordination between banks and FIs, mandatory participation by banks in the rehabilitation packages, designation of a nodal monitoring agency and devising a time frame for implementation of the rehabilitation package. The Reserve Bank evolved a single window concept for lending under the consortium arrangement for sick/weak units for disbursement of credit (working capital/rehabilitation/term loan). The Sick Industrial Companies (Special Provisions) Act (SICA), 1985 was amended in December 1991, widening its scope and coverage so as to bring public sector and government companies within the purview of the Act. The total number of sick units stood at 2,47,111 locking up an amount of ₹ 8,888 crore as on March 31, 1992.

THE PROCESS OF CONSOLIDATION

The efforts at bank consolidation continued to moderate branch expansion, while continuing to cover spatial gaps in rural areas, improving the financial viability of banks, introducing mechanisation and computerisation and inculcating a more effective management culture. The annual action plans covering the period April 1990 to March 1992 envisaged several measures to improve banks' operational efficiency, such as strengthening their organisational structure, upgrading the internal supervision and control system, placing greater focus on human resource development, improving customer service and housekeeping, reinforcing financial viability by better credit management, and raising productivity. The series of measures taken to improve banks' profitability and to provide them with a competitive edge included augmentation of banks' capital base, increase in coupon rates on government securities, withdrawal of the ceiling on lending rates for a sizeable part of their advances, an upward revision in service charges, introduction of new money market instruments, setting-up of subsidiaries to undertake para-banking activities, swapping of branches and opening of extension counters as also closure of branches in centres other than rural areas.

The low operating efficiency, growing NPAs and relatively inadequate capital base were, however, continued to cause concern. The increases in establishment expenses and narrowing interest spread had affected the profitability of the industry. The relatively high level of NPAs and the health code stipulations requiring provision for bad and doubtful debts resulted in a further deterioration in the banks' operating results. Until 1989–90, banks had the discretion to charge interest on accounts falling under health codes 4 and 5 (advances recalled) and carry them to income account. From 1990–91, this discretion was limited to accounts in health code 4 and banks were expected not to charge interest on accounts classified under health code 5.[16]

---

16. Banks had already been advised not to charge interest on accounts under health codes 6 to 8.

TABLE 17.3

Working Results of Scheduled Commercial Banks (1991–92)

(₹ crore)

Particulars	Public Sector Banks	Private Sector Banks	Foreign Banks
i) Interest Income	30,750	1,380	2,829
ii) Other Income	3,696	148	845
I. Total Income (i+ii)	34,446	1,528	3,674
II. Expenditure			
i) Interest expended	21,022	810	1,845
ii) Other operating expenses	7,884	424	570
iii) Provisions & Contingencies	4,737	212	939
III. Total expenditure (i+ii+iii)	33,643	1,446	3,354
IV. Profit for the year	803	82	320
V. Working Funds	3,01,717	14,069	25,103
VI. Profit as % to Working Funds	0.27	0.58	1.27

Source: Reserve Bank of India, *Report on Trend and Progress of Banking in India, 1992–93.*

While the spread between the cost of funds and the return on funds as reflected by the structure of interest rates was reasonable, bank profitability was under strain because of NPAs (debts recalled, suit-filed accounts, decreed debts and debts classified as bad and doubtful, all of which reflected an unhealthy assets portfolio of the bank). The NPAs of PSBs (under health codes 6 to 8) as a percentage of total advances amounted to 8.3 per cent as at the end of March 1991. In the context of added emphasis on asset liability management (ALM) and with a view to complying with the Basel Committee framework on international convergence of capital measures and capital standards, a risk-weighted capital ratio for banks (including foreign banks) in India was intended to be prescribed.

ASSESSING FINANCIAL HEALTH AND SOUNDNESS

In order to address these issues, several mutually reinforcing measures were initiated. To improve the health of the banking sector, internationally accepted prudential norms relating to income recognition, asset classification and provisioning, and capital adequacy were introduced in April 1992 in a phased manner. Banks were advised that they should not charge and take to income account interest on NPAs. For this purpose, NPAs were clearly defined based on objective criteria. Compared with the existing system of eight health codes, banks were required to classify their advances into four broad groups, *viz.*: (i) standard assets; (ii) sub-standard assets; (iii) doubtful assets; and (iv) loss assets.

In the old eight-category health code system, four categories were deemed as NPAs, *viz.*, debts recalled, suit-filed accounts, decreed debts, and debts classified as bad and doubtful and banks were not to recognise interest income on these categories.[17] However, in the absence of a clear definition of problem credits in actual practice, banks recognised interest income on all NPAs. The revised norms revealed the true position of banks' health. Aggregate domestic NPAs of all PSBs, which constituted 14.5 per cent of total outstanding advances at end-March 1992 based on the old health code system, worked out to 23.2 per cent as on March 31, 1993 based on the revised classification. This implied that about one-fourth of banks' advances were locked up in unproductive assets. This not only adversely affected banks' profitability, but also prevented recycling of funds, thereby constraining the growth of their balance sheets.

Banks were also required to make provisioning to the extent of 10.0 per cent on sub-standard assets and 20.0 per cent to 50.0 per cent on the secured portion of advances classified as 'doubtful', depending on the period for which the assets had remained doubtful. On the unsecured portion of 'doubtful' assets and on 'loss' assets, 100.0 per cent provisioning was required to be made. The health code system of classification of assets was to be pursued by banks as a management information tool.

The tentative provisioning required by banks was estimated at around ₹ 10,000 crore by the Reserve Bank. Further, banks needed additional resources to meet the capital adequacy norms.[18] The total resource requirement of banks was close to ₹ 14,000 crore. Of this, banks were able to provide about ₹ 4,000 crore from their own surplus generated over a two-year period and about ₹ 10,000 crore was required by the system as additional resources.

With a view to restoring and maintaining the financial soundness of banks, as also enabling them to meet the gap created by application of the first stage of prudential accounting standards and capital adequacy norms, the Government embarked on a recapitalisation programme of nationalised banks beginning from the financial year 1993–94. The total

---

17. Refer to chapter 7: Developments in Banking Supervision.
18. For details refer to the section on capital adequacy norms in this chapter.

capital contributed by the Government to nationalised banks up to March 1998 aggregated at ₹ 20,046 crore. Besides, the Government provided a sum of ₹ 1,532 crore during the year ended March 1997 to write-off the losses of two banks against their capital to cleanse their balance sheets so that they could make early public issues.

Since capital infusion by the Government was inadequate to enable banks to fulfil further provisioning norms and take care of additional capital needs while capital adequacy guidelines were fully implemented, the Government decided to allow PSBs to approach the capital market directly to mobilise equity funds from the public by amending the relevant acts. It was prescribed that the government ownership of the nationalised banks would remain at least at 51.0 per cent of the equity. However, in view of the oversized equity base, combined with the projected stream of earnings coming in the way of tapping the capital market by a number of nationalised banks, the Government allowed banks to reduce the paid-up capital. The paid-up capital, however, in no case was to be reduced below 25.0 per cent of the paid-up capital of a nationalised bank as on the date of the amendment. The aggregate capital allowed to be written-off by nationalised banks till March 31, 1997 was ₹ 3,038 crore. However, four banks returned to the Government the paid-up capital aggregating ₹ 842 crore during 1996–97 to improve their earnings per share.

By end-March 1998, nine PSBs raised capital (including premium) aggregating ₹ 6,015 crore from the market, including proceeds from the global depository receipt (GDR) issue of the SBI aggregating ₹ 1,270 crore raised during 1996–97. Besides, some banks also raised subordinated debt for inclusion in their tier II capital. The raising of capital by banks led to — diversification of ownership of PSBs, which made a significant qualitative difference to their functioning due to induction of private shareholding with attendant issues of shareholder value and representation of private shareholders on boards.

In order to contain fresh NPAs from arising on account of adverse selection, banks were put on guard against defaulters to other lending institutions. For this purpose, the Reserve Bank put in place a scheme for sharing credit data in April 1994. Apart from containing fresh NPAs, the issue was also to recover NPAs that had already accumulated. In this context, commercial banks were advised to increasingly make use of *lok adalats* (people's courts), which were conferred judicial status and had emerged as a convenient and low-cost method of settling disputes between banks and small borrowers. Further, The Recovery of Debts Due to Banks and Financial Institutions Act was enacted in 1993, which provided for the establishing tribunals for expeditious adjudication and recovery of such debts. Following the enactment, 29 debt recovery tribunals (DRTs) and 5 debt recovery appellate tribunals (DRATs) were established at several places in the country.

In August 1995, the Reserve Bank took a major decision to withdraw the credit information scheme that had been introduced in 1962. The scheme, which was intended to pool and supply information relating to the total banking commitments to the constituents of banks and notified FIs to help them make a realistic assessment of viability and credit needs of borrowers, was found irrelevant by Shri TNA Iyer, consultant, appointed by the Governor to examine, *inter alia,* the need for continuing the scheme. In fact, a detailed review note dated April 3, 1995 prepared on the scheme by the Reserve Bank highlighted that the non-involvement of banks and FIs delayed the submission of returns, there was a lack of demand for information, enormous efforts and costs were involved, faulty and incomplete information was furnished and there had been drastic changes in banking over a period; hence, there was no justification for continuing the scheme.

Various measures introduced had a favourable impact on the quality of banks' balance sheets. Within a short time, banks were able to bring down their NPAs significantly. The gross NPAs of PSBs as a percentage of gross advances, which was 23.2 per cent at end-March 1993, declined to 16.0 per cent by end-March 1998. Despite increased provisioning, the overall profitability of the banking sector in general, and PSBs in particular, improved. The soundness of the banking sector showed substantial improvement. Eight nationalised banks, six old private sector banks and three foreign banks could not attain the prescribed capital to risk weighted assets ratio (CRAR) of 8.0 per cent by end-March 1996. These banks were given one-year extension to reach the prescribed ratio, subject to certain restrictions, such as, modest growth in risk-weighted assets, containment of capital expenditure and branch expansion, among others. At end-March 1998, of the 27 PSBs, 26 banks attained the stipulated 8.0 per cent capital adequacy requirement. All banks, other than five banks (one PSB and four old private sector banks) were able to achieve the stipulated CRAR of 8.0 per cent (Table 17.4).

TABLE 17.4

CRAR Position

(End-March)

Bank Group	1996		1997		1998	
	No. of Banks with 8.0 per cent and above	*No. of Banks with CRAR less than 8.0 per cent*	*No. of Banks with 8.0 per cent and above*	*No. of Banks with CRAR less than 8.0 per cent*	*No. of Banks with 8.0 per cent and above*	*No. of Banks with CRAR less than 8.0 per cent*
(1)	*(2)*	*(3)*	*(4)*	*(5)*	*(6)*	*(7)*
Public Sector Banks	19	8	25	2	26	1
Private Sector Banks	28	6	30	4	30	4
Foreign Banks	28	3	39	-	42	-
Total	75	17	94	6	98	5

Note: - : Nil.

Source: Reserve Bank of India, *Report on Currency and Finance, 2006–2008*.

REMOVAL OF EXTERNAL CONSTRAINTS ON BANKS

A major factor that affected banks' profitability was the high pre-emptions in the form of CRR and SLR, which had reached a historic high level of 63.5 per cent in the early 1990s. These were progressively reduced as described elsewhere in this volume. The reduction in statutory pre-emptions not only removed the external constraints on banks and enhanced their profitability, but also augmented the lendable resources available to them. Further, with the more normal liquidity conditions in the money market, there was a further enhancement in the proportion of bank funds that were made available for financing growth and employment in the private sector. However, despite augmentation of lendable resources of banks, credit growth slowed in 1996–97, both on account of demand and supply-side factors. In view of application of prudential norms, banks became wary of enlarging their loan portfolio. The relatively high level of NPAs, in particular, had a severe impact on weak banks. Banks' capacity to extend credit was also impaired due to the little headroom available in the capital adequacy ratio (8.7% at end-March 1996). At the individual bank level, some banks, as indicated earlier, were not able to meet the capital adequacy requirements at end-March 1998.

The demand for funds by the corporate sector also slackened. In the wake of increased competition in the product market, the corporate sector shifted its focus from expanding capacity to restructuring. Increased competition also forced corporate entities to restructure their balance sheets, whereby they increased their reliance on retained earnings and reduced their borrowings. Rise in real interest rates caused by downward stickiness of nominal interest rates coupled with a falling inflation rate also contributed to slackness in credit expansion. Hence, despite the lowering of the statutory pre-emptions in the form of CRR and SLR, banks continued to invest in government securities, far in excess of the requirements. Banks' investment in SLR securities at end-March 1996 was 36.9 per cent of net demand and time liabilities (NDTL) as against the statutory requirement of 31.5 per cent.

TABLE 17.5

Movement of Interest Rates of Commercial Banks

(Per cent)

| Year (April-March) | Deposit Rates | | | Lending Rates |
	1 to 3 yrs	Over 3 yrs and up to 5 yrs	Above 5 yrs	Minimum Rate (General)
(1)	(2)	(3)	(4)	(5)
1990–91	9.00–10.00	11.00	11.00	16.00*
1991–92	12.00	13.00	13.00	19.00*
1992–93	11.00	11.00	11.00	17.00*
1993–94	10.00	10.00	10.00	14.00*
1994–95	11.00	11.00	11.00	15.00@
1995–96	12.00	13.00&	13.00&	16.50@
1996–97	11.00–12.00&	12.00–13.00&	12.50–13.00&	14.50–15.00@
1997–98	10.50–11.00&	11.50–12.00&	11.50–12.00&	14.00@

Notes: & : Refers to the deposit rates of five major public sector banks as at end-March;
@ : Lending interest rates were deregulated from October 1994. The rate indicated refers to the prime lending rates of five major public sector banks.

* : Key lending rate as prescribed by the Reserve Bank for commercial banks.

Source: Reserve Bank of India, *Handbook of Statistics on the Indian Economy, 2006–07.*

Banks were, as mentioned elsewhere in this volume, also provided with the freedom to fix their own deposit and lending rates. The structure of interest rates, which had become extremely complex, was first rationalised and then deregulated, barring a few rates, both on the deposits and lending portfolios. The information on the interest rates over the period is presented in Table 17.5.

The reduction in NPAs along with a reduction in CRR/SLR and deregulation of interest rates had a significant positive impact on the profitability of the banking sector (Table 17.6). With the application of objective prudential norms, 14 banks (12 PSBs) had reported net losses for the year ended March 1993. In 1996–97, the number of loss-making SCBs declined to eight (of which three were PSBs). Although in the following year, the number of loss-making banks increased to 11, the number of loss-making PSBs declined to two.

TABLE 17.6

Profitability Indicators of Scheduled Commercial Banks

Year (April–March)	No. of Profit-making SCBs	No. of Loss-making SCBs	Overall Profit/ Loss (−) (₹ crore)	Return on Assets (%)	
				SCBs	PSBs
(1)	(2)	(3)	(4)	(5)	(6)
1992–93	59 (15)	14 (12)	−4,150	−1.08	−0.99
1993–94	60 (15)	14 (12)	−3,625	−0.85	−1.15
1994–95	73 (19)	13 (8)	2,154	0.41	0.25
1995–96	80 (19)	14 (8)	939	0.16	−0.07
1996–97	92 (24)	8 (3)	4,505	0.67	0.57
1997–98	92 (25)	11 (2)	6,502	0.82	0.77

Notes: 1. SCBs : Scheduled Commercial Banks.
2. PSBs : Public Sector Banks.
3. Figures in parentheses indicate the number of PSBs.
Source: Reserve Bank of India, *Report on Currency and Finance, 2006–2008.*

BOARD FOR FINANCIAL SUPERVISION

The growing volume and complexity of the business conducted by banks and FIs in the country and the need for a sensitive and strong supervisory mechanism was increasingly recognised by the Narasimham Committee. It recommended that the supervisory functions of the Reserve Bank should be separated from the more traditional central banking functions and that a separate agency, which could pay undivided attention to supervision, should be set up under the aegis of the Reserve Bank. The committee underlined the advantages of having a single integrated system of supervision over different constituents of the financial systems, so as to avoid segmentation of supervisory functions and the associated problem of inadequate co-ordination among all the supervisory authorities.

The need for a strong system of supervision was felt early in the reform phase for the following reasons: (i) to ensure effective implementation of prudential regulations; (ii) the blurring of the traditional distinctions among the financial intermediaries; and (iii) the increased risks faced by banks in a liberalised environment. Keeping these considerations in view, the BFS was set up within the Reserve Bank to attend exclusively to supervisory functions and provide effective oversight in an integrated manner over the banking system, FIs and NBFCs. The proposal contained in the Deputy Governor's memorandum dated February 12, 1993, regarding the setting-up of the BFS, was approved by the Central Board in its meeting held on February 12, 1993.[19] The BFS was to be a separate body within the Reserve Bank. In terms of regulation 15 of the RBI (BFS) Regulations, 1994, the BFS was required to submit a half-yearly report on its activities to the Central Board of Directors of the Reserve Bank.

The BFS assumed supervisory responsibility for all-India FIs effective April 1995 and for registered NBFCs effective July 1995. The board consisted of the Governor as the chairman, the Deputy Governor as full-time vice-chairman and four members from the Central Board.

The scope of supervisory oversight by the BFS was initially restricted to banks, FIs and NBFCs. Subsequently, its scope was enlarged to include urban co-operative banks (UCBs), RRBs and primary dealers (PDs). The BFS initiated several measures to strengthen the supervisory systems. In order to have in place 'an early warning system' to take prompt corrective action, a computerised offsite monitoring and surveillance (OSMOS) system for banks was instituted in November 1995.

BANKING OMBUDSMAN SCHEME

While announcing the credit policy measures for the first half of 1993–94, the Governor indicated that effective grievance redressal machinery on the ombudsman model had to be introduced to attend to the large number of complaints emanating from the small scale industries (SSIs). Subsequently, in consultation with PSBs, it was felt that the proposed grievance redressal machinery should deal not only with grievances of the SSIs but with the

---

19. See Appendix 17.1 for details.

entire gamut of customer complaints regarding deficiencies in banking services and certain credit-related aspects. A scheme styled the banking ombudsman (BO) scheme, 1995 was drawn in consultation with the Government. The scheme and the operational guidelines envisaged setting-up offices of the BO at 15 centres to cover the entire country.

The Reserve Bank announced the BO scheme on June 14, 1995 under the provisions of the BR Act, 1949 for expeditious and inexpensive resolution of customer complaints in banking services. The scheme covered all SCBs and scheduled primary co-operative banks. It provided the public with an opportunity to approach the BO for grievances against a bank, provided the complaints pertained to a matter specified in the scheme. The BO scheme became operational with the appointment of a BO on a full-time basis in three centres — Mumbai, Delhi and Bhopal; it was then extended to several cities in subsequent years.

MARKET INTELLIGENCE

In 1992–93, an MIC was set up within the Reserve Bank on the recommendations of the Janakiraman Committee. The main objective of the MIC was to keep a track of market developments, especially those of a sensitive nature. This cell was constituted in addition to the Banking Intelligence Unit.

ESTABLISHMENT OF NEW BANKS IN THE PRIVATE SECTOR

The Narasimham Committee recommended, *inter alia*, that there be no bar to new banks in the private sector being set up, provided they conformed to the start-up capital and other requirements as may be prescribed by the Reserve Bank, the maintenance of prudential norms for accounting, provisioning and related aspects of operations.

The Central Board of Directors of the Reserve Bank considered this recommendation in their meetings held on September 11, 1992 and January 21, 1993 and agreed that the Reserve Bank would grant permission for the establishment of new private sector banks, subject to certain terms and conditions. Accordingly, the Reserve Bank issued a set of guidelines on January 22, 1993 for the entry of new private sector banks, heralding a new policy approach to foster competition. The minimum paid-up capital of a new private sector bank was to be ₹ 100 crore and it was expected to observe prudential norms and capital adequacy of 8.0 per cent from the time of its inception.

All three FIs, *viz.*, Housing Development Finance Corporation Ltd (HDFC), Industrial Credit and Investment Corporation of India Ltd (ICICI) and the UTI, to whom in principle approval was granted for setting-up new banks in the private sector, represented to the Reserve Bank for relaxation in the following conditions that formed part of the approval:

(i)   The chairman of the new bank shall be a whole-time professional. He shall not take up directorship of other companies as per the provisions of section 10B (2) and (4) of the BR Act, 1949.

(ii) There shall not be any common directors on the board of the FI and the new bank promoted by it.

(iii) Applicability of the provisions of section 12(2) of the BR Act, 1949 which restricted voting rights per shareholder to 1.0 per cent of the total voting rights of the banking company.

(iv) The FI should ensure and establish an 'arm's length' relationship organisationally and operationally with the proposed bank.

(v)   The FI shall accept the system of consolidated supervision by the Reserve Bank both for itself and the proposed bank.

It was considered necessary that the Reserve Bank took all appropriate steps to see that the new private sector banks were set up, to ensure that such banks were managed ably and that they were in a position to raise necessary capital from the market. Up to the end of February 1994, 143 applications/proposals were received for setting-up new private sector banks. Of these, only 23 were in the prescribed form under rule 11 of the Banking Regulation (Companies) Rules, 1949. The Committee of the Central Board had already approved the proposals received from HDFC Ltd, ICICI Ltd, UTI, Dr Jayanta Madhab & Associates, 20th Century Finance Corporation Ltd, Bennett Coleman & Co Ltd, Industrial Enterprises & Finance Ltd, Gujarat State Fertilisers Co Ltd, and the IDBI, subject to certain terms and conditions.

The proposal received from a former CMD, Punjab & Sind Bank (P&SB) was processed and it was proposed to give in principle approval to this proposal.

REVIEW OF NEW PRIVATE SECTOR BANKS AS ON MARCH 31, 1996

The total number of new private sector banks as on March 31, 1996 was nine. During the year, two more banks, *viz.*, Cox and Kings Bank Ltd and CRB Bank Ltd, were issued 'in principle' approval. All nine banks had complied with the capital adequacy norm of 8.0 per cent (of the risk-weighted assets stipulated by the Reserve Bank). As on March 1996, the nine new banks maintained a network of 76 branches and, of these, 16 were located in semi-urban and urban centres, while the remaining 60 branches were concentrated in metropolitan areas. None of the banks had opened branches in rural areas, although under the conditions of the licence these banks were required to establish 25.0 per cent of their branches in rural/semi-urban areas during the first three years after their inception. The aggregate deposits of these banks stood at ₹ 5,937 crore as on March 31, 1996, forming 1.3 per cent of deposits of all commercial banks. The advances of these banks stood at ₹ 4,890 crore as on March 31, 1996. The credit-deposit ratio averaged as high as 82.4 per cent against 58.6 per cent for all commercial banks.

The onsite assessment visits/inspections had revealed serious deficiencies, such as violation of the Reserve Bank instructions/guidelines on bill discounting, packing credit advances, consortium arrangements, stockinvest schemes and exceeding prudential exposure norms, apart from the banks not making a realistic assessment of the need-based requirements of borrowers. The new banks had generally adhered to the Reserve Bank norms relating to prudential guidelines on income recognition, asset classification and provisioning. However, show-cause notices were served to IndusInd Bank Ltd and HDFC Bank Ltd for irregularities in implementing the stockinvest scheme and for not complying with the regulatory requirements in bill financing.

All nine banks reported profits for the year ended March 31, 1996. Their net profits aggregated ₹ 165 crore and formed 1.8 per cent of their total working funds. Interest spread as a percentage of working funds worked out to 2.8 per cent for these banks. Of the nine banks, four banks, viz., IndusInd Bank Ltd, ICICI Banking Corporation Ltd, Global Trust Bank Ltd, and Bank of Punjab Ltd had declared dividends, while the other banks had ploughed back their net profits into their business.

All the new banks were attuned to the objective of providing high-class customer service backed by high-tech and sophisticated systems and networks and had gone in for comprehensive information technology plans with the latest technology for computerisation and networking. All their branches were networked and linked to the corporate/central office through very small aperture terminal (VSAT) systems of communication. This facilitated prompt submission of DSB 9 (offsite monitoring) returns by almost all the banks. In addition to installing ATMs and providing telebanking services, most of the banks had become members of the Society for Worldwide Interbank Financial Telecommunication (SWIFT).

PRUDENTIAL NORMS

A major reform in 1992 was the introduction of new norms for income recognition and provisioning for bad debts and the prescription of new capital adequacy requirements in line with the Basel Committee norms. The new norms would ensure that the books of the banks reflected their financial position more accurately and in accordance with international accounting practices. However, because of the new norms, banks were expected to make larger provisions for bad and doubtful advances in their portfolios. The impact, it was anticipated, would be felt in 1993 and 1994 and, to protect the viability and financial health of the banking system, the budget made provision for a capital contribution of ₹ 5,700 crore to nationalised banks in 1993–94 to meet the gap created by the application of the first stage of provisioning norms. There was no immediate net outgo from the budget, as the Government's contribution was in the form of government bonds, although interest payment on these bonds and other ultimate redemptions would place a burden on future budgets. However, in order to meet the additional capital needs arising out of the subsequent phasing in 1994–95 and 1995–96, the Government decided to allow the SBI as well as other nationalised banks access to the capital market to raise fresh equity, retaining at the same time the major ownership and, therefore, effective control of the PSBs. The legislation to give effect to it was to be introduced subsequently, but speedily.

CAPITAL ADEQUACY NORMS

In order to strengthen the capital base of banks, the Reserve Bank, following the Basel Committee recommendations, introduced in April 1992 a risk-weighted assets ratio system as the basis for assessment of capital for banks (including foreign banks) in India as a capital adequacy measure. It was stipulated that Indian banks that had branches abroad should achieve a capital adequacy norm of 8.0 per cent as early as possible and latest by March 31, 1994 (later extended by one year to March 31, 1995). Foreign banks were to achieve this norm of 8.0 per cent by March 31, 1993. Other banks were to achieve a capital adequacy norm of 4.0 per cent by March 31, 1993 and the 8.0 per cent norm by March 31, 1996.

In 1992–93, banks completed the first year of the three-year phased programme of implementation of prudential norms relating to income recognition, provisioning and capital adequacy. Several banks faced practical difficulties in implementing the norms within the stipulated period without incurring large capital losses. The Reserve Bank constituted an informal group in 1992 to look into these problems. As suggested by the group, relaxations were made with regard to the 'past due' status of an account, the treatment of non-performing advances for agriculture, the net worth of borrowers/guarantors or the value of security, the treatment of loss assets, consortium advances, the phasing of provisioning for NPAs and depreciation in the value of investments.

In respect of accounts with an outstanding balance of less than ₹ 25,000, provisioning to the extent of 2.5 per cent of the total outstanding was to be made in 1992–93 (which was raised to 5.0% from February 4, 1994). Advances under this category of lending aggregated at ₹ 19,845 crore. Again, provisioning for NPAs was scaled down during 1992–93 from 50.0 per cent of the provisions on sub-standard and doubtful assets and on advances with less than ₹ 25,000 to 30.0 per cent. Data based on the revised classification of advances with outstanding balance of ₹ 25,000 and above into sub-standard, doubtful and loss assets, placed the total of NPAs at ₹ 36,588 crore, forming 24.2 per cent of the aggregate outstanding advances (excluding those with an outstanding balance of less than ₹ 25,000) of the PSBs as at the end of March 31, 1993. Of these, sub-standard assets amounted to ₹ 12,552 crore, doubtful assets ₹ 20,106 crore and loss assets ₹ 3,930 crore.

Details in respect of CRAR of foreign banks for the year ended March 31, 1993 revealed that all 23 foreign banks operating in India had already reached the stipulated level of 8.0 per cent CRAR as on that day.

The private sector Indian banks had generally complied with prudential guidelines relating to asset classification, income recognition and provisioning. During 1992–93, 11 banks increased their paid-up capital through rights issues and one bank raised the same in 1993–94. Fourteen banks had achieved a CRAR of 4.0 per cent, while the position for the other banks was under review.

CREATING A COMPETITIVE ENVIRONMENT

One of the major objectives of reforms was to bring in greater efficiency by permitting the entry of private sector banks and new foreign banks, liberalising licensing of more branches of foreign banks, and providing increased operational flexibility to banks. These measures were intended to infuse competition in the banking sector.

First, the Reserve Bank announced the norms for entry of new banks in the private sector in January 1993. Second, in the context of the steps towards deregulation and the changed banking scenario in the country, it was decided in May 1992 to give greater freedom to banks in the matter of opening branches. While banks could not close down branches in rural areas, in order to enable them to rationalise their branch network in rural/semi-urban areas, they were allowed to relocate branches within the same block and service area of the branch, shift their branches in urban/metropolitan/port town centres within the same locality/municipal ward, open specialised branches, spin-off business, set up controlling offices/administrative units and open extension counters. It was decided in December 1994 that banks did not need prior permission from the Reserve Bank to install ATMs at licensed branches and extension counters. Banks, however, were required to report such installation to the Reserve Bank. Banks were also given the freedom to install ATMs at other places, in which case they could obtain a licence from the concerned regional office of the Reserve Bank before operationalising the offsite ATMs. Third, a commitment was made in the Uruguay Round to allow 12 licenses a year for new entrants and existing banks. However, India adopted a more liberal policy in permitting foreign banks to open branches in the country. Fourth, deregulation of interest rates was undertaken to infuse competition. Fifth, consistent with the policy of liberalisation, it was decided to allow full operational freedom to banks in assessing the working capital requirements of borrowers. Accordingly, all instructions relating to maximum permissible bank finance were withdrawn in April 1997. Banks were given complete independence to decide on the method of assessing working capital requirements. It was for corporate entities to convince banks about their working capital needs. They could choose to go through a single bank, set up a consortium arrangement or take the syndicate route. Sixth, all restrictions relating to project loans by commercial banks were withdrawn. Traditionally, project finance was the domain of term-lending institutions.

While competitive conditions were created, competition within the banking sector during this phase did not infiltrate enough. Though the number of new private sector banks and foreign banks increased during the period, there were only four bank mergers. The lack of sufficient competition was also reflected in the net interest margins of banks, which increased during this phase from 2.5 per cent in 1992–93 to 2.9 per cent in 1997–98. This was despite the fact that banks during this phase were in a disadvantageous position since interest rates during this phase declined significantly. It may be noted that the effect of a reduction in interest rates on lending was mostly instantaneous, while on deposit rates, it came into operation after existing deposits matured.

STRENGTHENING OF INSTITUTIONS

A fresh review of the banks' inspection system was undertaken and a new approach to onsite inspection of banks was adopted from the cycle of inspections commencing in July 1997. The focus shifted to the evaluation of total operations and performance of banks under the CAMELS system (capital adequacy, asset quality, management, earnings, liquidity systems and control) for domestic commercial banks and CALCS (capital adequacy, asset quality, liquidity, compliance systems and control) for foreign banks. The role of internal and external audit was also strengthened. Besides auditing the annual accounts, external auditors were required to verify and certify other aspects, such as adherence to statutory liquidity requirements, prudential norms relating to income recognition, asset classification and provisioning as also financial ratios to be disclosed in the balance sheets of banks. Thus, supervision now, apart from covering the supervisory process of the Reserve Bank, also focused on external audit and internal audit.

The significant financial improvement, however, posed two issues: how to ensure that the turnaround was real and durable; and what approach to adopt for weak banks. It was noted that banks must recognise that as their asset portfolio diversified, greater specialisation in the technical aspects of lending and credit evaluation was necessary. Attention needed to be given not merely to the size of assets, but also to their composition. Simultaneously, loan recoveries had to be substantial and speedy. Computerisation and upgrading of technologies, at least in critical branch offices with a large business turnover, were to be immediately implemented. Branches also needed to set up systems that were dedicated to sector-specific loan-making. Further, efforts at reducing NPAs were to be continued and the endeavour was to bring down the banking system's average of NPAs to about 10.0 per cent in the next couple of years. Reduction in costs, rationalisation of branch structure and staffing pattern and strengthening of risk management/corporate management strategies formed some of the essential elements of a sustainable turnaround.

As regards weak banks, the consultants' reports on the banks were submitted to each bank and the Reserve Bank. The diagnosis of the problems of weak banks carried several similarities: large staff complement; unviable branches; low productivity per employee; high NPAs ranging between 20.0 and 27.0 per cent of total advances; and several critical institutional weaknesses. While clearly there was no single remedy for these banks, a sound and a viable strategy oriented to the overriding objective of reducing and wiping out losses had to be formulated. Two areas where weaknesses were glaring and common both to weak and well-performing banks were: inter-branch reconciliation of accounts and occurrence of fraud. The progress in reconciliation was reviewed and the chairmen of PSBs were given a revised time frame within which arrears in reconciliation were to be cleared. Likewise, banks were advised to create a separate cell to regularly monitor the recovery and staff accountability of old cases of fraud and devise strategies and controls on an ongoing basis to prevent fraud. In this context, it was necessary to have a fresh review of the efficacy and adequacy of the internal control systems in banks. A working group was appointed to review the internal controls, inspection and audit system in banks.

TRANSPARENCY AND DISCLOSURE

One significant area of improvement in the banking system was greater accuracy and transparency in the financial statements of banks. The acceptance of the recommendations with regard to bringing Indian accounting standards closer to internationally accepted norms, coupled with requirements of fuller disclosure on sensitive aspects of operations had rendered greater credibility and transparency to the financial statements of banks. The refinement of accounting practices and disclosure requirements to bring them fully in line with international norms was also done from 1992–93. Regular communications, reporting changes in prudential norms, tracking of NPAs, focus on profitability and attaining specified capital adequacy ratios were the main features of this period.

PERFORMANCE OBLIGATIONS AND COMMITMENTS

To enable banks not to slip on the exacting standards that prudential accounting and capital adequacy norms entailed, the Reserve Bank laid down various performance indicators. The release of funds by the Government to augment their capital base was made subject to the fulfilment of the performance obligations/commitments in respect of the following:

(i)   Performance parameters: these were quantifiable targets to be attained with respect to deposits, advances, investments, increase in staff productivity, and interest spreads. In addition, upgrading technology at various levels was to be ensured.

(ii)   Management: the response of the top management towards an improvement in the areas of operational policies, organisational structures, inspection and supervision within a stipulated period would be elicited. Operational policies would cover plans for improving liability management, investment management, recovery management, human resource development, limiting capital expenditure and loan exposures.

(iii) Capital: detailed quarterly review of growth in risk-weighted assets to growth in capital would have to be undertaken.

(iv)   Customer service: periodic independent evaluation of customer satisfaction would be undertaken. Establishment of grievance redressal machinery could also be considered. These commitments would be reviewed by the banks on a quarterly basis at the board level and on a half-yearly basis at the level of the Reserve Bank.

RECAPITALISATION OF NATIONALISED BANKS

With a view to restoring and maintaining financial soundness of banks, particularly in the interests of depositors, as also enabling them to meet the gap created by application of the first stage of prudential accounting standards and capital adequacy norms, the Government contributed ₹ 5,700 crore as equity to recapitalise nationalised banks during the financial year 1993–94 (Table 17.7). As a result of recapitalisation, there was expected to be an improvement in the capital and reserves (including surplus) position of nationalised banks from ₹ 7,009 crore at the end of March 1993 to ₹ 12,709 crore at the end of March 1994. Bank-wise details of capital injection by the Government revealed that fresh capital injection was in the range of ₹ 45 crore and ₹ 705 crore. The recapitalisation of nationalised banks was undertaken to ensure that all banks were able to meet the minimum CRAR of 4.0 per cent as at the end of March 1993 and also maintained their capital unimpaired. The recipient banks were required to invest the Government's capital subscription in government bonds. In the past, the banks had been issued non-terminable, non-marketable special securities with a 7.7 per cent coupon rate. To strike a balance between fiscal adjustment and strengthening of bank capital, banks were allowed to invest in bonds of a finite tenor, so that, in addition to receipt of interest income, banks would receive a gradual inflow of principal over time.

The Government notified the issue of bonds, known as '10 per cent recapitalisation bonds, 2006' on January 1, 1994. Subscription to these bonds was limited to the extent of the amount allocated by the Government.

TABLE 17.7

Recapitalisation of Banks

(₹ crore)

S. No	Name of the Bank	Allocation of Capital
1.	Allahabad Bank	90
2.	Andhra Bank	150
3.	Bank of Baroda	400
4.	Bank of India	635
5.	Bank of Maharashtra	150
6.	Canara Bank	365
7.	Central Bank of India	490
8.	Corporation Bank	45
9.	Dena Bank	130
10.	Indian Bank	220
11.	Indian Overseas Bank	705
12.	Oriental Bank of Commerce	50
13.	Punjab National Bank	415
14.	Punjab & Sind Bank	160
15.	Syndicate Bank	680
16.	UCO Bank	535
17.	Union Bank of India	200
18.	United Bank of India	215
19.	Vijaya Bank	65
	Total	5,700

Source: Reserve Bank of India, internal records.

The important features of the bonds were that they: (i) would bear an interest rate of 10.0 per cent per annum, to be paid at half-yearly intervals; (ii) would be repayable in six equal annual instalments on the first day of January from the year commencing January 1, 2001 and onwards; (iii) would be transferable; (iv) would not be an approved security for purposes of SLR; and (v) would be considered as an eligible security for purposes of obtaining a loan from any bank or FI.

Since the capital infusion by the Government was not adequate to enable banks to fulfil further provisioning norms and take care of additional capital needs as capital adequacy guidelines were fully implemented, the Government decided to allow some PSBs to approach the capital market directly to mobilise equity funds from the public. For this purpose the SBI's provision for partial private holding in its statute was enhanced by an ordinance in October 1993, amending the State Bank of India Act, 1955. The SBI was the first PSB to access the capital market. It raised ₹ 2,210 crore in the form of equity and ₹ 1,000 crore through bonds. With this issue, the shareholding of the Reserve Bank in the equity of SBI came down to 68.93 per cent from 98.20 per cent. The Banking Companies (Acquisition and Transfer of Undertakings) Act, 1970 and 1980 were also amended with effect from July 15, 1994 to enable nationalised banks to raise capital funds from the market by public issue of shares. However, the holding of the Central Government would not be at all times less than 50.0 per cent of the paid-up capital of nationalised banks.

A few nationalised banks entered the capital market in 1994–95, but a number of them needed further injection of capital from the Government to clean up their balance sheets before they were in a position to approach the capital market.

The Oriental Bank of Commerce was the first nationalised bank that successfully accessed the capital market and raised ₹ 387 crore in October 1994, reducing the Government equity share from 100.0 per cent to 66.5 per cent. The equity base of several profit-making nationalised banks was oversized in relation to the projected stream of earnings, whereas banks with cumulative losses were not able to set off their losses against their capital. As this had come in the way of quite a few nationalised banks accessing the capital market and the loss-making banks in adjusting their cumulative losses, the Banking Companies (Acquisition and Transfer of Undertakings) Acts, 1970 and 1980 were amended, enabling banks to reduce their paid-up capital. The paid-up capital of nationalised banks could not be reduced at any time below 25.0 per cent of its paid-up capital as on the date of the amendment.

Of the 27 PSBs, 25 banks achieved the minimum CRAR of 8.0 per cent as at the end of March 1997. In order to shore up their earnings per share (EPS), three PSBs, viz., Bank of Baroda (BoB), Corporation Bank and Bank of India (BoI) together returned ₹ 504 crore of their capital to the Government, while three more PSBs, viz., Dena Bank (₹ 180 crore), BoB (₹ 850 crore) and BoI (₹ 675 crore) accessed the capital market during 1996–97. Four PSBs (PNB, State Bank of Mysore, State Bank of Travancore and State Bank of Bikaner and Jaipur) were also permitted to raise subordinated debt through private placement for inclusion under Tier II capital for capital adequacy purposes. The Government provided ₹ 1,532 crore during 1996–97 towards writing down the capital base against the accumulated losses of Allahabad Bank (₹ 532 crore) and Indian Overseas

Bank (₹ 1,000 crore). As regards recapitalisation of banks, the Government contributed during 1996–97, ₹ 1,509 crore towards the capital of six nationalised banks, *viz.*, Andhra Bank (₹ 165 crore), Central Bank of India (₹ 500 crore), P&SB (₹ 150 crore), UCO Bank (₹ 54 crore), United Bank of India (UBI) (₹ 338 crore) and Vijaya Bank (₹ 302 crore).

An important development in 1993–94 was entry of the SBI into the capital market with an equity-cum-bond issue of ₹ 2,532 crore. With a view to achieving the capital adequacy norm of 8.0 per cent by March 31, 1994, the SBI approached the capital market with a simultaneous public offer of 12, 40, 00,000 equity shares of ₹ 10 each at a premium of ₹ 90 per share and 50,00,000 bonds of the face value of ₹ 1,000 each. The public issue of equity was accompanied by a rights offer of 12,00,00,000 shares to existing shareholders in the ratio of three new shares for every five shares held and a preferential offer of 1,20,00,000 shares to SBI employees, both at a reduced premium of ₹ 50 per share. The SBI was permitted to retain 15.0 per cent over subscription in respect of the equity issue and 100.0 per cent over subscription in respect of the bonds issue. With this, the issued and paid-up capital of the SBI would be ₹ 456 crore as against the existing ₹ 200 crore. The rights entitlement of the Reserve Bank in the equity issue of SBI was 11,78,77,200 shares of ₹ 10 each at a premium of ₹ 50 per share, aggregating ₹ 707 crore. The bonds issued by the SBI were in the nature of promissory notes and constituted the direct, unsecured and subordinated obligation of the SBI. The bonds carried a floating rate of interest at 3.0 per cent over the maximum term deposit rate of the SBI, with a minimum coupon rate of 12.0 per cent annum and no maximum ceiling, subject to re-fixing at regular intervals of six months. If the deposits rates were completely deregulated, the maximum term deposit rate quoted by the Bombay main branch of the SBI would be the basis for the floating interest rate.

After making due provisions, the ratio of profit to working funds improved marginally in the case of the SBI and its associates, from 0.21 per cent in 1991–92 to 0.22 per cent in 1992–93. The banks in this group, however, could raise additional equity capital from the markets and strengthen their financial position. Given the need to meet the minimum capital adequacy norm of 8.0 per cent of risk-weighted assets by March 31, 1996 for the remaining Indian banks, the additional capital requirements of all the Indian banks were substantial. These large capital requirements were envisaged to be met by a combination of budgetary support, higher retained earnings and raising capital from the markets.

INCOME RECOGNITION, ASSETS CLASSIFICATION AND PROVISIONING

In response to suggestions regarding the practical difficulties that some banks faced in implementing the prudential system of income recognition and classification of assets as also the need to provide a longer period for compliance, an informal working group was set up in the Reserve Bank. As suggested by the informal group, it was decided to give certain relaxations, such as: (i) an amount under any credit facility should be treated as 'past due' when it remained outstanding for 30 days beyond the due date; (ii) for treatment as NPA of advances granted for agricultural purposes, where interest payment on half-yearly basis synchronised with the harvest; banks should adopt the agricultural season as the basis; (iii) the net worth of the borrower/guarantor need not be taken into account for the purpose of treating an advance as an NPA; (iv) negligible salvage value of the security may not be considered while providing for loss assets; (v) the reckoning for 'past due' in the case of project financing should commence only from the 'due' date for payment, i.e., the date after the completion of the moratorium or gestation period; (vi) credit facilities backed by the central and state government guarantees need not be treated as NPAs; (vii) the treatment of NPA had to be borrower-wise; and (vii) to comply with prudential accounting standards, credit facilities with an outstanding balance of ₹ 25,000 and above alone needed to be considered.

However, for advances with an outstanding balance of less than ₹ 25,000, aggregate provisioning was required to be made to the extent of 2.5 per cent, (later raised to 5.0% from February 4, 1994) of the total outstanding amount. Again, to refine the capital adequacy requirement, it was decided on February 8, 1994 to make further changes in this area, viz.: (i) all claims on banks were assigned a risk-weight of 20.0 per cent, irrespective of the banks having domestic or overseas operations or between funded and non-funded facilities. Further, certain transitions with a non-bank counterpart of the off-balance sheets would be treated as claims on banks; (ii) investments in subordinated debt instruments and bonds issued by other banks or public FIs would carry 100.0 per cent risk-weight; and (iii) advances covered by the guarantee of the DICGC/ Export Credit and Guarantee Corporation (ECGC) would be assigned a risk-weight of 50.0 per cent.

In order to enable banks to absorb the impact of prudential norms, it was decided to allow phasing of provisioning over two years. In terms of these guidelines, banks were required to provide for not less than 50.0 per cent of their aggregate provisioning requirement as on March 31, 1993 and the balance, in addition to the provisions needed for 1993–94, by March 31, 1994. When these guidelines were reconsidered, banks were advised in March 1993 to make 100.0 per cent provision in respect of loss assets, and not less than 30.0 per cent of the total provisioning needed in respect of sub-standard and doubtful advances and advances with an outstanding balance of less than ₹ 25,000 during the year ended March 31, 1993. The balance of provisioning for the above categories of advances, not provided for as on March 31, 1993, together with fresh provisioning needed for credit facilities identified in the year ending March 31, 1994, had to be made as on that date.

The introduction of new norms for income recognition and provisioning for bad debts and the prescription of new capital adequacy requirements were expected to ensure that the books of banks reflected their financial position more accurately and in accordance with international accounting practices. In order to protect the viability and financial health of the banking system, a large provision towards capital contribution to the extent of ₹ 5,700 crore was made in the Union Budget for 1993–94 to meet the gap created by the application of the first stage of provisioning norms. The Government's contribution was subject to specific commitments obtained from each bank to ensure that their future management practices ensured a high level of quality loan portfolio so that the problems of doubtful and bad loans did not recur. However, the amount of recapitalisation proposed by the Government was not sufficient to enable them to fulfil the provisioning norms and take care of additional capital needs on account of the implementation of capital adequacy guidelines.

If banks were to make provisions for bad debts, they would also be able to realise the security on their bad debts. The legal process for releasing banks' dues was not conducive for quick recoveries. The Government, therefore, decided to set up special tribunals to expedite legal action by banks to enforce recoveries and for this purpose, a bill, i.e., recovery of debts due to the banks and financial institutions bill, 1993 was approved by Parliament on August 17, 1993. The bill provided for the setting-up of special tribunals for the trial of claims for recovery of debts that were due to all commercial banks, including RRBs and FIs. The provisions of the bill were, however, not applicable if the amount of debt due to any bank or FI or to a consortium of banks or FIs was less than ₹ 10 lakh or such amount, being not less than ₹ 1 lakh, as the Government specified by notification.

As regards accounting standards for investments, investments in approved securities had to be bifurcated into 'permanent' and 'current' investments. Permanent investments were those that banks intended to hold until maturity and current investments were those that banks intended to deal in, *i.e.*, buy and sell on a day-to-day basis. To begin with, banks were to keep not more than 70.0 per cent of their investments in the permanent category from the accounting year 1992–93, but this ratio was to be brought down to 50.0 per cent in due course. While the depreciation in permanent investment was not likely to affect their realisable value and therefore did not need to be provided for, depreciation in the current investment was to be fully provided for. 'Permanent' investment could be valued at cost unless it was more than the face value, in which case the premium had to be amortised over the period remaining for the maturity of the security. Banks were not expected to sell securities in the 'permanent' category freely, but, if they did so, any loss on such transactions in securities in this category had to be written off. Besides, any gain was to be taken to the capital reserve account.

Foreign currency assets and liabilities and spot and forward foreign exchange transactions (not matured) were required to be revalued on a monthly basis. Spot and forward transactions were to be revalued at the prevailing spot and forward foreign exchange rates, respectively. Long/short positions were to be revalued as per regulations in force. Gains and losses arising from the above valuations were to be reported on a net basis in the income statement and were not to be aggregated with any other type of income or expenses.

OLD PRIVATE SECTOR BANKS

There were, in all, 28 Indian banks functioning in the private sector before the licensing of new Indian private banks. Bank of Karad was being taken into liquidation. The majority of these banks had their headquarters in the states of Tamil Nadu (6), Kerala (6), Maharashtra (5) and Uttar Pradesh (4). The remaining seven banks were in Karnataka (2), with one each in Jammu and Kashmir, Rajasthan, Sikkim, Haryana and Delhi. In terms of ownership, state governments held a substantial/major portion of capital in three banks and certain nationalised banks held substantial share capital in four other private sector banks. The deposits of these banks aggregated ₹ 11,912 crore as on March 31, 1992 and advances were ₹ 6,505 crore. Four of the private sector banks had deposits exceeding

₹ 1,000 crore. Following the rating norms of banks, the financial position of the 28 banks was classified as under (Table 17.8).

TABLE 17.8

Bank Ratings

Rating	Number of Private Sector Banks
Good	6
Satisfactory	14
Not Satisfactory	3
Unsatisfactory	5

Source: Reserve Bank of India, *Report on Trend and Progress of Banking in India, 1997–98.*

PROBLEMS AND CONSTRAINTS OF BANKS IN THE PRIVATE SECTOR

Apart from general problems like low capital base, large load of sticky advances/loan losses, low profitability and inadequate provisioning for bad loans, private sector banks were also beset with special problems that affected their performance and their ability to continue as viable units in the long run. Most banks in the private sector being small were not able to develop a managerial cadre from within the organisation. This was reflected in the sizeable number of banks (as many as 17) remaining weak. These banks had as their chairmen retired officers or officers on deputation from PSBs/state government/Reserve Bank.

In some of these banks, there was dissension within the board due to business rivalry of the dominant controlling groups, which affected the functioning of banks. In some banks, there was interference in day-to-day affairs by directors and it became necessary for the Reserve Bank to circulate instructions on the role of directors on the boards of private sector banks.

Most private sector banks had a low capital base. In fact, in eight of these banks, the ratio of paid-up capital and reserves to deposits was less than 2.0 per cent as against the desired norm of 2.5 per cent. Private sector banks were advised by the Reserve Bank to conform to the capital adequacy norms by raising their percentage of owned funds to risk weighted assets to 4.0 per cent by March 1993 and 8.0 per cent by 1996. Barring a few banks, almost all banks were able to improve their profitability during the year

1992. In the case of the old private sector banks, the level of sticky advances had gone up and it had a serious impact on their profitability and liquidity. In many of these banks the areas of concern were poor fund management, ineffective internal control, unsatisfactory credit appraisal, inadequate post-disbursal supervision, and lack of experienced and trained staff. Internal control mechanisms and the management information system (MIS) continued to remain unsatisfactory in most banks and the coverage of internal inspections continued to be deficient.

Among the old private sector banks, Bank of Karad Ltd, Bank of Madura Ltd, and Nedungadi Bank Ltd were affected by the irregularities in security deals. The Bank of Karad Ltd had undertaken large transactions in securities on behalf of some brokers without verifying the genuineness of transactions or the ability of the broker clients to honour commitments under bank receipts. In view of its small size and large liability, the bank had to be taken into liquidation, for which a petition was filed in the Bombay High Court. Although, Bank of Madura Ltd had not incurred any losses, the exposure of the bank to a potential risk of loss was high. The security transactions of Nedungadi Bank Ltd with ABFSL and FFSL were also not as per the Reserve Bank instructions.

There was an unusual incident of loss of cash held in an unassigned locker at the Madras (Mount Road) branch of Federal Bank Ltd. The money, according to the bank, belonged to its two constituents and the bank had initiated disciplinary proceedings against the officials involved. The bank also figured in the media in connection with its alleged dealings with FFSL. It was, however, affirmed that the bank's limited dealings with FFSL as a broker had not put the bank to losses.

There was adverse publicity in the press concerning the operations of Karnataka Bank Ltd as a sequel to the internal strife between the elected directors and the chairman of the bank. All the existing directors were replaced by a new set of directors by the shareholders at the annual general body meeting. The bank had extended certain credit facilities to FFSL and it had contended that the advances were fully secured.

In view of the liberalisation in the financial and economic spheres, several financial companies and industrialists were showing interest in joining the management of private sector banks. Substantial trading in banks' shares was taking place. Among others, the Narasimham Committee recommended that there be no bar to new banks being set up in the private sector, provided they conformed to the start-up capital and other requirements prescribed by the Reserve Bank. Most of the private sector banks were small and confined to limited areas of operations, but they served a useful purpose. It was, however, difficult for them to compete effectively with PSBs.

PROVISIONING FOR BANK ADVANCES OF LESS THAN ₹ 25,000

Banks were required to make provisioning to the extent of 5.0 per cent of the aggregate amount outstanding as on March 31, 1994 in respect of advances with balances of less than ₹ 25,000. Considering the proportion of NPAs in this category, the provisioning was considered inadequate and it was decided to increase the provisioning requirement for NPAs from the existing 5.0 per cent to 7.5 per cent of the aggregate amount outstanding in respect of advances with balance less than ₹ 25,000 for the year ending March 31, 1995 and further to 10.0 per cent for such balances for the year ending March 31, 1996.

Banks were required to maintain a margin of not less than 25.0 per cent for advances granted against deposits. To allow greater flexibility, the Reserve Bank gave banks the freedom to determine the margin on a case-by-case basis.

OFFSITE SURVEILLANCE AND MONITORING SYSTEM

In February 1995, the DoS introduced an OSMOS as the first step towards a new strategy of strengthening supervision of banks under the direction of the BFS. Prior to the introduction of OSMOS, the Reserve Bank was relying on onsite inspections to perform its supervisory role. With fast-paced changes in the financial environment and market orientation, data-based offsite surveillance was introduced to optimise supervisory resources and put in place a sound database for better supervision. This system depended on a package of prudential supervisory reports to be filed by banks on a quarterly basis, and was proposed to be introduced in two stages. These were used for prudential supervision of banks between onsite inspections in order to estimate the evolving financial condition of the banks and undertake prompt corrective action, if needed.

GOVERNMENT'S QUERY

In February 1995, the Ministry of Finance addressed a letter to the Reserve Bank stating that while the reforms in the financial sector had achieved the desired effect, the Government had received comments from various quarters highlighting some practical issues requiring attention in order to ensure efficient functioning of the financial system. The issues broadly related to CRR, bifurcation of credit facilities into a fixed loan and a fluctuating account, lending under consortium arrangement and installation of ATMs.

On the cash credit system of lending in Indian banking, it was pointed out that under this system, the volatility in the fund management exercise of banks increased and borrowers utilised cash credit limits to book arbitrage spreads in tight liquidity conditions. Conversely, banks lost out on interest when borrowers brought down cash credit drawals, when the market was flush with liquidity. It was, therefore, suggested that since companies had proved to be better managers of short-term liquidity than banks, a system based on bifurcation of credit facilities into a fixed loan and a fluctuating account, *viz.*, cash credit, appeared to be more useful than the cash credit system. It was also suggested that a higher interest rate should be charged on the cash credit component than on fixed loans.

In reply, the Governor in his letter of August 1995 clarified that as part of a historic reform of the credit delivery system, the Reserve Bank had introduced a loan system under which, for borrowers with maximum permissible bank finance of ₹ 20 crore and above, the cash credit component would be limited to 75.0 per cent of the maximum permissible bank finance, and if the borrower wished to avail of the balance 25.0 per cent of the maximum permissible bank finance, he had to necessarily take it in the form of a short-term loan. This was expected to bring about a measure of credit discipline.

In respect of consortium lending, the Secretary of the Ministry of Finance had observed that although the threshold limit for mandatory consortium lending had been raised from ₹ 5 crore to ₹ 50 crore, this did not seem to have made a substantial difference in the number of consortium borrowal accounts for the fear of loss of effective control over borrowers by banks. Also, borrowers were obtaining credit facilities from other banks either by not informing the lead bank or by waiting for a period of 10 to 15 days to lapse to get a no-objection certificate (NOC) from the lead bank. With the relaxation of the threshold limit for consortium lending, it had become mandatory for companies (with a net worth of ₹ 50 crore or so to begin with) to announce audited financial results half-yearly and later at quarterly intervals. It was added that companies should be asked to declare a schedule of all their borrowings from various sources along with details of securities charged, which would help banks keep better track of their borrowal accounts.

The Governor, in his reply highlighting the major relaxations made in the policy of consortium lending, stated that with deregulation of interest rates, the consortia arrangement would get replaced by syndication and borrowers would go in for multiple credit arrangements. As regards the suggestion to introduce mandatory audit on a quarterly basis for companies with a net worth of ₹ 50 crore and above, it was pointed out that as per the practice, banks were required to examine certificates obtained by borrowers from their statutory auditors regarding their borrowings from banks and FIs before a decision was taken on credit proposals. To keep track of borrowal accounts, a lending bank could obtain information audited or otherwise from its borrowers, particularly larger ones, about their borrowings and securities.

The Governor added that as competition became more intense among banks and institutions, consortia arrangement would gradually be dismantled and hence no further specific measures were warranted. On the Secretary's suggestion to remove the restrictions on grant of permission to banks to allow them to set up offsite ATMs to improve their popularity, the Governor replied that banks were permitted to install ATMs at places identified by them in addition to branches and extension counters for which they held licenses issued by the Reserve Bank subject to the condition that after the installation, banks should obtain a licence for the purpose from the concerned regional office of the Reserve Bank.[20]

DIVERSIFICATION OF ACTIVITIES BY BANKS: SETTING-UP OF SUBSIDIARIES

Some banks were given permission to set up subsidiaries to undertake para-banking and other incidental activities. In terms of the guidelines for primary dealers in government securities market issued by the Reserve Bank, the SBI, Canara Bank and PNB were given in principle approval to set up subsidiaries. The subsidiary of PNB would be wholly owned by the bank. The subsidiaries of SBI and Canara Bank were to be JVs with other PSBs. The Asian Development Bank (ADB) was contributing to the share capital of the SBI subsidiary to the extent of 15.0 per cent.

STOCKINVEST SCHEME

Four private sector banks and one foreign bank were allowed to introduce stocks schemes, bringing the total number of banks under the scheme to

---

20. Reserve Bank of India, circular no BP.BC 152/21.03.051/94 dated August, 29, 1994. This circular was also forwarded to the Government.

54. As per the extant instructions, stockinvests could be issued only to individuals and mutual funds. The scrutiny conducted by the DoS as also investigations by the Economic Intelligence Bureau of the Government revealed that corporate bodies/NBFCs/share brokers had misused the facility of stockinvest by using individuals as 'fronts'. The matter was followed up with the concerned banks (*i.e.,* Vysya Bank, IndusInd Bank and State Bank of Saurashtra) and, at the instance of the Reserve Bank, Vysya Bank took action against the erring staff and also stopped the issue of stockinvests from the erring branches. A show-cause notice was issued under section 47A of the BR Act 1949 to the State Bank of Saurashtra. In light of the irregularities, Reserve Bank made a proposal to SEBI to prescribe a ceiling of ₹ 1 lakh per individual per capital issue for the issue of stockinvests by banks.

EQUITY PARTICIPATION BY BANKS IN OTHER CORPORATES

Six PSBs and four private sector banks were allowed to participate in the equity capital of certain corporate that were being set up to provide specialised services. These specialised corporate were Canbank Computers Services Ltd, India Clearing and Depository Services Ltd, TAIB Capital Corporation Ltd, Weizmann Homes Ltd and Punjab Venture Capital Fund.

STUDY OF MANAGEMENT INFORMATION SYSTEM ON COMMERCIAL BANKING: OPERATIONAL AND REGULATORY ASPECTS

In view of the progressive liberalisation and deregulation of commercial banking operations, a need was felt to examine various returns called for by different departments of the Reserve Bank from banks so as to eliminate superfluous returns and streamline the reporting mechanism to conform to the new requirements. In January 1995, the Reserve Bank constituted a study group on review, rationalisation and redesign of returns relating to core commercial banking areas (Chairman: Shri T.N.A. Iyer). The group submitted its report on July 1, 1995 and recommended the following: (i) eliminating 120 returns; (ii) simplifying/redesigning/rationalising the remaining returns in terms of changing the frequency of submission; and (iii) immediate use of computer media for receipts, scrutiny and processing of returns. The follow-up on implementing the recommendations was initiated early to enable banks to reduce their workload and improve efficiency.

DEVELOPMENTS RELATING TO
URBAN CO-OPERATIVE BANKS

OVERVIEW

The co-operative system developed serious weaknesses over time and UCBs were no exception. The UCBs continued to be subjected to the Reserve Bank's regulatory policies and directions. A separate department handled matters relating to UCBs. By and large, whenever changes were introduced in the regulatory and supervisory policies for commercial banks, they were extended to UCBs, after a review with suitable modifications. Although these banks were functioning like commercial banks, in view of the nature of their ownership and regulatory structure, the Reserve Bank extended special dispensations to UCBs in the applicability of various norms, such as those relating to licensing, regulatory and supervisory guidelines, lending and prudential norms and statutory prescriptions on cash and liquidity requirements.

When the Narasimham Committee addressed the problems of the banking system in 1991 and suggested a road map for liberalising the banking sector, a similar need was felt to relook at the regulatory issues relating to the UCBs, *de novo*. Accordingly, the Reserve Bank appointed the Marathe Committee in 1991. The recommendations of this committee were far-reaching, particularly in the realm of bank licensing, branch licensing and areas of operation. The Marathe Committee suggested dispensing with the archaic 'one district–one bank' licensing policy and recommended that banks be organised based on the need for an institution and the potential for the bank to mobilise deposits and purvey credit. It also felt that the existence of a commercial banking network should not prevent the co-operative banking initiative.

The Reserve Bank also appointed a working group under the chairmanship of Shri Uday M. Chitale in December 1995 to review the audit systems in the UCBs. With a view to instilling professionalism in the audit of the UCBs, the group suggested that the audit of banks with deposits of ₹ 25 crore and above should be done by chartered accountants, thus ending the monopoly of the state government's audit of the UCBs. It also suggested a revised audit rating model for the UCBs. None of the states with a large presence of co-operative banks, however, implemented the recommendations of the working group.

Besides easing regulatory restrictions, the Reserve Bank made several policy pronouncements in the operational sphere. The UCBs were allowed to invest 10.0 per cent of their surplus funds outside the 'co-operative fold'. The ceiling on quantum of advances to nominal members was increased substantially and scheduled UCBs were allowed to undertake merchant banking forex operations. Effective November 1996, UCBs were given the freedom to finance direct agricultural operations. Interest rates on deposits of urban banks were deregulated. They could also install ATMs without the prior approval of the Reserve Bank.

In the post-Marathe Committee dispensation, there was a paradigm shift in the Reserve Bank's regulatory approach. An excessively controlled regime gave way to a fairly liberalised era. The shift in the policy of the Reserve Bank on UCBs was a natural corollary of its stance on the financial sector. Most of the state governments, who were co-regulators, had not brought out any significant parallel reforms in tune with the liberalisation process set in by the Reserve Bank. The notable exception was Andhra Pradesh, which brought in the Mutually-Aided Co-operative Societies Act, 1995 that freed co-operative societies registered under this Act from the government control as long as they did not raise share capital or seek guarantees from the state government. The enactment provided complete freedom to UCBs to frame and amend their bye laws, conduct elections to the boards, select auditors and take important decisions on day-to-day operations. It also permitted them to decide independently regarding amalgamation, liquidation, division and reconstruction with no prior approval from the Reserve Bank. As there was no provision regarding 'insured co-operative bank' in the Act, co-operative banks registered under this Act were not eligible for deposit insurance cover under the DICGC Act. The government of Andhra Pradesh was advised of the lacunae and asked to consider proposing suitable amendments to the new Act.

A meeting of the presidents of the national federation and some state federations of primary co-operative banks, the chairmen of select primary co-operative banks and the Registrars of Co-operative Societies of certain states was held on December 2, 1995 to discuss the problems that these banks faced. The Governor of the Reserve Bank presided over the meeting. The representatives of urban banks and their federations highlighted the problems such as dual control by the Reserve Bank and the state governments, the enrolment of nominal members, restrictions on mobilising share capital, donations for charitable purposes, extension of the areas of operation beyond the state of registration and allowing UCBs to take up leasing and hire purchase activities. The Governor indicated that the UCBs would be allowed opportunities to grow and diversify if they followed the prudential guidelines and norms prescribed by the Reserve Bank. Action on the part of the Reserve Bank, where necessary, on the issues deliberated at the meeting was taken.

IMPLEMENTATION OF MARATHE COMMITTEE RECOMMENDATIONS

The Reserve Bank accepted most of the recommendations of the Marathe Committee with certain modifications and came out with a new policy in May 1993. The emphasis of the new policy was on need-based and healthy growth of these banks. Certain relaxations were allowed in the entry point norms for new UCBs in the least developed, tribal and desert areas and less developed states as also for banks organised by women and scheduled castes (SCs)/scheduled tribes (STs). The revised viability norms were to be attained within three years. UCBs were allowed to extend their areas of operation to the entire district without specific approval from the Reserve Bank. Banks with deposits of ₹ 50 crore and above were permitted to cross the borders of the states of their registration. Banks complying with certain norms were also allowed to open extension counters.

Banks operating in metropolitan/urban/semi-urban centres were permitted to extend their areas of operation to the peripheral rural areas to meet non-agricultural financial needs of their members. Norms for issue of licenses to the existing unlicensed UCBs were also relaxed, and those for inclusion of urban banks in the second schedule to the RBI Act, 1934 were proposed to be revised.

Weak and non-viable banks were sought to be weeded out by merger/ amalgamation with stronger units and/or liquidation. The Reserve Bank urged the state governments to initiate measures in co-ordination with the former in this regard. State governments were advised to make appropriate amendments to the State Co-operative Societies' Law for promoting democracy and autonomy in the functioning of the co-operatives while also encouraging self-regulation and responsible action. Suitable legislative amendments to the BR Act, 1949 (as applicable to co-operative societies) were suggested to facilitate the merger/amalgamation of weak urban banks.

While accepting the recommendations of the Marathe Committee with regard to computerisation of UCBs, the Reserve Bank, on June 24, 1993 advised all UCBs, particularly those with working capital of ₹ 5 crore and above, to take appropriate measures to computerise their operations so as to render better customer service, enhance profitability and improve their overall efficiency.

LICENSING

A policy enunciated in 1986 to grant licenses to new UCBs in districts devoid of urban banking facilities continued through 1989–90. At the end of June 1990, there were 1,390 urban (primary) co-operative banks in the country, which included 36 *mahila* banks and 92 salary earners' banks.

Under the branch expansion programme for UCBs covering the three-year period 1991–1994, permission for opening branches was issued to a licensed bank that met the following requirements: (i) it was financially viable; (ii) it had deployed the stipulated level of credit to the priority sector; (iii) it had overdues within the prescribed limit; (iv) it had submitted proper compliance to the inspection reports; and (v) violations of directives, that had been pointed out, were complied with. Accordingly, during the branch plan period 1991–1994, of the proposals from 660 UCBs, those of 363 banks were approved and these banks were allotted 446 centres by the Reserve Bank for opening branches, as at end-June 1993.

On June 9, 1993, the Reserve Bank introduced relaxations in the guidelines regarding the opening of extension counters, shifting of offices and closure of branches; however, decisions on these had to be approved by the boards of directors of the respective banks under intimation to the Reserve Bank, obtaining post facto approval within one month of their implementation. With a view to giving greater freedom to financially strong and well-managed UCBs, banks that satisfied the prescribed norms were permitted to open branches at centres of their choice without prior approval from the Reserve bank.

UCBs were permitted to extend their areas of operation to rural centres, 10 kilometres beyond the boundaries of semi-urban/urban centres, subject to the condition that they provided financial assistance only for non-agricultural productive activities. In order to enable UCBs to freely extend their operation jurisdiction within the district of their registration, prior approval of the Reserve Bank was dispensed with, subject to their obtaining approval from the Registrar of Co-operative Societies. UCBs were, however, required to seek prior approval of the Reserve Bank for extension of field of operation beyond the district of registration. One UCB was deleted from the list of scheduled UCBs when it was converted into a commercial bank, while five UCBs were included in the second schedule of the RBI Act, 1934, which increased the total number of scheduled UCBs to 18.

A liberal policy of allowing new UCBs based on need, business potential and prospects of achieving viability within a specified time frame continued to be followed. The number of UCBs, including salary earners' societies, which stood at 1,653 at end-March 1997 increased to 1,811 at end-March 1998. Licensed UCBs whose demand and time liabilities were not less than ₹ 100 crore were qualified to be included in the second schedule to the RBI Act, 1934. The number of such scheduled UCBs stood at 29 at the end of March 1998. In 1997–98 (July–June), 388 centres were allotted to 54 UCBs. A total of 388 licenses were issued to 86 banks for opening branches.

REHABILITATION OF WEAK URBAN CO-OPERATIVE BANKS

Conscious of its responsibility to supervise, control and develop the urban co-operative banking system on a sound and viable footing, the Reserve Bank made special efforts to rehabilitate banks classified as weak. As on March 31, 1991, the number of UCBs classified as financially weak stood at 230. They were designated as 'weak' because of the heavy erosion in their owned funds, high level of overdues, non-compliance with minimum share capital required in terms of the provisions of section 11(1) of the BR Act, 1949 (as applicable to co-operative societies), not satisfying the viability norms prescribed by the Reserve Bank.

As a sequel to the adverse findings of inspection/investigation of complaints, indicating substantial deterioration in the financial position, directions under section 35A of the BR Act, 1949 (as applicable to co-operative societies) were issued to three primary urban co-operative banks, placing restrictions, among others, on payment to depositors incurring expenditure beyond specified amounts and prohibiting granting/renewal of loans and advances. With this, a total of 11 UCBs were working under such directions.

In view of serious irregularities/deficiencies observed in the functioning and/or their precarious financial position, directions were issued/ modified/extended to 11 UCBs under section 35A of the BR Act, 1949. Of the 1,811 primary urban co-operative banks, 53 co-operative banks and 2 salary earners' societies were under liquidation. The number of UCBs classified as 'weak' as at end-March 1997 stood at 242. The performance of weak banks was closely monitored by the regional offices of the Reserve Bank in close co-ordination with the respective state federations of UCBs/Registrars of Co-operative Societies. The Registrar of Co-operative Societies, Government of Maharashtra issued orders for liquidation of two weak banks in 1997–98 (July–June).

SOME PENAL ACTIONS

Winding up of Metropolitan Co-operative Bank Ltd

The involvement of Metropolitan Co-operative Bank Ltd in Maharashtra in issuing BRs to some banks, the outstanding amount of which exceeded ₹ 1,300 crore as against the bank's total working capital of less than ₹ 8 crore, came as a shock to the Reserve Bank. Considering the seriousness of the irregularities, the Reserve Bank in May 1992 asked the Registrar of Co-operative Societies, Maharashtra, in terms of section 110A (iii) of the Maharashtra Co-operative Societies Act, 1960 to immediately replace the board of directors of the co-operative bank by an administrator who would take charge and run its affairs. After consulting the authorities, the Reserve Bank accorded its sanction for winding up the bank on June 19, 1992. The DICGC was requested to stand ready to pay to the depositors the amount outstanding to their credit up to a maximum of ₹ 30,000 per depositor.

The Reserve Bank issued directions to four primary urban co-operative banks under section 35A of the BR Act, 1949 (as applicable to co-operative societies), placing restrictions, among others, on the maximum amount of withdrawal of deposits, on grant/renewal of loans and advances and incurring expenditure beyond specified amounts. Further, show-cause notices were issued to two banks for working to the detriment of interests of their depositors under the provisions of the BR Act, 1949, and their licence to carry on banking business in India was cancelled. In respect of six UCBs, the boards of directors were superseded. On the recommendation of the Reserve Bank, six banks were placed under moratorium by the Government during the year 1992–93, and all these banks were amalgamated or cleared for amalgamation with other stronger units.

Directions under section 35(A) of the BR Act, 1949 (as applicable to co-operative societies) were issued to five UCBs, placing restrictions on their functioning in view of deterioration in their financial position. In respect of eight banks that were earlier issued such directions, the validity was extended. Of 233 weak/non-viable UCBs as also UCBs that did not comply with the minimum capital requirements, four banks were identified by the Reserve Bank for amalgamation with stronger units. In view of serious irregularities in their working, the boards of directors of five UCBs were superseded by the respective Registrars of Co-operative Societies.

In 1994–95, 14 banks were classified as weak banks, 8 banks were amalgamated with stronger units and 5 were liquidated. 18 banks were deleted from the list of weak banks after they showed improvement in their financial position.

GUIDELINES RELATING TO ACCOUNTING AND OTHER REGULATORY PRESCRIPTIONS

Accounting Period

The accounting period of the co-operative banks was brought in line with that of commercial banks with effect from 1991–92. Section 29(i) read with section 56 of the BR Act, 1949 was amended for the Central Government to specify the date with reference to which annual accounts were to be drawn by co-operative banks. The Central Government issued a notification on January 29, 1992 specifying March 31 of each year as the date for co-operative banks to close their annual accounts. Some credit policy changes/restrictions on commercial banks, such as those relating to the prohibition of chit business, loans for purchase of consumer durables and other non-priority sector personal loans, credit to individuals against shares and debentures/bonds, selective credit controls and interest rates on deposits and advances were also made applicable, with suitable modifications, to the UCBs and central co-operative banks (CCBs).

Interest Rates on Deposits and Advances

The discretion enjoyed by the UCBs allowing additional interest at a rate not exceeding 1.0 per cent per annum on domestic savings and term deposits was reduced to not more than 0.5 percentage points, effective July 24, 1991 in view of the higher interest rates on term deposits. For non-scheduled UCBs, the same 0.5 percentage points' interest discretion was prescribed for the maximum maturity of deposits of 3 years and above; for other maturities, it was retained at 1.0 percentage point. The discretion given to UCBs to allow additional interest at a rate not exceeding one per cent per annum on all savings deposits and at rates not exceeding 0.5 per cent per annum on all term deposits of not less than 46 days was continued.

Following the rationalisation of interest rates on advances made by commercial banks, a similar exercise was undertaken for UCBs and a new interest rate structure, keeping in view their size and preponderance of small loans, was prescribed with effect from June 1, 1991. As a sequel to a further step-up in interest rates on advances made by commercial banks, increases of a similar nature were effected for interest rates on advances charged by UCBs, effective July 24, 1991. In respect of the general category (*i.e.,* other than the concessional rates), the increase was 0.5 percentage points each to a range of 15.0 per cent to 16.5 per cent for all sizes of advances up to ₹ 2 lakh and from 17.0 per cent (minimum) to 18.5 per cent (minimum) for advances over ₹ 2 lakh.

The interest rates on deposits and advances were revised at periodic intervals. With effect from October 1992, the single prescription on deposit rate was revised to not exceed 12.0 per cent per annum. Effective March 2, 1992 the lending rate on UCBs' credit limits of over ₹ 2 lakh was reduced by 1.0 percentage point, from 20.0 per cent (minimum) to 19.0 per cent (minimum), but the effective interest rate on discounting of bills of exchange was fixed at 18.0 per cent (minimum) per annum. Given the nature of the activity of co-operative banks, it was subsequently decided that the lending and deposit rates of all co-operative banks would be completely deregulated and co-operative banks would be given the freedom to determine their deposit and lending rates, subject to the prescription of a minimum lending rate of 12.0 per cent per annum.

In line with the instructions issued to commercial banks, UCBs were advised to afford credit of interest to customers if the amount of interest payable on account of delay in collection of outstation cheques worked out to 25 paise or more. Further, UCBs were allowed to extend immediate credit for more than one outstation cheque at a time within the overall limit of ₹ 2,500. They were also advised to sanction advances against the security of kisan vikas patra, taking into consideration the purpose of the advance and in accordance with the directives issued by the Reserve Bank on interest rates. Besides, they were allowed to sanction advances against the pledge of national savings certificates (viii issue), subject to the usual terms and conditions. At the end of June 1991, 58 UCBs were permitted to open and maintain non-resident (ordinary/external) [NR(E)R/NRO] accounts.

The Reserve Bank, on June 2, 1993, permitted UCBs to sanction advances against the security of gold bonds, 1998 and 10.0 per cent relief bonds, 1993. While the interest rate on such advances would depend on the directives on advances issued by the Reserve Bank, the banks should also satisfy themselves about the genuineness of the credit needs of the borrower and proper end-use of the funds provided as loan.

Limit on Advances

To curb kite-flying operations by their clients, UCBs were instructed that drawals allowed against cheques sent for collection (both local and outstation) would be treated as unsecured advances and would be subject to the directives issued by the Reserve Bank. Clearing house authorities at various places were also advised to ensure that members complied with the rules governing utilisation of favourable clearing balances so as to deny them the use of such funds before the returned cheques were adjusted. With effect from May 20, 1991, the maximum limits on unsecured advances to a director (including relatives) or any other single party/connected group for trade, commerce, cottage and small scale industry and identifiable purposes, were revised upwards to ₹ 25,000 and ₹ 50,000 for UCBs with demand and time liabilities of ₹ 1 crore to less than ₹ 10 crore, and ₹ 10 crore and above, respectively. UCBs with working capital funds of ₹ 25 crore and above were allowed to take up financing of leasing/hire-purchase companies in consortium with SCBs.

Licensed and unlicensed UCBs specifically recommended by the Reserve Bank were eligible for guarantee cover under the small loans (SSI) guarantee scheme, 1981 and small loans (co-operative banks) guarantee scheme, 1984 administered by the DICGC.

Non-Resident Accounts

UCBs were authorised to open and maintain NR(E)R/NRO accounts, and as at the end of June 1990, 49 banks were allowed to have non-resident accounts.

Priority Sector Guidelines

The UCBs were required to lend 60.0 per cent of their total advances to the priority sector, of which at least 25.0 per cent should be to weaker sections. Priority sector advances of co-operative banks aggregated at ₹ 1,703 crore, forming 63.1 per cent of their total outstanding advances in 1991.

The facility of refinance against the collateral of government and trustee securities was extended to scheduled UCBs for the purpose of clearing imbalances. The refinance limit was restricted to 1.0 per cent of demand and time liabilities of the concerned bank and the rate of interest on this refinance was 12.5 per cent.

Income Recognition and Asset Classification

Apart from prescribing entry point, viability norms and the guidelines relating to their operations, the Reserve Bank also placed stipulations on UCBs in respect of income recognition, classification of assets and provisioning along the lines stipulated for SCBs, with suitable modifications, that could be implemented in a phased manner over three years commencing from the accounting year beginning April 1, 1992. Accordingly, the Reserve Bank issued detailed guidelines on February 9, 1993, advising all UCBs to ensure that necessary provisions against sub-standard assets, doubtful assets and loss assets were reflected in their profit and loss accounts and balance sheets from the accounting year ending March 31, 1993.

Participation in Inter-bank Market

The UCBs were permitted to deal with the Discount and Finance House of India Ltd (DFHI) in the inter-bank market, both as lenders as well as borrowers. In view of this, deposits received by the UCBs from the DFHI were exempt from the provisions of the directives on interest rates issued by the Reserve Bank.

Cash Reserve Ratio

Effective the fortnight beginning July 17, 1991, 11 scheduled UCBs were required to maintain CRR of not less than 6.0 per cent of demand and time liabilities in India as against the 3.0 per cent minimum being maintained by them. The three remaining UCBs that were included in the second schedule of the RBI Act, 1934 were required to follow the same prescription from the fortnight beginning January 11, 1992.

DEVELOPMENTS RELATING TO NBFCs AND FIs

NBFCs were a growing segment of the Indian financial system and there was a pressing need for their orderly development along well accepted prudential lines. During the period 1991 to 1997, the Reserve Bank was actively engaged in introducing necessary legislative changes and prudential norms for the sound functioning of these institutions, based on recommendations of the expert groups. The Reserve Bank also introduced a system of registration and strengthened its supervisory practices.

REGULATION OF DEPOSIT ACCEPTANCE BY NON-BANKING COMPANIES

Effective July 27, 1991 the maximum rate of interest that NBFCs and miscellaneous non-banking companies could offer on their deposits was raised from 14.0 per cent to 15.0 per cent per annum. In September 1991, it was prescribed that interest could be paid or compounded at quarterly rests. From June 17, 1992, however, these companies were allowed to pay interest or compound interest at rests not shorter than monthly rests. The investment requirements in government and approved securities by hire-purchase and equipment-leasing companies was raised from 10.0 per cent to 15.0 per cent of the deposit liabilities, which could be achieved, in a phased manner, 1.0 per cent in each quarter commencing from November 1, 1991 and reaching 15.0 per cent on November 1, 1992. Of the 15.0 per cent liquid assets, a minimum of 5.0 per cent were required to be kept in the form of central and state government securities and/or central and state government-guaranteed bonds. The minimum and maximum period for which deposits could be accepted by loan and investment companies was raised from 6 months and 36 months to over 24 months and 60 months, respectively, as was the case with hire-purchase and equipment-leasing companies. It was stipulated that if a company was engaged in both hire-purchase finance and equipment-leasing activities, its business in both these activities would be considered in determining its principal business and classification. On a 3-year average, the company should hold at least 50.0 per cent of its assets in hire-purchase and equipment-leasing and should have at least one-third of its income from these two activities so as to be classified as a hire-purchase or leasing company.

OBSERVATIONS BY THE JPC

The JPC that enquired into irregularities in securities and banking transactions made certain observations and recommendations relating to NBFCs. The observations of the JPC, which acted as the trigger for the introduction of regulatory measures for effective monitoring, supervision and controls over NBFCs, were:

> The committee conclude that some non-banking financial companies played a dubious role in the scam. In this connection they note that the powers of the Reserve Bank of India to supervise and monitor the working of non-banking financial companies are derived from Chapter III B of the Reserve Bank of India Act. However, the control exercised by RBI in terms of the said provisions is not adequate being confined only to deposit taking activities. It is astonishing that no authority, either in the Government of India or in the Reserve Bank of India, appears to have taken stock of possible role of non-banking financial companies in securities and banking transactions nor of the limitations in the Reserve Bank of India Act to deal with such contingencies. Over a period of several years, an entirely new sector of financial activity was allowed to grow and flourish without

giving any thought to deleterious consequences of the activities of this new sector. In the light of the role of the NBFCs in the current scam, the committee are of the considered view that there is an imperative need to ensure that the financial companies follow prudent practices for inculcating healthy financial discipline and therefore their overall functioning, particularly the deployment of funds has to be brought within the purview of some guidelines. The committee, therefore, recommend that government should examine whether the provisions in Chapter III B of the RBI Act are sufficiently wide to cover the necessary regulation. If not, the question of re-enforcing the existing legislation or to enact a separate legislation for the non-banking financial companies be examined so as to ensure proper functioning of NBFCs and also to protect the interest of the depositors.

THE SHAH WORKING GROUP

The Narasimham Committee had recognised that NBFCs would have to be integrated within the mainstream of the overall financial sector reform. The committee observed that prudential norms and guidelines for conduct of business should also be laid down for these companies and a system of offsite supervision based on periodic returns should be instituted within the purview of the agency proposed to be set up to supervise the entire financial system.

In order to prepare a programme of reform for the financial companies, the Reserve Bank constituted a working group in May 1992 under the chairmanship of Dr A.C. Shah, which submitted its report in September 1992. The working group provided a comprehensive framework for reforms of the financial companies and sought to strengthen their operations by laying down prudential norms.

The Reserve Bank accepted the recommendations of the Shah Working Group with some modifications. As the reform process was likely to require adjustment by the financial companies, the measures were proposed for implementation in a phased manner. Accordingly, the Reserve Bank introduced several changes in the directions with effect from April 12, 1993.

As part of the measures in the first phase, the Reserve Bank made certain changes in the directions issued to NBFCs in April 1993, which were amended in May 1993. The duration of deposits of all NBFCs was uniformly stipulated at a minimum of 12 months and a maximum of 84 months; this implied that the maximum duration of deposits for residuary non-banking companies (RNBCs) was reduced from 120 months to 84 months, while the minimum for all other financial companies was reduced from over 24 months to 12 months. The rules for premature deposits were revised in tune with the bringing down of the minimum period for deposits. Thus, this brought into alignment the maturity range of deposits of different types of companies. Inter-corporate deposits of private limited companies and funds raised through the issue of debentures or bonds secured by mortgage of immovable property, which were earlier in the exempt category of deposits, were brought under the purview of the Reserve Bank's directions. However, inter-corporate deposits accepted by financial companies up to a period of 12 months to the extent of two times their NOFs were not subject to the stipulations on interest rate and minimum period.

Hire-purchase finance and equipment-leasing companies were required to maintain liquid assets at 10.0 per cent of deposits. Loan and investment companies were required to maintain liquid assets to the extent of 5.0 per cent of their deposits. Half the liquid assets, *i.e.,* 5.0 per cent of the deposits in the case of equipment-leasing and hire-purchase finance companies and 2.5 per cent of the deposits in the case of loan and investment companies, were required to be maintained in the form of government securities and/or government-guaranteed bonds.

The RNBCs were also required to maintain a minimum investment in government securities and/or government-guaranteed bonds to the extent of 10.0 per cent of their deposit liabilities, within the limit of 70.0 per cent investment in approved securities. NBFCs and RNBCs that had not attained the prescribed liquidity ratios were allowed time until the end of March 1994 to attain these stipulations. All financial companies including RNBCs that had NOFs of ₹ 50 lakh and above were required to register with the Reserve Bank. The registration would, in due course, be vital for companies that were expanding their operations. The other recommendations of the working group were implemented in a phased manner and legislative changes as required were suggested to the Government.

DIRECTIONS ISSUED TO RESIDUARY NON-BANKING COMPANIES

RNBCs that accepted deposits under certain schemes were governed by a set of directions known as the RNBCs (Reserve Bank) directions, 1987. Since most RNBCs did not have adequate NOFs (*vis-a-vis* the quantum of their deposits), unlike the directions issued to financial and miscellaneous non-bank companies, these directions stipulated that at least 10.0 per cent of their deposit liabilities should be kept in fixed deposits with PSBs and another 70.0 per cent of the deposit liabilities be held in the form of approved securities. The constitutional validity of these directions was challenged by some RNBCs. Some of these companies were not showing their entire liability to depositors and were transferring a portion of the deposits to their profit and loss account to meet their revenue expenditure. The Supreme Court in its judgement dated January 30, 1992 upheld the validity of the directions and ruled that the RNBCs could not use any portion of the deposits to meet their working capital expenses.

The RNBCs (Reserve Bank) directions, 1987 were amended on April 19, 1993 in order to prohibit some residuary companies from violating the directions by collecting substantial amounts from their depositors/ subscribers as processing/maintenance charges. One of the companies challenged this amendment in the Calcutta High Court. At the time of admission of the writ petition, the Reserve Bank gave the Court an undertaking that the relevant notification would not be enforced in respect of the petitioner company until further orders by the Court since there was not enough time for the Reserve Bank to file a counter-affidavit. In view of the delay in the disposal of the matter, the Reserve Bank made an application to withdraw this undertaking. The Court had, however, passed an order that the Bank would not enforce the provisions of the relevant notification until disposal of the petition.

THE CHIT FUNDS ACT

The Chit Funds Act was brought into force in 19 states/UTs in 1992–93. The other states and UTs were being persuaded to frame rules to bring the provisions of the Act into force. Here again, the validity of the Act was challenged in different courts and the Supreme Court; the case was heard in the Supreme Court in November 1992 and the Court, in its judgment dated July 17, 1993, upheld the validity of the Act in its entirety.

ACCEPTANCE OF DEPOSITS BY UNINCORPORATED BODIES

Several states/UTs had issued notifications authorising suitable officers to take action against unincorporated bodies as envisaged in sections 45T and 58E of the RBI Act, 1934. The number of such unincorporated bodies remained unaltered at 30 during 1992–93. The total number of unincorporated bodies that had to pay penalty was six; while one case was quashed by the concerned High Court. During 1994–95, the Reserve

Bank initiated proceedings against 19 unincorporated bodies under the legislation.

The constitutional validity of the stipulations regarding the ceiling on the number of deposit accounts to be accepted by individuals, firms and other unincorporated bodies as governed by chapter III-C of the RBI Act, 1934 was challenged, but the Supreme Court, in its judgment dated February 5, 1993, upheld the constitutional validity of chapter III-C of the Act.

PRUDENTIAL NORMS FOR NBFCs

A major step towards implementing the Shah Committee recommendations was taken by the Reserve Bank during 1994 when it decided to put in place the prudential norms on asset classification, provisioning, income recognition and capital adequacy requirements. However, the Reserve Bank felt that legislative changes in the provisions of chapter III-B of the RBI Act, 1934 were necessary, because without the enabling provisions in the Act, the prudential norms could be challenged in Court. The Governor, Dr C. Rangarajan, in a letter on December 31, 1993 to Shri Montek Singh Ahluwalia, Finance Secretary, stressed the need for these changes. This was followed by another letter by the Deputy Governor, Shri S.S. Tarapore to the Chief Economic Adviser to the Government of India.[21] These letters clearly established the rationale for the various prudential measures proposed by the Reserve Bank to ensure transparency in the operations of the non-bank financial sector. Accordingly, the Reserve Bank on June 17, 1994 issued detailed guidelines to be followed by registered financial companies having NOFs of ₹ 50 lakh and above on prudential norms for income recognition, accounting standards, provisioning for bad and doubtful debts, capital adequacy and concentration of credit and investments. The details of these guidelines are provided in Appendix 17.3.

The chronological developments in tightening the supervisory and regulatory norms over NBFCs were elucidated by the Deputy Governor, Shri S.P. Talwar:[22]

The recommendation of the committee (Chairman: Dr A.C. Shah) were implemented in a phased manner. While the scheme

---

21. The Reserve Bank of India and OUP (1998). *The Reserve Bank of India (1951–1967)*.

22. Talwar, S.P. (1997). *The Role and Regulations of NBFCs*. New Delhi: Associated Chambers of Commerce and Industry of India. August 27.

of registration was introduced in April 1993 for all NBFCs having NOF of ₹ 50 lakh and above, prudential norms/guidelines were issued in June 1994 for all registered NBFCs. These norms were more in the nature of guidelines which were not mandatory in the absence of necessary statutory powers. Subsequent to this in April 1995, underscoring the importance of setting out an effective supervisory framework, an expert group under the Chairmanship of Shri P.R. Khanna, Member of the Advisory Council for the Board for Financial Supervision was appointed to design an effective and comprehensive supervisory framework for NBFC sector. Most of the recommendations of the committee have been accepted and a supervisory framework comprising on-site inspection for bigger companies and offsite surveillance system for other companies has been designed and the same is being implemented in phased manner. As mentioned earlier, since mid-60s, legislative framework was structured mainly to regulate the deposit acceptance activities of NBFCs. However, in the changed scenario and in the light of the recommendation of the Shah Working Group as also the observations of the Joint Parliamentary Committee a comprehensive draft legislation was prepared in 1994 which however, required extensive discussion with Ministry of Finance and Law. Finally an ordinance was promulgated by the Government in January 1997, effecting comprehensive changes in the provisions of RBI Act. The ordinance has since been replaced by an Act in March 1997. The amended Act among other things provided for entry point norms of a minimum NOF of ₹ 25 lakh (even though the ordinance provides for the minimum limit at ₹ 50 lakh) and mandatory registration for the new NBFCs for commencing business, maintenance of liquid assets ranging from 5 to 25 per cent of deposit liabilities, creation of reserve fund by transferring not less than 20 per cent of the net profit every year, power to the Bank to issue directions relating to prudential norms, capital adequacy, deployment of funds etc., power to issue prohibitory orders and filing of winding-up petitions for non-compliance of Directions/Act.

Prudential norms were initiated for registered financial companies with NOFs of ₹ 50 lakh and above, whereby these companies were required to achieve a minimum capital adequacy norm of 6.0 per cent on their risk-weighted assets and off balance sheet exposures by March

31, 1995 and 8.0 per cent by March 31, 1996. Besides, they were advised to get themselves rated by a credit rating agency. During 1994–95 the Reserve Bank revised the requirement of maintenance of liquid assets by financial companies. The rates of liquid assets of 10.0 per cent of deposits (including intercorporate deposits and debentures/bonds) in the case of equipment-leasing and hire-purchase companies and registered financial companies was raised to 15.0 per cent effective June 30, 1995. The ratio for unregistered loan and investment companies was raised from 5.0 per cent to 7.5 per cent. The entire increase in the liquid assets for all finance companies would be in the form of investments in government securities/ government guaranteed bonds.

Effective July 8, 1996, the exemption granted to mutual benefit financial companies, popularly known as *nidhi* companies, in respect of interest rates and brokerage was withdrawn. Accordingly, *nidhi* companies could not invite, accept or renew deposits at a rate of interest exceeding 15.0 per cent per annum. They were also prohibited from issuing advertisements and paying any brokerage to solicit deposits. These measures were taken in view of aberrations noticed in the functioning of the *nidhis*.

In July 1996, the Reserve Bank took policy measures to free the interest rate ceiling on deposits and remove/increase the ceiling on the quantum of deposits for registered NBFCs, subject to the condition that they fully complied with the provisions of the NBFC directions, adhered to prudential norms and fulfilled the requirement of minimum investment grade credit rating to determine their own rate of interest on deposits. The minimum grade of credit rating requirement was fixed at the level of 'A' or equivalent for all credit rating agencies. Those not complying fully with the credit rating and prudential requirement as well as other directions/guidelines would continue to be subject to deposit rate regulation and, where compliance was clearly lacking, these companies would face a curtailment of the ceiling on the amount of deposits they could raise. The relaxations would be effective from the date of receipt of the specific certificate from the Reserve Bank by the individual company after the Bank's satisfaction of its compliance with the credit rating requirements, prudential norms and other regulations.

ACCOUNTING PRACTICES

Another dimension to the legislative changes was the presence of heterogeneous and sometimes questionable accounting practices being followed by NBFCs and the imperative need to bring uniformity in the accounting practices. A well-knit accounting practice in conformity with international standards was a pre-requisite to repose faith in the industry. There were several instances where NBFCs had capitalised on the absence or inadequacies of standard accounting practices. One example was leasing. It was noticed that the leasing route was being used as a tool to defer tax liabilities. Sale and lease-back transactions were rampant, supposedly on items in the 100.0 per cent depreciable category, which prompted the Government to come out with an amendment to the Income Tax Act. In light of the amendments and also against the backdrop of developments relating to CRB Capital Market Ltd, several policy changes were introduced after 1997.

REGISTRATION OF NBFCs

In pursuance of requirements under legislative amendments effective January 9, 1997, no NBFC would commence or carry on financial activity without applying for or obtaining a certificate of registration to/from the Reserve Bank. The industry responded promptly to the legal requirements and around 37,500 applications were received before the deadline. Of these, a preliminary scrutiny revealed that only around 8,300 NBFCs had a threshold limit of NOFs of ₹ 25 lakh and above. The onerous task of issuing certificates of registration was attended to on a war-footing. In terms of the provisions of the Act, the Reserve Bank, among other things, was required to ascertain that the NBFC was in a position to pay its depositors; the general character of the management of the NBFC was not prejudicial to the interests of the depositor/public; it had adequate capital structure and earning prospects and any other conditions specified by the Reserve Bank. With regard to the huge number of applications to be processed, it was proposed to utilise the services of chartered accountants as a one-time exercise to conduct a special audit of applicant companies and to help the Reserve Bank determine the suitability for a certificate of registration.

Another important point related to the role of statutory auditors in certifying the financial statements and other documents of NBFCs. Some instances were noticed where the assets and investments shown in the balance sheet did not reflect the existence of actual assets. Therefore, there was an urgent need for the accounting practices to be made transparent. The role of credit rating agencies in assessing the debt-servicing capacity of NBFCs assumed importance. The agencies were required to establish themselves with a more credible assessment of their clients.

Registered NBFCs were instructed to furnish half-yearly returns effective March 31, 1995 that indicated capital funds and risk assets ratio, calculation of risk-weighted assets ratio, off balance sheet exposure and certain other data.

With regard to concentration of credit, financial companies were advised not to lend in excess of 15.0/25.0 per cent of their owned funds to a single borrower/borrowers belonging to a single group, respectively. Financial companies were also advised not to invest more than 25.0 per cent of their owned funds in shares and debentures/bonds of another company. To ensure compliance with these norms, the Reserve Bank advised financial companies to submit half-yearly returns from March 31, 1995.

REGISTERED FINANCIAL COMPANIES

As a liberalisation measure, NBFCs, other than equipment-leasing or hire-purchase companies (such as a loan or an investment company), that were registered with the Reserve Bank were allowed a higher limit of acceptance of deposits (including money raised through the issue of non-convertible debentures/bonds) equal to their NOFs instead of 40.0 per cent of their NOFs and the directions issued to these companies were suitably amended. These companies were required to maintain liquid assets to the extent of 10.0 per cent of their deposit liabilities by the end of December 1994 as against the earlier requirement of 5.0 per cent.

UNREGISTERED FINANCIAL COMPANIES

It was proposed to bring down the quantum of deposits (including inter-corporate deposits/borrowings) in a phased manner for all categories of finance companies that were not registered with the Reserve Bank to the levels of 25.0 per cent and 15.0 per cent of their NOFs from the public and shareholders, respectively.

NON-FINANCIAL COMPANIES

The companies (acceptance of deposit) rules, 1975 framed under section 58A of the Companies Act, 1956 by the Government, which governed the acceptance of deposits by non-banking non-financial companies, were amended on December 10, 1993, whereby the maximum rate of interest payable by non-banking non-financial companies on deposits was brought down from 15.0 per cent per annum to 14.0 per cent per annum. Interest could be paid at rests that should not be shorter than monthly rests.

This brought the rate of interest payable by non-banking non financial companies on par with that payable by NBFCs.

LENDING TO NBFCs

There was an unduly large increase in credit from banks to NBFCs. As banks/FIs were now active in equipment-leasing/hire-purchase, substantial moderation had been brought about in the overall limits of borrowing by NBFCs from banks/FIs. For equipment-leasing/hire-purchase companies with not less than 75.0 per cent of their assets in equipment-leasing and hire-purchase and 75.0 per cent of their income from these two activities as per their last audited balance sheets, the overall limit on bank borrowings was reduced to three times the NOF from April 17, 1995, as against the earlier stipulation of four times the NOF. In respect of other equipment-leasing and hire-purchase companies, such limits, which were reduced to three times in September 1994, were further reduced to two times the NOF in April 1995. The overall limits for loan and investment companies and RNBCs, which were reduced to two times the NOF in September 1994, were made equal to the NOF in April 1995. These ceilings for bank lending to different categories of NBFCs were also made applicable to lending by FIs.

BRIDGE LOANS

The bridge loans/interim finance that banks/FIs were permitted to extend to all companies, including finance companies, against public issues and/ or borrowings from the market to a maximum extent of 75.0 per cent of the amount actually called up on each occasion in a capital issue was entirely withdrawn in September 1994 for NBFCs and in April 1995 for other companies. This was necessary in view of the possible misuse as well as the risk attached to this facility. In respect of loans that had already been sanctioned or disbursed, banks were instructed to ensure that such loans were utilised for the purpose for which they had been raised. Further, banks were to ensure timely repayment and not allow any extension for repayment of the existing loans.

Under the amended regulation announced by the Reserve Bank on July 24, 1996, NBFCs that fully met the requirements of registration, rating and prudential norms were free from interest rate ceilings on the quantum of deposits. Companies that did not fully comply with the directions/ guidelines continued to be subject to the regulations, and where compliance was clearly lacking, the companies faced a progressive reduction in their deposit-taking limits and also a curtailment of other relaxations provided by the Reserve Bank. NBFCs that did not observe the regulations in letter and spirit faced adverse action. NBFCs that were provided the freedom to determine their own interest rates were expected to be judicious and avoid escalation in interest rates, which would only invite problems associated with adverse selection. A need was felt to amend the RBI Act, 1934 chapter III-B on non-banking institutions to enable better regulation and supervision of the NBFCs and also chapter III-C on unincorporated bodies.

As already mentioned, on July 24, 1996, the Reserve Bank announced a package of measures relaxing its controls on NBFCs that complied with its directions and guidelines. In the case of companies where compliance was clearly lacking, a lower ceiling on deposit mobilisation was imposed. Pending a review of the measures, the period up to which the liberalised dispensation could be availed by the eligible NBFCs was extended to September 30, 1997. The restriction on lending by banks to NBFCs in certain multiples of the latter's NOFs was removed in April 1997 for NBFCs that complied with the registration, prudential norms and credit rating requirements stipulated by the Reserve Bank. Accordingly, the level of credit to be provided to NBFCs was left to the discretion of the banks.

An expert group (Chairman: Shri P.R. Khanna) was set up in April 1995 by the Reserve Bank to recommend a framework for supervision of the financial companies. The recommendations included, *inter alia*, supervision of NBFCs through an offsite surveillance system and the introduction of a supervisory rating system for NBFCs. Further, in order to regulate NBFCs effectively and to improve their financial health and viability, certain amendments to chapters IIIB, IIIC and V of the RBI Act, 1934 were made through the enactment of the RBI (Amendment) Act, 1997. The major features of this amendment are provided in Appendix 17.4.

In July 1996, the Reserve Bank introduced policy measures to free the interest rate ceiling on deposits and remove the ceiling/prescribe an enhanced ceiling on the quantum of deposits for NBFCs, subject to the condition that they would obtain a certificate from the Reserve Bank to the effect that they had fully complied with the Bank's directives and guidelines. In respect of registered equipment-leasing and hire-purchase finance companies that had complied with the credit rating requirement and prudential norms, the liberalisation measures included: (i) removal of ceiling on deposits, which were 10 times the NOFs; (ii) reduction of the liquid assets-to-deposits ratio from 15.0 per cent to 12.5 per cent, while continuing with the stipulation that at least 10.0 per cent of the deposits be maintained in government securities/government guaranteed bonds; and (iii) freedom to determine interest rates on deposits of 1–5 years.

As regards registered loan/investment companies that complied with credit rating requirements and prudential norms, the overall ceiling on deposits, which used to be equal to NOF, was increased to twice the NOF. The stipulation of 12.5 per cent of liquid assets ratio and the freedom to determine interest payable on deposits as in the case of equipment-leasing and hire-purchase companies also applied to these companies.

For registered equipment-leasing and hire-purchase as well as loan/investment companies that complied with credit rating or prudential norms, the ceiling interest rate of 15.0 per cent on deposits and overall ceiling on deposits alongside the stipulation of 15.0 per cent liquid assets ratio was to continue. In the case of non-compliance with both the credit rating and the prudential norms, the overall ceiling on deposits was reduced in relation to the NOF from 10 times to 7 times for registered equipment-leasing and hire-purchase companies, and for registered loan and investment companies from equal to NOF to 15.0 and 25.0 per cent of NOF for deposits from shareholders and public, respectively.

The Union Budget 1996–97 proposed amendments to the RBI Act, 1934 to strengthen its regulatory powers over NBFCs. During January 1997 the Government promulgated an ordinance to amend the RBI Act, 1934, for regulating the activities of unincorporated bodies and NBFCs. In view of the difficulties faced by *nidhi* companies in achieving the ratio of NOF to deposits not exceeding 1:20, the Reserve Bank decided that the ratio would be made applicable only on the incremental deposit liabilities over the level as on January 15, 1997. With a view to effectively regulating the activities of NBFCs and thereby improving their financial health and viability, the Government promulgated an ordinance bringing about comprehensive changes in the provisions of chapters IIIB and V of the RBI Act, 1934, effective January 9, 1997. The ordinance was replaced by the RBI (Amendment) Act, 1997 in March 1997, which also modified the provisions of chapter III-C of the Act relating to acceptance of deposits by unincorporated bodies, effective April 1, 1997. The Act stipulated that: (i) a new NBFC could not operate unless it was registered with the Reserve Bank and had a minimum NOFs of ₹ 25 lakh; (ii) all existing NBFCs were required to apply for registration by July 8, 1997; (iii) NBFCs with NOFs of less than ₹ 25 lakh were given three years (extendable by another three years at the Reserve Bank's discretion) to reach that level; (iv) the Reserve Bank was empowered to cancel the certificate of registration issued to any

NBFC; (v) NBFCs would have to maintain liquid assets of not less than 5.0 per cent of their deposits or such higher percentage not exceeding 25.0 per cent as may be fixed by the Reserve Bank; failure to do so would attract penalty from the Reserve Bank; (vi) every NBFC would create a reserve fund and transfer to it at least 20.0 per cent of its net profit every year before declaring a dividend; (vii) the Reserve Bank was authorised to issue directives relating to disclosures, prudential norms on income recognition, accounting standards, provisioning for bad and doubtful debts and credit concentration; (viii) the Company Law Board was empowered to adjudicate and pass orders in the case of non-repayment of deposits/ interest by NBFCs; and (ix) unincorporated bodies engaged in financial activities were debarred from accepting deposits from April 1, 1997.

Housing finance companies (HFCs) were exempted from all the provisions of chapter III-B of the RBI Act, 1934, as amended in terms of the RBI (Amendment) Act, 1997, as they are regulated by a separate regulatory authority, the NHB. Accordingly, the HFCs were not required to apply for a certificate of registration from the Reserve Bank as provided in section 45-1(A) of the RBI Act.

DEVELOPMENTS IN SUPERVISION

The BFS and the DoS exercised powers of integrated supervision in relation to commercial banks, all-India FIs and NBFCs. The emphasis of the BFS and DoS continued to be on broadening and sharpening supervision strategies and skills. The DoS with the approval of the BFS put in place a new supervisory strategy that retained the importance of onsite inspection, but also introduced offsite surveillance, strengthened the internal control system in banks and increased the use of external auditors in banking supervision. An offsite monitoring system that was introduced on a pilot basis was formalised.

The work on supervision of NBFCs was taken over by the DoS from the Department of Financial Companies (DFC) in July 1995 and the regional offices of the DFC were transferred to the DoS. A financial companies division was set up in the central office of the DoS and financial companies' wings were opened at all the 16 regional offices of the DoS. The financial companies division at central office dealt with the interpretation of policy matters, developing new supervisory mechanisms, evolving new guidelines for companies, providing directions and guidance to the regional offices and granting approval for registration of NBFCs. The regional office extensions of the division dealt with identification and classification/registration of companies, onsite inspection of companies and offsite surveillance through returns and complaints. The RBI (Amendment) Act, 1997 conferred wide powers on the Reserve Bank for exercising closer supervision over NBFCs. Accordingly, the Bank could prescribe the minimum level of NOFs, and ensure compulsory registration with the Bank as well as the maintenance of liquid assets on a daily basis. All companies that had financial business as their principal activity, whether registered or not, were required to apply afresh to the DoS for a certificate of registration by July 8, 1997. The Reserve Bank received 37,478 applications for registration. For more effective co-ordination between the regulatory and supervisory functioning relating to FIs, the financial institutions cell (FIC) concerned with the regulatory aspects started functioning within the DoS as a separate division effective from June 18, 1997.

The BFS adopted the recommendations of the reports submitted by three expert groups constituted by the DoS *viz.*, the group to review the system of onsite inspection of banks (Padmanabhan Committee), the group to review the internal control and audit system in banks (Jilani Committee) and the group for designing a supervisory framework for NBFCs (Khanna Committee). The Padmanabhan Committee had recommended far-reaching changes in the focus, scope and thrust of on-site inspections and follow-up. The main focus of the Jilani Committee was on the internal control and inspection/audit system in banks. The recommendations of the Khanna Committee were directed towards extensive supervision of NBFCs, mainly through an offsite surveillance system, and subjecting registered NBFCs to supervisory rating with the periodicity of their inspection being determined by their rating.

The recommendations of the Khanna Committee were accepted and implemented with modifications in keeping with the changing circumstances. Further, in light of the various recommendations made by Khanna Committee and the additional statutory powers vested in the Reserve Bank, a new manual for onsite inspection of NBFCs and offsite surveillance was prepared by a project group set up in the DoS.

BUDGET PROPOSAL TO DISCONTINUE RESERVE BANK'S
ANNUAL ALLOCATIONS TO FIs

The Reserve Bank had been making annual allocations out of its profits to FIs like IDBI, National Bank for Agriculture and Rural Development (NABARD), Small Industries Development Bank of India (SIDBI), Industrial Reconstruction Bank of India (IRBI) and Export-Import (Exim)

Bank. The Union Budget for 1992–93 made a significant announcement that no further allocations would be made to these institutions by the Reserve Bank and correspondingly a higher amount of profit would be transferred to the Government. This policy decision adversely affected the viability position, especially of NABARD, despite the Government continuing to make allocations for these institutions to float public sector tax-free bonds at attractive rates of interest. The Governor in his letter to the Finance Secretary dated April 6, 1992 elucidated the adverse impact of this decision, especially on NABARD.

In the past, select institutions, other than NABARD, were provided funds under the annual allocations by the Reserve Bank at interest rates of 8.0–9.0 per cent. However, NABARD was provided funds at a zero rate of interest because NABARD was in turn extending credit to the co-operatives at very low interest rates by blending these resources with market-raised resources. The main and perhaps the only reason for such support to the co-operatives was that the bulk of lending by co-operative banks was at very low rates of interest that were below their deposit rates. However, this special treatment made deposit-based expansion of credit by the co-operatives untenable and, more importantly, it became necessary to provide a subsidy to NABARD through reduced interest rates as long as the ultimate interest charged by the co-operatives was low. The Reserve Bank posed the dilemma inherent in the situation, namely, if the Government permitted NABARD to raise funds at the standing rate for public sector bonds, an interest rate subsidy was inevitable unless NABARD raised its lending rate to the co-operative banks and they, in turn, were allowed to raise their lending rates. The Government was requested to consider expeditiously this matter as it involved the viability issue.[23]

REGULATION OF CAPITAL MARKET INSTITUTIONS

In May 1990, the Ministry of Finance sought the views of the Reserve Bank on a proposal to convert the SEBI into a statutory body from its existing position as a non-statutory body. The Reserve Bank, in its reply dated May 18, 1990 addressed to the Finance Secretary, expressed the view that the regulation of the capital market should be its direct responsibility rather than that of SEBI. The various reasons adduced by the Reserve Bank in support of its standpoint are briefly discussed.

---

23. Also refer to chapter 18: Agriculture and Rural Development.

The Indian financial market was undergoing significant and rapid changes, and the financial sector had emerged as a key sector of the economy. The operations of FIs, the banking sector, NBFCs and the capital market were no longer confined to one segment of the market. In particular, the interface of banks and its subsidiaries with the capital market was on the increase. At the same time, non-bank financial institutions such as the UTI, Life Insurance of India (LIC) and General Insurance Corporation (GIC) had become lenders in the money market and insurance companies had entered activities like mutual funds and housing finance through their subsidiaries. The Reserve Bank averred that these developments, which were increasingly characterised by a de-segmentation of the financial market, had important implications for the kind and structure of the regulatory system that should be built.

Further, FIs were undergoing rapid changes, particularly in the multiplicity of financial services that they offered. This blurred the distinctions between institutions and market segments. The Governor noted, "More integrated markets would call for integrated supervision and avoidance of multiplicity of regulatory agency." In such a milieu, the Reserve Bank felt that the entire market, including the constituents in the capital market, should be made subject to the regulation by the central bank of the country since multiple authorities exercising supervision independent of each other over various overlapping segments of the market would inevitably lead to conflict of jurisdiction and confusion that should be avoided. The RBI Act, under chapter III-B, section 45L, empowered it to exercise 'comprehensive' oversight over the financial system. The Governor postulated, "Clearly, the intention of the law has been that the central banking authority of the country should exercise comprehensive oversight over the financial system as a whole." In countries where different supervisory authorities had evolved over time, there was a conscious effort to bring about greater co-ordination among them. In the Indian situation, instead of creating a new supervisory authority and finding ways to achieve co-ordination among different authorities, it was advisable for the central bank to exercise this power directly. The Reserve Bank proposed that it was in a position to undertake this work soon and it could also absorb whatever trained manpower was available in SEBI. The Government, however, went by its original plan.

PRUDENTIAL NORMS FOR FINANCIAL INSTITUTIONS

The Reserve Bank had advised the five all-India term lending institutions, *viz.*, IDBI, Industrial Finance Corporation of India (IFCI), ICICI, IRBI and Exim Bank, in March 1994 to implement prudential guidelines on capital adequacy and income recognition, asset classification, provisioning and other related matters in a phased manner from the accounting year commencing in April 1993. As against the stipulation of achieving a capital adequacy ratio of 4.0 per cent by March 31, 1994, all FIs achieved the ratio of 8.0 per cent by March 31, 1996. The provisioning requirements were also met by all FIs during 1993–94.

An important development during the year was the amendment to the IDBI Act, 1964 in October 1994 to enable it to restructure its capital, raise equity from the public and gain operational flexibility. Nevertheless, the equity holding of the Central Government at any time was not to be less than 51.0 per cent of the issued equity capital of the IDBI. The authorised capital of IDBI was increased from ₹ 1,000 crore to ₹ 2,000 crore which could be raised to ₹ 5,000 crore by a resolution in the general body meeting. The issued capital of ₹ 753 crore, which stood fully vested in and fully subscribed by the Central Government before the commencement of the IDBI (Amendment) Act 1995, was divided into 75.3 crore equity shares of ₹ 10 each.

The IDBI entered the capital market in July 1995 with the public issue of 16.8 crore equity shares of ₹ 10 at a premium of ₹ 120 per share, aggregating ₹ 2,184 crore. Besides, the IDBI, on behalf of the Government, offered for sale 144.2 lakh equity shares of ₹ 10 each at ₹ 170 per share, aggregating ₹ 187 crore. The issue was oversubscribed and after the public issue and the offer for sale by the Government, the Government's equity shareholding in IDBI declined from ₹ 500 crore to ₹ 486 crore which formed 72.7 per cent of the post-issue equity capital of IDBI as against 100.0 per cent before issue.

FIs had rationalised their interest rate structure in line with the overall economic environment. The IDBI, ICICI and IFCI introduced a variable interest rate loan scheme. They continued their efforts to widen their resource base and mobilised funds from domestic as well as international markets. In tune with the changing environment, they were diversifying their operations and reorienting their business strategies.

THE NATIONAL HOUSING BANK

The NHB augmented the flow of credit for housing activities by revising upwards its limit for refinance to SCBs to ₹ 5 lakh from ₹ 2 lakh, thus bringing its refinance eligibility on par with the specialised HFCs.

Cumulative disbursement on account of refinance to SCBs, HFCs and state-level apex co-operative housing finance societies in respect of eligible loans disbursed by them, along with subscription to special rural housing debentures floated by agriculture and rural development banks in respect of their eligible housing loans, amounted to ₹ 2,306 crore at the end of April 1995. Of the refinance provided, HFCs accounted for 81.9 per cent, co-operative sector institutions 11.1 per cent and the banking sector 7.0 per cent.

A significant policy by the NHB was the deregulation of interest rates charged by primary lending agencies on all loans above ₹ 1 lakh. The refinance rates charged by the NHB in respect of recognised and approved HFCs were revised downwards. The NHB also formulated prudential norms for income recognition and assets classification for the HFCs.

CONCLUDING OBSERVATIONS

During the period 1990–1997, as part of financial sector reforms, fundamental changes took place in banking and the financial system. While the liberalisation process commenced earlier in the mid–1980s, the reform measures gained momentum after the implementation of the report of the Narasimham Committee on the financial system. While the systemic shock due to irregularities in securities transactions jolted the financial system and the banking sector in particular, the lessons from the scam led to far-reaching reforms in market regulation and settlement practices. This also strengthened the bias towards a gradualist approach to financial sector reform and the continuation of public sector dominace in the financial system.

18

Agriculture and Rural Development

INTRODUCTION

In the field of rural credit, the Reserve Bank played a unique role since its inception. The critical importance of agriculture and rural development was also well recognised in the successive Five Year Plans, since growth in this sector helped to improve food security, nutritional standards and the supply of wage goods at reasonable prices. Around the turn of the 1980s, an urgent need was felt for broad-based agricultural and rural development that gave an impetus to allied activities in rural areas, both to generate employment and to alleviate poverty. This prompted the establishment of a specialised apex institution for agriculture and rural development, namely, the National Bank for Agriculture and Rural Development (NABARD) in 1982. Given its statutory responsibility, the Reserve Bank continued to guide the financial system and exercise overall regulation over rural financial institutions in co-ordination with the Government.

Apart from the massive expansion of banking in rural areas during the 1980s, banks were prompted to emerge as social institutions even at the cost of viability. Further, stress was laid on initiating programmes and schemes to develop agriculture and the rural segment with an emphasis on providing assistance to the weaker sections, particularly the scheduled castes (SCs) and scheduled tribes (STs). Programmes such as the integrated rural development programme (IRDP), new twenty-point programme and the differential rate of interest (DRI) scheme were intensified. The lead bank scheme (LBS) was introduced to ensure the flow of bank credit to the priority sector and to co-ordinate the activities of different entities, such as banks and the development agencies of the Government at various levels.

In the early 1980s, the over-emphasis on achieving quantitative targets resulted in weaknesses surfacing and raised concerns about the viability of the banking system. The later part of 1980s, therefore, focused *inter alia*, on the need for qualitative improvements in agriculture and rural credit. Thus, the service area approach (SAA) was introduced in 1989 to improve the quality of the delivery system in rural lending.

With the onset of wide-ranging reforms in the financial sector beginning in the 1990, including liberalisation and deregulation of interest rates based on the recommendations of the Narasimham Committee, the earlier rigour with which rural and priority sector lending was pursued by the Reserve Bank underwent some changes leading to the emergence of alternate models of the rural credit delivery system, such as micro-credit through self-help groups (SHGs) and non-government organisations (NGOs).

IMPACT OF REFORMS

The five year plan remained suspended during the period 1989–1991. Since the focus shifted to crisis management and the introduction of structural reforms in trade, industry and the financial sector, the intensity with which agricultural and rural credit targets and policies were pursued during the 1980s lost their momentum from the early 1990s. On the eve of the 1991 reforms, following the expansion phase during the 1980s, the rural credit delivery system was found to be rather inadequate. Despite the impressive geographic spread and consequent decline in the influence of informal sources of credit, the rural financial institutions were characterised by several weaknesses, *viz.*, a decline in productivity and efficiency and an erosion of repayment ethics and profitability.[1]

The significant increase in credit flow from institutional sources during the 1980s brought forth a strong sense of expectation from the banking system; in particular public sector banks (PSBs). However, this expectation could not be sustained since achieving quantitative targets was in focus through the decade. As a consequence, little attention was paid to the qualitative aspects of lending, resulting in loan defaults by all categories of borrowers and erosion of repayment principles. The result was a disturbing growth in overdues, which not only hampered recycling

---

1. Mohan, Rakesh (2004). "Agricultural Credit in India: Status, Issues and Future Agenda", *RBI Bulletin.* November.

of scarce bank resources, but also affected the operational efficiency of financial institutions.

Some significant measures in the area of agricultural credit as part of the overall structural reforms initiated in 1991 included: deregulation of interest rates by co-operatives and regional rural banks (RRBs); deregulation of lending rates by commercial banks for loans above ₹ 2 lakh; recapitalisation of select RRBs; introduction of prudential accounting norms and provisioning requirements for all rural credit agencies; increased refinance support from the Reserve Bank and capital contribution to NABARD; constitution of the rural infrastructure development fund (RIDF) in NABARD for rural infrastructure projects; and introduction of the kisan credit card (KCC).

The weaknesses in the performance of rural financial institutions since 1991 prompted the authorities to set up various committees/working groups/task forces to look into their operations. While the Narasimham Committee recommended revamping priority sector targets and rural lending policies, the Government and the Reserve Bank retained the emphasis on the social orientation of banking towards rural and the priority sector. Nevertheless, the overall financial reform measures were accompanied by rationalisation of rural banking policies. The definition of priority sector was expanded by raising the credit ceiling limit, and by widening the coverage to include many hitherto uncovered segments. At the same time, commercial banks were provided with the option of meeting the shortfall in achieving the priority sector target by investing in special bonds issued by certain specialised institutions. Except for a narrow segment of small borrower accounts, interest rate regulations under the priority sector were removed. The branch licensing policy, which had been instrumental in the expansion of commercial bank branches in rural areas, was modified to allow banks to rationalise their branch networks.[2]

As a result of the reform process, the financial health of commercial banks improved. However, commercial banks being more focused on operational viability tended to cherry-pick and give comparatively less priority to marginal and sub-marginal farmers.[3]

---

2. Bose, Sukanya (2005). "Rural Credit in India in Peril", in V.K. Ramachandran and Madhura Swaminathan (eds.), *Financial Liberalization and Rural Credit in India.* International Development Economics Associates and Tulika Books.

3. Thorat, Y.S.P. (2005). *Rural Credit in India and Concerns.* Presidential Address at the Indian Society of Agricultural Economics. Ludhiana: NABARD. November 24.

POLICY CONCERNS

Despite these shortcomings in the rural credit system, the agricultural performance during the 1990s was the equivalent of a long-term trend value. It was, however, moderate in the context of economic reforms, and could be considered as sustainable. The overall agricultural production index rose by 2.8 per cent and that of food grain production by 2.2 per cent. The growth rate in food grain production was close to the long-term growth rate in demand for food grains. A significant aspect of agricultural production in the 1990s was the minimal fluctuation in output, which was mainly due to a series of reasonably good monsoon seasons. Equally important was the fact that the increase in output, particularly in food grains, was contributed by a large number of states. The gradual opening up of agriculture to world markets, with its favourable impact on terms of trade for agriculture, created a progressively conducive environment for improvement in agricultural production. Further opening up of the economy, it was felt, required a sharp acceleration in the agricultural performance, which could be realised only with a strong policy package.

Public investment in rural development was constrained by the overall fiscal position, even though the Centre's budgets had allocated higher outlays for agriculture, rural development and irrigation and also raised the capital base of NABARD and RRBs. The state governments too had to make larger investments in rural infrastructure by managing their finances better through cost recoveries and resource mobilisation. Besides, private investment had to go up. The policy concern was about not merely sustaining the present rate of public investment in agriculture, but also improving the same, should there be a dip in private investment for any reason.

With the recapitalisation and adoption of prudential norms, attempts were made to strengthen RRBs. To create a favourable recovery culture, weightage was given to recovery performance in staff appraisals and attempts were made to evolve legal mechanisms for expeditious disposal of cases filed for recovery of dues. Strict observance of the memoranda of understanding (MoU) signed between NABARD, the state governments and the state co-operative bank/state land development bank (SLDB) and between the RRBs and sponsor banks was considered critical for strengthening the organisational base and the operating practices of rural financial institutions. The co-operative credit system was freed from interest rate controls except for the prescription of a minimum lending rate.

The policy instruments deployed to promote agricultural growth, *viz.*, prices, subsidies and procurement, were reviewed, and simultaneously other aspects, such as storage, technology and infrastructure needs relating to the agricultural sector, were addressed. The review showed that the major factors that constrained the capacity of the poor to borrow from organised credit institutions were lack of skills, lack of awareness about economic opportunities and markets and their inability to overcome intricate procedural requirements. In this regard, the role of voluntary agencies and NGOs in financial intermediation became increasingly important.

The annual growth rate in the output of food grains since the beginning of the 1990s at 1.7 per cent was marginally lower than the population growth rate at 1.9 per cent. Given the growth in the labour force, agricultural production had to expand at a secular rate of about 4.5 per cent per annum to maintain the momentum of the overall economic activity. Such an outcome would require productivity in agriculture to be enhanced. In this context, a number of considerations were evaluated by policymakers.

First, agriculture in India traditionally exhibited persistent, large inter-state differences in productivity levels across all crops. Such inter-state variations needed to be bridged quickly. Second, the expeditious creation of irrigation potential on so far un-irrigated lands and the holistic development of extensive rain-fed areas needed focus. Third, further opening up of agricultural product markets through removal of controls and regulations, such as those imposed on inter-state movement, exports, trade and storage, would empower farmers to realise more remunerative and profitable returns on their produce. To minimise price volatility in agricultural products, futures trading in specific commodities would need to be pursued vigorously. Further, agricultural products accounting for nearly 20.0 per cent of total exports would warrant a special thrust in overall export promotion efforts.

The long-term capital required for funding large and medium irrigation schemes and rural infrastructure had to flow from increased budgetary outlays at both the central and state levels. Further, the system of subsidising agricultural inputs required restructuring so that direct investment in productive assets, particularly in irrigation, power and rural roads could increase. Institutional credit agencies were required to support land improvement, irrigation projects and farm mechanisation on a larger scale. Commercial banks, on their part, had to meet the lending targets set for agriculture to help promote balanced development of all major sectors of the economy.

Regional imbalances in agriculture were a source of concern. Since rural lending was essentially risk-prone, the availability of finance and application of technology had to go hand-in-hand, and supplementing agricultural income by non-farm and farm-related activities was particularly important.

Environmental degradation reflected in the diminution of tree cover, growing scarcity of non-commercial energy resources and soil erosion received increasing attention during the 1990s. There was a need for developing better land use policies, encouraging social forestry and developing waste lands. The involvement of rural credit institutions in such activities was minimal. While a major part of these programmes was to be financed through budgetary resources, it was necessary for rural credit institutions to identify and support the projects that were bankable.

The lack of adequate marketing facilities was a major constraint in the rural economy, although over the years, roads and transportation facilities, public procurement and distribution systems, particularly for food grains and co-operative marketing for select produce, had shown marked improvement. However, the growth of agro industries and other non-farm activities required further strengthening of the linkages in production and marketing. It was, therefore, felt that the role of private trading and the services sector required special emphasis and consequently, the involvement of credit agencies with trade and marketing finance should increase.

Low credit-deposit ratios persisted in several regions, despite the efforts of the commercial banking sector. Areas that generated large deposits did not always have a correspondingly high credit demand. The high incidence of loan repayment defaults was also a constraint on lending. While bankers were prepared to lend, the low credit absorption capacity of deficient regions was a major handicap. This was an area of concern for policymakers.

Although the concern of the Government and the Reserve Bank to alleviate poverty was reflected in the policies, plans and their execution involving the banking system in the early 1990s, there was also a visible shift in their approach in the late 1990s when the need to run the banking system along professional lines was felt to ensure its viability and sustenance. The inadequacy of loan recovery continued to afflict the rural credit institutions, and the policy initiatives to make these institutions self-financing did not succeed. Their operational problems got aggravated, despite the increasing stability of agricultural production. The loan repayment record of large borrowers was particularly unsatisfactory. The question of the viability of institutions engaged in rural lending and related issues about their costs and the price of loans continued to receive the attention of the Reserve Bank and the Government.

FOLLOW-UP TO THE AGRICULTURAL CREDIT REVIEW COMMITTEE

Under the administered interest rate structure, the increase in lending at concessional rates and high reserve requirements had put considerable pressure on the operational efficiency of banks. The agricultural credit review committee (ACRC)[4] took the view that the lending rates were generally un-remunerative for credit institutions, especially the RRBs and co-operative credit institutions, and suggested that in the agricultural sector there should be two rates, *i.e.*, a concessional rate for small and marginal farmers and a general rate for others. The report also dealt with greater autonomy to banks in financing anti-poverty programmes, interest rates on agricultural advances, merger of RRBs with sponsor banks and setting-up a National Co-operative Bank of India (NCBI), Agricultural and Rural Development Corporations for the eastern and north-eastern regions and establishing a Crop Insurance Corporation (CIC). These were examined by the Reserve Bank and the issues were brought to the Government's notice through a communication dated April 28, 1990.

On the issue of autonomy of banks in financing anti–poverty programmes, the Reserve Bank agreed with the committee's recommendations and stated that there should be no upward revision in the targets set for such programmes. On interest rates, costs and margins, the Reserve Bank was of the view that the concessionality in the rate of interest should be extended to all small borrowers and the rate of interest on agricultural advances be raised to improve the viability of lending operations. The World Bank staff, while holding discussions on the committee's report with the Reserve Bank and NABARD in December 1989, also seemed to take this view, although they had reservations on some rates, which they felt were far below the market rates and might result in excessive demand and diversion of credit to unproductive purposes. The

---

4. The recommendations of the agricultural credit review committee (Chairman: Dr A.M. Khusro) have been dealt with in detail in chapter 8: Rural Credit Policy and in Appendix 8.1.

Reserve Bank, however, felt that the World Bank's reservations could be substantially overcome if the concessional rate was fixed at 11.5 per cent as per the committee's recommendations. The Reserve Bank also felt that the proposed interest rate structure would reduce, to some extent, the losses suffered by banks in their lending to weaker sections.

On the recommended scrapping of the DRI scheme, the Reserve Bank was agreeable to accepting it because the banks sustained a loss of ₹ 50 crore per annum on their DRI loans and the scheme had outlived its utility. The Reserve Bank was of the view that the beneficiaries eligible under the DRI scheme could be assisted under the IRDP in rural areas and the self-employment programme for urban poor (SEPUP) in other areas. On the recommendation of the committee to merge RRBs with their sponsor banks, the Reserve Bank was in agreement and opined that although the initial cost to commercial banks would increase as a result of the merger, the quality of operations would improve and the sponsor banks would be able to provide a measure of cross-subsidisation. The Reserve Bank, however, did not favour setting-up of an NCBI or ARDCs, in light of the fact that multiplicity of administrative agencies for discharging development functions could lead to an overlap. The Reserve Bank was apparently also not enthusiastic about the Government's proposal to merge all RRBs into a National Rural Bank of India (NRBI), since RRBs had continued to be non-viable.

Of the 196 RRBs, only 44 banks were able to achieve marginal profits, while 152 banks registered losses amounting to ₹ 550 crore and 134 banks suffered erosion in their deposits. The weakness of RRBs was further accentuated by the increase in pay and allowances of their employees on par with those of sponsor banks in terms of the award of the national industrial tribunal (NIT). On account of the NIT award, the pay and allowances of RRB employees were to increase by 60.0 to 65.0 per cent during 1993–94.

PROPOSAL FOR A NATIONAL CO-OPERATIVE BANK OF INDIA

The proposal to set up a NCBI was submitted to the Government and the Reserve Bank by the promoters of the bank. The principal objective envisaged for the NCBI was to function as a central financing agency for its constituents that would: (i) operate as a national balancing centre and spokesperson of the co-operative banking and finance system; (ii) act as a receptacle for surplus resources of the state systems; and (iii) deploy these and other resources through consortium and other arrangements. This was expected to provide systemic strength to the co-operative credit structure in the country. The proposal and the viability of the proposed bank were examined and a committee of the Deputy Governors also held detailed discussions with the promoters of the NCBI in September 1991.

It was observed that the main resources of the NCBI were to be raised through investment of 50.0 per cent of statutory liquidity ratio (SLR) of the state co-operative banks to be kept with it. The SLR consisted of investments in government and other approved securities and there was no reason to believe that the state co-operative banks would divert these resources to the NCBI. Apart from this, such banks would hardly have surplus resources to invest in the NCBI. Their reserve fund and other funds were locked up and, even if some state co-operative banks and larger co-operative organisations had funds to spare, it was likely that they would seek investment avenues that could fetch much higher returns than the 12.0 per cent that the proposed NCBI would offer. The promoters had also assumed that in due course ₹ 80 crore would be available from the state co-operative banks and ₹ 30 crore from other larger co-operative institutions. It was felt that these resources may or may not be available and such funds, therefore, could not form a firm resource base and would fetch the NCBI very little margin, if most of the return had to be passed on to the state co-operative banks and other organisations.

The Reserve Bank took the view that the proposed NCBI without the state co-operative banks investing 50.0 per cent of their SLR with it would not be a viable organisation, far less than the one with a strong resource base of its own that was worthy of a national bank. Another point made by the promoters was that the NCBI would bridge a systemic gap caused by the absence of a national-level institution. On examining the issue, which was also brought out in the ACRC report, it was observed that there was no significant systemic gap and certainly not any as to warrant the establishment of another bank. The Reserve Bank did not, therefore, accept the proposal for setting-up of an NCBI on the following grounds:

(i)   The so-called surplus resources of the state co-operative banks seemed to be illusory. The state co-operative banks that had surpluses were already participating in a food credit consortium and other consortia that were financing IFFCO and KRIBHCO.[5]

---

5. IFFCO: Indian Farmers Fertiliser Co-operative Ltd; KRIBHCO: Krishak Bharati Co-operative Ltd.

(ii) SLR and reserve funds were invested in an approved manner, and diverting these investments from government securities and re-routing them through another institution might not add substantially to the aggregate resources available to the system.

(iii) NABARD as the apex development bank had been providing financial assistance and taking several policy initiatives as per national priorities and programmes.

(iv) Regarding co-ordination and the need for a spokesperson of the co-operative movement at the national level, the existing federation of state co-operative banks and SLDBs could adequately serve the purpose.

PROPOSAL FOR A NATIONAL RURAL BANK OF INDIA

The salient features of the proposal for the NRBI included: (i) The NRBI was to be formed either as a company incorporated under the Companies Act as a subsidiary of NABARD or as a corporation through an Act of Parliament with a share capital of ₹ 200 crore, which would be contributed by NABARD (76.0 per cent) and employees of NRBI (24.0 per cent). (ii) To ensure its long-term viability, the NRBI would be allowed to finance 40.0 per cent of its incremental advances to non-target group borrowers in addition to part of the resources being deployed in 'corporate advances', *i.e.*, consortium lending such as agri-business consortium and food consortium. (iii) The staff of RRBs would be transferred to the NRBI. The deputed staff (from the sponsor banks) would continue for some time. (iv) To enable the NRBI to start on a clean slate, the accumulated losses (₹ 550 crore) and national industrial tribunal (NIT) award arrears (₹ 220 crore) would have to be neutralised. The proposal envisaged a write-off of sponsor bank refinance (₹ 367 crore), payment of ₹ 1 per RRB as nominal compensation to existing shareholders and meeting the balance of loss from new equity of NRBI. (v) In addition to the refinance from NABARD, the resource requirement of NRBI would be supplemented by:

(i) PSBs placing 10.0 per cent of their incremental rural deposits with the NRBI at the Bank Rate. This will be about ₹ 500 crore per annum.

(ii) Foreign banks and private sector banks transferring around ₹ 300 crore and ₹ 180 crore, respectively, annually to NRBI at the Bank Rate to cover the shortfall under their priority sector lending.

(iii) An annual contribution of ₹ 100 crore from the national rural credit (NRC) long-term operations (LTO) fund maintained by NABARD or an outright grant from the Government.

A meeting of representatives of the Government, major sponsor banks of RRBs and NABARD was convened at the Reserve Bank on August 28, 1992 to consider this proposal. It was decided that working groups would be formed, with representatives from the Government, NABARD, Indian Banks' Association (IBA) and major sponsor banks to consider the financial and organisational aspects of the proposal. The reports submitted by the groups were examined by a steering group at its meeting on September 21, 1992. The steering group, *inter alia*, highlighted the following points:

(i) NRBI should comply with capital adequacy norms. The issue and paid-up capital should be enlarged to ₹ 50 crore and should be held by the Government, NABARD, financial institutions (FIs)/PSBs and RRB employees in the proportion of 51: 25: 15:9, respectively.

(ii) In order that the new bank started on a clean slate, in addition to the losses at ₹ 550 crore worked out with reference to March 1992 working results, additional losses of RRBs during 1992–93 estimated at ₹ 300 crore would also have to be neutralised or made good by the Government in addition to the NIT award arrears estimated at ₹ 220 crore and bad debts of about ₹ 198 crore.

(iii) To enable NRBI to increase its corporate lending, SLR requirement could be reduced from 25.0 per cent to 20.0 per cent.

(iv) Regarding the organisational structure, it was felt that the head office of the NRBI should be either in Pune or Hyderabad and it should function through 15 zonal offices. The head offices of RRBs would function as the regional offices of the NRBI, with necessary adjustments regarding the number of branches under the control of each regional office. The group also recommended that the existing staff of sponsor banks should continue with the NRBI on deputation. If a prima facie view was taken to establish the NRBI, both the working groups and the steering group felt that it would be necessary to study various preparatory measures such as organisational/administrative set up, systems and procedures, motivational and work norms, legal aspects and financial structure and viability.

The viability of the NRBI was worked out on certain assumptions such as: a minimum lending rate of 13.5 per cent, as against the 11.5 per cent being charged earlier, NABARD to provide a return of 17.5 per cent on SLR deposits of the NRBI, provisioning for bad debts at an aggregate of 2.5 per cent only and availability of refinance from the Reserve Bank through a general line of credit (GLC). The steering group had expressed apprehensions about the realisation of these assumptions. It was concluded that the NRBI would not be viable.

APPROACH OF THE NARASIMHAM COMMITTEE

The Narasimham Committee made some strong recommendations on agricultural credit extended by the banking system. The committee felt that the institutional credit to the agricultural sector purveyed by commercial banks, co-operatives and RRBs was afflicted by the overdues syndrome that had over a period of time debilitated the process of recycling of funds. The implementation of the agricultural and rural debt relief scheme (ARDRS), 1990 further accentuated the problem of recovery and, with co-operative credit societies not being able to mobilise adequate deposits to meet credit needs, implied greater recourse to refinance from NABARD/ the Reserve Bank. This coupled with the fact that the rates of interest stipulated for agricultural advances were not only non-remunerative but also did not cover the cost of funds and other expenses incurred by the credit institutions, eroded their profitability.

While directed credit programmes played a useful role in extending the reach of the banking system to cover neglected sectors, there was a need to re-examine their continued relevance, at least with respect to sectors that did not require access to directed credit and, more so, at concessional rates. Accordingly, the committee recommended that the directed credit programmes be phased out. From the objective of redistributive justice, the committee opined that the instrument of the fiscal system rather than the credit system be used. The committee recommended that the priority sector could be redefined to comprise small and marginal farmers, tiny sector of industry, small business and transport operators, village and cottage industries, rural artisans and other weaker sections, and the credit target for this redefined priority sector should be fixed at 10.0 per cent of aggregate credit. To ensure the flow of credit to sectors excluded from the redefined priority sector, the committee recommended the introduction of a refinance facility from the Reserve Bank.

A detailed assessment by the Reserve Bank indicated that credit to the redefined priority sector would account for significantly more than 10.0 per cent of total advances. Hence, acceptance of the committee's recommendation would put a severe squeeze on the sectors within the redefined priority sector. For instance, if advances for farm mechanisation, advances over ₹ 10 lakh to small scale industries (SSIs), advances over ₹ 5 lakh to small road and water transport operators and advances to professional and self-employed persons were excluded from the priority sector, the ratio of the redefined priority sector advances to net bank credit as at the end of March 1990 would work out to a little less than 30.0 per cent. If advances over ₹ 2 lakh to agriculture, SSIs and transport operators and all advances to professional and self-employed persons were excluded from the priority sector, the ratio of residual advances to net bank credit would work out to 25.0 per cent.

There was little merit in drastically reducing the target for the priority sector and then meeting the requirements of these sectors through refinance from the Reserve Bank, as this would increase the amount of created money, thereby fuelling inflationary pressures. From a pragmatic viewpoint, it was essential to ensure that any change in the policy on priority sector credit did not disrupt the flow of credit for productive purposes. The stipulations on reserve requirements had implications for the actual credit available for priority sector lending. The incremental reserve requirements were reduced from 63.5 per cent in 1991–92 to 45.0 per cent in the first half of 1992–93 and further to an effective requirement of 25.0 per cent in the second half of 1992–93 (after adjusting for the release of SLR/CRR). For example, on the basis of the effective reserve requirements for the second half of 1992–93, an incremental priority sector allocation of, say, 30.0 per cent would imply that 22.5 per cent of banks' incremental deposits would be available for the priority sector. Similarly, 40.0 per cent allocation in 1991–92 implied an allocation of 14.6 per cent of incremental deposits to the priority sector.

It was, therefore, decided to continue with the existing targets for priority sector lending. Concessional finance was, however, limited to small loans below ₹ 2 lakh and for DRI advances. For advances above ₹ 2 lakh, banks were free to charge interest rates linked to the prime lending rate (PLR). The scope of priority sector lending was enlarged to include finance to state industrial development corporations (SIDCs)/ state finance corporations (SFCs), refinance to RRBs by sponsor banks and investments in bonds issued by certain specified institutions.

From a pragmatic viewpoint, it was felt that there was a case for reviewing the coverage and targets for priority sector lending. Once the micro-regulation of credit delivery was given up and banks were given freedom in matters relating to credit, the discipline of priority sector lending and the flow of credit to the needy and deserving on a timely basis could get neglected. The activities eligible for priority sector lending should, therefore, be enlarged. With interest rates deregulated and alternative avenues of investment permitted, priority sector lending would become far more flexible.

The Reserve Bank kept the overall stipulation of priority sector lending at 40.0 per cent of net bank credit and the sub-target at 10.0 per cent of net bank credit for weaker sections unchanged. However, some changes were effected in the composition of such lending. It was decided to club 'direct' and 'indirect' categories of advances for agriculture within the sub-target of 18.0 per cent for agricultural lending as a whole, subject to the stipulation that the 'indirect' category should not exceed one-fourth of the sub-target of 18.0 per cent, *i.e.*, 4.5 per cent of net bank credit. Indirect agricultural advances exceeding 4.5 per cent would, however, be reckoned as part of the overall priority sector lending while evaluating the bank's performance against the target of 40.0 per cent. With the revision in the definition of SSIs, it was decided to treat all advances granted to SSIs with investment in plant and machinery up to ₹ 60 lakh (₹ 75 lakh in the case of ancillary units and export-oriented units) as priority sector advances. In order to ensure adequate flow of credit to smaller units, it was decided that each bank should deploy at least 40.0 per cent of total credit to SSIs to cottage industries, *khadi* and village industries, artisans and tiny industries with investment in plant and machinery up to ₹ 5 lakh and other SSI units availing of credit limits up to ₹ 5 lakh.

INTEGRATED RURAL DEVELOPMENT PROGRAMME AND RELATED SCHEMES

The recovery performance of PSBs in respect of IRDP loans had been deteriorating over the years. The cumbersome lending procedures, inadequate supervision and, at times, the apathy of bank staff resulted in delayed and untimely credit, which was responsible for large-scale misutilistion and default of credit. Generally, the recovery to demand ratio with regard to these poverty alleviation programmes was very low. The recovery under IRDP was below 30.0 per cent. There were several reasons for the low recovery performance of the banks. Evaluation studies of the IRDP in particular revealed that the main reasons were incorrect identification of beneficiaries and activities, inadequate availability of proper infrastructure and lack of adequate marketing facilities. Several studies indicated that the percentage of beneficiaries of IRDP who might have crossed the poverty line was around 20.0 per cent. The 'target-oriented' approach had also compromised the quality of the programmes. Misutilisation of funds through diversion or non-creation of assets and selection of activities for financing without proper reference to their viability had also been observed.

MEHTA COMMITTEE

Several modifications were made in the IRDP to take care of some of these deficiencies. The Reserve Bank constituted a committee on September 29, 1993 (Chairman: Shri D.R. Mehta) to review the progress of the IRDP and recommend measures for its improvement. The terms of reference of the committee were: (i) to review the procedure for identification of beneficiaries under IRDP and suggest changes to ensure proper identification; (ii) to review the existing system of sponsoring loan applications; (iii) to examine the adequacy of forward and backward linkages, and the role of government agencies; (iv) to examine the procedure for sanction of loans by banks and suggest improvements to ensure timely and adequate credit; (v) to examine the causes of poor recovery and suggest measures for its improvement; and (vi) to examine the procedure for disbursement of subsidy under IRDP, i.e., a switch from front-end subsidy to back-end subsidy.

The expert committee in its report suggested far-reaching changes to make the IRDP more effective. The most significant recommendation of the committee was that since all the poor were not alike, they should be segmented into two categories. The category of extremely poor, with no experience in handling assets and who lacked skills should be helped initially through wage employment schemes. The other class of poor who were below the poverty line but slightly better-off and had skills and experience in handling assets could be put on the self-employment route under the IRDP. The other recommendations of the committee, inter alia, included: (i) a switch from a front-end to a back-end system of subsidy to avoid misutilisation of funds; (ii) linking a percentage of subsidy allocation to recovery performance; (iii) enhancing both the loan and the subsidy provided under IRDP; (iv) making a provision to extend credit for acquiring land or meeting working capital requirements; and (v) associating voluntary organisations and SHGs with the implementation of the IRDP. The recommendations of the committee were examined by the Government and the Reserve Bank.

Most of the recommendations were implemented. Further, the Government accepted the recommendation for a switch from a front-end subsidy to a back-end system of subsidy. The important measures undertaken in pursuance of the recommendations included the following: banks would provide loans to IRDP beneficiaries to acquire land; short-term credit to meet current farm expenditure and working capital requirements would be taken into account while sanctioning loans to IRDP beneficiaries; suitable cash credit limits would be sanctioned along with term loans; and the cash disbursement system might be extended throughout the country. The purchase committees where the cash disbursement system was in vogue were dispensed with. The repayment schedule was made realistic after giving due weight to the level of income generation and economic life of the assets and the minimum repayment period for an IRDP loan was raised from three years to five years. Initial moratorium was also provided, where required.

The banks would provide group loans for various activities under the IRDP, including assistance for infrastructure. The security required and the rate of interest on such loans would, however, be related to the per capita quantum of loan. Further, the Government decided to allow a subsidy of up to ₹ 1.25 lakh or 50.0 per cent of the project cost, whichever was lower, to a group of a minimum of five members belonging to below poverty line (BPL) families. The banks would provide a second dose of assistance to IRDP beneficiaries who could not cross the poverty line in the first instance and had not been in default. In 1994–95, banks assisted 22 lakh beneficiaries, of which 11 lakh beneficiaries belonged to SCs/STs and 7 lakh were women.

The Government abolished the cut-off point for IRDP assistance whereby any family with an income below the poverty line of ₹ 11,000 per annum would be eligible for assistance under IRDP, subject to fulfilling other pre-requisites such as motivation, entrepreneurial skill and aptitude. From 1995–96, the Government fixed credit targets rather than physical targets for the states/union territories (UTs) under IRDP.

The recovery performance of IRDP loans was generally poor, except for the year 1991 when loans were waived under the ARDRS and showed higher recovery. The advances from commercial banks under IRDP showed a decline during the 1990s. These advances, which grew steadily during the 1980s, reached a peak of ₹ 3,142 crore in 1987, and thereafter gradually declined to ₹ 1,112 crore in 1998.

CHANGE OF APPROACH IN INTENSIFYING RURAL CREDIT UNDER THE SERVICE AREA APPROACH

After the SSA scheme was introduced, the Reserve Bank advised banks in August 1993 to evaluate its impact at the grassroots level, identify operational difficulties and suggest ways to overcome the same. It was found that the SAA was generally acceptable with some modifications. The salient features of the modified SAA were: (i) block-wise grouping of service area branches without disturbing their service area identities; (ii) opening of mobile or satellite offices in large service areas; (iii) enlarging the area of operations of specialised branches to optimise their infrastructure facilities; (iv) re-aligning scattered service areas; (v) exempting large projects that covered several states or districts from SAA; and (vi) freeing RRBs with disbursals of less than ₹ 2 crore during 1992–93 from their service area obligations. However, the remaining RRBs were allowed to operate within the entire command areas (districts), subject to the obligation of extending financial assistance in their respective service areas.

To make the approach more effective, specific steps were taken during 1994–95: (i) commercial banks' designated branches were required to extend financial assistance to beneficiaries under the IRDP and priority sector up to March 31, 1996 wherever RRBs were unable to meet their obligations; (ii) the decision about whether or not a particular RRB was capable of meeting the obligation in disbursal of credit was to be taken by the concerned district consultative committee (DCC); (iii) RRBs that had branches in more than one district should convey decisions regarding their inability to meet the credit obligation to the Reserve Bank which, in turn, would identify designated branches of the commercial bank to meet their requirements; (iv) the unachievable IRDP targets of RRBs that were unable to meet their disbursal obligations should be included in the annual credit plans (ACPs) of the designated branches of the commercial bank.

The Reserve Bank made the reporting system more effective and useful under the service area monitoring and information system (SAMIS) by persuading banks to regularly submit their lead bank returns (LBRs). A provision was introduced in the returns for details on the advances to women beneficiaries. Besides, the designated branches of commercial banks would continue to extend financial assistance to beneficiaries under the IRDP and priority sector lending until end-March 1997 wherever RRBs were unable to meet their obligations of credit disbursal.

The essence of credit planning under the SAA was the thrust given to integrated development through full exploitation of the available resources and skills that could be created in the assigned area. Although government-sponsored programmes like the IRDP, self-employment scheme for educated unemployed youth (SEEUY) and state-level special programmes continued to dominate branch credit plans, it was reiterated that if the ultimate objective of SAA was to be achieved, bankers should convince the collaborative agencies in the Government about the imperative need to build the portfolio of productive programmes and projects for the target group beneficiaries instead of merely aiming at fulfilling numerical targets.

Besides the poverty alleviation and other government programmes, it was suggested that SAA should consciously plan and achieve channelling of credit for diversification of the rural economy. The Eighth Five Year Plan attached greater importance to market-oriented commercial agriculture. Horticulture, production of oilseeds and pulses, dry land farming and processing and marketing systems were envisaged to be upgraded and encouraged with a view to secure benefits of value addition for the farming community. Further, the pace of rural industrialisation was required to be accelerated to reduce growing unemployment in rural areas. The qualitative change in rural development should get reflected in the SAA and in the performance budget of the banks, it was proposed.

The lending programme of co-operatives had to be aligned with the service area plans prepared by commercial banks/RRB branches. Commercial banks should not ignore the lending programmes of co-operatives while preparing their credit plans, but should take into consideration the co-operatives' longer history of lending in rural areas, their familiarity with the rural environment and their volume of credit through both crop loans and term loans for agriculture and allied activities.

Major expectations from the decentralised credit planning through SAA included: organised and planned mobilisation of resources based on continuous assessment of potential in a homogeneous and compact area; eliminating the diffusion of resources and duplication of efforts by delineating the command area for each rural and semi-urban branch of a commercial bank including the RRB; integrating the role of co-operatives, RRBs and commercial banks in the delivery of credit by preparing a credit plan for each service area with the objective of better productivity in diversified economic activities and enlargement of rural income on a durable basis; close monitoring of the end-use of credit and assessment of its impact on production and income levels; and securing commitment, motivation and empathy for the rural community among the rural bankers on one hand and effective co-ordination with the other developmental agencies at the field level on the other. The SAA was expected to lead to better quality of lending in terms of higher productivity, income and, above all, efficient recycling of credit.[6]

OTHER WELFARE-ORIENTED PROGRAMMES

The Government and the Reserve Bank made several attempts to mitigate poverty and to create employment opportunities using the banking system in the 1990s through several programmes under the priority sector, which included: advances to weaker sections and special assistance programmes, the DRI, the Prime Minister's rozgar yojana for educated unemployed youth (PMRY), the scheme for urban micro-enterprises (SUME), SEEUY, Nehru rozgar yojana (NRY), urban basic services for the poor (UBSP) and the Prime Minister's integrated urban poverty eradication programme (PMIUPEP). These programmes were intensified/introduced, but they could not make much headway.

While presenting the budget for 1990–91, the Union Finance Minister observed that the economy's first priority was to create employment opportunities. In the 1980s, the economy grew at around 5.0 per cent. The employment statistics, however, presented a dismal picture. According to a report of the National Sample Survey Organisation (NSSO), the number of persons chronically unemployed increased from 8 million in 1983 to 12 million in 1987–88. Further, a vast number of persons were underemployed and their earnings fell well short of a decent minimum. In this context, the Finance Minister emphasised:

> Every citizen has the right to productive and gainful work in order to live meaningfully and with dignity. We would like to introduce an Employment Guarantee Scheme. However, the cost of doing so in all parts of the country are huge, and we do not have the necessary resources at this juncture. Nevertheless, it is proposed to make a beginning on an Employment Guarantee Scheme for the drought-prone areas and areas with an acute problem of rural unemployment. The allocation for the employment schemes of the Department of Rural Development will be supplemented, to the extent feasible, during the course of the year.

---

6. Malhotra, R.N. (1990). *Service Area Approach.* Valedictory Address at Trainers' Training Programme in Service Area Approach. Bombay: NABARD. August 18.

A new scheme was proposed in the Union Budget, 1995–96 to meet the credit needs of STs in predominantly tribal districts, for which NABARD would open an exclusive short-term seasonal agricultural operations (SAO) line of credit for central co-operative banks (CCBs) and RRBs. A sum of ₹ 400 crore was earmarked for this purpose during 1995–96. NABARD also earmarked ₹ 150 crore to provide refinance to commercial and co-operative banks for the development of SCs and STs, which was raised to 100.0 per cent from the earlier limit of 90.0–95.0 per cent.

The swarna jayanti shahari rozgar yojana (SJSRY) came into operation in January 1997 through a restructuring and streamlining of earlier urban poverty alleviation programmes.

PREPARING EX-SERVICEMEN FOR SELF-EMPLOYMENT (PEXSEM)

The basic objective of the PEXSEM scheme was to provide technical and financial assistance to retired defence personnel settled in rural areas so as to help them take up self-employment close to their homes. Financial assistance of up to ₹ 25,000 was made available under the scheme to trained service personnel by scheduled commercial banks (SCBs). The sainik boards gave a capital and interest subsidy under the scheme. The scheme was introduced in 1992–93 in certain districts of the country. The coverage of the scheme for each year was decided by the Ministry of Defence, Government of India.

PRIME MINISTER'S ROZGAR YOJANA FOR EDUCATED UNEMPLOYED YOUTH

The PMRY scheme was introduced in 1993 to provide sustained self-employment in micro-enterprises to both rural and urban unemployed youth who were resident in the area for more than three years, with family income not exceeding ₹ 24,000 per annum. The scheme was extended throughout the country from April 1, 1994. The SEEUY was subsumed under this scheme in April 1994. This scheme provided for reservation of 22.5 per cent and 27.0 per cent for SCs/STs and other backward classes (OBCs), respectively. Around 30,000 applications were sanctioned against the target of 42,040 as at the end of March 1994. The target for the year 1994–95 was fixed at 2.39 lakh beneficiaries. In 1995–96, commercial banks sanctioned ₹ 1,648 crore to 2.84 lakh applicants and disbursed ₹ 1,013 crore.

SMALL SCALE INDUSTRIES

THE NAYAK COMMITTEE

SSIs accounted for nearly 40.0 per cent of the gross turnover of the manufacturing sector, 45.0 per cent of manufacturing imports and 35.0 per cent of total exports from the country. The limited access of SSIs to institutional finance was a major policy concern. A committee set up by the Reserve Bank in December 1991 to look into the credit requirements of the SSI sector (Chairman: Shri P.R. Nayak) submitted its report in September 1992. The terms of reference of the committee included: (i) examining the adequacy of institutional credit (both for working capital and term loans) to the SSI sector; (ii) the need for modifications/relaxations in the norms prescribed by the Tandon/Chore Committees for SSIs; (iii) revision, if any, required in the existing Reserve Bank guidelines for the rehabilitation of sick SSI units; and (iv) any related matters.

The committee suggested that small unregistered units with credits limits of not more than ₹ 1 lakh should have the first claim on priority sector credit to SSIs, and the new priority sector credit dispensation, when adopted, should fully provide for the working capital requirement of all tiny units with credit limits up to ₹ 10 lakh. It also recommended that the working capital needs of other SSIs at 20.0 per cent of the output should be pre-empted by commercial banks through an annual budgetary exercise and, if necessary, a part of the resources that was flowing to the medium and large industries sector should be diverted to fully meet the demands of SSIs.

While the growth in the resources of the commercial banking system during the Eighth Plan period would, in the committee's view, adequately take care of the growth in working capital requirements as also the likely extent of a resources constraint, the committee recommended that various measures might be considered, such as a part of the freed SLR being used for SSIs, funds being provided by the Central Government, or a supplementary refinance window being provided by small industries development bank of India (SIDBI)/NABARD. The committee opined that the norms for inventory and receivables (as per the Tandon Committee), which had little relevance for a vast majority of SSIs, should not come in the way of SSI units getting at least 20.0 per cent of their turnover as working capital from the banks. Further, introducing special norms for SSI units in the north-eastern and hilly regions could also be considered.

To overcome the operational difficulties of SSIs, the committee had made detailed recommendations, the more important of which related to a system of annual budgeting for working capital requirements of SSI borrowers, computerisation of information on SSI borrowers, creation of an 'Ombudsman' type of authority within the banks to look into the grievances of SSI borrowers, revitalisation of the state-level forums and setting-up district level forums to oversee and monitor credit to SSIs, particularly units that came within the norms of the single-window scheme of SIDBI.

The committee recommended a modified definition of a sick SSI unit, the creation of cells within the banks at regional centres to deal with sick SSIs, the constitution of state-level inter-institutional committees (SLIIC) and a role for a district counterpart of SLIIC in monitoring and overseeing the bank's progress in the quick determination of the viability of sick units.

Other recommendations included: (i) indexing the value of investment in plant and machinery of units to ensure uniform application of the definition of SSI; (ii) moderating the interest rates charged to tiny units; (iii) reducing the service/collection charges and overdue interest charged by bank on the bills of their SSI clientele; (iv) abolishing the system of levying the DICGC credit guarantee fee separately for SSI borrowers; (v) creating a separate modernisation fund for SSIs; and (vi) setting-up factoring organisations in all parts of the country and allowing the private sector to enter this field. The implementation of the recommendations of the committee on financing SSI was monitored by the Reserve Bank by conducting sample studies. Besides, banks themselves were carrying out special studies on an annual basis and the Reserve Bank was kept informed of the findings and the steps taken to rectify the deficiencies in credit disbursal to SSIs.

MICRO-FINANCE MOVEMENT

In the past, several deficiencies had crept into the formal rural credit system, *viz.*, poor recovery of loans, high transaction costs in dealing with small borrowers at frequent intervals and the burden of subsidised interest rates. These had weakened the rural credit delivery system. Despite the Government's efforts to reach millions of poor through a variety of programmes for the priority sector, the reach of these programmes to the poorest of the poor was limited. Thus began the search for an alternative delivery mechanism that would meet the requirements of the poor, especially the women members of such households. It was then that the idea of organising SHGs began to take shape. An SHG is a group of about

10–20 persons from a homogeneous class (affinity group) who come together to address common problems. They collect voluntary savings on a regular basis and use the pooled resources to make small interest-bearing loans to their members. The process helps them imbibe the essentials of financial intermediation, including prioritisation of needs, setting terms and conditions and keeping accounts.[7]

The system of micro-finance offered as a viable alternative, following the example of the success of *grameen* banks created by Prof Muhammad Yunus in Bangladesh. Explaining the rationale behind the policy decision, Dr C. Rangarajan,[8] subsequently illustrated that despite the expansion of the organised banking system deep into rural areas, a very large number of the poor continued to remain outside the fold of the formal banking system. The extant banking policies, systems and procedures were not suited to enable the poor to approach the formal system.

The beginning of the micro-finance movement in India can be traced to the SHG- bank linkage programme, which was started as a pilot project in 1992 by NABARD in co-ordination with the Reserve Bank. The Reserve Bank provided policy support by advising banks to actively participate in the programme. In 1994, the Reserve Bank constituted a working group on NGOs and SHGs. On the recommendations of the group, the Bank advised that the financing of SHGs by banks would be reckoned as part of their lending to weaker sections, and that such lending should be reviewed by banks as well as the state-level bankers' committee (SLBC) at regular intervals. As a follow-up to the recommendations of another working group constituted by NABARD, the Reserve Bank took a series of measures in April 1996 to give a thrust to microfinance-based lending.

WORKING GROUP ON NGOs AND SHGs

The working group on NGOs and SHGs set up by the Reserve Bank in 1994 put forward a set of wide-ranging recommendations on SHGs and bank linkage as a potential innovation in the area of banking with the poor. In widening the credit delivery system, banks could extend credit to SHGs, NGOs and other intermediaries. Such organisations, in turn, could help identify and meet the genuine credit requirements of the rural

7. Chakrabarty, K.C. (2011). "Technology and the Financial Inclusion Imperative in India", in Sameer Kochhar (ed.), *Growth and Finance: Essays in Honour of C. Rangarajan.* New Delhi: Academic Foundation.

8. Rangarajan, C. (2005). "Microfinance: The Road Ahead". Inaugural Address at *The International Conference on Microfinance in India* organised by CARE. New Delhi. April 12.

poor. Attempts at rationalising the system of credit delivery had to be supplemented by a revamped system of credit recovery without which the rural credit system could not be sustained. While improving the recovery mechanisms, commercial banks, RRBs and co-operatives could consider appointing 'recovery facilitators', drawn locally, to help improve loan collections.

A systematic reform of rural credit had to aim at innovation and development consistent with the principles of efficiency and viability. Several factors continued to impede the ongoing efforts aimed at creating an efficient and viable rural credit delivery system. Overdues remained high. As a consequence, recycling of credit became a major casualty and the losers were prospective borrowers. Institutional reach to small and marginal farmers was not on the expected lines. There were complaints of inadequate and untimely credit availability on one hand and misutilisation of credit and defaults on the other. Any programme of rural credit reform needed an emphasis on: (i) institutional strengthening; (ii) appropriate changes in the policy framework; and (iii) mobilisation of larger financial resources. The existing multi-agency institutional structure had to continue, given the different stages of development of the institutions across the country in various states.

The three agencies involved in rural credit — rural branches of commercial banks, RRBs and the co-operative credit system — had, therefore, to be streamlined and strengthened so that they could become efficient disbursers and purveyors of credit. The Reserve Bank advised commercial banks to formulate specific plans for increasing their deployment in the agricultural sector and to ensure that lending to agriculture was considerably stepped up. The modifications in the SAA helped the banks in this direction. To ensure adequate and timely flow of rural credit, as also to meet the composite needs of farmers, the Reserve Bank allowed banks to extend cash credit facilities to farmers with irrigation resources for farming and to other farmers for undertaking non-farm/allied activities.

Banks were also asked to help farmers diversify into new areas, such as horticulture and floriculture, where the demand was more elastic than that of food grains. The early processing of the recommendations made by the expert committee on the IRDP, especially those dealing with issues such as procedures for selection of beneficiaries, mode of subsidy payment and effective recovery mechanisms, helped to bring about much needed change in the approach of the banks while lending under such programmes.

The Reserve Bank constituted another working group (Chairman: Shri S.K. Kalia) in 1996 to study the functioning of SHGs and NGOs with a view to expanding their activities and deepening their role in the rural sector. The recommendations of the working group were accepted by the Reserve Bank and the banks were advised to implement these as soon as possible.

IMPACT OF MICRO-FINANCE

Given that the poor, both in the rural and urban areas, did not have the necessary capabilities to approach and negotiate with organised credit institutions; the linking of formal credit institutions with the rural and urban poor through intermediaries, such as NGOs, was thought of as an alternative mechanism to meet the credit needs of the poor. The establishment of SHGs could be traced to the existence of one or more common problems around which the consciousness of the rural poor was built. The group, thus, was normally a response to a perceived need, besides being centred around specific productive activities. These groups also promoted savings among their members and used pooled resources to meet the needs of their constituents. It was felt that initiating and monitoring the credit programmes could be made more effective and less costly if banks made attempts to organise the poor into SHGs, whereby peer pressure could be used to ensure proper utilisation of credit and prompt repayment of loans. Apart from the powerful influence of peer pressure, the groups could also contribute towards improving the quality of lending by offering loans in a prompt and simple manner, ensuring extending only need-based loans and keeping the loan size within the repaying capacity of the borrowers.

The main advantage to the banks of the link with SHGs and NGOs was externalisation of a part of the work items of the credit cycle, *viz.*, assessment of credit needs, appraisal, disbursal, supervision and repayment, reduction in the formal paper work involved and a consequent reduction in the transaction costs. Improvements in recoveries led to wider coverage of the target group. A larger mobilisation of small savings was equally advantageous. The link was also useful to the groups due to access to larger quantum of resources compared with their meagre corpus generated through thrift, availability of better technology and skill upgrading through different schemes of the banking sector.

The role of voluntary organisations was somewhat distinct from SHGs. The NGOs had a role in organising the rural poor into SHGs and in ensuring their proper functioning. In the Indian context, NGOs focused on their activities in the areas of education and health and, to some extent, development in general. Their role in providing an effective link between organised credit disbursing agencies and those who had the need and were eligible to obtain credit from such institutions had been minimal. A fairly large number of programmes were formulated, which aimed at providing credit to the poor. Their effective utilisation by eligible borrowers could have been enhanced had the NGOs gained the necessary institutional strength to forge linkages with the formal credit agencies and reached out to the poor for their credit needs. Their mediatory role could go beyond facilitating securing credit and monitoring its effective use and recovery. The improvement in the recovery performance increased the credibility of these poverty alleviation programmes and resulted in effective recycling of credit.

Studies and surveys suggested that NGOs had a comparative advantage in making transfers to the poor because they had local contacts and consequently better information about the poor. Further, they could help reduce the leakage in delivery of benefits that resulted from the inefficiencies of the formal financial institutions. Additionally, the group dynamics and peer pressure could bring in excellent recovery from the members of SHGs.

THE RESERVE BANK, NABARD AND RURAL FINANCE

The resources of NABARD consisted mainly of NRC funds, capital, reserves, deposits and borrowings. In addition, the Government provided funds received from the World Bank and other external agencies under various credit projects supported by these agencies. With the contribution of ₹ 10 crore each from the Government and the Reserve Bank, the paid-up capital of NABARD increased from ₹ 100 crore to ₹ 120 crore during 1993–94. NABARD mobilised ₹ 78 crore through market borrowings by the issue of the 'thirteenth series of NABARD bonds' (at par) that had a maturity period of 10 years and carried an interest rate of 13.5 per cent per annum. NABARD revised the rates of interest on its refinance with effect from March 1, 1994, which would be applicable to all fresh lending/disbursements by banks. The interest rates prescribed for refinance were mostly specific rather than linked to the Bank Rate.

NABARD continued its efforts to identify thrust areas and priorities for credit support. The major thrust areas identified, *inter alia*, were minor irrigation, plantation and horticulture, post-harvest technology, tissue culture, export-oriented projects, agro-processing, dry land farming, wasteland development, forestry, fisheries and non-farm activities. For remunerative development of the resources of state co-operative banks and CCBs, NABARD decided to liberalise the norms for financing individuals by the banks. The facilities extended for the purpose included: (i) raising the maximum ceiling for loans against gold ornaments/jewellery per individual to ₹ 40,000; (ii) raising the ceiling for loans for purchase of consumer durables from ₹ 25,000 to ₹ 30,000; and (iii) sanction of cash credit facility to businessmen/traders against a collateral, pledge or hypothecation of stock-in-trade up to ₹ 2 lakh.

In terms of section 46 of the Reserve Bank of India (RBI) Act, 1934, the Bank was required to contribute every year such sums of money as it might consider necessary and feasible to the NRC (LTO) fund and NRC (stabilisation) [S] fund, which were maintained by NABARD. Accordingly, the Bank was contributing to the above funds every year before passing on the net surplus to the Government. These contributions were by way of grants to augment the resources of NABARD. The Reserve Bank's contribution to these funds at ₹ 4,780 crore formed 64.0 per cent of the total amount of the funds at ₹ 7,415 crore. During the years 1989–90, 1990–91 and 1991–92, the Reserve Bank contributed ₹ 340 crore, ₹ 385 crore and ₹ 420 crore, respectively, to these funds.

The Union Finance Minister, in his budget speech for 1992–93, announced that the Reserve Bank would transfer a larger share of its profits to the Union Government. In pursuance thereof, the Bank took a policy decision to discontinue appropriation of large sums from its profits for credit to the four statutory funds before transferring the surplus to the Government.[9] NABARD was accordingly advised that no contribution would be made to the above two funds from 1992–93. To ensure adequate availability of funds, NABARD was advised to take recourse to the market, and issue bonds akin to public sector bonds. The net effect was that the funds, which were being made available to NABARD free of cost by the Reserve Bank, were substituted by high-cost funds. NABARD was, therefore, with the restricted margin available to it, not in a position to continue to lend funds at low rates of interest and an upward revision could only be done in unavoidable circumstances.

During the statutory audit of the Reserve Bank for the year 1992–93, the auditors observed that according to section 46 A of the RBI, Act, 1934 it

---

9. For details refer to chapter 17: Reforms in Banking and Financial Institutions.

was a binding on the Bank to contribute to the two funds maintained every year, unless these provisions were suitably amended. The Legal Department opined that section 46 made it obligatory on part of the Reserve Bank to contribute to the NRC (LTO) and NRC [S] funds such sums of money as it considered necessary and feasible every year. Consequently, the Bank contributed a sum of ₹ 1 crore to each of these two funds from the surplus for the year 1992–93, pending necessary amendments to the section of the Act to give effect to the decision taken to discontinue such a practice.

As enunciated in the Union Budget for 1992–93:[10]

> ...the entire surplus profits of RBI were required to be passed on to Government of India. As such RBI did not contribute to National Rural Credit (LTO) Fund during the year. Considering the need for a substantial step up in the private capital formation in agriculture during the Eighth plan period to put it on a higher growth path, the flow of credit to agriculture and rural development from institutional sources have to be suitably expanded. In case the resources of NABARD are not suitably augmented, it may not be possible for it to meet the refinance commitment. Raising resources at market rates and providing refinance would not be a viable proposition for NABARD. There is therefore need for continued support to its resources through contribution from RBI to its NRC (LTO) fund.

No sooner did the Reserve Bank realise that it was violating the provisions of section 46(A) of the RBI Act, 1934 and section 42(I) of the NABARD Act, 1981, which made it mandatory for the Reserve Bank to contribute to this fund, the Bank considered various options in this regard. The alternative of adhering to the provisions of the Acts in letter, while not in spirit, was found by contributing a token amount of ₹ 1 crore every year. Had the Reserve Bank continued with the usual contribution, which worked out to an average of 31.14 per cent of its profits, the total transfers to the NRC (LTO) fund would have been much higher. To all requests for continuation and enhancement of the GLC, the Reserve Bank's stand was that: "since GLC is created money, it is by nature inflationary and therefore has to be discouraged." The stance of the Reserve Bank was a reflection of its association with monetary orthodoxy. Unless the economic policy contours of the country were freed from these orthodoxies, neither

---

10. NABARD, *Annual Report, 1992–93.*

of these institutions could appreciate the need for increased credit flow to agriculture by supporting the refinance operations of NABARD through regular transfers from Reserve Bank profits.[11]

In terms of the government policy, an amendment to the provisions of section 46 of the RBI Act, 1934 to make them 'enabling' rather than 'mandatory' provisions was carried out in 1994. In 1993–94, NABARD sanctioned total credit limits aggregating ₹ 557 crore for short-term purposes, which included credit limits for the SAO aggregating ₹ 396 crore sanctioned to 132 RRBs. Medium-term credit limits (non-schematic) were sanctioned to 88 RRBs for an aggregate amount of ₹ 58 crore as against ₹ 54 crore to 102 RRBs in the previous year. The rebate on income tax on the interest income of rural advances of commercial banks and the treatment of net funds provided by sponsor banks to RRBs as priority sector lending would also help improve the flow of rural lending. RRBs continued to avail of long-term refinance from NABARD. Up to March 1994, 5,547 schemes involving NABARD's commitment of ₹ 2,962 crore were sanctioned to RRBs and drawals against this commitment amounted to ₹ 2,672 crore as against 5,146 schemes involving NABARD's commitments of ₹ 2,577 crore and disbursements of ₹ 2,314 crore up to March 1993. A number of measures were taken to revitalise the co-operative banks.

For long-term improvement in rural credit, the Union Budget for 1994–95 provided ₹ 100 crore to augment the share capital of NABARD and a similar contribution would come from the Reserve Bank so that NABARD could play a leader in strengthening the system of rural credit. For the year 1995–96, the Reserve Bank sanctioned in June 1995 an aggregate limit of ₹ 4,950 crore, which was enhanced to ₹ 5,250 crore in January 1996.

Prudential accounting, guidelines of income recognition, asset classification, provisioning and other related matters were extended to NABARD in March 1996 with certain modifications, keeping in view the special nature of its operations. These guidelines were extended to RRBs, state co-operative banks and CCBs from the year 1996–97.

During 1995–96, the Reserve Bank enhanced its GLC (I and II) for NABARD by ₹ 300 crore to ₹ 5,250 crore and further to ₹ 5,500 crore in 1996–97. The share capital of NABARD was also raised during 1995–96 by ₹ 170 crore to ₹ 500 crore, with equal contributions from the Reserve Bank

---

11. Satish, P. (2010). "Funds for NABARD", *Economic and Political Weekly*. September 25

and the Government. As part of a plan to quadruple the share capital of NABARD from the existing level of ₹ 500 crore to ₹ 2,000 crore in the next five years, the Union Budget for 1996–97 proposed to double the share capital of NABARD to ₹ 1,000 crore in 1996–97 with a contribution of ₹ 400 crore from the Reserve Bank and ₹ 100 crore from the Government. To ensure that NABARD would adhere to the same financial discipline as banks and other term lending institutions, the prudential accounting standards as also the capital adequacy requirement of 8.0 per cent were extended to NABARD in March 1996 for implementation in phases.

RURAL INFRASTRUCTURAL DEVELOPMENT FUND

Many banks, both in the public and private sectors, were not able to meet their priority sector targets. Therefore, public and private sector banks with shortfalls in lending to the priority sector or to agriculture were required to contribute specified allocations to the RIDF. The Finance Minister announced in his budget speech on March 15, 1995 that a new RIDF would be established in NABARD to give loans to state governments and state-owned corporations for quick completion of ongoing projects on medium and minor irrigation, soil conservation, watershed management and other forms of rural infrastructure. The Union Budget for 1995–96, proposed that a new RIDF with a corpus of ₹ 2,000 crore would be established in NABARD. All SCBs (excluding RRBs and new private sector banks) would contribute to the RIDF an amount equivalent to the shortfall in achieving the priority sector sub-target of 18.0 per cent for agricultural lending, subject to a maximum of 1.5 per cent of net bank credit. The rate of interest paid by NABARD on the outstanding deposits placed by banks would be a floating rate equivalent to one-half of one percentage point above the maximum permissible rate on term deposits. The contribution to the fund made by banks would be reckoned as their indirect agricultural lending under the priority sector. The loans to be given by NABARD to the state governments/local bodies from the fund would be project-specific for a period up to 5 years. The concerned state governments would provide a government guarantee in respect of repayment of principal and payment of interest thereon. Further, state governments would execute an irrevocable letter of authority in favour of the Reserve Bank, authorising it to debit the state government account if the payment due under the scheme was made on the due date.

The first RIDF was established with NABARD in 1995–96 to provide loans to state governments for financing rural infrastructure projects. The

RIDF became the main instrument to channelise bank funds for financing rural infrastructure. By 1998, four tranches of RIDF were set, with a total corpus of ₹ 10,000 crore. The total amount disbursed from the four tranches of the RIDF aggregated ₹ 9,095 crore.

RELATED DEVELOPMENTS

Commercial banks were allowed in October 1994 to consider merit proposals for term loans/finance in the form of lines of credit to SIDCs and SFCs for extending loans to SSI units. Such loans to SSI units would be treated as part of priority sector lending. As a follow-up to the seven-point action plan announced in the Union Budget for 1995–96 to improve the flow of credit to the SSI sector, commercial banks were advised to set up 100 dedicated specialised branches during 1995–96 to serve the needs of 85 identified districts with a high concentration of SSI units.

The guidelines for setting-up banks in the private sector stipulated that they had to observe priority sector lending target as applicable to other commercial banks at 40.0 per cent. The new private sector banks were permitted to substitute the agricultural lending stipulation of 18.0 per cent by contributing partly or wholly to the deposit of NABARD and/ or the SIDBI for a period of three years from their inception. The interest rates payable on these deposits would be as stipulated by the Reserve Bank.

The rate of interest payable by SIDBI on deposits received from foreign banks to make good the shortfall in achievement of the overall priority sector lending target of 32.0 per cent as also the sub-targets of 10.0 per cent each in respect of SSIs and export credit were revised downwards in September 1994 to 8.0 per cent per annum.

The Union Budget 1995–96 took the initiative to increase the flow of credit to rural and SSIs. The contribution by commercial banks to such schemes, e.g., RIDF, loans to the khadi and village industries commission (KVIC), loans to weavers in the handloom sector and primary weavers co-operative societies (PWCS) and the lines of credit to SFCs for extending loans to SSIs would be reckoned as part of their priority sector lending. It was decided that the entire amount of refinance rather than the net funds hitherto provided by commercial banks to their sponsored RRBs would be reckoned as priority sector lending of the sponsor banks. Further, 50.0 per cent and 40.0 per cent of such refinance could be reckoned as indirect agricultural lending and advance to weaker sections, respectively.

In view of the crucial importance of non-farm activities, the Union Budget for 1995–96 proposed a scheme under which the banking system would provide ₹ 1,000 crore on a consortium basis to the KVIC to enable it to extend finance to viable *khadi* and village industrial units either directly or through state-level khadi and village industries boards (KVIBs). Accordingly, a consortium of select PSBs was formed, led by the State Bank of India (SBI), to provide credit to the KVIC. Banks that had not achieved the priority sector lending target of 40.0 per cent even after allocation of their contribution to the RIDF were included in the consortium. These loans, which would be provided at 1.5 per cent below the average PLR of five major banks in the consortium, would carry a government guarantee and would be reckoned as indirect lending of the concerned banks to SSIs under the priority sector. As proposed in the Union Budget for 1995–96, a consortium of 20 PSBs provided a sum of ₹ 325 crore as at end-June 1996 to the KVIC for lending to viable *khadi* and village industrial units. With the extension of NABARD's refinance facility to commercial banks, the latter were advised to provide working capital finance to the PWCS.

BANK FINANCE FOR PRIMARY WEAVERS CO-OPERATIVE SOCIETIES

A scheme announced in the Union Budget for 1995–96 envisaged increasing the flow of credit to the large number of weavers employed in the handloom sector. The refinance available from NABARD to the PWCS would be extended to commercial banks in addition to being routed through the co-operative sector, provided the societies to be financed had a satisfactory working record and were not indebted to the CCBs. NABARD would provide a line of credit to commercial banks for the production-cum-marketing activities of PWCS at 9.5 per cent per annum, which would be made available to the handloom co-operative at the same rate, provided that a subsidy of 2.5 per cent was received from the state government. The advances made by commercial banks to handloom co-operatives would be reckoned as indirect finance to the SSI sector and would form part of the banks' priority sector lending.

REGIONAL RURAL BANKS

With the introduction of financial sector reforms in 1991–92, the commercial viability of RRBs, which were an important element in the rural credit delivery system, emerged as the most crucial factor in deciding their role in the emerging economic scenario. The financial health of RRBs had turned weak due to limited business opportunities with little scope for expansion/diversification, smaller size of their loans with higher exposure to risk-prone advances and their professional inefficiency in financial deployment. RRBs had high credit-deposit ratios owing to low reserve requirements and liberal refinancing facilities.

The viability of RRBs had been under serious strain for quite some time as they extended credit only to weaker sections and consequently the return available to them was unsustainably low. Their loans were more risk-prone and recoveries somewhat lower than those of commercial banks. The average deposit per branch of RRBs was a fraction of the average for rural branches of commercial banks. RRBs were conceived of as low-cost institutions. However, the cost differentials between RRBs and commercial banks were narrowing over time.

A number of policy initiatives, therefore, were taken to improve the viability of RRBs. Considering that most of RRBs were weak and were incurring losses and that their target groups comprised weaker sections, the Reserve Bank exempted all RRBs from the proviso to sub-sections 1 and 1(A) of section 42 of the RBI Act, 1934 for a period of two years, up to December 31, 1994, allowing them to maintain the CRR at 3.0 per cent of their net demand and time liabilities (NDTL). Later, on December 22, 1993, the Reserve Bank, in consultation with the Government and NABARD, announced a package of measures for RRBs with a view to giving them greater freedom to rationalise their existing branch network and bring in operational efficiency. These included: (i) freeing 70 RRBs whose disbursals were below ₹ 2 crore during 1992–93 from their service area obligations, while permitting other RRBs to extend financial assistance in their entire command areas provided they met their service area obligations; (ii) increasing their non-target group financing from 40.0 per cent to 60.0 per cent of fresh loans; (iii) allowing RRBs to relocate the existing loss-making branches at new places like *mandis*/agricultural produce centres at block/district headquarters; (iv) giving them the freedom to open extension counters; and (v) upgrading and deepening the range of their activities to cover non-fund business. Besides, the Government took up the task of transforming the weak RRBs into financially viable and effective instruments of decentralised banking.

Of the 196 RRBs, the number of loss-making RRBs stood at 172 as at end-March 1993. Many had completely wiped out their equity and reserves, and in some cases the losses had eroded the deposit base. As this situation was unsustainable, there was a need for long-term structural measures. The 70 RRBs that had been freed from the SAA and were allowed to relocate their loss-making branches to specified centres within the same block were permitted to convert the loss-making branches into satellite/mobile offices and also consider mergers, wherever possible. These facilities were also extended to RRBs that adhered to the SAA, which, however, had to ensure that the conversions did not impair their continued performance of SAA obligations.

The Union Budget for 1994–95 announced several measures aimed at restructuring the rural credit delivery system and improving the credit flow to the agricultural sector. An important step taken in this direction was to resuscitate RRBs through comprehensive restructuring, which included cleaning up their balance sheets and infusing fresh capital. A committee was appointed under the chairmanship of Shri M.C. Bhandari, chief general manager, NABARD to identify RRBs for restructuring. The committee submitted its interim report identifying 50 RRBs based on their financial strength and also considering their regional representation. The Government accepted the recommendations of the committee to take up 49 of the 50 RRBs identified for restructuring. Forty-eight RRBs had already entered into an agreement with its respective sponsor banks. The Government contributed ₹ 150 crore as its share of 50.0 per cent for this purpose. Another 50 RRBs were taken up for restructuring during 1995–96, for which a sum of ₹ 300 crore was provided in the Union Budget for 1995–96.

The recipient RRBs for their part had to fulfil within a time frame certain performance obligations and commitments on a variety of indicators, including growth of deposits, a mix of various types of deposits, disbursement to target and non-target groups, investment in SLR and non-SLR categories, recovery targets, staff productivity, cost of funds, return on resources, improvement in spread and breakeven level. As part of the overall package of measures designed to improve the operational efficiency and profitability of RRBs, the Reserve Bank, in line with the recommendations of the Bhandari Committee, permitted RRBs in January 1995 to invest their non-SLR funds in specified investment avenues such as Unit Trust of India (UTI) listed schemes and fixed deposits of profit-making term lending institutions, or 25.0 per cent of the aggregate deposits as at the end of the preceding year, whichever was higher. The sponsor banks would continue to aid and advise RRBs regarding the choice of investment avenues until they developed the requisite technical expertise in funds management. Again in January 1995, RRBs were allowed to park part of their non-SLR funds in the credit portfolios of their sponsor banks through non-risk sharing participation certificates issued by the latter on mutually agreed terms and conditions. Such investments through the credit route were subject to a maximum of 15.0 per cent of fresh lending during the year and were to be reckoned within the ceiling fixed for non-target group lending.

In July 1995, the Reserve Bank constituted an expert group (Chairman: Shri N.K. Thingalaya) to examine the major policy issues concerning the managerial and financial restructuring of RRBs taken up during 1994–95 and continued in 1995–96, and to monitor the progress of this exercise. The group examined the progress of restructuring and suggested supplementary policy measures on an on-going basis.

Sixty-eight more RRBs were identified for restructuring in the second phase by a committee set up by NABARD in its report in December 1995 (Chairman: Dr K. Basu) in addition to two RRBs identified by the Government.

To widen the investment options of RRBs, the recommendations of the working group (Chairman: Shri K.K. Misra) on funds management in RRBs were considered and with a view to broad base their range of activities, RRBs were allowed to extend housing loans, subject to certain conditions.

The credit-deposit ratio of RRBs continued to decline from 67.0 per cent as at end-March 1993 to 56.0 per cent as at end-March 1995. Overdues as a percentage to advances outstanding, however, declined from 34.9 per cent as at end-March 1994 to 29.7 per cent in March 1995

In order to impart durability to the restructuring process, RRBs were advised to adopt income recognition, asset classification and exposure norms from 1995–96 and provisioning norms from 1996–97. As part of the restructuring process of RRBs, an amount of ₹ 200 crore was provided in the Union Budget for 1996–97 and a further allocation of ₹ 270 crore was made in the Union Budget for 1997–98. RRBs were permitted to open new branches that would be manned by redeploying their employees at centres that had business potential in the areas of their operation. In order to strengthen the capital base of rural financial institutions, a sum of ₹ 400 crore was released by the Government for recapitalisation of 90 RRBs in 1997–98, of which 15 were included for the first time. The Union Budget for 1998–99 earmarked an amount of ₹ 265 crore for further recapitalisation of RRBs.

The rebate on income tax on the interest income of rural advances of commercial banks and the treatment of net funds provided by sponsor banks to RRBs as priority sector lending also helped improve the flow of rural lending. These measures had the desired impact on the financial performance of RRBs. The number of profit-making RRBs increased sharply to 109 during 1997–98. RRBs, as a group, also earned a net profit of ₹ 43 crore during 1997–98 as against net losses of ₹ 589 crore incurred in 1996–97.

REVAMPING CO-OPERATIVE CREDIT INSTITUTIONS

Co-operative credit institutions accounted for the major share of total direct institutional credit for agriculture and allied activities. Loans extended by RRBs formed a relatively small proportion of the total rural credit. Commercial banks accounted for the rest, but a little over one-half of these loans were of a short-term nature. In response to the changing pattern of rural demand for credit, banks had been expanding their advances to allied activities at a more rapid pace than that for agriculture. The Reserve Bank facilitated the credit flow to agriculture and the rural segment by allowing flexibility in the interest rate and bringing in changes in the fund allocation methods of banks.

In general, the co-operative credit system suffered from a number of problems, such as: (i) excessive reliance on funds from higher-level structures; (ii) undue state control; (iii) poor deposit mobilisation; and (iv) poor recovery of loans. The major flaw of the co-operative system lay in the weakness of the base-level institutions, mainly because they neglected their basic responsibility of mobilising deposits. In the case of RRBs, the problem areas included low interest rates, high operating costs in handling small loans and loans to weaker sections in backward regions, and high salary structure, which resulted in very low and even negative margins.

To give greater freedom to financially strong and well-managed urban co-operative banks (UCBs), which fulfilled prescribed norms, were permitted to open branches at centres of their choice without having to obtain prior approval of the Reserve Bank. UCBs were permitted to extend their area of operation to rural centres even beyond 10 km from the boundaries of semi-urban/urban centres, subject to the condition that they provided financial assistance only for non-agricultural productive activities. Well-managed and financially strong UCBs with deposits above ₹ 50 crore that satisfied certain norms were permitted to extend the area of operation even beyond the state of their registration. In order to enable UCBs to freely extend their area of operation within the district of their registration, prior approval from the Reserve Bank was dispensed with, subject to their obtaining approval from the Registrar of Co-operative Societies. UCBs were, however, required to seek the prior approval of the Reserve Bank to extend their area of operation beyond the district of registration. One UCB was deleted from the list of scheduled UCBs when it was converted into a commercial bank, while five UCBs were included in the second schedule of the RBI Act, 1934, taking the total number of scheduled UCBs to 18.

Up to May 1995 the Reserve Bank issued licences to two state co-operative banks and 14 district co-operative banks under section 22 of the BR (as applicable to co-operative banks) Act, 1949, taking the total number of licensed state co-operative banks and district co-operative banks to 12 and 52, respectively. Licences were also issued to five state co-operative banks under section 23 of the BR (as applicable to co-operative banks) Act, 1949 to open five branches. With the granting of scheduled status to the Goa State Co-operative Bank Ltd by the Reserve Bank with effect from December 15, 1994, the total number of scheduled state co-operative banks rose to 15.

To re-orient the co-operative banking operations along commercial lines with cost effectiveness, the state co-operative banks, SLDBs, CCBs, and primary land development banks (PLDBs) were advised to prepare institution-specific development action plans and state action plans (SAPs).

A major shortcoming of the co-operative credit structure was the poor recovery rate of loans. Loan overdues as a percentage of loan demand was 53.7 per cent in 1992–93 for SLDBs, followed by 42.9 per cent for CCBs, 42.0 per cent for primary agricultural credit co-operative societies (PACS) and 16.2 per cent for state co-operative banks. The overdue rates for co-operatives in 1992–93 showed no improvement over the previous year in general, except for state co-operative banks and SLDBs

Some of the credit policy measures directed towards commercial banks such as those relating to loans and advances, credit to individuals against shares and debentures/bonds and interest rates on deposits and advances were also made applicable to UCBs with suitable modifications. The UCBs were allowed to offer at their discretion an additional rate interest not exceeding one-half of one percentage point per annum on term deposits of 46 days and above and one percentage point per annum on savings deposits over the rates prescribed for SCBs. The UCBs were allowed to accept term deposits for periods exceeding 10 years. Interest rates on term loans for three years and above were reduced by 0.5 per cent to 1.0 per cent per annum with effect from March 1, 1994. Further, in line with commercial banks, the PLR for advances above ₹ 2 lakh was made effective from October 18, 1994. For the first time, scheduled UCBs were considered for investing their surplus funds in certificates of deposit (CDs) and commercial paper (CP) with a credit rating of P1 or A1 from CRISIL/ ICRA.[12] Accordingly, during 1993–94, four of the scheduled UCBs were permitted to place their surplus funds in CP and six UCBs in CDs issued by SCBs and FIs that were authorised by the Reserve Bank.

While granting advances against units of mutual funds, UCBs were advised to follow broad guidelines on advances against shares and debentures and, in addition, ensure that: (i) units against which advances were made were listed on stock exchanges; (ii) the minimum lock-in period was over; (iii) the quantum of advance was linked to the need of the borrower as also the net asset value or market value, whichever was lower (not face value); and (iv) the prescribed margins were to be maintained and the advances were purpose-oriented, subject to the overall ceiling on borrowings by equipment-leasing and hire-purchase companies. The UCBs were allowed to lend to companies in consortium with commercial banks up to 4.0 per cent of the net owned funds (NOFs) of the individual company. In line with instructions to commercial banks, the UCBs were advised that advances secured against term deposits, national savings certificates (NSCs), Indira vikas patras and kisan vikas patras were exempt from the provisioning requirements. Further, the UCBs were permitted to take into account the amount of interest on the above types of advances on actual basis, provided that an adequate margin was available in the account.

With effect from May 16, 1994 the Reserve Bank permitted state co-operative banks/CCBs, (on a case-by-case basis) and all UCBs to invest 10.0 per cent of their deposits in public sector undertaking (PSU) bonds for deploying their surplus funds profitably, subject to certain conditions or safety measures, viz.: (i) the investments had already been made in PSU bonds and fresh investments should not exceed 10.0 per cent of their deposits; (ii) permission should be obtained from the concerned Registrar of Co-operative Societies; and (iii) instructions regarding investment policy and dealings in securities transactions should be complied with. Scheduled state co-operative banks were exempt from the provisions of

---

12. CRISIL: Credit Rating Information Services of India Ltd; ICRA: Investment Information and Credit Rating Agency of India Ltd.

the proviso to sub-sections (1) and (1A) of section 42 of the RBI Act, 1934 for a further period of two years up to December 31, 1996, whereby the cash reserves to be maintained by them would continue to be 3.0 per cent of their demand and time liabilities.

The Government proposed in the Union Budget for 1994–95 to initiate a series of measures for strengthening the co-operative structure. As part of this process, NABARD entered into MoU with state/district/CCBs and the concerned state governments to implement state-specific district action plans (DAPs) to revamp these banks and improve their viability. It also issued guidelines to co-operative banks for preparing the plans and actively assisted them in the implementation.

At the end of March 1995, NABARD signed such agreements with 17 state co-operative banks, and 13 SLDBs. The agreement envisaged, on the part of these banks, time-bound performance of specific actions for making the co-operative banks viable and strong.

NABARD extended support and guidance to the co-operatives in formulating their MoU, and made elaborate arrangements to monitor their implementation. The MoU contained various measures to be taken by banks and the concerned state governments in the areas of management, organisation, recovery, monitoring and the business plan over five-year period. The policy framework relating to rural credit was made conducive to maintain the economic viability of credit institutions. A major change brought about was total deregulation of interest rates in relation to co-operative banks. Co-operative credit institutions could access resources competitively and lend at remunerative rates of interest. Greater emphasis was placed on adequate and timely availability of credit from institutional sources than on subsidised rates of interest, which resulted in making the institutions viable.

It is relevant, in this context, to mention that periodic introduction of the schemes that waived the payment of principal or interest or both, damaged the loan recovery culture and credit discipline. While some of these schemes showed increased recovery in the year in which they were introduced, over time they adversely affected the borrowers' attitude towards repayment and, resultantly the practice of timely repayment suffered.

The process of signing MoU to revamp the co-operative credit structure, as discussed above, continued during 1995–96. In all, 28 state co-operative banks and 20 SLDBs were covered. MoU between NABARD, state co-operative banks and district central co-operative banks (DCCBs) were signed for 358 of the 363 DCCBs. To prepare the profit and loss account and balance sheet reflecting the bank's actual financial health, a proper system for recognition of income, classification of assets, and provisioning on a prudential basis was deemed as necessary. The feasibility of making income recognition and asset classification norms applicable to state co-operative banks/CCBs was examined by the Reserve Bank in consultation with NABARD and, accordingly, guidelines on prudential norms were issued to these banks for adoption effective March 31, 1997.

CO-OPERATIVE DEVELOPMENT FUND

NABARD set up the co-operative development fund (CDF) in 1994 to provide financial assistance through grants/loans to co-operative banks for human resource development with suitable training inputs, to build better management information systems (MIS) and infrastructure facilities for PACS to mobilise deposits.

COMMERCIAL BANKS

Undoubtedly, the presence of commercial banks expanded remarkably in the rural areas during the 1980s and they emerged as the leading agency for deposit mobilisation and lending to the rural sector. Apart from financing agriculture and village industries, they played a critical role in implementing poverty alleviation programmes, such as the IRDP. Despite these achievements, several deficiencies persisted in their operations. Their record in recovery of loans was only slightly better than that of co-operatives. The rural orientation of their staff, although improved over time, was often below desirable levels. Considering the high administrative and risk costs, the price of rural credit was inadequate. While cross-subsidisation from other borrowers such as from industry borrowers helped to some extent, it could not be stretched beyond a point.

The growth of rural commercial banking during the period 1989–1997 suffered in terms of number of bank offices, credit outstanding and credit-deposit ratio. During the period 1990 to 1996, the number of SCB bank offices declined from 34,867 to 32,981. The credit outstanding increased from about ₹ 17,000 crore to ₹ 29,000 crore, but its share in the total came down from 14.2 per cent to 11.0 per cent during the period. Rural deposits escalated from around ₹ 28,600 crore to ₹ 61,200 crore, but the credit-deposit ratio dropped from about 60.0 per cent to 47.0 per cent. The share of priority sector advances to the total also came down from 40.7 per cent to 32.8 per cent.[13] One of the main reasons for such developments appeared to be the risk aversion that developed due to the very low recovery performance.[14]

DEBT RELIEF

In his budget speech for 1989–90, the Finance Minister observed:

> Credit is a major input for agricultural production. In order to increase the flow of credit to agriculture, the target for direct finance to agriculture by Public Sector banks, which was raised from 16 per cent to 17 per cent of their total outstanding advances is being further raised to 18 per cent to be achieved by the end of 1989–90. With this change the total credit to be made available to agriculture by commercial banks, Regional Rural Banks and Co-operative banks will increase by over ₹ 4,000 crore in 1989–90. Hon'ble Members are aware that the rate of interest on crop loans up to ₹ 15,000 was reduced last year and the reduction varied between 1 1/2 per cent and 2 1/2 per cent. With a view to extending the scope of relief, the Reserve Bank of India is today issuing instructions reducing the rate of interest charged on crop loans between ₹ 15,000 and ₹ 25,000 to 12 per cent from the existing maximum rate of 14 per cent.

The high incidence of overdues in the rural credit system, which continued to increase over the years, was a matter of serious concern as it tended to erode the financial soundness of the system. The Finance Minister in his budget speech of 1990–91 highlighted this:

> Over the years, poor farmers, artisans and weavers have accumulated debt which they are unable to repay. They have been caught up in a vicious circle of indebtedness and low incomes which keeps them in perennial poverty. In order to relieve our farmers from the burden of debt, an assurance was given in the National Front's manifesto that relief will be provided to farmers with loans up to ₹ 10,000 as on October 2, 1989. I am glad to inform the House that we are now ready with the scheme of implementation of debt relief

13. Devaraja, T.S. (2011). *Rural Credit in India: An Overview of History and Perspectives.* Hassan: Department of Commerce, University of Mysore. May.

14. Shah, Mihir, Rangu Rao and P.S. Vijay Shankar (2007). "Rural Credit in 20th Century India: An Overview of History and Perspectives", *Economic and Political Weekly* 42(15). April 14–20.

to fulfill the promise, and redeem the pledge given to the kisans and artisans. It is proposed to introduce a scheme for providing debt relief which will have the following features. The relief will be available to borrowers who have taken loans up to ₹ 10,000 from public sector banks and Regional Rural Banks. The relief will cover all overdues as on 2nd October 1989 including short-term as well as term loans. There will be no limit on the size of the borrower's land holdings. However, willful defaulters, who in the past did not repay loans despite their capacity to do so, will be excluded. The Central Government will compensate the public sector banks and Regional Rural Banks suitably for the debts which are thus written off. Many of those who filed insolvency petitions and had taken loans below ₹ 10,000 which were overdue as of 2nd October, 1989 will also be covered under the scheme. The State Governments may also wish to introduce a scheme on the same lines in respect of co-operative banks within their purview. Subject to the constraint of resources, the Central Government will consider suggestions for helping State Governments in implementing a debt relief scheme on the same pattern in respect of co-operative credit institutions under their control. I consider the debt relief measure as a positive step which will enable our farmers, artisans and weavers to increase their productivity. It is at the same time necessary to ensure that there is no erosion of the credibility of the banking system. Once the past over-dues are cleared, it is reasonable to expect that loans taken for current operations will be serviced promptly. The Scheme should contribute to better agricultural recoveries and better identification of willful defaulters, who do not deserve any sympathy. Banks are being asked to set up a system of maintaining a proper credit history of their borrowers covered under the Scheme. The Government would also like to make it clear that the Scheme will not be extended nor will it be repeated.

In terms of the Finance Minister's budget indications, the Reserve Bank finalised and communicated to banks guidelines for implementation of the debt relief scheme effective May 15, 1990. The Central Government made a provision of ₹ 1000 crore towards the debt relief scheme and committed to underwrite the entire burden of the relief provided by commercial banks and RRBs. In addition, the Central Government assured to provide 50.0 per cent assistance for the relief to be provided by the co-operative credit institutions. After the scheme was implemented, the major challenge for the banking industry was to ensure that a multitude of fresh defaulters did not emerge again, choking the rural credit channels. It was essential that state governments effectively backed the efforts of commercial and co-operative banks in this regard. This was crucial in order to maintain the health of the rural credit system, so that it could continue to effectively support productive activity in the countryside.[15]

Under the scheme, debt relief of ₹ 10,000 was provided to eligible borrowers who fulfilled certain eligibility criteria. Accordingly, debt relief of ₹ 7,819 crore was provided under the scheme, of which public sector commercial banks provided ₹ 2,833 crore, the RRBs ₹ 793 crore and the co-operatives ₹ 4,193 crore. The Reserve Bank provided loans of ₹ 1,956 crore through NABARD to the state governments to meet their share of 50.0 per cent in the implementation of the scheme for the clients of co-operatives.

Banking in India had to operate under several constraints guided by socio-economic considerations that affected their profitability. These related primarily to rapid and vast expansion of banking facilities with associated costs, allocation of credit for priority needs and the element of cross-subsidisation to assist the preferred sectors. Banks were also subjected to a large pre-emption of funds by way of CRR and SLR, which also imposed constraints on their profitability. Several steps were taken to ease policy-related restrictions on profitability of banks. In the first phase, the measures aimed at directly improving profitability by increasing the administered rates, including an improvement in bond yields and interest on the eligible cash balances with the Reserve Bank. The second phase was marked by a move towards freeing the system, thus giving banks more discretion to set their rates competitively.

RATIONALISATION OF INTEREST RATES

On September 21, 1990, both the Department of Banking Operations and Development (DBOD) and the Rural Planning and Credit Department (RPCD) of the Reserve Bank issued a circular/directive at the instance of the Credit Planning Cell (CPC) on interest rates on advances to SCBs, including RRBs, and to the state co-operative banks/CCBs (Table 18.1). The notable feature of the new dispensation of lending rates announced was the linking of the interest rates to the size of the loan.

---

15. Malhotra, R.N. (1990). *Rural Credit: Issues for 1990s*. Inaugural Address at the seminar organised by the Institute of Development Studies. Jaipur. August 27.

TABLE 18.1

Interest rate Structure on Advances

(Per cent)

Size of limit	Rate of interest
Up to ₹ 7,500	10.0
Over ₹ 7500 and up to ₹ 15,000	11.5
Over ₹ 15,000 and up to ₹ 25,000	12.5
Over ₹ 25,000 and up to ₹ 50,000	14.0
Over ₹ 50,000 and up to ₹ 2 lakh	15.0
Over ₹ 2 lakh	16.0 (minimum)

Source: Reserve Bank of India, circular dated September 21, 1990.

This rate structure was revised in April 1991 and then in July 1991, but only for the last category, *i.e.*, the interest rates for credit facilities over ₹ 2 lakh was revised to 17.0 per cent effective April 13, 1991 and then again to 18.5 per cent effective July 4, 1991). Despite these revisions, the principle of linking interest rates to the size of the limit remained unchanged, which created a furore among co-operative banks.

The Reserve Bank received representations/references from NABARD, various co-operative banks, the national federation of state co-operative banks and SCBs that were providing finance to PACS ceded to them. They represented that the new dispensation, which linked interest rates to the size of the limit, did not take into account the differential in lending rates, which was earlier maintained between the on-lending agencies both in the co-operative structure as well as in state co-operative banks lending to PACS. The matter was taken up with the CPC, which, after a detailed discussion with the top management, advised the RPCD as below and a rate structure finally emerged (Table 18.2):[16]

To ensure uniformity of lending rates for ultimate borrowers, the SCBs would provide credit to the PACs at a rate 2.5 percentage points below the rate prescribed for direct lending by the SCBs for the relevant rate of advance by the PACs. In other words, if PACs lend for amounts up to Rs 7,500 per borrower at 10.0%, the PACs would be provided credit from the SCBs at 7.5%. The SCBs would be provided refinance from NABARD up to 60% of its lendings to PACs at the same rate at which the SCBs lend to PACs. The SCBs would limit their financing to only those PACs which are

---

16. SCBs in the quote refer to state co-operative banks and not scheduled commercial banks, as is the case in rest of the volume.

at present financed by them. The instructions to SCBs could be issued after DG (J) discusses this case with Chairman NABARD. The above discussions and the decisions were actually based on the writ petition filed by Andhra Pradesh High Court by Mulkanoor Co-operative Bank Ltd against State Bank of Hyderabad and the Reserve Bank challenging the application of interest rates revised with effect from 22nd September 1990. The issue was put up to the Governor and he gave his approval for revision. The interest rates had to be frequently revised and the objective was to reduce the interest rate gradually particularly in respect of loans beyond ₹ 2 lakh.

TABLE 18.2

Structure of Lending Rates

(Per cent per annum)

Category of Account	Rate Effective		
	October 9, 1991	April 22, 1992	October 9, 1992
(1)	(2)	(3)	(4)
Size of Credit Limit:			
Up to ₹ 7,500	11.5	11.5	11.5
Over ₹ 7,500 and up to ₹ 15,000	13.0	13.5	13.5
Over ₹ 15,000 and up to ₹ 25,000	13.5		
Over ₹ 25,000 and up to ₹ 50,000	15.5	16.5	16.5
Over ₹ 50,000 and up to ₹ 2 lakh	16.5		
Over ₹ 2 lakh	20.0*	19.0*	18.0*

Note: *: Minimum.

Source: Reserve Bank of India, internal documents.

PRODUCE (MARKETING) LOAN SCHEME

The scheme, initially introduced in 14 districts by the Government in December 1988 for loans not exceeding ₹ 10,000 to farmers by way of hypothecation of agriculture produce stored in a farmer's house or by pledge of the warehouse/rural godown[17] receipt, was kept in abeyance from

---

17. Godown is a storehouse in a village in which the farmer stores his produce.

April 1989 to March 1990. The scheme was, however, reintroduced for the 1990 *rabi* season and extended to eight additional districts in January 1991. By 1997, the scheme was in operation in 82 districts.

CASH CREDIT SYSTEM FOR AGRICULTURAL ADVANCES

Only a few banks provided cash credit facilities to a limited number of farmers subject to certain conditions. To ensure adequate and timely flow of rural credit as also to meet the composite needs of farmers, the Reserve Bank advised the banks in October 1994 to extend cash credit facilities to farmers for irrigation facilities and also for non-farm/allied activities.

Commercial banks were advised to set up at least one specialised agricultural finance branch (SAFB) in each state by the convenors of the respective SLBC to deal with high-tech agricultural loans. At end-June 1995, there were 735 specialised branches, of which 70 were SAFBs (Table 18.3).

TABLE 18.3

Number of Specialised Branches

(As on June 30, 1995)

Specialisation Category	Public Sector Banks	Private Sector Banks	Total
(1)	(2)	(3)	(4)
Industrial Finance Branch	85	10	95
Agricultural Finance Branch	69	1	70
SSI Branch	164	17	181
Capital Market			
Service Branch	15	–	15
Corporate Finance Branch	5	–	5
Overseas Branch	87	7	94
NRI Branch	49	15	64
Housing Finance Branch	2	–	2
Leasing Finance Branch	1	–	1
Others	204	4	208
Total	681	54	735

Note: – : Not available/nil.

Source: Reserve Bank of India, *Report on Trend and Progress of Banking, 1994–95.*

To promote investment in commercial or high technology agriculture and allied activities, state-level agricultural development financial institutions were proposed to be set up, with NABARD as the chief promoter. The Reserve Bank advised PSBs to prepare special agricultural credit plans. For the financial year 1995–96, disbursements under the plan were ₹ 10,173 crore as against the projection of ₹ 12,121 crore.

LOCAL AREA BANKS

In order to promote mobilisation and deployment of rural savings by local institutions, the concept of local area banks (LABs) with jurisdiction over two to three districts was evolved to cater to the credit needs of the local people and to provide efficient and competitive financial intermediation services in their areas of operation. This was expected to provide the much-needed competition to the existing financial institutions in those areas. As proposed in the Union Budget for 1996–97, guidelines were issued in August 1996 for setting-up new private LABs with jurisdiction over two or three contiguous districts in order to promote rural saving, bridge the gaps in credit availability and enhance the institutional credit framework in rural and semi-urban areas. A minimum paid-up capital of ₹ 5 crore was stipulated for such banks. The Reserve Bank granted in principle approval for the establishment of three LABs. These banks would be promoted by individuals, corporate entities, trusts and societies and should have a minimum paid-up capital of ₹ 5 crore, of which the promoters' contribution should be at least ₹ 2 crore. They would have to observe the priority sector lending target of 40.0 per cent of net bank credit and a sub-target of 10.0 per cent of net bank credit for lending to weaker sections as applicable to other domestic banks. They would also adhere to the prudential norms, accounting policies and other policies as laid down by the Reserve Bank. These banks would have to achieve capital adequacy of 8.0 per cent of the risk-weighted assets and norms for income recognition, asset classification and provisioning from their inception. The interest rates on advances in their case would be deregulated. LABs would be registered as public limited companies under the Companies Act, 1956. They would be licensed under the BR Act, 1949 and would be eligible for inclusion in the second schedule to the RBI Act, 1934.

CONCLUDING OBSERVATIONS

Although agriculture was recognised to be the backbone of the economy, the fact remained that over a period it lost its importance in terms of access to financial support. The regulatory and social compulsions with which banks had been providing assistance for agriculture and rural development were gradually disappearing. Although agricultural credit by various agencies rose from ₹ 15,169 crore in 1992–93 to ₹ 28,653 crore in 1996–97, the share of agricultural credit in the total was on the decline. Even after a significant increase in overall agriculture credit, there was a serious problem of overdues that dampened the flow of credit, besides adversely affecting the economic viability of lending institutions, especially the co-operatives and the RRBs. The recovery of agricultural advances by commercial banks, however, improved from 54.2 per cent in 1992 to 61.9 per cent in 1996.

Gross capital formation in agriculture increased from ₹ 4,729 crore (₹ 1,002 crore public share and ₹ 3,727 private share) in 1992 to ₹ 6,999 (₹ 1,132 public share and ₹ 5,867 private share) in 1997. The decline in share of public investment was attributed to the diversion of resources from investment to current expenditure. A large portion of public expenditure on agriculture in the early 1990s went into current expenditure in the form of increased output and input subsidies.

The Eighth Plan stipulated that the level of investment in agriculture should be raised to at least 18.7 per cent of the total investment. However, it could at best reach 11.0 per cent of the total investment. During the Eighth Plan, investments in the agricultural sector, particularly for the creation of irrigation potential, fell short of the target despite the efforts made to reverse the trend by introducing the accelerated irrigation benefit programme. As at end-March 1997, PSBs had exceeded their priority sector credit target with a total lending of ₹ 79,131 crore, which constituted 41.7 per cent of the net bank credit. As at end-March 1997, 353 specialised SSI bank branches were operationalised.

Disbursement to agriculture under the special agricultural credit plans, prepared on the advice of the Reserve Bank was ₹ 12,716 crore during 1996–97. The policy to channelise the shortfall in priority sector lending by banks into rural infrastructure investment continued during 1997–98. Apart from the RIDF-III corpus of ₹ 2,500 crore, the Union Budget for 1998–99 announced the establishment of RIDF-IV with a corpus of ₹ 3,000 crore.

The commercial banks were allowed to consider merit proposals for term finance/loans in the form of lines of credit to SIDCs and SFCs. The extent of such loans to SSIs was treated as a part of priority sector lending. The priority sector target was set at 40.0 per cent even for new private sector banks The Union Budget for 1995–96 took further initiatives to improve the credit flow to the rural sector and SSIs and announced several schemes, *viz.*, RIDF with a corpus of ₹ 2,000 crore, the scheme of loans to STs, a seven-point action plan for improving the flow of credit to the SSIs, ensuring availability of bank finance for PWCS and weavers in the handloom sector, instituting technology development and modernisation fund and extending bank credit to the KVIBs.

In order to align the priority sector lending of foreign banks operating in India with that of Indian banks, the target of priority sector lending by foreign banks was raised in October 1993 from 15.0 per cent to 32.0 per cent of their net bank credit, inclusive of two separate sub-targets of at least 10.0 per cent each in respect of advances to SSIs and exports to be achieved by the end of March 1994. Taking into account their difficulties in extending credit to the agricultural sector due to the lack of rural branch network, the composition of priority sector advances for foreign banks was enlarged to include export credit extended by them with effect from July 1, 1993. It was stipulated that in the event of any shortfall in the target at end-March 1994, the foreign banks would have to make good by placing a deposit with the SIDBI. Accordingly, nine foreign banks that could not meet the target deposited ₹ 310 crore with the SIDBI. As at end-March 1994, the advances to the priority sector by foreign banks stood at ₹ 3,177 crore, accounting for 32.0 per cent of their net bank credit. The overall target of priority sector lending in respect of foreign banks remained unchanged at 32.0 per cent of net bank credit, with a sub-target of 10.0 per cent in respect of advances to SSIs. The sub-target for export credit was, however, raised from 10.0 per cent to 12.0 per cent of net bank credit for the year ending March 1997. In case of any shortfall in priority sector lending from the targets and sub-targets, the policy prescription of placing deposits equivalent to the shortfall with the SIDBI (at an interest rate of 8.0 per cent per annum) was maintained.

Although the need to augment growth of agriculture and rural employment found expression in the policies of the Government, the economic reforms were largely confined to industry, trade and commerce. The balance of payments (BoP) crisis of 1991 induced economic reforms that, in a way, sidelined agriculture. The financial sector reforms placed emphasis on productivity, efficiency and profitability of banking, which compelled the banking system to focus on viability-based expansion of business and, at the same time, extend finance for agricultural and rural sector development as a fait accompli under policy compulsions of relaxed terms and conditions with reference to interest rates and other regulatory requirements. Several employment-linked programmes with subsidies, particularly to uplift weaker sections and micro-credit system of extending finance were attempted on an experimental basis, but the fact remained that agriculture and rural sector did not take-off as envisaged to support the growth process.

The Reserve Bank continued to play a key role in developing this sector by providing refinance and giving policy as well as regulatory support and guidance to NABARD, scheduled banks, including RRBs, and the co-operative sector. NABARD, established in 1982 as an apex national bank to exclusively cater to agriculture and rural development, continued to depend on the Government and the Reserve Bank for its resources and operations. It emerged as a refinancing body rather than a development agency. Despite being the backbone of the economy, agriculture and rural segment lagged behind other sectors in getting the focused attention. The reforms initiatives proposed in the report of the Narasimham Committee were centred at ensuring viability of banking and making it competitive and efficient.

The SAA focused attention on decentralised and micro-credit planning by rural and semi-urban branches of commercial banks and RRBs, with the support of NABARD. A small farmers' agri-business consortium was formed to provide better employment opportunities to farmers by way of diversified agricultural activities and improvement in efficiency of production through technological upgrading. A sharper thrust on improving agricultural production, which was sought to be achieved by various policy measures and institutional changes, concomitantly necessitated expanding and diversifying the operations of rural/agricultural credit delivery agencies, with the ultimate objective of enhancing the quality of rural lending.

Apart from strengthening commercial banks and RRBs, several measures were initiated to ameliorate problems in the flow of agricultural credit. First, the coverage of rural credit was extended to include facilities such as storage as well as credit through NBFCs. Second, procedural and transactional bottlenecks were sought to be removed by reducing margins, redefining overdues to coincide with crop-cycles, introducing new debt-restructuring policies and one-time settlement and relief measures for farmers indebted to non-institutional lenders. Third, the KCC scheme was improvised and its coverage widened, while some banks popularised general credit cards (GCCs), which was in the nature of a clean overdraft for multipurpose use, including consumption. Fourth, public and private sector banks were encouraged to enhance credit delivery while strengthening disincentives for shortfall in priority sector lending. Fifth, banks were urged to price the credit to farmers based on actual assessment of individual risk rather than on a flat rate, depending on the category of borrower or end-use, while ensuring that the interest rates charged were justifiable as well as reasonable. Other measures were also initiated that covered delegation of more powers to branch managers, simplification of applications, opening of more SSI specialised branches, an enhancement in the limit for composite loans and strengthening of the recovery mechanism. In a nutshell, the thrust was on improving credit delivery in a regime of reasonable costs within the existing legal and institutional constraints.

19

Conclusion: First Seven Years of the 1990s

INTRODUCTION

The Reserve Bank, one of the oldest central banks in the developing world, was formed primarily as a monetary institution in 1935. It was enjoined with the responsibility of maintaining the domestic and external value of the currency and overseeing and directing the credit system in a manner that worked to the country's advantage. The Bank was also entrusted to be the regulator, holder of foreign exchange reserves and guide of exchange rate management. Over time, its functions encompassed promotional and developmental roles in order to support economic development and the growth of the financial markets. As the economy was highly controlled until the late 1980s and the Government played a dominant role in managing the economy, the Reserve Bank as the monetary authority was supportive of government policies, while ensuring co-ordination in monetary, credit and foreign exchange policies.

The Reserve Bank grew in terms of size and complexity and witnessed continuous transformation in terms of organisational set up and management. The operations of the Bank emerged out of a diversity of roles played by it and were marked by flexibility. The organisational structure was continually modified to respond to domestic necessities and contemporaneous international developments. The Bank embarked upon technological transformation, and upgraded its systems and procedures to manage its functions effectively. The commitment of the employees in an environment of free expression and debate over emerging policy issues within the Bank, helped in arriving at solutions over the years with a good degree of success. These positive organisational features augured well for promoting productivity and improving the work ethos.

The decade of 1990s marked a new beginning in the organisational evolution of the Reserve Bank. While the Bank was not *de jure* an independent institution, the onset of wide-ranging reforms in the financial sector necessitated the Bank to gain some degree of autonomy, particularly in areas of monetary management and financial market regulation, although the process of close consultation with the Government continued. This chapter provides perspectives relating to the role played by the Reserve Bank in the post-reform period with particular focus on its functional areas, where sophistication for maintaining price and financial stability for sustainable growth was called for, as brought out in detail in chapters 11 to 18 of this volume.

A GRADUALIST APPROACH

The Indian economy was in the midst of several uncertainties as the decade of the 1990s dawned. The fragile economic situation resulted mainly from domestic macroeconomic imbalances and unforeseen economic events world-wide, apart from the uncertain political environment. It called for strong policy actions to correct the fiscal and external positions and help improve growth on a sustained basis.

While policy actions that flow from well-crafted comprehensive economic reforms are recognised the world over as essential, in India the consensus was on having the speed of policies to be gradual, orderly and well-sequenced. The gradualist approach entailed a fair-paced process of undertaking policy actions and balancing and rebalancing levers of control to realise the expected economic outcomes within a time frame perceived as reasonable. Transparency and involvement of all stakeholders had, in the process, become integral to imparting credibility to the reform measures.

The interesting aspects of the evolution of the policy framework in respect of the financial sector reforms were: first, financial sector reforms were undertaken early in the reforms cycle; second, the process was not driven by any banking crisis, but was home-grown and coincided with the structural adjustments taken under arrangements that were backed by the International Monetary Fund (IMF) and the World Bank; third, the reforms, facilitated as they were by domestic expertise, took onboard the international experiences as well.

India's approach to reforms was guided by five principles, *i.e.*, cautious sequencing of reform measures, introduction of mutually reinforcing norms, initiating complementary reforms across sectors (monetary, fiscal, external and financial sectors), development of financial institutions, and growth and integration of financial markets. The financial sector reforms were led by strengthening prudential and supervisory measures that were introduced early in the reforms agenda. This was followed by interest rate deregulation and a gradual lowering of statutory pre-emptions. The more complex aspects of legal and accounting measures were brought in subsequently, once the basic tenets of reforms were already in place.

The gradualist and prudential management of the external sector including the commitment to maintain orderly conditions in the foreign exchange market through 1991 to 1996 helped the country to tide over the potential contagion of the South-East Asian crisis that jolted emerging market economies (EMEs) in the mid-1997.

THE CRISIS BUILD-UP AND RESPONSE

The fiscal position, both of the Centre and the state governments, remained precarious in the late 1980s and posed a major challenge. The combined deficit of the central and state governments, as per cent of gross domestic product (GDP), increased substantially, from 8.8 per cent during 1984–85 to 9.4 per cent during 1990–91. In addition, the critical external payments position and elevated inflationary pressures contributed to the build-up of macroeconomic imbalances. The structural rigidities and the instability in the economic system constrained the sustainability of the growth process to a certain extent. There was consistent deterioration in merchandise trade, almost entirely attributable to a rise in petroleum, oil and lubricants (POL) imports, which registered a sizeable increase in volume as well as in value terms due to escalating international oil prices. Massive loss of foreign exchange reserves during the early 1990s considerably slowed the pace of broad money expansion. This combined with a sluggish real economy on account of transport and other infrastructure constraints led to moderation in savings and investment rates.

The reforms programme of the 1990s was preceded by some significant measures, in particular in trade, industry, taxation and exchange rate management areas. The early reform initiatives introduced since the mid-1980s had lacked an overarching framework and led to the emergence of macroeconomic distortions. A sizeable component of monetised deficit in the already large fiscal deficit resulted in rapid growth of monetary liquidity that was far out of alignment with real economic growth, thus generating severe demand pressures and accelerating the pace of inflation.

Such imbalances, in turn, were reflected in the build-up of a large and unsustainable current account deficit (CAD). The persistently high levels of fiscal deficit and CAD led to the accumulation of sizeable public debt, both domestic and external. By 1990, there was a realisation among policymakers that the widening fiscal deficit and associated money growth had high inflationary potential, besides posing risks to the balance of payments (BoP). Such concerns were communicated by the Reserve Bank to the Government from time to time.

The serious external payments crisis that struck in the 1991 was the result as much of highly expansionary fiscal policy pursued since the mid-1980s as of some serious distortions in macroeconomic policies pursued in the domestic and external sectors, combined with geopolitical developments. A confluence of economic and political factors was at play in the build-up of the external payments crisis. The turmoil in the world oil market in the aftermath of the gulf war had adverse implications for India's external balance.

By the early 1990s, concessional aid had dried up. This meant resorting to commercial borrowings as a major source of external finance, which resulted in escalation of the debt-service ratio to 35.3 per cent in 1990–91. The incipient signs of a crisis on the external account were visible in the second half of 1990–91, when the gulf war led to a sharp increase in oil prices. The official reserves, which were relatively stable between 1982 and 1989, slid to a level equivalent to 1.3 months of imports by March 1991. This, in quantity terms, was approximately US$ 5.8 billion. The effect of the rise in oil prices was aggravated by the events that followed. Indian workers employed in Kuwait had to be airlifted back to India and their remittances ceased to flow in. Loss of confidence in the Government's ability to manage the situation exacerbated the crisis. The composition of external debt shifted from the official to commercial debt. More importantly, external debt tended to be short-term, an aspect acknowledged as a sign of external vulnerability. Short-term credit dried up, imposing a severe strain on the BoP position. In addition, the outflow from non-resident Indian (NRI) deposits was substantial, which were in effect a form of short-term debt. With effect from October 17, 1990, the Reserve Bank in consultation with the Government commenced the practice of revaluation of the gold holdings from time to time in accordance with international price movements in order to present a more realistic picture of India's foreign exchange reserves.

India, for the first time in several decades, was faced with the risk of a default on its external obligations during the early months of the fiscal 1991–92. To avoid risking a default, India sold 20 metric tonnes of government gold with a re-purchase option to the Union Bank of Switzerland (UBS) through the State Bank of India (SBI), yielding a little more than US$ 200.0 million. Subsequently, as a part of the reserves management policy and as a means of raising resources, the Reserve Bank pledged 47 metric tonnes of gold with the Bank of England (BoE) and the Bank of Japan (BoJ) and raised a loan of US$ 405.0 million in July 1991. Criticism about pledging the gold to recover from the crisis was countered by the argument that the action was necessary to garner international support and it also provided an opportunity to address the reforms process that, in fact, went well beyond the management of the BoP crisis.

The strain on external and internal resources, the threat to monetary stability and the resultant inflationary pressures had begun to hamper investment plans. The situation called for strong stabilisation efforts in the form of fiscal correction, monetary tightening, inflation control and strengthening the competitiveness of India's exports.

The period was characterised by considerable political uncertainty that halted the steady progress being made towards reforms since the mid-1980s. The country had three unstable governments in a span of two years prior to the point when the BoP position reached a crisis level. It was left to the Government formed under the Prime Minister, Shri Narasimha Rao to tackle the situation. Dr Manmohan Singh, as the Finance Minister, carried forward the much needed reforms in close co-ordination with the Reserve Bank, facilitated by the multilateral institutions.[1]

With the CAD reaching 3.0 per cent of GDP in 1990–91 and dwindling foreign exchange reserves, the Government felt it necessary to effect exchange rate adjustments, undertake fiscal reforms and counter destabilising market expectations as immediate policy responses. Devaluation of the Indian rupee, an emergency measure, was implemented in two stages: on July 1, 1991 and, after confirmation of the positive market reaction, on July 3, 1991. The two step downward adjustment in the value of the rupee worked out to 17.38 per cent in terms of the intervention currency, i.e., the pound sterling and about 18.7 per cent in US dollar terms.

---

1. Also refer to chapter 1: Introduction and Overview.

The Government followed up the devaluation process with wide-ranging reforms that set in motion the course of liberalisation of the Indian economy and its financial sector. The reforms process comprised, *inter alia*, abolition of licensing for all except 18 industries; removal of investment caps on large industrial houses; retention of only 6 industries in the public sector; liberalised access to foreign technology; abolition of import licensing; sharp reduction in import duties; and grant of permission to exporters to open foreign currency accounts.

Both the Government and the Reserve Bank were involved in executing measures needed to bring about these adjustments since the late 1989 and through 1990. However, it was only when the country faced the threat of a default in its external payments that it was felt necessary to shore-up international confidence by embarking on a 20-month IMF programme of stabilisation and structural adjustment from 1990–91 to 1992–93. The support of the IMF lent credibility and the arrangement set structural benchmarks to be achieved in stages by May 1993, that were widely regarded as realisable given the strong commitment of the authorities to reforms.

EXTERNAL SECTOR DEVELOPMENTS

The successful mobilisation of external finance and a marked improvement in the external payments situation as well as the debt indicators was experienced after the agreement with the IMF. As a result, there were positive developments in the economy, which included an increase in reserves to US$ 9.8 billion and recovery in the economic growth to 4.0 per cent by the end of 1992–93. This provided the basis for further liberalisation of trade, tariff, export credit and foreign investment policies during the ensuing period, *i.e.*, 1992–93 to 1996–97.

During 1992–93, export performance remained subdued and the increase in import demand was moderate. The collapse of trade with the erstwhile USSR, one of India's principal markets in 1993, led to a marked shift in the destination of exports and sources of imports between general currency area (GCA) and rupee payment area. During the subsequent three years, *i.e.*, from 1993–94 to 1995–96, export performance was robust. India's exports also exhibited substantial structural changes in favour of manufactured goods. The shift in the composition of merchandise imports, however, was not as perceptible. Further, a rebound in India's imports from the contraction of 1990–91 and 1991–92 was strong in the year 1992–93. The significant expansion in imports during 1994–95 and 1995–96 can be attributed to the marked buoyancy in the industrial sector. The trade deficit widened due to an increase in imports but growth in invisibles came to the rescue to a significant extent. At this point thus, the Indian economy was much less vulnerable than most East Asian economies. Debt service payments on past debts were high; the debt-service ratio, however, declined gradually but significantly from 30.2 per cent in 1991–92 to 23.0 per cent in 1996–97. The CAD to GDP ratio also declined to (-)1.25 per cent in 1996–97. Further, short-term debt was 7.2 per cent of total debt and foreign exchange reserves climbed to US$ 26.4 billion in 1996–97.

Drawing lessons from the crisis of 1991, the high level committee on BoP chaired by Dr C. Rangarajan observed that the CAD should be maintained at 1.6 per cent of GDP over the medium term, which could be financed with normal capital flows. The IMF obligations under Article VIII were accepted by India and, in pursuance of this, current account convertibility was introduced in August 1994.

The capital account was dominated by foreign investment inflows, which met more than half the financing needs of the country. A welcome development was the spurt in foreign direct investment (FDI) from 1995–96. During 1997–98, inflows of FDI far exceeded that of portfolio investment. There was also a steady improvement in inflows arising from investment proposals made by NRIs. The US continued to be the largest direct investor, followed by the UK.

EXCHANGE RATE MANAGEMENT

The dual exchange rate arrangement instituted on March 1, 1992 under the liberalised exchange rate management system (LERMS) was a successful transitional step to move in an orderly manner from a managed float regime to a market-determined system. The spread between the official and market rates moved in a narrow range, except in the month of February 1993, when speculative activity resulted in some turbulence in the inter-bank exchange market. LERMS, however, created conditions for transferring an augmented volume of foreign exchange transactions on to the market. It imparted stability, resulted in significant deceleration in the rate of inflation and a build-up in the level of foreign exchange reserves. At this point, the Reserve Bank evaluated three options for modification of the extant mechanism of LERMS. These were: (i) to maintain the status quo; (ii) to change to an 80:20 ratio; and (iii) to have a unified exchange rate regime with a few exceptions, with no requirement for authorised dealers (ADs) to surrender any part of foreign exchange receipts to the Reserve Bank. The Bank went for the third option.

Accordingly, the unified exchange rate management system came into effect from March 1, 1993. A number of measures were put in place that enabled a smooth transition to a regime under which the external value of the rupee was determined by market forces. The unification of the dual exchange rate system into a single floating exchange rate imparted a significant degree of flexibility to the exchange rate regime in BoP adjustment. The experience with the free floating market-determined exchange rate was found to be satisfactory. Contrary to the speculation, remarkable stability was achieved in the exchange rate of the rupee. This also enabled the foreign exchange market to grow further and to mature. The Reserve Bank's interventions in such a regime were passive and occasional, motivated primarily by the need to protect export competitiveness by containing the potential appreciation of the rupee.

Following the success of the unified market determined exchange rate system introduced in 1993 and the accumulation of foreign exchange reserves to a comfortable level, the Reserve Bank further simplified the procedures and delegated greater autonomy to ADs in respect of a number of current account transactions. While the linkage between the money market and foreign exchange market was weak in the pre-LERMS period, the switch to the market-determined exchange rate and the growing importance of the forward market in the foreign exchange transactions strengthened the conduits of transmission of impulses between the short-end of the money market and the foreign exchange market. Several measures were taken by the Reserve Bank to deepen the foreign exchange market in India.

The Reserve Bank set up an expert group (Chairman: Shri O.P. Sodhani) in November 1994 to recommend measures for the growth of an active, efficient and orderly foreign exchange market and to suggest introduction of derivative products. The group made wide-ranging recommendations concerning removal of market constraints, development of derivative products and propositions for risk management, accounting and disclosure standards. It also dealt with aspects such as information systems and clearing mechanisms relating to the market. This was followed up with the Reserve Bank introducing institutional measures directed towards widening and deepening the exchange market and providing greater functional autonomy to market participants. The efforts resulted in increasing the average monthly turnover of merchant transactions.

MONETARY MANAGEMENT

The objectives of monetary policy of the Reserve Bank in the 1990s continued to be multi-dimensional, with as much emphasis on growth as on price stability. Towards this end, the Reserve Bank perceived that monetary growth should be consistent with the estimated output growth and a tolerable inflation rate. In pursuit of these objectives, the monetary policy had to be flexible enough to make strategic adjustments to any market disequilibria as also the surge in foreign capital inflows. Thus, in the eventful post-liberalisation phase, monetary management was also vested with the responsibility of maintaining orderly conditions in money, credit, securities and foreign exchange markets.

Monetary policy had to bear the brunt of external adjustment in the initial years of reforms when the stringent performance criteria of the IMF were to be met. Once inflation was under control and the external payments position improved, progressive rationalisation and deregulation of the interest rate structure became integral to the process of refining the operating procedures of monetary policy. Broad money (M_3) continued to act as an intermediate target, while the level of bank reserves served as the operating target. There was nevertheless a marked shift in emphasis from direct to indirect instruments of credit control. It was expected that the flexibility provided to policy formulation would improve the functioning of the financial markets and, in the process lead to close alignment in the interest rates and greater market integration. Open market operations (OMOs) and repos were, therefore, actively deployed to influence the level of reserves with commercial banks and thereby adjust liquidity in the system. The Reserve Bank made efforts to develop the financial markets to serve as an efficient transmission mechanism of monetary policy impulses.

The historic agreement signed in September 1994 between the Reserve Bank and the Government to phase out automatic monetisation of budget deficit, afforded a good degree of manoeuvrability to the Reserve Bank in the conduct of its monetary and credit policy. The phenomenon of continuous and large inflows of foreign capital since 1993–94 and the resultant accretion to the foreign exchange reserves posed new challenges to monetary policy, since the external payments position impinged strongly on the domestic economy. The period witnessed the integration of monetary policy with debt management policy, as also between the money, gilt-edged and foreign exchange markets.

ACTIVE PUBLIC DEBT MANAGEMENT

The decade of the 1980s was an era of tightly regulated interest rates, including those on government securities. The government securities market during the decade was characterised by administered interest rates, high statutory liquidity ratio (SLR) requirements for banks and administrative directions to insurance and investment institutions and provident funds (PFs) that provided a captive market. As a result, a liquid and a transparent secondary market for government securities could not develop. The borrowing costs of the Government were kept artificially down by offering low coupon rates. The automatic accommodation to the Central Government by the Reserve Bank led to voluminous expansion of short-term government debt, through the mechanism of issue of *ad hoc* Treasury Bills. As a result, the debt management practised by the Bank remained passive.

With the implementation of the Narasimham Committee recommendations, the interest rates on government borrowing were progressively made market related, which were expected to help reduce SLR. Against the backdrop of the emphasis on moderation of gross fiscal deficit (GFD) in the reforms period in the early 1990s, it was envisaged that an active internal debt management policy would facilitate the integration of debt management policy with monetary policy. An Internal Debt Management Cell (IDMC) carved out of the Secretary's Department in April 1992 was converted into a full-fledged inter-disciplinary and independent department in October 1992. The move was aimed at strengthening delivery capabilities in developing both the primary and secondary segments of the government securities market.

The developments in public debt management in the initial reforms period included introduction of auction-based issuance of 91-day Treasury Bills, auctions of dated government securities, introduction of longer maturity 364-day Treasury Bills, repos in government securities by the Reserve Bank for efficient liquidity management, launch of innovative debt instruments such as zero coupon bonds, floating rate instruments, partly paid stocks and conversion of Treasury Bills into dated government securities to reduce roll-over risk of the government debt. In effect, the market had to be groomed and nurtured during this phase through continuous dialogue with the treasury managers and by organising workshops.

These efforts led to the emergence of a market based yield curve. Since the growth of the secondary market was rather slow initially, primary yields through auctions served as proxies in the attempt to evolve a yield curve. The manoeuvrability of the Reserve Bank to set in place public debt management practices consistent with monetary policy received a stimulus with the agreements signed between 1994 and 1997 for a phased reduction in issuance of *ad hoc* Treasury Bills and the ultimate discontinuation of such bills with effect from April 1997, to be replaced by a system of limited ways and means advances (WMA) from the Reserve Bank. The transition from *ad hoc* Treasury Bills to the WMA mechanism was a major milestone in fiscal, financial and monetary policy reforms. It led to substantial improvement in fiscal discipline and ensured greater flexibility to the conduct of public debt management consistent with monetary policy objectives.

The move towards the strengthening of public debt management operations by the Reserve Bank in co-ordination with the Government during 1992 to 1997 proved to be extremely beneficial in terms of the high proportion of market absorption of government securities and lower devolvement of such securities on the Reserve Bank. This facilitated competitive pricing of securities, and gradually led to the emergence of a market responsive yield curve that resulted in greater attention to treasury management and interest rate risk management by bankers and investors.

DEVELOPMENT OF FINANCIAL MARKETS

The Indian financial system grew rapidly over the decades of the 1980s and 1990s and comprised an impressive network of institutions. The deepening and widening of the financial system was most significant in the case of banking and term-lending institutions. But, until the close of the 1980s, markets were subject to a plethora of controls. While the equity market got a boost beginning in the 1980s, the money, debt and credit markets suffered on account of a plethora of controls. Nevertheless, the mid-1980s witnessed early liberalisation in the money market and a few new short-term instruments were introduced in the market.

Financial market evolution was guided by the recommendations made by the Chakravarty Committee (1985), Vaghul Committee (1987), Narasimham Committee (1991) and Sodhani Committee (1994). In addition, the Reserve Bank followed a consultative approach to the development of financial markets by constituting internal working groups and committees with participation from other institutions and market players from time to time.

Financial sector reforms also included policies and measures directed towards improving the allocational and functional efficiency of the economic system. The implementation of the reforms process and supervision under the aegis of the Reserve Bank strengthened the interplay of market forces and fostered the process of integration among various segments of the financial markets. Towards this end, efforts were made to develop institutions and instruments, and put in place the operating procedures for smooth functioning of the markets. These measures resulted in relative rates of return on various instruments in different market segments moving in alignment, within a narrow range. Further, the development of a liquid and deep market for government securities infused vigour into the entire financial system and imparted flexibility to the conduct of monetary policy.

By the year 1996–97, the role of the financial markets had become critical in more than one way, *i.e.*, in mobilising and apportioning savings in the economy, transmitting signals for policy formulation and facilitating liquidity management consistent with the overall short and medium-term policy objectives. While the long-term goal of achieving integration among different segments of the financial markets was continuously kept in view, the main thrust of the Reserve Bank's policies was on eliminating the factors that constrained the free flow of resources among various market segments and facilitating opportunities for arbitrage across segments and maturities in order to achieve efficient pricing. These inter-linkages added another dimension to the conduct of monetary policy, *i.e.*, the necessity to access, on a continuous basis, the liquidity available in the system and adopt appropriate measures for minimising volatility in the financial markets.

The Reserve Bank evolved a combination of liquidity management tools, such as repo operations and management of refinance facilities, to absorb and inject liquidity at discretion and provide greater stability to the short-term money market. Attempts were made to activate Bank Rate as the benchmark rate, and a system of prime lending rate (PLR) was introduced to impart efficacy to the interest rate channel of monetary policy. This met with limited success, and Bank Rate was posited to eventually become a signalling rate. There were also, in parallel, attempts to deepen and diversify the money market by introducing new instruments in the form of auctioning of Treasury Bills of varied maturities, commercial paper (CP) and certificates of deposit (CDs). For structural reasons, such as the high cash reserve ratio (CRR) and limits on the maturity structure of deposits, the money market continued to be dominated by the overnight call money market. The term money market was a non-starter. As a result, while a term structure of interest rates evolved with the deepening of the government securities market, attempts to develop a short-term yield curve and benchmarks along the lines of the London interbank offered rate (LIBOR) did not take off.

BANKING AND FINANCIAL INSTITUTIONS

The early 1980s were characterised by continuation of expansionary policy towards the banking system combined with intensification of efforts to promote priority sector credit at the cost of operational efficiency. This resulted in the surfacing of several weaknesses, such as poor quality of lending and an increase in non-performing loans (NPLs), thereby necessitating a rethink on the credit delivery system. The consolidation measures were thus introduced, beginning in the mid-1980s. The policies towards regulation and prudential supervision gained momentum from the late 1980s, with the Reserve Bank gradually bringing the financial system in alignment with international best practices.

The Reserve Bank kept a constant vigil over international developments, since a wave of breakdown of the fixed exchange rate system, liberalisation and deregulation was sweeping across its Asian counterparts, especially in the financial sector. The Bank learnt from international experiences, imbibed and internalised new policies and practices that it adapted to Indian conditions, against the backdrop of constraints, such as, government ownership of major FIs and banks, directed lending practices, regulated interest rate structure, pre-emption of bank resources under the reserve requirements and exchange controls. The Reserve Bank, nevertheless, in co-ordination with the Government facilitated rapid deregulation of the sector, beginning in the mid-1980s to make the financial system more efficient and competitive.

During the period 1991–1997, as part of financial sector reforms, a significant transformation took place in the banking and financial system. The implementation of the Narasimham Committee report gave a fillip to the process. While the systemic shock due to irregularities in securities transactions in 1992 affected the financial system and the banking sector in particular, the lessons from the episode led to far-reaching reforms in market regulation and settlement practices. This also strengthened the bias towards a gradualist approach to the reforms process and continuation of public sector dominance in the financial sector.

The banking reform measures encompassed, *inter alia*, strengthening and consolidating banks, prescribing prudential norms relating to asset classification and income recognition, provisioning for bad and doubtful assets, introducing a system of capital to risk-weighted asset ratios and establishing a strong supervisory system. The entry of new banks, including private sector banks, mergers, putting in place supervisory and surveillance mechanisms and in house strengthening of banks also formed part of the reforms package. The implementation of prudential norms and guidelines was a significant step towards the introduction of transparency in accounting practices and brought the norms in line with international best practices. A Board for Financial Supervision (BFS) was set up under the aegis of the Reserve Bank on November 16, 1994, to give a specialised and independent focus to supervision of banks and FIs.

The banking system withstood a major set-back which came in the form of the securities scam of 1992. The Janakiraman Committee was appointed to investigate the irregularities in funds management by commercial banks and FIs, especially their dealings in government securities, public sector bonds, units of the Unit Trust of India (UTI) and similar instruments. The committee report pointed to several deficiencies in the functioning of treasuries in banks and FIs, the absence of necessary internal controls, raising money without backing of genuine securities, diversion of call money funds to current accounts of chosen brokers, massive collusion between officials and the brokers involved in government securities dealings and the breakdown of necessary discipline regarding issue and recording of bankers' receipts (BRs).

The committee made a series of recommendations that included introduction of proper control systems, strengthening monitoring mechanisms and removing lacunae in the existing systems and procedures to avoid recurrence of such irregularities. The Reserve Bank and the Government, in light of these suggestions, took concerted action to restore public confidence in the country's financial system. Several follow-up measures were initiated by the Reserve Bank in close co-ordination with the Government to unearth ramifications of the scam, recover bank dues, impose penalties on the guilty and put in place preventive measures to avoid recurrence of such events.

The 1990s witnessed, in parallel, strengthening of the regulatory role of the Bank over non-banking financial companies (NBFCs) which came often into disrepute on account of cheating and fraud on trusting depositors. Prudential norms were strengthened across all categories of non-banking companies, in particular those accepting deposits from public. The Reserve Bank attempted to bring the supervisory and regulatory standards by and large in harmony with those applicable to the banking system.

AGRICULTURE AND RURAL DEVELOPMENT

The Reserve Bank, since its inception, had a unique role statutorily carved out in the field of agriculture and rural development. It initiated the All-India Rural Credit and Investment Survey in 1951 and nurtured the rural co-operative credit institutions through a specialised Agricultural Credit Department (ACD). It also formed the Agricultural Refinance Corporation (ARC) as a development finance institution in July 1963, later known as the Agricultural Refinance and Development Corporation (ARDC). It created the institution of regional rural banks (RRBs) in the late 1970s. In 1982, spanning out of the ACD and ARDC was the apex institution for agriculture and rural development, namely, the National Bank for Agriculture and Rural Development (NABARD). In the post-nationalisation period after 1969, directions for bank lending to agriculture and rural development schemes through priority sector norms were issued, thereby significantly improving organised lending to agriculture and relieving the farm sector from the control of money lenders.

Following an expansionary phase during the 1980s, the intensity of efforts towards increasing agricultural productivity and providing rural credit in the aftermath of the external sector crisis and its resolution, however, lost much of its momentum. Thus, at the advent of the economic reforms in 1991, the rural credit delivery system was relatively weak. From the early 1990s, the rural credit system had been on the downslide, afflicted with mounting overdues that dampened the flow of funds. This trend adversely affected the economic viability of lending institutions, especially the co-operatives and RRBs. Despite the impressive geographic spread of the formal channels of finance, and the diminishing influence of informal channels, the rural financial institutions showed several weaknesses, such as low productivity, inefficiency, poor recovery culture and diminishing profitability.

In pursuance of the recommendations of the Narasimham Committee, measures were initiated to ameliorate the problems related to flow of agricultural credit, apart from strengthening commercial banks and RRBs. The thrust of the approach was to improvise credit delivery at reasonable interest rates within the extant legal and institutional constraints. First, the coverage of rural credit was expanded to include additional facilities such as storage. Second, procedural and transactional bottlenecks were removed, reducing margins, redefining overdues to coincide with crop-cycles, and announcing new debt-restructuring policies, as also one-time settlement and relief measures for farmers who owed debt to non-institutional lenders. Third, the kisan credit card (KCC) scheme was improvised and its coverage widened, while some banks also floated general credit cards (GCCs) that offered overdraft for multipurpose use, including consumption. Fourth, public and private sector banks were encouraged to enhance credit delivery while promoting disincentives for shortfall in priority sector lending. Fifth, banks were urged to price credit for farmers on the basis of actual assessment of individual risk rather than on a flat rate, depending upon the category of borrower or end-use, while ensuring that interest rates charged were justifiable. Other measures introduced included delegation of more powers to branch managers, simplification of applications, opening of more small scale industries (SSI) specialised branches, enhancement in the limit for composite loans and strengthening of the recovery mechanism.

In order to align the priority sector lending of foreign banks operating in India with that of the Indian banks, the target for priority sector lending by foreign banks was raised in October 1993 from 15.0 per cent to 32.0 per cent of their net bank credit, inclusive of two separate sub-targets of at least 10.0 per cent each in respect of advances for the SSIs and exports to be achieved by end-March 1994. Taking into account their difficulties in extending credit to the agricultural sector due to the lack of rural branch network, the composition of priority sector advances for foreign banks was enlarged to include export credit extended by them with effect from July 1, 1993. The overall target of priority sector lending in respect of foreign banks remained unchanged at 32.0 per cent of net bank credit with a sub-target of 10.0 per cent in respect of advances for SSIs. The sub-target for export credit was, however, raised from 10.0 per cent to 12.0 per cent of net bank credit for the year ending March 1997. In the event of shortfall in priority sector lending from the stipulated targets and sub-targets, the policy of requiring foreign banks to place deposits equivalent to the shortfall with the Small Industries Development Bank of India (SIDBI) at an interest rate of 8.0 per cent per annum was maintained.

Though the need to augment the growth of agricultural and rural employment was part of the Government's policy, the fact remained that economic reforms were largely confined to industry, trade and commerce. The financial sector reforms stressed the productivity, efficiency and profitability of banking, which compelled the banking system to focus on viability-based expansion of business, while at the same time extending finance to agriculture and the rural sector at relaxed terms and conditions. In forward-looking initiatives, several subsidised employment-linked programmes, particularly those to uplift weaker sections, and the micro-credit system of extending finance were attempted on an experimental basis.

The Reserve Bank continued to play a key role in development of the agricultural and rural sector by providing refinance, and extending policy and regulatory support to NABARD and scheduled banks, which included RRBs and the co-operative sector. NABARD, established in 1982 as an apex national bank to exclusively cater to agriculture and rural development, continued to depend on the Government and the Reserve Bank for its resources and operations. Though agriculture was the backbone of the economy, it did not get the focused attention that it deserved in view of the need to ensure the viability of the banking sector combined with the necessity of providing low-cost funds to this segment.

As a result of weaknesses in credit delivery through conventional priority sector norms, a new model in the form of the micro-finance movement was ushered in following the example of the grameen bank of Bangladesh. NABARD spearheaded this movement through a self-help group (SHG)-bank linkage programme in 1992 on a pilot basis. This programme was extended countrywide subsequently. The model was further expanded with the foray of non-government organisations (NGOs) and microfinance institutions (MFIs) into the field. This paved the way for a new approach to financial inclusion that aimed at providing access to financial services at the doorstep for women and other vulnerable sections in the rural sector.

COMMUNICATION PRACTICES

While the practices of communication evolved over time, it remained by and large one-way until the 1980s, as the policies were centralised and mostly encompassed directions in a tightly regulated financial regime.[2] Communication, however, emerged as an important central banking function in the 1990s, as with the liberalisation and financial sector reforms, the Reserve Bank adopted an active communication strategy and started to influence markets through its announcements. Besides, the Bank's withdrawal from the micro-management of FIs and allowing them more operational flexibility helped to make communication a two-way process. Through the communication practices, the Bank discharged its responsibility of keeping various segments of society informed about its role in the financial system.

The Reserve Bank's communication, although broadly categorised as external and internal, can be viewed in three dimensions in terms of channels, namely, publications, speeches, and other modes. While periodic publications, *viz.*, bulletins, reports, newsletters and pamphlets provided a wealth of information on macroeconomic and policy developments within and outside the Bank, the speeches delivered by the top executives provided insights into the Reserve Bank's thinking and policy stance on various issues. There was a noticeable increase in such addresses made by the top executives since the mid-1980s. This was necessitated in order to foster financial education in the country. The Reserve Bank, in tune with the revolution in information and communication technology, operationalised its website with the URL *http://reservebank.com* on September 17, 1996. The site helped to host the publications, speeches and notifications/circulars of the Bank.

Market intelligence took centre-stage in pursuance of the recommendations of the Janakiraman Committee. Market intelligence cell (MIC) was set up in the Bank in 1992–93 to track market developments to co-ordinate with the departments within the Bank and to collect sensitive information on areas of concern to the Bank, thereby providing important market-related inputs for policy evolution. All these endeavours resulted in evolving a gradual but integrated network to connect with markets, other stakeholders and public and yielded agreeable results.

TO CONCLUDE

The robust financial system built up over the years and further strengthened during the 1990s, combined with prudential management of monetary, exchange rate and capital account policies, helped India to

---

2. Chapter 20: Communication Practices gives a more detailed account of this aspect.

overcome the potentially unfavourable impact of a series of currency, banking and capital account crises that plagued emerging markets in the mid-1990s. India came out rather unscathed from such adversities. Besides, the unique handling of exchange rate management and management of the capital account by the Reserve Bank, much against the paradigm advocated by multilateral institutions and a number of economists, served as a model for the EMEs after the South-East Asian crisis struck.

III
ORGANISATIONAL ASPECTS

20

Communication Practices

INTRODUCTION

Transparent and consistent communication[1] strategies hold the key for a central bank to enhance the efficacy of its policies, especially the monetary policy. They help reduce uncertainty and information asymmetry across sections of stakeholders, thereby strengthening the formation of expectations in the financial markets. There are two facets of communication, namely, external and internal. The latter involves exchange of information and dialogue between departments and communication between the management and staff. While external communication shapes market expectations, internal communication facilitates trust building and inculcates a sense of belonging among the employees, thereby leading to increased productivity and efficiency. Further, central banks disseminate a variety of macroeconomic data and information through the electronic media as well as through publications. The large variation in

---

1. The Reserve Bank had been entrusted with the responsibility to prepare its Annual Report (RBI Act, 1934) and the Report on Trend and Progress of Banking in India (Banking Regulation Act, 1949). Besides, from its early years, the Bank had been publishing the Report on Currency and Finance (RCF) and the monthly bulletin (1947). During the 1960s and 1970s, the Bank's new publications included, Reserve Bank of India: Functions and Working (1941, 1958, 1970 and 1983) and the RBI history [(1935–1951), (1951–1967) and (1967–1981)]. No doubt, there was early recognition on the part of the Reserve Bank to disseminate information about its functions but it was only in the 1990s that serious efforts were made to develop a communication policy and strategy, especially after the launching of the economic and financial sector reforms. This is the first time that the topic of communication is being dealt with as a separate chapter. Therefore, while the main focus of this chapter is on developments in this area during 1981–1997, the events of earlier period have also been covered in brief, wherever found necessary.

communication strategies across central banks suggests that a consensus is yet to emerge on what constitutes an optimal communication strategy.[2]

Communication is not just about transparency. It is also about publicising, guiding and steering matters in the desired direction. Communication is effective in conditions where markets are well-developed and the regulatory framework is strong. In this, the central bank can be an honest channel between the Government and the public and even Parliament.[3] Historically, central bank communication is known to guide market perceptions and reactions. Mr Alan Greenspan, Chairman, Federal Reserve Board was known for being adept at guiding the Board to consensus on policy issues and his public statements and comments influenced the behaviour of participants in the financial markets in the manner intended by the Fed. Following the stock market crash of October 19, 1987 in the US, Chairman Greenspan issued a statement before the start of trading on October 20, 1987:[4]

The Federal Reserve, consistent with its responsibilities as the nation's central bank, affirmed today its readiness to serve as a source of liquidity to support the economic and financial system.

The market rallied immediately, posting a record one-day gain of 102.27 points the very next day and 186.64 points on October 22, 1987. By September 1989, the market had regained all of the value that it lost in the crash.[5]

The consequences of central bank communication can be decisive for the markets. It was historically construed that central bank communication needed to be understood in terms of 'constructive ambiguity', a term popularised by President Gerald Corrigan of the Federal Reserve Bank of New York. It was believed that the financial markets watched for pauses

---

2. Blinder, Alan S., Michael Ehrmann, Marcel Fratzscher, Jakob De Haan, David-Jan Jansen (2008). "Central Bank Communication and Monetary Policy: A Survey of Theory and Evidence", *NBER Working Paper* No. 13932.

3. Dr I.G. Patel's address to the SAARC Governors' meeting on Communication in Central Banks, which was scheduled for December 2004, was cancelled due to the tsunami and quoted in remarks by Dr Y.V. Reddy, Governor, Reserve Bank of India at the 7th Bank for International Settlements (BIS) Annual Conference at Lucerne, Switzerland on June 26, 2008.

4. *www.federalreserveeducation.org.* "History of the Federal Reserve 1990s: The Longest Expansion". Federal Reserve Education.

5. Itskevich, Jennifer (2002). "What Caused the Stock Market Crash of 1987?", *George Mason University's History News Network*, July 31.

in central bank communication, and some punctuation marks in the text statement had the possibility of getting transmitted through the movement of a few points in the yield curve. Against the backdrop of plausibility of such consequences, which could be measured in millions of rupees or dollars, communication in central banking indeed was a serious matter.[6]

Monetary policy communication is particularly important. One of the most significant developments of the Greenspan era was the evolution towards greater transparency and therefore, more attention was devoted to communication in formulating the US monetary policy. He transformed the Federal Reserve into an institution that embraced the benefits of transparency. In 1994, under Mr Greenspan's leadership, Fed began to publicly disclose its policy actions.[7]

Even much earlier, in the early 1980s, the Governor, Dr Manmohan Singh, had highlighted the importance of communication for the central banks in their functioning. Speaking at a seminar organised by the Maharashtra Economic Development Council,[8] he averred that the policies of a country's central bank and monetary authority had profound implications for the functioning of any modern economy and, therefore, it was appropriate that these policies should be a subject matter of public concern and debate. He further emphasised:

> Unfortunately, central bankers are often a very shy group of people. They are particularly not adept in techniques of mass communication. As a result, central banking policies are not always well understood and appreciated even when they are based on sound logic and empirical analysis.

Dr Manmohan Singh's successors went a step further in explaining the rationale of the policies of the Bank through speeches delivered at different forums. It was during the latter half of the 1980s that there was a noticeable rise in the number of speeches and such orations became an important element of the communication strategy at the Reserve Bank.

---

6. Mohan, Rakesh (2005). "Communications in Central Banks: A Perspective". *SAARCFINANCE Governors' Symposium*. Mumbai. September 9.

7. Macklern, Tiff (2005). "Central Bank Communication and Policy Effectiveness". Commentary at the symposium *The Greenspan Era: Lessons for the Future*. Sponsored by the Federal Reserve Bank of Kansas City. August 25-27.

8. Singh, Manmohan (1982). *Credit Policy of the Reserve Bank of India*, Inaugural Address at a seminar organised by the Maharashtra Economic Development Council, Bombay, November 18.

THE INDIAN SETTING

Communication has remained a significant aspect of central banking in India since the inception of the Reserve Bank in 1935. Although the role played by communication was recognised, there existed practices of communication, but a formal policy in this regard does not appear to have been in place until recently.[9] Communication took the form of information dissemination either through official circulars to banks, publications or speeches by the top executives. Over time, with the organisational evolution of the Reserve Bank in response to its functional progression, the role played by the Reserve Bank in the Indian economy expanded. This led to the streamlining as well as the fanning out of modes of communication. Communication practices, as a matter of fact, were still evolving and improved communication was accorded a special focus in the Reserve Bank in relatively recent years. The technological improvements through the years facilitated faster communication, thus saving time and enhancing productivity and efficiency.

EARLY HISTORY

The beginning of information dissemination could be traced to publishing of the first Annual Report in 1936, which had a limited scope and presented the financial accounts of the Reserve Bank. In 1937, the statistical section of the Agriculture Credit Department (ACD) brought out the first issue of the Reserve Bank's RCF, covering the years 1935–36 and 1936–37. This report presented an account of the major developments in different sectors of the economy during these years. The report was, thereafter, put out annually and was one of the first steps in evolving a communication strategy for the Bank. The efforts in this domain received a stimulus in 1945 with the setting-up of the Department of Research and Statistics (DRS), which was entrusted with the task of publishing various reports and research papers on issues of economic interest. These were essentially meant for publicising central bank perceptions and other information. The DRS embarked upon the publication of the Reserve Bank of India monthly bulletin along with its weekly statistical supplement (WSS) in January 1947. This endeavour reflected the fact that the Reserve Bank was well ahead of its contemporaries in the matter of communication and information dissemination. There was further progress when, under the provisions of the Banking Regulation (BR) Act, 1949, the Reserve Bank

---

9. The communication policy of the Reserve Bank of India was framed in July 2008.

was assigned the responsibility of submitting the Report on Trend and Progress of Banking in India to the Central Government as a statutory annual publication.

To strengthen the Bank's efforts in communication, a separate cell was carved out within the Economic Department in 1969 (erstwhile DRS), under the charge of a Press Relations Officer (PRO). The PRO, for which the first incumbent was appointed in September 1970, not only looked after the dissemination requirements of the Reserve Bank but also that of the Industrial Development Bank of India (IDBI), the Agricultural Refinance and Development Corporation (ARDC) and the Deposit Insurance and Credit Guarantee Corporation (DICGC). The office of the PRO was moved to the Secretary's Department in 1970 to handle matters relating to public and press relations and in 1972, it was converted into a full-fledged press relations section.

Prior to the formation of an equipped division, the division of publications and press relations in the Economic Department of the Bank handled matters relating to communication. The division was delegated with the charge of bringing out various publications of the Bank such as the Annual Report, RCF, Report on Trend and Progress of Banking in India and the monthly bulletin, among others. It also issued press releases relating to various departments of the Bank and promulgated policy changes, as and when required. The reach of these releases was, however, limited to select newspapers and journals published from Bombay.

In March 1978, the post of the PRO was upgraded and the section was renamed the press relations division (PRD). The officers, except for the head of the division, were drawn from various departments of the Reserve Bank. The PRD also monitored media reports relating to the Reserve Bank and the banking and financial system, and provided an account of the same to the top executives of the Reserve Bank. The PRD published brochures, leaflets and booklets for exposition of various schemes introduced periodically by the Bank to the staff. Specific initiatives taken by the PRD were, *inter alia*, a special handout issued on the anniversary of the nationalisation of banks that highlighted the progress made by commercial banks in expanding their branch network, mobilising deposits and providing credit facilities to the priority sector. During 1981–82, the PRD released a revised edition of the booklet, Exchange Control: Non-Resident Indians and five brochures on various staff amenities, such as the leave fare concession scheme, medical facilities for workmen employees, the housing loan scheme, medical facilities for officers, and facilities on tours and transfers. A leaflet on Know Your Bank and a folder on ledger posting machines for familiarisation of the mechanisation being undertaken in the Reserve Bank were also prepared and circulated by the PRD.

CHANNELS OF COMMUNICATION

The Reserve Bank's communication network can be grouped into three major categories: internal communication, communication between the Reserve Bank and the banking system, and external communication. In terms of channels, communication took place through: (i) publications (including circulars/notifications); (ii) speeches; and (iii) others.[10] While periodic publication of the monthly bulletin, reports, newsletters and pamphlets provided a wealth of information on macroeconomic developments and the working of various schemes supported by the Reserve Bank, the speeches by the Governors and Deputy Governors gave insights into the Reserve Bank's perspectives on varied issues. Other endeavours included the creation and maintenance of a Reserve Bank website, improving internal communication by encouraging the publication of in house magazines and bringing out handouts on various welfare schemes promoted by the Bank.

There was lack of effective inter-department communication in the Reserve Bank prior to the 1990s. This limitation was in fact perceived to be one reason for the delayed recognition of the irregularities in the transaction of government securities leading to the securities scam in 1992. The Janakiraman Committee[11] on irregularities in government securities' transactions recommended that the Reserve Bank should strengthen its market intelligence mechanism for timely detection of such events to enable initiating early action. Pursuant to the recommendations of the committee, a market intelligence cell (MIC) was set up in the Bank in 1992–93 to follow market developments. The cell was created as a separate entity and in addition to the banking intelligence unit within the Department of Banking Operations and Development (DBOD). The cell communicated with various departments of the Bank and collected sensitive information from the markets on areas of special interest to the

---

10. Others consist of reports of the committees/working groups set up by the Reserve Bank from time to time and research studies on policy-related issues (Development Research Group [DRG] studies) by the staff and outside expert(s). The Annual Report from 1993 onwards and the RCF subsequent to 1993 contained critical evaluation of economic developments.

11. For details refer to chapter 17: Reforms in Banking and Financial Institutions.

Reserve Bank. Further, the Bank formed inter-department groups to share sensitive information related to the markets and to monitor the flow of funds.

RESERVE BANK OF INDIA PUBLICATIONS: CANVAS AND CONTENT EXPANDED

ANNUAL REPORT

The Annual Report of the Reserve Bank is a statutory publication that carries the Reserve Bank's financial accounts and a review of the macroeconomic situation. The first Annual Report, published in 1936, was primarily a statement of accounts of the Bank to its shareholders. The report became bilingual (Hindi and English) in keeping with the requirements of the Official Languages Act (OLA), 1963. Beginning in 1980–81, the Annual Report of the Bank contained two sections: one that presented the macroeconomic analysis and the other that highlighted banking and other developments; transmitted the balance sheet of the Bank and profit and loss accounts for the year ending June. In the successive reports, the section on assessment and prospects gained prominence because the analytics and perspectives contained therein reflected the Bank's views on emerging economic issues. The report was strengthened over the years in terms of coverage and content, supplemented by graphs and tables.

Apart from reporting the status of accounts, the Annual Report also put forth the Reserve Bank's assessment of public policies, including fiscal and external sector policies. During the late 1980s, on several occasions the report provided a review of fiscal issues. On one occasion, it also emphasised that the Bank was not mandated to provide ways and means advances to the Government and that this was only an enabling provision in the Reserve Bank of India (RBI) Act.[12]

In 1988–89, there was a rearrangement of the contents in terms of presentation and the overall coverage of the developments and policy issues in the report. An overview presented a brief on the macroeconomic backdrop, followed by a discussion on the sector-wise economic situation. A special feature in this issue was a detailed analysis of the monetary inter-relationships, such as the money multiplier, which was an important addition. An innovation was furnishing the highlights of banking and other developments, which was a welcome feature. Illustrations in the form of

---

12. Reserve Bank of India, *Annual Report, 1989–90*.

tables and charts came to occupy a much larger space in the successive reports. The coverage of organisational issues remained a prominent aspect in all the reports.

In accord with the advent of economic liberalisation, a point of departure in the report for 1991–92 was that the first part, the economic review, captured policy developments and perspectives. The second part of the report was rechristened working and operations of the Reserve Bank of India, which focused, *inter alia*, on commercial bank operations, co-operative credit structure, non-banking financial and non-financial companies, the DICGC, exchange management and exchange control, organisational matters and the Bank's accounts for the year. The report for the year also carried detailed appendix tables on various macroeconomic variables, which was an addition. Another important insertion was an annex on notes to accounts and significant accounting policies, which followed the profit and loss accounts statement. This became a regular feature in later issues of the report. These changes considerably enhanced the information content relating to the working of the Bank.

The Annual Report for 1994–95 was notable for the introduction of boxes on the issues of contemporary economic debate. This was a novel feature, was well received by the readers and formed an integral part of the successive reports.

It is worth mentioning that in 1995–96, an annex on chronology of events for the period April 1995 to July 1996 was introduced. The supplement encapsulated the significant events in various spheres of economic policymaking and was a useful reference for researchers, journalists, academics and other readers. These features were an essential part of various Annual Reports of the Bank in the years that followed.

REPORT ON CURRENCY AND FINANCE

The RCF, though not a statutory report, constituted a major communication and dissemination channel for the Reserve Bank. The report contained a comparative review of macroeconomic developments and served as an important source of time-series data on various macroeconomic aggregates. The report comprised two volumes, namely the Economic Review (Volume I) and the Statistical Statements (Volume II). Over the period 1981 to 1997, the format, coverage and contents of the report followed a traditional style and over the years, it earned the distinction of being a comprehensive source of information for researchers and academics in colleges, libraries, institutions and universities.

The analysis in the report was synthesised with graphs and tables to enhance presentation and readability. An important addition was the introduction of a chapter on some important developments in states and union territories in 1990–91. This was expected to bridge the gap in the analysis of the economic developments in the states and the union territories (UTs).

The statistical data presented in volume II of this report were used extensively by researchers, students and academics. Although most of the data were on a financial year basis, certain statements were presented on a calendar year basis, wherever source agencies compiled these on such a frequency. The statistics on the variables such as, area and production of agricultural commodities, financial assistance sanctioned and disbursed, IDBI liabilities and assets, the operations of National Bank for Agriculture and Rural Development (NABARD) and Unit Trust of India (UTI), and consumer price index (CPI) for agricultural labourers, related to July-June period. The scope of the volume was strengthened by expanding its coverage and by modifying the contents through the years 1981 to 1997.

Though the report gained immense value and popularity among its users over time, it was felt necessary to alter its structure. Consequently, the report was revamped after 1996–97 along specific themes. With this, volume II of the report containing statistical statements was discontinued, while a succinct review of the macroeconomic developments was retained in an otherwise single-volume thematic composition. The discussion on macroeconomic issues was maintained for the benefit of the public and researchers, who were accustomed to using the report for studying such developments in the Indian economy. To avoid information loss with the discontinuation of volume II, most of the statistical tables and statements were included in the Handbook of Statistics on the Indian Economy that began to be published subsequently by the Reserve Bank on an annual basis.[13]

REPORT ON TREND AND PROGRESS OF BANKING IN INDIA

The first issue of the statutory report titled: Trend and Progress of Banking in India was brought out by the DBOD under section 36(2) of the BR Act, 1949. The DRS took over the publication of the report in 1953. Further, in pursuance of the OLA, 1963 the Hindi version of the report was first published in 1967.

---

13. *Handbook of Statistics on the Indian Economy* was first published in December 1998 and provided time-series data on various economic aggregates.

The coverage and scope of the report contained, *inter alia*, developments in commercial banking, credit policy measures announced by the Reserve Bank, trends in credit deployment, details of various special credit schemes and facilities, such as the differential rate of interest (DRI) scheme and credit authorisation scheme (CAS), features of export finance, branch expansion, various committees and working groups set up in the area of banking, details of amendments in banking legislation and regulation, operations of co-operative banks, schemes relating to non-agricultural credit, functioning of NABARD, and other financial institutions (OFIs). Major changes in the contents of the report were undertaken from time to time keeping in view the necessity of putting out relevant additional information on matters relating to banking operations in India, as also to enhance the presentation and readability of the report.

With the setting-up of the Discount and Finance House of India Ltd (DFHI) in April 1988, a new section on developments in the short-term money market within the chapter on commercial banking was introduced in the report for the year 1988–89. In light of the changing banking scenario and fast-paced developments in the system, it was decided to incorporate information on topics of contemporary relevance, as and when warranted. From 1992–93, such reviews were captured in boxes to highlight the issues. Over the years, the emphasis was to make this report more focused. The analysis was supplemented with graphs and tables on various indicators to enhance its style and presentation.

RESERVE BANK OF INDIA BULLETIN

The history of the Reserve Bank of India, Volume 1 (1935–1951) stated:

In January 1947, the Department of Research and Statistics (DRS)[14] also embarked on the publication of a monthly economic and financial journal called the Reserve Bank of India Bulletin. In this, the Bank was very much ahead of some of the older central banks and followed the pattern of the newer banks like the Federal Reserve. The contents of the Bulletin generally included a monthly

---

14. The Department of Research and Statistics was later bifurcated into two departments, namely, Economic Department and the Department of Statistics, which were subsequently reorganised as the Department of Economic Analysis and Policy and the Department of Statistical Analysis and Computer Services. More recently the two Departments were rechristened the Department of Economic and Policy Research and the Department of Statistics and Information Management.

review of economic and financial conditions, articles based on the studies and surveys conducted by the Bank and a statistical section presenting monetary and economic data. Over the years, the range of the material published in the Bulletin was enlarged and it became an important source of reference on current monetary and economic problems.

The objective of publishing the bulletin was set out in its first issue as:

The aim of the Reserve Bank of India Bulletin, which will be published monthly, is to present in summary form statistics and other information which may help to portray the changing pattern of economic activity of the country. This task, however, must be necessarily limited by the inadequate character of the data now available. But, wherever possible, advantage will be taken of such information as may be in the possession of the Bank or is easily accessible to it, but which the public has no means of acquiring. The Bulletin will also embody, where permissible, the results of the studies and investigations made by the Bank, in particular by its Department of Research and Statistics. It incorporates the Reserve Bank of India's statistical summary, which will, consequently, cease with the December 1946 issue. Its contents will include, in addition to current statistics now published in the summary, a monthly review of business and financial conditions, articles on economic problems, notes on current events, book reviews and recent legislation, Indian and foreign, relating to finance and banking.

Accordingly, the bulletin contained the Reserve Bank's analysis of macroeconomic developments and analytical articles by the staff, details of the regulatory environment in which the Bank functioned and relevant data. Over the years, while there was no major deviation from the original mandate, the contents of the bulletin were expanded to include speeches of the top executives, important press releases, empirical articles, and circulars on regulatory and foreign exchange developments. It is worth mentioning that there was a noticeable increase in the number of speeches of the top executives from the mid-1980s, and this reflected greater importance being attached to the need for more effective communication.

The contents of the section on statistics in the monthly bulletin were revised over time to capture the changes taking place in the economy and markets. The initial mandate of the Reserve Bank bulletin was to publish statistics on money, banking and balance of payments for which the Reserve Bank was the primary source. However, over the years, the bulletin also began to incorporate secondary data that were considered important for analysing macroeconomic developments in the economy. The scope and contents of the bulletin were expanded as information dissemination became vital, particularly in the context of deregulation and liberalisation of the economy from the 1990s. Transparency in policy formulation and operations became imperative to enhance efficiency in the functioning of the markets and transmission of policy, thus making such modifications necessary.

Major Changes Effected in the Monthly Bulletin During 1981–1997

An exercise to examine the evolving structure of the contents of the monthly bulletin for the period 1981 to 1997 revealed interesting results. It was found that since the beginning of 1980, the bulletin had carried a monthly financial and economic review that covered various developments in the economy. Further, the monetary and credit policy measures announced from time to time by the Governor were summarised in the relevant monthly review from 1980 up to 1996. Other regular features covered in the bulletin included, quarterly commodity reviews; highlights of the Union Budget (as finances of the Government of India); articles on the economic and functional classification of central government budget; highlights of the railway budget; finance commission recommendations; highlights of the finances of state governments; and corporate finance studies. Trends in the wholesale price index (WPI), the prices of securities and bullion and analyses of trends in the index of industrial production (IIP) and the index of agricultural production were discussed as and when such data/revisions were released by the Government.

The bulletin, as a matter of convention, incorporated circulars issued by the Reserve Bank, especially to various banks, indicating policies relating to banking and any changes therein. The bulletin also covered various committee/working group reports, as and when these were released.

Various departments of the Reserve Bank contributed articles in their areas of interest/specialisation in the bulletin. Further, reviews were prepared on the policies announced periodically by the Government, such as the Exim policy. Articles of topical relevance were published from time to time, which included viability of regional rural banks (RRBs), statistics on the working of the foreign currency non-resident (FCNR) deposit scheme and estimates of state domestic product released by the Central Statistical Organisation (CSO). Special articles prepared by senior executives of the Bank on policy issues were also published (with the usual disclaimer) in the bulletin.

The regular articles comprised, *inter alia*, flow of funds accounts of the Indian economy', for which the Reserve Bank was a primary source, (published intermittently and usually covering a period of five years); investments of scheduled commercial banks (annual feature); centre-wise distribution of offices opened/closed by commercial banks in India and monthly seasonal factors of selected economic time series (published every year in January).

The results of surveys conducted by the Reserve Bank, covered in the bulletin, were a noteworthy feature. The periodic surveys included, finances of medium and large public limited companies, finances of large public limited companies, finances of medium and large private limited companies, India's international investment position, foreign collaboration survey, composition and ownership pattern of bank deposits, performance of financial and investment companies, finances of government companies, growth of deposits with non-banking companies, ownership of government debt, all-India debt and investment survey, and survey of ownership of shares in joint-stock companies. *Ad hoc* surveys comprised a survey of traders and transporters conducted by the Reserve Bank in collaboration with commercial banks (1979–80) and a study of the deposit acceptance activities of hire-purchase finance companies.

The monetary and credit policy measures announced by the Governor from time to time were not reproduced in the monthly bulletin. Instead, the policy announcements found a prominent place in the Monetary and Credit Information Review (MCIR) and the RBI Newsletter, published monthly and fortnightly, respectively, by the PRD. These brochures were time-bound publications with a wide reach. Such information sources were handy at times when the bulletin was released with a lag.

Another modification in the contents of the bulletin was that the monthly financial and economic review was discontinued in January 1990, and a quarterly financial and economic review was introduced in June 1990 in its place. Further, since the other publications carried a detailed examination and analysis of such macroeconomic aspects, the quarterly review too was done away with from May 1995; the last such review appeared for the period October–December 1994 in the April 1995 issue of the bulletin.

A column entitled, news and notes, covering policy announcements and short notes on significant developments was brought in. This section was of immense relevance as it contained important details. To illustrate, the October 1991 issue of the bulletin carried memoranda/resolution for the constitution of the following committees and their terms of reference: the committee on the financial system (Chairman: Shri M. Narasimham); the high level committee on trade policy reform (Chairman: Shri Montek Singh Ahluwalia); and the high level committee on tax reforms (Chairman: Dr Raja J. Chelliah). In the January 1995, the news and notes section carried details of the historic agreement signed between the Reserve Bank and the Government on phased discontinuation of issuing of the *ad hoc* Treasury Bills.

In April 1995, publication of press releases was commenced, which included releases issued not only by the Reserve Bank but also by the Government, for the benefit of readers and users. From June 1994, abstracts of the major research journal, *i.e.*, the Occasional Papers, were incorporated for wider reach of the in house research by Reserve Bank officials.

It was only in October 1996 that the practice of reproducing the monetary policy[15] announcements in the monthly bulletin was introduced. Since then, the policy statements for the first half and second half of the year became a regular feature. The policy measures announced between the two major announcements also found a prominent place in the bulletin.

CURRENT STATISTICS

A regular constituent of the bulletin was the section on current statistics. This segment not only contained data for which the Reserve Bank was the primary source, (*e.g.*, money supply, money stock measures and balance of payments) but also included statistics released by other official agencies (*i.e.*, price indices).

The current statistics section was expanded and reorganised in April 1996. Six new tables covering data on the capital market, money market and the government securities markets were introduced. Certain tables were modified in view of transformation in the available data and the changing requirements of data users. This considerably improved the information content of the statistics.

---

15. The policy circular for the second half of 1996–97 was reproduced in the RBI Bulletin, October 1996.

WEEKLY STATISTICAL SUPPLEMENT

The WSS to the Reserve Bank monthly bulletin was intended to disseminate high-frequency data on a weekly basis, such as the main constituents of the balance sheet of the Reserve Bank, data on foreign exchange reserves held by the Reserve Bank, scheduled commercial bank business in India, the cash reserve ratio (CRR) and interest rates, data on money stock, reserve money, repo/reverse repo and auctions of the *ad hoc* Treasury Bills. The handout continued to be a source of important data to its users through the years. Changes were introduced in the statistics contained in the supplement from time to time to reflect the evolving market conditions and to suit user requirements.

MONETARY AND CREDIT POLICY ANNOUNCEMENTS

Monetary and credit policy measures were, as per the convention, announced twice a year by the Governor — for the slack season (*i.e.*, the first half of the year) generally in April and for the busy season (*i.e.*, the second half of the year) in October. The practice of using slack and busy seasons was based on the fact that the Indian economy was essentially agrarian. The slack season policy took into account budget proposals of the Central Government to a certain extent. The busy season policy, on the other hand, was intended to meet the demand for credit for productive activities in sectors such as agriculture, industry and exports.

The official circular to commercial banks announcing the monetary and credit policy for the six-month period was issued to all scheduled commercial banks (SCBs, excluding RRBs). Just before announcement, the Governor convened a meeting of the chairmen of select commercial banks where the envisaged credit policy measures were unveiled. This practice continues even today in its essential aspects.

The communication from the Governor at times contained governance matters. In the slack season policy of 1985, the Governor, Shri R.N. Malhotra, urged commercial banks to revamp their management functions, promote staff discipline and reinforce customer service with a view to improve the image of the banking system. The management functions, the Governor felt, had suffered erosion. While emphasising the discipline aspect, the Governor expressed that the morale of the large majority of bank officers and staff, who were able and honest, was not only to be maintained but also enhanced. At the same time, it was necessary to discipline those who were less co-operative. This was pertinent since better discipline meant improved customer service. The credit policy statements thus facilitated such communication.

Increasing transparency in monetary policy communication became more relevant in the market-oriented environment of the 1990s. Such statements not only put forth the Reserve Bank's perceptions about the macroeconomic scenario, but also conveyed the policy decisions and their objectives to the markets. The pronouncements also informed the rationale for such decisions.

Monetary policy during the decade of 1980s was essentially in the form of credit policy. In the 1990s, with the process of implementation of financial sector reforms, the scope of credit policy was widened to monetary and credit policy. Thus, the policy, which was known as credit policy for a long time, was modified to monetary and credit policy to highlight the fact that monetary policy was much more than mere credit dispensation and flows.[16]

RESERVE BANK OF INDIA: FUNCTIONS AND WORKING

The Reserve Bank of India: Functions and Working was first published in 1941. The book aimed at informing the public about the functions performed by the Reserve Bank, as also its governing and organisational structure. This was, for the times, a novel initiative at sharing with the masses the role played by the Bank in the economy. The second edition of the book was released in 1958. In his Foreword to this issue, the Governor, Shri H.V.R. Iengar stated:

A Bulletin entitled 'Functions and Working of the Reserve Bank of India' was first published in 1941. Since then, as a result of constitutional developments as well as continuous adaptation to the needs of a rapidly developing economy, a great many changes have taken place both in the structure of the Bank as well as in the scope of its functions. The Bulletin has, therefore, been entirely re-written and is now presented to the general public in the hope that it will enable them to understand the broad working of an institution which is so closely concerned with their general welfare.

The edition that followed was updated and published in 1970, and it captured the evolution of the functions of the Reserve Bank over the

---

16. Transcript of the interview with Dr C. Rangarajan, former Governor, December 2006.

years. Dr Manmohan Singh, Governor, in the preface to the fourth edition (1983),[17] expressed:

> The object of this book, 'Reserve Bank of India: Functions and Working', which enters its fourth edition, is to present a concise and updated narration of the responsibilities and functions of the Bank in the areas of central banking, banking and financial regulation, international finance and other related areas. Supplemental information on the structure of the Indian banking system and money market and some theoretical aspects of central banking have been included to provide the reader with a better understanding of the role of the Bank in the nation's economic and financial well-being.

RESERVE BANK OF INDIA OCCASIONAL PAPERS AND STAFF STUDIES

The occasional papers through 1981 to 1997 were a means of apprising the academia with the technical research carried out mainly in the research and the statistics departments of the Bank. This journal facilitated transmitting well-researched articles forging a link between the theoretical developments and empirical information to a community of researchers. It had, over time, established itself as a journal of repute among the economic research community and academics. The Reserve Bank staff studies were another medium to communicate the work done largely on non-technical issues relevant to the Bank. Both these publications reflected views of the staff rather than those of the Bank.

DATA DISSEMINATION PROCESSES

The monthly bulletin and its WSS, apart from other regular reports as explained earlier in the chapter were widely used media for meeting data requirements of the public.

Publishing of Statistical Tables Relating to Banks in India began well before the establishment of the Reserve Bank and the report was brought out first by the Department of Statistics, Government of India in 1915. The work relating to its preparation was transferred to the Reserve Bank in 1939 that brought out the issue in 1941.[18] This publication offered

---

17. The updated fifth edition of the book was published in 2001.

18. This publication is presently brought out annually by the Department of Statistics and Information Management (DSIM), Reserve Bank of India.

key statistics relating to operations of banks, covering bank-wise and bank group-wise data on major indicators such as liabilities and assets, income and expenses, non-performing assets (NPAs), financial ratios, spatial distribution of offices, number of employees and priority sector advances. It also provided bank group-wise monthly statistics on variables, such as aggregate deposits, liabilities of the banking system, assets with the banking system, investments, bank credit and sector-wise and industry-wise gross bank credit.

The basic statistical returns (BSR) system was introduced in the year 1972 based on the recommendations of the committee on banking statistics (Chairman: Shri A. Raman) constituted by the Reserve Bank in April 1972. The BSR system comprised a framework of returns relating to advances, deposits and investments of SCBs. Under the BSR system, the publication titled Basic Statistical Returns of Scheduled Commercial Banks in India[19] presented comprehensive data on the deposits and credit of SCBs and also statistics on number of employees of these banks as at end-March annually. Detailed occupation-wise credit data on different dimensions, *viz.*, type of account, organisation, interest rate range and size of credit limit besides statistics on population group, bank group and state-wise credit by type of occupation were also put out. A unique feature of this publication was that it covered the spatial distribution of credit sanctioned as well as credit utilised. The data were collected through the annual statistical surveys, BSR 1 & 2, from the offices of SCBs including RRBs.

The Reserve Bank, with the focus on collating information on the geographical distribution of aggregate deposits and gross bank credit, collected statistics on aggregate deposits and gross bank credit of SCBs (including RRBs) on a monthly basis through BSR 7, which was introduced in August 1974. These data were disseminated from the year 1981 through

---

19. The first publication of *Banking Statistics*, volume 1, December 1972 was published in November 1973. The earlier title of the publication, *i.e., Banking Statistics* was changed to *Basic Statistical Returns of Scheduled Commercial Banks in India* from Volume 29 in March 2000. This was done to highlight the source and the nature of the data published in the volume and to distinguish it from the banking statistics presented in the *Statistical Tables Relating to Banks in India*, which is based on data collected through various statutory returns and other statistical returns. BSR 1A/1B present credit data (annual); BSR 2 covers deposit data (annual); BSR 3 collects sectoral credit (monthly); BSR 4 collects data on the composition and ownership pattern of deposits (annual); BSR 5 gives data on the investment portfolio of scheduled commercial banks (annual); BSR 6 presents debits to deposit and credit accounts with scheduled commercial banks (once every five years) and BSR 7 gives quarterly statistics on the deposits and credit of scheduled commercial banks.

the publication titled Banking Statistics: Monthly Return on Aggregate Deposits and Gross Bank Credit. The periodicity of the return was changed to quarterly from the quarter ended March 1984. Accordingly, the data were published under the title Banking Statistics: Quarterly Handout with effect from March 1984.[20]

SPEECHES OF TOP EXECUTIVES

Speeches of the top executives of the Reserve Bank have been an influential and informative communication medium. It is well recognised that the information content of the address delivered by the management is backed by sound research and profound thinking. The management speaks on an array of issues at various forums and conveys to the banking and financial system as well as to public at large, the rationale and intent behind various policy decisions. They often influence the behaviour of the markets and induce the desired changes in the banking and financial system. Signals sent through such address systems are captured by the markets quickly, and help bring about the required changes in their operations.

During the period 1981 to 1997, some of the speeches of the top executives framed market perceptions and helped transmit the intended message to the system. In this connection, it is relevant to quote the Governor, Shri R.N. Malhotra, who emphasised the vital role that had been assigned to monetary and fiscal policies in maintaining a stable price environment and in resource allocation since the commencement of the planning era. This role acquired a different tenor as the economy moved to higher stages of economic development. He, therefore, felt that it was important to reassess the role played by monetary policy periodically to be able to focus on the emerging economic scenarios. He further noted with concern:[21]

> In an economy characterised by wide disparities, an important objective is that growth should be accompanied by distributive justice...A delicate balance has, therefore, to be achieved in the pursuit of the twin objectives of promoting growth and maintaining price stability.

---

20. The name of the publication has further been changed to *Quarterly Statistics on Deposits and Credit of Scheduled Commercial Banks* from September 2003.

21. Malhotra, R.N. (1985). *Monetary Policy for Dynamic Growth*. Speech at a seminar organised by the Indian Chamber of Commerce. Calcutta. December 12.

In a speech by Shri S. Venkitaramanan, Governor, sensitivity to the use of gold in India was highlighted and he observed:[22]

Only a year ago, we had started the dialogue with Bank of England and Bank of Japan to use our gold to raise resources to meet our balance of payment crisis. There was an atmosphere of secrecy in which we had to operate. Preference for gold holdings appears to be an important characteristic of every national psyche. Use of gold holdings, even in a time of deep crisis, has provoked strong reactions in India. Indirectly, it also signalled the seriousness of the balance of payment crisis to the average Indian...Even the elite in our society considered the movement of gold an act of national humiliation...Ultimately a developing economy cannot depend only on its gold stocks. It has to grow based on its macroeconomic performance, its exports, its productivity and its inflation management. To these tasks India assigns the highest importance.

The Kutty Memorial Lecture[23] in this context focused on the issue of the autonomy of central banks. In this address, Governor Rangarajan forcefully put forth the arguments in favour of independence for central banks. Excerpts throw light on how this speech communicated the need for ensuring fiscal prudence on the part of the Government:

Historically speaking, the concept of independence of central banks is associated with the concern that in the absence of such independence, Government would finance itself without limit, through money creation... While this concern is still a potent factor in several countries, more attention is now being paid to the broader issue of the impact of political influence on the pursuit of monetary policy.

He further noted:

In the discussion on policy effectiveness, a point that is often made is that effectiveness of policy depends upon how the public perceives policy maker's commitment and behaviour. Based on this premise, it is argued that an independent central bank would

---

22. Venkitaramanan, S. (1992). "Gold Mobilisation and its Use for External Adjustment". Keynote Address at the *World Gold Conference*. Montreux. Switzerland. June 22.

23. Rangarajan, C. (1993). "Autonomy of Central Banks". *Tenth M.G. Kutty Memorial Lecture*. Calcutta. September 17.

tend to impart greater credibility to monetary policy and therefore improve its effectiveness.

In an endeavour to make the public aware of the role of the Reserve Bank in the economic system, as also to address a range of themes, communication in the form of speeches by the top executives continued to grow over the years. The speeches were topical and rich in content and remain a source of vital information and policy communication by the Bank till date.

OTHER INITIATIVES

ENDEAVOURS IN EXTERNAL COMMUNICATION

Monetary and Credit Information Review

The PRD publishes an MCIR[24] to disseminate information on matters relating to central banking, banking, monetary and other issues relevant to the banking industry and the general public. The MCIR, launched in August 1979 as Credit Information Review, set out its objectives and outreach as follows:

> The past few years have witnessed a significant expansion of commercial banks' branch network especially in the unbanked rural areas. There has also been an increasing involvement of banks in providing credit to the economically disadvantaged borrowers in priority sectors. Even so, a vast number of such persons have yet to benefit from the various measures which have been initiated. Lending policies of the banks to benefit the weaker sections of the community are under constant review. One of the important impediments in the way of further progress in this direction is the lack of timely and adequate information regarding such facilities. This monthly publication Credit Information Review has been launched with the object of filling this gap and conveying to the public the banking and credit policy decisions of the Reserve Bank without delay.

> The Review will explain in simple language the circulars issued by the Reserve Bank from time to time. Copies of the Review will be sent directly to all branches of banks, besides head offices,

---

24. In two languages, *i.e.*, Hindi and English.

regional offices and zonal offices. While the review will provide ready information on the policy decisions taken by the Reserve Bank, the head offices of banks will issue instructions separately to the regional zonal branch offices for the proper implementation of advices, instructions contained in the Reserve Bank's circulars. Copies will also be sent to the General Managers of District Industries Centres, Block Development Officers, District Collectors and other concerned Central and State Government Departments.

In order to facilitate easy dissemination of credit information among borrowers, the Review will be distributed widely among trade associations and chambers of commerce, AIR offices, news agencies and newspapers (English and local language papers) throughout the country.

The MCIR became a means for quick transmittal of a plethora of news and reports across cross-sections of society.

History of the Reserve Bank of India

Institutional histories are significant as they pen the role that institutions play in moulding events. The histories also corroborate how influential and effective the institutions have been. The history of the Reserve Bank is not just the history of an institution; it is part of the economic history of the country. As the apex institution of the financial system, the Bank played a critical role in steering the economy through the years. As an important source of communication and to familiarise the public with the role performed by the Reserve Bank in the economic system of the country, the history of the Bank was recorded, covering about 16 years in each of the three volumes published so far. The Bank's history is a record of events and decisions evolving in the context of a time and environment, reflecting, in large part, socio-political realities. The history is based on official records and a number of published sources, as well as discussions with various people who were closely involved with different events during the period covered. The effort was an exercise in transparency and accountability through an objective scrutiny, as far as possible, of the functioning of the Reserve Bank in retrospect.

In line with this, the first volume of the history for the period 1935–1951, published in March 1970, dealt with the formative years of the Bank and critical issues faced by the country and the Reserve Bank in the post-independence period. The volume covered the preparatory years, and provided a brief but comprehensive account of the developments in the areas of money, banking and exchange in India for almost a century prior to the establishment of the Reserve Bank in 1935. The 16 years covered in this volume, divided into three parts, *i.e.*, 1935–1939 (the formative years), 1939–1945 (the war years) and 1945–1951 (the post-war years), treated the matter in both chronological order and by subject. The account of the Bank's working is sufficiently detailed to be of practical use to those responsible for shaping and administering India's monetary policy in the years to come. In a sense, this is more than a history of the Reserve Bank and is, to some extent, a financial history of India.[25] The Reserve Bank, one of the oldest central banks in the developing world, had eventful formative years. Its efforts to adapt central banking functions and techniques to an economy in which modern banking was neither deep-rooted nor widespread, the special responsibilities including those of exchange control that it was called upon to shoulder with the outbreak of the World War II in the very first decade of its existence, its transformation from a privately owned institution to a nationalised undertaking and its new role in the economy with the advent of independence — all these made the Bank's initial years of special interest.[26]

In order to take this effort forward, it was decided to publish the subsequent volumes. Towards this end, a separate history cell was set up in the Reserve Bank. A committee of direction was constituted to oversee the preparation of these volumes. The compilation of the history of the Reserve Bank for the period 1951–1967 (Volume 2) progressed under the guidance of the committee. The second volume published in 1998, the fiftieth year of India's independence, dealt with the issues of economic development and management of the financial system in a period marked by several crises of shortages. 1951 was a watershed year in the economic history of India, since it witnessed the launch of the First Five Year Plan. The volume thus covered an important era in India, *i.e.*, the advent of planning, when initiatives were taken to strengthen, develop and diversify the country's economic and financial structure. The Reserve Bank played a notable role in bringing about these changes, especially through its pioneering efforts in public policy and institution-building in about the first one-and-a-half

25. Sir C.D. Deshmukh, Chairman, Editorial Committee in the "Preface" to *The Reserve Bank of India (1935–1951)*. Volume 1.

26. Shri L.K. Jha, Governor, Reserve Bank of India, in "Foreword" to *The Reserve Bank of India (1935–1951)*. Volume 1.

decades of planned economic development. The volume not only narrated the history of an important public institution in the process of change, but also shed light on the country's economic development during these crucial years.[27] It essayed the Bank's role in mobilising resources for the central and state governments, regulating the banking system, establishing an institutional infrastructure for agricultural and long-term industrial credit in India. It also covered developments in India's external sector, including the initiatives to raise long-term foreign assistance for development and the rupee devaluation of 1966. The volume concluded with an extensive survey of evolving relations between the Reserve Bank and the central and state governments in India during this period.

The third volume covering the period from 1967 to 1981 was released in 2006. This period was not only marked by political and economic upheavals, but also by far-reaching changes in the financial system. The volume spanned over the period of bank nationalisation and consolidation of the banking system, which changed the face of banking in India. The decision revamped the fundamentals of banking in terms of its orientation and operations, and was thus flagged as a defining event of the period. The dominance of fiscal policy over the monetary policy, the breakdown of the Bretton Woods system and the emergence of a new international financial order characterised by a floating rather than a fixed exchange rate system were highlights of the period. The time frame of volume 3 was marked by phenomenal expansion and diversification of the financial sector, and attempts to closely align financial and regulatory practices with Plan and development priorities. Aiming at the correction of market failures, it was an era of heightened regulation and direction in every sphere of financial activity. As an institution charged with maintaining the financial health of the country, the Bank was at the centre of spreading banking from a few urban centres to semi-urban and rural areas, including remote parts of the country. The Bank significantly impacted the economic life of the masses by deepening the financial system and, through detailed directions, shaped the behaviour of banks and financial institutions (FIs). It thus became the responsibility of the Reserve Bank to ensure that the poor and the vulnerable participated in the novel financial experiments that were undertaken. As a central bank, responsible for the conduct of monetary policy, it attended to the task of maintaining price stability. Although

---

27. Dr C. Rangarajan, Chairman, Committee of Direction in the "Foreword" to *The Reserve Bank of India (1951–1967)*. Volume 2.

dominated by fiscal imperatives and considerations arising out of central planning, the Bank was able to contain strong inflationary pressures twice in the 1970s, which were partly driven by large and unanticipated external shocks. Against the backdrop of a chronic shortage of foreign exchange, the Bank made significant contributions to the management of India's external relations.[28]

These three volumes of history became a permanent record of the Reserve Bank's functions and policies and provided insights into the Bank's relations with the Government through the years.

Library

A library was set up in the Reserve Bank in the year 1938 and the first lot of books was purchased in January, 1938.[29] The Central Library of the Reserve Bank, maintained by the Department of Economic and Policy Research (DEPR)[30] historically offered a rich collection of books, documents, reports, working papers and journals. It acted as a means of communication for the Reserve Bank staff, researchers, academicians and others, pursuing various interests. Revamped in 1982, the library adopted an internationally accepted classification and cataloguing system in 1993. Computerisation of library records using LIBSYS software for housekeeping functions was commenced during 1994. Collection of the Central Library comprised 66,917 books, 544 journals and 900 CD-ROMs. CD NET system was facilitated in 1995 to enable access to CD-ROMs thorough LAN in Central Library. The library subscribed to proquest online database in December, 1997.

Technology

The Reserve Bank of India website (*http://reservebank.com*) went live on September 17, 1996. The site regularly hosted the publications brought out by the Bank, *viz.*, the monthly bulletin, its WSS, the Annual Report and other reports. The site also had a section on press releases and put

---

28. Dr Y.V. Reddy, Governor, Reserve Bank of India in the "Foreword" to *The Reserve Bank of India (1967–1981)*. Volume 3.

29. The first accession register, showing the column for date of purchase of books, recorded date of purchase of books as January 6, 1938.

30. Department of Economic Analysis and Policy (DEAP), to which the Central Library is attached was subsequently rechristened Department of Economic and Policy Research (DEPR).

into the public domain speeches delivered by the Governor, Deputy Governors and other senior executives of the Bank. The site worked as a dissemination point for data on the Indian economy, particularly for data on the banking and financial sectors. The website served a useful purpose in communicating statistics under the special data dissemination standards (SDDS) of the International Monetary Fund (IMF).

Economic Editors' Conference

An annual conference of economic editors from all over India was convened by the PRD to promote better understanding of the Reserve Bank's policies through an informal exchange of views between the media, the Governor and other senior executives of the Bank. This emerged as a meaningful forum for the exchange of perspectives between the top brass of the media and the Bank. The PRD continued its endeavours to co-ordinate publicity and press relations work and served as a focal point for disseminating information to the public.

Memorial Lectures

The C.D. Deshmukh memorial lecture series was instituted in 1984 in the Reserve Bank in commemoration of memory of the first Indian Governor of the Reserve Bank, Sir C.D. Deshmukh (August 11, 1943 to June 30, 1949). The first lecture in the annual series was delivered by Lord Nicholas Kaldor, Professor Emeritus of Cambridge University on January 18, 1984 in Bombay. Lord Kaldor spoke on the subject of The Failure of Monetarism. The event became an important communication stage for the exchange of views on topics of contemporary debate and relevance to the Bank.

In reverence to the services of Shri L.K. Jha, former Governor of the Reserve Bank (July 1, 1967 to May 3, 1970), the Bank instituted a lecture series in the year 1990. The inaugural address in this annual series was delivered by Mr Robin Leigh-Pemberton, Governor, Bank of England on October 16, 1990 in Bombay. The subject of his talk was Economic Liberalism, Central Banking and the Developing World. This occasion added another dimension to sharing knowledge and opinions on the economic issues confronting the world.

Banking Chintan-Anuchintan

Another development was the launch of a quarterly journal titled: Banking Chintan-Anuchintan. This magazine was published by the Bankers'

Training College (BTC), in association with the Indian Banks' Association (IBA). The periodical was envisaged to promote original writings in Hindi on banking and disseminate information, know-how and terminology on banking-related issues. The journal was meant for circulation within the Reserve Bank and in the banking industry, and its first issue was brought out during 1987–88. The journal was received well in the circles of reach. In a related initiative, a committee consisting of officers of the Reserve Bank's Rajbhasha Division and heads of departments of some public sector banks (PSBs) revised and updated Banking Shabdavali, a glossary of Hindi terms for better communication on issues relating to banking in Hindi.

RBI Legal News and Views

In April 1995, the Governor suggested that the Legal Department should circulate from time to time important judgments of the Courts and other legal developments in matters related to banking. Thus was born the idea of institutionalising an in house legal information system that took the form of a quarterly journal published by the Legal Department of Reserve Bank. In the Foreword to the first issue, brought out in 1996, the Governor, Dr C Rangarajan expressed:

> Law has an important role in the success of any reform process. Every reform brings with it a new host of legal issues. Any mismatch between policy intention and the legal framework could defeat the entire effort at reform. Thus, the need for a continuing review of legal principles and a system of dissemination of legal information has indeed become more pronounced in the wake of the on-going structural reforms in the banking and financial sector. I am therefore happy that the Legal Department of the Reserve Bank is coming out with an in-house Law Journal to meet this gap. I am confident that it will go a long way in clarifying the various legal nuances and provide a proper legal institutional perspective to the changes in the banking and financial sector. I wish the journal all success and compliment all persons who have been responsible for this initiative.

The journal continued to provide the much needed support and received an impressive response, while striving to serve the objective of sharing valuable information that was dependable and qualitative.

CAB Calling

CAB Calling[31] started as a quarterly newsletter in 1977 and its first issue was published on November 15, 1977. As mentioned therein, the newsletter was started 'in response to persistent requests from the participants of various CAB Programmes to have continuing liaison and dialogue with the College'.

The newsletter contained details of the forthcoming programmes of the college and also reports on the various other activities of the CAB. Over time, the scope of the newsletter expanded to include gist of important circulars issued by the Reserve Bank and developments in the field of banking.

The newsletter was published in the form of a quarterly magazine in the year 1987 and the first such issue was published on August 15, 1987. Besides the write-up on the activities of the CAB and gist of circulars issued by the Reserve Bank, it also included short articles relating to the programmes conducted at the CAB and the essence emerging from the group discussions that formed a part of these programmes.

INTERNAL COMMUNICATION PROCEDURES

Managers' Conferences

An important platform to facilitate internal communication within the Reserve Bank was the managers' conferences held annually. This forum, chaired by the Governor or a Deputy Governor, was an effective medium for formal as well as informal discussions among the top executives of the Bank, managers of the regional offices and heads of departments. The agenda for such conferences was well thought out and covered a vast canvas of functions of the Bank, while assessing the work environment and industrial relations on a regular basis. This convention also provided in-charges of offices at various centres with an opportunity to highlight the achievements of their centres and share concerns on problems with the top executives of the Bank. The approach offered speedy and feasible solutions to the predicaments and issues placed before the participants.

The conferences acted as a medium for the exchange of ideas between the central office and the regional offices and facilitated understanding of points of view of the officials from both sides on varied subjects in an attempt to work towards improving the functioning of the Bank. In the two-way dialogue, several policy issues were emphasised and discussed, apart

---

31. Published by the College of Agricultural Banking (CAB), Pune.

from purely procedural items that invariably formed part of the schedule. While participative management was always underlined as the theme of the conferences, the areas of debate included, *inter alia*, discipline, efficiency, reduction in overtime, industrial relations, organisational restructuring, problems faced by the Bank from time to time, currency management practices, matters relating to computerisation and mechanisation and customer service.

Internal Manuals

The internal manuals of the Reserve Bank provided guidelines in respect of functioning of various departments. The Issue Department manual was first brought out in 1937.[32] It communicated to the staff necessary instructions and procedures for dealing with notes and coins and other work of the department. The intent remained ensuring that service to the public was both prompt and efficient in respect of provision of adequate supply of coins and bank notes.

The guidelines for the operations of the Banking Department were in place at the inception of the Reserve Bank. The Banking Department manual (1957) contained practices and processes for accounting, establishment and administrative procedures to be followed by all departments of the Reserve Bank. These instructions as also changes which came about in the scope of Bank's activities and operations with time were compiled in the form of General Administration Manual 1988 (Volume I and Volume II), published for the first time in 1988.

Within the Banking Department, the PDO manual for apprising the staff about operational procedures for public debt administration and management of public debt on behalf of the central and the state governments was first published in 1936.[33] The PAD manual, for which practices were in place in the late 1930s, a published version of 1957[34] is in the archival records. A cyclostyled DAD manual for 1957 also forms a part of the archival material.

Further, laying down the procedures for exchange control and regulation, the exchange control manual was first published in 1940 and revised with the expansion of the scope in the area.[35]

---

32. This was revised in 1952, 1972 and 2004.
33. This was revised in 1951, 1977 and 1999.
34. This was revised in 1981.
35. The manual was revised in 1943, 1949, 1959, 1965, 1971, 1978, 1987 and 1993.

RBI Newsletter

The RBI Newsletter was first published on November 15, 1974 as an exercise in developing internal communication. In a message to the introductory issue, the Governor, Shri S. Jagannathan, expressed:

> There is a clear need to keep the staff of the Reserve Bank continually informed about the developments taking place in the different departments of the Bank, as well as in its affiliate institutions. This is the object which the fortnightly RBI Newsletter seeks to fulfil. I hope it will be found useful by the officers and other staff.

Published fortnightly, the focus of the brochure was to inform employees on various policy issues and guidelines released by the Reserve Bank. It also covered highlights of various reports of the Bank, government publications and international releases. The newsletter, through time, became much sought after and immensely important source for in house learning. It apprised readers about research publications of the Bank, various internal matters and decisions such as senior management appointments, portfolio allocation, information about new offices, details of training/workshops conducted by the Bank, proceedings of managers' conferences and other internal meetings and excerpts from management speeches, among others.

In October 1985, a new column, miscellany and montage, was introduced that culled snippets of information on diverse subjects from domestic and international sources. Though high in information content, this column was dropped in April 1986 due to space constraints. There was a practice to publish data on money, banking and price trends in the brochure for the benefit of the Reserve Bank community. The table containing such data was, however, discontinued in December 1989 in order to make space for other notifications.

During 1985, in its already vast scope, details of staff welfare measures were added. The content was further enhanced by incorporating clips of information on developments in international banking and use of computers in banks abroad. This kept the staff updated on the inroads being made by technology the world over. Topical matters, such as increase in the assistance provided by banks due to political uncertainty and disturbances in various regions of the country, issue of fresh notes, need for public to handle bank notes with care to avoid soiling of notes and apprising the staff about the added security features of bank notes were discussed in the newsletter.

Without Reserve

Back in 1959, Shri H.V.R. Iengar, Governor, recorded a note:

> Several business houses have 'House Magazines' *e.g.*, I.C.I., Dunlop, Hindustan Lever, Martin Burn. These magazines are believed to help materially in improving staff relations, apart from their general educational effect. I would like the point to be examined as to whether we may start a house magazine in the Reserve Bank.

While examining the proposal, it was noted that the magazines brought out by various entities had self-serving objectives and were issued as an exercise in public relations. It was also recognised that for the Reserve Bank house magazine to be a success, it could not merely be a mouthpiece of the management. This tenet was pursued through the years and it helped establish Without Reserve as a credible journal.

The Without Reserve[36] was launched in 1968 and aimed to improve communication standards within the Reserve Bank. In his message in the inaugural issue of the journal, the Governor, Shri L.K. Jha expressed:

> There are occasions when we need to shed our formal mode of address and talk about things of concern to us all in a free and informal manner. 'Without Reserve' seeks to do just this...all of us...give it the support it deserves so that it becomes a live and continuing instrument of our mutual communication and contact.

The periodical won an award in the house magazine category in the annual awards competition of the Association of Business Communicators of India for the year 1979 and a special award in the category of 'house magazines' in a contest conducted by the Thiruvananthapuram Press Club in 1996.

CAPACITY BUILDING

RESERVE BANK'S TRAINING ESTABLISHMENTS

The training establishments[37] of the Reserve Bank provided a platform to conduct programmes, courses, workshops and host seminars.

---

36. The title for the journal was suggested by Shri G.I.S. Pais, deputy chief accountant of the Calcutta office, at the time of its launch.

37. BTC and CAB also received candidates from other domestic as well as from the institutions abroad.

The Bankers' Training College (BTC)[38] was a conduit for bridging capacity-building gaps, primarily for executives of commercial banks, and imparted training in practical banking to the supervisory staff of commercial banks. It served the important purpose of addressing professional skill upgrading among Reserve Bank employees, besides offering courses to upscale the proficiencies of participants from commercial banks, co-operative banks, RRBs, the central and state governments and foreign trainees to enable them to meet their work requirements. These courses included, managerial programmes on personnel management, courses in industrial relations, human resources development modules, housekeeping, computer appreciation, creativity, organisational excellence, managerial effectiveness and value systems. In line with the government policy on promoting the official language, the BTC also conducted programmes in Hindi. The BTC acted as a communication platform to help Reserve Bank officers prepare for promotion to higher grades. It also conducted programmes designed to meet specific requirements of the sponsoring institutions.

The Reserve Bank Staff College (RBSC) served as the introductory communication medium for officers joining the Reserve Bank. Participants were apprised of the operations of various departments of the Bank, and courses were designed to augment the technical, supervisory and human relations skills of newly recruited and promotee officers. Middle management officers were also trained at the RBSC. Special programmes on communication skills and seminars and workshops on time management and executive health hazards were handled by the RBSC for senior officers of the Reserve Bank. Computer appreciation programmes were conducted for officers across various grades. The college also provided training to central bankers from other developing countries. These included officials from Bhutan, Botswana, Ghana, Kenya, Macau, Malawi, Nepal, Sudan, Tanzania, Uganda and Zambia. This widened the communication network of the RBSC beyond national boundaries.

The Zonal Training Centres (ZTCs) of the Reserve Bank facilitated capacity-building among the clerical cadres. The ZTCs also trained tellers and coin/ note examiners of the Cash Department on a regular basis. Class IV staff of the Bank were trained at the ZTCs in various fields, especially in the area of security awareness. Certain courses were undertaken in the

---

38. BTC was closed and in it place Centre for Advanced Financial Research and Learning (CAFRAL) was inaugurated by Dr Manmohan Singh, the Prime Minister, in March, 2006.

local languages to ensure proper understanding of issues, which ensured better internal communication.

The college of agricultural banking (CAB) focused on providing training in banking policies, practices and procedures exclusively for co-operative banks. The curriculum of the programmes underwent changes with the multi-agency approach and the introduction of commercial banks into the realm of agricultural and rural credit, particularly after nationalisation. Further, officers from various states and the central government development departments associated with the preparation and execution of agricultural projects also received training at the college. The programme design, in accordance with its widening scope, was modified and the emphasis shifted from co-operative banks to the broader sphere of agricultural development, banking and finance. With the establishment of RRBs in 1976, CAB introduced development programmes in rural finance exclusively for the officers of RRBs. Programmes were added for IES probationers and chief executives of co-operative banks. The initiation of highly specialised programmes, such as high-tech agriculture, plantation and horticulture, animal husbandry, forestry and waste water management made CAB a unique institution in terms of range of specialisation offered. The CAB conducted several programmes on behalf of organisations such as the Food and Agricultural Organisation in Rome, the Commonwealth Secretariat in London, the Asia Pacific Rural and Agricultural Credit Association in Manila, the Economic Institute, the World Bank and the IMF Institute in Washington. Programmes were also designed and conducted to suit the specific requirements of clients from Afghanistan, Nepal and Sri Lanka.

CONCLUDING OBSERVATIONS

Communication remained an important aspect of central banking in India since the inception of the Reserve Bank in 1935. The communication efforts in the Reserve Bank received a stimulus in 1945 when the DRS was set up to undertake publication of reports and research papers on issues of economic interest. To strengthen the communication practices, a separate cell was operationalised within the Economic Department in 1969, headed by a PRO. In March 1978, the post of the PRO was upgraded and the section was renamed the PRD.

The Reserve Bank's communication initiatives could be classified in terms of communication channels into three parts, namely, publications, speeches, and others. While periodic publication of bulletins, reports, newsletters and pamphlets furnished a wealth of information on macroeconomic developments and the working of various schemes supported by the Reserve Bank, speeches by Governors and Deputy Governors provided glimpses of Reserve Bank's thinking and stance on an array of issues. Besides being a rich source of knowledge and information, views expressed by the top executives, it was believed, could influence market sentiments. Other endeavours towards this end included the creation and maintenance of a Reserve Bank website, strengthening internal communication by encouraging in house magazines and circulating handouts on the various welfare schemes promoted by the Bank.

In the aftermath of the securities scam in the transaction of government securities, there was a conscious attempt to improve intra-departmental communication to assess the signs of incipient strains in the financial system, so that such events could be addressed on time. In pursuance of the recommendations of the Janakiraman Committee, an MIC was set up in the Bank in the year 1992–93, to strengthen market intelligence mechanisms.

In response to the revolution in information technology, the Reserve Bank of India website was put into operation on September 17, 1996. The site regularly hosted publications brought out by the Bank, besides disseminating press releases and speeches of the top executives of the Bank. The site was also a propagation point for data on the Indian economy, particularly data on the banking and financial sectors, apart from serving the useful purpose for communicating statistics under the SDDS of the IMF.

To a considerable extent, the economic liberalisation and financial sector reforms of the 1990s were responsible for the Reserve Bank adopting a more active communication strategy and with good results. This was evident from rich content and analytical review of the policy perspectives contained in the bi-annual credit policy circulars, the increasing number of speeches of the top executives of the Bank to express the rationale of monetary policy measures as also reforms in the banking sector and constant refining of the contents and scope of the publications with the aim of communicating the Reserve Bank's stance on various issues in a purposeful manner.

21

Institutional Changes

INTRODUCTION

At its inception, the organisational set up of the Reserve Bank more or less followed the Bank of England (BoE) pattern. In the planning era, which commenced from the 1950s, the Reserve Bank played a developmental role in promoting economic growth along with achieving price stability. The growth and spread of banking and also rural credit were its major responsibilities. In the 1990s, a new dimension was added in implementing the financial sector reforms. Moreover, the large inflow of external funds called for reorientation of its policies *inter alia* in the areas of monetary policy, management of foreign exchange reserves and public debt. Accordingly, the range of its functions expanded both in scope and diversity. In discharging these functions, the Reserve Bank's organisational structure and set up underwent significant changes. The Bank laid stress on meeting these challenges through higher productivity, computerisation, adoption of mechanisation and new technology and active communication practices. However, the relations with its staff experienced stresses and strains for some time in the early 1980s.

The evolution of the Reserve Bank took place in response to domestic circumstances and the international practices. Flexibility was a characteristic of this transformation over the decades. The organisational progression not only enhanced the structure of the Reserve Bank in terms of size but also went hand-in-hand with functional changes that were necessitated by the evolving economic and financial conditions.

This chapter is thematic and captures the developments in the organisational set up from 1981 to 1997 against the backdrop of changing economic circumstances.

ORGANISATIONAL EVOLUTION

The decade of the 1980s began with both restructuring and expansion of the administrative machinery of the Reserve Bank as its responsibilities multiplied with the changing economic scenario. In 1981, the Department of Administration and Personnel (DAP) was split into two departments namely, the Department of Administration (DA) and the Personnel Policy Department (PPD) with the objective of redefining operations, besides enhancing the focus on policy matters concerning the staff. The PPD sought to improve industrial relations in the Bank. The Department of Accounts and Expenditure (DAE) was recast into three departments in order to reallocate its activities and strengthen human resource management. The departments that emerged were, the Department of Currency Management (DCM), which was assigned the task of attending to policies and matters relating to currency circulation; the Department of Expenditure and Budgetary Control (DEBC) established for drawing the annual budget of the Bank, besides handling provident and pension funds and the housing loans of employees of the Bank; and the Department of Government and Bank Accounts (DGBA), constituted for managing public debt (central and state governments), acting as banker to the governments and preparing the profit and loss account and the balance sheet of the Reserve Bank.

The Industrial Finance Department (IFD) was amalgamated into the Industrial Credit Department (ICD) in 1981. The composite unit looked after the provision of bank credit to industry, sick industrial units and export finance and also administered the credit authorisation scheme (CAS). After this expansion, the ICD was merged into the Industrial and Export Credit Department (IECD), which performed the function of financing small scale industries (SSIs) besides monitoring export finance and the district industries centres (DICs).[1] The work relating to the SSIs was later transferred to the priority sector wing of the Department of Banking Operations and Development (DBOD) and that concerning credit guarantee was taken over by the Deposit Insurance and Credit Guarantee Corporation (DICGC). The authorised capital of the DICGC was raised from ₹ 10 crore to ₹ 15 crore on January 1, 1981, thus reaching

---

1. Based on the recommendations of an expert committee, the functions of IECD were merged with DBOD, DBS and MPD in July 2004 (*Report on Currency and Finance, 2004–05*).

the maximum permissible limit under the Deposit Insurance Corporation Act, 1961. The additional capital of ₹ 5 crore was contributed by the Reserve Bank. Later, the authorised capital of the DICGC was further increased to ₹ 50 crore to augment its resources. Effective May 1, 1993, the deposit insurance cover was enhanced to ₹ 1,00,000 per bank account. The premium was also revised to ₹ 0.05 per ₹ 100 in July 1993. These efforts underscored the intent to further promote the interests of the depositors.

Records and archives are the backbone of the information system of any organisation. The archival records are important because they provide insights into the decision-making processes and governance mechanisms in an organisation over time. In a pioneering effort to preserve the records for posterity, the archives of the Reserve Bank, *i.e.*, the Central Records and Documentation Centre (CRDC)[2] was set up in Pune on August 24, 1981 to function under the joint charge of the Management Services Department (MSD) and the DAP. The College of Agricultural Banking (CAB), Pune, provided administrative support to the CRDC[3] since its inception. The mission of the centre was to identify, acquire, preserve and make available non-current permanent records of historic value to the interested institutions, individuals and the Reserve Bank, especially for writing the history of the Reserve Bank.

In 1982, with the shift in policy focus on intensive research on economic issues, the Economic Department and the Department of Statistics were revamped and rechristened the Department of Economic Analysis and Policy (DEAP) and the Department of Statistical Analysis and Computer Services (DESACS), respectively. This facilitated leveraging the available expertise in the areas of economic analysis and statistics, besides encouraging research on contemporary issues. The DEAP emerged as a primary source of data on monetary aggregates, balance of payments (BoP), household financial savings, state finances and capital markets; prepared weekly economic and financial reports for the Committee of the Central Board of the Reserve Bank; and maintained the management information system (MIS) for the top executives as well as the operational departments of the Reserve Bank.

In an endeavour to reach out to various sections of society, the department was entrusted with the responsibility of bringing out Reserve

---

2. From May 8, 2000, the CRDC came under the purview of the history cell (DEPR), Reserve Bank of India.

3. The CRDC was renamed as RBI Archives (RBIA) effective September 29, 2006.

Bank's major publications. It began publishing the Reserve Bank of India bulletin in January 1947 — a monthly economic and financial journal signifying that the Bank was well ahead of some of its contemporaries in this area.[4] Over time, the department also prepared and released various reports and research journals. These included the Annual Report, Report on Trend and Progress of Banking in India, Report on Currency and Finance, Statistical Tables Relating to Banks in India[5] and Finances of the State Governments; weekly statistical supplement (WSS) to the monthly bulletin, and Reserve Bank of India Occasional Papers (a tri-annual research journal).

Between 1981 and 1997, the DEAP was expanded and regional offices were set up. In 1988, five regional offices were established in Bangalore (now Bengaluru), Bhopal, Guwahati, Jaipur and Patna, thus marking a significant expansion of the department during the year.

Against the backdrop of economic and financial sector reforms launched in 1991, several concerns caught the attention of researchers and policymakers. To address these problems and bridge the gap in this area, the development research group (DRG) was set up within the DEAP in November 1991. The mandate of the group was to prepare research papers on policy issues and areas of interest to the Reserve Bank. This initiative was a collaborative effort between the Reserve Bank and external experts to address contemporary economic issues. The DRG studies were published for wider dissemination.

The DESACS was entrusted with the responsibility of conducting all-India surveys, analysing corporate financial accounts, compiling security price indices, preparing flow of funds accounts of the economy and undertaking studies in econometrics.[6] In 1985–86, three regional offices of DESACS became functional at Madras (now Chennai), Calcutta (now Kolkata) and New Delhi, to facilitate the collection and transmission of important data to the central office of DESACS.

With the creation of National Bank for Agriculture and Rural Development (NABARD)[7] in July 1982, the Agricultural Credit Department

---

4. Reserve Bank of India. "The Evolution of Central Banking in India", *Report on Currency and Finance, 2004–05.*

5. The work relating to publication of this report was later taken over by the Department of Statistics and Information Management.

6. Some of these functions were later transferred to the DEAP.

7. For details, refer to chapter 8: Rural Credit Policy.

(ACD) of the Reserve Bank ceased to function. Most of the supervisory functions pertaining to rural credit were transferred to NABARD and the obligations cast upon the Bank under the Reserve Bank of India (RBI) Act, 1934 in respect of agricultural credit were modified. A separate department, Rural Planning and Credit Department (RPCD), was set up in the Reserve Bank. The RPCD was assigned the overall regulatory role in respect of rural credit.

In an initiative relating to banking, a special investigation cell was constituted in the Reserve Bank in May 1983 to facilitate speedy investigations of the major frauds coming to the notice of the Reserve Bank.

In pursuance of the recommendations of an inter-institutional group,[8] the national clearing cell (NCC) was set up in the Reserve Bank in November 1983 to help introduce magnetic ink character recognition (MICR) technology for facilitating mechanised cheque processing. The cell was commissioned in the four metropolitan cities of Bombay (now Mumbai), New Delhi, Calcutta and Madras, and replicated in all state capitals and other important centres in phases. At this time, the Premises Department of the Reserve Bank was re-organised into three distinct functional units connected with projects, maintenance and administration to earmark individual responsibilities for preserving and maintaining the Reserve Bank's properties. To administer and safeguard Reserve Bank's properties and manpower, including customers on the premises, the Governor, Shri R.N. Malhotra, constituted a committee in October 1982 under the chairmanship of Dr M.V. Hate, Deputy Governor. Further, in pursuance of the recommendations of the committee on security arrangements (COSA), the central security cell (CSC) was established in the Reserve Bank on June 2, 1986. The role of the CSC was meant to be advisory. It offered its views and advice on security arrangements in the Reserve Bank and public sector banks (PSBs).

The urban banks cell, which was attached to the ACD that became part of NABARD, was merged with the DBOD and began to function as the urban banks division. The division was expected to handle all matters regarding urban banks including licensing and compliance. However, a full-fledged Urban Banks Department (UBD) was constituted in 1984 to cater to the needs of the urban co-operative banks (UCBs).

---

8. The group also recommended standardisation of cheque forms, paper/printing specifications, and organisational arrangements for national cheque clearing.

Against the backdrop of the growing currency demand in the economy and the strains arising from recurrent currency shortages,[9] sub-office of the Reserve Bank at Guwahati was converted into a full-fledged issue office, taking the total number of issue offices in the Bank to 14.[10] Further, the Department of Non-Banking Companies was rechristened the Department of Financial Companies (DFC) on August 24, 1984.

With the growing focus on managing India's foreign exchange reserves and the external sector, the Department of External Investments and Operations (DEIO) was organised by converting the foreign accounts division into a full-fledged department in 1986. This department was entrusted with the responsibility of managing the country's external reserves, maintaining the external value of the rupee, transacting external operations of the Government including settlement with the International Monetary Fund (IMF), the World Bank and the Asian Development Bank (ADB) besides managing the membership of the Bank for International Settlements (BIS), as also co-ordinating banking business between India and Russia.

The Reserve Bank took a keen interest in promoting economic research and learning and for this purpose, it established the Indira Gandhi Institute of Development Research (IGIDR) in Bombay (now Mumbai). The institute began functioning from December 28, 1987. Registered as an autonomous society on November 14, 1986, the institute became a public trust on January 15, 1987, and was inaugurated by the Prime Minister, Shri Rajiv Gandhi, on December 28, 1987. The institute was later recognised as a deemed university and encouraged economic research with a multi-disciplinary approach.

A separate history cell was set up within the DEAP in the Reserve Bank during 1990–91. The Bank also constituted a committee of direction (COD) to guide the preparation of history of the Reserve Bank. Prior to setting-up of the cell, the work on history compilation was undertaken under the guidance of an editorial committee constituted for the purpose (Volume 1). Since the history for the period 1935–1951 (Volume 1) had already been published, the Bank planned to bring out subsequent volumes and the cell began to draft the developments from 1951 to 1967.

---

9. Details are available in the section on Issues in Currency Management in this chapter.

10. Including those at Ahmedabad, Bangalore, Bhubaneswar, Bombay, Byculla, Calcutta, Hyderabad, Jaipur, Kanpur, Madras, Nagpur, New Delhi and Patna.

In the process of functional transformation, certain departments were either merged or wound up. One such department was the Securities Department, which started as a unit of the Banking Department when the Reserve Bank was established in 1935. Its areas of operation included the purchase and sale of government securities on behalf of the Government, foreign banks or provident funds (PFs) and acting as the custodian of securities held by the Reserve Bank in the Issue and the Banking Department as well as those deposited by insurance companies with the Government in compliance with the statutory investments under the Insurance Act. Over time, these functions were transferred to the Public Debt Office (PDO), Deposit Accounts Department (DAD) and the Public Accounts Department (PAD) and by 1990 the Securities Department ceased to exist.

During 1990–91, the financial institutions cell (FIC)[11] was set up in the DBOD to serve as a nodal unit for better co-ordination among various segments of the financial system. For more effective co-ordination of the regulatory and supervisory functions in the financial system, the FIC was merged with the Department of Supervision (DoS) and operated as a separate division from June 18, 1997.

As monetary policy had to contend with several issues and adapt to the evolving environment by influencing economic activity through indirect methods, an imperative need emerged for reinforcing the internal debt management policies and operations. The Internal Debt Management Cell (IDMC) was created within the Secretary's Department in April 1992 by merging the public borrowing, open market operations (OMOs) and ways and means sections of the Secretary's Department with an aim of activating and strengthening the debt management practices. The objective of the cell was to promote an active and efficient government securities market. However, the cell was turned into an independent unit within the Reserve Bank on October 1, 1992.[12] Further, in a move to develop an institution for fostering an active secondary market in government securities and public sector bonds, the Securities Trading Corporation of India Ltd (STCI) was established at Bombay in May, 1994 as a subsidiary of the Reserve Bank.

The role played by gold in the management of the external payments crisis in early 1991 underscored the need to mobilise domestic gold for

---

11. For details refer to chapter 6: Banking and Finance and chapter 17: Reforms in Banking and Financial Institutions.

12. The IDMC was upgraded to a department (IDMD) in May 2003.

external adjustment in times of crises as well as to evolve policies to improve the availability of gold within the country through legal channels. In this context, issues dealing with liberalisation of gold and silver imports, market regulations, augmentation of the refining capacity within the country, and the orientation of jewellery exports to international markets needed to be reviewed. In response to such considerations and the possibilities of using gold for external adjustments, the gold management division was formed in the DEIO in 1992. The division was entrusted with keeping track of developments in the local and international bullion market by collecting relevant data; examining policy issues concerning the bullion market in India; making suitable recommendations; and devising schemes to mobilise unused gold from the public.

The Janakiraman Committee on irregularities in government securities' transactions recommended that the Reserve Bank should strengthen its market intelligence structure so that early action could be initiated, whenever warranted. Pursuant to its recommendations, a market intelligence cell (MIC) was set up in the Bank in 1992–93, to monitor market developments. This cell collected information on areas of concern to the Reserve Bank and which was sensitive. It was constituted in addition to the banking intelligence unit handled by the DBOD. On October 9, 1995, another MIC began operations in the Exchange Control Department (ECD) in order to closely study and monitor forex market developments.

The Board for Financial Supervision (BFS) was constituted based on the recommendations of the committee on the financial system (Chairman: Shri M. Narasimham) in terms of the RBI (BFS) Regulations 1994. This was done to strengthen the supervisory mechanism and the board was entrusted with the responsibilities of supervising and inspecting the financial system including banks, non-banking financial companies (NBFCs), development finance institutions (DFIs), UCBs and primary dealers (PDs). Prior to the setting-up of the BFS, in an effort to segregate the regulatory and the supervisory functions of the DBOD, the DoS was constituted in 1993 and designated as an executive wing of the BFS. The DoS began operations on December 22, 1993 with its central office in Bombay and 16 regional offices at various centres. The new department set out to recast supervisory practices and augment necessary skills.

With the growing recognition of management of human resources within the Reserve Bank and to pay adequate attention to the administrative necessities arising on account of increased responsibilities, the erstwhile DA and PPD were both re-organised into two departments in 1995. Thus, the Department of Administration and Personnel Management (DAPM) and Human Resources Development Department (HRDD) were created. This ensured focusing squarely on improved human resource policies, protection of employee interests and finding people-sensitive solutions to problems. The accepted recommendations of the Marathe Committee were reflected in this reorganisation. The Reserve Bank's vigilance unit was strengthened to function within the DAPM on a two tier basis with central vigilance cell in central office, and branch vigilance cells in other central office departments at Mumbai[13] as well as in the regional offices of the Bank.[14] The cell dealt with the implementation of the action plan on vigilance and anti-corruption rules of the Government. It also dealt with the complaints, matters relating to vigilance, acquisition, disposal and holding of assets by officers of the Reserve Bank. The cell worked in association with the Central Bureau of Investigation (CBI), Central Vigilance Commission (CVC), Ministry of Finance (MoF) and Enforcement Directorate (ED).

In 1995, the Department of Information Technology (DIT) was constituted, bringing about another structural change in the DESACS. The creation of a separate department provided the required drive to technology upgrading in the Reserve Bank. This was essential given the changes that had come about in technology the world over by this time. Two divisions of the DESACS namely, the computer operations division and the systems and programming division were merged with the erstwhile MSD to form the DIT, and the MSD ceased to exist.

The increasing concern about customer service reflected in the setting-up of a complaints redressal cell in August 1996 to address the grievances of the general public. Similar cells started operations later at the regional offices of the Reserve Bank. The employee concerns were given equal importance, and in this context, grievances redressal cell was instituted in April 1997 by amending the Reserve Bank of India Services Board Regulations. This cell looked into the grievances of the officers of the Reserve Bank against the decisions of the Bank. The complaints referred to the cell related to issues such as remuneration, tenure, leave, continuation of service, amenities and facilities, working conditions and crossing of efficiency bar. The Reserve Bank of India Services Board was constituted

---

13. Bombay was renamed as Mumbai in November 1995.
14. A vigilance cell also operated in DICGC, which is a subsidiary of the Reserve Bank.

in July 1968, under the Reserve Bank of India Services Board Regulations, 1968 to attend to recruitment of staff to the officers' cadre and promotion to such services and posts in the Bank or under the associate institutions.[15]

The advisory board on bank frauds (Chairman: Shri S.S. Tarapore) was set up to advise the Reserve Bank on cases referred to it by the CBI and to register cases against the erring bank officers of the rank of general manager and above. The board began operations from March 1, 1997.[16]

GOLDEN JUBILEE OF THE RESERVE BANK

The Reserve Bank celebrated the golden jubilee[17] of its establishment in 1985. During the year, it appointed a steering group, which prepared a book on the role played by the Reserve Bank in the field of rural credit. The Reserve Bank set up additional chairs in some universities to mark the occasion and to enhance its role as a knowledge-building institution. The celebrations underlined the contribution of the Reserve Bank to the growth and development of the country and its reaffirmation of the commitment to uphold the same.

The Prime Minister, Shri Rajiv Gandhi inaugurated the formal ceremony to mark the golden jubilee of the Bank. In his address, the Prime Minister observed that the Reserve Bank had been "changing with the times and helping our country to progress." He hailed the role of the Reserve Bank as "one of the prime movers of the development process." The Government issued commemorative coins to mark the celebrations. Setting-up of the IGIDR at Bombay was announced at this event. During the ceremony, two monographs were released: Reserve Bank of India: Fifty Years (1935–1985) and The Reserve Bank and Rural Credit. The former highlighted landmarks in the development of the Reserve Bank and its major contributions in various fields and the latter reflected on the crucial role played by the Reserve Bank in the field of rural finance.

INDUSTRIAL RELATIONS

The Reserve Bank in its relations with its staff had all along adopted a positive and helpful attitude in terms of service conditions, emoluments

---

15. *Reserve Bank of India: Functions and Working, 2001.*

16. In August 2000, the Board was renamed the Advisory Board for Bank, Commercial and Financial Frauds (ABBCFF) and its scope was extended to cover financial and commercial fraud in central PSUs and financial institutions.

17. Also refer to chapter 3: Monetary-Fiscal Interface.

and employee welfare schemes. This contributed in a good measure to build up favourable industrial relations environment in the Bank, except on a few occasions in the early 1980s.

In terms of the Justice C.T. Dighe Award, the Reserve Bank increased the daily quota of note examination by its note examiners by 15.0 per cent. The award was accepted by both the Government and the Bank in totality, and the Reserve Bank immediately sought to confer additional monetary benefits, while at the same time increasing the work quota from April 12, 1982. This led the All-India Reserve Bank Employees' Association (AIRBEA) to launch an instant agitation to protest the increased work quota in the cash department and the mechanisation of certain functions in the Reserve Bank. In the national industrial tribunal award (interim) pronounced on June 17 and December 4 of 1981, monetary perks were extended to class III employees, while upholding the Bank's right to increase the quota of work in the note examination and verification sections. The objective was to eliminate wasteful and restrictive practices and introduce mechanical aids subject to observing the prescribed safeguards. The agitation, however, did not elicit the expected response from the staff except in the Calcutta office of Reserve Bank, where it continued till August 1982 and resulted in work arrears. To resolve the issue of work arrears, the Government and the Reserve Bank partnered with nationalised banks at Calcutta to ensure the smooth conduct of government business.

The Nagpur Bench of the Bombay High Court had struck down certain provisions of the Reserve Bank's scheme for promotion to staff officers (grade A) in March 1981. The Reserve Bank moved the Supreme Court on this issue. The Supreme Court directed the Bank to modify certain features and draw a revised scheme in consultation with the recognised AIRBEA. The Court also directed the Bank to ascertain acceptability of the revised scheme among its employees holding a referendum. The referendum was held in July 1984 and 67.7 per cent of the employees approved. Based on the results, the Supreme Court permitted the Reserve Bank to conduct examination for promotion to staff officers (grade A) purely as an interim measure, and accordingly the examination took place in August 1984. The Court observed:[18]

> In matters of service conditions, it is difficult to evolve an ideal set of norms governing various conditions of service and in the grey area where service rules operated, if more than one view

---

18. Reserve Bank of India, *Annual Report, 1985–86.*

is possible, without sacrificing either reason or commonsense, the ultimate choice has necessarily to be conditioned by several considerations that would ensure justice to as many as possible and injustice to as few.

As a result of the agitations and strained industrial relations in 1981–82, the Bank terminated services of some employees. However, in 1983–84, it was decided to reinstate the dismissed members of staff. The Governor, Dr Manmohan Singh, expressed that the act to reinstate the employees could begin a fresh chapter in the industrial relations between the Bank and various associations. In his view, while revoking dismissal orders was fraught with risks, these risks were worth taking. He reiterated that all employees of the Reserve Bank whether in class I, III or IV were members of a large family and it would be impossible for the Bank to function without their dedicated and sustained co-operation. Therefore, rather than taking vindictive action, the Bank had to give each employee a fair chance to correct himself/herself. The erring staff members, at the same time, had to be dealt with firmly. The spirit behind this, the Governor said, was to carry the workforce along to achieve the goals and objectives set for the institution.[19]

During 1984–85, negotiations on the charter of demand submitted by the Employees' Association and the Workers' Federation to the Bank were successful and the dialogue resulted in wage-settlement. Following this, the issue of pay revision for officers was taken up with the officers' associations. Consequently, the revision in scale for officers was announced on September 27, 1985. The revised scales were made effective from February 1, 1984.

In the presence of multiple associations and unions — some recognised and others unrecognised — the Reserve Bank, in 1983–84, decided to take a middle course by meeting with the recognised associations within office hours and the others after office hours. This ensured that the associations/unions which were not recognised did not feel ignored. However, the management was clear that negotiations could take place only with the recognised associations/unions. The Bank had accepted the code of discipline evolved under the aegis of the labour ministry, which stipulated that only a single class III association could be recognised at each centre. The AIRBEA, however, did not accept the code of discipline.

---

19. Reserve Bank of India, internal records relating to proceedings of managers' conferences.

In February 1986, the dismissal of an officer triggered agitations. A call for an indefinite strike was given by the Hyderabad office. The concerned officer was charged with misconduct and breach of the RBI (Staff) Regulations, 1948. The strike was, however, called off after the management handled the situation firmly. The central office supported the Manager, in-charge of the Hyderabad office, in resolving the crisis and the essential services remained available during the strike. The dismissed officer later appealed to the Governor against the order of dismissal. The Reserve Bank accepted his appeal and reinstated him in view of the fact that he regretted his actions and showed an inclination to work. The reinstatement, however, came with a severe penalty imposed on the officer.

Employer-employee relations remained by and large cordial during 1987. There was, however, an agitation on account of the Government's decision to ban recruitment. Later, the Government took positive steps to release some vacancies and allowed the appointment of 147 candidates for the 1983–84 waiting lists at six centres, including Calcutta. This helped in diffusing the situation. Another issue that invited sporadic agitations by class IV staff related to compassionate appointments in view of the fact that some senior class IV staff, who had been working part-time for long were awaiting regular appointment. Proposals were put up to the top executives to address this problem.

During 1987, in an incident, some employees violated the rules of conduct. The agitation began in the Bangalore office initiated by office bearers and activists of the local AIRBEA on August 18, 1987 to protest the Manager's decision of deputing a grade I clerk for short-duration training in the central accounts section, Nagpur. The deputed employee was a member of the rival Reserve Bank Workers' Organisation (RBWO) affiliated to the National Organisation of Bank Workers (NOBW). The local AIRBEA accused the Manager of favouritism and demanded that he reverse his decision, but the Manager expressed his inability to do so. As a result, on August 19-20, 1987, class III employees representing the local AIRBEA held demonstrations. This led the Manager to serve suspension orders on August 21, 1987 on one officer and two class III employees for their conduct. To oppose the suspension, class III employees of the local AIRBEA went on a strike from August 21 to September 30, 1987. The strike was called-off on September 30, 1987 after a settlement between the Reserve Bank and the AIRBEA, signed before the Chief Labour Commissioner in New Delhi on September 30, 1987. The striking employees resumed duty on October 3, 1987 (October 1 and 2 were holidays). Charge sheets were issued to 17 employees, including 3 employees, who faced suspension after an internal enquiry; the penalty of a pay reduction was imposed on all concerned. The suspension orders of three employees were, however, revoked.

A joint study team comprising six members each from the AIRBEA and the Reserve Bank was set up in August 1990 to analyse the issue of offering promotion avenues to class III employees in order to meet organisational needs and achieve greater flexibility in staff deployment. The Reserve Bank accepted the report, and implemented its recommendations on the Cash Department. Another joint study team comprising representatives from the All-India Reserve Bank Workers' Federation (AIRBWF) and the Reserve Bank examined the issues such as recruitment to base cadres and regularising part-time employees. The team submitted its report in November 1992 and its major recommendations were accepted by the Reserve Bank.

During 1992–93, an agitation was launched by the joint action committee, spearheaded by the AIRBEA over their demands, which included a pension scheme as a third retirement benefit and early settlement of their charter of demands. This resulted in a settlement between the Indian Banks' Association (IBA) and the unions over the pension issue. During the same period, the Reserve Bank signed two agreements with the AIRBWF in pursuance of the recommendations of the joint study team, one on the recruitment procedures and the other on an increase in leave reserves and the abolition of the *Ticca* system.[20] The All-India Reserve Bank Staff Officers' Association (AIRBSOA) was registered as a trade union.

Barring sporadic incidents as discussed above, industrial relations within the Bank, by and large, remained cordial.

ISSUES IN CURRENCY MANAGEMENT

During the early 1980s, the currency management practices of the Reserve Bank came under severe criticism. There was a recurrent shortage of coins and notes in circulation in the entire country. The top executives of the Reserve Bank felt that although the shortages did not result from

---

20. *Ticca mazdoor* (labourer), referred to a daily wage worker, who helped the coin-note examiners perform their duties. They were appointed by the Bank on a temporary basis and were required to report to the Bank regularly before business hours to ascertain if they would get work for the day and had to wait till noon to be deployed. On some days no work was assigned to them. The practice of engaging *ticca mazdoors* was discontinued due to litigation.

its policies, the responsibility for resolving the problem lay with the Bank, since the supply and distribution of currency was one of its core functions. The Deputy Governor, Dr C. Rangarajan, expressed concern over the situation in the managers' conferences and felt that the Reserve Bank must redeem its reputation and resolve the issue.

The banks came to face a difficult situation regarding the accumulation of soiled notes awaiting removal at various currency chests, and this number had escalated to 3,639 million pieces as at end-December, 1981. About 1/9th of the soiled notes were lying in the Kanpur office alone. There was resistance on the part of the staff in handling these notes. The number of notes at various Reserve Bank offices that awaited examination and verification amounted to 3,576 million pieces and 1,493 million pieces, respectively (March 1, 1982), verified notes awaiting destruction amounted to 394 million pieces, and the number of defective notes stood at 2 million pieces. To address these issues, the Reserve Bank set up two sub-offices at Trivandrum (now Thiruvananthapuram) and Lucknow. Another sub-office at Bhopal was also opened. The central office of the Reserve Bank issued instructions on a regular basis about modified/special procedures in currency management to minimise the backlog of accumulated soiled notes.

The Reserve Bank of India (note refund) rules were liberalised so that half the face value of mutilated notes of denominations ₹ 10, ₹ 20, ₹ 50 and ₹ 100 were payable at Reserve Bank offices subject to certain conditions. PSBs were authorised to pay in specified categories of mutilated notes. The Reserve Bank also considered reducing printing of one rupee and two rupee notes and replacing them with coins as they were more durable.

In another initiative, the Reserve Bank advised nationalised banks to open additional currency chests at various centres to meet the increasing demand for currency but progress on this front was slow. At this point, the issue of understaffed chest offices emerged as a major constraint. The Deputy Governor took stock of the situation in order to sensitise the senior management of nationalised banks on this issue. In another move, the Deputy Governor advised the concerned department to make provisions for capacity expansion of the incinerators in the Reserve Bank and to open new note examination sections. He reiterated that one way to address the problem was to open the sanctioned additional note examination sections with immediate effect. In a background note on the subject, the Deputy Governor set out the objective that by December 31, 1983, no branch office should have an accumulation exceeding 3 months' capacity of currency notes for disposal through chain examination, verification and destruction. Accordingly, note destruction was undertaken under the special procedures.[21]

Despite the best efforts, the accumulated soiled notes continued to pose an acute problem and the solution required a longer-term perspective. In fact, it was viewed as a national problem. The issue again came up for a serious debate at the managers' conference in 1984. It was recognised that mints and printing presses were not being able to cope with the demand for coins and currency notes. Long queues of customers at the counters of the Reserve Bank at centres like Bombay had become a common sight. The shortage of small denomination notes was attributed to a shortage of paper and it was felt that this could be solved by augmenting the capacity of the printing presses. Another solution was to retrieve the soiled notes and keep them in circulation for as long as possible.

The shortage of small denomination notes was, however, not as acute as that of coins. The Reserve Bank, at the instance of the Government, made projections of the estimated requirement of coins for the period 1985–86 to 1994–95. This forecast was revised at the request of the long-term coinage policy committee set up by the Government. The revised forecast indicated an increase in the volume of coins required from 3,200 million pieces to 4,650 million pieces.[22] In this context, the finance ministry noted:[23]

> With the three mints in Bombay, Calcutta and Hyderabad having been put on overtime working (54 hours per week) and with an incentive scheme in operation, the production achieved during the year 1984–85 was approximately 1400 million pieces only. With the addition of a few coining presses in the three mints, the possible production for the year 1985–86 has been estimated as 2000 million pieces. There is thus, a wide gap in demand and supply position. The capacity of the three mints will not be adequate to meet the increasing demand for coins. Further, there is already a

21. Reserve Bank of India: internal documents, records and proceedings of managers' conferences.

22. Reserve Bank of India (1985). *Mintage of Coins: Establishment of New Mint*, Department of Currency Management, September 3.

23. Government of India (1985). *Project Report–New Mint: Noida (U.P.)*. Ministry of Finance. July 23.

shortage of coins in circulation due to the cumulative effect of gap in the demand and supply over the last few years. There is also an intention of the Government to dispense with the printing of one rupee and two rupee currency notes and replace them with coins of much longer circulation life. It may also become necessary to introduce five rupee coins for circulation within next three to four years as per indications of the RBI.

The Reserve Bank advised the Government to set up additional mints as a long-term solution, and to import coins as an interim measure, which did help to ease the immediate shortage. Some reasons behind the coin shortage were identified. The problem was being aggravated by public sector institutions holding coins and notes; it was found that BEST was no longer re-depositing the coins and notes that it received. The Government, therefore, undertook to commission the Noida mint and modernise the mints at Calcutta, Bombay and Hyderabad. It was emphasised that the techniques of projecting requirements and anticipating demand should be constantly reviewed and revised. Staff had to be alert, especially in the areas of public contact, and officials were repeatedly sensitised about peoples' needs in this matter. Managers at all Reserve Bank offices were advised to personally supervise the cash counters and their direct contact with the public was advocated. In addition, managers were counselled to maintain cordial relations with the railways as well as the police authorities to ensure efficient management of distribution of the available stock of coins. Another concrete measure was re-organising the note examination section, so that it would consist of six groups, each with seven examiners, apart from the ancillary staff; if there were 28 note examiners, one assistant treasurer would be in charge and where the strength exceeded 28, there was a provision for two assistant treasurers. This arrangement was put into effect on a trial basis.

Some solutions that were considered to meet shortages were, *inter alia*, transfer of currency from other parts of the country to Calcutta or other centres to meet festival-specific or seasonal currency requirements, a restriction on issue of coins per person equivalent to ₹ 19 or ₹ 20 only, specific solutions to deal with the racketeers and hirelings, who cornered the supply of coins and making the issue of licences for opening new bank branches conditional on opening new currency chests. Further, there were reports that some cash department staff were colluding with professional dealers, but it was difficult to take action against such employees as there were no witnesses or any concrete evidence. One suggestion was to hire private detectives to gather proof against the erring employees. The Union Minister of State for Finance wrote to the state governments to invoke the Essential Commodities Act to deal with the culprits. As a long-term solution, the rotation of staff in such critical seats of public interaction was exercised.

In an attempt to ease the coin shortage, the Government increased the working hours in the mints from 48 hours to 54 hours a week, besides introducing incentive schemes to improve staff productivity. At the Calcutta mint, a second shift was introduced to increase coin production.

From 1982 through 1986, the state government of Tripura repeatedly approached the Reserve Bank to set up a sub-office at Agartala. The Reserve Bank office, Guwahati, was responsible for supplying notes and coins to Tripura. The state government was of the firm opinion that unless an office of the Reserve Bank was set up in Tripura, the problems of shortages of notes and coins in the state could not be resolved. The reasoning given was that the state had a locational disadvantage, being a landlocked area, and with 13 currency chests and 4 small coin depots of various bank branches supplying coins and notes that they received from the Guwahati depot of the Reserve Bank, it always faced shortages. The Chief Minister emphasised that hoarding and melting of coins by unscrupulous elements, as was happening in other parts of the country, did not occur in Tripura, as a strict watch was kept in the state to avoid any such malpractices.[24] The Reserve Bank, however, took the considered view that the north-eastern region, and especially Tripura was always given priority in currency management and the needs of the region were given greater attention by the Reserve Bank when it distributed notes and coins. The Reserve Bank thus declined to establish an office at Agartala.[25]

The shortages continued through the second half of the 1980s. In 1985–86, the Issue Department of the Reserve Bank undertook an exercise for 'intensive monitoring of resource operations' across its offices. The demand for currency was the crucial variable being tracked, since demand analysis was seen to be the key to proper distribution of supplies. The

---

24. Letter D.O. No. F. 10(5)-FIN (TRY)/81 dated February 21, 1986 from the Chief Minister, Tripura to Shri Janardhana Poojary, Minister of State for Finance, Government of India, New Delhi.

25. Letter D.O. DCM. No. 7461/PN.9-85/86 dated April 4, 1986 from the Chief Officer, Department of Currency Management, Reserve Bank of India to the Ministry of Finance, Government of India.

shortage in the supply of coins assumed such serious proportions from August 1985 that the Union Minister of State for Finance issued instructions that he be briefed every Friday by the officials of the DCM in the Reserve Bank to enable him to constantly review the situation. At this point, the Reserve Bank initiated measures to tide over the supply shortages in coins. The Noida mint (Ghaziabad, Uttar Pradesh) commenced production in July 1988 to enhance the supply of coins. Other measures included opening several small coin depots at PSB branches, importing coins and running four dedicated trains from mint-linked offices to expedite the movement of coins.

The Guwahati office of the Reserve Bank faced a peculiar problem in transfer of remittances. In February 1986, insurgents intercepted a truck loaded with remittances, but the attempt was thwarted by the security personnel. The next remittance, therefore, was sent by air, which prompted the staff to demand that this mode of remittance transfer should be continued.

The attempts to solve the currency crisis finally paid off. The co-ordinated efforts of the Government and the Reserve Bank went a long way in resolving the issues in currency management and conditions were brought under control. The crisis, however, led to some vital decisions such as setting-up a new mint with the combined capacity of three mints. The production capacity of the existing mints was also augmented by replacing the machinery. A second security printing press was established with twice the capacity, which had modern machinery and the latest security features. It was also decided that the Reserve Bank must at all times maintain a reserve stock of notes and coins for three to six months to meet seasonal demands during festivals.

A need was felt to review all existing rules on currency management, and replace these with practical solutions. As a result of the Reserve Bank's efforts to improve the availability of coins, the number of small coins issued in the quarter ended December 1983 represented a 100.0 per cent increase over the quantity issued in the first quarter; in addition there was a substantial increase in the availability of other coins. As a long-term strategy, it was decided to involve commercial banks that had a wide network of branches, in currency distribution on a much larger scale. As a result, by the year 1986–87, there was a comfortable availability of notes and coins. Shortages were eliminated and distribution improved facilitated by co-operation from the railways and police authorities. In fact by the year 1988–89, there was surplus availability of coins in the system.

The committee on currency management (Chairman: Shri P.R. Nayak) was set up by the Reserve Bank in 1988 to examine the issues involving management of currency. The committee submitted its report on September 30, 1989. The Nayak Committee made several recommendations regarding rationalising systems and procedures in the cash department including simplification of functions for receipt and distribution of fresh notes, coinage of notes of smaller denominations and modernising currency management practices.

Implementation of recommendations of the committee led to a revamp of the extant practices and new procedures were adopted for higher productivity and an improved work environment. The Government entrusted implementation of its recommendations to a standing group that finalised the specifications and design of coins as suggested by the committee. The group also decided to bring out a new family of notes of reduced sizes, commission the two note presses at Mysore (Karnataka) and Salboni (West Bengal) and optimally utilise the existing production capacity of the Nasik (Maharashtra) press and the bank note press at Dewas (Madhya Pradesh). Similarly, the Reserve Bank assigned the task of executing the recommendations concerning the Reserve Bank to a small in house committee and held discussions with the Government to sort out the policy issues in this regard. The Bank also initiated action to change the systems and procedures involved in cash handling within the Bank in pursuance of the committee's recommendations.

Currency notes of ₹ 500 denomination were issued for the first time by the Reserve Bank in 1987–88 in order to contain the volume of ₹ 100 notes in circulation. Printed with a portrait of Mahatma Gandhi, the note was issued in the Ashoka Pillar watermark series. The earlier ₹ 500 denomination notes had been issued by the Government in the pre-independence period. Against the backdrop of a phenomenal growth in currency circulation in the 1980s, there was a steep rise in demand for fresh currency/bank notes in the early 1990s. Supply constraints were acute in the case of higher denomination notes. The production capacities of the two note-printing presses at Nasik and Dewas had, however, remained static, and hence these presses were unable to meet the indent for fresh notes. The Government, therefore, initiated the process to modernise the two printing presses and the Reserve Bank took steps to set up two additional note printing presses at Mysore and Salboni. The Reserve Bank advised all currency chests to sort the notes and salvage the maximum number of re-issuable notes on a continuing basis. The currency chests were also asked to identify surplus/deficit chests to effect inter and intra-circle diversions. Further, there was a move for coinage of ₹ 1, ₹ 2 and ₹ 5 denomination notes, which constituted the bulk in circulation, in phases by 1995. To facilitate error-free and quick flow of data on currency chest transactions between bank branches that maintained chests and the issue offices; advanced computerised communication technology was put in place. The new reporting system was to be implemented in phases so as to cover the transactions of all the currency chests spread across the country. The satellite-based network, NICNET, of the National Informatics Centre (NIC) of the Government was selected as the carrier of the data. These measures were aimed at enhancing the availability of fresh notes.

The work of forecasting currency requirements was entrusted to the Indian Statistical Institute (ISI), Calcutta, which submitted its report to the Reserve Bank. Further, a wholly-owned subsidiary company of the Reserve Bank, namely, the Bharatiya Reserve Bank Note Mudran Private Ltd (BRBNM) was set up under the Companies Act, 1956 to take over the new note press project from the Reserve Bank on February 3, 1995. The company had authorised capital of ₹ 800 crore and its registered office was established at Bangalore. The task of commissioning the new printing presses came under the purview of the BRBNM Ltd. While the mini-press at Mysore was commissioned on June 1, 1996 and began to print new ₹ 100 notes, the press at Salboni commenced printing new ₹ 10 denomination notes (Mahatma Gandhi series[26]) from December 11, 1996. The series had additional security features to prevent forgery.

As proposed, the lower denomination notes were phased out as per the schedule. In addition to denominations of ₹ 10 and ₹ 100 in the Mahatma Gandhi series, the Reserve Bank introduced notes of ₹ 50 denomination in the new series in March 1997. A significant step forward was that except for ₹ 10 notes, all other denominations contained an additional feature to assist the visually impaired to identify denominations. Other key initiatives taken by the Reserve Bank to improve currency management practices included, *inter alia*, setting-up a forged note vigilance cell in the DCM for effective monitoring of banknote forgeries, releasing an educational film

---

26. A new series of bank notes, the Mahatma Gandhi series, was issued in June 1996 with additional security features. In this series, the watermark was changed from the Ashoka Pillar to a portrait of Mahatma Gandhi.

highlighting the differences between genuine and forged notes telecast by the Doordarshan, stopping stapling of notes to prolong their durability, treating notes torn into two pieces as soiled rather than mutilated and authorising all PSBs to accept such notes in exchange, as also towards deposits and against payments.

COMPUTERISATION AND MECHANISATION

Interestingly, the Reserve Bank installed its first set of computers (Honeywell) not within the Bank but at the premises of the Bhabha Atomic Research Centre (BARC) in 1967 in Bombay under police supervision in order to avoid confrontation with the trade unions. The Governor, Shri L.K. Jha inaugurated these computers. From time to time, the unions launched agitation against computerisation in the Reserve Bank. Beginning in 1968, when the Employees' Association in Calcutta office protested the computerisation in the Bank, there were violent demonstrations against the move in Jaipur office in 1977 and 1979.

Pursuant to the Dighe Tribunal Award, the Reserve Bank undertook detailed studies in systems research and development during 1981–82 to assess the viability of introducing electro-mechanical devices/mini-computers for facilitating maximum utilisation of available resources and increasing the overall productivity. This was done to improve services, specifically in the areas of public interest. As a result, a decision was taken to computerise cheque clearing operations and introduce ledger-posting machines. Note-shredding machines were also installed to ease the destruction of accumulated soiled notes. During staff agitations, disruption was largely noticed in the functioning of clearing houses. With the installation of micro-mini computers, the situation on this front was expected to ease.

Major initiatives were taken during 1981–1997 to computerise crucial areas of operation of the Reserve Bank. Though the resistance from the unions and the associations did not abate, the management endeavoured to take the workforce along, addressing their concerns and assuring them that the intent was to protect the interests of the employees. Dr Manmohan Singh, Governor, while inaugurating the managers' conference of 1982–83, stated that the process of computerisation had begun in the Reserve Bank clearing houses and ledger postings. He, however, reiterated that the Reserve Bank was not resorting to mechanisation to destroy jobs, as the unions and associations feared; instead the Bank was exploring areas where the dislocation would be minimal. He pointed out that the world economy was expanding fast and technical progress was rapid; hence, to mechanise and computerise was the way to survive. He added that the Reserve Bank wished to carry the workforce along and was willing to explain to them the compulsions of computerisation and the public interest involved in mechanisation. Computerisation, as expressed by Governor Manmohan Singh, was a means to improve productivity and efficiency and not a way to snatch jobs.

CHEQUE CLEARING OPERATIONS

As a prelude to introducing national clearing of outstation cheques, an inter-institutional group was set up to finalise its report for the introduction of MICR technology, which mechanised cheque sorting. The group also recommended standardising cheque forms, setting paper printing specifications and making organisational arrangements for national clearing. To put these processes into operation, the NCC was set up in the Reserve Bank in November 1983. Clearing operations were initially computerised in Bombay, Madras, New Delhi and Calcutta and extended to Ahmedabad, Hyderabad, Bangalore and Kanpur offices during 1984. At this juncture, however, there was resistance from commercial banks, who were reluctant to adjust to the timing of computerised clearing. In the meantime, within the Reserve Bank, a computer was installed in the DICGC for operations connected with the settlement of non-industrial claims and accounting of premium/fees. Work areas related to the maintenance of government accounts and remittance clearance account at the Nagpur office were subsequently computerised and were ready for a parallel run in August 1983.

The national clearing of inter-city cheques commenced on July 6, 1986 under the MICR national clearing project at select centres that included Bombay, New Delhi and Madras; the system had also been put in place in Kanpur and Calcutta. By this time, operations in eight clearing houses of Ahmedabad, Bangalore, Bombay, Calcutta, Hyderabad, Kanpur, Madras and New Delhi had been computerised. Computerisation was extended in phases to the other centres[27] through a national grid. Bombay was the first centre to get the benefit of a high-speed reader/sorter system that could help clear a large volume of local cheques. The system was initially run on

---

27. The remaining six centres were Bhubaneswar, Guwahati, Jaipur, Nagpur, Patna and Trivandrum, where clearing houses were managed by the Reserve Bank.

a trial. After a successful trial-run, it was extended to Madras, New Delhi and Calcutta. The total cost of the clearing operations at the three centres of Bombay, New Delhi and Madras worked out to ₹ 180 lakh. At this point, a decision was taken to introduce uniform regulations and rules (URR) for bankers' clearing houses.

By 1986–87, considerable progress had been made in computerising critical areas, such as clearing house settlement operations, for which a microprocessor system had already been introduced in eight centres. A move was already on to provide mini-computer systems at six more centres under a plan that not only covered clearing house settlements but also other processes, such as pay-roll, currency chest operations, and government receipts and payment transactions.

One-way inter-city cheque clearing was extended during 1990–91 to connect Trivandrum and Baroda to Bombay; and Coimbatore, Salem, Trichy, Madurai and Trivandrum to Madras. An electronic clearing service was introduced that facilitated crediting of the Reserve Bank employee salaries through the clearing house mechanism. The scheme was operationalised in Madras and one salary-disbursing unit was also active in the central office. Pension credit through the clearing house mechanism commenced at Madras, Calcutta and Bombay. The NCC at Madras also processed electronic clearings for the monthly interest payment transactions of Madras-based financial companies.

MICR clearing was made functional at all four metropolitan centres in a phased manner from 1989 and the process was completed by 1992. As a continuation of the process, settlement work was computerised at seven other clearing houses managed by the Reserve Bank. Besides, the settlement operations of the clearing houses at Pune and Baroda, managed by the State Bank of India (SBI), were also computerised.

By 1992, the Reserve Bank succeeded in connecting four metros, *i.e.*, Bombay, Madras, Calcutta and New Delhi, in two-way clearing for speedy collection of out-station cheques. The Bank also established connections of four centres, namely, Ahmedabad, Bangalore, Hyderabad and Nagpur, to the four metros for one-way clearing. The concept of regional grid clearing, whereby commercially important centres in a region were connected to the nearest metro in one-way clearing, was taken up by the Bank for implementing in a phased manner. In this process, Kanpur was connected to New Delhi; Pune and Indore were connected to Bombay; Patna was connected to Calcutta; and Trivandrum was connected to Bombay and Madras. Baroda was connected to all four metros. In Tamil

Nadu, as many as 24 centres were connected to Madras by 1993–94 under a plan to connect all district headquarters in the state to Madras. Kolhapur and Surat were identified to be brought under the regional grid scheme with the NCC, Bombay.

Apart from the MICR clearing, which was functioning successfully at all four metros since 1989, computerisation of other clearing operations, such as return clearing, high-value clearing and inter-bank clearing was also commissioned at New Delhi, Calcutta and Madras, and was in the process of being put in place at Bombay. Special clearing of high-value transactions (above ₹ one lakh) was introduced in Bombay from October 1988 and in Madras from March 1989. This facilitated receipt of credit for high-value cheques by customers in their account on the same day.

COMPUTERISATION OF OFFICES AND DEPARTMENTS

In the Calcutta office, computerisation had to be undertaken cautiously, as it was a sensitive issue at this centre and the Reserve Bank did not want to face the problems as it did in Bombay. In the New Delhi office of the Bank, computerisation proceeded smoothly. At Nagpur, the response of the staff to computerisation was encouraging, despite opposition from the association. The Reserve Bank management, however, was resolved to go ahead with computerisation, despite resistance from the Employees' Association and this message was sent out time and again at the conferences of managers that were held during this period.

In the initial efforts at computerising various departments of the Reserve Bank, in 1984–85, a mini-computer system was set up in the Bombay and Byculla offices for efficient handling of the work of the foreign accounts division, MIS for the top executives, the Reserve Bank of India Services Board, and for the resource operations in the Issue Department.

By this time, the processes that had been computerised included foreign exchange rate determination, resources accounting, portfolio/swap deal evaluation in the DEIO, commercial banks' borrowings, mechanisation of the pay-roll system for which software was developed by DESACS, mini-computer installation in the DBOD covering the operations of overseas commercial bank branches, branch licensing and periodic returns. At the central accounts section, Nagpur, an enhanced memory mini-computer system was installed to systematise work of the Central Board of Excise and Customs (CBEC), the Central Board of Direct Taxes (CBDT) and the accounts of the railways, defence and posts & telegraph department.

Systems design and analysis was taken up for computerising the operational work of the seven sections of the DEBC.

Computer systems were set up in the Bangalore and New Delhi offices of the DFC as had been done in the central office in Bombay. Personal computers (PCs) were also provided to the PPD, CAB in Pune, the DEAP and the Credit Planning Cell (CPC) for effective data management. Further, the training establishments of the Bank, namely, the Bankers' Training College (BTC), the Reserve Bank Staff College (RBSC) and the Zonal Training Centre (ZTC) at Bombay were equipped with computers for more effective training facilities. All along, however, the emphasis of management was that though the Reserve Bank was going ahead in adopting new technology, it did not intend to retrench any employee.

During 1988–89, a super-mini system for the central office of the Exchange Control Department (ECD) was set up in the Reserve Bank to computerise non-resident Indian (NRI) investments and foreign accounts. Further, the Reserve Bank acquired personal computers for nine major regional offices of the ECD. The software packages were developed in house for select items, such as, deferred payment projects, foreign collaboration in India, joint venture (JV) projects, turnkey projects and caution listing of exporters. Personal computers were also installed in the DGBA, DEBC, Premises Department, MSD, DA (training division), Claims section and the DCM. The Reserve Bank also decided to provide word processing facilities in the DBOD, ECD, Secretary's Department, MSD and history cell of the DEAP to expedite correspondence and the preparation of documents. A mini-computer system was also installed at the central office of the UBD. Further, the secretarial offices of the Deputy Governors and Governor were computerised. Additional systems were provided to the DEIO and the RBSC, Madras. Systems installed at the Issue Department offices at Byculla (Bombay), Ahmedabad, Nagpur and New Delhi were upgraded. The Issue Department was also provided computers at its Bangalore, Hyderabad, Kanpur, Trivandrum, Jaipur, Madras and Patna offices. A significant development was installation of a mini-computer system in the Legal Department for storage and quick retrieval of legal decisions. The pilot project to develop software for the legal department was installed in the mini-computers and operationalised in 1992. To facilitate the processing of dealing room transactions of the DEIO, a software package was developed.

The process of replacing the CII-Honeywell bull mainframe computer system in DESACS by a state-of-the-art large mainframe computer system with online data communication facility was underway and was completed by March 31, 1994. Plans to replace the existing BDP-100 microprocessor system used for payrolls of Bombay-based employees by a pair of state-of-the-art mini-computers were at an advanced stage. The process of acquiring PCs for the central office of the IECD, FIC and seven more regional offices was in progress.

In the immediate past, due to the phenomenal increase in public debt, services pertaining to the issue of scrips, repayment of loans and payment of interest posted an alarming increase that required a thorough overhaul of the Reserve Bank's systems and procedures. An inter-departmental committee was constituted to prepare an operational plan for introducing computers in the PDOs to improve customer service and streamline internal procedures. The committee submitted its report in June 1990. Based on its recommendations, in the first phase the subsidiary general ledger (SGL) transfers (local) in respect of central government loans were computerised on July 2, 1992 and work on the remaining segments progressed. Computerisation of SGL transactions (including interest calculation) for both central and state government loans was operationalised at Bombay, Madras, Calcutta, New Delhi, Ahmedabad, Bangalore, Hyderabad and Kanpur. The software package for processing the auction of 91-day Treasury Bills and the OMOs of the IDMC were put into operation during 1992–93. In addition to the eight centres of the PDO, SGL transactions were computerised at six more centres during 1993–94. The scope of the system for computerisation of such transactions was being enhanced to provide prompt customer service and to prevent the accumulation of arrears. In the next phase, computerisation of the processes relating to interest payments, debt operations and new loan applications was taken up.

The Reserve Bank installed a software package on debt management developed by the debt management section of the Commonwealth Secretariat, London, in 1988 with the objective of procuring an efficient database and ensuring its integration with the database on external debt maintained by the Ministry of Finance. The software package, i.e., CS-DRMS (Version 4.3) to be used for processing external commercial loans was installed in pursuance of this objective and through this; the details of all loans up to March 1990 were captured. An advanced version to speed up the processing was proposed to be installed and for this purpose, sophisticated computer hardware was acquired.

By 1990–91, the internal accounting and chest accounting modules were running live at the Issue Departments in Ahmedabad, Byculla (Bombay), Nagpur, Madras, Hyderabad, Bangalore, New Delhi and Kanpur. Similar systems were also being put into operation at Jaipur and Trivandrum. This process was completed during 1993–94. It was also decided that the modern computer-based communication technology of BANKNET/NICNET/DIAL-UP[28] facilities would be put to the maximum use for currency chest transactions. The computerised payroll module was fully functional at Bangalore, Ahmedabad, Madras and Kanpur. The payroll package was also loaded in the Issue Department at Nagpur and Hyderabad offices and was on a parallel run at Nagpur. Next in line were the Issue Department systems at New Delhi and Trivandrum for installing the payroll software. The upload was scheduled to be done in phases in the rest of the offices of the Reserve Bank. A back-up payroll application package was developed and installed in the computer system of the NCC to avoid any dislocation of the sensitive payroll application in the event of a breakdown of the existing mainframe system, which was prone to frequent failures.

To streamline the operations for the preparation of various reports, weekly statements, profit and loss accounts, balance sheet of the Reserve Bank and to reconcile the Reserve Bank general accounts, three PCs run on a UNIX[29] operating system were provided in the DGBA. Five additional PCs were installed in the DEAP. By 1993–94, the accounting system of the Reserve Bank in respect of various advances, such as time, general accounting, pension processing, advances for consumer articles and housing loan sanctions and disbursements to the employees had been computerised.

During 1991–92, there was a drive to equip the regional offices of the DEAP at New Delhi, Calcutta, Madras, Thiruvananthapuram, Bangalore, Hyderabad and Bombay with PCs. The press relations division (PRD) at Bombay was also computerised.

By 1992, the banking industry began adopting new technology by computerising its operations. The use of computers in the Reserve Bank,

---

28. BANKNET: Banking Network; NICNET: National Informatics Centre Network; DIAL-UP: Internet access facility to establish a dialled connection to an internet service provider (ISP) *via* telephone lines.

29. A multitasking, multiuser computer operating system.

which was so far restricted to research activities and certain functions, was envisaged to be spread to the operational areas in an attempt to improve customer service standards. The early 1990s saw the Reserve Bank using computers for the following important purposes:

(i) The main computer, essentially for the computation of a large flow of BoP data or tabulation of other banking data.

(ii) Increasing use of mini-computers or PCs in various departments to collect information for their own purposes.

(iii) Computers in the areas of public interaction for improved customer service and to apprise the public that they were benefiting through the use of technology.

By 1993–94, the Reserve Bank had installed 271 word processor systems in its various offices to promote computer literacy and awareness among its employees.

The Reserve Bank introduced a system of electronic clearance settlement and depository (ECSD) in November 1992 for electronic data processing (EDP) in operations involving recording, clearing, settlement, and payments relating to securities transactions. This was expected to ensure early detection of any irregularities in the securities transactions by banks and financial institutions. After the acceptance of the Joint Parliamentary Committee (JPC) report, a need was felt for an effective functional transformation within the Reserve Bank to be able to cope with the pressures of work that fell on the regulator with the unearthing of the securities scam. The Janakiraman Committee report had pointed out that the absence of such a system had led to the occurrence of the securities scam.

The Reserve Bank set up a committee on technology issues pertaining to payment system, cheque clearing and securities settlement in the banking industry (Chairman: Shri W.S. Saraf) on June 1, 1994. The committee submitted its report to the Bank on December 9, 1994. The recommendations of the committee provided a broad framework for the process of computerisation and information technology applications, including modern communication network in the years to come in the Reserve Bank and the banking industry. In pursuance of these recommendations, the Reserve Bank created a separate department, *i.e.*, the DIT in January 1995, to carry forward the agenda of computerising and modernising systems and procedures within the Bank. This department brought the focus squarely on the issue of quick introduction of new technology in the Reserve Bank. The advanced technology for inter-office communication, such as, the file transfers and electronic mail (e-mail) was increasingly being used within the Reserve Bank, making communication faster, easier and more effective. It resulted in expeditious delivery of circulars to various offices within the Bank and outside and ensured streamlining of the statement of accounts. The Reserve Bank also instituted an electronic fund transfer (EFT) system and set up a committee chaired by Smt K.S. Shere in August 1995 to study all aspects concerning EFT transfers as also to propose the EFT legislation. The thrust of all these efforts was to improve customer service in various areas of operation of the Reserve Bank.

Subsequent to these developments, the Bank assigned top priority to full computerisation of the DoS. The accounts of the Issue Department were computerised at 11 offices of the Bank, and computerisation was proposed to be extended to the remaining three accounting offices. The application of computerised communication facilities for daily reporting of currency chest transactions was implemented using the satellite-based data communication network, NICNET. It was decided to create a separate computer division in the DCM to supervise the functioning of the computer cells at various Issue offices. Computerisation of the PAD was taken up and it progressed in line with the recommendations of the committee chaired by Shri Jagdish Capoor set up for the purpose.

A customised software package was loaded on the LAN system of the DAD in the Chandigarh office of the Reserve Bank. It started operations in April 1995. It was decided to replicate this system in the first phase at the other offices, *viz.*, Hyderabad, Calcutta, New Delhi, Bombay, Ahmedabad and Madras, and subsequently at the remaining offices of the Bank.

After the installation of 271 word processor systems at various locations in the Reserve Bank, LAN systems were installed at 16 sites in Bombay, regional offices and training centres to handle the requirements of the MIS, the processing activities in the PDO, Bombay and ensure connectivity with other PDOs and banks, the dealing room activities of the DEIO, the processing and transaction of Treasury Bills in the IDMC and to facilitate research and analysis work in the DEAP.

Recognising the urgent need to replace its obsolete systems, the Reserve Bank decided to replace the ICIM 6060 system at the central accounts section, Nagpur with the RISC-based HCL-HP 9000/E55 system. The CII-Honeywell bull mainframe computer system in DESACS was also replaced with an HCL-HP 9000/170 system for acting as a server for reader-sorters for cheque clearing. This was not only to share the burden of cheque clearing at Bombay but was also supposed to provide a back-up facility.

During 1996–97, the focus of the Bank was to computerise with the purpose of improving housekeeping and customer service and streamlining the payment system. The PDO, DAD, PAD, Issue Department and the central accounts section, Nagpur had been taken up for technological upgrading. It was expected that full computerisation of banking departments would be completed during 1996–97. Besides, with the introduction of off-site surveillance system in banking supervision, the computerisation of DoS and DBOD assumed priority. Computerisation of ECD also made rapid strides with the finalisation of the forex clearing system.

As recommended by the Saraf Committee, the DIT took over the computerisation process in earnest, with a thrust on improving customer service and house-keeping, and creating an information base for decision-making by the management. In this endeavour, the cash receipts counters and the outward clearing work of the PAD was also computerised. The DAD was computerised in almost all the offices. The system of delivery *versus* payments (DvP) in settlement of the SGL transactions in government securities was operationalised in Bangalore and Chennai, besides at Bombay. The process for servicing relief bonds was computerised at the Byculla (Bombay), Calcutta and Bangalore offices. An integrated solution for the PDO, encompassing a centralised SGL system and a localised system for book debt and relief bonds using the proposed VSAT network, was being envisaged. Computerisation of UBD and CRDC, Pune was underway. Software for settlement of claims of soiled/mutilated notes was designed on a SCO-UNIX platform and was being installed.

The Reserve Bank initiated measures in July 1996 to address the problem of Y2K, both within the Reserve Bank and for the banking industry as a whole. The computer application systems in the Reserve Bank supported the change of only a two-digit year in the dd-mm-year format. With the advent of the year 2000 AD, most of these old programmes would either fail to recognise 2000 as a valid year as the last two digits would be '00' or recognise the year as 1900. Hardware components were replaced and the software was made compatible so that the computer systems of the Reserve Bank would adapt to the year 2000. In response to these measures, the transition to the year 2000 was smooth and unhindered.

TRAINING IN COMPUTERS AT RESERVE BANK COLLEGES

With the advent of computers and developments in communication technology, the Reserve Bank's training establishments, *viz.*, BTC at Bombay, RBSC at Madras and CAB at Pune re-oriented their training methods to meet the emerging challenges in the areas of computer applications and technological upgrading. The BTC at Bombay, besides imparting training on a general understanding of computers and technology applications, also touched on the other areas to suit the imminent requirements. In 1986–87, the BTC conducted a new programme on systems analysis, computer appreciation programme for Reserve Bank officers and senior officers of commercial banks and a faculty development programme on computerisation. Computer input programmes and computer management modules were also introduced at the BTC. In 1989–90, the BTC incorporated computer inputs in most of its programmes and also added customer service applications in its curriculum.

The RBSC initiated a programme on UNIX, 'C' programming language and a programme on structured systems analysis and design. Besides the regular programmes, new programmes such as faculty development (computers), computer orientation and mechanisation in banks were also conducted. In 1990–91, the RBSC included programmes on SWIFT[30] for officers posted in NCC, and PC application and d-base programmes for other officers.

OFFICE AUTOMATION AND COMMUNICATION

The Reserve Bank made essential arrangements in the spheres of technology and communication[31] systems to foster financial services by adapting itself to emerging technological developments across the world. A significant move was made towards achieving technological finesse in the banking system, in general, and in the Reserve Bank in particular. To support the technological upgrading, the Bank established a specialised institution, namely the Institute for Development and Research in Banking Technology (IDRBT), in March 1996 at Hyderabad. For wider benefits, the Reserve Bank collaborated with other institutions in the country and abroad to leverage technological advantage.

---

30. Society for Worldwide Interbank Financial Telecommunication.

31. The communication aspect has been dealt with in detail in the chapter 20: Communication Practices.

Towards upgrading the technology in various departments, during 1983–84, Itelec II electronic ledger posting machines were installed in the DAD in the offices at Bangalore, Bombay, Madras and New Delhi. This was followed up with their introduction at Calcutta and other centres.

The Reserve Bank was also in the process of developing two specialised telecommunication networks, *viz.*, the Store and Forward Telegraph (SFT) network and the Integrated Network (speech, facsimile and data transmission) for faster inter-office communication among Reserve Bank offices all over the country. These applications facilitated faster transmission of telegraph/telex messages as well as telephone/facsimile and computer data messages. The SFT system was initially provided at five centres, namely, Bombay, Madras, New Delhi, Calcutta and Nagpur, and was commissioned at the other centres later. Twenty centres of the Bank were, by September 1987, inter-connected by the SFT tele-printer network, for which leased lines were hired from the post and telegraph department. About 80.0 per cent of the total telex/tele-printer traffic was routed through the tele-printer network. A special network of telephone communication between the central office and other offices of the Bank was in the process of being developed. Of the 22 telephone circuits needed for this network, 17 were already commissioned and were working on a point-to-point basis. The Department of Economic Affairs (DEA), Ministry of Finance, was also connected to this network during 1987–88.

During 1988–89, a sign bank system was introduced in the DAD, Bombay on an experimental basis to enable the storage of signatures for retrieval and verification. A signature capture and retrieval system was also installed at the Byculla office of the Reserve Bank for speedy signature verification. This application was a step forward in the area of customer service. Such systems were also operationalised and adopted for retrieving and verifying signatures in the Nagpur and Bangalore offices.

Further, it was decided in principle to replace the ledger posting machines by installing advanced ledger posting machines (ALPMs) with local area network arrangements at Bombay, New Delhi, Madras, Bangalore and Hyderabad. The ALPMs connected to a LAN were initially introduced in the DAD at Bombay, Madras and New Delhi during 1988–89. Later, ALPMs were installed and put into operation in Hyderabad. While the application ran live at the Madras, New Delhi and Hyderabad offices of the Reserve Bank, it was put on test and parallel runs at Bombay. There was also a proposal to install the ALPM at the Bangalore office.

Further, the Reserve Bank decided to install 19 LAN systems with 110 terminals at 16-locations in Bombay, at regional centres and at its training establishments to facilitate efficient handling of important work. The work on replacing 6060 system at the central accounts section, Nagpur with a RISC-based system had been initiated. As a temporary measure, to facilitate data entry operations, 4 PC-ATs with the necessary software and connectivity to a 6060 system was provided.

Facsimile machines were installed exclusively for the DEIO and the PPD, and were also being set up in the Bombay, New Delhi, Madras and Calcutta offices. Further progress was made on office equipment in the Reserve Bank, and, in addition to the fax machines, introduced in 1988–89, 34 additional fax machines were installed in 8 central office departments, 3 training colleges and 21 offices across the country during 1990–91. By 1991–92, fax machines were provided in the Reserve Bank in all the offices and training colleges, with the exception of the Srinagar office. Fax modem cards were also provided in the PCs at the NCC at the central office, the Bombay regional office, and the PDO and DESACS offices in Bombay.

The Reserve Bank, in recognition of the space constraints in the central office and in view of the need for better records management, examined the feasibility of microfilming its records. A beginning towards this end was made during 1988–89 by microfilming the records of a few departments in the central office.

RBINet was inaugurated on December 3, 1994, covering all the offices and departments of the Reserve Bank. RBINet enabled free-format messaging, transferring ASCII and binary files, error-free messaging and secured messaging. RBINet was being developed as a way to introduce an e-mail culture in the Reserve Bank. By 1996–97, RBINet had been set up in all central office departments, regional offices and training establishments for e-mail and file transfers within the Bank. It had become a primary source for the banks for EFT data transmission. Staff of commercial banks was trained to transmit statutory returns through RBINet.

Internet technology revolutionised the process of information collection and knowledge sharing. The Reserve Bank put up a home page and periodically uploaded news and current events relevant to central banking. It instantly became an important source of interaction with the rest of the world. At this point, the Reserve Bank was also planning to set up its own website so that its policy framework could be given a wider reach. The Reserve Bank website with the URL *http://reservebank.com* was finally operationalised on September 17, 1996.[32]

TRAINING

The Reserve Bank remained fully aware of the need to upgrade the skills of its employees in order to keep up with the challenges of the changing economic and banking circumstances. With transformations in the system, there was a need to enhance professional competence. The Reserve Bank took steps to revitalise the available expertise and filled the gaps in the training content and coverage. It revised the training modules, methodology and curriculum. New programmes were designed and introduced every year at various levels to suit the needs of the system and courses of contemporary relevance were started to upgrade proficiency. In a two-way process, the Reserve Bank also provided training to foreign participants at its institutes on request or otherwise. Such participants were mainly officials from various central banks or foreign commercial banks.

To enhance the professional ingenuity of its officers, the Bank deputed them to participate in seminars, workshops and training programmes in India and abroad. Further, to motivate the employees to work in a computerised environment, the Reserve Bank offered its staff various incentives for acquiring professional qualifications and encouraged them to join computer courses. The details of various aspects of training are given in Annex 21.1.

BANKERS' TRAINING COLLEGE

The training establishments of the Reserve Bank provided a platform for conducting programmes, courses, seminars and workshops. The BTC[33] was set up in as early as 1954 with technical assistance from the UK under the Colombo Plan and two officials from Midland Bank extended their services for this initiative.

RESERVE BANK STAFF COLLEGE

The staff training college was established in August 1963 at Madras and later this was renamed as the RBSC.[34] The college was set up as a venue

---

32. For details refer to chapter 20: Communication Practices.
33. Ibid.
34. Ibid.

for induction programmes for new recruits in officer cadre and for those promoted to the officer cadre.

In 1989, the RBSC celebrated its silver jubilee and to commemorate the occasion, a book on the history of the college titled Reserve Bank Staff College: Evolution and Development was released.

COLLEGE OF AGRICULTURAL BANKING

The CAB[35] was set up as the co-operative bankers' training college (CBTC) at Pune on September 29, 1969. The CBTC attended exclusively to the training requirements of co-operative banks, focusing on banking policies, practices and procedures in this category. The multi-agency approach advocated by the all-India rural credit review committee (Venkatappiah Committee) and the introduction of commercial banks into the realm of agricultural and rural credit after nationalisation led to a shift in the structure of the CBTC programmes. Programmes were also designed for the officers from various state and the central government departments associated with the preparation and execution of agricultural projects. The curriculum was, over time, modified and the emphasis was placed on the broader sphere of agricultural development, banking and finance. To reflect its focus on the widening area of the training activity, the college was renamed the CAB on February 16, 1974. The CAB occupied a pivotal position on the international training map, especially in the Asia-Pacific region.

ZONAL TRAINING CENTRES

The ZTCs,[36] established by the Reserve Bank in August 1962 at the four metropolitan cities, namely Bombay (Byculla), Calcutta, New Delhi and Madras, facilitated capacity building among the clerical cadre in the Reserve Bank. The induction programmes for the clerical grades were conducted at these centres before posting to various departments. Class IV staff of the Bank were also trained at the ZTCs in various fields. Preparatory courses for scheduled caste/scheduled tribe (SC/ST) candidates in class III for promotion to the officer cadre were held regularly at the ZTCs.

---

35. Ibid.

36. Ibid.

NATIONAL INSTITUTE OF BANK MANAGEMENT

The National Institute of Bank Management (NIBM) was established in 1969 by the Reserve Bank, in consultation with the Government, as an autonomous apex institution with the mandate of playing the role of a think-tank for the banking system. The NIBM formed part of the vision of giving a new direction to the banking industry in India and making the industry a more cost-effective instrument for national development. Therefore, helping the managers in their endeavour to make their organisations competitive in both domestic and international markets was the mission of the institute.

INSTITUTE FOR DEVELOPMENT AND RESEARCH IN BANKING TECHNOLOGY

During the first phase of reforms in the Indian financial sector, a need was felt to develop an institute of higher learning that would also provide operational service support in the field of information technology to banks and financial institutions (FIs). The foundation for the induction of computer technology in the Indian banking sector was laid by two reports in the years 1984 and 1989 (Chairman: Dr C. Rangarajan). The two reports recommended computerising banking industry operations at various levels, while also suggesting the appropriate architecture. In 1993, the employees' unions of banks signed an agreement with the management under the auspices of the IBA. This agreement was a major breakthrough in the introduction of computerised applications and development of communications network in the banking industry. In the two years that followed, substantial work was done and bank managements realised the urgent need for training, research and development activities in the area of technology. Banks and FIs set up technology-based training centres and colleges. A need was, however, felt for an apex-level institute that could be the brain trust for banking technology and would spearhead technology absorption in the banking and the financial sectors.

In 1994, a committee was constituted by the Reserve Bank on Technology Up-gradation in the Payment Systems. The committee recommended a variety of payment applications that could be implemented with appropriate technology upgrading and the development of a reliable communications network. It recommended setting-up an information technology institute for research and development that could also provide consultancy in the application of technology to the banking and the financial sector in India. As a result, the Institute for Development and Research in Banking Technology (IDRBT) was established by the Reserve Bank in March 1996 at Hyderabad as an autonomous centre for development and research in banking technology.

STAFF WELFARE AND OTHER MATTERS

At the managers' conference in 1988, it was noted that in the matter of providing staff facilities, especially housing facilities, the Reserve Bank had set the best record in the country. The continued good service conditions were not a sign of extravagance but an essential element in keeping the morale of the staff high. The Reserve Bank introduced measures from time to time, which enabled continual progress in staff welfare.

HOUSING LOAN

In 1981, in pursuance of the national industrial tribunal award, which came into effect on December 6, 1981 the minimum loan for class III staff was raised by the Reserve Bank from ₹ 25,000 to ₹ 48,000. The rate of interest charged on the loan was also changed from 3.0 per cent to half of the Bank Rate prevailing on July 1 every year. Since the Bank Rate stood at 9.0 per cent on July 1, 1981, the rate on housing loans during the period December 6, 1981 to June 30, 1982 worked out to 4.5 per cent. Further, effective February 1, 1982, the limit of the loan admissible to class I was enhanced from ₹ 72,000 to ₹ 1,00,000. Simultaneously, the interest rate charged was altered from 3.0 per cent to 6.0 per cent on the first ₹ 25,000, 8.0 per cent on the next ₹ 25,000 and 10.0 per cent on the remaining amount of ₹ 50,000.

Major changes made in the housing loan rules and regulations during the early 1990s included:
  (i)   Effective March 1, 1991, the minimum limit of housing loan for class III employees was revised to ₹ 1,25,000 from ₹ 1,00,000. The minimum limit of housing loan for class IV employees was also raised from ₹ 75,000 to ₹ 88,000 effective July 1, 1990 and further to ₹ 1,13,000 effective April 1,1991.
  (ii) Effective November 15, 1990, the minimum service put in for availing of a PF advance for a housing loan was reduced from 5 years to 3 years of continuous service, including service on probation/temporary service.

(iii)   Effective September 1990, the aggregate ceiling on housing loan
        and PF advance/withdrawal together for acquiring/constructing
        houses/flats to employees in class III and IV was increased from
        ₹ 2,25,000 to ₹ 3,00,000 with a further discretion to the extent of
        25.0 per cent of the aggregate ceiling to the sanctioning authority.
(iv)   The construction cost of a garage as also stamp duty/registration
        charges had not been considered admissible under the Reserve
        Bank's housing loan scheme. From September 1990, these
        items were considered admissible under the scheme, provided
        they formed part of the original plan/project and stamp duty/
        registration charges were included in the total cost of acquiring
        the flat.

The Reserve Bank raised, with effect from July 20, 1992, the aggregate
ceiling on housing loans and PF advances/withdrawals together for
the acquisition/construction of houses/flats for the employees in
class I and class III/IV from ₹ 4,00,000 to ₹ 6,00,000 and ₹ 3,00,000 to
₹ 4,00,000, respectively, with a further discretion to the extent of 25.0 per
cent of the aggregate ceiling to the sanctioning authority. The subscriber
was permitted to avail of the PF withdrawal after 10 years of service (instead
of 15 years stipulated earlier), provided it was for the purpose of acquiring
a new house or a new flat.

As directed by the Committee of Central Board, an in house group
was constituted that attempted, within the extant monetary parameters
of the scheme, to redraft the housing loan rules and simplify them, study
the procedural requirements in the Reserve Bank *vis-a-vis* other banks and
suggest measures that would encourage employees to avail of the housing
loan facility. As per the recommendations of the in house group, the RBI
employees' housing loans rules were replaced by a new set of rules called
the RBI employees' housing loans rules, 1995. Many changes were effected
to simplify the procedures. Monetary parameters like the quantum of loan
and rate of interest, however, remained unchanged.

The eligibility for housing loan was raised from 50 months' pay to 70
months' pay for all categories of staff with the maximum and minimum
limits remaining unchanged from November 26, 1993. For the benefit of
a larger number of employees acquiring a second property, the Reserve Bank
allowed PF withdrawal to employees having less than 10 years of remaining
service as against less than 5 years of remaining service, as designated
earlier.

PENSION SCHEME

Perhaps one of the most beneficial measures was the introduction of long-awaited pension scheme for its employees by the Bank. The Reserve Bank, at a meeting with the representatives of the recognised associations of workmen employees and officers of the Bank, held on January 16, 1990, announced that a pension scheme was being introduced in lieu of the contributory provident fund (CPF). The scheme was optional for serving employees, but compulsory for new entrants. Designed along the lines of the pension scheme applicable to employees of the Central Government, the modalities of the scheme were under the consideration of the Bank at this point. On receipt of the approval from the Government, the scheme came into effect from November 1, 1990. While all employees joining the Bank on and from November 1, 1990 were governed by the RBI pension regulations, 1990, employees in service as on November 1, 1990 were given the option of continuing with the CPF, if they so desired. Former employees of the Reserve Bank who were in service and had retired on or after January 1, 1986 were covered by the pension scheme, though the pension was payable to them with effect from November 1, 1990 only if they chose to surrender the CPF benefits already drawn by them along with the interest.

Certain amendments were effected to the RBI pension regulations during 1991–92, which included an important amendment providing for the grant of premature retirement pension to employees seeking voluntary retirement after rendering 20 years of qualifying service and an addition up to a maximum of 5 years to qualifying service for such retirement. Employees opting for the CPF were allowed to exercise fresh option in favour of pension. A decision was also taken to give the benefit of past service in the PSBs/SBI/central and state governments/central autonomous bodies as qualifying service for pension, broadly along the lines of similar provisions in the central government pension scheme.

MEDICAL ASSISTANCE FUND

During 1986–87, the Reserve Bank introduced a new scheme to provide medical assistance to serving as well as retired employees. A fund named the Reserve Bank of India Medical Assistance Fund (MAF) was instituted for the purpose effective January 1, 1987. The objective of this fund, which was contributory, was to facilitate provision of financial assistance to meet a part of the medical expenditure incurred by serving employees or their families and retired employees or their spouses for hospitalisation and treatment of serious ailments in India. Under the provisions of the scheme, known as the MAF, the assistance available to serving employees was over and above the reimbursement admissible under the Reserve Bank's medical facilities. Membership to the fund was optional and the Bank contributed ₹ 15 lakh initially to the corpus of the fund.

The benefits under the MAF facility, which were available to spouses of members only during the lifetime of the member, were extended with effect from January 1, 1993 to spouses even after the death of the member. An advisory committee headed by the chief manager and consisting of a representative from each of the four recognised associations of officers and workmen employees was set up on January 1, 1993 to suggest improvements in the MAF scheme.

SCHEMES FOR HIGHER STUDIES FOR OFFICERS

To encourage officers in the DEAP to specialise and upgrade their professional competence, it was decided in 1990-91 to sponsor up to four officers (two each in two semester programmes) every year at the Indian Institute of Technology (IIT), Bombay and two additional officers at the IGIDR, Bombay for a Ph.D. degree in Economics. A new scheme was later made applicable for other departments for a Ph.D. in various areas of interest to the Reserve Bank.

In 1989, the Reserve Bank announced a scheme to enrol in the Chartered Financial Analyst (CFA) Programme conducted by the Institute of Chartered Financial Analysts of India (ICFAI), Hyderabad, in pursuance of its policy to encourage the staff to acquire professional qualifications in various spheres. The total number of employees benefitting from this scheme stood at 213 as of the year 1994–95 and the total number of beneficiaries stood at 222 during 1995–96.

With effect from April 1, 1994, based on the recommendations of the Marathe Committee on human resources development, the Reserve Bank structured and introduced a new scheme to grant study leave to officers for higher studies in India and abroad. A maximum of 10 officers were to be selected under the scheme every year. Confirmed officers, who had put in a minimum of five years service, were eligible for study leave for post-graduate courses, such as MBA and Ph.D. at the reputed universities in India and abroad on the subjects directly related to the Bank's main functions.

Apart from training and upgrading the professional competence of its own officers, the Reserve Bank extended professional enhancement facilities to 68 officials during 1993–94 from 12 different countries. These included Bhutan, Botswana, Kenya, Mauritius, Nepal, Nigeria, Russia, Sri Lanka, Sudan, Tanzania, Uganda and Zambia. During 1995–96, a total of 229 officials from 14 countries, *i.e.,* 57 from Bangladesh, 10 from Bhutan, 3 from Botswana, 2 from China, 1 from Ghana, 2 from Indonesia, 4 from Malaysia, 3 from Mauritius, 22 from Nepal, 3 from the Philippines, 1 from Russia, 106 from Sri Lanka, 6 from Tanzania, and 9 from Uganda were provided training facilities in the Reserve Bank's training establishments/ offices.

A scheme for study leave was introduced by the Reserve Bank in 1994, and during 1995–96, two officers were granted study leave for higher studies abroad. The scheme of sponsoring officers for M.Phil. programmes offered by the Department of Humanities and Social Sciences at IIT, Bombay, was initiated in December 1994. During 1995–96, one officer was nominated under the scheme for acquiring specialisation.

OFFICE AND RESIDENTIAL PREMISES

The new central office building (NCOB)[37] of the Reserve Bank was formally inaugurated by the Union Finance Minister, Shri R. Venkataraman, on November 7, 1981. The work on the office buildings of Trivandrum and Bhubaneswar was completed and the offices were occupied in September 1981 and February 1982, respectively. The office buildings at Jaipur and Chandigarh were readied for occupation in December 1982.

A major highlight during the year 1983–84 was that a five-year plan for the construction of office buildings and residential quarters covering the period 1983–84 to 1987–88 was drawn and approved by the Central Board in September 1983. The thrust of the plan was to provide adequate residential facilities for Reserve Bank employees at all centres. It was expected that a total of 2,279 flats for officers, 2,319 for class III and 1,553 for class IV employees would be completed under the plan; a budget of ₹ 161 crore was earmarked for the five-year period that was to be utilised under the supervision of three zonal cells of the Premises Department set up at Bombay, Calcutta and Madras. Another cell at New Delhi also came up for the purpose.

During the first three years of the five-year plan, the total expenditure amounted to ₹ 71 crore, as against the envisaged outlay. During 1985–86, the office building at Nagpur was completed and the expansion scheme

---

37. For details also refer to *The Reserve Bank of India (1967–1981).* Volume 3.

at the BTC also concluded. In the pipeline was the construction of office buildings at Chandigarh and Cochin, and the completion of work at the Kanpur office and Bandra-Kurla complex in Bombay. Office premises had also been planned at Bhopal, Jammu and New Bombay.

The total expenditure on the office and residential complexes of the Bank under the five-year plan was estimated at ₹ 114 crore during the first four years of the plan. The expansion of the Bangalore office by adding new floors to the office building was completed during 1986-87. As regards the residential quarters, a total of 1,317 flats and 27 single rooms were completed during 1986–87 comprising 600 flats and 27 single rooms for officers, 575 flats for class III staff and 142 flats for class IV staff.

With an additional expenditure of ₹ 30 crore on construction and acquisition of office premises and residential quarters, additions/ alterations to the existing buildings and purchase of land, the total outlay under the five-year plan escalated to ₹ 144 crore as against the budgeted expenditure of ₹ 161 crore during 1983–84 to 1987–88. During 1987–88, the construction work on the office buildings at the Bandra-Kurla complex (Bombay), Chandigarh office and Kanpur was completed.

A total of 306 flats and single rooms comprising 96 flats and 4 single rooms at Bhubaneswar, 120 officers' flats at Patna, 8 flats at Bombay and 78 flats at Bangalore for class III staff were made ready for occupation. Overall, during the five-year period of 1983–84 to 1987–88, a total of 4,181 flats and 67 single room flats were completed for various categories of staff.

SECURITY AND DISCIPLINE

In a significant move, the Reserve Bank introduced a system of issuing identity cards to its employees in 1982. The measure was aimed at tightening security within the Reserve Bank. Identity cards were issued at all centres of the Bank, except Calcutta and Madras, where there was resistance from the local associations. The issue was, however, addressed and the process of issuing the cards began in these offices also. Staff members were advised to wear identity cards in the office premises and metal detectors were installed for better security, initially in eight offices including at the NCOB at Bombay during 1987.

Staff discipline and reduction in overtime formed an integral part of the agenda at all internal conferences of the management. One concern was that many officers, when promoted, did not give up their office bearer or member status in unions/association of workmen employees. This resulted in maintaining dual interests. To solve the problem, it was decided to obtain a declaration from the officers promoted from clerical cadres before promotion that they would not be a member or office bearer in any of the workmen unions or associations. The two of the Reserve Bank offices where this was a common problem were Kanpur and Hyderabad.

At the managers' conference in 1986, a review of pending disciplinary cases was undertaken. It was reiterated that the tenets to be upheld while dealing with such cases included a reasonable opportunity be given to the employee to defend himself/herself in case of disciplinary action and that the principles of natural justice and fairness must be observed. This reflected the management's endeavour to maintain an employee-friendly atmosphere in the Reserve Bank, wherein there was objectivity and integrity in resolving cases of disciplinary proceedings.

SCHOLARSHIPS FOR WARDS

A scholarship scheme for employees' wards with outstanding academic performances was introduced by the Reserve Bank as part of the golden jubilee celebrations. In 1991–92, the scheme was liberalised and the limit on the number of scholarships was done away with, so that all eligible wards were covered under the scheme. Further, the Reserve Bank decided to provide financial assistance for the purchase of books to wards of the workmen employees, who were awarded the scholarship.

HOLIDAY HOMES

The decision on selecting properties to be converted into holiday homes for staff members at Lonavala near Bombay and Mussoorie was taken during 1986–87. The year 1988–89 saw the culmination of acquisition of properties at Lonavala, Mussoorie and Ootacamund for developing holiday homes for Reserve Bank staff. These three holiday homes were commissioned in June 1988. Also, the construction of additional rooms in the holiday home at Ootacamund was taken up, and acquisition of property for a holiday home at Darjeeling was also initiated. The Reserve Bank's holiday home at Shimla with 20 rooms was inaugurated in September 1995.

COMMITTEES FOR STAFF WELFARE

From time to time, the Reserve Bank set up various committees to address human resources issues, which were of considerable importance in enhancing the productivity and welfare of employees.

The expert committee on human resources development was set up in the Reserve Bank (Chairman: Shri S.S. Marathe), which submitted its report in 1992. The committee made extensive recommendations covering all important aspects of human resource development, *viz.*: (i) direct recruitment of officers; (ii) placement; (iii) promotion; (iv) training; and (v) performance appraisal. During 1992–93, the recommendation on direct recruitment of officers was accepted by the Reserve Bank, the age ceiling was relaxed and the requirement of a minimum period of service for staff members who wished to apply for the direct recruitment in grade B was waived.

IMMUNITY FROM ROBBERIES AND TERRORIST ATTACKS

In the early 1990s, in the context of a spate of robberies and terrorist attacks on banks and their employees, the Reserve Bank, as outlined by the Government, made available a package of compensation/reward for its employees who were injured or killed in such incidents. As per this package, the family of the deceased was eligible for compensation in the range of ₹ 1 lakh to ₹ 5 lakh, besides other benefits. This scheme, along with the Reserve Bank's own scheme of compensation for injuries/death due to accident while on duty, adequately provided for employees and their families in case of any untoward incidents.

OTHER MEASURES

The grievance redressal procedure (GRP) and the scheme of joint consultation, which were submitted by the Reserve Bank to the national industrial tribunal, were approved during 1982–83. The Bank implemented these schemes to the extent possible.

In 1985, the Reserve Bank instituted the golden jubilee scheme for awarding scholarship for higher studies abroad. Over the years, a number of officers availed of the scheme and by 1994–95, the number of officers benefitting from the scheme stood at 35. In 1994–95, 3 officers were pursuing higher studies abroad and in 1995–96, 4 more officers were selected, bringing the total number of beneficiaries to 39.

As a welfare measure for employees, the Reserve Bank introduced a group savings-linked insurance scheme administered by the Life Insurance Corporation of India (LIC) for the benefit of its full time employees from November 14, 1988. The scheme received an overwhelming response, and 91.0 per cent of the employees immediately subscribed to it.

During 1990–91, to commemorate the birth centenary of Bharat Ratna Dr B.R. Ambedkar, the Reserve Bank constituted a fund with a corpus of ₹ 50 lakh for the benefit of its SC/ST employees. The interest earned on the fund was to be spent on enhancing the educational qualifications of the Reserve Bank's SC/ST employees, including scholarship schemes for their wards. A professional chair designated the Dr B.R. Ambedkar Professorship at the Department of Economics was also set up as part of the celebrations at the University of Bombay.

During 1991–92, the Reserve Bank decided to grant *ex-gratia* payment of ₹ 150 per month to the widow/widower/eligible child of a deceased employee who had retired from the Bank's service or died while in service prior to January 1, 1986. Dearness relief was also payable on the *ex-gratia* payment at the rate admissible for family pension. The *ex-gratia* amount was payable from January 1, 1986.

During 1993–94, the Reserve Bank effected several improvements in the staff welfare schemes such as granting advances for the purchase of PCs, relaxing the stipulation on leave encashment for employees who died in harness, and raising the entitlement for maternity leave to six months from four months. Further, the benefit of an advance for purchase of consumer articles was extended to part-time workmen employees in 1994–95.

The Reserve Bank reviewed in 1995–96 the recruitment policy for officers. It decided on direct recruitment only at grade B level and no such recruitment at grade A level. Also, a transparent transfer policy was put in place to avoid hardships, which were integral to transfers. These decisions were taken after wide-ranging consultations with all concerned and after careful scrutiny of the issues. The outcomes were well received.

A revised performance appraisal system (PAR) was introduced in January 1987. The objectives of this system remained the same as earlier, *i.e.,* monitoring the efficiency and performance of officers from the organisational point of view. The revised PAR system was the outcome of laborious exercises, such as, responses to a questionnaire, followed by discussions between the Governor and heads of departments and a study conducted by an in house committee. The new features of this system included issuing an appreciation letter on getting two consecutive A+ reports and the introduction of a self-appraisal system. During 1996–97, a revised PAR for grades C, D and E was put in place that was more transparent than the existing system. Further, a working group was set up to review career progression opportunities of the protocol and security officers, lounge supervisors, Rajbhasha officers and technical staff in the Premises Department. Another study group was constituted to review the opportunities for the career growth of the class III staff.

There was frequent representation from the SCs/STs in different categories of the cadres in class I, class III and class IV employees. The Bank recruited physically challenged persons at various levels from time to time. By 1989–90, the total number of such personnel in the Reserve Bank stood at 377 and the number reached around 450 in December 1996. Certain posts in class IV grade were also offered to partially blind persons (who were not deaf and/or dumb). The Reserve Bank also recruited ex-servicemen in class III and class IV grades on a regular basis.

PROMOTION OF HINDI IN THE RESERVE BANK

In compliance with the provisions of the Official Languages Act (OLA), 1963, the Reserve Bank took measures from time to time to ensure the progressive use of the official language in the daily work. Attempts were made by devising annual time-bound programmes. To assess the progress with regard to adopting Hindi as a functional language, the Official Language Implementation Committee (OLIC) in the central office held quarterly meetings with various departments and offices of the Reserve Bank. Various reports, brochures, press communiquйs, notifications, licence agreements and publications meant for in house communication were released in Hindi in addition to the English version for wider dissemination of information. From January 1986, the monthly bulletin of the Bank started being published in bilingual form. The training establishments of the Bank also conducted several courses in Hindi for staff at various levels. Reserve Bank offices hosted elocution competitions, poets' gatherings and essay competitions to popularise Hindi.

The Reserve Bank conducted regular Hindi workshops for employees to train them in Hindi noting, drafting and correspondence. This was aimed at improving the proficiency of the staff in their daily work. Such workshops were also introduced for senior officers of the Bank. Employees were also nominated to Hindi typewriting and Hindi stenography classes held by the Government. There was a progressive increase in the honorarium for passing the examination organised by the Government as also for passing the Prabodh, Pravin and Pragya examinations. Hindi-medium was allowed by the Reserve Bank for recruitment and promotion examinations for officers' and other posts. Bilingual agenda notes were introduced for the meetings of the Central Board. All these developments paved the way for installing bilingual word-processors in the Hindi division of the central office of the Bank and some bilingual electronic typewriters were also purchased.

In recognition of the outstanding work done in various areas in promoting the official language, the rajbhasha trophy was awarded every year. In 1989–90, a reference section was set up in the rajbhasha division of the central office for the employees. Hindi Saptah and Hindi Divas were organised by all departments in the Reserve Bank in September each year. The display of Hindi terms and sentences was also introduced in the Bank to raise awareness. The RBSC published a glossary of computer terms titled Computer Sandarbha Sulabha in 1994–95. All these initiatives resulted in the increased strength of officers and other staff proficient in the use of Hindi in the Bank, resulting in the expansion of the Rajbhasha Department.

CONCLUDING OBSERVATIONS

The decades of the 1980s and 1990s were notable for the challenges faced by the central bank and the new tasks performed by it in a period of fiscal dominance and later, in an environment of economic liberalisation and financial sector reforms. These developments were the major reasons for the significant transformation that took place in the organisational structure of the Reserve Bank. This took the form of re-organisation of some departments, creation of new departments and assuming additional responsibilities, especially in the areas of economic research and publications, banking supervision, settlement of securities transactions and improvement in payment systems. The two major achievements of the Reserve Bank were the rapid and successful computerisation both within the Bank and the banking industry in general and achieving large scale mechanisation of banking operations. Internally, the launching of a pension scheme for its employees; reviewing and improving the avenues of promotion from time to time; providing opportunities for staff at various levels to acquire professional skills and knowledge through training and scholarships as also enabling study and research in India and abroad; and instituting a wide range of welfare schemes for the benefit of staff and their wards went a long way in building cordial industrial relations in this premier institution.

ANNEX 21.1
Staff Training

Year	Domestic (Nos.)	Foreign (Nos.)	Countries of Deputation	Training for Foreign Participants	Other Important Training Programmes/ Professional Qualifications
(1)	(2)	(3)	(4)	(5)	(6)
1983–84	201	19	US, UK, France, Switzerland, Korea, West Germany, Malaysia, Japan, Singapore, Philippines, China, Indonesia and Thailand.		
1984–85	150	22	US, England, Switzerland, West Germany, Japan, Malaysia, Indonesia, Thailand, Zimbabwe, Hong Kong, Nepal and the Philippines.	Participants from foreign central and commercial banks were given training in response to specific requests.	

contd...

contd...

Year	Scholarships Awarded to Officers	Training in Computer Technology
(1)	(7)	(8)
1984–85	Introduced in 1985 as a part of the golden jubilee celebrations of the Bank; 4 officers were selected every year for higher studies abroad for a period not exceeding one year.	

contd...

contd...

(1)	(2)	(3)	(4)	(5)	(6)
1986–87	263	29	US, UK, Switzerland, West Germany and Japan.	Special programmes on health of the Executives were initiated by RBSC, Chennai and foreign participants from Bhutan, Botswana, Kenya, Macau, Malawi, Sudan, and Tanzania attended some of the programmes conducted by the RBSC.	Two officers from DEAP were deputed to CDS, Trivandrum for an M.Phil. course in applied economics, which became an annual feature, thereafter.

contd...

contd...

(1)	(7)	(8)
1986–87	Under the golden jubilee scheme 4 officers were selected for higher study abroad for 1 year in 1986 and another batch of 4 officers in 1987.	To implement Bank's scheme of computerisation and mechanisation at a faster pace incentives were offered for acquiring skills in computer technology. The Bank encouraged class III and all officers to take up short-term diploma/ certificate courses in computers at approved institutions. On successful completion of the course an honorarium of ₹ 500 was given in addition to reimbursement of the fee.

...contd

contd...

(1)	(2)	(3)	(4)	(5)	(6)
1987–88	230	19	US, UK, Switzerland, West Germany and Japan.		Two officers completed CDS course and 2 more were attending the course.
1988–89	358	25	US, UK, Switzerland, West Germany and Japan.	Sixty-five foreign participants, 12 from Sri Lanka, 8 from Bhutan, 7 from Kenya, 6 each from Afghanistan and Iran, 5 from Tanzania, 4 each from Nepal, Zambia and Somalia, 3 from Botswana, and 1 each from Uganda, USSR, Nigeria, Sudan, Ethiopia and Malawi were trained in response to specific requests from these countries.	Two officers were attending the M. Phil. course at CDS, Trivandrum.

contd...

contd...

(1)	(7)	(8)
1987–88		The response to the scheme of computerisation was very encouraging and therefore its scope was enlarged.
1988–89	Four officers completed their studies under the golden jubilee scholarship scheme. The third batch of 4 officers was studying at various universities abroad and 4 more officers had been selected for the year.	The scheme of incentives designed for acquiring computer qualifications evoked an encouraging response from the staff.

contd...

contd...

(1)	(2)	(3)	(4)	(5)	(6)
1989–90	Officers continued to be sent on training.	Officers continued to be deputed for training abroad.		Bank also continued to extend training and study facilities to officials from foreign central and commercial banks, on request.	Two more officers were deputed to take up M.Phil. courses at CDS, Trivandrum.
1990–91	275	23	US, UK, France, Switzerland, Germany, Japan, Singapore, China, Bangladesh, Thailand and South Korea.	Forty-eight foreign officials including 9 from Afghanistan, 7 each from Kenya and Iran, 5 each from Nepal and Ethiopia, 2 each from Gambia, Sri Lanka, Zimbabwe, Nigeria and Bhutan, 1 each from Somalia, Uganda, Tanzania, Germany and an economist from the ADB were provided training and study facilities by the Reserve Bank.	One hundred and three employees completed the CFA programme conducted by ICFAI, Hyderabad.

contd...

contd...

(1)	(7)	(8)
1989–90		The Bank made constant efforts to encourage staff to acquire additional computer qualifications. Therefore, the scheme was made more flexible and employees were allowed to enrol in institutions of their choice, subject to certain stipulations.
1990–91	As a part of the golden jubilee celebrations, the scheme of higher studies abroad was availed of by 4 officers during the year.	The scheme to encourage participation in computer courses continued.

contd...

contd...

(1)	(2)	(3)	(4)	(5)	(6)
1991–92	314	26	During the decade 1981 to 1991, 813 officers were trained.		
1992–93	349	38	14 countries		IGIDR continued to conduct workshops and conferences on topical issues. It enrolled the third batch of research scholars to the Ph.D. programme in August 1992. By now the Bank had granted 171 employees permission to join the CFA programme.

contd...

contd...

(1)	(7)	(8)
1991–92	As part of the golden jubilee celebrations of the Bank 4 officers were selected every year to pursue higher studies abroad for a period of 1 year. 24 officers had benefited from the scheme till 1991–92.	The North Eastern Institute of Bank Management (NEIBM), Guwahati established in 1980 to cater to training needs of the north-eastern region had a funding share of 30.0 per cent from the Reserve Bank.
1992–93		Incentives for computer training were continued by the Bank.

contd...

contd...

(1)	(2)	(3)	(4)	(5)	(6)
1993–94	389	51	US, UK, Switzerland, Germany, Japan, Thailand, France, South Korea, Philippines, Iran, Malaysia, Austria, Singapore and Taiwan.	The Bank extended professional enhancement facilities to 68 officials from Sri Lanka, Mauritius, Nepal , Nigeria, Tanzania, Kenya, Zambia, Botswana, Sudan, Bhutan, Russia and Uganda.	
1994–95	412	42	Canada, Malaysia, France, Germany, Hong Kong, Philippines, Singapore, Switzerland, Thailand, US and UK.	Sixty officials from 11 countries were provided training at various colleges of the Bank. They included 25 from Nepal, 14 from Sri Lanka, 5 from Uganda and Kenya, 3 from Mauritius, 2 each from Ethiopia, Jordan, Indonesia and Nigeria.	Two more employees joined the CFA Programme at Hyderabad, taking the total number of such employees to 213. Two programmes on bank supervision with emphasis on off-site surveillance were organised with faculty support from Bank of England. Another programme was conducted on on-site surveillance with the Fed Reserve, New York.

contd...

contd...

(1)	(7)	(8)
1993–94	Based on the recommendations of the committee on human resource development, 10 officers were selected every year for grant of study leave for pursuing post-graduate courses such as MBA and Ph.D. at well known universities in India and abroad. The Bank also continued to depute 1 officer for Ph.D. at IIT, Bombay.	
1994–95	Total number of officers who had benefited from the scheme of award of scholarship for higher studies abroad stood at 35. A new scheme for officers from departments other than that of research, was introduced for Ph.D. in various areas of interest to the Bank.	Twelve officers and 127 clerical staff joined computer courses raising the number of beneficiaries to 179 and 764, respectively.

contd...

contd...

(1)	(2)	(3)	(4)	(5)	(6)
1995–96	132	39	Australia, Belgium, France, Germany, Hong Kong, Israel, Italy, Japan, Pakistan, Philippines, Singapore, South Korea, Sri Lanka, Switzerland, UK, and the US.	Two hundred and twenty nine officials from 14 countries—57 from Bangladesh, 10 from Bhutan, 3 from Botswana, 2 from China, 1 from Ghana, 2 from Indonesia, 4 from Malaysia, 3 from Mauritius, 22 from Nepal, 3 from Philippines, 1 from Russia, 106 from Sri Lanka, 6 from Tanzania, and 9 from Uganda were given training in the Bank's establishments/offices.	Total number of beneficiaries in the CFA programme stood at 222.

contd...

contd...

(1)	(7)	(8)
1995–96	Four officers were selected under the golden jubilee scholarship scheme for higher studies abroad. Total number of beneficiaries stood at 39. Under the scheme of study leave 2 officers pursued higher studies abroad. One officer was nominated to the M.Phil. programme in IIT, Bombay.	Two hundred and nineteen officers and 899 clerical staff were given training in computer technology. Basic computer training for officers and class III employees was introduced to cope with the increasing training needs in the area. Till June 1996, 540 officers and 1,698 clerical staff were identified for training in a phased manner.

contd...

contd...

(1)	(2)	(3)	(4)	(5)	(6)
1996–97	145	63	Bahrain, China, Germany, Hong Kong, Indonesia, Iran, Italy, Japan, Malaysia, Netherlands, Philippines, Singapore, South Africa, Sri Lanka, Switzerland, Thailand, UK and the US.	Eighty-one officials from 11 countries—1 each from Kuwait, Oman, Sierra Leone and Uganda, 2 from Bhutan, 3 from Nepal, 4 from Tanzania, 6 from Nigeria, 7 from Sudan, 16 from Sri Lanka, and 39 from Bangladesh were provided training in various institutes of the Bank.	

contd...

concld.

(1)	(7)	(8)
1996–97	Four officers were selected under the golden jubilee scholarship scheme and the total number of beneficiaries stood at 43. Four officers were granted study leave for higher studies abroad.	Twenty-eight officers and 48 clerical staff attended computer training, raising the total number to 247 and 957, respectively. Further, 2,515 in class III and 870 officers were identified for Basic computer training in a phased manner.

Source: Reserve Bank of India, *Annual Report,* various issues.

ANNEX 21.2

Residential and Office Complexes[38]

During 1981, the Bank facilitated the occupation of readied 336 staff quarters (48 for class III employees at Trivandrum and 288 for class III and class IV at Jaipur). In addition, 60 flats for officers were almost ready for occupation at Ahmedabad. The Reserve Bank had entered into three agreements to purchase 315 flats (144 flats for officers at Parel, Bombay, 155 flats for class III and class IV staff at Bangalore and 16 flats for class III staff at Pune) on a package deal basis. The purchase of 623 flats on a package deal basis (200 flats for officers and 250 flats for class III staff at Goregaon, Bombay; 17 flats for officers at Pune; and 156 flats for officers at Madras) was approved by the Bank. Further, the Reserve Bank purchased 6 acres of land at Bhubaneswar and 2.87 acres at Chandigarh for the purpose of housing for officers and other employees.

During 1982, a total of 306 new flats, including 64 officers' flats at Ahmedabad, and 100 flats for officers and 112 for class III and IV at Bhopal, were occupied. Also 100 officers' flats at New Delhi and 56 class IV quarters at Trivandrum were ready for occupation.

The Jaipur office building of the Reserve Bank was completed and occupied in March 1984. While Chandigarh office building construction had entered Phase II, the work on the office buildings at Nagpur and Kanpur was progressing. Also, the pending construction on the office building at Bandra-Kurla complex was nearing completion.

During 1983–84, 248 flats and 8 single rooms were completed at Hyderabad and Bombay. These included 108 flats and 8 single rooms for officers and 140 flats for class III staff. The Bank, well aware of the acute shortage of housing facilities for its employees, was making all efforts to ease the situation by identifying new centres, purchasing land or going for package deals to buy flats to alleviate the pressure.

The construction of 734 flats and 8 single rooms was concluded during 1985–86. This included 136 flats and 8 single rooms for officers, 196 flats for class III staff and 402 flats for class IV employees at various centres. Under the five-year plan, a total of 2,560 flats and 36 self-contained single rooms were completed in the first three years of the plan for various categories of staff. Several other residential projects were in the pipeline and also at the planning stage, reflecting the emphasis being placed in the Reserve Bank to provide these facilities at the earliest to its employees.

During 1988–89, an amount of ₹ 20 crore was spent on construction or acquisition of office buildings and residential quarters, renovation of the existing premises and purchase of land. The year 1988–89 also witnessed the construction

---

38. The Reserve Bank of India, *Annual Report*, various issues.

of 174 flats for officers, 240 for class III staff and 80 for class IV staff in Bangalore, Bombay, Chandigarh, Jammu and Kanpur.

During 1989–90, a sum of ₹ 21 crore was spent on construction or acquisition of office buildings and residential facilities; renovation of existing facilities and purchase of land. The office buildings at Cochin and coin vault at Noida (U.P.) were ready for occupation. Further, 365 officers' quarters and 918 staff quarters were completed at Trivandrum, Cochin, Bangalore, Calcutta, Kanpur, Chandigarh and Bombay.

During 1990–91, an amount of ₹ 17 crore was spent on various activities relating to construction or renovation of the buildings and acquisition of land. The construction of an office building at Bhopal and an annexe to the office building at New Bombay were finished during the year. In terms of creating housing facilities for the staff, the Reserve Bank constructed 92 officers' quarters at Bombay and 224 staff quarters for class III and IV at Lucknow were ready to be occupied during the year.

In 1991–92, an amount of ₹ 14 crore was spent on construction and upkeep of the office buildings, including purchase of land. Fifteen flats for the officers and 92 staff quarters were readied to be occupied during the year.

During 1992–93, a sum of ₹ 17 crore was spent by the Bank on capital account towards construction and renovation of office and residential buildings.

An expenditure of ₹ 25 crore was incurred during 1993–94 on capital account towards construction of office buildings, residential quarters, additions/alterations and renovations of various properties of the Bank. During the year the office building at Jammu, 102 flats for officers at Ahmedabad, 28 flats for officers at Bombay and 132 flats for staff at Jaipur were completed and occupied.

IV

MISCELLANY

Select Photographs

GOVERNORS OF THE RESERVE BANK OF INDIA: 1981–1997

Dr I.G. Patel
(December 1, 1977 to September
15, 1982)

Dr Manmohan Singh
(September 16, 1982 to January 14,
1985)

Shri A. Ghosh
(January 15, 1985 to February 4,
1985)

Shri R.N. Malhotra
(February 4, 1985 to December 22,
1990)

Shri S. Venkitaramanan
(December 22, 1990 to December
21, 1992)

Dr C. Rangarajan
(December 22, 1992 to November
22, 1997)

Appendices

Committee to Review the Working of the Monetary System: Recommendations and their Implementation

Set up as a monetary institution, the Reserve Bank was enjoined with the responsibility of operating the currency and credit system to the country's advantage. Till the mid-1980s, the Bank operated only a credit policy, the focus of which was on regulating the quantum and flow of credit particularly between the Government and the commercial sector, given the estimated resources of banks and FIs. The monetary system, as such, was not comprehensively reviewed. In 1982, the Governor, Dr Manmohan Singh set up a committee under the chairmanship of Prof Sukhamoy Chakravarty to undertake a comprehensive review of the working of the monetary system in India.[1] The committee submitted its report in April 1985.

The mandate to the committee covered almost every aspect of the monetary system that required a review of the relevant policy issues, bearing in mind the need for long-term changes. The terms of reference included: (i) a critical review of the structure and operation of the monetary system in the context of the basic objectives of planned development; (ii) an assessment of the interaction between monetary policy and public debt management in so far as they had a bearing on the effectiveness of monetary policy; (iii) an evaluation of various instruments of monetary and credit policy in terms of their impact on the credit system and on the economy; and (iv) recommend measures for improvement in the formulation and operation of monetary and credit policies and suggest specific areas where the policy instruments needed strengthening.

---

1. The other members of the committee were Shri M.P. Chitale, Shri R.K. Hazari (former Deputy Governor), Shri F.A. Mehta and Dr C. Rangarajan (Deputy Governor) with Shri J.C. Rao as the Secretary.

BACKDROP

The Governor, Dr Manmohan Singh, in his inaugural address at a seminar organised by the Maharashtra Economic Development Council, Mumbai in November 1982, had hinted at the forthcoming committee. Mentioning that India had a large number of instruments that had a bearing both on the management of aggregate demand and the allocation of resources among different sectors, he posed several questions: how did monetary and credit policy fit into this; how much weight ought to be placed on monetary and credit policies to achieve our national objectives; how could monetary planning be harmonised and co-ordinated with national planning; how effective were various instruments of monetary control in achieving the given objectives; what were the implications of the growing number of financial instruments and intermediaries for the success of our monetary and credit policies; and how did the increasing openness of our economy impinge on the effectiveness of monetary and credit policies. He believed that the time had come for a detailed and comprehensive analysis and evaluation of these and related issues. Dr Manmohan Singh, "after considering all the relevant factors," came to the conclusion that a thorough review of the functioning of the monetary system in India was called for. His concluding statement confirmed that monetary policy was looked upon more as an instrument of planning in a closed and controlled economy rather than as an independent instrument to achieve the objective of price stability.

Prof Sukhamoy Chakravarty,[2] a year after the submission of the report, explained that since the mid-1960s, several major changes had taken place in the economic management of the country, which had a significant impact on the monetary and financial system. The combined effect of these changes, partly structural and in part conjectural implied that a careful look was called for at the functioning of the monetary system, especially from the point of view of ensuring non-inflationary planned development in the years to come. He also observed that in an increasingly open economy, there was the added need to heighten export competitiveness, which depended, among other things, on the rates of domestic inflation relative to world inflation and that inflation in India had rarely been coupled with favourable redistribution effects.

Prof Chakravarty[3] stated in the context of the committee that:

It should be obvious that the terms of reference before the Committee, while far ranging, had a very definite focus on planning and the role of public debt in financing the plans. In addition, the problem of evolving an appropriate credit policy, which will help best in raising productivity

---

2. *Sir Purushotamdas Thakurdas Memorial Lecture* delivered in 1986.

3. Chakravarty, S. (1993). *Selected Economic Writings of Sukhamoy Chakravarty*. New Delhi: Oxford University Press.

of resources use as well as expanding resource base, was highlighted as a major conceptual problem. Finally, there was the operational dimension having to deal with instrumentalities of formulating monetary and credit policies.

MAJOR RECOMMENDATIONS

The major areas covered by the committee were the objectives of monetary policy, co-ordination between monetary policy and fiscal policy, regulation of money supply, maintenance of price stability, interest rate policy and regulatory measures pertaining to bank credit.

MONETARY POLICY OBJECTIVES

The committee concluded that the monetary system must necessarily be supportive of the national development strategy as articulated in the successive Five Year Plans and should seek to perform the following tasks:

(i)   Mobilise savings of the community and enlarge the financial savings pool.

(ii) Promote efficiency in allocating savings of the community to relatively more productive purposes in accordance with national economic goals.

(iii) Enable the resource needs of the major 'entrepreneur' in the country, *viz.*, the Government, to be met in adequate measure.

(iv) Promote price stability.

(v)   Promote an efficient payments system.

Although the committee viewed monetary policy as an arm of the economic policy and agreed that its objectives could be no different from the overall objectives of the economic policy, the effectiveness of various instruments of economic policy in pursuing different objectives was not always the same. The committee recognised that price stability was a major concern for monetary policy, since monetary policy instruments were more effective than other policy instruments in achieving this objective. Another reason was that in a society in which a significantly large proportion of the population was in the unorganised sector, price rise went against social justice. Against the background of historical experience, the committee suggested that an average annual increase in the WPI of no more than 4.0 per cent should be the objective. Dr C. Rangarajan later termed this guideline as 'reasonable', the achievement of which would require considerably improved demand and supply management.[4]

4. Rangarajan, C. (1988). *Issues in Monetary Management.* Presidential Address at the Annual Conference of the Indian Economic Association. Calcutta. December 29.

MONETARY TARGETING

Besides suggesting a certain degree of co-ordination between the Government and the Reserve Bank in evolving and implementing the agreed policy, the committee recommended that the regulation of M_3 should be undertaken in a framework of monetary targeting in terms of a range, using feedback with necessary support from an appropriate interest rate policy. The choice of M_3 was based on the fact that money multiplier relating to M_1 was prone to sudden and large movements as a result of seasonal shifts between currency and deposits. Such influences over M_3 were not significant and hence money multiplier for M_3 was relatively more stable.[5]

The committee stated that a constant money supply growth was not feasible in the Indian context where supply shocks were frequent and where significant structural changes were sought to facilitate the growth process. According to Dr Rangarajan, this did not, however, take away the need for regulating the overall growth in M_3 over a period of time, and a scheme of monetary targeting with feedback would ensure the necessary co-ordination between the fiscal and monetary authorities in steering the growth of money supply consistent with real growth and an acceptable order of increase in prices.[6]

Based on the relationship between money, output and prices, the committee suggested that the target for monetary expansion should be set at 14.0 per cent or in a range around 14.0 per cent, based on the assumption that the real output would expand by 5.0 per cent, income elasticity of demand for broad money at 2.0 per cent and the acceptable rise in prices at 4.0 per cent.

CO-ORDINATION BETWEEN MONETARY POLICY AND FISCAL POLICY

The committee pointed out that the major cause of the substantial growth in M_3 since the 1970s had been the rise in Reserve Bank credit to the Government. The main reason for the high degree of monetisation of debt was the relatively low yields on government securities and the low discount rate on Treasury Bills, which had remained unchanged since 1974 at 4.6 per cent per annum. It, therefore, recommended that a proper framework for the regulation of Reserve Bank credit to the Government be evolved through co-ordination between the Reserve Bank and the Government by suitable restructuring of yields on government securities and by revising the discount rate on Treasury Bills. These measures were also expected to facilitate greater participation in the government's borrowing programme by the non-bank sector of the public and hence reduce the growth in reserve money attributable to Reserve Bank credit to the Government.

5.	Pages 104–105 of the report.

6.	Rangarajan, C. (1987). *An Analytical Framework of the Chakravarty Committee Report on the Monetary System.* Lecture delivered at the meeting sponsored by the Society of Auditors. Madras. August 29.

The committee suggested a change in the definition of budgetary deficit to 'net RBI credit to Government', so that an economically meaningful and definite measure of the monetary impact of fiscal operations became available.

INTEREST RATE POLICY

The report envisaged a role for the interest rate policy as supportive of the regulation of M_3, but did not make any significant departure from the position where important interest rates were administered. Nonetheless, as the principal participants in the money and capital markets were in the government sector, certain guidelines with regard to the determination of interest rates were presented in the report. The report clearly recognised that borrowings by the Government should be at a slightly lower rate compared with the other organised sectors, but had to be positive in real terms. Assuming a rate of growth of the economy of the order of 4.0 to 5.0 per cent, which could be taken as a ceiling on the pure rate of interest for the economy as a whole, the maximum real interest rate on long-term government borrowings was suggested at 3.0 per cent per annum. Along with Treasury Bills, for which only a marginally positive real interest rate was recommended, the average interest rate on the entire spectrum of government borrowings from the market was expected to be even lower than 3.0 per cent.

Another point made was that even when interest rates did not play an allocative role, there was need to see that the interest rate structure of the organised financial system was in reasonable correspondence with market perceptions. On the understanding that interest rates on bank deposits should be positive, after adjusting for inflation to encourage small savers, the committee suggested a maximum real rate of interest of 2.0 per cent on bank deposits. In the case of lending rates, the committee suggested that the maximum lending rate could be fixed at 3.0 per cent above the maximum nominal deposit rate, so that banks had a reasonable margin over cost of raising funds and could thus function as viable economic units even though an element of cross-subsidisation could be built into the lending rate structure. In order that the credit requirements of the productive sectors were adequately met within the overall limits set for monetary expansion, the committee recommended that banks should have greater freedom in determining their lending rates.

OTHER IMPORTANT RECOMMENDATIONS

The committee examined various aspects of bank credit and made recommendations regarding credit policies and procedures to facilitate more efficient use of bank credit. It stressed the importance of providing bank credit in the form of loans and recommended promoting bill finance instead of cash credit. It also highlighted the disruptive effect on credit flows arising from tardy payments to suppliers by large public sector and private sector units as also the Government, and recommended that interest on delayed payments should be provided for in the purchase contracts. The committee also expressed the view that problems associated with improving the effectiveness of priority sector lending were principally related to organisational re-orientation and effective communication and monitoring. It emphasised the importance of strengthening the credit delivery system in the area of priority sector lending, so that adequate and timely credit could be made available to this sector.

PROCESS OF IMPLEMENTATION

The Governor, Shri R.N. Malhotra, set up a task force in the Reserve Bank, with one member drawn from the Ministry of Finance. The task force set out to examine the recommendations of the committee from the viewpoint of implementation and its report was submitted at end-1985. Based on the report, the Governor apprised the Finance Minister, Shri V.P. Singh, in a detailed letter dated January 14, 1986 of the proposals for implementation, which were prefaced with the following important observation:

> While the Committee has set out a logical framework of the monetary system towards which we should ultimately work, the current milieu would require that any changes should be undertaken in full recognition of their implications and after careful preparation. In considering the Committee's recommendations, the Task Force has adopted a pragmatic approach. In the light of the views of the Task Force on such matters as are of direct concern to the Government, I am setting out my own recommendations for your kind consideration.

Both the Reserve Bank and the Government acted promptly in implementing the recommendations.

REDEFINITION OF THE CONCEPT OF BUDGETARY DEFICIT

The committee suggested a change in the definition of budgetary deficit to 'net RBI credit to Government' and Governor Malhotra commended the suggestion as it 'fully reflected' the increase in net Reserve Bank credit to the Government and also put the extent of monetisation of Government debt into 'sharper focus'. He urged an early changeover to the new definition of budgetary deficit, as it would be of considerable advantage in the effective co-ordination between monetary and fiscal policies. This had one important implication in that the increase in Reserve Bank holdings of government securities would be reflected in the budgetary deficit. The correct course would, therefore, be not to assume any Reserve Bank support to dated securities when determining the size of the market borrowing programme, the letter added.

MONETARY TARGETING

For a number of years, the Reserve Bank and the Government were engaged in a dialogue on a consistent set of projections for the deposit and credit aggregates, against a backdrop of certain perceptions of the real growth of the economy and the expected inflation rate, and it was in this context that the market borrowing programmed was finalised. For the fiscal year 1986–87, the Governor stated in his letter dated January 7, 1986 to the Finance Secretary that the Reserve Bank would suggest that for 1986–87 the key aggregates set out by the Bank be given serious consideration, and after discussions these could be given the status of agreed targets between the Government and the Reserve Bank, and as the year progressed, policy responses could be developed with reference to these targets. The Governor recommended that specific targets be worked out for: (i) net Reserve Bank credit to the Government; (ii) total net bank credit to the Government; and (iii) overall liquidity (M_3). The Reserve Bank was of the view that these three aggregates could be given a 'trial run' in 1986–87 as internal targets and after a successful outcome, there could be a move to a system where the targets were made public.

GOVERNMENT SECURITIES: MATURITY PATTERN AND COUPON RATES

While endorsing the committee's recommendation that the maximum maturity period for government securities should be reduced from 30 years to 15 years as part of a gradual adjustment, the Reserve Bank was of the view that the maximum maturity period could initially be reduced to 20 years in 1986–87 and, in light of this experience, a further reduction to 15 years could be considered in 1987–88. Shri Malhotra also suggested that the current coupon rate need not be raised, though there was need for increasing the coupon rates on maturities up to 20 years. Accordingly, for maturities of 5, 10, 15 and 20 years the existing coupon rates of 9.0 per cent, 9.5 per cent, 10.0 per cent and 10.5 per cent per annum, respectively, were proposed to be raised by one percentage point, *i.e.*, to 10.0 per cent, 10.5 per cent, 11.0 per cent and 11.5 per cent, respectively.

A related point was that even though the coupon rates on various maturities up to 20 years would go up, the enhanced rates would still be highly concessional, since banks, which were the major investors in these securities, paid a rate of 11.0 per cent on 5-year deposits. This change was also expected to improve the prospects of floatation of securities of state governments, as there had been some difficulties in successfully floating securities of state governments and other institutions.

TREASURY BILLS: DISCOUNT RATE AND FUNDING

The committee recommended that the discount rate on Treasury Bills should be marginally above the short-term inflation rate. Based on the average inflation rate over the past five years of about 7.0 per cent, the Governor urged: "early implementation so that in 1986–87 the discount rate on 91-day Treasury Bills would be raised from 4.6 per cent to 7.5 per cent." The Reserve Bank viewed the higher rate as substantially lower than the rates applied to WMA of the state governments, which were provided at rates varying from 9.0 per cent for the first 90 days to 12.0 per cent beyond 180 days. Moreover, it was pointed out that as on July 19, 1974 the Treasury Bill rate was 4.6 per cent, while the coupon rate on central government securities of the longest maturity was 6.25 per cent, *i.e.*, the difference between the two rates was only 1.65 percentage points as against the prevailing difference of 6.9 percentage points. Under the new proposal, this difference would be reduced to 4.0 percentage points, which would still be quite large. To drive home his proposal, the Governor stated:

> I am aware of the impact of this change on the Government budget, but am afraid that correction of this historical distortion is long overdue and the longer this adjustment is postponed, the greater the future adjustment problem. To minimise the burden on the budget, I would suggest that towards the end of the current financial year or in early 1986–87, there should be a funding of existing Treasury Bills into securities of the order of Rs. 20,000 crore (or more depending on the outstandings at the time of the funding) at a rate of 4.6 per cent; this funding operation should be considered as a one-shot operation.

In the context of the committee's repeated stress that monetisation of the government debt must be kept to the minimum, the Reserve Bank expressed the view that it was essential to explore techniques of placing the short-term debt of the Government outside the Reserve Bank. In this connection, the increase in the discount rate on 91-day Treasury Bills from 4.6 per cent to 7.5 per cent would certainly be 'a step in the right direction', the Reserve Bank averred, though this by itself would not be sufficient to enable an absorption of the short-term government debt outside the Reserve Bank in the immediate future. Therefore, the Governor proposed that an attempt should be made in 1986–87 to place at least a part, say, about 20.0 per cent, of the total Treasury Bills to be generated during that year outside the Reserve Bank. With this objective, two measures were proposed. The first was to effect an increase in the discount rate for 91-day Treasury Bills from 4.6 per cent to 7.5 per cent immediately after the proposed funding operation. Holders of these bills would be provided rediscounting facilities as hitherto. The second proposal was the introduction in 1986–87 of 180-day Treasury Bills on auction basis offered outside the Reserve Bank on which there would be no rediscounting facilities with the Reserve Bank, which by itself would encourage development of a secondary market in these bills. The discount rate would be determined at the auctions, subject to such regulations as the Reserve Bank might consider necessary.

The strategy of funding outstanding Treasury Bills was also expected to benefit the Government's fiscal operations by smoothening the process of filling the budgetary gap. The Reserve Bank reasoned in the following manner:

Under the present arrangement, the Government has to seek Parliamentary authorisation for a high turnover of Treasury Bills (Rs. 1,50,000 crore in 1985–86) and erroneous adverse publicity results from such a large turnover. A major part of this high turnover is caused by the fact that, in the absence of funding, the outstanding Treasury Bills are unduly large and, illustratively, an outstanding of Rs. 25,000 crore would necessitate an annual turnover of Rs. 1,00,000 crore. The funding of a large part of the outstanding bills will largely relieve this problem. I am aware that, in addition, the rapid rediscounting of bills by banks also unnecessarily increases the turnover of Bills. I propose to increase the administrative charges on rediscounting bills and we are also exploring the recycling of bills, which would significantly reduce their turnover. Again, the introduction of the 180-day Treasury Bill on auction basis without rediscounting facility with the Reserve Bank would also reduce the turnover of Treasury Bills.

DEPOSIT AND LENDING RATES OF BANKS

The committee recommended that there should be rationalisation of deposit and lending rates and that these rates should be, to some extent, deregulated. The Reserve Bank found that the bankers who were consulted appeared to be apprehensive of deregulation of the rates. The committee's formula of a 2.0 per cent real rate and an average long-term inflation rate of 9.0 per cent gave a deposit rate of 11.0 per cent for five years, which incidentally was the current 5-year deposit rate. The 1-year deposit rate of 8.5 per cent also appeared to be in line with the committee's recommendations. The Reserve Bank conveyed its desire to continue with the prevailing structure of interest rates on deposits.

The Reserve Bank was not in favour of deregulating deposit rates as it felt that if deposit rates were deregulated, they might rise, and this might not be in alignment with the policies aimed at bringing down the overall structure of lending rates as inflation abated. The communication from the Bank stated: "An increase in deposit rates would warrant increases in lending rates, and it would hardly be feasible to have uncontrolled increases in lending rates to preferred sectors."

The committee recommended that the minimum lending rate of banks should be 3.0 percentage points above the maximum deposit rate, and that there should be only one concessional rate below the minimum lending rate. The task force had pointed out that prescribing only one concessional rate below the minimum lending rate and freeing all rates above the minimum lending rate would neither be feasible nor desirable. The chairmen of some of the banks, who were consulted, were also not in favour of any major deregulation of lending rates. There was a likelihood that freeing the rates above the minimum lending rate could result in large borrowers using their strong bargaining power to lower lending rates to levels that would adversely affect banks' profitability. While conceding that it was necessary to rationalise lending rates and avoid multiple prescriptions, the Reserve Bank felt that such rationalisation could be considered at an appropriate stage when interest rates were reviewed and that any changes in the deposit-lending rates of banks would need to take into account the impact on banks' profitability.

OTHER MATTERS

The committee made a number of other recommendations regarding the mode of lending, recovery of advances made to the priority sector, instruments of monetary policy and development of the money market. The Reserve Bank was of the view that these were matters related essentially to the banking system and, hence, consultation with banks and proper study would be necessary to bring about well-planned implementation of some of these changes. The question of the need for discount houses and the development of the money market were matters that needed further detailed examination. Therefore, the Governor, Shri R.N. Malhotra, advised the Government that he proposed to set up a working group to report on these matters and added that the introduction of Treasury Bills of the type suggested would have an important bearing on the development of the money market.

Governor Malhotra's 8-page letter to the Finance Minister, Shri V.P. Singh, concluded that he would be glad to discuss these issues with him at his convenience. A copy of the letter was endorsed to the Finance Secretary and the Chief Economic Adviser.

THE GOVERNMENT'S RESPONSE

The response of the Government was prompt and positive. The Governor discussed the recommendations of the Chakravarty Committee with the Finance Secretary on January 30, 1986. This was followed by a letter dated April 3, 1986 from Shri K.S. Sastry, Joint Secretary (Budget) to the Deputy Governor, Dr C. Rangarajan, conveying the Government's approval to the proposals made by the Reserve Bank. First, the Reserve Bank's proposal to revise the interest rate structure for government and government-guaranteed loans was approved in toto. Second, the Government agreed to the issue of 180-day Treasury Bills on auction basis for subscription by outside parties subject to a maximum interest rate of 7.5 per cent per annum. However, *ad hoc* Treasury Bills issued to the Reserve Bank or other Treasury Bills discounted with the Reserve Bank would carry an interest rate of only 4.6 per cent. Third, the Government was agreeable to the funding of Treasury Bills held by the Reserve Bank as special securities at that point carrying interest at 4.6 per cent. The amount to be funded was to be decided with reference to savings available in the budget provision made for the discharge of Treasury Bills.

The Government showed its earnestness in implementing the recommendations. In the 1986–87 Union Budget, it was announced that the Government had accepted in principle the recommendations of the Chakravarty

Committee with regard to the measurement of budgetary deficit, by accounting changes in the entire Reserve Bank credit to the Government, including changes in the Reserve Bank's holdings of long-dated securities on the basis of modalities worked out in consultation with the Reserve Bank. Further, to bring about better co-ordination between fiscal and monetary policies and make their overall management more scientific, the Government decided to set overall monetary targets and monitor them regularly. This arrangement was put in place in 1986–87 on an experimental basis.

IMPLEMENTATION PROBLEMS

The Economic Survey for 1986–87 revealed that within the first year of implementation of the recommendations, it was noticed that *ex ante* there were several problems in the estimation of Reserve Bank credit to the Government, particularly where the budget for the next year was under preparation in the months of January/February every year and it became necessary to have as firm an estimate of the deficit as possible at the RE stage. On an analysis of the past data of variations in the net Reserve Bank credit to the Central Government, it was found that there was no stable and predictable relationship between the full year credit extended by the Reserve Bank to the Central Government and that extended in the first nine months of that year. Transactions in Treasury Bills and the long-dated securities by parties other than the Reserve Bank showed wide swings during the course of a fiscal year. In fact, the week-to-week fluctuations in the holdings of Treasury Bills by the banks were particularly pronounced. In the case of long-dated securities, the factors causing fluctuations were variations in the liquid assets of banks, as also the transactions in securities by financial institutions under the buy-back arrangement, especially by institutions that kept their accounts exclusively with the Reserve Bank.

In addition to absorption by the Reserve Bank of dated securities floated under the market borrowing programme, Reserve Bank credit to the Central Government included rupee coins and special securities issued by the Central Government to the Reserve Bank for borrowings against collections under the compulsory deposit (IT payers) scheme and for payment of charges on drawings from the IMF. There were also disparate practices with regard to the valuation of Treasury Bills and dated securities, which in the monetary data were based on the Reserve Bank's book value (*i.e.*, purchase price), whereas in the fiscal accounts, the transactions were based on the face value of the securities. The different methods of recording the transactions by the Government and the Reserve Bank resulted in an asymmetry in the fiscal and monetary data, according to the Economic Survey, 1986–87. In view of the technical problems in achieving 'a one-to-one correspondence' in the fiscal and monetary accounts, the Government decided to show Reserve Bank net credit to the Central Government as a 'memorandum item' in the budget documents.

INTRODUCTION OF 182-DAY TREASURY BILLS

The Chakravarty Committee recognised the need to explore new financial instruments that could provide alternative avenues for short-term investments for which an active secondary market could develop in future. Specifically, the committee recommended that Treasury Bills should be developed as a monetary instrument with flexible rates, which would enable the banks to better manage their short-term liquidity. Following this, from November 28, 1986, Treasury Bills of 182-day maturity were issued on a monthly auction basis.

MONETARY TARGET EXERCISE

In developing this exercise, several technical problems connected with the choice of variables, the volatility in the variables and their seasonal variations were required to be resolved. The choice of variables was necessarily influenced by the fundamental objectives of controlling aggregate fiscal and monetary outcomes, and the feasibility of predicting the full year outcome based on available information. On the basis of these criteria, three monetary variables, namely, aggregate monetary resources (M_3), net Reserve Bank Credit to Central Government (NRBICG), and net Bank Credit to Government (NBCG), were selected as early warning signals with respect to growth in M_3 in the economy. NRBICG, a key component of the stock of reserve money, although volatile, served as the single most important explanatory variable for year-to-year changes in M_3 in the economy. NBCG had the virtue of including the full recourse to bank borrowing by the Government and, being less volatile than the NRBICG, it provided a better indicator of within-year trends. M_3 was considered as the appropriate indicator of the degree of overall liquidity in the economy, as it exerted a substantial influence on the rate of inflation in the economy.

APPENDIX 5.1

Exchange Control : Operations and Regulations

DEVELOPMENTS IN FOREIGN TRADE POLICY

In recognition of the need to maximise export earnings in a situation of rising trade deficit and a continuing unfavourable trading environment around the world, the emphasis of the export strategy during the 1980s was to keep export controls at the minimum. Broadly, the policy in vogue in the late 1970s was continued during the 1980s, and controls were imposed only on select commodities whose supply position demanded export restrictions in the larger national interest.

The foreign trade policy for 1982–83 emphasised the reduction of the technology gap, particularly in the export sector, through a system of liberal import allocations for upgrading and developing technology. Another noteworthy feature was establishing administrative machinery for effective monitoring and evaluation of the flow and utilisation of imports, particularly under the export promotion schemes.

Substantial procedural changes were introduced, designed primarily at enabling actual users to obtain inputs expeditiously, maximise production and improve productivity. Keeping in view the need to encourage investment and facilitating timely execution of production programmes, 100 new items of raw materials, components and consumable were put under the OGL for import by actual users. A noteworthy procedural liberalisation was that a number of items could now be imported under the OGL by both actual users and others. The waiver of the actual user stipulation was intended to assist small industrialists who could now buy them off-the-shelf and thus cut down on the cost of holding inventory. The restrictions on imports of several commodities were kept under close and constant review in light of the output performance of the domestic industry. The facilities for import of capital goods and equipment available to NRIs returning home to settle or residents abroad investing in India through foreign exchange remittances were further liberalised.

Export trading houses were henceforth entitled to bulk advance licences. The scheme of duty-free import of raw materials by manufacturers against their replenishment (REP) licences, which had been in operation for two years in respect of select products, was further expanded to cover several new export products.

In the interests of continuity and stability, the Exim policy for 1984–85, announced on April 12, 1984, maintained the general framework as in the preceding year. Thus, the policy for import of raw materials, components and spares and the facilities for supplementary and automatic licences including repeat licences to actual users to import raw materials, components and consumables continued and remained unaltered. The OGL list was enlarged by adding 149 new items, including 94 items of industrial machinery. Simultaneously, 53 items were removed from the OGL in light of developments in the domestic industry, bringing the net addition of items to the OGL to 96. Export promotion continued to be an important facet of the foreign trade policy. The 1984–85 policy carried the progressive liberalisation in the policy witnessed since 1979–80 a step further.

FOREIGN TRADE POLICY: 1985–1988

The Government announced the Exim policy for three years ending March 1988, instead of one year, as had been the practice. The licensing, however, continued to be on an annual basis. The Government's new economic philosophy, namely, liberalisation, updating/upgrading the technology to international standards and exposing Indian industry to global competition, were visible in the policy during the period 1985–1988.

Restrictions were placed on free OGL imports by the ONGC, OIL and the GAIL. Henceforth, they had to obtain prior clearance from the empowered committee on indigenisation of the Ministry of Petroleum and Natural Gas. On the other hand, the long-term import policy for export/trading houses was liberalised in June 1986, allowing these houses to import non-OGL capital goods, except for restricted items against their REP additional licences.

FREE TRADE ZONES SET UP DURING THE 1980s

MEPZ[1] was established in 1984. As a multi-product zone, it dealt in export of engineering goods, garments, perfumes, electronics, leather products, plastics and rubber, toys and musical instruments. Total exports from the zone during the year 1988–89 rose by 46.3 per cent to ₹ 24 crore from ₹ 16.4 crore in the previous year. However, exports were still short of the targeted amount for the year.

NEPZ[2] was established in 1984 with an investment of ₹ 16.2 crore. In the second phase, development of additional 200 acres of land was taken up. Principal exports from the zone include computers-cum-electronics, readymade garments, and light engineering goods. During 1988–89, exports from the zone increased by 33.0 per cent to ₹ 21.3 crore from ₹ 16 crore in 1987–88, but were still lower than the target of ₹ 30 crore stipulated for the year, mainly due to non-utilisation and delays in installing the capacities on account of power shortages.

FEPZ,[3] located on the eastern bank of the river Hooghly at Falta, was established in 1984. The Central Government and the West Bengal Government spent an aggregate amount of ₹ 28.1 crore on developing the infrastructure for the zone. In all, 64 export proposals were approved for Falta by March 1989.

CEPZ,[4] a multi-product zone, was established in 1984. By end-March 1989, 62 units had been given licences. Exports from the zone were higher by 58.0 per

---

1. Madras Export Processing Zone.
2. Noida Export Processing Zone.
3. Falta Export Processing Zone.
4. Cochin Export Processing Zone.

cent during 1988–89 over that in the previous year. An export target of ₹ 15 crore was set for the year 1989–90.

TRADE AGREEMENTS AND ECONOMIC AND TECHNICAL CO-OPERATION WITH OTHER COUNTRIES

The most common features of these agreements were that: (i) MFN treatment would be extended to the other nation for both commodities and services in mutual trade; (ii) payments for transactions would be settled in freely convertible currencies through normal banking channels in accordance with the foreign exchange regulations in force in the respective country; (iii) the agreements would initially be operative for an year or two with provisions for renewal as also for modifications or termination on the prescribed notice being served by either of the signatories; (iv) the agreements would be reviewed periodically by joint committees set up for monitoring progress, discussing problems arising in the process, identifying areas that offered scope for increased trade and co-operation between India and these countries and helping to exchange information of interest to each other; and (v) each country would provide facilities for organising and/ or participating in exhibitions in its territory and arrange for mutual visits by technical, commercial and business delegations.

India maintained cordial and close economic and commercial relations with other countries, thus paving the way for trade agreements and protocols. During 1984–85, India signed fresh long-term trade and payments agreements with the USSR, the GDR, Poland and Romania for the period 1986–1990, when the earlier agreements expired. Another agreement on mutual deliveries of goods and commodities for 1986–1990, envisaging an increase in the trade turnover with the USSR by 1.5 to 2 times, was signed during 1984-85. A salient feature of the agreement was export of machinery, equipment, materials and services from India for civil and industrial projects in the USSR. A protocol on the delivery of machinery and equipment to India from the USSR on DPT was also signed for the period 1986–1990. A trade and payments agreement was signed with Poland for a five-year period from January 1986 to December 1990 on February 22, 1986 at Warsaw. Along with the agreement, a long-term trade plan on reciprocal delivery of goods and essential commodities between India and Poland during 1986–1990 was also put in place.

The trade and payments agreements with Romania and the GDR were renewed for five years till December 31, 1990. The agreement with Romania covered important commodities, such as, import of steel products, fertilisers/ chemicals, capital goods and railway equipment from Romania and export of manganese, iron ore, bauxite, cotton, coffee, pepper and engineering goods from India. The trade protocols for 1986 were signed with all the five countries, with whom India had long-term trade and payments agreements.

The trade protocol with China providing for exchange of goods worth US$ 100.0–160.0 million during 1986 was signed in November 1988. Under the protocol, China would import from India iron ore, chrome ore, steel products, tobacco, finished leather, mining and building machinery, instruments and tools. The protocol of the Indo-Finnish Joint Commission signed in April 1985 identified products for special thrust for export to Finland from India, which included agricultural products, leather goods, engineering goods and electronic components. Important items of import from Finland included newsprint, pharmaceuticals, fertilisers, hot and cold steel, coils and non-ferrous products. India signed a protocol for co-operation in trade and other fields of activity with Egypt in November 1985. A trade protocol on transfer of technology, which would help boost India's exports, was signed with Switzerland in September 1985 at Indo-Swiss Joint Commission. In October 1985, India signed an agreement with Sweden for assistance of S. Kr. 30.0 million for an integrated programme for technical co-operation in trade promotion. The focus of this programme was on developing exports of select labour-intensive products produced by SSIs in specific geographic areas.

India signed a MoU with Pakistan on January 10, 1986, containing a number of provisions to boost mutual trade. Pakistan, under this MoU, allowed the private sector to import 42 items from India.

MoU were also signed with Afghanistan and Ethiopia. The bilateral textile agreement with Norway allowed, for the first time, free access for export of traditional folklore textile products and products made from handloom fabrics to Norway markets. The agreement was initially effective for 18 months from July 1, 1985 but had provisions for extension for one more year. In February 1986, a bilateral agreement on economic and technical co-operation was signed between India and Maldives.

RELAXATIONS/SIMPLIFICATION OF PROCEDURES AND OTHER DEVELOPMENTS

INVESTMENT BY NON-RESIDENTS OF INDIAN NATIONALITY OR ORIGIN

The facility for portfolio and direct investment in equity shares of Indian companies available to non-residents of Indian nationality or origin (including overseas bodies owned by such persons to the extent of at least 60.0 per cent) was extended to investment in preference shares and debentures (convertible and non-convertible). The portfolio investment scheme for NRIs was modified in light of the experience gained in its operation. Under the modified scheme, designated banks could purchase equity shares and convertible debentures without the Reserve Bank's specific approval for each transaction, to the extent of 1.0 per cent per non-resident investor, subject to an overall ceiling of 5.0 per cent of the total paid-up equity capital of the investee company and 5.0 per cent of the total paid-up value of each series of convertible debentures issued by the company.

EXPERT COMMITTEE ON EXPORTS AND IMPORTS

The Reserve Bank appointed an expert committee to review the exchange control regulations relating to exports and imports and to suggest measures to simplify and streamline the documentation and procedures in November 1982. In terms of the recommendations of the committee, the process for simplification and rationalisation of exchange control procedures and also for improving the quality of customer service was undertaken in consultation with the Government.

ACU: PAYMENT FOR
TRANSACTIONS THROUGH ACU

To encourage intra-regional trade between member countries of the ACU,[5] it was decided that all eligible payments on account of current international transactions (other than payments relating to travel) between India and other member countries in the ACU, except Nepal, be settled compulsorily through the ACU mechanism. The new arrangement was brought into force from January 1984. Export and import transactions involving settlement of DPT were kept outside the purview of compulsory settlement procedure. In such cases, however, there was no bar on the advance/down payment against shipping documents being settled through the ACU.

With effect from August 1, 1985, the Reserve Bank arranged to announce its rates for purchase and sale of the ACU currencies on a daily basis. This was in response to the decision taken by the ACU that exchange rates for ACU currencies against the domestic currencies of the participating countries should be quoted by the respective central banks on a daily basis to overcome the problem of divergence between the rates fixed for the accounting period and the actual daily rates.

The seventeenth meeting of the board of directors of the ACU was hosted by the RBI in Bombay on March 2 and 3, 1989. The board noted with satisfaction that only 26.0 per cent of the total transactions among the participants were settled in foreign exchange in 1988 as compared with 36.0 per cent in 1987. Further, ways and means to expand the scope of ACU's activities and its membership was also discussed. A noteworthy outcome of the meeting was the decision to introduce swap arrangement amongst ACU members as a temporary facility for members facing deficit at the time of bi-monthly settlements.

SALE/TRANSFER OF SHARES OF INDIAN COMPANIES BY NRIs

To facilitate the sale and transfer of shares of Indian companies held by non-residents of Indian nationality or origin to citizens of India or PIO, the Central

---

5. The ACU was established in December 1974 on the initiative of the ESCAP with the objectives of providing a facility to settle, on a multilateral basis, payments for current international transactions, promoting use of the participants' currencies in current transactions and promoting monetary co-operation among the participants.

Government issued a notification on May 4, 1983 exempting such transfers from the provisions of the FERA, 1973. The exemption covered cases where: (i) the shares were purchased by the transferee from the stock market through a member of a recognised stock exchange in India; and (ii) the proceeds of the shares sold by the transferor were credited to his NRO account with an AD in India, with no right of repatriation outside India.

ORDINARY NON-RESIDENT ACCOUNTS FOR CORPORATE BODIES

A measure of liberalisation of investment facilities available to OCBs/trusts in which at least 60.0 per cent ownership/beneficial interest was held directly or indirectly, but ultimately by non-residents of Indian nationality or origin was introduced in April 1984. ADs were permitted to open and maintain NRO accounts in rupees in the names of such OCBs/trusts, subject to the condition that the initial deposits for opening such accounts should be made by remittance from abroad in an approved manner or out of rupee funds originating in India, which were otherwise eligible for credit to such non-resident accounts.

INDIANISATION OF FOREIGN COMPANIES

As on June 30, 1984, the number of cases in which final orders under section 29 (2)(a) of the FERA, 1973 were passed requiring dilution/Indianisation of foreign companies to specified levels came to 379. During the year, 17 more companies complied with the directive, bringing the total number of such companies to 349. The remaining 30 companies were at various stages of compliance.

As at the end of June 1987, final orders under section 29(2) of FERA requiring indigenisation/dilution of foreign equity to a specified level were issued to 389 companies including 14 companies, which opted for winding up their activities in India instead of indigenisation. Of these, 368 had complied with the FERA directives by that date. The remaining 21 companies were at various stages of compliance.

FORWARD EXCHANGE COVER

In view of the changing external trade and payments scenario and emergence of new lines of activities, a review of the regulations relating to forward sale and purchase contracts of foreign currencies undertaken by ADs was made. It was found necessary to enlarge the scope and coverage of some of the existing facilities and introduce forward cover facilities for some emerging business activities. Accordingly, the Reserve Bank introduced a number of changes in the package of forward cover facilities with effect from December 28, 1985. The new areas where forward cover facilities were introduced included: (i) roll-over forward cover for repayment of foreign currency loans; (ii) cross-currency forward cover for payments towards imports financed out of foreign currency loans where the goods were invoiced for payment in a currency/currencies other than the currency of the loan; (iii) cross-currency forward cover in respect of repayment of instalments of a loan obtained in one foreign currency by an Indian airline or a shipping company for acquisition of aircrafts/ships from out of revenue earnings in other foreign currencies; (iv) forward cover for charter hire payments by Indian airline and shipping companies/shippers; (v) forward cover for remittance of technical know-how fees; (vi) forward cover for remittance of erection and commissioning charges; and (vii) forward cover for re-transfer abroad of funds temporarily brought into India by Indian companies/firms executing turnkey/civil construction/service contracts abroad.

RIFEE SCHEME

Under the RIFEE scheme, prior to December 26, 1985, eligible non-residents of Indian nationality or origin returning to India for permanent settlement were entitled to avail of foreign exchange up to 25.0 per cent of the total amount repatriated to India and balances held in their NR(E)A or FCNR (A) at the time of transfer of residence. The limit for foreign exchange entitlement under the scheme was raised from 25.0 to 50.0 per cent with effect from December 26, 1985.

EXPORT-IMPORT PASS BOOK SCHEME

The Government of India introduced an export-import pass book scheme for manufacturer-exporters to provide duty-free access to imported inputs for export production. This scheme, broader in its coverage than the advance licensing scheme, was intended to help regular registered manufacturer-exporters to obtain their requirements of imported articles, such as raw materials, duty free to suit their production/export time schedules.

WORKING GROUP ON EXCHANGE CONTROL

The working group on exchange control constituted by the Reserve Bank submitted its report in January 1986. Several recommendations made by the working group for simplification and selective liberalisation of exchange control policies for better customer service were accepted and implemented by the Bank. These related, *inter alia*, to foreign travel under the special travel schemes, remittance facilities available to non-residents of Indian nationality or origin, remittance of dividend by non-FERA companies and agency commission on exports.

SALE OF US DOLLARS BY THE RESERVE BANK

The Reserve Bank introduced a scheme for sale of US dollars to ADs effective February 2, 1987. Earlier, the Bank was selling only spot pound sterling while it bought, both on spot and forward basis, four currencies, *viz.*, pound sterling, US dollar, DM and Japanese yen from ADs. The scheme, which was confined to Bombay, was intended to assist the healthy growth of the local exchange market as also to help importers get finer rates from ADs. There was no ceiling on the amount of dollar purchases.

REMITTANCE OF DIVIDEND TO NON-RESIDENT SHAREHOLDERS OF INDIAN COMPANIES

Prior to July 31, 1986, ADs could remit dividend to non-resident shareholders without the prior approval of the Reserve Bank, if the equity shares held by non-resident shareholders in a non-FERA company did not exceed 25.0 per cent of the total issued equity capital of ₹ 5 lakh in face value. To facilitate prompt remittance of dividend to non-resident shareholders, the Reserve Bank granted general permission to ADs with effect from July 31, 1986 to make remittances towards equity dividends to non-resident shareholders of all non-FERA companies, irrespective of the face value of equity shares or percentage of the issued capital held by the non-resident shareholders. Applications of only FERA companies were now required to be submitted to the Reserve Bank for prior approval.

INVESTMENT BY NRIs

To provide further incentives to NRIs and overseas bodies, owned directly or indirectly to the extent of at least 60.0 per cent by NRIs, for investing in Indian companies with the benefit of repatriation of capital and income earned, certain additional facilities were offered. These included: (i) bulk investments up to 100.0 per cent of equity capital in sick industrial units; (ii) investments in new issues of Indian shipping companies and companies engaged in the development of computer software or oil exploration services under the 40.0 per cent scheme; (iii) investments in medical diagnostic centres under the 40.0 per cent and 74.0 per cent schemes; and (iv) investments in private limited companies under the 40.0 per cent scheme.

RELAXATION IN EXCHANGE CONTROL PROCEDURES RELATING TO EXPORTS

To render prompt service to exporters, the powers delegated to ADs in certain exchange control areas were enhanced from April 23, 1987. These included: (i) Permission to allow reduction up to 10.0 per cent of the invoice value of an export shipment or ₹ 10,000, whichever was less, on account of disputes about quality and quantity on behalf of all regular exporter-clients. Earlier, ADs could consider such applications only from exporters who held blanket permits. (ii) Permission to remit commission or agree for deduction of the commission amount from the invoice of the relative export shipment up to ₹ 1 lakh in respect of shipments of goods included in the select list of export products and up to ₹ 50,000 in respect of shipments of other export products, provided the rates at which commission was paid were within the prescribed ceiling rates. (iii) Permission to effect remittances towards export claims up to 10.0 per cent of fob value of the shipment or ₹ 30,000 whichever was less. (iv) Grant of pre-bid clearance for bids/offers for export of engineering goods on DPT and execution of turnkey/civil construction contracts abroad up to the value of ₹ 5 crore. The monetary ceiling on the powers delegated to the Exim Bank to grant such pre-bid clearances was raised from ₹ 5 crore to ₹ 20 crore.

SCHEMES FOR EXPORT OF SILVER JEWELLERY AND ARTICLES

The Government introduced from December 8, 1986 a scheme for export of silver jewellery and articles against silver supplied by foreign buyers. Under the scheme, silver required for the manufacture of articles/jewellery had to be supplied free of charge by foreign buyers so that there was no net export of silver from India. Export of jewellery and articles (including studded ones) was permitted only if the value added in the export was at least 20.0 per cent. Under a second scheme introduced the same day, exports of jewellery and articles (other than coins) made of silver were entitled to the benefit of replenishment of silver, provided they satisfied the value added and other requirements laid down by the Government.

SCHEME FOR EXPORT OF SILVER JEWELLERY

To obviate the need for the HHEC and STC to approach the Reserve Bank for permission each time silver was to be imported or silver jewellery was to be exported under the scheme for export of silver jewellery, the Bank granted special permission to the HHEC and STC to import silver metal and export silver jewellery/articles under the scheme initially for a period of one year effective December 30, 1987.

SCHEME FOR MANUFACTURE AND EXPORT OF GOLD AND SILVER JEWELLERY AND ARTICLES

The Government introduced the scheme for export of gold and silver jewellery and articles from EPZs and 100.0 per cent export-oriented complexes. The Government permitted the SBI to make available to such units gold imported by it under the gold jewellery export promotion and replenishment scheme, and the MMTC was also permitted to import gold into India for supply to such units to enable them to manufacture jewellery for export. In order to obviate the need to secure specific export licences from the Reserve Bank as required under section 13(2) of FERA, the Reserve Bank granted special permission to these units to send out Indian gold/silver jewellery under the provisions of the scheme.

PROJECT EXPORTS

During 1986–87 (July–June), the working group on project exports accorded approvals to 107 proposals involving an aggregate value of ₹ 3,703 crore. These comprised 23 proposals for civil construction contracts (₹ 1,464 crore), 44 proposals for turnkey contracts (₹ 1,747 crore), 10 proposals for deferred payment contracts for supply of engineering goods (₹ 168 crore) and 30 proposals for consultancy contracts (₹ 323 crore).

JAPANESE YEN AND DEUTSCHE MARK PURCHASES BY THE RESERVE BANK

The facility of spot sale and sale for delivery up to one month of Japanese yen and Deutsche mark to the Reserve Bank was restored to ADs effective November 2, 1987 to cover their spot purchases from their overseas branches and correspondents for crediting rupee funds to their accounts in India.

FORWARD DELIVERY RATES FOR POUND STERLING: REVISION IN FORWARD MARGIN

Effective December 7, 1987, the forward margin charged by the Reserve Bank on its purchases of pound sterling was changed to a slab basis, depending on the Reserve Bank's rupee-pound sterling rate, to make the forward margins more consistent with changes in the rupee-pound sterling rates. The forward discount was fixed at GBP 0.0040 per ₹ 100 per month instead of GBP 0.0060 hitherto. Extension of forward purchase contracts in pound sterling continued to be permitted by the Reserve Bank on payment of a charge of GBP 0.0075 per month over the contracted rate.

FOREIGN TRAVEL SCHEME

Travel under the foreign travel scheme could now be combined with travel abroad for any other purpose, except for tours on export promotion or business grounds, *Haj* pilgrimage and travel under the NTS.

FOREIGN TRAVEL UNDER SPECIAL TRAVEL SCHEME

Under the FTS, Indian residents were eligible to undertake visits to any country (other than Bhutan and Nepal) once in two calendar years and were entitled to draw foreign exchange up to the equivalent of US$ 500 per capita. Similarly, under the NTS, Indian residents were eligible to visit any country in the group of eight neighbouring countries (*viz.*, Bangladesh, Burma, Malaysia, Maldives, Mauritius, Pakistan, Seychelles Islands and Sri Lanka) once in two calendar years and could draw foreign exchange up to the equivalent of US$ 250 per capita. According to changes made with effect from April 7, 1986, foreign travel under these schemes could be undertaken only once in three calendar years instead of two. Further, a combination of FTS and NTS for the purpose of drawing exchange was not permissible.

FOREIGN EXCHANGE CONSERVATION (TRAVEL) TAX

Effective October 15, 1987, persons drawing exchange for travel abroad were required to pay, unless specifically exempted, foreign exchange conservation (travel) tax at a rate of 15.0 per cent of the rupee equivalent of the foreign exchange released to them, under the provisions of the Finance Act, 1987. The foreign exchange conservation (travel) tax rules, 1987 laid down the detailed procedure for collection of the tax and its deposit into government account, refund of the tax following surrender of unutilised exchange, exempted categories of travel and allied matters.

LEVY OF CESS ON PAYMENTS TOWARDS IMPORT OF TECHNOLOGY

Under the Research and Development Cess Act, 1986, a cess at the rate of 5.0 per cent was levied on every industrial concern on all payments made towards such import of technology effective December 1, 1987. The proceeds of the cess collected by the Central Government were transferred to the IDBI, which would administer the above Act by crediting the amounts to a venture capital fund to be used for providing equity capital or any other form of financial assistance to industrial concerns attempting commercial application of indigenous technology or adapting imported technology to wider domestic applications.

SURRENDER OF UNSPENT FOREIGN EXCHANGE TRAVELLERS ON RETURN TO INDIA

Under a notification issued by the Reserve Bank on February 27, 1988, the maximum period allowed for surrender of any amount of unspent foreign exchange brought back to India was uniformly fixed at 90 days from the date of return in respect of all travellers, as against the earlier condition of surrender to an AD not later than 60 days from the date of return of the traveller, if the amount was within US$ 200 or its equivalent and within 30 days if the amount exceeded US$ 200 or its equivalent.

GUIDELINES FOR EXPORT OF CONSULTANCY/TECHNICAL SERVICES ON DPT

In the past, Indian companies/firms undertaking execution of overseas consultancy and technical service contracts were required to stipulate the terms of payment under which the full contract value was payable against progress bills before completion of the contract. The Bank evolved broad guidelines for exporters of such services under which they were able to bid for overseas service contracts on DPT, on a selective basis.

LIBERALISATION OF INTERNATIONAL CREDIT CARD FACILITY

Effective November 23, 1987 liberalisation measures were introduced in the international credit card facility available to holders of blanket exchange permits issued by the Reserve Bank. The facility of holding international credit cards was also extended to firms/companies holding exchange permits issued under the CAFEX scheme.

EXPORTS TO OVERSEAS INDIAN-OWNED WAREHOUSES APPROVED BY THE RESERVE BANK

During 1987–88, the Bank permitted the Electronics Trade and Technology Development Corporation Ltd, a Government of India undertaking, to establish a warehouse in the US for promoting the exports of Indian electronic goods to the US. Considering the longer time required for sale of goods on 'stock and sell' basis, the statutory time limit prescribed for realisation of proceeds of exports made to Indian-owned warehouses established abroad with the approval of the Reserve Bank was fixed at 15 months as against the period of 6 months prescribed for normal exports.

ENGAGEMENT OF FOREIGN NATIONALS

Before August 1988, companies/firms were required to obtain prior permission from the concerned administrative ministry of the Government to engage foreign technicians/technical experts, except in cases where the engagement was for a short period not exceeding three months for attending to an emergency or breakdown of plant/machinery. This procedure was modified and the Reserve Bank dealt with all types of applications for engaging foreign technicians/technical experts by companies and firms in India, subject to compliance with the following conditions: (i) the total duration of the engagement of the foreign technician/s or technical expert/s by any Indian company/firm should not exceed 12 months in a calendar year; (ii) the payment towards fees/remuneration to any single foreign technician/technical expert should not exceed US\$ 500 per day; and (iii) in the case of payments in foreign exchange on a company-to-company basis, the total payment by any Indian company to all foreign companies/firms taken together on account of services of foreign technicians/ technical experts should not exceed US\$ 50,000 in a full calendar year.

Further, companies/firms holding blanket exchange permits were permitted to utilise these permits to meet expenditure in foreign exchange to engage foreign technicians/technical experts, provided they had obtained the Reserve Bank's prior permission for such engagement.

RUPEE LOANS/OVERDRAFT TO NRIs FOR DIRECT INVESTMENT IN INDIA

To encourage investment in India by NRIs, the Reserve Bank started considering, on merit, applications by ADs for grant of rupee loans/ overdrafts to non-residents of Indian nationality/origin against security of fixed deposits in their NRE/FCNR accounts for making direct investments in India, on non-repatriation basis, in the following areas in addition to manufacturing activities and export-oriented trading activities: (i) hospitals (including diagnostic centres); (ii) hotels with 3, 4 or 5 star rating; (iii) shipping companies; (iv) development of computer software; (v) oil exploration services; and (vi) any industry listed in appendix I to the Ministry of Industry's press note dated February 2, 1973 or any other export-oriented industry.

NRI BOND ISSUE BY SBI

The NRI bond issue opened on November 14, 1988 and closed on February 15, 1989. The maturity period of the bonds was seven years and they carried 11.5 per cent per annum interest compounded at half-yearly intervals. The principal amount of the bonds on maturity and the periodic interest thereon was payable to the bond holders after converting the amounts into rupees at the SBI at the telegraphic transfer (TT) buying rate for US dollar prevailing on the date of payment. To enable holders of NRI bonds to raise rupee funds to meet their genuine financial requirements in India, they were granted the facility of obtaining rupee loans against the security of the bonds for specified purposes.

EXCHANGE RISK ADMINISTRATION SCHEME

With a view to provide a measure of protection to the sub-borrowers of the ICICI, IDBI and IFCI, against the exchange risk inherent in their medium and long-term borrowings in foreign exchange, these three FIs launched the ERAS with effect from April 1, 1989. The benefit of cover under the scheme was available to foreign currency sub-loans disbursed on or after April 1, 1989 by the FIs out of their ECBs.

The repayment obligations in respect of the principal amounts of the sub-loans were rupee-tied at the rates prevailing on the dates of disbursement. The interest liability of the sub-borrowers, the spread of the FIs and the exchange risk premium was merged into a 'composite cost' with ceiling and floor rates. The actual rate within the band was announced from time to time and was payable at quarterly intervals. The exchange risk premium in the composite cost was credited to the exchange risk administration fund set up and administered by the IDBI.

NEW BLANKET EXCHANGE PERMIT SCHEME

The Reserve Bank introduced a single broad-based permit scheme for exporters in place of the separate blanket permit schemes, namely, the Reserve Bank and the ITC (import trade control) blanket permit schemes. The main features of the new scheme were: (i) the list of approved purposes for which foreign exchange could be availed by holders of blanket permits was expanded considerably to obviate frequent applications from exporters to the Reserve Bank; (ii) monetary ceilings prescribed for foreign exchange expenditure for the approved purposes were either removed or considerably enhanced to afford greater freedom to exporters; and (iii) the quantum of exchange entitlements was related to specific percentages of realised fob value of goods exported and their classification in accordance with product lists prepared by the Government. The scheme was further liberalised in 1988–89. The 100.0 per cent export-oriented units holding green cards issued by the Ministry of Commerce were eligible for blanket permits during the initial period of two years of their operations, irrespective of their export performance. This facility was extended to new units operating in the export processing zones, even if such units did not have to their credit the required minimum export performance during the initial two years of operations. Besides, the number of approved purposes for which exchange could be drawn against blanket permits was considerably enlarged to cover more items, which stood at 24 in 1988-89.

APPENDIX 6.1
Committees and Working Groups

BANKING

COMMITTEE TO CONSIDER FORMATS OF PUBLISHED ACCOUNTS OF BANKS AND FULL DISCLOSURE IN SUCH ACCOUNTS

The Reserve Bank appointed a committee in March 1982 under the chairmanship of Shri A. Ghosh, Deputy Governor. The committee had representatives from banks, the NIBM, the Government, the Reserve Bank, and a chartered accountant to examine the formats of the published accounts of banks and consider the need, if any, for full disclosure by banks of their liabilities/assets.

The terms of reference of the committee included:

(i)   to examine the desirability of greater or full disclosure in the published accounts of banks, public accountability of banks, requirement of maintaining confidentiality between banker and customer and the requirement of maintaining the image, reputation and credit-worthiness of banks;

(ii)   to suggest whether it was necessary to make any further provisions in the existing laws if greater or full disclosure was not considered necessary or appropriate;

(iii)   to suggest suitable changes/amendments in the formats of the balance sheets and profit and loss accounts, having regard to: (a) the need for greater or full disclosures, (b) the expansion of banking operations both area-wise and sector-wise, (c) the need for improving the presentation of accounts, and (d) the presentation of accounts of other companies;

(iv)   to look into the practices broadly followed by banks in accounting/classifying various items of liabilities and assets and income and expenditure, and to suggest standard accounting concepts, which would facilitate a uniform and comparable presentation of such items in the published accounts, and compliance with various statutory requirements; and

(v)   to consider evolving suitable norms for creation of provisions for income tax and other taxes, bad and doubtful debts and depredation in government securities on a scientific basis.

The committee held several meetings with the chairmen of banks and representatives of regional councils of the ICA, the ICWA, the Chambers of Commerce and management institutes before finalising its recommendations.

WORKING GROUP TO REVIEW THE EXISTING SYSTEM OF INSPECTIONS

The Reserve Bank appointed a working group, in December 1981, under the chairmanship of a retired senior officer of the Bank to review the existing system of inspection of commercial banks in the public and private sectors and to suggest improvements/modifications. The group was asked to review the existing system of inspection of UCBs and RRBs. The terms of reference also covered an examination of: (i) the question of in-class as well as on-the-job training of inspection staff of the Reserve Bank; and (ii) the existing machinery for monitoring the progress of inspections and the follow-up of their findings.

Pursuant to the recommendations made by the working group on simplification of inspection forms and synchronisation of the inspection system in banks with the basic data required for purposes of inspection, the inspection forms were revised and forwarded to regional offices for their use.

WORKING GROUP TO REVIEW THE ACCOUNTING SYSTEM AT BANK BRANCHES

The Reserve Bank constituted on July 11, 1981 a working group to review the accounting system at bank branches in the context of generating data for various statutory and other returns relating to deployment of credit, particularly data relating to priority sector lending. The terms of reference of the working group were:

(i)   to look into the existing systems of maintenance of accounts at the branch level, including maintenance of the main books of accounts like general ledgers and loan ledgers, as also various systems of maintenance of sub-day/supplementary books, loan balancing and other records, particularly at the rural and semi-urban branches and suggest changes that would facilitate: (a) generation of summary data regarding deployment funds and lending to various categories of priority sectors, (b) generation of data for compiling the returns and schedules prescribed by the Reserve Bank and for furnishing information required by the Reserve Bank, central and state governments, returns required by the head office/controlling offices of banks for control and supervision as well as for statistical purposes;

(ii)   to review the information system introduced by the Reserve Bank and examine the feasibility of integrating the system with the control/statistical returns required to be submitted by banks;

(iii)   to suggest other measures necessary to ensure the availability of data on a regular basis and without delay; and

(iv)   to any other matters that are incidental or related to the terms of reference.

The group could appoint study groups, comprising bank officers who had sufficient operational experience, which could be assigned specific tasks. It could also conduct sample studies of the existing system of accounting in a few banks, and such studies could be entrusted to individual banks and/or the NIBM, Pune.

The report of the working group was examined and processed. Banks were asked to implement the recommendations relating to maintenance of separate subsidiaries for different segments of priority sector advances, separate loan ledgers for different segments of priority sector borrowers and introduction of the loose-leaf system of maintaining loan ledgers.

STANDING CO-ORDINATION COMMITTEE FOR
TRAINING ARRANGEMENTS IN BANKS

To strengthen the training arrangements in banks with a view to providing motivated and trained manpower, a standing co-ordination committee under the chairmanship of a Deputy Governor of the Reserve Bank was constituted in March 1986 to co-ordinate, monitor and guide the training arrangements in banks on an on-going basis. The third meeting of this committee was held on June 20, 1988. The important decisions taken at the meeting were as follows:

(i) banks should conduct an evaluation test for trainees at the end of the induction programme for base-level officers (both direct recruits and promotee officers);

(ii) the model course design for induction training programme for base-level officers was finalised for adoption by banks; and

(iii) while drawing up the training programme for officers, banks were advised to keep in mind the views of the Parliamentary Consultative Committee attached to the Ministry of Personnel, Public Grievances and Pension. The proposals reiterated that bank officials at all levels needed to be suitably briefed about the nature, scope and details of various development programmes of the Government by suitable training inputs. Further, there was even greater need for these functionaries to overcome their mistrust of the poor and to engender suitable attitudinal changes to make them take a genuine interest in the sphere of development administration rather than treat these activities as unwelcome but unavoidable chores.

WORKING GROUP ON OPERATIONS OF INDIAN BANKS ABROAD

There was a quantum jump in the volume of business as also diversification of such business during the 1970s in the overseas sector of Indian banks. Against the backdrop of the need for banks to focus on developing sound marketing and business strategies and to take fresh initiatives, which were deemed necessary to give a sense of direction to their international operations, the Reserve Bank set up a working group to appraise the operations of Indian banks operating abroad, assess their growth potential and make recommendations for improving the business performance of banks. The working group was appointed on July 29, 1988 with chief officers and executives from the SBI, BoI, BoB and NIBM in addition to the controller, ECD, Reserve Bank, as members.

SMALL GROUP TO CONSIDER NATIONAL CLEARING
OF OUTSTATION CHEQUES

The Reserve Bank examined the feasibility of introducing national clearing of outstation cheques in consultation with the IBA with a view to reducing the time involved. Accordingly, the Bank appointed a small group of representatives from the Government of India (Ministry of Finance), the Electronics Commission, the IBA and the Reserve Bank to consider:

(i)   the feasibility of introducing MICR/OCR technology for cheque writing and to recommend a suitable system for national clearing of outstation cheques;

(ii)   details on standardisation of the cheque form with reference to size, quality of paper and printing specifications;

(iii) tentative schedules for introducing the system; and

(iv)   related matters, particularly those relating to the feasibility of introducing the giro system as part of national clearing for quicker remittance of funds, which also required mechanisation.

INDUSTRIAL SECTOR

COMMITTEE OF DIRECTION

The COD had been constituted by the Reserve Bank in 1975 to consider and advise, on an on-going basis, on problems arising from the implementation of the recommendations of the Tandon Study Group on follow-up of bank credit and other related matters. The committee had representatives from the Reserve Bank, IDBI and commercial banks. The committee had set up five sub-committees: four to review the inventory/receivable norms for various industries, *viz.*, engineering, electrical, textiles, glass and leather and the fifth to evolve lending norms for units in the trading group. The recommendations of the sub-committee on the textiles group were accepted by the COD and the Reserve Bank with some modifications and banks were advised of the revised norms in June 1984. The recommendations of the sub-committee on the electrical group were also accepted by the COD.

The COD served as a forum to examine on an ongoing basis the problems arising from the implementation of the recommendations of the Tandon, Chore and Marathe Committees.

WORKING GROUP TO REVIEW THE SYSTEM OF CASH CREDIT

The report of the working group, which was submitted in September 1979, was accepted by the Bank with certain modifications, and commercial banks were advised on December 8, 1980 to implement the accepted recommendations. The major decisions taken by the Reserve Bank on the recommendations made by the working group were:

(i) Enhancement of borrowers' contribution

The contribution from borrowers towards working capital out of their long-term sources should hereafter be not less than 25.0 per cent of the current assets required for the estimated level of production, which would mean a minimum current ratio of 1.33:1 (as against 25.0 per cent of working capital gap, *i.e.*, total current assets minus current liabilities other than bank borrowings). In case a borrower was not in a position to comply with this requirement immediately, the existing need-based credit limits already enjoyed by the borrower should not be curtailed; the excess over the credit limits permissible to the borrower should be segregated and treated as WCTL, which would be made repayable in half-yearly instalments within a definite period, not exceeding five years. The WCTL should carry a rate of interest that should in no case be less than the rate charged for the relative cash credit and banks may, at their discretion, even charge a higher rate of interest not exceeding the ceiling. In addition, suitable provision should be made for charging the penal rate of interest in the event of any defaults in the timely repayment of WCTL.

In respect of such borrowers, if additional limits became necessary on account of increased production, banks were asked to ensure that the WCTL component was not enhanced and additional limits were allowed on the basis of an incremental current ratio of 1.33: 1.

(ii) Separate limits for peak level and non-peak level

Separate limits should be fixed, wherever feasible, for peak level and non-peak level credit requirements, indicating the periods during which the relative limits would be utilised by borrowers.

(iii) Ad hoc or temporary limits

Banks should consider very carefully requests from borrowers for *ad hoc* or temporary limits in excess of the sanctioned limits, which should be allowed only for a pre-determined short duration and given through a separate demand loan or non-operable cash credit account. As such, additional accommodation would put the bank's credit planning out of gear, and banks should charge additional interest of one per cent per annum over the normal rate. However, in exceptional circumstances, such as natural calamities, banks may not charge any additional interest.

(iv) Drawal of funds to be regulated through quarterly operative limits

Borrowers should indicate before the commencement of each quarter the funds required during the quarter, *i.e.*, the operative limit, which should be within the limit sanctioned for peak level/non-peak level periods. The quarterly statements should form the basis for a quarterly review of the account and the operative limit indicated by the borrower should eventually set the level of drawings in that quarter, subject to a tolerance limit of 10.0 per cent either way. Excess or under-utilisation of the operative limit beyond the tolerance level should be considered as an irregularity in the account and banks should initiate necessary corrective steps, including dialogues with the borrowers, to prevent recurrence of such irregularities.

If a borrower did not submit the returns within the prescribed time, banks may charge penal interest of one per cent per annum on the total outstanding for the period of default in the submission of quarterly returns. In case the default persisted, banks should review the position, and where they were satisfied that action was necessary, the accounts of such borrowers may be frozen.

The measures suggested under items (i) to (iv) above were applicable to all the borrowers without exemption, having aggregate working capital limits of ₹ 50 lakh and above from the banking system. Sick units under the nursing programme, or where rehabilitation measures were under active consideration by banks, would not be covered by the measures indicated in items (i) and (iii) above.

(v) Encouragement of bill finance

Banks were advised to discourage the sanction of cash credit against book debts and take steps to review all such accounts and convert such cash credit limits into bill limits, wherever possible.

(vi) Drawee bill system

In respect of borrowers with aggregate working capital limits of ₹ 50 lakh and over from the banking system, banks were required to extend at least 50.0 per cent of the cash credit limit against raw material inventory to the manufacturing units, whether in the public or private sector, by way of drawee bills.

(vii) Dues of PSUs to SSIs

Banks should insist that PSUs and large borrowers maintained control accounts in their books to give precise data regarding their dues to small units and furnished the data in their quarterly information system. This would enable banks to take suitable measures for ensuring payment to small units without delay.

As various problems/issues arising from the implementation of the recommendations of the group were brought to the notice of the Reserve Bank, it organised a seminar in July 1981, where senior executives of banks, representatives of the IDBI, ICICI and NIBM participated. In light of the consensus reached at the seminar, the following relaxations were made by the Reserve Bank:

(i)   As some of the borrowers, for instance: (a) new companies floated prior to December 8, 1980; (b) companies showing signs of incipient sickness; and (c) companies having finalised modernisation/expansion programmes prior to the implementation of the Chore Committee recommendations might not be in a position to switch to the second method of lending recommended by the Tandon Committee (according to which the borrowers' contribution from owned funds and long-term resources to meet the working capital requirements should be at least 25.0 per cent of the total current assets), banks were instructed to assess the credit requirements of such borrowers without applying the second method of lending. Such relaxation was, however, to be permitted for a period not exceeding three years.

(ii) Banks were advised to adopt a flexible approach in respect of exporters who were unable to bring in additional contributions required under the second method of lending in respect of additional credit limits sanctioned for specific export transactions. In view of the concessional rate of interest applicable to export packing credits in the case of exporter-borrowers, banks may identify the working capital term loan where required on a notional basis and not carve it out from the relative account. Banks were also advised that additional interest of one per cent per annum on *ad hoc* temporary limits may be charged only on limits other than pre-shipment/post-shipment credit finance; as such finance was governed by ceiling rates of interest prescribed under the directives issued by the Reserve Bank from time to time.

(iii) To calculate the current assets/current liabilities and contributions to be made by borrowers, the net amount relating to income tax paid for the previous years, years for which assessments were pending and the corresponding provision may be taken into account. The advance tax paid for the current year and the corresponding provision may be taken as current assets and current liabilities, respectively, for the purpose of assessment and not the net position.

(iv) To compute permissible bank finance, banks were advised to include under current assets the amount of excise duty levied on the permissible level of inventory to be held by the borrower. Such amounts of excise duty may, however, be shown under other current assets and should not be treated as cost of production. Further, where the receivables of the borrower included an element of sales tax paid, banks could include such element of sales tax under other current assets.

COMMITTEE ON REHABILITATION OF SICK INDUSTRIAL UNDERTAKINGS

The Reserve Bank constituted a committee on May 14, 1981 to examine the legal and other difficulties faced by banks and FIs in rehabilitating sick industrial undertakings and suggest remedial measures. The terms of reference were:

(i) to review the policy framework within which banks/FIs could bring about a change in the management of assisted industrial units, and recommend changes;

(ii) to review the existing criteria adopted by banks/FIs for determining the suitability of a sick unit for revival and recommend appropriate modifications;

(iii) to identify the main constraints in the rehabilitation of sick units and suggest remedial measures including amendments to statutes;

(iv) to suggest measures for facilitating the restructuring of the capital base of the assisted units;

(v) to identify concessions that should normally be made by various agencies for reviving sick units and consider whether sick units should be burdened with obligations like payment of minimum bonus and implementation of wage awards; and

(vi)   to identify the factors inhibiting expeditious merger of sick units with healthy ones and suggest measures for expediting such mergers.

The committee submitted its interim report in November 1981 on the issue of special legislation for creating a special authority, *i.e.*, the Board for Industrial Revival, with an indicative draft legislation suggesting suitable legal measures for expeditious rehabilitation of sick industrial undertakings. The interim report was examined by the Reserve Bank and its views were forwarded to the Government for its consideration.

COMMITTEE TO REVIEW THE WORKING OF CAS

In pursuance of the decision taken at the meeting between the Governor, Reserve Bank and the chairmen of major banks on October 25, 1982, the Bank appointed a committee in November 1982 to review the working of CAS from the point of view of its operational aspects. The terms of reference of the committee were:

(i)   to examine the objectives, scope and content of the scheme and suggest modifications, if any, given the changing economic situation;

(ii)   to examine the adequacy of credit appraisal machinery/procedures in commercial banks and suggest modifications, if any, in their modalities;

(iii)   to study the existing set up for compliance with the requirements of the scheme within the commercial banks, both at the head and regional office levels, and suggest necessary modifications to facilitate proper appraisal and expeditious disposal of applications and monitoring;

(iv)   to examine the existing database used by banks to make recommendations to the Reserve Bank for authorising a given level of credit for a particular party and suggest modifications/simplifications;

(v)   to examine the existing format used by banks to submit applications to the Reserve Bank in respect of seeking authorisation, and suggest necessary modifications;

(vi)   to study the desirability of introducing time-bound guidelines to be observed by commercial banks and the Reserve Bank to speed-up the processing and disposal of applications; and

(vii)   to make any other relevant recommendations.

The committee submitted its report in July 1983.

COMMITTEE ON FINANCING OF THE TEA INDUSTRY

The Reserve Bank of India constituted a committee on October 3, 1980 to examine problems relating to the financing of the tea industry. The terms of reference were:

(i)   to review the existing norms for providing working capital to the tea industry recommended by the Reserve Bank to SCBs in March 1972 on the basis of the report of the study group under the chairmanship of Shri B.K. Dutt and suggest suitable modifications in the changed circumstances;

(ii)   to examine the credit requirements of the tea industry (both working capital and term loans) in the wider context of the need to expand output to meet the sustained rise in domestic consumption without impinging on the exportable surplus;

(iii)   to enquire into the problems faced by the industry in obtaining finance (both working capital and term loans) from commercial banks, OFIs and the Tea Board;

(iv)   to consider other problems faced by commercial banks in providing credit to the tea industry; and

(v)   to make recommendations on these and any other related matters.

Based on the recommendations of the working group, guidelines were issued to banks in June 1982 for assessing the working capital requirements of borrowers. For this purpose borrowers were classified into four categories:

Large borrowers:[1] Cash credit/bills limits should not exceed 75.0 per cent of the peak deficits as reflected in the cash budgets of borrowers. Banks were required to fix the limits for the entire season/year on the basis of monthly cash budgets.

Small borrowers:[2] Working capital limits should be fixed on the basis of per acre scale of finance as determined by area committees (to be constituted by the Tea Board). No minimum contribution by way of net working capital was stipulated, but banks had to take into account the owned funds that could be brought in by the more affluent among the tea planters and determine the limits accordingly.

Bought-leaf factories:[3] Advances to factories holding registration certificates as SSI units should be eligible for classification as priority sector advances. The working capital needs should continue to be assessed on the basis of Tandon/Chore Committee discipline.

Tea traders:[4] Need-based finance should continue to be extended to tea traders, keeping in view the Tandon/Chore Committee discipline, except where specially relaxed by the Reserve Bank, as in the case of *ad hoc* increase in packing credit limits to meet large unforeseen export orders.

STANDING COMMITTEES FOR SELECTED INDUSTRIES

The Reserve Bank appointed standing committees on co-ordination of institutional finance for four major industries, *viz.*, jute, tea, sugar and fertilisers

---

1.   Units having their own processing factories, and those which did not have processing factories but whose holdings were over 100 hectares.

2.   Units with holdings up to 100 hectares and which did not have processing factories of their own.

3.   Units which buy green leaves from neighbouring small planters for processing.

4.   Those engaged in buying tea at auctions in bulk and eventually selling/exporting it.

to study their financial problems on an on-going basis. The standing committees for the jute and tea industries were set up on November 20, 1982 and those for the sugar and fertiliser industries on January 8, 1983. The members of the committees were drawn from the Reserve Bank, term-lending institutions, the concerned industries, the Central Government and experts/technologists. Each committee was to discuss financial and other problems of the respective industries that were referred to it.

STANDING COMMITTEE ON CO-ORDINATION OF INSTITUTIONAL FINANCE

Sugar

The SCCIF for the sugar industry, which had been in existence for the past few years, was set up to take a co-ordinated view on credit requirements and related problems of the sugar industry. The committee met as and when the need arose to discuss problems affecting the sugar industry. A sub-committee headed by the chairman of IFCI was also set up to suggest broad measures for the rehabilitation of the sugar industry. The recommendations of the sub-committee were considered at the final meeting of the SCCIF held on May 20, 1986 and follow-up action was initiated.

Based on the recommendations of the sub-group constituted by the standing committee, banks were advised by the Reserve Bank in October 1986 to classify the sugar mills financed by them into four categories according to the norms evolved, viz., viable, potentially viable, marginally viable and non-viable. Based on the data provided by banks, detailed instructions for working out rehabilitation packages and giving concessions to potentially/marginally viable and non-viable sugar mills were issued to banks in July 1987.

Tea

The standing committee for the tea industry in its sixth meeting held in September 1986 discussed, among others, issues relating to the allotment to tea estates of land rendered surplus under the Land Ceiling Act in Assam and West Bengal, the classification of small tea growers under the priority sector, overdues of sick tea gardens and norms for financing the tea industry. There had been complaints that there was no uniformity among banks in applying the prescribed norms, resulting in the adoption of divergent assessment methods by banks. Therefore, a small sub-group comprising representatives of the Reserve Bank, commercial banks, the Tea Board and the tea industry was formed to study the problem in its entirety and suggest necessary modifications. The sub-group submitted its report.

Textiles

In pursuance of the textile policy statement announced by the Government in June 1985, a standing advisory committee on modernising the textile industry was constituted by the Government. The committee, comprising representatives from the textile industry, textile machinery manufacturers, handlooms, power looms and exports, the Reserve Bank and officials from the Government, was to give its recommendations on planning and implementation of modernisation of the textile industry. The committee held two meetings. Further, the Government constituted working groups to review the position of closed/sick cotton textile mills in the country. The Government also created a nodal agency to look into the problems of closed/sick textile mills and consequently the earlier working groups were disbanded.

Export Finance

The standing committee on export finance, a high-powered policy-making body, set up by the Bank in 1975 to periodically discuss problems and policies relating to export finance, held frequent meetings. In December 1983, the Bank issued detailed guidelines to banks based on the suggestions made by the sub-group appointed by the standing committee for elongated suppliers' credit facilities for certain categories of goods to promote exports to various African countries. Also pursuant to the sub-group's recommendations, a working group was constituted consisting of representatives of the Reserve Bank, Exim Bank, ECGC, the concerned banks and a government nominee to consider proposals to extend credit terms beyond 180 days for targeted African countries as well as other countries for the export of selected commodities.

The committee met on November 15, 1985 and discussed problems faced by the export community. Important decisions taken by the committee included the following:

(i) Although the sub-group had recommended that the banks' practice of resorting to rediscounting/acceptance facilities abroad to raise resources was accepted in principle, it was decided that, in view of the liquidity in the banking system, the Reserve Bank might review the position.

(ii) The commerce ministry agreed to the Reserve Bank's proposal to make available an enhanced subsidy at 3.0 per cent to banks on rescheduled instalments of deferred payment exports, on a conditional case-by-case basis, where an agreement at the government-to-government level existed.

(iii) Post-supply credit facilities at a concessional rate of interest were granted for 'deemed exports' up to 30 days and a circular to this effect was issued.

INTEREST RATE ON EXPORT CREDIT

The committee to study the structure of interest rates on export credit comprising members from the NIBM, the SBI, Exim Bank, the Government of India (Ministry of Commerce) and the Reserve Bank was set up on January 11, 1986.

To provide a fillip to exports by extending the period for which concessional interest was offered and also to simplify the prevalent structure, the rates of interest for pre-shipment credit were fixed uniformly for all commodities as below:

		(Per cent per annum)
Period	March 1, 1986	August 1, 1986
(i) Up to 180 days	12.0	9.5
(ii) Beyond 180 days but not exceeding 270 days (with prior RBI approval)	14.0	11.5
(iii) Beyond 270 days	Not exceeding 16.5	

The interest rate on post-shipment credit up to 180 days was brought down from 12.0 per cent to 9.5 per cent. Consequent to these changes, the Reserve Bank reduced its interest rate on export refinance from 10.0 per cent to 9.0 per cent, with effect from the same date.

ALL-INDIA EXPORT ADVISORY COMMITTEE

The AIEAC Committee had been constituted by the Reserve Bank in October 1983 in order to have a continued dialogue and receive feedback from the export community on problems of export credit and foreign exchange. The export advisory committee, consisting of Reserve Bank officials, representative from banks and people from all-India export promotion councils/organisations, met at frequent intervals. Various recommendations of the committee were brought to the notice of the standing committee on export finance for information/decisions.

COMMITTEE ON TOBACCO EXPORTS

A consultative committee was set up with officials drawn from the Reserve Bank and commercial banks, tobacco exporters, representatives of the Tobacco Board and Indian Tobacco Association to look into the export credit requirements of tobacco exporters. The committee held its first meeting at Guntur on January 27, 1984.

STANDING CO-ORDINATION COMMITTEE

The standing co-ordination committee, appointed in January 1979 to consider issues pertaining to co-ordination between banks and term-lending institutions following the recommendations of the inter-institutional group, was reconstituted in August 1983. The reconstituted committee was expected to provide a standing forum to sort out inter-institutional problems relating to term lending based on past experiences. It would also review the involvement of banks and term-lending institutions in extending term credit besides dealing with compilation and sharing of information on term credit and other issues that may be referred to it.

The committee, which served as a standing forum to consider co-ordination between banks and term-lending institutions in project finance and allied matters, met in August 1985 and April 1986. It considered the following issues:

(i) detection of sickness at the incipient stage and proper co-ordination between commercial banks and term-lending institutions in formulating and implementing rehabilitation programmes;

(ii) parameters for providing relief/concessions by banks under rehabilitation packages evolved for potentially viable sick units;

(iii) sharing of expenses for protection, preservation and disposal of security where a receiver was appointed;

(iv) operational issues with regard to implementing the provisions of the SICA, 1985; and

(v) adoption of a common definition for a 'sick industrial unit'.

Necessary instructions were issued to banks on the decisions taken by the committee.

WORKING GROUP TO REVIEW THE NORMS FOR CONSORTIUM ADVANCES

In accordance with the suggestion made by the NFCC in its meeting in December 1986, a working group was set up by the Reserve Bank in January 1987 to examine the system and formulate norms for advances made to both healthy and sick units by banks in consortium, with or without the participation of FIs, to make appropriate recommendations to speed up the decision-making process and to provide timely and adequate credit to borrowers. Based on the first report of the group, detailed instructions were issued to banks in June 1987 which, envisaged a major role to be played by the lead bank and the second largest financing bank or two major banks (under a multiple financing arrangement) and covered issues such as carrying out viability studies, formulating and implementing rehabilitation packages within a specified time frame, adhering to the commitment there under, exchange of information between banks and FIs, carrying out joint reviews, adopting a unified stand on recall of advances, vesting bank officials with larger discretionary powers, upgrading skills and training staff. These measures were expected to ensure greater co-ordination between banks and FIs in financing sick and weak industrial units to expedite decisions on measures for their rehabilitation and implementation.

RURAL SECTOR

HIGH LEVEL STANDING COMMITTEE TO REVIEW THE FLOW OF INSTITUTIONAL CREDIT TO THE RURAL SECTOR AND RELATED MATTERS

A high level standing committee was appointed in 1985 under the chairmanship of a Deputy Governor of Reserve Bank to review the flow of institutional credit to the rural sector and related matters. The committee was also asked to suggest measures to improve the credit delivery system for the greater benefit of farmers, artisans, landless labourers and other weaker sections, particularly SCs/STs. The committee comprised representatives from the Reserve Bank, the Government of India, NABARD, the IBA, SBI, GIC, Agricultural Finance Corporation Ltd, Planning Commission, State Governments, National Federation of State Co-operative Banks Ltd, National Co-operative Land Development Banks Federation Ltd, Indian Council of Agricultural Research, Indian Institute of Science, Punjab Agricultural University, National Co-operative Development Corporation, KVIC and the Indian Agricultural Research Institute.

At its second meeting held on March 6, 1986, the committee decided to constitute a working group: (i) to consider problems relating to non-availability of credit to new and non-defaulting members of co-operative credit institutions and to suggest measures to ensure smooth flow of credit to these borrowers; and (ii) to recommend measures to assist the co-operative credit structure in areas susceptible to repeated natural calamities to insulate itself and its members from the increasing burden of overdues. Accordingly, a working group was constituted under the chairmanship of a former Union Minister for Agriculture.

The committee at its fourth meeting held in May 1987 considered the recommendations of the study team on banking development in the north-eastern region. For rapid economic development of this region along the lines suggested by the study team, it was decided to set up a separate task force in each state in the region and the SLBCs in these states would constantly review the performance under action plans. It was decided that an integrated plan for developing at least one block would drawn up on a pilot basis for each state.

WORKING GROUP ON THE MODALITIES OF IMPLEMENTATION OF PRIORITY SECTOR LENDING AND TWENTY-POINT ECONOMIC PROGRAMME BY BANKS

The working group constituted by the Reserve Bank on implementation of priority sector lending and the twenty-point programme submitted its report, and its recommendations were accepted by the Government and the Reserve Bank. The group, which identified the beneficiaries who required assistance from the banking system in pursuance of the twenty-point programme, spelt out ways in which such assistance could be rendered. As most of the beneficiaries under the programme fell in the relatively under-privileged groups within the priority sector, the group suggested changes in the approach to priority sector lending, including refining the definition of 'priority sector'. In particular, it introduced the concept of 'weaker sections' within the priority sector and recommended separate sub-targets for lending to such weaker sections in the two main categories within the priority sector, namely, agriculture and SSIs. The total enhanced target of 40.0 per cent for lending to priority sector was to be reached by the end of the Sixth Plan period. Consumption loans and housing loans for the poor were also brought within the priority sector lending. The need for a schematic and integrated approach to assisting the beneficiaries in consultation with state development agencies was emphasised. At the field level, the DCPs prepared by banks had to explicitly provide for the beneficiaries under the twenty-point programme. With the large number of borrowers involved, the group recommended routing credit to the weaker sections through state-sponsored corporations/agencies (besides functional co-operatives) specifically set up for the benefit of such persons.

Based on the recommendations by the group, the Reserve Bank issued detailed instructions in October 1980 to all commercial banks for their implementation. In particular, the targets for lending to weaker sections and priority sector, placed before the banks, were: (i) The overall assistance to the priority sector should constitute 40.0 per cent of total advances by March 1985. (ii) At least 40.0 per cent of the advances to the priority sector should be extended for agriculture and allied activities; in other words this sector would account for at least 16.0 per cent of total advances by 1985. (iii) Direct advances to 'weaker sections' in agriculture and allied activities should constitute at least 50.0 per cent of total direct lending to agriculture (including allied activities) by March 1983. 'Weaker sections' in this sector comprised small and marginal farmers and landless labourers. Persons engaged in allied activities whose borrowing limits did not exceed ₹ 10,000 were also included in 'weaker sections'. (iv) Advances to 'weaker sections' in SSIs, *i.e.*, those with credit limits up to and inclusive of ₹ 25,000, should constitute 12.5 per cent of total advances to SSIs by 1985.

The state governments were separately advised by the Reserve Bank, indicating the vital role they had to play in facilitating banks' assistance under the twenty-point programme. The main areas where supportive action from the state government was required related to identification of beneficiaries, provision of infrastructure and technical facilities, input supply and marketing, training support and assistance for recovery of loans.

A new information system for monitoring the implementation of the DCPs and financing of twenty-point programme at the district and state levels was introduced by the Reserve Bank in January 1981, based on the recommendations of the working group.

In pursuance of the guidelines issued by the Reserve Bank, commercial banks took measures to implement the recommendations for assisting beneficiaries under the programme. These included arranging seminars for branch managers/ staff to impress on them the importance of the programme, discussions and lectures at training centres, setting-up special cells for monitoring performance, arranging credit camps and mass loan programmes and co-ordinating activities with government agencies at the district and state levels for integrated action.

WORKING GROUP ON MODALITIES OF IMPLEMENTATION OF THE NEW TWENTY-POINT PROGRAMME

Consequent upon the announcement of the new twenty-point programme by the Prime Minister in January 1982, it was decided at the Finance Minister's meeting with the chief executives of PSBs on February 15, 1982 that the Reserve

Bank would appoint a working group to formulate the modalities for banks to implement the new twenty-point programme. Accordingly, on March 11, 1982, the Bank appointed a working group under the chairmanship of Shri A. Ghosh, Deputy Governor, comprising senior officers of banks, the Ministry of Finance, Ministry of Rural Development, ARDC, AFC and the Reserve Bank. The terms of reference of the working group were: to identify the tasks for the banking system for effective implementation of the new twenty-point programme; to review the targets and sub-targets within the priority sector with special reference to the needs of the weaker sections; to examine the scope for modifications in the definitions of priority sector; to review the reporting and monitoring system regarding the flow of credit to the new twenty-point programme with a view to simplifying and expediting the flow of information and making evaluation more effective; and to make any other recommendations that were incidental or related to the terms of reference.

WORKING GROUP ON PROBLEMS OF BANK CREDIT IN THE NORTH-EASTERN REGION

Major banks operating in the north-eastern region were advised in December 1980 to take immediate steps to strengthen their existing set up in the region, so as to enable them to undertake, besides conventional functions, development banking to supplement the efforts of the central and state governments. Such development banking would imply not only granting term loans more liberally, but also assisting in project identification, formulation and appraisal. These banks opened or upgraded their regional offices at Guwahati so that they could be proactive in accelerating the flow of credit for implementation of the development schemes for the region.

In the fifth meeting of the regional consultative committee for nationalised banks, it was decided that the state governments and the lead banks in the states would co-ordinate their efforts to increase the flow of credit in the north-eastern area, particularly for the implementation of IRDP and DCPs. It was also decided that all states in the region would bring in legislation to empower village councils to borrow from banks and that all banks would adopt the procedures of the SBI for extending agricultural credit to farmers in areas where land was vested in the community; the SBI had decided to grant advances up to ₹ 10,000 to individual cultivators against hypothecation of agricultural machinery and/or crops and group guarantee of not less than three persons.

NABARD continued its efforts to effect various recommendations of the committee on agricultural productivity in eastern India (Chairman: Shri S.R. Sen). Some of the decisions taken and conveyed to the banks/state governments for implementation as also the follow-up action taken were:

(i)   The need for preparing normal credit limit statements for all members by the PACS (including non-borrowers and defaulters) was emphasised.

(ii) State governments were advised to prepare a list of selected dealers/ suppliers of agricultural inputs, such as fertilisers, pesticides and farm equipment, so that the credit societies would be in a position to introduce a voucher system for disbursement of the in-kind component as recommended by the committee.

(iii) The committee's recommendation to use the services of local voluntary organisations on a commission basis in the special drive to collect overdues was accepted and recommended for implementation, subject to the banks bearing the entire operational costs.

(iv) The Planning Commission was requested to keep in view the recommendations of the committee on problems of irrigation, drainage and water management during the formulation of the Eighth Five Year Plan and also to help states initiate a systematic action programme and make provisions for it in their budgets when approving their annual plans. It was decided to discontinue the practice of appointing expert group/ state-wise consultants. Various development efforts were, henceforth, to be spearheaded by the regional offices of NABARD.

Considering the general backwardness of the north-eastern region and the need for accelerated development in view of its vulnerable position, it was decided to undertake a study of the steps needed for banking development in the region. Accordingly, a study team chaired by an Executive Director of the Reserve Bank was deputed to the region in May 1986. The study team met the representatives of banks, state governments and other institutions and held discussions. The recommendations of the study team in the report submitted in October 1986 covered four major aspects, *viz.*, provision of infrastructure facilities, banking facilities, extension facilities, and monitoring and follow-up of the action programme.

WORKING GROUP ON DATA COLLECTION RELATING TO CREDIT SUPPORT TO RETAIL OUTLETS OF THE PDS

The Ministry of Food and Civil Supplies considered it expedient to have detailed information on the extent of credit support to retail outlets of the PDS, comprising mainly private retail traders dealing in essential commodities (fair price shops), consumer co-operative stores, and suggested that the Reserve Bank set up a small group to look into the data sources and suggest improvements. Accordingly, the Reserve Bank set up a working group in December 1984 to examine the issue with the following terms of reference:

(i) To look into the available data under the existing reporting system and estimate the credit support to retail trade and distribution of essential commodities.

(ii) To formulate suitable format for making available adequate data on the above aspects to the Reserve Bank and the Government.

(iii) Any other relevant matters.

WORKING GROUP ON BANK CREDIT TO THE STATE HANDLOOM DEVELOPMENT CORPORATION

The working group appointed by the Reserve Bank in June 1984 to study operational problems of the State Handloom Development Corporations in relation to bank credit met three times and also undertook field visits to Karnataka, Tamil Nadu, West Bengal and the north-eastern region during early 1985. The field visits helped the working group understand various operational problems, such as supply and distribution of yarn to weavers, marketing of handloom products and raising finance for production and marketing under local conditions.

STUDY GROUP ON FLOW OF CREDIT TO IRDP BENEFICIARIES

A study group was set up by the Reserve Bank in November 1985 headed by the chairman of NABARD, with the objective of streamlining arrangements for the flow of credit and supply of inputs and assets to IRDP beneficiaries so that they would draw the full benefit of the anti-poverty programmes. Based on the recommendations of the study group in its interim report, which were accepted by the Government, banks were advised to implement, on an experimental basis, a system of cash disbursement of IRDP assistance for specified purposes in 22 selected blocks all over the country with effect from April 1, 1986, viz.: (i) when the asset was of a standard type, make or brand name marketed by reputed suppliers; (ii) when the loan was for Industries, ISB sector activities and a number of sundry items were to be bought, disbursement up to ₹ 3,000 may be made in cash in such cases; and (iii) to purchase animals. In all these cases, the borrowers were to provide documentary evidence to the bank for having purchased the asset/s, and banks were to verify the acquisition of the same by inspection.

STUDY GROUP ON THE FLOW OF INSTITUTIONAL CREDIT TO THE SSI SECTOR AND RELATED MATTERS

The study group appointed by the Reserve Bank under the chairmanship of a Deputy Governor of the Reserve Bank submitted its report in 1987. The report set out the background and features of the SSIs, analysed the causes of its sickness, identified the problems of credit institutions in nursing sick SSI units, reviewed the available facilities, explored the need to set up another fund in view of the existing gap and discussed the resources for such a fund. The recommendations of the group were forwarded by the Reserve Bank to the Government.

COMMITTEE TO CONSIDER PROBLEMS IN IDENTIFYING AND REHABILITATING SICK SSI UNITS

In February 1986, the Reserve Bank appointed a committee under the chairmanship of an Executive Director to consider problems in identifying and rehabilitating sick SSI units. The committee was to examine the following and make recommendations:

(i)   Definition of a sick SSI unit.

(ii)   Identification of incipient sickness in SSI units.

(iii) Establishment of a suitable machinery for identifying sickness, preparing rehabilitation packages in the case of potentially viable units, and follow-up and monitoring of implementation.

(iv)   Formulation of parameters to provide relief/concessions by commercial banks, SFCs, state governments and other agencies under rehabilitation packages evolved for sick SSI units considered as potentially viable.

Based on the recommendations of the committee, guidelines stressing the need for adequate and intensive relief measures and their speedy application were issued to banks in 1987. An illustrative list of working signals of incipient sickness and a list of reliefs/concessions that could be extended to sick units according to certain norms were issued along with the guidelines.

The standing advisory Committee reviewed the flow of bank credit to the SSI sector and also the measures taken by the Reserve Bank to improve co-ordination between banks and term-lending institutions that were found to be satisfactory. The committee, however, expressed concern over the increasing number of SSI units falling sick and made the following recommendations:

(i)   The state government and federations/associations concerned with the development of SSIs may take up sample studies of SSI units to identify problems/causes leading to industrial sickness and to make suitable arrangements to improve the information system.

(ii)   Measures should be taken to popularise customer service centres to reduce delays in the flow of credit.

(iii) SLIICs should be used to sort out policy issues concerning the flow of credit to the SSI sector.

In connection with the financing of the SSI sector in the north-eastern region, the committee felt that the relatively low credit absorption capacity of the region should be gradually increased by providing infrastructure facilities, entrepreneurial development, assured supply of inputs and technology and adequate marketing support.

STUDY GROUP ON NORMS FOR INVOLVEMENT OF RESOURCES BY STATE AND CENTRAL CO-OPERATIVE BANKS IN AGRICULTURAL LENDING

The study group constituted by NABARD in June 1983 to recommend norms for involvement of resources by state co-operative banks/CCBs in agricultural lending submitted its report in June 1984. The important recommendations of the committee included, inter alia, fixing the minimum involvement of ILR of state co-operative banks and CCBs in short-term agricultural lending (25.0 per cent for state co-operative banks and 40.0 per cent for CCBs) and modifying the scheme of linking borrowings from NABARD with efforts at deposit mobilisation by CCBs. The recommendations of the study group were accepted by NABARD and implemented from 1985–86.

COMMITTEE TO EXAMINE ISSUES RAISED BY THE NATIONAL FEDERATION
OF URBAN CO-OPERATIVE BANKS AND CREDIT SOCIETIES

The committee set up to examine the issues raised by the National Federation of Urban Co-operative Banks and Credit Societies submitted its report in February 1987. Almost all the recommendations of the committee were accepted and the Reserve Bank took the necessary follow-up action. A significant outcome of these recommendations was the decision to accord scheduled status to select UCBs. The Government issued orders to publish the notification in the official gazette describing UCBs that were licensed and whose demand and time liabilities were not less than ₹ 50 crore as FIs under sub-clause (iii) of clause (a) of sub-section 6 of section 42 of RBI Act, 1934. Other recommendations related to relaxing the norms for reckoning advances towards priority sector/weaker sections, enhancing the ceiling on housing loans by UCBs and increasing the limit on advances in certain categories.

The terms of reference of this group included, to identify the main market segments that banks should concentrate on and work out a plan for the immediate future, to assess and estimate their assigned capital, provisioning and infrastructure requirements and suggest modalities for raising such capital, to study personnel policy and suggest norms for selection, placement, transfer and training in respect of overseas branches, and to review the control and monitoring systems and suggest suitable changes wherever required.

WORKING GROUP TO EXAMINE THE SCOPE AND FUNCTIONS OF SLDBs

A high level working group was constituted by NABARD on January 2, 1985 to study the problems of LDBs, suffering from structural, financial and legal disabilities that tended to impede their growth, and to suggest measures for their orderly growth.

STANDING ADVISORY COMMITTEE FOR UCBs

The standing advisory committee for UCBs, after considering the views expressed by the state governments/co-operation departments on the uniform norms suggested by the Reserve Bank for audit classification of UCBs, recommended the adoption of standard norms for classifying UCBs in the country. It also suggested that the audit of bigger banks with working capital of ₹ 2 crore and above be entrusted to qualified auditors/chartered accountants to improve the quality of audit. As suggested by the standing advisory committee, urban banks with working capital of ₹ 25 crore and above were advised to ensure that at least 10.0 per cent of the liquid assets required to be maintained by them under SLR were held in the form of government and other trustee securities with a view to involving larger UCBs in the development activities of the Government. The committee also discussed the revised proposals on norms of viability of UCBs/

branches and recommended that a committee be constituted to conduct an in-depth study and suggest suitable norms of viability for its consideration.

The seventh meeting of the standing advisory committee for UCBs held on May 31, 1988 discussed, among others, the appointment of chief executives and other key personnel in UCBs, the rationalisation of recruitment procedures, the desirability of chartered accountants conducting the audit of UCBs, the supersession of the board of directors, selection of administrators, and progress in the rehabilitation of 'weak' and 'non-viable' banks.

COMMITTEE ON TERM LENDING THROUGH CO-OPERATIVES

The COTELCOOP met on six occasions after its formation; the final meeting was held on April 4, 1985. The committee continued to review the progress in implementing the rehabilitation of weak CCBs (evaluation studies). A sub-committee of COTELCOOP was set up in June 1983 to study the problems of rehabilitating primary units in the LDB structure and prepare broad guidelines for various state governments, which they could follow for drawing up individual rehabilitation plans. The sub-committee submitted its report to the committee for its consideration in its meeting held on October 29, 1984. The recommendations of the sub-committee, as approved by the COTELCOOP, were communicated to all SLDBs and the state governments for consideration and implementation.

APPENDIX 6.2

Banking and Allied Laws

BANKING LAWS (AMENDMENT) ACT, 1983

The banking laws (amendment) bill, 1983 proposing amendments to the laws affecting banking, mainly contained in the RBI Act, 1934 and the BR Act, 1949 was passed by both houses of Parliament in December 1983, and consequent on the President giving his assent to the bill, it became the Banking Laws (amendment) Act, 1983. The provisions of the Act, except sections 6, 7, 21, 26, 37 and clauses (V) and (IX) of section 42 came into force from February 15, 1984 in terms of Government of India notification No.F.1/15/83-B.O.I. dated February 14, 1984. The important amendments related to:

(i) Imposing restrictions on individuals, firms and unincorporated associations in accepting deposits from public to protect the interests of the vast multitude of small and uninformed depositors.

(ii) Enabling banks to undertake innovative measures, such as leasing and factoring business.

(iii) Providing nomination facilities to depositors/persons keeping articles in safe custody and those hiring lockers with banks to save legal heirs from hitherto cumbersome and expensive legal procedures to get deposits of the deceased depositors/parties from banks.

(iv) Changing the weekly return showing demand and time liabilities of a bank into a fortnightly return for computing CRR and basing SLR to be maintained by banks on demand and time liabilities as on the last Friday of the second preceding fortnight to which it related, so as to give banks time to visualise their liabilities and arrange for proper maintenance of CRR and SLR.

(v) Imposing a penalty for non-compliance with SLR.

(vi) Authorising the Reserve Bank to determine the mode of valuation of approved securities (one of the components of SLR) in accordance with the monetary policy.

(vii) Protecting the rates of interest charged by banks in pursuance of Reserve Bank of India directives from being challenged in courts as usurious.

(viii) Restricting the tenure of directors of banks to eight continuous years.

(ix) Widening the scope of consideration, which the Reserve Bank may take into account while examining applications for opening of banks.

(x) Giving statutory backing to the arrangements made by PSBs regarding nomination of directors on the boards of assisted units.

(xi) Raising the authorised capital of the DICGC to ₹ 50 crore.

(xii) Enabling the amalgamation of private sector banks with nationalised banks.

The concept of average daily balance, as per the Banking Laws (Amendment) Act, 1983, came to be linked to balances held at the close of business on each day of a fortnight instead of a week, and scheduled banks were required to file fortnightly returns on alternate Fridays of a month instead of each Friday of the month as hitherto. This would give banks more time to visualise their liabilities and arrange for proper maintenance of cash reserves. The change of periodicity for maintenance of average daily balance for CRR purposes from week to fortnight came into effect on March 29, 1985 (the first such fortnight commencing from March 30, 1985). Changes were made in the basis for calculating demand and time liabilities for the purpose of maintenance of SLR. The Reserve Bank was empowered to levy penalty for non-compliance with SLR. A special return in form A was to be filed if the alternate Friday was not the last Friday of the month. Section 7, which amended section 43 of the RBI Act, 1934 provided for the issue of a fortnightly (instead of weekly) press communiquй by the Reserve Bank.

Further, the definition of 'deposit' was widened to include any receipt of money by way of deposit or loan or in any other form, but specifically excluding certain types of deposits so as to enable individuals and unincorporated associations and firms to obtain funds or advances for their legitimate business. Earlier, there were no restrictions on acceptance of deposits by individuals or firms or unincorporated associations of individuals. In the larger interest of the public, and more particularly the vast number of small and uninformed depositors, it was felt necessary to curb the capacity of such unincorporated bodies to accept deposits from the public. Accordingly, the new provisions stipulated that no individual or firm or an unincorporated association of individuals should at any time have deposits from more than the specified number of depositors.

The amendment to the Banking Regulation Act applied to a wide range of provisions. It enabled banking companies to take up business activities specified by the Central Government in addition to those already undertaken as per the BR Act, 1949. It placed a limit on the tenure of directors of a banking company, empowered the Reserve Bank to decide if a change was permissible in the number of directors as also to appoint a chairman when a vacancy arose, if such an appointment was deemed necessary. It enabled the calculation of CRR of non-scheduled banks and SLR of all banks based on demand and time liabilities as on the last Friday of the second preceding fortnight. The amendment precluded granting loans to a company when the banking company's director was a director or any other office holder of such a company or its subsidiary or holding company in which he held a substantial interest. It enabled the Reserve Bank to raise the maximum SLR that it required a bank to maintain to 40.0 per cent and to call for a daily return from any banking company apart from other statutory returns. The Reserve Bank was further empowered to impose penal interest on banking companies that defaulted in maintaining SLR and to carry out a scrutiny of the affairs of a banking company in addition to regular inspections. The amendment also provided for nomination facilities to bank customers for deposit accounts and articles kept in safe custody/safe lockers. Some of these amendments to the two Acts came into force with effect from February 15, 1984.

BANKING LAWS (AMENDMENT) ACT, 1985

The Banking Laws (Amendment) Act, 1985 amending various statutes, mainly the Banking Companies (Acquisition and Transfer of Undertakings) Act, 1970 and 1980 and the Reserve Bank of India Act, 1934, was enacted in December 1985. Some of the provisions of the Act were brought into force with effect from December 30, 1985 and others with effect from May 1, 1986. The more important amendments were: the limit on the borrowing powers of the SFCs was raised from 90.0 per cent of the paid-up share capital to twice the paid-up capital; the ceiling on the paid-up capital and reserves of nationalised banks was raised from ₹ 15 crore to ₹ 100 crore to improve their debt-equity ratio and profitability; and the name of United Commercial Bank was changed to UCO Bank in view of the existence of a bank with the same name in Bangladesh.

By amendment to the relevant sections of the BR Act, 1949 (as applicable to co-operative societies), the above provisions were also made applicable to state co-operative banks/CCBs and RRBs. Further, loans taken by a scheduled state co-operative bank from the NCDC and by an RRB from its sponsor bank would be excluded from 'liabilities' for the purpose of calculating CRR. In terms of section 21, every non-scheduled bank was required to maintain on a daily basis a cash reserve, the amount of which should not be less than 3.0 per cent of its demand and time liabilities in India as obtaining on the last Friday of the second preceding fortnight.

Section 26 led to the amendment to section 24 of the BR Act, 1949. It provided for a change in the basis of calculating the demand and time liabilities for the purpose of maintenance of SLR. Before the amendment, advances, if any, taken by a bank from the Reserve Bank, the SBI and its associates, the IDBI, or the Exim Bank were excluded. After the amendment, the special status for borrowing from the SBI and its associates was removed. Banks now had to calculate the net liability to the banking system.

Several banks were making double use of cash balances — one to meet CRR and again to meet SLR requirements. Banks took advantage of SLR being monitored only on Fridays and computed the excess cash for the purposes of SLR as the difference between the average cash balance required to be maintained and the cash balance actually maintained on Friday, irrespective of the level of balances held on other days of the week, which were generally small. As per the amendment, banks were advised that average excess cash balance was to be computed as the difference between the average cash balance actually maintained and the average cash balance required to be maintained under CRR and this average excess cash balance figure was to be included in the daily SLR position.

The Reserve Bank was empowered to levy penalty for non-compliance with SLR requirements. The rate of penalty for non-compliance was fixed on the same basis as for CRR, that is, first default at 13.0 per cent (3.0 per cent over the Bank Rate) and subsequent continuous default at 15.0 per cent (5.0 per cent over the Bank Rate). The percentage of SLR above the statutory minimum of 25.0 per cent but not exceeding 40.0 per cent of the demand and time liabilities was henceforth governed by the issue of a notification in the official gazette by the Reserve Bank.

Section 37, which incorporated new sections 45Y and 45Z in the BR Act, 1949, provided for framing rules for the period of preservation of banks' records and nomination facilities to bank customers. A banking company was enabled to make payment to the nominee of a deceased depositor the amount of his deposits, to return the articles kept by a deceased person in safe custody to his nominee and to release the contents of a safety locker to the nominee of the hirer of such a locker.

BANKING LAWS COMMITTEE'S REPORT

The banking laws committee, appointed by the Government to review and codify commercial laws affecting banks, had submitted five reports. Of these, the recommendations contained in the committee's report on *hundis* were processed earlier but were not accepted by the Reserve Bank. The Bank's views on the draft warehouse receipts bill, contained in the report on documents of title of goods, were forwarded to the Government during the year. The bill intended to give the status of negotiability to warehouse receipts and, once passed, it was expected to facilitate liberal bank credit against the security of warehouse receipts. As regards the other three reports, the position was:

(i) *Report on Negotiable Instruments Law*

The report was examined by the Bank in consultation with the IBA. Since the recommendations contained in the report were mainly based on the uniform commercial code of the US, which was not suitable for India, it was decided to reject the report and to review the draft negotiable instruments bill, 1960 in light of the laws of the UK and other commonwealth countries, whose legal systems are similar to the Indian legal system. Accordingly, the draft bill *vis-à-vis* the recommendations of the banking laws committee in its report having a direct bearing on the bill were discussed at several meetings of the legal committee convened by the IBA. The draft negotiable instruments bill, 1960 was revised in light of the IBA's views and then forwarded to the Government for its consideration.

(ii) *Report on Personal Property Security Law*

The draft personal property security bill recommended by the banking laws committee in its report on this subject was examined by the informal group comprising representatives from the Reserve Bank and the IBA. As the proposed bill could bring about radical changes, a final decision by the Bank in the matter was envisaged to be taken in light of the reconsidered views received from the IBA.

(iii) Report on Real Property Security Law (RPSL)

The committee had submitted its report on the RPSL, examining lacunae in the law relating to credit and security of immovable properties and the special law relating to extension of rural credit by institutional agencies, the legal framework pertaining to investigation of title to immovable property and the scheme of registration.

SPECIAL LEGISLATION FOR RECOVERY OF BANKS' DUES

The Government accepted the recommendations of the Tiwari Committee to set up special tribunals to adjudicate on issues relating to the recovery of banks' dues. A committee of legal experts was constituted to prepare the draft of the legislation for this purpose. It was decided to vest special powers in favour of banks and FIs similar to those conferred on the IFCI and SFCs under their respective statutes.

BANKING, PUBLIC FINANCIAL INSTITUTIONS AND NEGOTIABLE INSTRUMENTS LAWS (AMENDMENT) BILL, 1988

The banking, public financial institutions and negotiable instruments laws (amendment) bill was passed by Parliament in December 1988 and received the assent of the President in December 1988. The provisions of the Act, except for three sections, were brought into force with effect from December 30, 1988. A notification was also issued by the Government on December 30, 1988 by which banks were required to close their accounts on the expiry of a period of 12 months ending March 31, instead of at the end of the calendar year as hitherto. Accordingly, banks closed their accounts on March 31, 1989, covering the 15-month period from January 1, 1988 to March 31, 1989. The other more important provisions which came into force on December 30, 1988 related to:

(i)   Uniform tenure for directors of nationalised banks, associate banks and other FIs, such as, the IDBI, NABARD, Exim Bank, DICGC and IRBI.

(ii) Increase in the limit of paid-up capital of nationalised banks from ₹ 100 crore to ₹ 500 crore.

(iii) Vesting authority in the Reserve Bank to direct special audits of banks.

(iv) Increase in the rate of interest specified in sections 80 and 117 (C) of the Negotiable Instruments Act, 1881, from 6.0 per cent to 18.0 per cent.

(v)   Removal of legal lacunae in the Nationalisation Act to provide for the amalgamation of one nationalised bank with another nationalised bank and to enable transfer of part business.

Subsequently, the Government by issue of a notification gave effect to the provisions of section 4 of the Amendment Act. The section provided for penalties in the case of dishonour of cheques for insufficient funds in the drawer's account. With effect from April 1, 1989, where any cheque drawn by a person on any account maintained by him with a banker for payment to another person for discharge in whole or in part of any debt or liability was returned by the bank unpaid due to insufficient funds in the account or because it exceeded the arrangements with the bank, such personnel were deemed to have committed an offence and were to be punished with imprisonment for a term that may extend to one year or with a fine that was to extend to twice the amount of the cheque or with both. The section also provided certain safeguards to save harassment to unwary drawers of cheques. It had been, *inter alia*, provided that the drawer could make payment within 15 days on receipt of the notice of return and only if he failed to do so could prosecution be launched. It was also provided that the complaint could be made only by the payee or holder in due course.

APPENDIX 7.1

Commercial Banks: Issues in Customer Service,
Internal Control and Housekeeping

WORKING GROUP ON CUSTOMER SERVICE IN BANKS

The Government set up a group in 1975 to examine the recommendations of the working group on customer service in banks under the chairmanship of Shri R.K. Talwar (Chairman, SBI) and implement the recommendations expeditiously. The Government assessed the appraisal notes prepared by the Reserve Bank and took the following decisions:

(i)   All banks should ensure that the customer should not be asked to go from counter to counter and as far as possible the waiting time should be curtailed.

(ii) All PSBs should take steps to introduce suitable arrangements to encash travellers' cheques issued by any PSB.

(iii) Bankers' cheques issued by PSBs should be freely used to make local inter-bank payments and these should be given the same status as cash for accounting purposes.

Further, the Government asked PSBs to implement 136 of the 176 recommendations of the working group. The Reserve Bank vigorously pursued with commercial banks the issue of improving customer service. The banks, in turn, took steps, such as extending the teller system to more branches, 10 banks introduced regional collection centres at the metropolitan centres for collection of outstation instruments and large-sized branches with poor customer service were allowed to be split on a functional or segment basis.

The performance of banks in the public sector was reviewed in respect of all 136 recommendations of the working group, including those contained in the interim report of the group. The review revealed that 85 recommendations had been implemented by more than 75.0 per cent of the PSBs (excluding the nationalised banks), *i.e.,* 17 banks. Further, progress reports from the banks revealed that the SBI and its associates had implemented more than 100 recommendations, while 14 nationalised banks had implemented more than 90 recommendations. In accordance with the decision of the group, private sector banks, that had implemented only 54 recommendations, were also advised to implement 136 recommendations.

In October 1982 the Reserve Bank called a meeting of the senior executives, in-charge of customer service cells in PSBs and the IBA to discuss critical areas of banking services where concerted efforts were needed to improve customer service. Banks were asked to pay special attention to introduction of the teller system; issue/payment of bank drafts; arrangements for payment of travellers' cheques; collection of outstation cheques and immediate credit against the lodging outstation cheques for collection up to an amount of ₹ 2,500 (of only one cheque at a time), subject to charging normal collection charges. Salary cheques of up to ₹ 2,500 issued by government/quasi-government bodies were to be brought under the purview of the scheme, as were timely submission of statements of accounts to customers; attitude of the staff and general discipline; follow-up action on complaints/suggestions from bank users; and overseeing/monitoring the implementation of the recommendations of the working group on customer service at the bank's level. Banks were also instructed to issue demand drafts to all customers without insisting on their having an account with them, to ensure that teller counters were kept open throughout banking hours, and to ensure the implementation of nomination facilities to deposit holders in all their branches.

Further, all PSBs were advised in August 1987 to ensure that drafts drawn on their branches were paid immediately without waiting for the receipt of relative advice from the issuing branches. They were also advised to pay interest on delays in collection of instruments beyond 14 days from the date of receipt of the instrument for collection and to pay interest beyond a period of 10 days if the instruments lodged and drawn on state headquarters were not collected within 10 days. However, for state capitals in the north-eastern region and Sikkim, where two-way postal transit time was not less than 5 days, the earlier norms of 14 days would remain unchanged. Following the decision by the Government, banks were advised that they should not insist upon a succession certificate when settling the accounts of deceased depositors where the amount of credit did not exceed ₹ 25,000; nevertheless, while settling such claims, banks were advised to observe the usual safeguards, including obtaining an indemnity bond wherever required. All scheduled banks in the private sector, including foreign banks, were also to take appropriate action. Further banks were advised: (i) that payment of drafts should be made promptly, and a passport or postal identification could be accepted as evidence of identity; (ii) to issue cheque books with a larger number of leaves, if customers requested them and to maintain adequate stocks of such cheque books at branches; and (iii) that the Reserve Bank had no objection to their affording immediate credit to more than one outstation cheque to a customer at a time within the overall limit of ₹ 2,500.

From an institutional standpoint, many of the problems afflicting the banking industry, including deterioration in customer services, were traced to shortcomings inherent in the manual system of operations. The deficiencies in the system encouraged bank fraud, which had been growing fast.

To cater to the growing volume of transactions as well as to improve customer service, banks were making concerted efforts to install and operationalise ALPMs in identified larger bank branches. The banks also installed mini-computer systems in their regional/zonal offices to improve control over branches and to monitor their performance. To speed up mechanisation at various levels, industry-level AAPs were drawn for the years 1988 and 1989, and progress was closely monitored by both the Reserve Bank and the Government. Further progress was made during the year in mechanised cheque processing and computerisation of clearing house settlement operations. Mechanised cheque processing at all four metropolitan centres, *viz.*, Bombay, Calcutta, Madras and New Delhi, was completed. The national clearing of MICR outstation cheques was in operation in the four metropolitan centres and one-way clearing of MICR outstation cheques was in operation at another four centres, *viz.*, Ahmedabad, Bangalore, Hyderabad and Nagpur.

CLEARING HOUSES

In the context of frequent disturbances and suspension of clearing house operations in the country on one pretext or another, causing inconvenience to trade and industry, a need was felt to assist the functioning of the clearing houses, with some statutory backing. As the clearing houses were autonomous bodies subject to the rules framed by their members, it was considered necessary to have uniform rules and regulations governing all the clearing houses in the country. With this in view, the IBA appointed a working group to frame draft model rules, with representatives from the DBOD and DGBA of the Reserve Bank.

The idea of a night clearing system or an additional clearing house offered only a short-term solution to the clearing problems. The IBA proposed the establishment of a national clearing authority.

INTERNAL CONTROLS AND SAFEGUARDS FOR PREVENTION OF FRAUD AND MALPRACTICES

The Governor, in a meeting with the chief executives of PSBs on February 25, 1983, expressed concern at the dwindling image of the banking system, the growing number of complaints about poor service, the prevalence of corruption/ malpractice in banks and the increasing incidence of fraud. Banks were, therefore, advised to review and revamp the vigilance machinery, take urgent steps to tone control and supervision, strengthen the MIS, follow-up/inspection/audit arrangements, draw a time-bound programme to clear arrears in balancing of books and take up reconciliation of inter-branch and other accounts. Also, detailed guidelines were issued to the banks in April 1983 for prevention of fraud. Banks were advised to strengthen control mechanisms including the internal audit/inspection machinery, take note of warning signals, such as non-submission or irregular submission of control returns and arrears in housekeeping.

A special investigation cell was set up in the Reserve Bank in May 1983 to carry out, *inter alia*, special investigations into major frauds that came to its notice and to closely monitor the implementation of the guidelines to prevent fraud. The cell carried out investigations of frauds/complaints on a selective basis in banks' offices and findings were communicated to the concerned banks for corrective action and examination of the cases from the staff-angle. The outcome of the scrutiny was also brought to the notice of the Government, wherever necessary. As a sequel to the follow-up action on the reports of the scrutiny/sample surveys, the cell issued instructions/guidelines to banks suggesting safeguards to prevent recurrence of such irregularities.

In terms of the guidelines, advances should not ordinarily be granted beyond the discretionary powers of the authorities or by verbal/telephone instructions. For unavoidable exigencies, a proper record of such sanctions/instructions should be maintained and confirmation from the competent authority obtained within a week. There should be proper investigation into the identity of borrowers, credit granted in accordance with the borrowers' requirements and frequent excess drawals in accounts should be prevented. There should also be supervision to ensure proper end-use of credit.

Regional/zonal offices should be made accountable for lapses by their branches. A system should be introduced to periodically review the working of controlling offices on the effectiveness of their control over branches, submission of periodic returns and the general working of branches.

In view of several complaints of fraudulent withdrawals from savings bank accounts, banks were advised to instruct branches to follow the rules and procedures regarding opening of accounts, withdrawals and maintenance of passbooks. The procedure for reporting instances of fraud from banks to the regional offices of the Reserve Bank and from the latter to the Bank's central office was specified. The banks' attention was drawn particularly to certain aspects of advances against merchandise/bills, which were fraud-prone.

APPENDIX 7.2

Review of the Working of PSBs for the 15-Month Period Ended March 31, 1989

The weak area in banks' functioning was identified as credit administration, resulting from poor or inadequate credit appraisal. Banks carried an increasing load of sticky advances. The incidence of industrial sickness was on the increase and so was the volume of bank advances made to sick units. Consequently, banks' profitability was constantly under strain.

Credit facilities were often extended without regard for the actual need for funds or a realistic assessment of the quantum. Extraneous considerations, such as the connections of the borrowers and the promise of deposit support, often influenced credit decisions. An equally inadequate or neglected area was post-disbursement supervision. Timely receipt and scrutiny of stock statements and periodic verification of securities charged to banks were also not attended to at several branches, particularly the larger ones, where there was the need for close monitoring was crucial.

Banks were continuously exhorted by the Reserve Bank to bring down the level of sticky advances. They were also advised to settle problem accounts on reasonable terms to the extent possible. The health code classification of advances that had almost stabilised was an important instrument for self-monitoring of advances by banks. The quality of the credit portfolio was continuously monitored, both during action plan discussions and also when bank executives called on the Deputy Governor/Executive Director of the Reserve Bank for discussions on inspection findings.

Another area causing concern was profitability. The overall deterioration in the profitability of PSBs is evident from the following table:

TABLE 7.2.1

Indicators of Profitability

(Annualised figures)

	1986	1987	1988–89
Percentage of gross profit to working funds	1.19	1.10	1.00
Percentage of profit after tax to working funds	1.01	0.89	0.80

Source: Reserve Bank of India, *Report on Trend and Progress of Banking in India*, various issues.

Both indicators point to a fall in profitability. While the yield on investments were picking up (it was 7.7 per cent in 1986 and 8.7 per cent during 1988–89) and the average cost of deposits had marginally declined between 1987 and 1988–89, the other two main indicators, *viz.*, average yield on advances and interest spread, did not show any encouraging signs and were declining. Yield on advances declined from 13.0 per cent in 1986 to 12.2 per cent in 1988–89. The average interest spread declined from 3.0 per cent in 1986 to 2.6 per cent in 1988–89. The increasing volume of NPAs was a major constraint on improving profitability.

As a result of heavy loan losses, as revealed by the Reserve Bank's annual financial review, the financial position of eight nationalised banks was considered unsatisfactory. In these cases, even a portion of their deposits had been eroded. In order to strengthen the net worth of nationalised banks, the Government was contributing substantial amounts to their capital. But it was primarily for the banks themselves to streamline their credit administration, improve the quality of their credit portfolio and strengthen their reserves.

A summary position showing the number of branches, domestic deposits (excluding inter-bank deposits), advances, working funds and published net profits of PSBs as at the end of 1987 and March 1989 is given below:

TABLE 7.2.2

Select Indicators of PSBs

(Amount in ₹ crore)

	No. of Branches		Working Funds	
	31.12.1987	*31.3.1989*	*31.12.1987*	*31.3.1989*
SBI and its associates	10,958	11,493	44,270	58,469
Nationalised banks	26,080	27,388	89,754	1,09,866
Total	37,038	38,881	1,34,024	1,68,335

	Domestic Deposits		Domestic Advances		Published Net Profits	
	*25.12.87**	*31.3.89**	*25.12.87**	*31.3.89**	*1987*	*1988–89*
SBI and its associates	32,786	39,923	20,987	26,770	54.83	110.74
Nationalised banks	74,136	91,820	39,983	51,633	206.99	254.16
Total	1,06,922	1,31,743	60,970	78,403	261.82	364.90

Note: * Last Friday of 1987 and March 1989.

Source: Reserve Bank of India, *Report on Trend and Progress of Banking in India*, various issues.

The financial position for March 1989 of all PSBs based on the findings of AFRs is summarised below:

TABLE 7.2.3

Public Sector Banks (March 1989)

	Good (Paid-up capital & reserves intact)	Satisfactory (Reserves affected)	Not Satisfactory (Paid-up capital affected)	Unsatisfactory (Deposits affected)
(1)	(2)	(3)	(4)	(5)
State Bank Group	8	-	-	-
Nationalised Banks	2	3	7	8

Source: Reserve Bank of India, DBOD, internal records.

APPENDIX 8.1

Agricultural Review Committee
(Chairman: Dr A.M. Khusro), August 1989: Key Observations
and Recommendations Pertaining to Rural Credit

INTRODUCTION

The emerging agricultural technologies and secular shifts in the agricultural sub-sectors in favour of commercially-oriented activities were expected to create a robust agricultural economy in India. It was to these changes and the associated problems that the rural credit system was expected to effectively respond. Judging from the steep increase in the quantum of institutional credit over the past two decades and its coverage of the rural population, the objective of weaning away poor peasantry from money lenders had been achieved. The credit pattern that emerged in the process was, however, skewed in favour of larger farmers to the neglect of others. The future thrust had, therefore, to be on preserving the vitality of the credit structure, which showed signs of weakness in the very process of quantitative expansion. The only two structural changes visualised were: merger of RRBs with their sponsor banks and creation of a national apex co-operative bank. To correct regional imbalances, a comprehensive crop insurance scheme and a separate corporation to administer this as well as the ARDCs in certain states were also recommended. These were intended to reinforce the prevalent system of credit delivery.

In a poverty-ridden economy, financial institutions have a responsibility towards the weaker sections, but it was necessary to recognise the limitations of credit as the principal instrument of poverty alleviation. A sharper focus on the selection of beneficiaries and greater transparency in concessions and subsidies was important to avoid leakages. Better co-ordination between development planning and credit planning through a graduation of the 'service area scheme' into a more comprehensive 'development area scheme' became necessary. The 'multi-agency approach' needed to be sharpened where commercial banks and co-operatives supplemented and supported each other. The relative freeing of interest rates, a new and greater thrust on deposit mobilisation and more effective lending and recovery were meant to make the credit system more responsive to emerging development needs.

All these could be achieved only if greater autonomy was given to the credit institutions. The growing inroads into the commercial banking system through excessive directions, controls and interference with the democratic management of co-operatives, which debilitated these systems over the years, were disturbing trends. There was a need to reverse this trend.

COMMERCIAL BANKS AND RURAL CREDIT

With the introduction of social controls in 1967 and the nationalisation of major commercial banks in July 1969, commercial banks started to play a substantive role in dispensing rural credit and began opening branches in rural areas. After nationalisation, rural people came to be served quite extensively by commercial banks.

Commercial banks were mandated to achieve certain targets and sub-targets under priority sector lending. All these targets were achieved by banks by March 1988. The commercial banks' involvement in various poverty alleviation programmes such as IRDP, DRI, SEEUY and SEPUP increased substantially after nationalisation. There was a sharp increase in the number of branches of commercial banks in all states and regions of the country. Since the main objective of branch expansion was largely fulfilled within 15 years after nationalisation, there was a shift in policy from further expansion to consolidation and from quantitative to qualitative improvement.

With the rapid expansion of commercial bank branches in the rural areas, it was felt necessary to emphasise the deployment of deposits mobilised by rural branches locally in the rural areas. The banks were, therefore, advised to achieve a credit-deposit ratio of at least 60.0 per cent in rural and semi-urban branches. An analysis of the regional distribution of commercial bank deposits and advances showed a marked variation in the deployment of credit and mobilisation of deposits.

Commercial banks found that sanctioning and monitoring large numbers of small advances in rural branches was time-consuming and manpower-intensive, and hence a high-cost proposition. Partly because of this, banks were reluctant to post sufficient supervisory and other staff in rural branches. Consequently, supervision of rural advances was neglected. In addition, the staff in rural branches of the commercial banks lacked motivation to work in these areas for various reasons. In such a scenario, it was felt that monetary and non-monetary incentives were necessary to encourage staff to work in rural and semi-urban branches. It was found that efforts by commercial banks to gear up their organisational structure, adopt schematic lending, improve pre-lending appraisal of schemes and launch recovery drives had yielded results.

Under the LBS, 1969, the lead bank acted as a consortium leader to co-ordinate the efforts of all credit institutions in the allotted districts for branch expansion and met the credit needs of the rural economy. Various mechanisms designed under the LBS created better understanding of the problems at the ground level. However, many of the committees under the LBS tended to become more ritualistic than functional.

To improve the quality of rural lending by commercial banks, the Reserve Bank initiated a new approach called the 'service area scheme' in April 1989. The committee preferred to modify this 'service area approach' into a 'development area approach', especially since the scheme had emerged out of the development plan and development-linked credit plan.

The overall profitability of commercial banks had been under strain due to a rise in the cost of deposits, declining yield on advances and rise in establishment expenses. Low interest rates on agricultural advances, lending under IRDP, relatively poor deposit mobilisation in rural branches and lower staff productivity contributed to declining profitability of rural business. However, commercial banks were able to absorb the losses of their rural branch operations through earnings from more profitable businesses. The bottom line was that commercial banks were the only system that was capable of lending to rural and weaker sections at concessional rates, and had the capacity for cross-subsidisation. A major problem associated with such rapid expansion was deterioration in the quality of lending due to various factors.

The committee sounded a note of concern on these issues, such as, tardy scheme preparation, particularly under the anti-poverty programmes; a heavy housekeeping workload without a commensurate increase in support staff; a tendency to rely on walk-in business or sponsoring of loan applications by the branch managers; lack of detailed instructions on several aspects of rural lending contributing to a decline in professionalism in rural branches; and insufficient discretion to the branch managers in taking credit decisions even within the overall framework of guidelines and for which they could be made accountable.

REGIONAL RURAL BANKS

The intent behind creating RRBs was to develop an institutional framework combining the local feel and familiarity with respect to the rural problems and the business organisation skills and modernised outlook of commercial banks. RRBs succeeded in taking banking services to very remote areas that were unbanked and made institutional credit available to weaker sections in these areas.

The working groups periodically set up on RRBs brought out the deficiencies in their working and, in particular, their inability to operate on a viable basis. A closer look at their performance to evaluate their impact on the rural credit structure revealed that the RRBs had developed serious organisational problems. These critical areas related to a steep decline in profitability, poor recoveries and problems relating to management and staff.

Major factors that contributed to erosion of RRBs' profitability included lending exclusively to weaker sections, low interest rate margins and high operating costs involved in handling small loans. In the absence of loans that could yield higher returns, they did not have any scope for cross-subsidisation. Further, wilful defaults, misuse of loans, lack of follow-up, wrong identification of borrowers, extension of *benami* loans, and staff agitations contributed to poor recoveries in RRBs. It was proposed that RRBs should be merged with the sponsor banks. The merger recommendation did not imply dilution of the concern for the common man. On the contrary, the intention was to give the common man a stronger institution to serve his needs more efficiently. The proposed merger involved the question of absorbing the accumulated losses of the RRBs. It was recommended that net loss of each RRB should be shared between the Government of India, the sponsor bank and the state government in the same proportion as their shareholding.

CO-OPERATIVE BANKING SYSTEM

A major weakness of the co-operative credit system was the neglect of the base-level institutions and the tendency of higher-level institutions to look after their own interests, often at the cost of the primaries. The co-operative credit system had neglected its basic responsibility of mobilising deposits, with the lower tiers looking up to the higher tiers for refinance at all levels. Organisational and financial ties in the co-operative system had to be redesigned so that each tier strengthened the other. This meant larger reliance on resources mobilised locally and a lower dependence on higher credit institutions. Dependence on outside funds had made the members less vigilant on the one hand and led to greater outside interference and control on the other. The states had come to gain almost total financial and administrative control over the co-operatives and in the process stifled their growth. This trend had to be reversed.

Some of the results of politicisation were interference in the recovery of co-operative dues or promises to write-off the dues if elected to power and the determination of interest rates on considerations other than financial returns, *i.e.*, operating on populist appeal. Such actions generated a psychology of non-repayment, vitiating the recovery climate and jeopardising the financial interest of credit agencies. Another lever for greater politicisation was the incorporation of certain undesirable provisions in the Co-operative Societies Acts and Rules of various states. Paradoxically, state partnership, which was conceived as an effective measure to strengthen the co-operative credit institutions, paved the way for ever-increasing state control over co-operatives, virtually depriving the co-operatives of their democratic and autonomous character.

SHORT-TERM CO-OPERATIVE CREDIT STRUCTURE

The concept of a three-tier hierarchy in the short-term co-operative credit structure had been accepted and the committee did not see any advantage in abolishing any of the tiers. Although the co-operatives ceased to be the sole purveyor of agricultural credit with the entry of first the commercial banks and later RRBs, they continued to occupy a leading position in disbursing production finance for agriculture.

The profitability of the co-operatives caused considerable concern. The programme of re-organising the PACS based on viability norms had not been completed in some states. Unsatisfactory recovery of dues, low margins and the non-viable nature of many societies were affecting the operations of PACS. The position of the DCCBs and the state co-operative banks was slightly better. Measures to remove the weaknesses of PACS and strengthen them in order that they could function effectively were grouped under: (i) viability; (ii) strengthening of share capital; (iii) mobilisation of deposits; (iv) improving lending policies and procedures; (v) management; (vi) office premises and godowns; (vii) loans for non-productive purposes; (viii) allocation of repayments; and (ix) audit of PACS.

The committee recommended the following lines of action:

(i) An action programme, not extending beyond five years, should be drawn for each of the PACS. All PACS that had not reached a loan business of ₹ 1 lakh should be taken up for specific attention. The programme of development for each PACS should deal with increasing loan business, enlarging its package of profitable non-credit activities, augmenting resources (deposits) and reducing overdues. The Eighth Five Year Plan should, in fact, become the period for the revival of PACS. The states of Maharashtra, Gujarat and Jammu & Kashmir must also undertake the programme or re-organisation at the earliest.

(ii) Each PACS must have at least one full-time, paid and properly trained official, to handle the business activities on a regular basis. Further, the managing committees of PACS must play an important role. The committees would determine the overall policy, appoint the secretary, decide on loans and credits and were accountable to the general body of the society for management of all its affairs.

(iii) The process of re-organisation was envisaged to be in tune with the dynamics of economic development. It was, however, not the intention to recommend another state-sponsored programme of re-organisation of PACS (except in the three states referred to earlier). Further, re-organisation was meant to be voluntary.

(iv) The share capital of PACS in many cases needed to be augmented to meet the growing responsibilities and challenges devolving on them. Most PACS were completely dependent on finance provided by the DCCBs and if the DCCBs were weak, the PACS were starved of finance. While the branches of commercial banks and RRBs were able to mobilise rural savings, the PACS largely failed in this area, with some exceptions, such as those in the states of Kerala and Punjab.

(v) The state co-operative banks/DCCBs could help build infrastructure facilities such as bank counters. As recommended by CRAFICARD, the state co-operative banks/DCCBs should create a co-operative development fund to help the PACS acquire bank counters and safe deposits.

(vi) The PACS should preferably mobilise low-cost deposits, such as savings bank deposits. The PACS should maintain 15.0 per cent (of deposits) liquidity with DCCBs in a special account.

(vii) The crop loan limits of members of PACS may be prepared once in three years, subject to certain precautions, to ensure that any subsequent changes in the crop acreage of members were taken note of. The existing scales of finance fixed by the district-level technical committees of the DCCBs and accepted by commercial banks were found to be inadequate.

Further, PACS should extend credit from their own resources for non-productive purposes, such as consumption loans, up to prescribed limits but only against tangible security. This would greatly help the poor who needed occasional consumption loans. The audit of the PACS should be done by the Registrar of Co-operative Societies free of cost or at a nominal fee.

The following areas were critical to the overall development of the state co-operative credit structure: (i) development of the leadership role of higher tiers; (ii) greater deposit mobilisation; (iii) development of project formulation and investment-planning capability for better and diversified project lending; and (iv) rehabilitation of weak banks.

LONG-TERM CO-OPERATIVE CREDIT STRUCTURE

The structure of the LDBs was not uniform across the country. In some states it was unitary, in other states it was federal, and in two states it was both unitary and federal. The overall performance of LDBs in reaching the plan targets was satisfactory and their progress in lending was steady. After the adoption of multi-agency approach in agricultural lending and the entry of commercial banks in the field, the share of LDBs in agricultural lending showed a decline. Like the short-term co-operative credit structure, this structure for rural lending faced problems that included: (i) overdues; (ii) restricted lending eligibility of units; (iii) inability of banks to become viable because of restricted lending; (iv) consequent deterioration of the profitability of the banks; (v) high cost of raising ordinary debentures and lower margins available on non-schematic lending; and (vi) external interference and government intervention in management.

Another problem that these banks faced was the uneconomical cost of interim finance required for issue of loans before debentures were floated. It was, therefore, recommended that NABARD should provide adequate interim finance at a concessional rate of interest. In most LDBs there was no definite policy with regard to recruitment, appointment, career planning and development of the staff, and they depended on transitory personnel sent on deputation.

THE OVERDUES SYNDROME

The high incidence of overdues in the agricultural credit system had become a major constraint on the expansion and smooth delivery of credit. However, the bulk of the overdues got recovered over time, leaving only a small proportion ultimately becoming irrecoverable. The overall position on recovery of loans continued to be unsatisfactory in respect of all types of credit agencies, although it varied among the different agencies and different regions/states. Recoveries in aggregate were relatively better in the LDBs than in PACS, commercial banks and RRBs (which had the poorest rate). By state, the recovery of agricultural credit was consistently better in Punjab, Kerala and Haryana irrespective of the type of agency dispensing credit, whereas it was far from satisfactory in states such as Manipur, Tripura, Assam and Meghalaya. Similarly, recoveries were better in irrigated areas and where high-value crops were grown. Since recycling was as important as mobilisation of additional resources, effective measures were called for to bring down overdues to the minimum level within a definite time frame.

The dual legal framework for recovery, *viz.*, legislation along the lines recommended by the Talwar Committee in the case of commercial banks and RRBs and the Co-operative Societies Acts in various states for co-operative credit institutions suffered from various shortcomings. Administrative arrangements for recovery through legal measures, such as recovery staff, were inadequate, resulting in heavy arrears in disposal of recovery cases. Besides making the existing legal framework more effective and augmenting the government staff for effecting recoveries, a single common legal framework that covered both co-operatives and commercial banks for the country as a whole, special tribunals at the state level and a single government department in each state to execute the awards obtained through such tribunals were needed.

Providing loans to groups of persons or associations of farmers for a common purpose needed to be facilitated and in fact encouraged. Unlike individual loans, group loans besides being secured by the joint and several liabilities of those constituting the group/association, were also backed by their responsibility, including the moral one to discharge the loan liability. Similarly, there was an imperative need to educate borrowers about the correct use of bank credit and the commercial discipline that went with it.

There was a growing tendency to use agricultural credit as an instrument to achieve short-term populist objectives. Government measures such as write-off of agricultural dues, concessions/relief announced by political functionaries from public platforms, stay orders on legal processes of recovery and disbursement of loans/assets at the hands of political dignitaries in loan *melas* had vitiated the recovery climate. The need for a strong political will could not be over-emphasised if politicisation of the agricultural credit institutions was to be checked. A consensus was also needed among all political parties to ensure that agricultural credit was not used for political purposes. The Government of India and the state governments had to evolve a concrete long-term policy for recovery of agricultural dues and take a firm and objective view on wilful defaulters.

Factors internal to the credit system that directly affected recoveries included defective loan policies and procedures, inadequate supervision over credit and unsatisfactory management. These related to unrealistic scales of finance/unit costs, delays in sanction and disbursement of loans, fixing defective repayment schedules, failure to provide working capital to borrowers under term credit and over-emphasis on the target approach. Several recommendations on streamlining the crop loan system were made by earlier committees and policy decisions taken, but these were not implemented. More attention and effort also needed to be given to linking credit with marketing and processing.

APPENDIX 12.1

Liberalisation Measures Introduced by the Reserve Bank:
1991–92 and 1992–93

TRADE LIBERALISATION

FINANCING OF IMPORTS: SPECIAL REGULATIONS

In view of the difficult foreign exchange reserves position, the Reserve Bank issued a series of instructions stipulating minimum cash margins against LCs and generally regulating the financing of imports. These included the requirements for obtaining prior approval from the Reserve Bank for remittances to be made against imports beyond certain limits or under certain other circumstances.

ROLL-OVER ON FORWARD COVER FOR DEFERRED PAYMENT OF EXPORTS AND IMPORTS

ADs were permitted to enter into forward purchase contracts on a roll-over basis in cases of exports on DPT and for forward sale contracts on a roll-over basis in cases of imports under import licenses issued on DPT as well as for repayment of foreign currency loans. The initial contract could be for six months and thereafter, as each deferred instalment was taken up, the outstanding balance of the forward contract could be extended for a further period of six months. It was decided to allow ADs, on specific requests from customers, to undertake roll-over at shorter intervals to reduce the costs payable by the customer.

DESPATCH OF SHIPPING DOCUMENTS DIRECT TO CONSIGNEES/OVERSEAS AGENTS OF CONSIGNEES

Exporters of precious/semi-precious stones and non-gold jewellery were granted general permission to dispatch shipping documents directly to consignees for consignments not exceeding US$ 25,000 or equivalent in value as against the earlier limit of US$ 15,000.

PERMITTED METHODS OF EXPORT PROCEEDS

Exporters were not normally permitted to receive payments for exports directly from overseas buyers in the form of bank drafts, pay orders, bankers' cheques, personal cheques, foreign currency notes or foreign currency travellers' cheques. The Reserve Bank permitted ADs to handle export documents in cases where their exporter customer had received payment, in the form of bank draft, pay order, banker's cheque or personal cheque drawn by the overseas buyer in favour of the exporter, not exceeding US$ 7,500 per shipment, directly from the overseas buyer, subject to the conditions: (i) the instrument was tendered to the AD within seven days from its receipt and was meant for payment for exports; (ii) export documents were routed through the AD/branch to whom the instrument was presented for realisation; (iii) payment was received in an approved manner; and (iv) export was made only on realisation of the instrument. Applications involving amounts above US$ 7,500 or equivalent per shipment or applications for receiving payments in the form of foreign currency notes or foreign currency travellers' cheques tendered by overseas buyers while on a visit to India required a reference to the Reserve Bank for its consideration.

PROJECT EXPORTS

Between July 1, 1990 and June 30, 1991, the working group on project exports approved 104 proposals valued at ₹ 5,027 crore. These comprised 68 proposals for turnkey contracts valued at ₹ 4,089 crore, 25 proposals for civil construction contracts valued at ₹ 770 crore and 11 proposals for consultancy service contracts valued at ₹ 168 crore. The working group also cleared 33 proposals valued at ₹ 810 crore at the post-award stage.

SUBSIDIARIES/JVs ABROAD AND OPENING OF OFFICES IN INDIA/ABROAD

Between July 1, 1990 and June 30, 1991, five proposals allowing Indian companies to establish their subsidiaries abroad and 25 proposals enabling Indian companies to enter into JVs abroad were cleared. Indian companies were granted approval for opening 32 trading offices and 64 non-trading offices, and posting representatives abroad in 42 cases.

Approval for opening 70 liaison offices, 16 representative offices and 12 project offices in India were granted to foreign companies.

MEASURES TO ATTRACT NRI DEPOSITS

CREDIT TO NON-RESIDENT ORDINARY RUPEE (NRO) ACCOUNTS

The regulations governing operations on NRO accounts by non-residents of Indian nationality/origin and OCBs predominantly owned by such persons were revised as below:

(i)   ADs were permitted to freely allow credit of rupee funds without any limit to NRO accounts maintained by NRIs/OCBs that were lawfully due to the account holder as against the previous limit of ₹ 4,000 a month, with individual credit not exceeding ₹ 1,500, up to which the ADs could allow such credits without prior approval from the Reserve Bank.

(ii)   ADs were advised to call for documentary evidence for individual credits that exceeded ₹ 10,000 in order to ascertain that the transaction was bonafide.

(iii) ADs were also advised to get an undertaking from both existing and new account holders that they would not make available to any person in India any foreign currency against reimbursement in rupees or in any other manner.

NRO ACCOUNT HOLDERS

The limit up to which ADs were empowered to grant loans and overdrafts to their NRI constituents for purposes other than investment, against the security of fixed deposits held in NRO accounts, was increased from ₹ 2 lakh to ₹ 5 lakh.

NRE ACCOUNT HOLDERS

The limit for grant of loans/overdrafts to NRE account holders against the security of their fixed deposits held in NRE/FCNR accounts was raised from ₹ 2 lakh to ₹ 5 lakh and later to ₹ 10 lakh for purposes other than investment. Repayment in such cases was, however, to be made either by adjustment of the NRE/FCNR deposit or by fresh inward remittance from abroad.

ADs were empowered to grant, subject to certain conditions, rupee loans/overdrafts up to ₹ 10 lakh to their NRI customers against security of fixed deposits held by them in NRE/FCNR accounts for the purpose of making direct investment in India on non-repatriation basis in the capital of Indian companies that were either engaged or proposed to engage in manufacturing/industrial activities, hospitals, hotels of three-star or higher grades, shipping, development of computer software and oil exploration services. Earlier, such applications were required to be referred to the Reserve Bank.

LOANS TO RESIDENTS AGAINST SECURITY OF NRE FIXED DEPOSITS

ADs were hitherto required to refer to the Reserve Bank applications for grant of loans/overdrafts to resident individuals/firms/companies in India against collateral of fixed deposits held in NRE accounts. Powers were delegated to ADs permitting them to grant such loans/overdrafts without any limit, subject to the following conditions:

(i) There should be no direct or indirect foreign exchange consideration for NRI depositors who agreed to pledge their fixed deposits to enable the resident individual/firm/company to obtain such loans/overdraft.

(ii) The period of loans should not exceed the unexpired period of maturity of NRE/FCNR fixed deposits accepted as security. In addition, the NRI depositor should furnish an irrevocable undertaking to the AD not to withdraw the deposit during the period of the loan/overdraft.

(iii) The loan/overdraft to be granted should conform to the regulations relating to normal margin, rate of interest depending on the purpose of the loan as stipulated by the Reserve Bank from time to time.

(iv) The loan could be used for personal purposes or for business activities other than agriculture/plantation and real estate.

TRANSFER OF FUNDS BETWEEN NRE ACCOUNTS OF NRIs

Hitherto, the Reserve Bank approval had been required to transfer funds from the NRE account of one person to the account of another person if the two people were close relatives. Powers were delegated to ADs to undertake such transfers if the transfer was for genuine personal purposes, *e.g.*, education of children, gift or personal expenses and the transferor and transferee account holders were resident in the external group of countries or in the same bilateral group country.

If the funds were to be transferred from one bank to another, the transferor bank had to certify the NRE status of the account from which the funds were to be transferred. Transfer of funds as gifts were allowed subject to payment of gift tax, if applicable.

FCNR (A) DEPOSITS

ADs were permitted to pay commission not exceeding one per cent of the deposits mobilised under the FCNR (A) scheme with effect from November 26, 1990. The payment of brokerage was restricted to: (i) deposits mobilised under the pension scheme; and (ii) other deposits of US$ 25.0 million each under the FCNR (A) scheme. Such deposits were required to be kept for a minimum period of two years.

FCNR SPECIAL DEPOSIT SCHEME FOR THE MIDDLE EAST

To meet the requirements of NRIs/OCBs resident in countries of the Middle East, the FCNR special deposit scheme was introduced on August 20, 1990. Under the scheme, ADs were permitted to open accounts only in US dollars in the name of NRIs/OCBs resident in countries of the Middle East, provided the funds for the purpose were transferred to India in an approved manner from the country of residence of the prospective account holder or from any other country in the external group. The accounts could also be opened either by transfer of funds from the existing FCNR/NRE accounts of account holders or by tendering foreign currency notes and/or travellers' cheques, subject to conditions. No restrictions were placed on the number of withdrawals that could be made from these special accounts and, accordingly, no interest was payable on the balances in these accounts. Loans/overdrafts could not be granted against the security of the funds held in these accounts. The other provisions that applied to FCNR accounts were applicable, *mutatis mutandis,* to these special accounts.

Subsequently, it was decided that banks could pay interest on such deposits in cases where there were no further deposits or withdrawals in the same account and the deposits remained with the bank for a minimum period of six months. In other words, such deposit accounts were in the nature of term deposits. In such cases, the rates of interest were the same as was applicable to deposits denominated in US dollars for the period for which the deposits remained with the banks.

FOREIGN CURRENCY (ORDINARY NON-REPATRIABLE) DEPOSIT SCHEME

To provide further incentives and give wider options to NRIs and OCBs for making investments in India, the Reserve Bank introduced with effect from June 17, 1991 a new deposit scheme, *viz.,* the foreign currency (ordinary non-repatriable) deposit scheme. Deposits accepted under the scheme were denominated in US dollars for a fixed period of five years. The rate of interest was one per cent above the ruling applicable rate for FCNR dollar deposits for three years. Certain benefits, such as availability of loans/overdrafts against the security of the deposit and tax exemptions under the Income Tax Act and the Wealth Tax Act, were also available to the depositors. The deposits were also free from gift tax for one-time gifts. Premature withdrawals of the deposit were permissible and the interest rate payable in such cases was the rate ruling on the date of deposit for the period for which the deposit remained with the bank. However, the rupee equivalent of the amount withdrawn or the maturity proceeds of the deposit including interest would be credited to the NRO account of the deposit holder.

INDIA EQUITY FUND UNIT SCHEME: 1990

The UTI was granted permission to enter into an agreement with India Equity Fund Inc. to raise funds abroad up to US$ 100.0 million for investing in units of UTI under its special unit entitled 'India Equity Fund Unit Scheme: 1990'.

NRI BONDS II SERIES BY THE SBI

The SBI was granted permission to issue a second series of NRI bonds to NRIs on non-repatriation basis. The special features of the scheme were:

(i) ADs in India were permitted to grant rupee loans for certain purposes to NRI bondholders against the collateral of the above bonds held by them.

(ii) These bonds could be gifted without restriction and without attracting the provisions of the Gift Tax Act only once, either by the original holder or an NRI transferee to any individual of Indian nationality or origin, whether or not he was resident in India, or to any charitable Trust in India that was recognised under the Income Tax Act, 1991.

(iii) Joint holdings were allowed between NRI and a resident Indian who was not a close relative.

INDIAN OPPORTUNITIES FUND

Indian Bank was granted permission to establish an off-shore fund, *i.e.*, the IOF in the Netherlands in collaboration with Perpetual Chescor, UK to raise funds abroad to the extent of US$ 200.0 million for investing in India in the units of Indbank (off-shore) Mutual Fund established by the Indian Bank.

IDBI CAPITAL BONDS

The IDBI was granted general permission to issue 3-year IDBI Capital Bonds to NRIs on non-repatriation basis, subject to the following conditions:

(i) Neither the capital invested nor the income earned was allowed to be repatriated outside India at any time in future; and

(ii)   All interest accruals and maturity proceeds of the bonds were to be credited to the investor's NRO account maintained with a bank authorised to deal in foreign exchange in India.

RELAXATION IN REMITTANCES FOR MISCELLANEOUS PURPOSES

RELEASE OF FOREIGN EXCHANGE FOR VISITS TO BILATERAL GROUP OF COUNTRIES

Persons visiting the bilateral group of countries for business, study tour, or attendance at a conference, seminar/symposium were allowed to draw their entire exchange quota in free foreign exchange even though *per diem* scales of exchange and the permits issued by the Reserve Bank continued to be expressed in rupees. In the case of permits issued for medical treatment and higher studies, the conversion facilities on a limited scale allowed at that time were continued. Remittances for registration, admission, examination and membership fees continued to be allowed in rupees without any conversion facilities.

MCO FACILITY FOR TRAVELLERS VISITING MAURITIUS UNDER NTS

Indian residents visiting Mauritius under the NTS were permitted to avail of the facility of miscellaneous charges order (MCO) to cover expenses for surface transportation. This facility could be availed of by people travelling in a group of 15 or more, up to a limit of US$ 150 per person.

REFUND OF FOREIGN EXCHANGE CONSERVATION TRAVEL (FECT) TAX

In terms of sub-rule (1) of rule 5 of the FECT tax rules 1987, refund of FECT tax could be claimed within a period of one month from the date of return from foreign travel, for which exchange was released. This time limit for claiming the refund was increased to 90 days from the date of return from abroad.

FOREIGN EXCHANGE FOR HIGHER STUDIES

With effect from June 1, 1990 powers to release exchange for higher studies abroad were delegated to designated branches of PSBs. The total number of branches designated by these banks was 328.

SPECIALISED TRAINING

The period for release of exchange for advanced training in highly specialised medical fields at reputed overseas institutions for medical practitioners/specialists was enhanced from six months to a maximum of twelve months.

ENHANCEMENT OF RIFEE FACILITY AGAINST REPATRIATION
OF MONTHLY PENSION

From April 1990, Indian nationals and persons of Indian origin receiving pension
in foreign exchange from their erstwhile foreign employers and also regularly
repatriating the entire pension amount to India were allowed to utilise up to
25.0 per cent of the pension amount drawn and repatriated to India for purposes
specified under the Returning Indians Foreign Exchange Entitlement Scheme
(RIFEES). The percentage of entitlement for pension amounts drawn prior to
April 1990 and repatriated to India remained unchanged at 10.0 per cent under
the scheme.

DEVELOPMENTS DURING 1992–93

FOREIGN EXCHANGE REGULATION (AMENDMENT) ACT OF 1993

To simplify and remove regulations that hindered the free flow of foreign capital
into India as also investments by Indian companies in JVs overseas, comprehensive
amendments were effected to FERA, 1973 under the following broad categories:

(i)   Some provisions governing the operations of FERA companies in India
       were amended, with the result that the restrictions placed on these
       companies under FERA, 1973 were removed. FERA companies were thus
       placed on par with domestic companies that did not have any foreign
       equity participation or had foreign equity participation up to a level of
       40.0 per cent and did not attract the restrictive provisions of FERA, 1973.

(ii)   Several provisions that imposed restrictions, which hampered the move
       towards convertibility of the rupee, were amended or deleted. Two
       important developments were the deletion of the provision requiring
       foreigners to pay their hotel bills in India in foreign currency and deletion
       of the provision that required payment in rupees for travel to/from India
       by NRIs.

(iii) Certain provisions relating to the enforcement of the Act were amended
       to prevent harassment of people suspected of having violated the
       provisions of the Act.

(iv)   Two new provisions, viz., sections 18A and 73A, were introduced to
       provide better regulation of export of goods on lease or hire and to
       ensure better compliance by ADs of the directions issued by the Reserve
       Bank. Section 73A empowered the Reserve Bank to impose penalties on
       ADs without prejudice to the powers and jurisdiction of the Enforcement
       Directorate.

SIMPLIFICATION OF PROCEDURES UNDER FERA

In another important step, the authority to ADs was simplified in several areas of
remittances, such as: (i) surplus collections of foreign airline companies operating

in India; (ii) remuneration payable to foreign technicians engaged by Indian companies; (iii) advance remittances for import of goods; and (iv) remittances for sundry purposes, such as advertisements, membership fees, examination fees and legal expenses. ADs were permitted to offer forward cover to their overseas investors for direct foreign investment in India, subject to certain conditions, and relaxations were given on dividends from their shareholdings and to residents on balances held in bank accounts with ADs in India, designated in foreign currencies. Remittance of dividend to foreign investors on their shareholdings in FERA companies, which earlier required authorisation by the Reserve Bank, were now permitted to be effected directly by ADs.

The regulations relating to travel abroad for business visits including travel abroad of delegations sponsored by trade bodies, such as the Associated Chambers of Commerce and Industry of India (ASSOCHAM) and Federation of Indian Chambers of Commerce and Industry (FICCI) for conferences/seminars, study tours, training and higher studies and for medical treatment were further liberalised and the procedures and documentation were simplified. ADs were empowered to deal with all these applications directly, without seeking approval from the Reserve Bank.

GENERAL PERMISSION IN SELECT AREAS

EXEMPTION FROM DECLARATIONS/SURRENDER OF FOREIGN CURRENCY ASSETS BY RETURNING INDIANS

Indian nationals and foreign nationals of Indian origin were required to declare to the Reserve Bank all their foreign currency assets, acquired while they were non-residents, on their return to the country permanently. They were also required to close their bank accounts aboard and were permitted to hold other forms of foreign currency assets only with the permission of the Reserve Bank subject to its terms and conditions. Where such persons desired to continue to maintain foreign currency accounts abroad, they had to obtain permission from the Reserve Bank. Non-residents with a minimum stay abroad for a period of one year were exempt from declaring their foreign currency assets to the Reserve Bank even after their return to the country permanently and were permitted to use them without any restrictions. The facility included switching of their foreign investments and investing abroad the income earned on their lawfully acquired foreign assets. As an incentive, such persons bringing foreign currency funds into the country were permitted to transfer their foreign currency funds into the country and maintain foreign currency accounts with banks in India (RFC accounts), and use the funds in such accounts freely without any exchange control restrictions.

LIBERALISED BAGGAGE RULES

The Government reduced the rate of customs duty applicable to 35 specified baggage items from 255.0 per cent to 150.0 per cent *ad valorem*. There was no prescribed condition relating to minimum stay aboard for availing of the concessional rates and the total value of goods eligible for these rates was fixed at ₹ 1.50 lakh.

DEVELOPMENTS IN THE DOMESTIC FOREIGN EXCHANGE MARKET

There were several developments in the domestic foreign exchange market. The regulations relating to the provision of forward exchange cover by ADs were relaxed. They were permitted to: (i) provide forward cover for all genuine transactions; (ii) provide cover for longer periods, *i.e.*, even beyond 180 days, on outright basis without going in for periodic roll-overs after obtaining the Reserve Bank's approval; (iii) undertake fully covered swaps in any convertible currency, against one of the FCNR currencies, with NRI depositors; and (iv) do such swaps between two FCNR currencies.

To ease the pressure on the rupee, banks were advised that the overnight oversold position in the rupee should not exceed US$ one million or its equivalent at the close of business each day. For the purpose of this limit, however, customer purchases and foreign currency purchase for *vostro* funding were excluded.

FOREIGN INVESTMENTS

During the year, foreign investment proposals in high-priority areas were freed of non-tariff restrictions embodied in export obligations to balance dividend repatriation (except for 22 consumer goods industries). Keeping in view the ever-expanding frontiers of global technology, a scheme was introduced that provided for 100.0 per cent foreign equity participation, duty-free import of capital goods and a 5-year tax holiday relating to corporate and income tax. One hundred per cent foreign equity participation in power generation units was also permitted. Indian firms/companies were free to engage the services of foreign technicians without seeking permission from the Reserve Bank, provided the terms of their engagement conformed to certain guidelines. Reservations for the public sector in the areas of mining and mineral extraction were done away with. The new national policy envisaged foreign equity participation up to 50.0 per cent in Indian companies engaged in mining activities and even beyond that in the case of non-captive mines, on a case-by-case basis.

GUIDELINES FOR INVESTMENTS IN PRIMARY AND SECONDARY MARKETS FOR FIIs

In continuation of the process of developing a market-friendly environment for foreign investment, guidelines were set out for FIIs, *i.e.*, pension and corporate or institutional portfolio managers. FIIs were allowed to invest in all the securities traded in the primary and secondary markets, provided they were registered with SEBI, for which SEBI would seek general permission from the Reserve Bank before initial registration was granted. Simultaneously, the FIIs were to file an application, in a specified format, with the Reserve Bank seeking approvals under FERA. Further, the concerned FIIs had to hold a registration of Securities and Exchange Commission or the regulatory organisation for the stock market in the country of domicile/incorporation. SEBI's initial registration was valid for five years and could be renewed.

The general permission from the Reserve Bank, as per the guidelines, would enable FIIs to: (i) open foreign currency-denominated accounts in a designated bank; (ii) open a special non-resident rupee account to which all receipts would be credited; (iii) transfer sums from the foreign currency accounts to the rupee account and vice versa; (iv) make investments in securities in India out of the balances in the rupee account; (v) transfer/repatriate (after tax) proceeds from the rupee account to the foreign currency account; (vi) repatriate the capital, capital gains, dividends and interest income; and (vii) register FII holdings without any further clearance under FERA.

The guidelines also stated that there was no restriction on the volume of investment for the purpose of entry of FIIs in the primary/secondary market. In addition, there was no lock-in period prescribed for the purposes of such investments made by FIIs. Portfolio investments of FIIs in primary or secondary markets were, however, subject to a ceiling of 24.0 per cent of issued share capital for the total holdings of all registered FIIs in any one company, The holding of a single FII in any company was also subject to a ceiling of 5.0 per cent of total issued capital, and for this purpose the holdings of a group of FIIs was counted as holdings of a single FII.

According to the guidelines, disinvestment was permitted only through exchanges in India. All secondary market operations of FIIs were conducted only through recognised intermediaries on the Indian stock exchanges.

INTRODUCTION OF STOCKINVEST FACILITY IN PRIMARY CAPITAL MARKET FOR NRIs/OCBs

The stockinvest facility was provided by ADs to resident Indians. ADs were allowed to issue stockinvest with certain conditions to NRIs and OCBs predominantly owned by the non-residents. NRIs and OCBs could thus avail of the facility to apply for shares/debentures with repatriation benefits.

INVESTMENTS ABROAD BY ADs

The Reserve Bank permitted ADs from August 16, 1993 to invest their funds held in all foreign currency accounts in their books in Treasury Bills and with banks abroad rated for short-term obligations as A1+ by Standard and Poor's or P1 by Moody's. They were also allowed to lend the foreign currency amounts standing in their EEFC and RFC accounts to residents towards their genuine foreign exchange requirements as in the case of funds mobilised under the FCNR (B) Scheme. However, ADs were advised to ensure that the maturities of such deposits and placements were taken into account, along with the maturities of foreign exchange transactions when computing gaps, and to make sure that aggregate gap limits were not exceeded. They had to ensure that investments were made such that the deposit liabilities were promptly met on maturity/demand. The details of investment in Treasury Bills and deposits placed abroad as well as the total balances held by customers in their foreign currency accounts were to be reported periodically.

FOREIGN EXCHANGE RATE QUOTATION SWITCHOVER TO DIRECT QUOTATION SYSTEM

The Reserve Bank and ADs had been using the indirect quotation system for their sale/purchase transactions in foreign exchange. The Reserve Bank decided to switch to the direct system of quotation of exchange rates. Accordingly, from August 2, 1993, the Reserve Bank started to express its exchange rates in terms of rupees per US dollar instead of US dollar per ₹ 100. Simultaneously, the inter-bank and merchant quotations of the ADs were changed to the direct quotation system.

EXTENSION OF FACILITY TO OPEN NRE/FCNR ACCOUNTS

In view of relaxations in the policies and in order to attract more foreign investment, it was decided to extend the facility to open NRE/FCNR accounts, making available the schemes relating to investments in shares and debentures of Indian companies under various investments account schemes to NRIs and their foreign-born spouses.

INVESTMENT BY NRIs IN HOUSING AND REAL ESTATE DEVELOPMENT

To encourage NRI investments, it was decided to allow existing or new private or public limited companies engaged or proposing to engage in the development of plots and construction of residential and commercial premises, including business centres and offices, development of townships, urban infrastructure facilities and manufacture of building materials to issue equity shares and convertible debentures to NRIs up to 100.0 per cent of the new issue with repatriation benefits. OCBs were, however, not eligible for this facility.

Persons of Indian nationality/origin, who were permitted to acquire residential properties only on non-repatriation basis, were now allowed to repatriate the original investment in equivalent foreign exchange in residential properties subject to a maximum of two houses, provided the properties were purchased on or after May 26, 1993, and the properties were not transferred or disposed of by way of sale for a period of three years from the date of purchase.

General permission was granted to NRIs and foreign citizens of Indian origin, whether resident in India or not, to acquire through purchase, inheritance and transfer or disposing of by sale commercial immovable property in India. Repatriation of the original investment in equivalent foreign exchange was also allowed, subject to certain conditions.

General permission was also granted under section 31(1) of FERA, 1973 to foreign citizens of Indian origin, whether resident in India or not, to acquire, transfer or dispose of residential properties (up to two houses) situated in India by way of gift from or to a relative who may be an Indian citizen or a person of Indian origin, whether resident in India or not, subject to the condition that gift tax, if any, will be paid. The above general permission, however, was not available for acquisition of agricultural land/farm house/plantation property situated in India.

SILVER IMPORTS

The Government of India notified on February 8, 1993 a scheme to allow import of silver into the country along the lines for gold imports. NRIs and Indians returning after a stay of six months abroad were allowed to bring in 100 kg of silver as personal baggage after paying duty of ₹ 500 per kg in foreign currency

APPENDIX 13.1

Liberalisation in Exchange Management and Exchange Control

The liberalisation process in the sphere of exchange management and control was continued with vigour during the period from 1993–94 to 1996–97. Simplification of procedures and delegation of authority to ADs were extended in many more areas of operation. There were a number of policy changes with far-reaching implications for the foreign investment, foreign currency non-resident account schemes, euro issues, and portfolio investment by FIIs, which are discussed briefly below.

TRADE LIBERALISATION

REDISCOUNTING OF EXPORT BILLS ABROAD

During 1993–94, ADs were permitted to negotiate BAF with the overseas banks and discounting agencies; or make a similar arrangement with other agencies, including a factoring organisation abroad, without the prior approval of the Reserve Bank for the purpose of rediscounting export bills abroad, provided the rate of interest on the BAF or similar arrangement did not exceed 1.0 per cent over the six-month LIBOR in the case of rediscounting with recourse and 1.5 per cent over the six-month LIBOR in the case of rediscounting without recourse. If the facility was availed of from an overseas factoring organisation, it could only be 'without recourse'. Similarly, exporters were permitted to arrange for lines of credit with overseas banks or any other agency abroad with whom their export bills were discounted without the prior approval of the Reserve Bank, provided the rate of discount did not exceed the spread indicated above and the exporter undertook to get the export bills discounted from the overseas bank or agency only through the branch of an AD in India designated by him for this purpose. ADs were, however, required to advise the Reserve Bank about the terms and conditions of such lines of credit as soon as they were finalised. If the export bills were not paid on the due date, ADs were permitted to remit the amount, equivalent to the value of the bill earlier discounted, to the overseas bank or agency that had discounted the bill, without the prior approval of the Reserve Bank.

REGULATIONS RELATING TO FORWARD CONTRACTS

The regulations governing forward exchange cover were further liberalised during 1993–94. The decision on the period and extent to which an exposure in genuine permissible transactions was to be covered was left to customers. ADs were permitted to book roll-over forward cover as necessitated by the maturity period of underlying transactions, market conditions and the need to reduce the cost to the customer. They were also permitted to substitute orders after satisfying themselves with the circumstances under which the original sale/purchase contracts could not be performed by the customer. In cases where the foreign currency amounts to be covered could not be quantified, ADs were permitted to book forward contracts based on reasonable estimates.

ACU TRANSACTIONS

Settlement of payments towards the import of sugar, fertiliser and pulses from any ACU country was allowed to be made outside the ACU mechanism in any permitted currency. During 1994–95, Indian exporters were permitted to accept payment in free foreign exchange in respect of their exports to ACU countries, provided such payment was voluntarily offered by the importer in the ACU country.

EXPORT FACTORING SERVICE

In 1994–95, the ECGC was permitted to provide non-fund-based export factoring services to exporters holding its policies. The Reserve Bank also approved the scheme evolved by the SBI Factors and Commercial Services Pvt Ltd, Bombay, for providing international factoring services on a 'with recourse' basis.

UTILISATION OF FUNDS IN EXCHANGE EARNERS' FOREIGN CURRENCY (EEFC) ACCOUNTS

Export/trading/super-star trading houses were permitted, with the Reserve Bank's permission, to make advance payments to their overseas suppliers by utilising funds in their EEFC accounts up to 5.0 per cent of their export realisation of the previous year, through a branch of an AD to be designated by them for this purpose.

OVERSEAS JOINT VENTURES/WHOLLY OWNED SUBSIDIARIES

Until 1992–93, Indian companies that wanted to establish JVs/subsidiaries abroad were required to approach the Government for clearance of their proposals. While applications involving equity in the form of cash and/or capitalisation of export proceeds/other receivables up to certain ceilings were cleared by the Ministry of Commerce under the automatic route, the remaining applications were considered in the inter-ministerial committee constituted for the purpose. The Government decided to transfer the work to the Reserve Bank and the procedural details and modalities in this regard were worked out.

CROSS-CURRENCY OPTIONS

To provide greater flexibility to the corporate for managing their foreign currency exposures, it was decided to selectively permit banks to write cross-currency options on a fully covered basis from January 3, 1994. The operational guidelines were laid down by the FEDAI in consultation with the Reserve Bank.

LOANS/OVERDRAFTS BY INDIAN BANKS

The limit for grant of loans/overdrafts in the rupee accounts (*vostro* accounts) maintained with ADs by overseas branches was raised from ₹ 50 lakh to ₹ 150 lakh. Simultaneously, the limit of ₹ 50 lakh for availing of loans and overdrafts by ADs from overseas branches was raised to US$ 5,00,000.

PROJECT EXPORTS

The value limits up to which ADs and Exim Bank could grant approvals at the pre-bid and post-award stages for proposals for project exports were enhanced from ₹10 crore to ₹ 25 crore for the former and from ₹ 50 crore to ₹ 100 crore for the latter.

DELEGATION OF POWERS TO ADs

The broad areas of simplification and delegation of greater autonomy to ADs during the year 1993–94 were as under:

TRAVEL

(i)   ADs were permitted to release exchange for higher studies abroad in all cases where the student had secured admission in an overseas educational institution.

(ii) Powers were also delegated to full-fledged moneychangers to release foreign exchange to Indian businessmen going abroad on business.

(iii) The FTS and NTS under which Indian nationals could avail of exchange facilities up to US$ 500 and US$ 250, respectively, for private visits abroad once in three years were replaced by a scheme of basic travel quota of US$ 2,000 in a year, which could be availed of for one or more visits abroad for private purposes.

OTHER CURRENT ACCOUNT TRANSACTIONS

(i)   Powers were delegated to ADs to write-off outstanding export bills that could not be realised for reasons beyond the exporters' control, subject to certain limitations.

(ii) The monetary ceiling up to which ADs were allowed to make remittances on behalf of their constituents towards cost of services rendered by overseas parties was increased substantially.

(iii) A new scheme for providing non-fund-based export factoring service to exporters who were ECGC policyholders was introduced by ECGC with the approval of the Reserve Bank.

(iv) Value limits for allowing remittances by ADs towards advance royalty or lump-sum royalty on books was enhanced from US$ 500 to US$ 3,000.

(v)   ADs were permitted to allow remittance of commission to buying agents abroad who had been appointed by Indian companies. The scope of powers delegated to ADs to allow remittance of surplus freight collections by airline/shipping companies was widened.

(vi)   The scope of powers for ADs to allow remittances towards remuneration of foreign nationals engaged by Indian companies was widened and the *per diem* rates as well as annual ceilings were dispensed with.

(vii) ADs were permitted to allow remittance facilities for maintenance of non-trading overseas offices of Indian exporters who complied with the stipulated criteria.

(viii) The value limits of ₹ 250 for dispatch of samples of journals and periodicals by airfreight, ₹ 200 for dispatch of other goods by airfreight and postal packets not involving foreign exchange transactions were raised to ₹ 10,000.

(ix)   Powers were also delegated to ADs to allow remittances of gifts/donations up to US$ 500 a year.

(x)   Foreign citizens of Indian origin (whether resident in India or not), holding residential/commercial properties, were granted general permission to let out their properties, subject to the condition that the rental income or proceeds of any investment from such income would not be repatriable.

During 1994–95, the process of delegation of authority by the Reserve Bank to ADs regarding the release of foreign exchange was carried forward and the existing ceilings on various categories of outward remittances were raised. These were: (i) Release of exchange at the rate of US$ 500 *per diem* under the special scale for senior executives and US$ 350 *per diem* under the general scale for others. (ii) The limit for the release of exchange to Indian firms/companies for participation in trade fairs/exhibitions abroad was raised from ₹ 2 lakh to US$ 20,000 or its equivalent. This was also applicable to private printers and publishers. (iii) The limit on remittances by Indian shipping companies towards solicitor's fees/ average adjuster's fees was raised from US$ 5,000 to US$ 10,000. (iv) Remittance for accessing information from international databases up to US$ 10,000 to foreign data service vendors was permitted. With effect from July 5, 1995, ADs were permitted to release exchange for visits abroad for business, participation in overseas conferences/seminars, specialised training, medical treatment and studies, even beyond the scales and the duration prescribed by the Reserve Bank, provided that they were satisfied about the bonafide of the applicant and the need for releasing exchange at the higher rates.

During 1995–96, ADs were permitted to export their surplus stocks of foreign currency notes and coins for realisation of proceeds to private moneychangers abroad in addition to their overseas branches or correspondents. They were allowed to remit commission in cases where an Indian exporter secured an export order through an overseas agent for which payment was made from an escrow account designated in US dollars under the counter-trade arrangement. The ceiling of ₹

15 crore of the aggregate overnight open position to be maintained by ADs was removed with effect from January 1, 1996 and ADs were given the freedom to fix their own open exchange positions, subject to approval from the Reserve Bank. ADs were permitted to renew NRNR deposits along with the interest accrued with effect from October 1, 1994 for a further period ranging from six months to three years. ADs were permitted to allow EEFC account holders to utilise funds held in such accounts for making remittances in foreign exchange connected with their trade and business-related transactions of a current account nature. Banks were accorded the freedom to fix their own aggregate gap limit (AGL) for more efficient management of their assets/liabilities. It was decided to permit select banks with adequate dealing expertise and infrastructural facilities to initiate positions overseas in cross-currency transactions. ADs were now permitted to offer forward cover for interim dividend due to overseas investors on account of direct foreign investment in India and provide forward cover for a period not exceeding two months in respect of new remittable freight collections due to foreign shipping companies. ADs were also permitted to allow the corporate to substitute orders under forward contracts, irrespective of whether or not the original order against which the cover was offered was cancelled.

The process of liberalisation in the external sector that focused on giving greater freedom to banks and the corporate in respect of current account transactions was continued during 1996–97. Besides, ADs were permitted to offer various hedging products to the corporate for hedging loan exposures without prior reference to the Government/Reserve Bank. ADs were permitted to offer cost-effective and risk-reduction option strategies like range forwards and ratio range forwards, subject to the condition that there was no net inflow of premium to the customers. ADs were permitted to use FCNR(B) funds to lend to their resident constituents for meeting their foreign exchange as well as the rupee needs. ADs were also allowed to remit dividend/interest on shares/debentures/bonds held by non-residents on repatriation basis, subject to fulfilment of certain conditions. They were empowered to release exchange/allow remittances on actual basis without the prior approval of the Reserve Bank for: (i) legal expenses; (ii) postal imports; (iii) imports of design and drawings; (iv) establishment of overseas offices; (v) electronic database costs; (vi) maintenance expenditure for journalists stationed abroad; (vii) advertisement costs; and (viii) solicitors' fees. ADs were permitted to (a) borrow up to US$ 10.0 million from their overseas offices/correspondents without any conditions on end-use and repayment of such borrowings, and (b) invest funds in overseas money market instruments up to US$ 10.0 million. To impart flexibility to the corporate and improve liquidity in the forward markets for longer periods (beyond six months), ADs were permitted to book forward cover for exporters and importers based on a declaration of an exposure by the customer. They were allowed to arrange forex-rupee swaps between the corporate and run a swap-book within their open positions/gap limits.

FACILITIES FOR NRIs AND OCBs

INVESTMENT IN INDIAN COMPANIES ENGAGED IN DEVELOPMENT OF HOUSING AND REAL ESTATE

OCBs predominantly owned by NRIs were permitted to invest up to 100.0 per cent in the new issues of equity shares/convertible debentures of Indian companies engaged or proposing to engage in housing and real estate development. Repatriation of the proceeds on disinvestment was permissible after the lock-in period of three years to the extent of the original investment in foreign exchange with the Reserve Bank's approval. In addition, they were permitted to repatriate net profit up to 16.0 per cent arising from the sale of such investment. Repatriation of dividend/interest on equity shares/debentures was permissible without any lock-in period. Earlier, this facility had been available to persons of Indian nationality/ origin outside India for whom the repatriation of proceeds on disinvestment continued to be restricted to the original investment.

INVESTMENT IN SHARES AND BONDS

NRIs and OCBs were allowed to: (i) invest in the schemes of all domestic public sector and private sector mutual funds and also to invest through the secondary market on a repatriation basis after complying with certain conditions; (ii) invest in the bonds issued by PSUs in India with repatriation of both the principal and interest; and (iii) purchase shares of Indian public sector enterprises on a repatriation basis after complying with the necessary stipulations. Also, NRIs in Nepal were permitted to invest in India for which the funds needed to be remitted in free foreign exchange through banking channels. The repatriation or otherwise of such investments was, however, not subject to the existing terms and conditions.

RAISING OF FOREIGN EQUITY THROUGH PREFERENTIAL ALLOTMENT

The Reserve Bank issued revised guidelines in June 1995 for determination of the issue price in respect of shares issued to non-residents by existing Indian companies through preferential allotments, to bring them in line with those issued by the Government of India and SEBI. Accordingly, every preferential allotment of shares by listed companies to foreign investors was to be made at the market price of the shares. As per the revised guidelines, the valuation of such shares, effective 30 days prior to the shareholders' general meeting, was required to be at least the higher of the average of the weekly highs and lows of the closing share prices quoted on a stock exchange for the preceding fortnight or an average of the weekly highs and lows of the closing prices on a stock exchange during the previous six months. For this purpose, the share prices of the stock exchange on which the highest trading volume in respect of the shares of the company were recorded were to be taken into account. The shares allotted on preferential basis were not transferable in any manner for a period of five years from the date of their allotment.

WORKING GROUP ON NRI INVESTMENTS

Six recommendations of the working group on NRI Investments (Chairman: Shri O.P. Sodhani) were implemented during the year 1995–96 to further facilitate NRI/OCB investments: (i) General permission for sale of shares acquired under the portfolio investment scheme was extended to OCBs. (ii) The general permission to NRIs for subscribing to the memorandum and articles of the association of Indian companies engaged in industrial activities was extended to cover other permissible activities. (iii) General permission was granted to ADs to remit sale proceeds of shares kept under pledge for liquidation of outstanding loans. (iv) Housing loan to NRI staff of Indian companies was granted under the staff housing loan scheme. (v) General permission was given for crediting interest on delayed refunds of share application money. (vi) The scope of safe custody of securities on behalf of NRIs was extended to institutional custodians.

NRIs were permitted to invest funds on non-repatriation basis in MMMFs floated with prior authorisation from the Reserve Bank/SEBI.

The following recommendations of the working group on NRI investments were accepted for implementation during 1996–97 to further liberalise investment by NRIs/OCBs: (i) liberalisation of the scheme for 100.0 per cent investment by NRIs in sick units; (ii) general permission for interest free non-repatriable loans from NRI relatives for personal purposes and for business activities; (iii) permission for fund transfers between NRE account holders; (iv) permission to NRIs/OCBs to establish schools and colleges on the same terms and conditions as a resident individual/corporate body; (v) permission for NRIs/OCBs to invest in unlisted companies in non-annexure III industries with full repatriation benefits; (vi) permission for NRIs/OCBs to remit income/interest on investments and deposits in India subject to clearance from the income tax authorities; (vii) permission for NRIs to participate in venture capital activities on the same terms and conditions as foreign investment; (viii) grant of housing loans to NRIs for acquisition/improvement of existing houses on the terms and conditions applicable to residents; and (ix) placing all information relating to NRI/foreign investment on the internet.

JVs/WHOLLY OWNED SUBSIDIARIES ABROAD

The Reserve Bank commenced functioning as the single-window agency for receipt and disposal of proposals for overseas investments by Indian companies from December 1, 1995. Subject to certain conditions, the Reserve Bank processed and cleared, under the fast track route (FTR), within 21 days from the date of receipt of application, proposals involving Indian investment up to US$ 4.0 million contributed through cash remittance and/or capitalisation of exports and the technical know-how fees. Proposals that did not qualify under the FTR were processed by a special committee constituted by the Reserve Bank.

The guidelines for Indian direct investment in JVs and wholly owned subsidiaries abroad under the FTR clearance scheme were further modified in 1996–97. Foreign exchange earnings other than from exports and export/foreign exchange earnings (track records) of parent/subsidiary companies were also to be taken into account for determining eligibility under the FTR. The other conditions regarding fulfilment of prudential norms, eligibility criteria and feasibility reports, were, however, kept in view while considering proposals under the FTR.

REMITTANCE OF INCOME ON INVESTMENTS

The remittance of current income/interest earned by NRIs and OCBs on investments made in India and deposits with Indian companies and banks, which was of non-repatriable nature, was permitted in a phased manner over a three-year period.

REMITTANCE OF SURPLUS PASSAGE COLLECTION

Off-line carriers and their general sales agents in India, with appropriate permission from the Reserve Bank, were permitted to stock and sell their tickets to travellers in India and also remit surplus fare collection without limit.

OTHER RELAXATIONS

CAPITAL ACCOUNT TRANSACTIONS

(i)   The limit up to which the Reserve Bank permitted repatriation of capital assets at the time of retirement of foreign nationals who were resident in India on grounds of employment was raised from ₹ 5 lakh to ₹ 10 lakh. The ceiling on annual instalments for remittance of the remaining assets was increased from ₹ 2.5 lakh to ₹ 5 lakh.

(ii)   The monetary ceilings on proposals for project exports and export of services on cash terms by Exim Bank and ADs were revised substantially.

(iii)   The limit of US$ 1.0 million or its equivalent on oversold position of rupees against foreign currencies was raised to ₹ 15 crore. The ceiling was also applicable to over-bought positions.

HOLDING OF FOREIGN CURRENCIES BY RESIDENTS

The Government of India on January 5, 1994 granted general permission to persons resident in India to hold for personal purposes, in addition to the amount allowed to be held for numismatic purposes, foreign currencies up to an equivalent of US$ 500 held or acquired by them. Accordingly, the Reserve Bank granted general permission to residents to take out of India foreign currencies equivalent to US$ 500.

INTER-BANK FOREX CLEARING SYSTEM

The Reserve Bank initiated the process of establishing a clearing house for inter-bank foreign exchange transactions that initially took up transactions in US dollars for clearing followed by other major currencies. Trial runs for the clearing system, based on actual data, commenced in September 1995 with initial participation by six ADs.

MARKET INTELLIGENCE CELL

The Reserve Bank set up a market intelligence cell to study and closely monitor developments in the Indian foreign exchange market. The cell received from the ADs, on a daily basis, information on forex transactions, which were analysed and followed up.

APPENDIX 13.2

Features of United Exchange Rate System

LERMS, which came into effect from March 1, 1992, was replaced by unified exchange rate system with effect from March 1, 1993. The salient features of the new arrangement were:

(i)   Effective March 1, 1993, all foreign exchange transactions (receipts/ payments), both under current and capital accounts of the BoP, would be put through by ADs at market-determined rates of exchange. Foreign exchange receipts/payments would, however, be subject to exchange control regulations; foreign exchange receipts should be surrendered by residents to ADs except where residents had been permitted, either under a general or special permission of the Reserve Bank, to retain them either with banks in India or abroad. Foreign exchange would be sold by ADs for permissible transactions.

(ii)   The regulations laid down in the exchange control manual, as amended from time to time, would continue to remain in force. In terms of the instructions contained in paragraph 8.2 of the exchange control manual (volume I), ADs should maintain, at the close of business each day, square or near-square positions in each foreign currency. Further, ADs should not have an oversold position in rupees against foreign currencies in excess of US$ 1 million or its equivalent (subject to the relaxations related to customer purchases and purchases for funding *vostro* accounts) at the close of business on each day. If any AD was observed to have violated these provisions or had built up balances in his *nostro* accounts in violation of the provisions of paragraph 8.3 of the manual, the Reserve Bank would take appropriate action.

(iii)   The Reserve Bank's sale of foreign exchange to ADs was to be only for purposes approved by the Government. ADs would be free to retain the entire foreign exchange receipts surrendered to them for being sold for permissible transactions and were not required to surrender to the Reserve Bank any portion of such receipts.

(iv)   The Reserve Bank would sell US dollars to any authorised person at its offices/branches for meeting foreign currency payments at its exchange rate based on the market rate only for purposes that were approved by the Central Government. The Central Government had approved the following purposes for sale of US dollars by the Reserve Bank:

(a)   Debt-service payments on government account.

(b)   As an arrangement in transition:
  •   to meet 40.0 per cent of the value of imports under advance licences, imprest licences and replenishment (REP) licences for the import of raw materials for gem and jewellery exports, as per

instructions to be issued by the Department of Economic Affairs (DEA), and

- to meet the full value of imports under Exim scrips and REP licences and other licences treated on par with Exim scrips.

(v) The Reserve Bank would buy spot US dollars from any authorised person at its offices/branches referred to in the aforesaid order at its exchange rate. The Reserve Bank would not ordinarily buy spot pound sterling, deutsche mark (DM) or Japanese yen. It would not ordinarily buy forward any currency. Any offer of foreign currency to the Reserve Bank would be governed by the provisions of paragraph 9.6 of the exchange control manual. If the offer was not covered by the aforesaid provisions, the AD could approach the Department of External Investments and Operations (DEIO) at Bombay.

(vi) No forward sale in any currency would be made by the Reserve Bank to ADs. It would, however, be prepared to enter into swap transactions under which it would buy US dollar spot and sell forward for two to six months.

(vii) The purchases/sales of US dollars would be made by the Reserve Bank in multiples of US\$ 5,000 with a minimum of US\$ 25,000. The procedure for such sales/purchases would be the same as was being followed, except that for purchases from the Reserve Bank, a revised format had to be used.

(viii) Forward commitments/swaps: All outstanding forward commitments and swap liabilities in respect of transactions in the inter-bank market and with the Reserve Bank as on February 27, 1993, would be honoured at the contracted rates. Customer forward contracts would also be honoured at the contracted rate unless cancelled by the customer.

(ix) FCNR accounts: There was no change in the regulations relating to FCNR deposits. The Reserve Bank would continue to provide exchange risk cover.

(x) Other non-resident accounts: There was no change in the regulations relating to these accounts. The operations on these accounts would be at market-determined exchange rates.

(xi) RFC accounts: The existing instructions in terms of which foreign currency accounts with banks in India were allowed to be maintained would continue. No rupee finance was admissible on the security of funds in these accounts.

(xii) Exim scrips/REP licences/Advance licences: The purchase of Exim scrips and other eligible licences valid for import from Caucasus and Central Asia (CCA) at a reasonable premium might be considered.

(xiii) Asian Clearing Union (ACU): The rates of exchange for transactions with countries belonging to the ACU would be at rates announced by the

Reserve Bank. Such rates would be determined based on the prevailing market rates.

(xiv) Bilateral trade arrangements: Rupee trade and payment arrangements, wherever they existed, would continue for the period announced by the Reserve Bank from time to time.

(xv) Market intervention: The Reserve Bank might also undertake, at its discretion, purchases/sales of foreign exchange in the market.

APPENDIX 17.1

Constitution of the Board for Financial Supervision

I. COMPOSITION

Chairman	*Governor*
Full-time Vice-Chairman	Deputy Governor
Ex officio members	Other Deputy Governors
Four full-time members of the	(i) Two from the Reserve Bank.
rank of Executive Directors	(ii) Two from the fields of finance, banking, law or audit.

The BFS[1] was to be assisted by the newly set up Department of Supervision (DoS), an independent department within the Reserve Bank that would report directly to the BFS. The department would draw its personnel from the Reserve Bank, but also take personnel from outside to the extent necessary, either on deputation or through direct recruitment. This way, the expertise available within the Reserve Bank as also outside could be blended and taken advantage of.

The BFS would undertake supervision over different segments of the financial sector comprising commercial banks, FIs, NBFCs and para-banking organisations, such as subsidiaries and mutual funds of banks.

II. SUPERVISION

(i)   Prepare independent inspection programmes for different institutions.

(ii)   Undertake scheduled and special onsite inspections and offsite surveillance, and ensure follow-up and compliance.

(iii) Determine the criteria for the appointment of statutory and special auditors and appoint them, and also assess audit performance.

(iv)   Undertake special studies, write reports, analyse data and provide resource support.

(v)   Collect, process and disseminate market trends and developments (business intelligence).

(vi)   BFS would have the powers to inspect a gamut of activities of banks, FIs and NBFCs. It would be expected to comment on their compliance with the laws, rules, regulations, policies, directives, guidelines and instructions applicable to them. It would, however, carry out supervisory intervention only in the implementation of the regulations in the areas of credit management, asset classification, income recognition, provisioning, capital adequacy, treasury operations and financial viability

---

1. As approved by the Central Board of Directors, Reserve Bank of India on February 12, 1993.

of banks, institutions and other segments of the financial sector. It would also deal with financial sector fraud. After inspection on matters other than these, the relevant points would be conveyed to other departments of the Reserve Bank for information and necessary action.

III. SUPERVISORY POWERS

(i)   Removal of managerial and other persons excluding top personnel, such as the chairman, managing director, executive director and director, under section 36 AA of the BR Act, 1949.

(ii)   Recommend suspension of business.

(iii)   Recommend to the Reserve Bank about amalgamation, merger or winding up.

(iv)   Call for information and returns.

(v)   Issue directives and impose penalties in areas referred to in [II(vi)] above.

(vi)   These supervisory functions, however, would not include powers of rescheduling, de-licensing and other matters not listed in (III) above. These shall continue to be exercised by the concerned departments of the Reserve Bank.

(vii)   The supervision would not extend to co-operative banks. In the case of the exchange control functions of the Reserve Bank, however, the BFS might conduct inspection but would not, on its own, exercise the power of supervisory intervention.

(viii) The BFS, being only a supervisory body, shall deal only with supervision and not with credit and monetary policy or the regulatory and development functions of the Reserve Bank as also monitoring, thereof.

(ix)   The Reserve Bank would frame regulations regarding the conduct of business of the BFS.

(x)   The Annual Report on the functioning of the BFS would be submitted to the Central Board of Directors of the Reserve Bank. Supervision by such a quasi-autonomous Board, exclusively dedicated to supervision, was proposed to be undertaken with greater professional expertise, paying focused attention to compliance.

APPENDIX 17.2

Statement on Irregularities and Fraudulent Transactions in Banks and Other Financial Institutions During 1991-92: Chronology of Events

March 20, 1991	The Governor, Reserve Bank of India, orders scrutiny of operations of certain banks with reference to the practice of dealing in securities through pieces of paper — Bankers' Receipts — without actually holding securities against them.
April–May 1991	The Reserve Bank inspectors carry out scrutiny in these banks and recommend issuing guidelines to banks to ensure that the practice of Bankers' Receipts is not misused. The Governor orders immediate issue of instructions.
July 26, 1991	Detailed guidelines for securities transactions are issued. The circular, among other things, calls on banks to form an internal investment policy, keeping in view the Reserve Bank guidelines. Banks are also asked to confirm compliance with the guidelines after getting the policy approved by their Board.
July–December 1991	Banks, including Standard Chartered Bank and the SBI, indicate compliance with the Reserve Bank guidelines. Standard Chartered Bank issues three letters (August 26, 1991, September 4, 1991 and December 20, 1991) indicating its Board's acceptance. The SBI confirms compliance on October 8, 1991. (It is normal practice for the Reserve Bank of India to follow up compliance of circulars during the course of annual inspection or through annual statutory audit. In fact, individual banks are expected to have their own internal control systems to ascertain, *inter alia*, compliance with the Reserve Bank circulars). By December 1991 as many as 51 banks acknowledge and 24 banks forward their investment policies to the Reserve Bank. Ten more banks formalise their investment policies, but do not forward their compliance to the Reserve Bank.
January 27–February 4, 1992	Reports are received regarding possible violations of the Bankers' Receipts circular. Investigations are undertaken, at the Governor's instance, of the Bank of Karad, Bank of Madura and Andhra Bank.

February 1–29, 1992   BSE Sensitive Index goes up from 2302 to 3017.

March 1–9, 1992   BSE Sensitive Index further goes up from 3017 to 3547.

March 3, 1992   Investigations indicate continuance of practice of Bankers' Receipts in these three banks. The Governor expresses displeasure and suggests drastic action. A decision is taken to issue a final warning to the erring banks.

March 9, 1992   The Governor expresses concern at a meeting in Hyderabad at the sharp rise in share prices.

March 10, 1992   Against the background of the information available on banks' wrongdoings, the Governor holds a meeting of the chief executives of financial institutions and the SBI. He urges them to consider appropriate steps to identify the sources of funds that were fuelling speculation.

March 13, 1992   The Governor reiterates, in Madras, the need for corrective measures to cool the overheated market due to excessive speculation.

March 16, 1992   At the Governor's instance, the Executive Director, Kum. V. Visvanathan obtains from the Chairman, SBI, a statement of the current account of Shri Harshad Mehta maintained at the SBI's Bombay main branch. Kum. Visvanathan informs the Governor, who, in turn, advises the SBI Chairman to monitor the transactions of Shri Harshad Mehta. The Chairman places Mehta's account under continuous monitoring.

March 30, 1992   Bank of Karad, Bank of Madura and Andhra Bank, where irregularities of Bankers' Receipts and securities operations were uncovered, are cautioned. They are given a final opportunity to improve their position.

April 1, 1992   Shri Harshad Mehta meets the Governor. He mentions certain difficulties he has been facing with the SBI. The SBI Chairman explains that the difficulties were because he had not allowed roll-over to Mehta. The Governor concurs with the SBI's stand.

April 2, 1992   The Reserve Bank deputes an officer to the SBI, to investigate, *inter alia*, the purchases of government securities by SBI on the eve of the hike of coupon rates. The officer asks for the reconciliation statement for the bank's investments as at March 31, 1992. The bank indicates that investments were reconciled only up to January 1992. The SBI is asked to reconcile accounts as on March 31, 1992 and furnish the statement to the Reserve Bank. The Chairman and his officers arrange for the reconciliation, as a result of which a gap of nearly ₹ 1,022 crore is uncovered between the books in the PDO and the SBI. Shri Harshad Mehta is summoned by the officers of the SBI to reconcile the account. He pays ₹ 622 crore between April 13 and April 24, 1992.

April 23, 1992	The press breaks the story on irregularities in securities transactions relating to the SBI and the broker Shri Harshad Mehta.
April 23–May 4, 1992	The Reserve Bank trails the cheques through which Shri Harshad Mehta paid the SBI and finds that the funds had come via ANZ Grindlays Bank. On examining further, the Reserve Bank finds that the cheques were issued by the National Housing Bank (NHB).
April 30, 1992	The Governor appoints a committee under the Deputy Governor, Shri R. Janakiraman, to look into the securities irregularities. The Finance Minister announces the same.
May 4 and 5, 1992	The Reserve Bank's follow-up of cheques reveals that in 1992, the NHB had engaged in arbitrage transactions. The Chairman, NHB declares that he was unaware of these transactions on May 4, 1992. The NHB submits details of the transactions, which indicate that Shri Harshad Mehta was to deliver certain securities or pay a corresponding amount on May 5, 1992. Roll-over was not permitted to the broker.
May 18 and 19, 1992	The Reserve Bank convenes a bankers' roundtable for Bankers' Receipts reconciliation.
May 31, 1992	Janakiraman Committee submits its first interim report.
April 1993	Janakiraman Committee submits its final report.

APPENDIX 17.3
Prudential Norms for NBFCs

In pursuance of the recommendations of Shah Committee, 1993, the following prudential norms for NBFCs were put in place.

INCOME RECOGNITION

The policy on income recognition to be objective, it had to be based on a record of recovery. Income from NPAs might not be recognised merely on the basis of accrual. An asset would become non-performing when it ceased to yield income. Income past due but not received within a period of six months was not to be booked until income was actually received. Assets were to be classified as non-performing based on recovery record. Interest on NPAs should not be booked as income if the interest had remained outstanding for more than six months on and from March 31, 1995. The basis of treating a credit facility as NPA should be as under:

TERM LOAN BEYOND ONE YEAR

If the interest amount remained past due for six months, the term loan was to be treated as an NPA. Where the instalment was overdue for more than six months, the entire outstanding loan inclusive of unpaid interest, if any, should also be treated as an NPA.

LEASE RENTAL, HIRE-PURCHASE INSTALMENT

Where lease rentals/hire-purchase instalments were past due for six months, the entire dues from the lessee/hirer were to be treated as an NPA. A bill was to be treated as an NPA if it remained overdue and unpaid for six months. All other credit facilities in the nature of short-term loans were to be treated as NPAs if any amount to be received in respect of such a facility remained past due for a period of six months,

ACCOUNTING FOR INVESTMENTS

All investments in securities were to be bifurcated into current investment and long-term investment. Current investment was readily realisable and intended to be held for not more than one year from the date on which the investment was made. Current investment was to be valued at the lower cost and market value for each individual investment. A long-term investment was defined as one other than current investment, which should be valued at cost. However, provision for diminution should be made to recognise a decline other than temporary. In the value of long-term investment, such reduction should be determined for each individual investment. Unquoted shares were to be valued at cost or break-up value of the share as per the last audited balance sheet of the company concerned, whichever was less. Investments in units of mutual funds that were not quoted in the market should be valued at the lower cost or the latest NAV declared by the mutual fund for each scheme. Commercial paper and Treasury Bills should be valued at carrying cost. Unquoted debentures, depending on the tenor, were to be treated as long-term loans or other credit facilities for the purpose of income recognition and asset classification.

CAPITAL ADEQUACY

The ratio of capital to risk-weighted assets and off-balance sheet items should be a minimum of 6.0 per cent by March 31, 1995 and 8.0 per cent by March 31, 1996.

CREDIT RATING

The NBFCs and RNBCs were required to get rated at least once every year for fixed deposits by one of the following three credit rating agencies and secure a minimum rating as indicated below:

Name of the Credit Rating Agency	Minimum Rating
CRISIL	FA –
ICRA	MA –
CARE	CARE BBB(FD)

Source: Reserve Bank of India, Department of Non-Banking Supervision (DNBS).

While companies with NOFs of ₹ 2 crore and above had to get the rating by March 31, 1995, those having NOFs below ₹ 2 crore had the option to get the rating by March 31, 1996.

As per the instructions issued by the Reserve Bank, the capital of these companies would comprise two tiers. Tier I would consist of paid-up equity capital and free reserves, and tier II capital of preference shares, revaluation reserves, general provisions and loss reserves in excess of the required amounts, and hybrid debt capital instruments/subordinated debts, if any. Preference shares had characteristics similar to equity capital, as the shareholders' funds were subordinated to the claims of creditors. Revaluation reserves served as a cushion against unexpected losses, but these were less permanent and could not be considered as core capital. Revaluation reserves arose from revaluation of assets, such as premises and marketable securities. The extent to which the revaluation reserves could be relied upon as a cushion for unexpected losses depended only upon the estimates of the market value of the relevant assets, subsequent deterioration in the market value or forced sale. Therefore, the Reserve Bank thought it prudent to consider revaluation reserve at a discount of 55.0 per cent for inclusion in tier II capital. It was advised by the Reserve Bank that if general provisions and loss reserves were not attributable to actual diminution in the value of specific assets and were available to meet unexpected losses, they could be included in tier II capital. However, general provisions and loss reserves would be admitted up to a maximum of 1.25 per cent of weighted risk assets. Hybrid debt capital instruments comprised a number of capital instruments that combined certain characteristics of equity and debt, and they could be included in tier II capital.

SUBORDINATED DEBT

To be eligible for inclusion in tier II capital, the instrument should be fully paid-up, unsecured, subordinated to the claims of other creditors and not redeemable without the consent of the supervisory authority of the NBFCs. These instruments carried fixed maturity; they should be subjected to progressive discount in tier II capital as under:

Where the date of maturity is beyond 5 years	50.0 per cent
Beyond 4 years but does not exceed 5 years	60.0 per cent
Beyond 3 years but does not exceed 4 years	70.0 per cent
Beyond 2 years but does not exceed 3 years	80.0 per cent
Beyond 1 year but does not exceed 2 years	90.0 per cent
Where date of maturity does not exceed one year	100.0 per cent

Source: Reserve Bank of India, Department of Non-Banking Supervision.

Subordinated debt capital would be limited to 50.0 per cent of tier I capital and tier II capital would not exceed Tier I capital.

Assets classified as NPAs were based on recovery record and needed to be classified as standard assets, sub-standard assets, doubtful assets and loss assets. Norms had been prescribed for provisioning of the last three categories of assets.

RISK-WEIGHTED ASSETS AND OFF-BALANCE SHEET ITEMS

Risk-weighted assets mean the weighted aggregate of funded and non-funded items as furnished below. The degree of credit risks expressed as percentage weights was assigned to the balance sheet and conversion factors to off-balance sheet items. The value of each asset item was to be multiplied by the relevant weights to arrive at risk-adjusted assets and off-balance sheet items as detailed below:

On-Balance Sheet Items	*Percentage Weights*
Cash and bank balance including FDs and CDs	0.0
Investment in government and approved securities	0.0
Shares, debentures, bonds, units of mutual funds	100.0

contd...

concld.

Current assets	
Stock on hire, inter-corporate deposits, other secured loans and advances considered good, bills purchased/discounted and others to be specified	100.0
Loans and advances fully secured by company's own deposits, loans to staff	0.0
Fixed assets net of depreciation	
Assets leased out, premises, and furniture and fixtures	100.0
Other assets	
Income tax deducted at source, advance tax paid	0.0
Interest due on government securities, and others to be specified	0.0

Source: Reserve Bank of India, Department of Non-Banking Supervision.

OFF-BALANCE SHEET ITEMS

The credit risk exposure attached to off-balance sheet items had to be calculated by multiplying the face amount of each item by the credit conversion factor as indicated in table below.

Nature of Item	*Credit Conversion Factor*
Financial and other guarantees, partly-paid shares and debentures, bills discounted/rediscounted, lease contracts entered into but yet to be executed	100
Shares, debenture underwriting obligation, other contingent liabilities	50

Source: Reserve Bank of India, Department of Non-Banking Supervision.

APPENDIX 17.4

Reserve Bank of India (Amendment) Act, 1997: Major Features

In pursuance of Khanna Committee recommendations, the Reserve Bank of India (Amendment) Act, 1997 with regard to the NBFCs was characterised by:

(i)   NBFCs were clearly defined. Institutions carrying on agricultural or industrial activity as their principal business were excluded from the definition.

(ii)   The minimum NOFs of ₹ 25 lakh and Reserve Bank registration were prescribed as entry point norms.

(iii)   Existing NBFCs had to apply for registration by July 8, 1997. Their business could, however, be carried on, unless registration was refused.

(iv)   NBFCs with NOFs of less than ₹ 25 lakh were given three years to reach that level; the three-year period was extendable by three more years at the Reserve Bank's discretion.

(v)   The Reserve Bank had powers to cancel registration, but NBFCs had the right to appeal to the Central Government.

(vi)   NBFCs had to maintain liquid assets in specified securities on a daily basis; liquid assets were to be maintained as per the existing norm of 5.0 and 10.0 per cent of their deposits outstanding as at the end of the last working day of the second previous quarter, depending on the category and regulatory status of NBFCs. The Reserve Bank penalised NBFCs for any shortfall. The percentages were increased in a phased manner to 10.0 and 15.0 per cent effective January 1 and April 1, 1998, respectively.

(vii)   NBFCs had to create a reserve fund and transfer not less than 20.0 per cent of their net profit to the reserve fund every year.

(viii)   The Reserve Bank could direct NBFCs on issues such as disclosures, prudential norms, credit and investments.

(ix)   For violation of any provisions of the RBI Act, the Reserve Bank not only could prohibit NBFCs from accepting deposits, but also ask them not to sell or, transfer their properties and assets without its prior permission for a period of six months.

(x)   The Reserve Bank could file a winding-up petition against an NBFC if it failed to pay its debt or was disqualified from carrying on business.

(xi)   The Company Law Board could adjudicate and pass orders in case of non-repayment of deposits/interest by NBFCs.

(xii)   Nomination facility was made available to depositors of non-banking institutions.

(xiii)   Unincorporated bodies engaged in financial activities could not accept deposits from April 1, 1997. They could, however, accept deposits from their relatives and borrow from specified institutions. Existing deposits were to be repaid within three years from April 1, 1997 extendable by one more year on merit.

(xiv) Unincorporated bodies could not issue advertisements for soliciting deposits.

(xv) NBFCs could be penalised for carrying on business without a registration certificate and non-compliance with directions/orders of the Reserve Bank and Company Law Board. Similarly, unincorporated bodies could also be subjected to pecuniary penalty and imprisonment for committing a breach of the provisions of the Act.

Enclosures

ENCLOSURE 1

The Reserve Bank of India (1981–1997)

I. GOVERNORS

Name	Period	
	From	*To*
Dr I.G. Patel	01–12–1977	15–09–1982
Dr Manmohan Singh	16–09–1982	14–01–1985
Shri A. Ghosh	15–01–1985	04–02–1985
Shri R.N. Malhotra	04–02–1985	22–12–1990
Shri S. Venkitaramanan	22–12–1990	21–12–1992
Dr C. Rangarajan	22–12–1992	22–11–1997

II. DEPUTY GOVERNORS

Name	Period	
	From	To
Shri P.R. Nangia	29–12–1975	15–02–1982
Shri M. Ramakrishnayya	02–01–1978	31–01–1983
Shri A. Ghosh	21–01–1982	20–01–1992*
Dr C. Rangarajan	12–02–1982	20–08–1991
Dr M.V. Hate	12–03–1982	11–03–1985
Shri R.K. Kaul	01–10–1983	30–09–1986
Dr P.D. Ojha	29–04–1985	28–04–1990
Shri P.R. Nayak	01–04–1987	31–03–1992
Shri R. Janakiraman	16–05–1990	15–05–1993
Shri S.S. Tarapore	30–01–1992	30–09–1996
Shri D.R. Mehta	11–11–1992	21–02–1995
Shri S.P. Talwar	07–11–1994	30–06–2001
Shri R.V. Gupta	02–05–1995	30–11–1997
Dr Y.V. Reddy	14–09–1996	31–07–2002
Shri Jagdish Capoor	01–01–1997	30–06–2001

* From 15–01–1985 to 04–02–1985 Shri A. Ghosh was Governor.

III. DIRECTORS OF THE CENTRAL BOARD

Name	Date of first nomination	Date of retirement
Shri S.L. Kirloskar	15–01–1969	18–03–1983
Shri M.P. Chitale	06–09–1972	18–03–1983
Dr V. Kurien	06–09–1972	18–03–1983
Prof M.L. Dantwala	23–02–1973	21–07–1981
Shri A.N. Haksar	23–02–1973	18–03–1983
Dr Bharat Ram	23–02–1973	18–03–1983
Dr D.P. Singh	13–11–1975	18–03–1983
Shri Akbar Hydari	13–11–1975	18–03–1983
Dr B. Venkatappiah	22–07–1977	18–03–1983
Shri Jehangir P. Patel	22–07–1977	18–03–1983
Air Chief Marshal P.C. Lal (Retd.)	22–07–1977	21–07–1981
Shri M.V. Arunachalam	22–07–1977	28–03–1994
Shri Chhedi Lal	02–04–1979	01–04–1983
Dr K.N. Raj	02–04–1979	01–04–1983
Shri R.N. Malhotra	19–04–1980	12–10–1982
Shri M. Narasimham	12–10–1982	01–07–1983
Shri Jaharlal Sen Gupta	18–03–1983	28–03–1994
Dr S.R. Sen	18–03–1983	28–03–1994
Shri Ashok Kumar Jain	18–03–1983	28–03–1994
Shri R.P. Goenka	18–03–1983	28–03–1994
Dr A.S. Kahlon	18–03–1983	28–03–1994
Shri Raghu Raj	18–03–1983	28–03–1994
Shri A.V. Birla	18–03–1983	28–03–1994
Shri R. Ganesan	18–03–1983	28–03–1994
Shri P.N. Devarajan	18–03–1983	28–03–1994
Shri P.K. Kaul	11–07–1983	08–02–1985
Dr K.A. Naqvi	29–11–1983	23–04–1984
Shri S. Venkitaramanan	11–03–1985	06–04–1989
Shri S.S. Marathe	16–01–1986	28–03–1994
Shri M.S. Patwardhan	16–01–1986	28–03–1994
Shri G.K. Arora	06–04–1989	08–01–1990

contd...

concld.

Name	Date of first nomination	Date of retirement
Dr Bimal Jalan	09–01–1990	02–01–1991
Shri S.P. Shukla	03–01–1991	05–11–1991
Shri Montek Singh Ahluwalia	06–11–1991	31–08–1998
Shri Y.H. Malegam	28–03–1994	Continuing
Dr J.J. Irani	28–03–1994	27–11–2000
Shri P.N. Dhar	28–03–1994	27–11–2000
Shri E.A. Reddy	28–03–1994	27–11–2000
Shri R.N. Tata	28–03–1994	27–06–2006
Shri K.L. Chugh	28–03–1994	27–11–2000
Shri Mumtaz Ahmad	28–03–1994	27–11–2000
Dr Sardara Singh Johl	28–03–1994	27–11–2000
Dr C.H. Hanumantha Rao	28–03–1994	27–11–2000
Dr Bhai Mohan Singh	28–03–1994	27–11–2000
Dr M.L. Shahare	28–03–1994	27–11–2000
Dr Amrita Patel	28–03–1994	27–06–2006
Shri Gopala Ramanujam	28–03–1994	29–07–1994
Shri Vipin Malik	28–03–1994	27–11–2000
Shri G. Ramachandran	10–05–1995	27–11–2000

Source: Reserve Bank of India, internal records.

IV. MAJOR PORTFOLIOS HELD BY DEPUTY GOVERNORS

Name	Period of office	Major portfolios held
Shri P.R. Nangia	29–12–1975 to 15–02–1982	Department of Administration, Personnel Policy Department, Exchange Control Department, Bank's Training Establishments, Inspection Department, Legal Department, Management Services Department, DICGC and Premises Department.
Shri M. Ramakrishnayya	02–01–1978 to 31–01–1983	Agricultural Credit Department, Agricultural Refinance and Development Corporation, Rural Planning and Credit Department, Department of Currency Management, Department of Government and Bank Accounts (excluding Foreign Currency Accounts), Department of Expenditure and Budgetary Control and Management Services Department.
Shri A. Ghosh[1]	21–01–1982 to 20–01–1992	Department of Banking Operations and Development, Industrial Credit Department, Department of Administration, Personnel Policy Department, Exchange Control Department, Inspection Department, Legal Department, Premises Department, Department of Financial Companies, Management Services Department, DICGC, Secretary's Department and Department of Expenditure and Budgetary Control.

contd...

---

1. From 15–01–1985 to 04–02–1985, Shri A. Ghosh was Governor.

contd...

Name	Period of office	Major portfolios held
Dr C. Rangarajan	12–02–1982 to 20–08–1991	Department of Economic Analysis and Policy, Credit Planning Cell, Department of Statistical Analysis and Computer Services, Secretary's Department, Department of Government and Bank Accounts (Foreign Accounts Division), Department of External Investments and Operations, Rural Planning and Credit Department, Urban Banks Department, Management Services Department and DICGC.
Dr M.V. Hate	12–03–1982 to 11–03–1985	Rural Planning and Credit Department, Urban Banks Division of DBOD, Premises Department, Inspection Department, Department of Government and Bank Accounts (except Foreign Accounts Division), Department of Expenditure and Budgetary Control, Department of Non-Banking Companies, DICGC and Department of Financial Companies.
Shri R.K. Kaul	01–10–1983 to 30–09–1986	Department of Currency Management and Management Services Department.

contd...

contd...

Name	Period of office	Major portfolios held
Dr P.D. Ojha	29–04–1985 to 28–04–1990	Rural Planning and Credit Department, Urban Banks Department, Department of Financial Companies, DICGC, Department of Expenditure and Budgetary Control, Inspection Department, Premises Department, Department of Government and Bank Accounts (except Foreign Accounts Division) and Department of Currency Management.
Shri P.R. Nayak	01–04–1987 to 31–03–1992	Department of Currency Management and Rural Planning and Credit Department.
Shri R. Janakiraman	16–05–1990 to 15–05–1993	Department of External Investments and Operations, Industrial and Export Credit Department, Exchange Control Department, Department of Expenditure and Budgetary Control, Department of Government and Bank Accounts, Inspection Department, Management Services Department, Department of Financial Companies, Urban Banks Department, Rural Planning and Credit Department, Premises Department, DICGC, Department of Currency Management, Personnel Policy Department and Department of Administration (including Training).

contd...

contd...

Name	Period of office	Major portfolios held
Shri S.S. Tarapore	30–01–1992 to 30–09–1996	Department of Economic Analysis and Policy, Credit Planning Cell, Department of Statistical Analysis and Computer Services, Internal Debt Management Cell, Department of Financial Companies, Secretary's Department, Legal Department, Department of External Investments and Operations, Financial Institutions Cell, Bank's Training Establishments, Rural Planning and Credit Department, Department of Expenditure and Budgetary Control, Industrial and Export Credit Department, Premises Department, Management Services Department, and Urban Banks Department.
Shri D.R. Mehta	11–11–1992 to 21–02–1995	Department of Banking Operations and Development, Industrial and Export Credit Department, Urban Banks Department, Premises Department, Rural Planning and Credit Department, Management Services Department, DICGC, Setting-up of the Board for Financial Supervision, Financial Sector Reform Cell, Exchange Control Department, Inspection Department, Central Security Cell,

contd...

contd...

Name	Period of office	Major portfolios held
		Supervision, Department of Administration, Personnel Policy Department, Department of Currency Management and Premises Department.
Shri S.P. Talwar	07–11–1994 to 30–06–2001	Department of Banking Operations and Development, Department of Banking Supervision, Industrial and Export Credit Department, Department of Information Technology, Department of Administration and Personnel Management, Human Resources Development Department, Inspection Department, Management Services Department, Urban Banks Department, Premises Department, Department of Currency Management, DICGC, Central Security Cell, Department of Financial Companies, Financial Institutions Cell, and Legal Department.
Shri R.V. Gupta	02–05–1995 to 30–11–1997	Rural Planning and Credit Department, Exchange Control Department, Legal Department, Department of Information Technology, Department of Currency Management, DICGC, Premises Department, Central Security Cell, Urban Banks Department, Department of Administration

contd...

concld.

Name	Period of office	Major portfolios held
		and Personnel Management, and Human Resources Development Department.
Dr Y.V. Reddy	14–09–1996 to 31–07–2002	Department of Economic Analysis and Policy, Credit Planning Cell (later known as Monetary Policy Department), Department of Statistical Analysis and Computer Services, Internal Debt Management Cell, Department of External Investments and Operations, Department of Government and Bank Accounts, Department of Expenditure and Budgetary Control and Secretary's Department.
Shri Jagdish Capoor	01–01–1997 to 30–06–2001	Industrial and Export Credit Department, Central Security Cell, Department of Administration and Personnel Management, Human Resources Development Department (including Training), Rural Planning and Credit Department, Exchange Control Department, Urban Banks Department, Department of Currency Management and DICGC.

Source: Reserve Bank of India, internal records.

ENCLOSURE 2

Ministry of Finance (1981–1997)

I. FINANCE MINISTERS

Name	Period	
	From	*To*
Shri R. Venkataraman	14–01–1980	15–01–1982
Shri Pranab Kumar Mukherjee	15–01–1982	31–12–1984
Shri Vishwanath Pratap Singh	31–12–1984	24–01–1987
Shri Rajiv Gandhi	24–01–1987	25–05–1987
Shri N.D. Tiwari	25–05–1987	25–06–1988
Shri S.B. Chavan	25–06–1988	02–12–1989
Prof Madhu Dandavate	06–12–1989	10–11–1990
Shri Chandra Shekhar	10–11–1990	21–11–1990
Shri Yashwant Sinha	21–11–1990	21–06–1991
Dr Manmohan Singh	21–06–1991	16–05–1996
Shri Jaswant Singh	16–05–1996	01–06–1996
Shri P. Chidambaram	01–06–1996	21–04–1997

Source: Government of India, Ministry of Finance.

II. MINISTERS OF STATE FOR FINANCE

Name	Year/s
Shri Jagannath Pahadia	1980–81
Shri S.S. Sisodia	1980–81
Shri Maganbhai Barot	1980–82
Shri R.B. Pattabhi Rama Rao	1982
Shri Janardhana Poojari	1982–88
Shri S.M. Krishna	1984
Shri B.K. Gadhvi	1986–89
Shri Brahm Dutt	1987
Shri Ajit Panja	1988–89
Shri Edwardo Faleiro	1988–89
Shri Rameshwar Thakur	1991
Shri Dalbir Singh	1991
Shri Shanta Ram Potdukhe	1991
Dr Abrar Ahmed	1993–94
Shri M.V. Chandrashekara Murthy	1993–95
Dr Debi Prosad Pal	1995–96
Shri M.P. Virendra Kumar	1997
Shri Satpal Maharaj	1997–98

Source: Government of India, Ministry of Finance.

III. FINANCE SECRETARY/SECRETARY (EA)

Name	Year/s
Shri R.N. Malhotra, Finance Secretary	1980–82
Shri M. Narasimham, Finance Secretary	1982–83
Shri P.K. Kaul, Finance Secretary	1983–85
Shri S. Venkitaramanan, Finance Secretary	1985–89
Shri G.K. Arora, Finance Secretary	1989
Dr Bimal Jalan, Finance Secretary	1990
Shri S.P. Shukla, Finance Secretary	1990–91
Shri Montek Singh Ahluwalia, Secretary (EA)	1991
Shri Montek Singh Ahluwalia, Finance Secretary	1993–98

Source: Government of India, Ministry of Finance.

IV. CHIEF ECONOMIC ADVISER

Name	Year/s
Dr Bimal Jalan	1986–88
Shri Nitin Desai	1988–90
Dr Deepak Nayyar	1990–91
Dr Ashok Desai, Chief Consultant and Secretary	1991–93
Dr Shankar N. Acharya	1993–98

Source: Government of India, Ministry of Finance.

ENCLOSURE 3

Chronology of Major Events (1981–1997)

1981

March	The committee to review arrangements for institutional credit for agriculture and rural development (CRAFICARD) in its report recommended establishment of a National Bank for Agriculture and Rural Development (NABARD).
July 11	Bank Rate revised from 9.0 per cent to 10.0 per cent, forming a package of anti-inflationary measures.
August 24	Central Records Documentation Centre (CRDC) set up in Pune.
November	Government of India negotiated with IMF for a loan facility of SDR 5 billion under the EFF to tide over the balance of payments crisis.
November 7	New central office building (NCOB) of the Reserve Bank at Bombay (now Mumbai) was inaugurated by the Union Finance Minister, Shri R. Venkataraman.

1982

March	The new bank branch licensing policy for three fiscal years, *i.e.*, from 1982–83 to 1984–85, came into operation.
July 12	NABARD was established.
September 15	Dr I.G. Patel relinquished office as Governor.
September 16	Dr Manmohan Singh assumed charge as Governor.
December	A committee to review the working of the monetary system set up by the Reserve Bank (Chairman: Prof Sukhamoy Chakravarty).

1983

May	A special investigation cell was constituted in the Reserve Bank to facilitate speedy investigation of major frauds/complaints which came to its notice.
September	Detailed guidelines were issued to commercial banks by the Reserve Bank regarding their role in implementation of the scheme for providing self-employment to the educated unemployed youth (SEEUY).

November   National Clearing Cell (NCC) was set up.

December   The expert committee on exports and imports appointed by the Reserve Bank submitted its final report.

1984

January 1   The system of prescribing a sterling rate schedule was abolished. ADs were permitted to quote exchange rates for merchant transactions in pound sterling on the basis of market conditions as in the case of other currencies.

February 1   Urban Banks Department (UBD) was set up in the Reserve Bank.

February 15   Various provisions of the Banking Laws (Amendment) Act, 1983 came into effect. The remaining provisions came into effect from March 29, 1985.

May 1   Government of India terminated the extended fund facility (EFF) borrowal arrangement with the IMF, six months ahead of its date of expiry.

August 24   DNBC renamed as the Department of Financial Companies (DFC).

August   The committee on mechanisation in banking industry submitted its report.

December 31   The committee on agricultural productivity in Eastern India set up by the Reserve Bank in March 1983 submitted its report.

1985

January 14   Dr Manmohan Singh relinquished office as Governor on his being appointed as the Deputy Chairman of the Planning Commission.

January 15   Shri A. Ghosh took over charge as Governor and relinquished charge on February 4, 1985.

February 4   Shri R.N. Malhotra assumed the office of Governor. Shri A. Ghosh reappointed as Deputy Governor.

March 31   Reserve Bank of India completed 50 years of service to the nation.

April 10   The committee to review the working of the monetary system (Chairman: Prof Sukhamoy Chakravarty) submitted its report.

June 1	The golden jubilee celebrations of the Reserve Bank of India inaugurated by the Prime Minister, Shri Rajiv Gandhi.
December 19	The long term fiscal policy (LTFP) announced by the Government.
December 30	Some provisions of the Banking Laws (Amendment) Act, 1985, were brought into force. The other provisions were made effective from May 1, 1986.

1986

June 2	Central Security Cell (CSC) established in the Reserve Bank.
November	The first auction of 182-days Treasury Bills held.

1987

January 13	Working group on money market (Chairman: Shri N. Vaghul) submitted its report.
June	Magnetic ink character recognition (MICR) technology introduced in Bombay (now Mumbai).
December 28	Indira Gandhi Institute of Development Research (IGIDR) set up and started functioning.

1988

April 12	Securities and Exchange Board of India (SEBI) constituted by the Central Government.
April 25	Discount and Finance House of India Ltd (DFHI) commenced business operations.
July 9	National Housing Bank (NHB) set up.
October 8	Credit authorisation scheme (CAS) replaced by credit monitoring arrangement (CMA).

1989

April 1	A new strategy of rural lending, namely, service area approach (SAA), became operational.
August	The agricultural credit review committee (ACRC) submitted its report.
August 29	The Reserve Bank signed a wage settlement with the AIRBEA (class III employees).

September 30   Committee on currency management (Chairman: Shri P.R. Nayak) submitted its report.

November 27   The Reserve Bank signed a wage settlement with the AIRBWF (class IV employees).

1990

January 16   The Reserve Bank announced its decision to introduce a pension scheme in lieu of CPF on an optional basis for serving employees. The scheme came into effect from November 1, 1990.

August   The financial institutions cell was set up to function as a nodal unit for matters pertaining to financial institutions.

July-September   An amount of SDR 487 million in the reserve tranche of the IMF was drawn in three instalments on July 20, August 14, and September 4, 1990.

October 17   Gold held by the Reserve Bank as its assets revalued closer to international market price in contrast with the erstwhile statutory price of ₹ 84.39 per 10 fine grammes.

December 22   Shri R.N. Malhotra relinquished charge of the office of the Governor.

                  Shri S. Venkitaramanan took charge as Governor with effect from the same day.

1991

January 23   As part of concerted efforts towards liquidity management, India negotiated with the IMF a drawal of SDR 717 million under the CCFF and SDR 552 million under the first credit tranche of IMF's stand-by arrangement.

May   Government of India sold 20 tonnes of gold with a repurchase option to the Union Bank of Switzerland (UBS) to enable it to borrow US$ 200.0 million for six months.

July onwards   The Government and the Reserve Bank initiated far-reaching policy initiatives to achieve macroeconomic stabilisation through fiscal correction, structural adjustment and financial sector reforms. The Centre's regular budget for 1991–92 laid the foundation for the process of fiscal adjustment, including a number of non-fiscal reform measures.

July	India shipped 47 tonnes of gold to the Bank of England (BoE) to raise US$ 405.0 million.
July 1	BCCI (Overseas) Ltd, Bombay, suspended all its banking operations in India.
July 1 and 3	The exchange rate of the rupee was adjusted downwards in two stages. In terms of pound sterling (*i.e.,* the intervention currency) it worked out to 17.38 per cent and 18.7 per cent in US dollar terms.
July 3	Bank Rate revised to 11.0 per cent from 10.0 per cent.
August	Government of India appointed a high level committee on the financial system (Chairman: Shri M. Narasimham).
August 21	The Government of India entered into a 20-month stand-by arrangement with the IMF for an amount equivalent to SDR 1,656 million.
October	Government negotiated a structural adjustment loan (SAL) with the World Bank for US$ 500.0 million, and a hydrocarbon sector loan for US$ 250.0 million with the ADB.
October 8	Bank Rate revised to 12.0 per cent.
November	The committee on the financial system (Chairman: Shri M. Narasimham) submitted its report.

1992

January 1	A scheme of post-shipment export credit denominated in foreign currency (PSCFC) was introduced.
February	SEBI reconstituted as a Board with statutory powers by the Government.
March 1	The liberalised exchange rate management system (LERMS) (*i.e.,* a dual exchange rate system) was introduced.
April	Internal Debt Management Cell (IDMC) was created within the Secretary's Department in the Reserve Bank.
April	The Reserve Bank announced detailed guidelines on a phased introduction of norms for capital adequacy, income recognition and provisioning for banks.
April 21	Credit policy circular for the first half of the year 1992–93 enunciated adoption of an active internal debt management policy.

April 30	The Reserve Bank set up a committee (Chairman: Shri R. Janakiraman) to investigate the irregularities in funds management and securities transactions by commercial banks and financial institutions, and in particular, in relation to their dealings in government securities, public sector bonds, UTI units and similar instruments. In all, the committee on securities operations of banks and financial institutions submitted six reports, the last one being in April 1993.
May 5	Memorandum of agreement signed between India and the Russian Federation for rupee-rouble debt retirement.
May 20	The committee on licensing of new co-operative banks (Chairman: Shri S.S. Marathe) submitted its report.
August 1992	Joint Parliamentary Committee (JPC) constituted to look into the irregularities in the securities operations of banks and financial institutions.
October 1	IDMC became an independent policy-making unit within the Reserve Bank.
November	A system of electronic clearance settlement and depository (ECSD) introduced by the Reserve Bank.
December 10	Repos auctions of central government securities commenced.
December 21	Shri S. Venkitaramanan relinquished office as Governor.
December 22	Dr C. Rangarajan took over as Governor.

1993

January	The Reserve Bank issued guidelines for grant of licences for opening new banks in the private sector.
January 8	The Foreign Exchange Regulation Act (FERA), 1973, was amended through an ordinance promulgated on January 8, 1993, which was replaced on April 2, 1993 by the Foreign Exchange Regulation (Amendment) Act, 1993.
March 1	A unified exchange rate system was introduced by merging dual exchange rates under the LERMS.
March 15	The gold bond scheme, 1993, (introduced by the Government of India) opened for public subscription and it closed on June 14, 1993.
April	The high level committee on the balance of payments (Chairman: Dr C. Rangarajan) submitted its report.

June 13	Guidelines were issued to NBFCs on prudential norms, income recognition, accounting standards and provisioning for bad and doubtful debts.
July 17	The Supreme Court in its judgment upheld the validity of the Chit Funds Act in its entirety.
December 22	A new department, *i.e.*, Department of Supervision (DoS), was set up in the Reserve Bank.

1994

January 17	Government of India floated zero coupon bonds of five-year maturity on auction basis.
June 1	Reserve Bank set up a committee on technology issues relating to payments system, cheque clearing and securities settlement in the banking industry (Chairman: Shri W.S. Saraf).
June 27	In order to develop a vibrant secondary market in government securities, the Securities Trading Corporation of India Ltd (STCI) was set up.
June 30	National Stock Exchange (NSE) commenced trading operations in debt securities.
August	India's external current account convertibility was formalised through declaration of Article VIII status in the IMF.
September 9	The first supplemental agreement between the Government of India and the Reserve Bank signed on September 9, 1994 placed a limit on the former's access to the Reserve Bank for accommodation through issue of *ad hoc* Treasury Bills. This agreement also envisaged discontinuation of the automatic monetisation of budget deficit through issue of *ad hoc* Treasury Bills over a period of three years.
November	An expert group on foreign exchange market (Chairman: Shri O.P. Sodhani) set up to recommend measures for the growth of an active, efficient and orderly foreign exchange market and to suggest introduction of new derivative products.
November 16	The Board for Financial Supervision (BFS) was constituted under the aegis of the Reserve Bank, with the Governor as the chairman, for an integrated and efficient supervision over banks, financial institutions and financial companies.
December	RBINet was inaugurated.

1995

January 1	Two new departments, namely, Human Resources Development Department (HRDD) and Department of Information Technology (DIT), were formed in the Reserve Bank.
February	Department of Supervision (DoS) introduced an offsite computerised monitoring system (OSMOS) as a first step towards a new strategy of strengthening supervision of banks under the direction of BFS.
February 3	Bharatiya Reserve Bank Note Mudran Private Ltd (BRBNM) was established as a fully-owned subsidiary of the Reserve Bank, with registered office at Bangalore (now Bengaluru). It commenced printing of currency notes at the Mysore press on June 1, 1996 and December 11, 1996 at Salboni (West Bengal).
March 1	DFHI and STCI started functioning as PDs in government securities market.
April 12	BFS took up supervisory responsibility for all-India financial institutions.
June 1	Four more PDs became operational. These were, the SBI Gilts Ltd, PNB Gilts Ltd, Gilts Securities Trading Corporation Ltd, and ICICI Securities.
June 14	Banking Ombudsman Scheme was introduced by the Reserve Bank under the provisions of the Banking Regulation Act, 1949 for an expeditious and inexpensive resolution of complaints about deficiency in banking services.
July 7	BFS with the assistance of DoS started supervising NBFCs.
July 14	The share capital of NABARD was increased from ₹ 330 crore to ₹ 500 crore, with contribution of ₹ 85 crore each from the Government of India and the Reserve Bank.
July 17	A system of delivery *versus* payment (D*v*P) for transactions in government securities was introduced in Mumbai to synchronise the transfer of securities with cash payment.
September 20	The expert group to review internal control and inspection/ audit system in banks (Chairman: Shri Rashid Jilani) submitted its report.
November 23	Private sector was allowed to set up MMMFs to provide greater liquidity and depth to the money market.

1996

January 7 — Banks were granted freedom to decide their own foreign exchange overnight open position limits subject to approval by the Reserve Bank. Earlier, a uniform limit of ₹ 15 crore was applicable for each bank irrespective of the nature and volume of business and the structure of the bank's owned funds.

January 18 — The committee on electronic fund transfer system (Chairperson: Smt. K.S. Shere) submitted its report.

April 3 — The Reserve Bank set up a foreign exchange market technical advisory committee.

July 1 — The Institute for Development and Research in Banking Technology (IDRBT) was established at Hyderabad by the Reserve Bank as an autonomous centre.

July 2 — Banks were given the choice to fix their own interest rates on domestic term deposits with a maturity of over one year with a view to provide them greater flexibility in determining their term deposit rates.

July — Measures were initiated to address the problem of Y2K both within the Reserve Bank and banking industry as a whole.

October — Reserve Bank became a shareholding member of the Bank for International Settlements (BIS), Basel, Switzerland.

October 9 — A market intelligence cell was started in the Exchange Control Department of the Reserve Bank to closely study and monitor the developments in the foreign exchange market.

December 31 — Guidelines for setting-up satellite dealers (SDs) announced with the aim of strengthening the infrastructure in the government securities market, enhancing liquidity and turnover and providing a retail outlet.

1997

January 27 — A technical advisory committee on government securities market was constituted by the Reserve Bank.

January 30 — Government decided to permit foreign institutional investors (FIIs) to invest in government dated securities.

March 26 — In terms of the second supplementary agreement signed between the Reserve Bank and the Government of India, the system of *ad hoc* Treasury Bills to finance budget deficit was discontinued from April 1, 1997.

March 31   Government of India introduced (from April 1, 1997) 14-day Intermediate Treasury Bills to provide state governments, foreign central banks and special bodies with an alternate arrangement for investment of their temporary cash surpluses.

Documents

List of Documents

(1) D.O. letter No. 295-SSEA/82 dt. 14/2/82 from Ministry of Finance to the Governor Dr. I.G. Patel

(2) Telex message no. COF (CPC)11969 dt. 25/5/85 from Dy. Governor Dr. C. Rangarajan to Shri S. Venkitaramanan, Finance Secretary.

(3) D.O. letter No. DEIO.4149/177(25-88/89) dt. 10/9/88 from the Governor Shri R.N. Malhotra to Shri S. Venkitaramanan, Finance Secretary, Utilisation of Gold Reserves.

(4) Letter No. G.Sec.158/88 dt. 23/12/88 from the Governor, Shri R.N. Malhotra to Hon. Shri S.B. Chavan, Minister for Finance.

(5) D.O. letter No. CPC. 1880/279A-89 dt. 7/1/89 from the Governor, Shri R.N. Malhotra to Hon. Shri S.B. Chavan, Minister for Finance, Government Budget Deficit and Monetary Policy.

(6) D.O. letter No. CPC. 1368/279A-89 dt. 6/6/89 from the Governor, Shri R.N. Malhotra to Shri G.K. Arora, Finance Secretary, Introduction of Commercial Paper in the Indian Money Market.

(7) D.O. letter No. G Sec 115/89 dt. 18/12/89 from the Governor, Shri R.N. Malhotra to Shri Madhu Dandavate, Hon. Minister for Finance, Measures

for Preventing Automatic Monetisation of the Government Budget Deficit.

(8)   D.O. letter No.RPCD.No.791/NB3 (J)-89/90 dt. 28/4/90 from the Governor, Shri R.N. Malhotra to Dr. Bimal Jalan, Finance Secretary, Report of the Agricultural Credit Review Committee.

(9)   Letter No. G. 20/561/90 dt. 18/5/90 from the Governor, Shri R.N. Malhotra to Dr. Bimal Jalan, Finance Secretary, Legislation on the Securities and Exchange Board of India (SEBI)- Regulation of Capital Market.

(10) IMF document dt. 27/8/91-Stand-By Arrangement- Letter of Intent.

(11) Letter dt. 11/11/91 from Dr. Manmohan Singh to Mr. I.T. Preston, President, The World Bank.

(12) Suo moto Statement by the Prime Minister in Parliament dated July 9, 1992.

(13) Supplemental Agreement between the Reserve Bank of India and the Government of India dated September 9, 1994.

(14) D.O. letter No. 1855 (I)/FS/95 dated February 24, 1995 from Shri M.S. Ahluwalia to the Governor, Dr. C. Rangarajan.

(15) D.O. letter No. 2739/FS/96 dated April 5, 1996 from Shri M.S. Ahluwalia to the Governor, Dr. C. Rangarajan.

(16) Supplemental Agreement between the Reserve Bank of India and the Government of India dated March 26, 1997.

SECRET/BY BAG

GOVERNMENT OF INDIA
MINISTRY OF FINANCE
DEPARTMENT OF ECONOMIC AFFAIRS
NEW DELHI

D.O.No.295-SSEA/82

February 14, 1982

Dear Dr. Patel,

I am writing this in response to a letter dated February 4, 1982 addressed to me by Tambe suggesting certain changes in interest rates for fixed deposits with maturities of one to three years. The Finance Minister has no objection to the Reserve Bank giving effect to these proposals.

2. While considering the Report of the Working Group on foreign remittances into India by Indian nationals resident abroad and foreign nationals of Indian origin, the Finance Minister has approved the Group's proposal that deposits with maturities of one year and above held in the two non-resident external accounts should carry interest at 2 per cent above the rates permissible on local currency deposits of comparable maturities. The higher rates would apply only to fresh deposits and on renewals of maturing deposits. In this connection, I had mentioned to the Finance Minister the reservations of the Reserve Bank and its suggestion that the Government should subsidiese the banks for the extra cost they would incur in paying additional interest on this account. While the Finance Minister did not favour the payment of the proposed subsidy to the commercial banks, he agreed that the banks could be compensated by a somewhat higher return on Government borrowings under the SLR.

3. It is suggested that the changes in the interest rates referred to above may be brought into effect from March 1, 1982. An announcement in this behalf could be made by the Reserve Bank immediately after the Finance Minister presents his Budget.

With best regards,

Yours sincerely,

Sd/- R.N. Malhotra

Dr. I.G. Patel,
Governor,
Reserve Bank of India,
Bombay.

Pl.see what follow-up action is necessary. I tried
to reopen our old idea of going all the way. But Econ.
Secy.was not prepared to change his view and F.M.
though let us see how far the present proposal works.
We may have to be clear about what Govt. would do on
'A' - and whether we also should in any case raise the
return on impounded segment.

Id. IGP.
17/2

E.D.(T)

P. see this. We will discuss tomorrow at 12.30 noon
along with CO(DBOD) and C.E.

Ad(M)

11 5673 COFS IN   EDX BY 1-31390 25.05 13:19 GA
313546+
31 3546 FINE IN
11 5673 COFS IN

FROM DR.C.RANGARAJAN, DEPUY GOVERNOR, RBI BOMBAY
FOR (1) SHRI S.VENKITARAMANAN, FINANCE SECRETARY
        ECOFAIRS
        ND
        REPEAT
    (2) DR. BIMAL JALAN, SECRETARY(BANKING) AND CHIEF
        ECONOMIC ADVISER, MINISTRY OF FINANCE, NORTH
        BLOCK, GOVT. OF INDIA
        ND
    WE TELEX BELOW THE TEXT OF GOVERNOR'S LETTER TO
SCHEDULED COMMERCIAL BANKS ISSUED TO-DAY. YOU MAYLIKE
TO BRING THIS TO THE NOTICE OF THE FINANCE MINISTER.

QUOTE:

    WITH EFFECT FROM APRIL 8,1985 SCHEDULED COMMERCIAL
BANKS WERE GIVEN THE DISCRETION TO FX++ FIX INTEREST
RATES ON DEPOSITS OF MATURITIES OF LESS.THAN ONE YEAR
WITHIN A CEILING OF 8 PER CENT. IT WAS EXPECTED THAT
WITH REASONABLE RATES OF INTEREST, ON SUCH MATURITIES,
BANKS WOULD BE ABLE TO MOBILISE HITHERTO UNTAPPED
RESOURCES AND THEREBY WIDEN THEIR DEPOSIT BASE. A
SUITABLE INCREASE IN INTEREST RATES FOR SHORTER
MATURITIES WAS ZL++ALSO EXPECTED TO ACHIEVE A BETTER
DISTRIBUTION OF TERM DEPOSITS INSTEAD OF THE PRESENT
HIGHLY SKEWED DISTRIBUTION WITH CONCENTRATION AROUND
THE LONGER MATURITIES AT RELATIVELY HIGHER COSTS.

2. IT WAS HOPED THAT IN THE EXERCISE OF THE DISCRETION
GIVEN TO THEM, INDIVIDUAL BANKS WOULD SO FIX THE RATES
AS TO SAFEGUARD THEIR CURRENT AND SAVINGS ACCOUNTS
AND AT THE SAME TIME BRING ABOUT BETTER PORTFOLIO
MANAGEMENT. HOEWEVER, THE APPROACH OF BANKS HAS BEEN
SUCH AS TO PREVENT THE EMERGENCE OF SUCH EFFICIENT
PORTFOLIO MANAGEMENT. THE MAJOR BANKS INITIALLY FIXED
UNIFORM RATES FOR FIVE MATURITIES BELOW ONE YEAR ++
YEAR AT A LEVEL OF ONE PERCENTAGE POINT ABOVE THE
RATES PREVAILING PRIOR TO APRIL 8, 1985. HOWEVER,
WHEN A FEW BANKS STARTED OFFERING A RATE OF 8 PERCENT
EVEN FOR MATURITIES OF 15 DAYS, ALL BANKS SIMPLY

FOLLOWED SUIT AND, 'WITHOUT REGARD TO CONSIDE-RATION
OF PROFITABILITY, SET A SINGLE RATE OF 8 PERCENT FOR
MATURITIES STARTING FROM 15 DAYS AND BELOW ONE YEAR.
SOME OF THE BANKS ARE MANAGING THEIR 15-DAY DEPOSITS
ALMOST LIKE CURRENT ACCOUNTS. MOREOVER, RESORT TO
MATURITIES ABOVE 15 DAYS BUT BELOW ONE YEAR HAS
GREATLY DIMINISHED. THE CONSQEQUENCE HAS BEEN A SHIFT
OF DEPOSITS FROM 'CURRENT ACCOUNTS AND, TO A LESSER
EXTENT, FROM SAVINGS ACCOUNTS TO 15-DAY DEPOSITS.

3. IN VIEW OF THESE DEVELOPMENTS, WE HAVE REVIEWED THE
POSITION. WITH EFFECT FROM MAY 27, 1985, THE RATES
FOR MATURITIES UPTO 90 DAYS ARE BEING RESORTED TOTHE
LEVELS PREVAILING PRIOR TO APRIL8,1985, THE RATE FOR
MATURITIES OF 91 DAYS TO LESS THAN 6 MONTHS IS FIXED
AT 6.5 PERCENT AND THE RATE FOR 6 MONTHS TO LESS THAN
ONE YEAR IS FIXED AT 8 PER CENT. THE REVISED STRUCTURE
OF INTEREST RATE ON DEPOSITS WILL BE AS FOLLOWS:

SCHEDULED COMMERCIAL BANKS1 INTEREST RATES ON DEPOSITS

	EXISTING (EFFECTIVE APRIL 8,1985 (PER CENT	NEW (EFFECTIVE MAY 27,1985) PER ANNUM)
1. CURRENT ACCOUNTS	NIL	NIL
2. SAVINGS ACCOUNTS	5.0	5.0
3. TERM DEPOSITS		
(A) 15 DAYS TO 45 DAYS		3.0
(B) 46 DAYS TO 9Q DAYS		4.0
(C) 91 DAYS AND ABOVE BUT LESS THAN 6 MONTHS	Not Exceeding 8.0	6.5
(D) 6 MONTHS AND ABOVE BUT LESS THAN 1 YEAR		8.0
(E) 1 YEAR AND ABOVE BUT LESS THAN 2 YEAR	8.5	8.5
(F) 2 YEARS AND ABOVE BUT LESS THAN 3 YEARS	9.0	9.0
(G) 3 YEARS AND ABOVE BUT LESS THAN 5 YEARS	10.0	10.0
(H) 5 YERARS AND ABOVE	11.0	11.0

NOTE: BANKS WHICH ARE AUTHORISED DEALERS IN FOREIGN
EXCHANGE AND WHO ACCEPT TERM DEPOSITS HAVING
A MATURITY PERIOD OF ONE YEAR AND ABOVE UNDER
THE FOREIGN CURRENCY(NON-RESIDENT. ACCOUNTS
SCHEME (FCNR) AND THE NON-RESIDENT(EXTERNAL)
RUPEE ACCONTS SCHEME(NRE) SHALL PAY, ON SUCH
DEPOSITS, INTEREST AT RATES 2 PERCENTAGE POINTS
PER ANNUM ABOVE THE RATES PERMISSIBLE ON. LOCAL
CURRENCY DEPOSITS OF COMPARABLE MATURITIES.

THE RELEVANT DIRECTIVE IS BEING ISSUED SEPARATELY

XKUMSX   UNQUOTE

TLX MSG NO.COF(CPC) 11969   25-5-85   14.50HRS+
31 3546 FINE IN
11 5673 COFS IN PSE ACK AND PASS ON IMMEDIATELY

11 5673 COFS IN   EDX BY 1-40138 25.05 14:43 GA
313546+
31 3546 FINE IN
11 5673 COFS IN

FOR (1) SHRI S.VENKITARAMANAN, FINANCE SECY ECOFAIRS
        ND
        REPEAT
    (2) DR. BIMAL JALAN, SECRETARY (BKG) AND CHIEF
        ECONOMIC ADVISER MINISRY OF FINANCE, NORTH
        BLOCK, GOVT.OF INDIA ND.

FROM NXIOX DR.C.RANGARAJAN, DY GOVERNOR RBI BOMBAY

REFERENCE OUR TLX MSG NO.COF(CPC)-11969COF.+
11 5671
      5,' 8-31
+++

REFERENCE OUR TLX MSG NO.COF(CPC)-11969

DATED 25TH MAY 1985. KINDLY ADD IN PARAGRAPH 1 LINE
NO.8 XX AFTER DISTRIBUTION "OF TERM DEPOSITS INSTEAD
OF THE PRESENT HIGHLY SKEWED DISTRIBUTION".
AND PARA 2 LINE NO.6 AFTER MANAGEMENT 11THE MAJOR
BANKS INITIALLY FIXED UNIOFORMEEE UNIFORM RATES FOR
FIVE MATURITIES".

TLX MSG NO.COF.11972   25.5.1985   1455HRS+
31 3546 FINE IN
11 5673 COFS IN
PSE ACK +?
AFTD POSITIVELY

SECRET

D.O.DEIO.NO.4149/177(25)-88/89   10th September 1988.

Utilisation of Gold Reserves

You may recall that during the course of our review
of deployment of foreign exchange reserves by the
Reserve Bank on 5th July 1988, I had made a suggestion
that a part of our gold reserves, which as of now do
not earn any income, could be leased out to earn an
income. Both you and Bimal agreed that it was a good
idea. My detailed proposal in this behalf is described
in the following paragraphs.

2. The practice of gold lending is not uncommon
with central banks, a large number of whom have
arrangements with Bank of England, Federal Reserve
Bank of New York, Swiss National Bank, and also some
private institutions to store a proportion of their
gold reserves which are deployed in international gold
markets. The most convenient and expedient method of
utilising gold reserves would be to lease out certain
proportion of the reserves and earn a return thereon.
This, however, requires physical shifting of gold to
an acceptable depository abroad. In terms of Section
33(5) of the RBI Act , 1934, out of the gold held
by the Bank, not less than 17/20th, i.e., 85 per
cent shall be held in India. The Bank's official gold
holdings are 324.988 tonnes (10,449 million ounces
troy), all of which are held in India itself. It is
thus permissible for the Bank to transfer about 48.7
tonnes of gold out of the country within the existing
parameters of the law. Such a movement would, however,
be reflected in the weekly statement of affairs of the
Bank whose format requires the Bank to show separately
the gold held in India and outside India. Any shifting
of gold from India will, therefore, automatically come
to the knowledge of the public and Government will
have to be prepared to explain the reasons.

3. The gold acceptable in international markets has
to conform to specifications of good delivery bars
weighing approximately 400 ounces troy (12.5 kgs.)

and of minimum assay 995 from acceptable Melters and
Assayers. The physical possession of gold has to be
given by the Bank to the lessee/s' ex-vault, say,
Bank of England or any gold depository. (The title
to the gold will continue to vest with Reserve Bank
of India). We are ascertaining the quantity of good
delivery gold bars held by the Bank and, if necessary,
the India Government Mint standard bars may have to be
reassayed at a nominal cost.

4. In return for use of gold for a specified period,
the lessee will pay a lease fee which, historically,
has been around 0.5 per cent per annum but varies
on demand and supply conditions obtaining in
international markets. Lease fee is calculated on spot
value of the quantity of gold deployed on the lease
date and is payable in either US dollar or in gold. At
the end of the lease period, an equivalent quantity
of gold in fine ounces/grams is returned to the Bank's
account with its depository. The only risk involved in
this transaction is that of a default by the lessee.
Such risks, even otherwise, exist for currency deposit
transactions and can be minimised by spreading out
gold deposits amongst institutions in our approved
list within the overall exposure limits that have
been/may be assigned to them. We can also utilise the
services of the Bank for International Settlements,
Basle for the purpose of placement of deposits since
they have developed the requisite expertise over the
years.

5. The physical movement of gold from Bombay to say,
London, would involve a one time cost which would
decline asymptotically over the period during its
employment and retention in.-London. The cost of
transportation and insurance from Bombay airport to
"in vault" Bank of England is estimated at about 40
cents (US) per ounce, or say $12,900 (approximately)
per metric tonne. The 1987 average London. P.M. fix
works out to $446.41 per troy ounce. The 1988 half
year average is $452.80 per troy ounce. Assuming a
conservative price of $400 per troy ounce, one tonne
of gold will have a deployable value of $12,860,400,

say, $12.86 million which will yield an income stream of $64,300 per tonne per annum.

6. Taking into account the absorbtive capacity of the markets, their logistics and the practical difficulties involved, it is deemed advisable to shift about 40 tonnes to Bank of England, London. Depending upon the actual amount leased, the annual income that would accrue to us would be about $2.5 million or say Rs. 3.5 crores.

7. The proposal set out above may kindly be examined by the Government. I shall be glad to have Government's approval in principle before proceeding further in the matter.

    With regards,

                                        Yours sincerely,

                                        (R.N. Malhotra)

Shri S. Venkitaramanan,
Finance Secretary,
Government of. India,
Ministry of Finance,
New Delhi

गवर्नर
GOVERNOR

भारतीय रिज़र्व बैंक
केन्द्रिय कार्यालय,
बंबई
RESERVE BANK OF INDIA
CENTRAL OFFICE
BOMBAY

SECRET
G.Sec.158/88   23rd December 1988

Dear Shri Chavan,

Kindly recollect the brief discussion we had on developments in the balance of payments when I called on you recently in Delhi. This letter sets out in some detail the position as it has evolved in the current fiscal year against the background of developments in recent years. A note on the "External Debt Position as on March 31, 1988" is also enclosed.

The balance of payments has been under severe strain during the current financial year. Foreign exchange reserves comprising foreign currency assets of Reserve Bank of India, gold and SDRs during the current financial year upto December 9, 1988 declined by Rs.1064 crores, as compared with a fall of Rs.1025 crores in the corresponding period of 1987-88. However, excluding valuation changes, i.e., net appreciation in the value of foreign currency assets of RBI and SDRs, reserves would show a larger fall of Rs.1966 crores as compared with a fall of Rs.1383 crores in the corresponding period of 1987-88 (Table 1). The present level of reserves at Rs.6623 crores is quite low, constituting less than 2.8 months of imports. This is the first time since 1974-75 that the level of reserves is less than 3 months of imports, the earlier low being at the end of 1974-75, when reserves level was equivalent of 3 months of imports.

The real loss in reserves is much higher than is indicated above. If special transactions (that is, funds brought in, receipts from India Supply Mission, Washington and Indian Embassy, Tokyo and sales of foreign currencies to RBI by ICICI/IDBI/IFCI out of their commercial borrowings) are .excluded, the fall in reserves this fiscal year so far upto December 9, 1988 works out to Rs.3752 crores. This is more than twice the fall of Rs.1714 crores (after excluding special transactions) in the corresponding period of 1987-88. Besides, we increased our resort to the use of short-term credits, the outstandings of which went up by Rs.1441 crores to Rs.2855 crores between end March 1988 and December 2, 1988, nearly twice the rise of Rs.767 crores in April-November 1987.

The main factor for the sharp fall of reserves this year was larger net sales of foreign currencies to Authorised Dealers by RBI, reflecting mainly higher import payments. Although aid receipts were somewhat higher, the debt service payments were much more than in the last year. Repurchases from the IMF under External Fund Facility were also higher this year. On the other hand, net inflow of funds under Foreign Currency Non-resident Account (FCNRA) Scheme was much stronger (Table 2).

Detailed balance of payments data for the current financial year are not yet available. According to provisional DGCIS data, during April to September 1988, while exports went up by 21.3 per cent over April to September 1987, this was more than offset by a sharp rise of 26.6 per cent in imports over the same period. It is disquieting to note that the export growth this year in rupee terms was lower than the growth of 26.5 per cent achieved during April to September 1987, while the import growth was substantially higher than the growth of 12.6 per cent in April to September 1987. In terms of SDRs, while the growth in exports during April-September 1988 was only 9.1 per cent as compared with a growth of 13.1 per cent in April-September 1987, the rise in imports during the two reference periods was 13.9 per cent and 0.6 per cent respectively. Because of a larger rise in imports than in exports, the trade deficit in rupee terms widened sharply by 39.8 per cent from Rs.2988 crores in April to September 1987 to Rs.4177 crores during April to September 1988. The estimated current account deficit during April-November 1988 worked out from known capital transactions would be over Rs.7250 crores, about 70 per cent higher than that estimated for the same period of 1987-88 (Table 3).

The balance of payments has been under considerable pressure since the beginning of the Seventh Plan. Foreign Exchange reserves, excluding valuation changes, declined continuously during the first three years of the Seventh Plan by Rs.707 crores, Rs.732 crores and Rs.954 crores, respectively despite a sharp increase in aid flows and commercial borrowing. In SDR terms, foreign exchange reserves steadily declined from SDR 6,004 million at the end of March 1985 to SDR 3443 million by the end of December 9, 1988, about SDR 750 million lower than the level a year ago (SDR 4196 million). The order of current account deficits experienced during the Seventh Plan has been very large. The current account deficit more than doubled from Rs.2852 crores in 1984-85 to Rs.5927 crores in the first year of the Seventh Plan. Although it came down somewhat in 1986-87, it went up once again in 1987-88. The available indicators, as stated above, show that the current account deficit in 1988-89 would be even more than in 1987-88. It is clear that the current account deficits have been running at a much higher rate than postulated in the Seventh Plan document. The annual average ratio of current account deficit to GDP of over 2 per cent in the first three years of the Seventh Plan, as against the targeted average of 1.6 per cent for the Plan period, underscores the pressure on balance of payments.

The large order of current account deficits has been financed partly by drawing down reserves, but mainly through a larger inflow of capital both on concessional and commercial terms and by way of NRI deposits. As a result, India's medium` and long-term debt has reached high proportions. As can be seen from the note on the External Debt Situation (Appendix), India's medium and long-term external debt which was around Rs.13300 crores at the end of March 1980, increased to nearly Rs.55000 crores by end-March 1988 (vide Annexure I of Appendix). In addition, we have also contracted short-term debt which is estimated to have gone up from Rs.750 crores at end-March 1980 to Rs.3700 crores by the end of March 1988. India's external debt (short,medium and long term) as a proportion of exports and current invisible receipts has consequently gone up from 135 per cent at the end of 1979-80 to 240 per cent at the end of

1987-88. Even if allowance is made for the increase in debt due to exchange rate factors, there has been a substantial rise in external debt over the last few years. At the same time, NRI deposit liabilities have gone up from Rs.855 crores at end-March 1980 to Rs. 3819 crores by the end of the Sixth Plan and to Rs. 11775 crores by the end of September 1988.

Some estimates place the external debt at an even higher level than the figures indicated above. According to the September 1988 Report of the Institute of International Finance (IIF), India's outstanding external debt (medium and long-term) at the end of March 1988 is $45.1 billion (as against our figure of $42.3 billion) and inclusive of short-term debt and NRI deposits, the external debt is placed by the IIF at $57.6 billion as against our figure of $53.0 billion (Annexure V of Appendix). The higher figure of external debt given by the IIF seems. to be mainly due to exchange rate adjustments under IBRD, IDA and bilateral credits as well as due to a higher estimation of short-term debt.

Consequent to increase in external debt, the debt service obligations have steadily gone up over the last few years. India's debt service ratio on medium and long-term debt rose from 8 per cent in 1980-81 to 13.6 per cent in 1984-85, 21.6 per cent in 1986-87, in 24 per cent in 1987-88 and in expected to rise further to nearly 26 per cent in 1988-89. In this context, it may be mentioned that if debt service payments (on economic credits) and exports to rupee payment area countries are excluded from the calculations, the debt service ratio would be higher. If the instalment payments on defence credits from the USSR which are financed by way of export of goods but not included under debt service, are also considered, the ratio would be even still higher. Even without making these adjustments, if interest payments on NRI deposits and short-term debts are taken into account under debt service, India's debt service ratio in 1988-89 would go up to 30.8 per cent. The country's debt service ratio is now fast approaching a level of the "countries with recent debt servicing problems" as a group according to IMF World Economic Outlook, 1988, whose debt service ratio was

30.4 per cent and is expected to touch 32.4 per cent in 1988. It is necessary to reverse as quickly as possible the rising trend in debt service ratio.

The present level of reserves in SDR terms (SDR 3443 million) is the lowest reached since March 1978 and there is hardly any scope for further drawdown on the reserves. Our debt service liabilities are mounting. Over the next two years, we have to make repayments to the Fund amounting to SDR 1698 million (SDR 1486 million under EFF and SDR 212 million against Trust Fund loans).

The pressure on balance of payments and the mounting burden of external debt can be contained only through a reduction in current account deficit in absolute terms quickly. The Department of Economic Affairs of the Finance Ministry had drawn up an action plan sometime in July this year to reduce the deficit. However, looking to the developments and trends, since then, more efforts need to be made not only to `attain a higher volume growth in exports but to carefully examine the scope for containment, of imports in the areas of defence, POL and edible oils. There has been some softening in crude oil prices, but the situation is uncertain and the scope for limiting the growth rate in oil consumption may have to be explored. There has been a fairly sharp increase in non-bulk OGL imports. The possibilities of raising duties on products covered by the OGL as a means of restricting their imports may be considered. The current account deficit on the external account is intimately related_ to the budgetary deficit. The reduction of budgetary deficit would help to contain the current account deficit.

With kind regards,

Yours sincerely,

(R.N. Malhotra)

Hon. Shri S.B.Chavan,
Minister for Finance,
Government of India,
New Delhi.

Encls : 1 Note and 4 Tables.

गवर्नर
GOVERNOR

भारतीय रिज़र्व बैंक
केन्द्रिय कार्यालय,
बंबई
RESERVE BANK OF INDIA
CENTRAL OFFICE
BOMBAY

SECRET

D.O.No.CPC.1880/279A-89   7th January 1989

Dear Shri Chavan,

Government Budget Deficit and Monetary Policy

    Monetary Policy has to ensure the twin objectives of
maintaining reasonable price stability and meeting the
genuine credit requirements necessary to support the
growth of output. The large and recurring Government
budget deficits have been contributing to strong
monetary expansion and, over time, there has been a
serious erosion in the effectiveness of monetary policy
instruments. In the context of the large budget deficits
it is difficult to control monetary expansion which,
in turn, contributes to inflation. Government's market
and other borrowings have also been rising rapidly and
interest payments are now very large. A disturbing trend
has been the steep increase in the ,Government's revenue
deficit which has grown from Rs.384 crores in 1981-82 to
Rs.4,224 crores in 1984-85 to Rs.9,842 crores in 1988-
89(BE). This means that Government has been borrowing
heavily to meet current expenditure. While the need
for corrective action is well recognised, effective
measures have not yet materialised. Postponement of the
needed adjustment would, however, lead to more acute
problems.

2. The overall budgetary deficit of the Government of
India has been growing over the years. Between 1977-
78 and 1987-88, the overall budgetary deficit of the
Government of India grew at an annual compound rate of
over 20 per cent. The deficit is budgeted to increase by
another 23 per cent during 1988-89. Upto December 16,
1988, however, the deficit is already 36 per cent more
than the budget estimate for the full financial year and

also over a fourth more than the comparable deficit at this point of time last year. On current indications, the actual deficit during 1988-89 is likely to exceed the budget estimate unless immediate measures are taken to contain the deficit.

3. Over the years the practice has grown by which the entire budget deficit of the Central Government is taken up by the Reserve Bank of India through the acceptance of ad hoc Treasury Bills issued in its favour. Since these budget deficits are not temporary, the huge amount of Treasury Bills outstanding is being continuously rolled over. A part of the outstandings has recently been converted into long-term securities at the rate of interest applicable to Treasury Bills. In addition, the Reserve Bank continues to provide support to the Central Government's market borrowing programme. The automatic monetisation of large and growing budgetary deficits has led to excess liquidity in the system with serious inflationary implications.

4. Treasury Bills are meant to provide short-term accommodation but this has become a permanent form of financing the Government. The longer term requirements of the Government should, quite properly, be met from the market and not the Reserve Bank. I hardly need mention that automatic monetisation of the budgetary deficit by the central bank is not a healthy practice and it would be desirable, over a period of time, to move away from such monetisation. As a first step, this calls for reducing the budget deficit, in a phased manner, from the level of 2.3 per cent of GDP in 1988-89 to 1 per cent of GDP say by 1992-93. The eventual aim should be that only temporary accommodation to the Government is provided by the Reserve Bank, the long term needs being met from the market.

5. Over the years, the expansionary impact of the large budget deficits has been partly neutralised and the consequent inflationary impulse moderated through the pursuit of a cautionary monetary policy. The main instrument Of monetary restraint has been the use of the cash reserve ratio which has virtually reached its statutory limit of 15 per cent of Bank's net demand and time liabilities. This statutory limit would not

have posed much of a problem if the fiscal deficit had remained low. As the currently high deficits can be brought down only in a phased manner we have been constrained to suggest to the Government an enhancement of the statutory limit for the cash reserve ratio from 15 per cent to 20 per cent. We have already written to the Ministry of Finance in this context and an early action in the matter is urged.

6. The use of the interest rate instrument for monetary control has limitations in our context because of substantial concessional lending to the priority sectors and the below-market rates at which Government borrows from the market. The insulation of Government borrowing from market rates also prevents the Reserve Bank from undertaking open market operations to mop up excess liquidity.

7. I would like to point out that the large current account deficit in the balance of payments has had a moderating impact on monetary growth and prices. This deficit, however, has considerably increased our external indebtedness and sharply raised the debt service ratio. A reduction in the current deficit which is urgently needed, would, however, put pressure on both money supply and prices. Under the circumstances, a substantial moderation of the fiscal deficit has become inescapable. In the absence of such moderation, the inflationary situation could become serious and there could be further pressures on the balance of payments.

8. While the monetary targetting and borrowing programme exercise for 1989-90 is being worked out separately, I thought it would be useful to set out the broad framework for this exercise. On the assumption of a 5 per cent rate of real growth and an objective of containing the inflation rate to within 5 per cent, we should ensure that the growth of M3 in 1989-90 does not exceed 15.0 per cent as against a projected 16.3 per cent increase in 1988-89. Consistent with this would be a growth of aggregate deposits of scheduled commercial banks. in 1989-90 of Rs.23,300 crores (16.8 per cent) as against a working estimate of Rs.20,500 crores (17.4 per cent) for 1988-89. To contain the growth of liquidity within the abovementioned limits, the overall market borrowing programme of the Centre, States and institutions would

need to be limited to Rs.12,200 crores in 1989-90 as against Rs.11,721 crores in 1988-89. This itself would require Reserve Bank support to dated securities of Rs.1,200 crores. The overall growth of liquidity can be contained within a limit of 15 per cent in 1989-90 only if the RBI net credit to Central Government is limited to an increase of Rs.8,200 Crores. Since the support to the borrowing programme would be of the order of Rs.1,200 crores, the budget deficit of the Centre in 1989-90 should not exceed Rs.7,000 crores.

9. To sum up, may I suggest that the following broad parameters be accepted as part of a programme to adjust the budgetary gap:

(i)   The Government of India should ensure that its deficit during 1988-89 does not exceed the budget estimate of Rs. 7,484 crores.

(ii)   The budget deficit for 1989-90 should not exceed Rs.7,000 crores (equivalent to 1.9 per cent of GDP) and net RBI credit to the Central Government should be limited to Rs.8,200 crores. The overall borrowing programme of the Centre, States and institutions should be limited to Rs.12,200 crores in 1989-90; this would mean an increase of about Rs.500 crores over 1988-89.

(iii)   There should be a programme for a phased reduction in the absolute size of the budget deficit so that by 1992-93 it is reduced to 1.0 per cent of GDP, which could approximate to Rs.5,000 crores.

10. I do appreciate that these suggestions imply the beginning of an adjustment process calling for action on controlling expenditures and raising revenue. I would like to discuss these matters with you at an early date.

With kind regards,

Yours sincerely,

(signature)

(R.N. Malhotra)

Shri S.B. Chavan,
Finance Minister,
Government of India,
New Delhi.

<u>CONFIDENTIAL</u>

D.O.NO.CPC.1368/279A-89   6th June 1989

My dear Gopi,

Introduction of Commercial Paper in the Indian Money Market

As you are already aware, the question of introducing Commercial Paper (CP) in the Indian money market had been under consideration for quite some time. The CP would enable highly rated corporate borrowers to diversify their sources of short-term borrowing and also provide an additional instrument to investors. You would recall that I had discussed this matter with the Finance Minister and yourself and in March 1989, as part of the credit policy for the first half of 1989-90, I had announced the decision to introduce Commercial Paper together with the salient features of the new instrument. We are at present finalising detailed guidelines in consultation with the Indian Banks' Association (IBA) and others concerned and the detailed scheme is expected to be ready for implementation very shortly.

2. While announcing the salient features of the scheme, we had set out that certain exemptions would have to be obtained from the Government before CPs can be issued. In the scheme of things, CP would be in the form of unsecured promissory notes with the maturity period ranging from three months to six months. However, under the Companies (Acceptance of Deposits) Rules 1975, framed by the Government of India under Section 58A of the Companies Act, 1956, companies are prohibited from accepting deposits which are repayable on demand or on notice or repayable after a period, except where such deposits are repayable after the expiry of six months from the date of acceptance of deposits.

3. To enable companies to issue CPs, it would be necessary to either (i) exempt CPs from the provisions of Section 58A of the Companies Act or (ii) the Companies (Acceptance of Deposits) Rules 1975 could be amended to exempt deposits raised through CPs from the

definition of deposits. In our view, the first alternative seems preferable. It is therefore requested that the Government of India may kindly agree to grant exemption for the issue of Commercial Papers from the provisions of Section 58A(8) of the Companies Act, 1956. I am forwarding a copy of the draft exemption order for the consideration of the Government and it would facilitate the introduction of CPs if the exemption order could be issued by an early date. (draft 1 attached). If for some reason the second alternative is preferred a draft for giving effect to that is also attached. (draft 2).

With Regards,

Yours sincerely,

(R.N. Malhotra)

Shri G.K. Arora,
Finance Secretary,
Ministry of Finance,
Government of India,
New Delhi.

गवर्नर
GOVERNOR

भारतीय रिज़र्व बैंक
केन्द्रिय कार्यालय,
बंबई
RESERVE BANK OF INDIA
CENTRAL OFFICE
BOMBAY

SECRET

D.O.No.G SEC 115/89   18th December 1989

Dear Shri Dandavate

Measures for Preventing Automatic
Monetisation of the Government
Budget Deficit

As you are well aware, an important objective of
monetary policy is to ensure price stability. With the
large and recurring budget .deficits of the Government,
and their monetisation by virtue of these deficits being
automatically financed by the Reserve Bank of India, the
efficacy of monetary policy has been greatly attenuated.
It is, therefore, desirable to move away from such
monetisation. While the longer term needs of the
Government should be met from the. market, the Reserve
Bank should provide only temporary accommodation to
the Government. This question was also addressed in
the Report of the Central Board of Directors on the
working of the Reserve Bank of India for the year ended
June 30,1989, wherein it was argued that an effective
monetary policy Would require the avoidance of the
automatic monetisation of the budget deficits and that
over the medium term, beyond a mutually agreed Ways and
Means accommodation from the Reserve Bank, Government
should aim at placing its entire debt in the market at
appropriate interest rates (extracts from the Report
are attached as Annexure I for ready reference). In
this letter I am setting out the genesis of the existing
practice of monetisation of the budget deficit by the
Reserve Bank of India and make certain specific proposals
for avoiding this in future.

Genesis of the Problem

2. Before considering measures to prevent automatic monetisation of the Government budget deficit it may be useful to briefly recapitulate the genesis of the existing procedures of financing the budget deficit. In terms of Section 17(5) of the Reserve Bank of India Act, 1934, the Bank is authorised to grant to the Central and State Governments, advances repayable in each case not later than three months from the date of making the advance. These "Ways and Means" advances were granted to the Central Government to ensure that the balances of the Government did not fall below the agreed minimum level to be kept with the Bank. The provisions of Section 17(5) are enabling and not mandatory, and they do not require the Reserve Bank to finance unlimited deficits of the Government. While the Central Government did not avail of Ways and Means advances during the period 1944-54, from 1954-55 onwards the Central. Government sought accommodation through sale of ad hoc Treasury Bills under Section 17(8) of the Act which authorises the Reserve Bank to undertake purchase and sale of securities of the Central Government. In January 1995, the Government and the Reserve Bank agreed that if the balances of the Government fell below the stipulated minimum of Rs.50 crores, the Reserve Bank would create ad hocs to replenish the cash balances of the Government. While the practice of creating ad hocs for replenishing the balances with the RBI commenced only in 1955, right from the inception of the Bank, the Reserve Bank purchased ad hocs from the Government for providing eligible assets to facilitate currency expansion; however, such expansion was very modest and as late as 1948 the total outstanding Treasury Bills were only Rs.99 crores of which the holdings by the Reserve Bank amounted to a mere Rs.6 crores.

3. I may draw your attention to the fact that as far back as 1957, the then Governor, the late Shri H.V.R. Iengar, expressed concern at the prevailing arrangement regarding automatic creation. of ad hocs to finance the Government deficit and in his letter dated July 5, 1957 to the then Finance Minister, the late Shri T.T. Krishnamachari, he said:

"Ever since I came to the Reserve Bank, I have been exercised over the fact that under the arrangements in force for the last five years or thereabouts, currency is expanded against the creation of ad hoc Treasury Bills as a merely mechanical process depending on the weekly closing balance of the Central Government. There is no check against the volume of currency that could be so expanded. If Government want to go on increasing their expenditure without regard to the available resources, there would be nothing to stop them, so far as ways and means are concerned; the currency would be provided automatically. The process is in fact so mechanical that it is operated by my Calcutta Manager and I hear about this action subsequently ..... The reason I am exercised in my mind is that the present arrangement, as a standing arrangement, is defective The Reserve Bank, under the Statute, is charged with responsibility of regulating the issue of bank notes and the keeping of reserves with a view to securing monetary stability in India. (Please see the preamble to the Act). As matters now stand, with an automatic expansion of currency at the will of Government, the Bank, in my judgement, is not really in a position to discharge its responsibility."

In reply, the Finance Minister vide his letter No.8340/PSF/57 dated July 27, 1957 said:

"What to my mind is necessary is to ensure that Government policy is formulated in this respect after very full discussion with the Reserve Bank and that the latter is kept informed from time to time of any changes that Government feel called upon to make before they are made. Thus, it would be the duty of the Finance Ministry to formulate their proposals for borrowing as also for deficit financing in consultation with the Reserve Bank. These programmes of borrowing and deficit financing are incorporated in the Budget and placed before the Parliament for its approval. The subsequent creation of ad hoc Treasury Bills when the

Government's cash balances fall below a certain level is done within the limits thus prescribed. If in the course of the year it is found that these limits are likely to be exceeded, revised arrangements may become necessary and these would certainly also be formulated in consultation with the Reserve Bank. The Reserve Bank thus would have every opportunity of discharging its responsibility of regulating the issue of Bank Notes and keeping of reserves with a view to securing monetary stability in India."

It will thus be seen that what started off as a mechanism for providing temporary accommodation to the Central Government to enable it to maintain a minimum balance with the Reserve Bank became an open-ended monetisation of budgetary deficits, thus substantially undermining the role and effectiveness of monetary policy. What is more, the Treasury Bill which is a short term instrument for meeting temporary needs has been used for financing the long-term requirements of the Government.

Impact of Monetisation of the
Deficit in Recent Years

4. In recent years, the budget deficit has been large and apart from monetising this deficit, the Reserve Bank has also had to provide support to the Government's market borrowing programme through purchase of long-term bonds. As a result, the pace of monetary expansion has been unduly high and this has put inevitable pressures on prices. It is pertinent to note that as on December 1, 1989 the outstanding reserve money (i.e. the money created by the Reserve Bank) amounted to Rs.69,462 crores of which the net claims of the Reserve Bank on the Central Government accounted for Rs.70,948 crores. The overall liquidity in the system (M3) as on December 1,1989 was Rs.215,318 crores and this M3 expansion is almost exclusively the secondary impact of the increase in net Reserve Bank credit to the Central Government. As on December 1, 1989, the Reserve Bank's holdings of Treasury Bills amounted to Rs.24,435 crores and its holdings of other securities was Rs.46,522 crores; of the holdings of other securities, as much

as Rs.36,000 crores of holdings relate to three large fundings of Treasury Bills undertaken in the current decade (Rs.3,500 crores in March 1982, Rs.15,000 crores in March 1987 and Rs.17,500 crores in March 1988) at a low rate of 4.6 per cent. At the end of March 1989 the net Reserve Bank credit to Central Government was equivalent to 51.2 per cent of the net domestic debt of the Central Government. This epitomises the impact of the automatic monetisation of the .Central Government budget deficit.

5. Despite the large automatic monetisation of the budget deficit the expansionary impact has been partly neutralised, and inflation moderated, particularly in the 1980's, by a strong regime of monetary restraint which was only possible because of the frequent use of the instrument of the cash reserve ratio (CRR). But this instrument is no longer available to us as the statutory ceiling of 15 per cent of banks' net demand and time liabilities has already been reached. I had, over a year ago, urged the Ministry of Finance to initiate early action to raise this statutory ceiling from 15 per cent to 20 per cent. I would urge immediate action to amend the Reserve Bank of India Act so that we are in a position to impound a part of the excess liquidity whenever necessary. I must, however, stress that the cash reserve ratio cannot be effective for very long if the Government continues the present arrangement of automatic monetisation of the budget deficit. This is because high cash reserve ratios entail payment of interest to banks to maintain their profitability and such interest payments materially reduce the effectiveness of the CRR instrument. Besides, a situation is created where resources tend to move away from banks to non-bank financial intermediaries which are not subject to such reserve requirements. What the cash reserve ratio would provide (if the ceiling is raised) is breathing time until a fundamental restructuring is undertaken of the arrangements for financing the budget deficit.

6. The trends in the budget deficit in the current financial year have been, to say the least alarming. As against an estimated budget deficit of Rs.7,337 crores for 1989-90, the deficit as on December 1, 1989 was

Rs.13,025 crores and the budget deficit has been above Rs.10,000 crores for the past 22 consecutive weeks. The increase in the net Reserve Bank credit to the Central Government in 1989-90, as on December 1, 1989, was Rs.12,748 crores. The growth of overall liquidity (M3) in 1989-90 between March 24, 1989 and December 1, 1989 was Rs.23,244 crores (12.1 per cent) as against Rs.18,377 crores (11.3 per cent) in the comparable period of last year. The growth of M1 (demand deposits and currency) was Rs.9,233 crores (13.9 per cent) this year as against Rs.3,907 crores (6.8 per cent) last year. The Cabinet Committee on Economic Affairs had approved an M3 target of 16.1 per cent as against last year's expansion of 17.3 per cent (on March 31 basis); current trends indicate that we could well exceed even last year's high monetary growth. Wholesale prices on a point-to-point basis in the current financial year upto December. 2, 1989 indicate an increase of 6.2 per cent as against 4.6 per cent last year. Unless some measures are taken to bring about a drastic reduction in the budget deficit, prices would show a sharp upsurge in the remaining months of the year. If the administered price adjustments, which are overdue, are put through we could well have a double digit inflation rate in 1989-90.

Financing of the Government in
Other Countries

7. Before setting out a specific scheme for financing the budget deficit of the Central Government, I thought it would be pertinent to mention that in developed countries the central banks do not automatically monetise the budget deficit. A limited amount of the government's borrowing is in the form of Treasury Bills and these bills are placed in the market outside the central bank at market related interest rates. The central bank in the course of its open market operations freely buys or sells government securities bearing in mind its objectives of controlling liquidity in the system. In such a milieu, the central bank is able to have a far better control over liquidity as it can determine how much of primary liquidity to inject into the system. A basic precondition for such operations necessarily has

to be flexible interest rates on Government securities. In some countries, as part of a conscious policy, a budget surplus is planned so as to enable a net repayment of the outstanding public debt. In some other countries plans are afoot to direct the central bank, by an Act of Parliament, to hold inflation within a low rate of say two per cent and the central bank has the freedom to take such action as may be necessary to achieve this objective. Several developing countries have also moved away from automatic monetisation of the budget deficit.

8. A perusal of the provisions, in various countries, on central bank statutes on lending to Government reveal a common strand: (i) that the provisions are enabling and not mandatory, (ii) that the advances are essentially of a short-term nature to be repaid within clearly specified periods, (iii) that there are ceilings on outstanding borrowings from the central bank.

Legislative Aspects on Monetisation
of the Budget Deficit in India

9. As already indicated in paragraph 2 above, the provisions in the RBI Act regarding the financing of the Government are enabling and not mandatory. At the present time, however, a practice has evolved under which the budget deficit is automatically monetised by the Reserve Bank. In view of the prevailing practice it is necessary to consider an explicit amendment to the Reserve Bank of India Act whereby the Reserve Bank shall not be subject to any directions by the Central Government regarding the Bank's holdings of Government securities (including Treasury Bills). This must be so notwithstanding any powers the Central Government may have to give_ directions to the Reserve Bank under Section 7 of the Act. Incidentally, to underpin the autonomy of the Reserve Bank, it is necessary to provide that any directive under Section 7 of the Reserve Bank of India Act would be issued with the consent of the Cabinet and that a copy thereof, along with a statement setting out the circumstances leading to the issue of the directive, shall be placed before Parliament within a stipulated time. If these proposals are agreed to in principle, a suitable amendment to the Act can be drafted.

Proposed Scheme for Financing
the Central "Government

10. In pursuance of the objective of phasing out the
current system of automatic monetisation of the budget
deficit, an understanding needs to be worked out between
the Central Government and the Reserve Bank. The main
ingredients of such an understanding could be as follows:

(i)   The Central Government should adopt a medium-
term strategy of bringing about a decisive turnaround in the overall budget deficit. As part of
a phased programme, the overall budget deficit
in 1990-91 should not exceed Rs.6,000 crores.
During the subsequent three years the overall
budget deficit should be progressively reduced
till the budget deficit, as presently defined,
comes close to zero. The longer term resource
requirements of the Government should be met
through floatation of dated securities and not
Treasury Bills. The needs of the Government
to cover temporary requirements for mismatches
within the year between revenue receipts and
expenditures could be met through Ways and Means
advances from the Reserve Bank and Treasury
Bills raised from the market. A limit must be
set on the outstanding level of Ways and Means
advances and once this limit is reached, further
utilisation will be possible only to the extent
of repayments. The arrangements regarding Ways
and Means advances should be put in place from
1993-94 when the budget deficit is expected to
reach the level close to zero.

(ii)   The Reserve Bank of India should not be required
to provide any support to the Government market
borrowing programme starting from 1990-91. The
Government should move towards a system of
market related rates on Government securities
and the rates of interest on bonds should be so
adjusted as to enable the Government to place
the entire debt in the market.

(iii) As part of the progressive effort towards
placing the Treasury Bills outside the Reserve

Bank, the rate of interest on 182-day Treasury Bills should be allowed to move up from the present level. When the budget deficit reaches a point close to zero as envisaged earlier, the 182-day Treasury Bills auctions can be replaced by 91-day Treasury Bills auctions with market determined interest rates. At that point, the existing stock of 91-day Treasury Bills held by the Reserve Bank could be entirely funded into longer term securities.

11. I do recognise that the scheme I am recommending implies a fundamental change in the present system of financing of the Government. If, however, we are to keep inflation under control, you will kindly appreciate that there is an urgent need for an early cessation of automatic monetisation of the budget deficit. If the proposals set out above meet your broad agreement, the Ministry of Finance and the Reserve Bank could draw up a detailed programme of action. I would be glad to discuss this matter with you at your earliest convenience.

With best regards,

Yours sincerely,

(R.N. Malhotra)

Shri Madhu Dandavate,
Hon'ble Finance Minister,
Government of India,
New Delhi.

Extracts from the Report of the
Central Board of Directors on the
Working of the Reserve Bank of India
for the year ended June 30, 1989

11.37 Broadly, the three major objectives of economic policy are growth, social justice which implies a more equitable distribution of income, and price stability. While all of these objectives are relevant for monetary policy, price stability has to be its chief focus. This does not, however, mean that it cannot contribute to the attainment of other objectives. Credit and bank¬ing policy, particularly during the past two decades, through the various schemes of direct credit allocation and interest rate changes, has helped to promote such objectives as the promotion of the weaker sections of society and balanced regional development. Nevertheless, monetary policy is able to make a more effective contribution towards the objective of price stability than to the other objectives. The importance of price stability as an objec¬tive of economic and monetary policy is not, always, well appreciated. In some situations there is perhaps a trade-off between growth and inflation in the very short run. Over a longer time period growth cannot however be bought with the aid of higher prices and there is no evidence to show that a higher growth rate is associated with a higher inflation rate. In India quite the contrary is the case. In fact, it is price stability which provides the appropriate environment in which healthy and sustainable growth can occur. In an economy where a predominant proportion of the population operates in the unorganised sector with little protection against inflation, maintenance of price stability is intimately linked with social justice.

11.38 For regulating money supply, which in conjunction with real out¬put, determines the general price level, there has to be a reasonable degree of control over the creation of reserve money. Over the years, the practice has grown under which the entire budget deficit

of the Central Govern¬ment has been financed by the
Reserve Bank leading. to an automatic monetisation of
the deficit. This is in addition to whatever support
the Reserve Bank may provide to the market borrowing
programme. The Reserve Bank has, therefore, to address
itself continually to the task of neutralis¬ing, to the
extent possible, the expansionary impact of deficits.
The increasing liquidity of the banking sector resulting
from rising levels of reserve money has to be mopped
up on a continuous basis. The task of absorbing the
ex¬cess liquidity in the system has been done in the
past mainly by increasing the cash reserve ratio. With
the frequent and sharp increases, the cash reserve
ratio has now reached its statutory limit.

11.39 An effective monetary policy would require the
avoidance of the automatic monetisation of the budget
deficits. As a step in this direction, the level of
fiscal deficits as a proportion of GDP needs to be much
lower than what it is now. This would enable better
control over the regulation of money supply. Over the
medium. term, however, beyond a mutually agreed ways and
means accommodation from the Reserve Bank, Government.
should aim at placing its entire debt in the market
at appropriate interest rates. The attainment of this
objective would be greatly facilitated by a substantial
reduction of the Centre's revenue deficit. The overall
economic policy framework would then improve and it
would give to the Reserve Bank the necessary freedom
to determine the level of reserve money creation and
therefore the money supply depending on how the real
factors in the economy are evolving, thus enabling it
to play a more effective role in con-tributing to the
objective of growth with price stability.

SECRET

D.O.RPCD.No.791/NB3(J)-89/90   28th April 1990

Report of the Agricultural
Credit Review Committee

Please refer to your D.O.letter No.7(60)/89-1N, dated 21st March 1990. A Task Force constituted under the Chairmanship of Dr.Ojha, Deputy Governor which included three representatives of Government of India (Additional Secretary, Banking and two Joint Secretaries from the Departments of Rural Development and Agriculture) had examined the draft final report of the Agricultural Credit Review Committee. The final report has been submitted by the Committee after taking into account the observations made by the Task Force. The major issues dealt with in the final report requiring priority considerations are (a) greater autonomy to the banks in financing anti-poverty programmes, (b) interest rates on agricultural advances, (c) the merger of the Regional Rural Banks with the sponsor banks, and (d) the suggestions for the setting up of the National Co-operative Bank of India, Agricultural and Rural Development Corporations for the Eastern and North Eastern Regions and a Crop Insurance Corporation. We have had the major recommendations examined in the Reserve Bank and your comments are contained in the statement enclosed. On some of the important issues we have the following views to offer.

2. Autonomy of banks in financing
    anti-poverty programmes

The Committee has observed progressive deterioration in the autonomy of commercial banks particularly in regard to financing of anti-poverty programmes. The commercial banks have been subject to several external pressures in the form of loan melas etc. According to the committee, mandatory credit by commercial banks which entails target setting, should not result in dilution of the accountability of the banks and to this end it is necessary that once policies have been laid down and targets set, there should be no interference by any external authority in decision making so far as appraisal and sanction of projects and steps initiated for recovery of loans are concerned. It is also necessary to ensure that the targets set to subserve social objectives are within the bank's financial capacity to bear the risk involved. We are in agreement with the observations made by the committee. We must ensure greater autonomy to the banks in their lending decisions. Banks have already over-fulfilled the target of 40 per cent of their outstanding credit to the priority sectors. It is important that new targets for such lending are not fixed and that the tendency to require banks to lend under new special programmes at the highly unremunerative rate Of 10 per cent is eschewed. Practices like loan melas need to be eliminated. The present arrangements regarding recovery of bank dues are unsatisfactory inasmuch as State Governments' machinery for recovery is inadequate. Further, periodical announcements by various governments regarding across-the-board write-offs/reductions of dues vitiate the environment for recovery. Unless effective steps are taken to reverse these trends the viability of the rural lending system will remain under serious threat. It is also necessary to improve legal and administrative arrangements for recovery of dues.

3. Interest rates

The Committee has estimated the financial and transaction costs and the income realizable in agricultural lending by commercial banks, RRBs and co-operatives based on the interest rates existing before the budget of 1988 (when the interest rates were reduced to a minimum of 10 per cent on crop loans) and has recommended the gross margins required by each type of institution to provide for risk costs and a minimum surplus. These are summarised at item 2 of the statement enclosed herewith.

4. The deficit in the margins available in the case of commercial banks has been estimated by the Committee at 2.86 per cent on their agricultural advances (this would have risen by about 1.5 per cent after the March 1988 reduction in the minimum short term interest rate from 11.5 per cent to 10 per cent and the increase in

guarantee fee charged by the Deposit Insurance and Credit Guarantee Corporation). The Committee's approach is that the gross margin recommended by it is necessary for the institutions to attain viability in their agricultural credit operations. They also feel that the institutions capable of cross-subsidisation from other operations should be able to live with somewhat lower gross margins. The Committee has, therefore, recommended raising the interest rates and in doing so has stated that there should only be two sets of rates of interest as far as agricultural loans are concerned. The concessional rate of interest for small and marginal farmers should be at 1.5 per cent above the highest rate of interest on deposits allowed by scheduled commercial banks (this would work to a minimum rate of interest of 11.5 per cent) and that the higher rates of interest with a ceiling of 15.5 per cent (which is the existing maximum rate of interest for short-term agricultural advances) be charged to other borrowers. It is to be presumed that the Committee expects a substantial reduction in the deficit in the margins by raising the interest rates as above and also that the remaining deficit, if any, will be made good through cross-subsidisation from other than agricultural advances. If the Committee were aware that the deficit in the gross margin would in the event turn out to be higher, they might have suggested further jacking up of. the interest. The present interest rate structure for Short-term agricultural advances varies from 10. per cent to 15.5 per cent. The rates of interest for term loans for agricultural advances are 10 and 12.5 per cent. In the case of DRI loans the rate of interest is four per cent per annum.

5. In the light of the detailed examination made by the Committee we agree with it that interest rates on agricultural advances have to be raised to improve the viability of lending institutions. We also agree that under our conditions a degree of concessionality in interest rates to the weaker sections is unavoidable. The World Bank staff who have had discussions on the report with the RBI and NABARD in December 1989 also seem to have taken this view, though they have expressed reservations on some rates which they regard too far

below market rates on the ground that they might result in excessive demand and diversion of credit to unproductive purposes. They seem to feel that the minimum rate should not be below 12.5 per cent, provided the overall margin in agricultural lending could be protected through higher rates for other borrowers. We, however, feel that the World Bank's reservations could be substantially overcome, if the concessional rate is fixed at 11.5 per cent, as recommended by the Committee. This was the rate applicable to the lowest slab of short-term agricultural advances till it was reduced to 10 per cent in March 1988. We are of the opinion that the proposed interest rate structure would reduce to some extent the losses suffered by the banks in their lending to the weaker sections.

6. We also feel that the benefit of concessionality in interest rates should be extended not only to small and marginal farmers but also to all categories of small borrowers including artisans. Accordingly, all advances both short-term and term loans, granted to all categories of borrowers including those assisted under special programmes like IRDP, SEEUY and SEPUP upto an amount of Rs.25,000 could carry a rate of. interest of 11.5 per cent.

7. In my detailed D.O. letter NO.CPC.2197/279A-90 dated 16th February 1990 addressed to you on the restructuring of scheduled commercial banks' lending rates we have suggested an alternative system of administered lending rates wherein the present practice of prescribing specific rates for specific programmes/ lending would be discontinued and the element of concessionality would be directly and exclusively linked to the size of the loan while determining the structure of lending rates. In that letter too a uniform rate of 11.5 per cent has been suggested for loans upto Rs.25,000. You would recollect that this matter was subsequently discussed by us and we came to the tentative conclusion that if Government find it difficult to raise the present rate of 10 per cent to 11.5 per cent, one way could be to charge 10 per cent on loans upto Rs.7,500 and 12 per cent on the next slab upto Rs.25,000. Another conclusion was that on higher slabs

the interest rates suggested by us could be prescribed. The adoption of such rates would generally be less than those proposed by the Khusro Committee but could, nonetheless, afford a reasonable basis for discussion of future World Bank/IDA loans to NABARD.

8. The Committee has recommended the abolition of the DRI Scheme because of the anomalous situation under which commercial banks are required to lend to weaker sections under two parallel programmes, one at the higher rate of 10 per cent under IRDP with subsidy and the other at the lower rate of four percent under the DRI Scheme. The banks sustain a loss of about Rs.50 crores per annum on their DRI loans. The DRI Scheme has out-lived its utility and we may accept the recommendation of the Committee to discontinue it. The beneficiaries eligible under DRI Scheme may be assisted under IRDP in rural areas and the SEPUP in other areas.

9. The Committee has recommended that if the interest rates for any category of borrowers are fixed, in pursuance of Government policy, at below the financial costs plus transaction costs, the shortfall in the interest actually charged and the economic rate should be made good to the institutions by the Government. While there may be no need to provide a subsidy to the commercial banks under the proposed interest rate structure, the subsidy to be provided by the Government, assuming no change in the pre-March 1988 deficit level of 2.86 per cent in the margin on outstanding direct agricultural advances of Rs.13,500 crores would be of the order of Rs.400 crores.

10. In the case of RRBs the deficit in margin available is high at 5.45 percent. As the RRBs lend exclusively to the weaker sections, their ability to cross-subsidise is practically non-existent and according to the Committee, the RRBs' economic rate of lending would be 16.45 per cent. Since this will not be possible, the RRBs would hardly ever become viable.

11. The Committee has estimated the deficit in the gross margin available to the primary agricultural credit co-operative societies at 3.81 per cent and the primary land development banks at 2.61 per cent. The

short-term co-operative credit structure represented by the State Co-operative banks, the District Central Co-operative Banks and the Primary Agricultural Credit Societies depends largely for their resources on the refinance provided by RBI through NABARD. Over the years the general line of credit extended by the RBI to NABARD has increased -- from Rs.1,200 crores in 1982-83 to Rs.3,350 crores in 1989-90 -- and nearly 40 per cent of the outstanding short-term loans of the primary agricultural credit societies is out of the refinance availed of by them from NABARD. In March 1988 when the interest rates on short-term agricultural advances were reduced by 1 to 2.5 percentage points, as desired by the Government of India, the Reserve Bank/NABARD had to reduce the rate of interest on the general line of credit to the State Co-operative Banks from seven to three per cent for compensating the losses incurred by the short-term co-operative credit structure.

12. As the rate of interest to the ultimate borrowers, whether they borrow from the commercial banks or co-operative banks or RRBs, is uniform, the modification in the interest rate structure now proposed by us would also apply to the co-operatives. The raising of the lending rate to 11.5 per cent for loans upto Rs.25,000 would make it possible for the co-operatives to increase their involvement in agricultural loans because of better return and our estimate is that their involvement in the short-term agricultural loans could go up by Rs.750 crores to Rs.1000 crores(However, if only 10 per cent is charged on loans upto Rs.7,500 the return to the co-operative institutions will get considerably reduced). As a substantial portion of the loans in the case of co-operative banks would come within the range of Rs.25000, their ability to cross-subsidise by charging higher rates of interest on larger advances is limited. Hence, the deficit in the interest margin in their case even after raising the rate of interest to 11.5 per cent would be around Rs.300 crores on the present level of their advances. It would be around Rs.200 crores in the case of the RRBs. It would be necessary for the Central and State Governments to make good the deficit by way of subsidy to these institutions. The quantum of

subsidy would go up with the increase in agricultural advances which are growing at about 15 per cent per annum in the case of co-operatives.

13. Regional Rural Banks

The financial viability of a vast majority of RRBs has been seriously eroded and they are increasingly unable to deliver credit to the target groups. The accumulated losses of RRBs have been going up every year. They have increased from Rs.133 crores at the end of' December 1987 to Rs.180 crores in respect of 183 reporting RRBs out of a total of 196 RRBs at the end of 31st March 1989. As a result, the paid up capital and reserves of 153 RRBs amounting to Rs.59 crores and deposits of 103 RRBs amounting to Rs.121 crores have been eroded. Besides, but for a few RRBs which have worked well the functioning of most such banks leaves much to be desired. In this context we had urged an early decision in regard to the merger of RRBs with the sponsor banks (vide copies of my D.O.letters RPCD.No.NB.799/RRB.10-88/89 dated 10th April 1989 addressed to Shri S.B.Chavan, the then Finance Minister and RPCD.No,NB.273/RAB.10-89/90 dated 19th October 1989 addressed to Shri G.K.Arora, the then Finance Secretary). Although the initial cost to the commercial banks would go up as a result of the merger, the quality of operations will improve and the sponsor banks would be able to provide a measure of cross-subsidisation.

14. Setting up of new Institutions

We do not accept the Committee's recommendations for establishing the National Co-operative Bank of India and the Agricultural and Rural Infrastructure Development Corporations and the concept of only one commercial bank branch for each block. Our detailed comments on these and other major recommendations of the Committee are given in a statement enclosed.

15. The World Bank/pre-appraisal mission which had held discussions with NABARD in December 1989 had given the impression that they would be willing to consider a funding arrangement of approximately $ 700 million for three years. They seem to have left hints that their main concern would be for viable interest

rates which they would prefer to be not less than 12.5 per cent at the minimum. Although it may be difficult for the Government at this stage to give any advance assurance of a minimum interest rate for agricultural and rural development lending, Government may like to inform the World Bank that it is confident of arriving at a mutually acceptable position regarding this issue when the appraisal mission enters into discussions with Government. I suggest that an invitation may be extended to the World Bank for a pre-appraisal mission.

    With best regards

                                            Yours sincerely,

                                            (R.N. Malhotra)

Dr. Bimal Jalan,
Finance Secretary,
Government of India,
New Delhi.

गवर्नर
GOVERNOR

भारतीय रिज़र्व बैंक
केन्द्रिय कार्यालय,
बंबई
RESERVE BANK OF INDIA
CENTRAL OFFICE
BOMBAY

G.20.561/90   18th May 1990

My dear Bimal,

Legislation on the Securities and Exchange Board of India (SEBI) - Regulation of Capital Market

With a view to ensuring the growth of the capital market along healthy lines the Government has been considering measures to strengthen the regulatory framework relating to Stock Exchanges and the Securities industry. Some time back, the Securities and Exchange Board of India (SEBI) was set up as a non-statutory body. I understand it is now proposed to convert this Board into a statutory body. Meanwhile, the question of the regulation of the financial system including the securities market has also been engaging the attention of the Reserve Bank of India and I would like to share with you some of our views on the subject.

2. In recent years, the Indian financial market has been undergoing significant and rapid changes. The financial sector is emerging as a key sector of the economy and the market, from the short end to the long end, is developing into a continuum. Though the sector is loosely divided into (a) the banking sector, (b) non-banking financial companies (including leasing, hire purchase and investment companies, most of which are deposit takers) and (c) the capital market (including stock exchanges, brokers, market makers and other intermediaries), financial institutions are no longer confined to operations in any one segment of the market. Banks and their subsidiaries have extended their activities into new areas such as merchant banking, underwriting, investment, leasing, mutual funds, portfolio management

and venture capital funds. Some subsidiaries of banks have become corporate members in the stock exchanges. The interface of banks with the capital market, whether directly or through subsidiaries or associates, is increasing. I have no doubt that as the capital market develops iris size and sophistication, the number and role of institutional members of stock exchanges - mainly banks or their subsidiaries or other associated companies - will grow. At the same time, non-banking financial institutions such as the Unit Trust of India, the Life Insurance Corporation, the General Insurance Corporation etc. have also become lenders, usually in combination with term lending institutions, but also on their own, particularly in the money market. Insurance companies too have entered activities like mutual funds and housing finance through their subsidiaries. Private sector financial companies offering a variety of services are also springing up. These developments which are increasingly characterized by desegmentation of the financial market have important implications for the kind and structure of the regulatory system which we should build.

3. The regulatory systems for overseeing the financial markets in various countries have traditionally developed in the context of the rigid segmentation of financial institutions and activities. For instance, in the United States the Glass Steagall Act provided for almost total separation of commercial banks from investment and securities companies. This separation was also replicated in Japan in the post-war period. It is therefore not surprising that in these countries there are different regulators for the securities businesses and banks. In the United Kingdom the stock exchanges were the concern of the Department of Trade while the Bank of England and the commercial banks were associated with the Treasury. This again appears to have influenced the dichotomy in regulatory institutions for the banking sector and the securities businesses. In several countries the regulation of capital markets has been left essentially to stock exchanges acting as self regulating organisations. There have been, however, conflicts between different regulatory agencies necessitating resort to coordination mechanisms such as

the development of the concept of lead regulator for the Bank of England in respect of bank subsidiaries and deposit taking companies. The conflicts have, however, not been easy to resolve and in any case entail confusion and delays. Perhaps some difficulties have already been encountered in devising the scope and role of SEBI.

4. The need to regulate the securities market in the interest of investors, to specify and enforce disclosure requirements and to prevent insider trading and fraudulent and unfair trade practices, is well recognised. In setting up an appropriate regulatory system, however, we must take into account the fast changinq nature of the financial markets, particularly the multiplicity of financial services which financial institutions are increasingly undertaking and the blurring of distinctions between institutions and market segments. More integrated markets would call for integrated supervision and avoidance of multiplicity Of regulatory agency. It is desirable that the entire market, including the constituents in the capital market, is subject to regulation and supervision by a common authority which appropriately is the central bank of the country. Multiple authorities exercising supervision independent of each other, over various overlapping segments of the market will inevitably lead to conflict of jurisdiction and confusion which can be avoided.

5. While the supervision and control of the banking sector has been the major pre-occupation of the Reserve Bank of India, it has also been given wide powers under Chapter IIIB, Section 45L, of the Reserve Bank of India Act to enable it to exercise a comprehensive oversight over the financial system. I enclose a copy of Section 45L ibid for ready reference. According to that Section, if the Reserve Bank is satisfied that for the purpose of enabling it to regulate the credit system to its advantage it is necessary so to do, it may require financial institutions to furnish statements, information or particulars relating to the business of such financial institutions and to give such institutions directions relating to the conduct of business by them. In issuing such directions to any financial

institutions, the Reserve Bank shall of course, have due regard to the conditions in which, and the objects for which, the institution has been established, its statutory responsibilities, if any, and the effect the business of such financial institution is likely to have on trends in the money and capital markets. Section 45L empowers the Reserve Bank to carry out inspection of any non banking institution, including a financial institution, if it is necessary or expedient to do so. The expression "Financial Institutions" has been defined in Clause (C) of Section 45(1) of Reserve Bank of India Act. A copy of the aforesaid clause (C) is also enclosed for ready reference. It will be seen therefrom that the expression "Financial Institutions" has been widely defined and covers any non-banking institution carrying on the activities, inter alia, of financing by way of making loans or otherwise of any activity other than its own, the acquisition of shares, stocks, bonds, debentures, letting goods on hire purchase and insurance business.

6. The statement of objects and reasons for the amendment introducing Chapter IIIB in the Reserve Bank of India Act inter alia states:

> "The Reserve Bank of India should also be empowered to give to any financial institution or institutions directions in respect of matters, in which the Reserve Bank, as the central banking institution of the country, may be interested from the point of view of the control of credit policy."

While moving the Bill in the Lok Sabha on December 19, 1963, the then Minister of Planning observed:

> "We also intend that the activities of loan, investment and hire-purchase companies or firms, or other financial institutions, which grant loans and advances for a variety of purposes, or purchase securities or shares and thereby influence or affect the money and capital markets, should be controlled by the central bank of the country, so far as these activities are concerned.....".

(emphasis supplied)

Clearly the intention of the law has been that the central banking authority of the country should exercise comprehensive oversight over the financial system as a whole. Since the Reserve Bank authorised the establishment of bank subsidiaries carrying out merchant banking, investment and other financial services, it has been exercising its powers of supervision under Section 45L ibid through inspections. There is a growing consensus among bank supervisers the world over that banks and their subsidiaries or associates should be subjected to consolidated supervision and the Reserve Bank of India has already initiated steps in that direction. As regards other financial institutions the Reserve Bank of India has so far confined itself to informal discussions with them. However, considering the large size of operations of several financial institutions and their impact on the credit and monetary area and the capital market, it has become essential to exercise a more structured supervision over them. A committee of the Reserve Bank is currently devising formats for calling periodical information from selected financial institutions. These formats will be discussed with the heads of _the institutions concerned shortly. I also intend to have consultations with the heads of these institutions on a structured basis at suitable intervals. The quality of assets of many financial institutions, the cost of their funds and rates of interest charged by them also call for a close look for assessing their financial health so that they continue to perform their functions under the relevant statutes effectively. For this purpose, we intend to institute a system of annual financial reviews of important institutions. Another objective would be. to improve, where necessary, co-ordination of these institutions with commercial banks.

7. Considering the scope of the Reserve Bank's powers over commercial .banks as well as financial institutions (as explained above) two different authorities laying down prescriptions in relation to securities industry and financial institutions providing various services can create areas of conflict. Thus, from the point of view of overall credit policy as well as the need to avoid supervisory overlap, it is my view that the regulation of the security industry as envisaged under

the contemplated legislation of SEBI should become a direct responsibility of the Reserve Bank. Even from the operational point of view, there is an advantage in the Reserve Bank of India being entrusted with this responsibility. The Offices of the Reserve Bank of India are located at all important State capitals and there is already a well developed machinery for inspection operating in the Bank which can easily handle the additional tasks with some limited re-organisation. Instead of creating a new institution, it will be economical to use the facilities that now exist in the Reserve Bank. With the authority of the Reserve Bank behind it, there would be greater compliance of the directives and regulations issued. As I have already indicated, in countries where different supervisory authorities have evolved over time, there is a conscious effort now to bring about greater co-ordination among them. The Indian situation is different. In relation to some segments of the financial is system like the securities markets, there is as yet no comprehensive supervisory authority. Instead of creating a new one and then finding ways and means for achieving co-ordination among different authorities, it will be advisable to let the central bank exercise directly this power. The Reserve Bank is in a position to undertake this work soon. It can also absorb whatever trained manpower has been developed in the SEBI. I suggest that the Government may consider these recommendations early. I would like to discuss the matter with yourself and the Finance Minister.

    With kind regards,

                                        Yours sincerely,

                                        (R.N. Malhotra)

Dr.Bimal Jalan,
Finance Secretary,
Ministry of Finance,
Government of India,
Department of Economic Affairs,
New Delhi.

Available to the Public
        DOCUMENT OF INTERNATIONAL MONETARY FUND
              AND NOT FOR PUBLIC USE

                                              FOR
                                              AGENDA

                                      EBS/91/143

                                      CONFIDENTIAL

                                   August 27, 1991

To: Members of the Executive Board

From: The Secretary

Subject: India - Request for Stand-By Arrangement -
           Letter of Intent and Memorandum on Economic
           Policies

   Attached for consideration by the Executive
Directors is the letter of intent from the Indian
authorities requesting a stand-by arrangement
equivalent to SDR 1,656 million, together with a
memorandum on economic policies for 1991/92-1992/93.
The staff report for the 1991 Article IV consultation
with India and its request for a stand-by arrangement
will be circulated later.

   Mr. Neiss (ext. 7604) or Mr. Goldsbrough (ext.
4735) is available to answer technical or factual
questions relating to this paper prior to the Board
discussion.

        Att: (1)

New Delhi, India
August 27, 1991

Dear Mr. Camdessus,

The attached Memorandum on Economic Policies sets out the economic program of the Government of India for the period 1991/92-1992/93. In support of this program, the Government requests an 18-month stand-by arrangement in an amount equivalent to SDR 1,656 million. The Government also intends shortly to request an additional purchase under Section V of the decision on the compensatory and contingency financing facility (CCFF) with respect to any remaining excess in oil import costs or shortfall in merchandise and remittance earnings for the shortfall year that ended July 31, 1991. At a later stage, the Government intends to enter into discussions on a comprehensive medium-term structural adjustment program, supported by an arrangement under the extended Fund facility.

The following quarterly performance criteria for 1991/92 are proposed to monitor progress under the program (Table 1): (a) ceilings on the overall borrowing requirement of the Union Government; (b) ceilings on the net domestic assets (NDA) of the Reserve Bank of India (RBI); (c) a subceiling on RBI credit to the Union Government; and (d) floors on net official international reserves. Indicative magnitudes of these variables for 1992/93 are also proposed and, at the time of the first review, quarterly performance criteria for 1992/93 will be established. During the course of the program, the Government will refrain from imposing new or intensifying existing restrictions on payments and transfers for current international transactions, or introducing or modifying multiple currency practices, or concluding bilateral payments arrangements with Fund members inconsistent with Article VIII, or imposing new or intensifying existing import restrictions for balance of payments reasons.

Three reviews of the program will be conducted. The conclusion of the first review, which is to be completed by March 31, 1992, will depend, inter alia, on the reaching of understandings on the 1992/93 budget, on the establishment of quarterly performance criteria for the remainder of the program period, as well as understandings on: (i) the formulation of a program for tax reform, including concrete measures proposed for the 1992/93 budget and a timetable of action for the medium term; and (ii) the introduction of a detailed tracking system for all categories of expenditures and a system of quarterly expenditure reviews. The second and third reviews of the program will be completed by September 30, 1992 and March 31, 1993, respectively.

The Government of India believes that the policies set forth in the Memorandum are adequate to achieve the objectives of the program, but will take any additional measures appropriate for this purpose. In addition, the Government will consult with the Fund on the adoption of any measures that may be appropriate in accordance with the policies of the Fund on such consultations.

                                        Sincerely yours,

                                        Manmohan Singh
                                        Minister of Finance

Attachment

Mr. Michel Camdessus
Managing Director
International Monetary Fund
Washington, D.C. 20431
U.S.A.

Memorandum on Economic Policies for 1991/92-1992/93

1. The new Government that took office on June 21, 1991 inherited an economy in deep crisis. The balance of payments situation was precarious, with reserves at a low level and the weakening of international confidence having resulted in a sharp decline in capital inflows through commercial borrowing and nonresident deposits. Inflation had reached double digits, hurting most the poorer sections of our society; and there were signs that economic growth had begun to slow somewhat as the shortages of imports and political uncertainty began to affect production and investment. The origins of these problems are directly traceable to large and persistent macroeconomic imbalances, most notably the unsustainably large fiscal deficits, and to the low productivity of past investments. The crisis in the Middle East had exacerbated the situation by contributing to a higher oil import bill in 1990/91 and the temporary loss of export markets and remittance earnings.

2. The new Government, recognizing that there was no time to lose, immediately adopted a number of stabilization measures that were designed to restore internal and external confidence. Thus, monetary policy was tightened further through increases in interest rates, the exchange rate of the rupee was adjusted by 18.7 percent, and a major simplification and liberalization of the trade system was announced. It is the Government's intention, as announced in the Budget speech to Parliament on July 24, 1991, to complement these initial measures by a comprehensive program of economic adjustment. The centerpiece of the economic strategy will be a substantial fiscal correction in the remainder of the current fiscal year and in 1992/93, to be followed by continued fiscal consolidation thereafter. The reduction in fiscal imbalances will be supported by reforms in economic policy that are essential to impart a new element of dynamism to growth processes in the economy. The thrust will be to increase the efficiency and international competitiveness of industrial

production, to utilize foreign investment and technology to a much greater degree than in the past, to improve the performance and rationalize the scope of the public sector, and to reform and modernize the financial sector so that it can more efficiently serve the needs of the economy. During the inevitable period of transition, it is the Government's firm intention that the poorest sections of society are protected to the maximum extent possible from the costs of adjustment.

3. Key macroeconomic objectives (Table 2) will be (i) economic growth in the range of 3-3 1/2 percent in 1991/92 followed by a gradual recovery in 1992/93; (ii) an inflation rate of no more than 9 percent by end-1991/92 and no more than 6 percent by end-1992/93; indeed, the Government will strive for an even more rapid reduction in inflation during the course of 1991/92; and (iii) an easing of the present critical payments situation and a rebuilding of gross international reserves from the extremely low level of about three weeks of imports at end-July to over 1 1/2 months by the end of 1992/93. 1/ In particular, there is an urgent need to rebuild foreign exchange reserves from their current critically low level ($1.3 billion) to about $2.2 billion by end-1991/92.

4. Taking account of the sizable new investments and related imports that will be needed to support the restructuring of the economy, the external current account is targeted to decline from about 3 1/2 percent of GDP in 1990/91 to about 2 1/2 percent of GDP in 1991/92 and 1992/93. 2/ In order to provide room for an expansion in private investment to take advantage of the new opportunities created by the structural reforms, and to allow for a likely

---

1/ According to the IMF definition, i.e., including SDR holdings and with gold valued at SDR 35 per ounce.

2/ These targets refer to the IMF definition of the external current account. According to the official Indian definition, the external current account would decline from 2.5 percent of GDP in 1990/91 to about 2.1 per¬cent in 1991/92 and 2.0 percent in 1992/93.

temporary decline in the private savings ratio, the
reduction in the public sector deficit, which will
initially be brought about by a reduction in the fiscal
deficit of the Central Government, will be larger than
the adjustment in the external current account.

Fiscal policy

5. Our medium-term objective is to progressively
reduce the overall public sector deficit 3/ from an
estimated 12 1/2 percent of GDP in 1990/91 to about
7 percent of GDP in the mid-1990s, a level that we
judge to be consistent with external viability and the
goal of ensuring adequate private sector resources to
respond dynamically to the opportunities created by
the structural reforms. In line with this objective,
we aim to reduce the Union Government deficit 4/ to 6.5
percent of GDP in 1991/92 and 5 percent in 1992/93,
which will include a substantial decline in Union
Government net transfers to the rest of the public
sector, most notably to central public enterprises.

6. The interim budget presented to Parliament in
March 1991 aimed for a deficit of about 6.5 percent of
GDP, but a number of the measures needed to attain
this target were not formulated. Consequently, the
postponement of the regular budget has made fiscal
adjustment in 1991/92 even more difficult because
almost four months of the financial year have elapsed
without a comprehensive fiscal correction effort. The
required adjustment is about 2 1/2 percentage points
of GDP. We expect a swing from deficit to surplus
in the accounts of the Oil Coordination Committee
as a result of higher domestic petroleum prices to
contribute about 0.4 percentage points of GDP. About
half of the remaining adjustment will be achieved by

3/ Defined to include the Union Government, the
Oil Coordination Committee (O.C.C.), States, Union
Territories and internal and extrabudgetary resources
of central and state enterprises for financing their
capital expenditure.

4/ Including the balance in the accounts of the Oil
Coordination Committee.

lowering expenditures and about half from higher tax
and nontax revenues.

7. Total expenditures and net lending are targeted
at a little over 19 percent of GDP in 1991/92--a
decline of about one percentage point. The bulk of the
savings are to be achieved from lower expenditures
on subsidies, moderation in defense spending, cuts
in transfers to public enterprises, and restraint
on other current and capital spending. Cash export
subsidies on new shipments were eliminated with effect
from July 3, 1991; fertilizer prices were raised by
30 percent in August (with special arrangements to
cushion the impact on small and marginal farmers); the
subsidy on sugar was eliminated by raising the issue
price under the public distribution system by about
16 percent; and subsidies on foodgrains will be held
broadly unchanged as a share of GDP. In all, these
measures will reduce the major subsidy payments from
1.9 percent of GDP in 1990/91 to 1.5 percent of GDP
in 1991/92; on a full-year basis, the savings will
be considerably greater (about 1 percent of GDP).
Budgetary support to central public enterprises is
budgeted to decline from 1.5 percent of GDP in 1990/91
to 1.2 percent of GDP in 1991/92. Two considerations
will guide our approach to expenditure policy. First,
no area of government spending should be exempt from
scrutiny in the effort to achieve fiscal correction.
Second, the benefits of the recent exchange rate
adjustment should not be eroded by inflation. At the
level of the departments, no additional budgetary
provision has been made for cost-of-living increases
("dearness allowance"); any increases will have
to be financed from savings on departments' other
expenditures.

8. During the remainder of the financial year, there
will be no net additions to expenditures through
supplementary appropriations, other than those
supported by matching savings or additional receipts.
Beyond this, we plan to have strengthened expenditure
monitoring and control procedures in place by the time
the 1992/93 budget is presented to Parliament.

9. Total revenue as a share of GDP is targeted
to rise by over one percentage point (to about 12
1/2 percent) in 1991/92. Additional tax measures
with an estimated gross revenue yield equivalent to
0.5 percent of GDP have been adopted in the 1991/92
budget. Important new measures include a 5 percentage
point increase in the corporate tax rate; a reduction
in generous depreciation allowances that have tended
to encourage capital-intensive methods of production;
a tax on the gross interest receipts of banks; and
increases in excise duties, especially for consumer
durables and other products that are purchased
primarily by the affluent sections of society. At
the same time, we have taken some initial steps to
rationalize the structure of import tariffs and to
broaden the base and strengthen the collection of
direct taxes. The ad valorem rate of basic plus
auxiliary customs duties has been reduced to a maximum
of 150 percent; many of the increases in auxiliary
customs duties introduced in December 1990 have been
partially or fully rolled back; and rates of import
duty on general capital goods and their components
have been reduced by 5 percentage points (to a range
of 65-80 percent). To strengthen tax collection, the
system of deduction at source is being extended to
cover interest income, commissions,and withdrawals
from the National Savings Scheme; and a major loophole
in the wealth tax has been plugged. With regard to
nontax receipts, Rs.25 billion (0.4 percent of GDP)
will be generated from the planned sale to mutual
funds of shares in a number of public enterprises
(paragraph 30).

10. In order to ensure that the objective of
reducing the fiscal deficit of the Central Government
to 6.5 percent of GDP in 1991/92 is achieved,
notwithstanding any unanticipated adverse developments
during the course of the year, the Government intends
to take additional measures, on both the revenue
and expenditure sides, resulting in an estimated
adjustment of Rs 20 billion (0.3 percent of GDP).
These additional measures will be implemented in
stages, in the light of budgetary developments, and

will be in place by December 31, 1991. The nature of
the additional measures will be in keeping with the
Government's policy of achieving a sustainable fiscal
deficit reduction.

11. Our target for reducing the fiscal deficit of the
Union Government to 5 percent of GDP in 1992/93 is
an ambitious one, but we are determined to take all
possible measures to achieve this objective. Reduction
of the fiscal deficit would yield desired results only
when the method of bringing about such reduction is in
harmony with reforms in economic policy and economic
management. We intend, therefore, to formulate
policy proposals in a number of areas. We intend
to initiate a process of comprehensive tax reform
with the object of broadening the base of taxation,
reducing levels of and dispersion in import duties,
improving compliance and modernizing the entire
system of tax administration. We will take a fresh
look at the whole area of expenditure, and no major
category should be exempt from scrutiny. Particular
emphasis would be given to transfers and loans to
public enterprises. The aim is to tighten their budget
constraint and improve their efficiency and viability.
We hope that norms of fiscal discipline being set by
the Central Government would find acceptance by the
State Governments as well. There is need for further
rationalization and reduction of subsidies. Our aim
should be to move to a more objective system of
administered prices, as indicated in paragraph 16,
that takes into account world market developments and
domestic supply conditions. We would have a major
thrust for a more efficient expenditure control system.
With this end in view, a thorough review of the
existing system will be undertaken to remove existing
deficiencies and to significantly strengthen its
effectiveness. Thus, fiscal adjustment in 1992/93 will
not only be of a substantial magnitude, but will also
be anchored to measures and policies that would have a
sustainable impact on future fiscal consolidation.

12. In consonance with the fiscal consolidation
of the Union Government, it is our hope that the
State Governments will move in a similar direction

to correct their fiscal imbalances. We will encourage
them to take steps to improve their fiscal performance
and streamline the working of their enterprises. In
particular, renewed efforts will be made to address
the financial difficulties of the State Electricity
Boards through improved efficiency and a rationalized
tariff structure. This would also enable them to
ensure prompt payment of dues to central public
sector undertakings, especially the power generation
companies. Our overall strategy for the central
public enterprises is outlined in paragraph 29.
As a result of these efforts to improve efficiency
and profitability, we expect the internal resource
generation of the central public sector enterprises to
improve significantly in 1991/92. This will permit a
reduction in budget support even while their capital
spending is expected to increase. The aggregate deficit
of all central public enterprises is projected to fall
from 3 1/2 percent of GDP in 1990/91 to 3 percent in
1991/92. As part of our endeavor to introduce a hard
budget constraint for the enterprises, no increase in
budget support 1/ during 1991/92 beyond the budget
figures will be considered, barring exceptional
circumstances where matching savings would be found.

Monetary policy

13. A restrictive monetary policy will be pursued
in order to reduce inflationary pressures and support
the targeted balance of payments improvement. Such
a policy, in conjunction with the lowering of the
public sector's claims on resources, is both an
essential corollary of exchange rate stability and the
only way to achieve a lasting reduction in interest
rates. Monetary policy has already been tightened
considerably during 1991. Thus, in April a number of
interest rates were increased, the incremental nonfood
credit-deposit ratio was lowered, and an additional
10 percent cash reserve requirement was imposed on
increases in deposits. A further across-the-board

1/ Net of the impact of exchange adjustments on
the rupee value of aid receipts.

increase of one percentage point in deposit interest
rates was implemented in July, and the minimum loan
rate for nonpreferred credits was also raised from
17 percent to 18 1/2 percent. For 1991/92, broad
money (M3) growth of 13 percent has been targeted,
consistent with the output and inflation targets.
Taking account of the impact of the new incremental
cash reserve requirement, reserve money has been
targeted to rise by 15 1/2 percent. A further slowdown
in the growth of broad and reserve money (to 11-
12 percent) will be sought in 1992/93. The monetary
program for 1991/92 specifies quarterly ceilings on
the net domestic assets (NDA) of the Reserve Bank of
India (RBI) as well as on net RBI credit to the Union
Government (Table 1). The projected NDA levels are
consistent with a targeted improvement of about $1
billion in gross official foreign exchange reserves
between end-June 1991 and end-March 1992. Quarterly
floors for net official international reserves in
1991/92 have also been established.

14. In implementing its monetary and credit
policies, the, RBI uses both indirect, market-oriented
mechanisms that operate through their effect on
reserve money growth and commercial bank liquidity
as well as the existing instruments that influence
more directly the overall magnitude and composition
of credit growth. In line with the overall thrust of
financial sector liberalization, described in paragraph
32, the RBI intends to rely increasingly on indirect
policy instruments. Therefore, interest rate policy
will be used flexibly to manage the balance of payments
and to achieve the desired deceleration in inflation.
In particular, the RBI will act decisively to tighten
monetary policy should net official international
reserves fall below the targeted floors.

Pricing policies

15. With a view to reducing budgetary subsidies
and promoting a more flexible price structure, the
Government recently announced increases in a number
of administered prices including for important inputs
(petroleum products and fertilizer); for services
(such as railway fares); and for agricultural

commodities (such as sugar). Beyond this, our pricing
policies will aim at imparting greater flexibility
in all areas, and public enterprises will be given
greater freedom in setting prices according to market
forces--a step that will need to be coordinated with
the phasing of trade liberalization and the promotion
of increased domestic competition. Detailed plans will
be announced at the time of the first review.

16. Average domestic petroleum prices were
increased by a cumulative 38 percent in 1990 and were
not lowered again as world market prices fell in
early 1991. Further price changes were announced at
the time of the presentation of the 1991/92 Budget to
Parliament: a 20 percent increase for motor spirit
(gasoline), aviation fuel, and LPG for nonindustrial
use; no change for diesel; a 10 percent reduction for
kerosene for nonindustrial uses; and a 10 percent
increase for all other petroleum products. The
reduction in kerosene prices reflects the importance
of this item in the consumption basket of the poor
and the Government's determination to cushion the
impact of the adjustment process on this segment of
Indian society. On a weighted average basis, the price
changes amount to a 7 percent price increase and are
sufficient to ensure that, at prevailing world market
prices, total oil-related fiscal receipts, 1/ will not
be reduced as a result of the recent exchange rate
action. The accounts of the Oil Coordination Committee
are now projected to record a small surplus. In line
with the general policy described in paragraph 15, the
Government intends to evolve a system for the pricing
of petroleum products that provides for periodic
adjustments in the light of developments in the world
market and domestic supply conditions.

External policies

17. An exchange rate policy that safeguards
competitiveness is a crucial element of our economic
program. Shortly after the new Government assumed
office, the RBI adjusted downward in two steps the

1/ Accruing to the Union budget and the Oil
Coordination Committee.

value of the rupee by 18.7 percent against the
U.S. dollar in order to improve the international
competitiveness of exports and to bring about a more
orderly compression of imports. This adjustment
will help check the flight of capital, encourage the
repatriation of outstanding export receipts and
remittances, and thereby help to stabilize the balance
of payments. Following this realignment of the rate,
the Government intends to hold the nominal effective
exchange rate stable by relying primarily on monetary
and fiscal policy to maintain competitiveness and
ensure the balance of payments objectives.

18. The Government's stabilization and import
compression measures are expected to reduce the
external current account deficit to 2.7 percent of
GDP in 1991/92. 1/ Import volumes would decline by
about 5 percent, while export earnings are expected
to gradually resume the growth that was interrupted
in 1990/91, in reflection of the improvement in
competitiveness, the resumption of exports to
the Middle East, and better demand conditions in
industrial countries. The capital account, however,
is expected to deteriorate substantially in 1991/92
because of the curtailment in access to commercial
capital markets and the outflow of nonresident deposits
and short-term capital that took place during the first
quarter of the fiscal year. As a result, despite the
improvement in the current account, an exceptional
financing need of about $4 billion is expected for
1991/92. 2/ Part of this amount ($870 million) has
already been covered from various sources, including

1/ To 2.1 percent of GDP according to the official
Indian definition.

2/ The size of the remaining compensable amount
under the CCFF, and hence the size of the requested
purchase, are larger than anticipated at the time
of the discussion on the program (SDR 468.9 million
compared with an earlier estimate of SDR 314.4
million). Under the program, the difference, amounting
to $220 million, has been added to the targeted gross
reserve accumulation, with a corresponding increase in
total exceptional financing.

the recent CCFF drawing from the Fund, and exceptional
assistance already disbursed by multilateral and
bilateral creditors. The remainder of about $3 billion
is expected to be covered by a further CCFF drawing,
purchases under the stand-by arrangement, and by
additional financing from multilateral and bilateral
sources, including a Structural Adjustment Loan and
two sector loans from the World Bank as well as
additional quick-disbursing support from the Asian
Development Bank and bilateral donors. A meeting of
the aid donor's consortium is scheduled for mid-
September.

19. The current account deficit is expected to
remain broadly unchanged in 1992/93, at 2.6 percent
of GDP. Export growth is projected to continue its
recovery (with an 11 percent volume increase) as a
result of improved competitiveness and a further
pickup of demand in world markets. However, imports
are also expected to rise significantly (by about
7 percent in volume terms) from the low level of
1991/92 as the special import compression measures
are removed. The capital account is expected to
register a significant improvement (from a surplus
of $2.8 billion in 1991/92 to about $4.4 billion in
1992/93) as a result of a moderate reversal of the
previous year's net outflow of nonresident deposits,
some increase in normal net aid disbursements, and a
reversal in net short-term flows. Given the need for a
further restoration in official reserves, there would
still be a need for exceptional financing from the Fund
and other multilateral and bilateral creditors, but
we estimate that the need (about $2.8 billion) would
be considerably smaller than in the current year. A
further sizable adjustment in the external current
account will be needed over the medium term. The pace
at which India's external viability can be restored
would depend, however, on how quickly access to normal
commercial borrowing can be resumed. In this respect,
the Government envisages that, in 1993/94¬-1994/95,
covering the external financing gaps would continue to
require some additional assistance from multilateral
sources, including the Fund, as well as access to

financing from official bilateral and commercial sources. We also expect a significant expansion in foreign direct investment inflows as a result of the new policy measures discussed in paragraph 25. Our aim is to eliminate the need for exceptional financing by the mid-1990s.

20. The targeted buildup in gross official reserves to about 1 1/4 months of imports at end-1991/92 and a little over 1 1/2 months of imports at end-1992/93 would still leave reserves at a low level in comparison with earlier years. Hence, India's external position will remain vulnerable to adverse shocks or to any unexpected slippages. Therefore, the Government will act quickly and decisively to correct any shortfall from the targeted path for reserve increase through a further tightening of monetary policy. The Government intends to pursue prudent debt management policies, and higher-than-anticipated commercial borrowings will be used for an additional rebuilding of reserves. Specifically, any unanticipated borrowing from commercial markets by the public sector will be matched by a corresponding increase in the floors for net official international reserves.

Social policies

21. The Government is aware that the process of macroeconomic adjustment is bound to be painful. All sections of the community have to make sacrifices to preserve our economic independence and to restore the health of the economy. Our endeavor would be to minimize the burden of adjustment on the poor. We are committed to adjustment with a human face; therefore, a steadfast adherence to the objective of poverty alleviation is an integral part of our conception of the adjustment process. We expect the structural reforms that have been initiated to generate long-lasting benefits in the reduction of poverty by promoting greatly increased employment opportunities. In the interim, any adjustment process that widened social and economic disparities would, in our view, be self-defeating. With this principle in mind, the Government has provided in the 1991/92 budget for

higher outlays on elementary education, rural drinking water supply, assistance to small and marginal farmers, programs for women and children, programs for the welfare of scheduled castes and scheduled tribes and other weaker sections of the society, as well as for increased spending on infrastructure and employment-creation projects in the rural areas.

22. India continues to have a deep commitment to environmental conservation, drawn both from her ethos and traditions as well as her experience in the last two decades. We share the global concern for adverse environmental changes induced by economic and technological activities. Our commitments and concerns are reflected in our present and projected policies and legislation relating to air and water pollution control, forestry, and to conservation of natural resources, including wasteland and water resource development. We shall endeavor to obtain a greater quantum of peoples' involvement and association of nongovernment organizations in their implementation. The objective will be to attain ecologically sound and sustainable development.

Structural policies

23. Our adjustment strategy is predicated upon a comprehensive program of structural reforms that are designed to promote faster economic growth. The broad thrust of these reforms as well as the initial concrete policy measures are described below. In the areas of industrial deregulation, trade policy, public enterprises, and aspects of financial sector reform, we expect that policy changes already introduced, combined with further action to implement and strengthen policy reform, would also form the basis for World Bank support in the context of a structural adjustment loan.

24. While over the years a well-diversified industrial structure was established, barriers to entry and limits on growth in the size of firms led to a proliferation of licensing arrangements and an increase in the degree of monopoly. There was inadequate emphasis on reduction of costs, upgradation

of technology, and improvement of quality standards. With a view to fostering increased competition between the firms in the domestic market so that there are adequate incentives for raising productivity and reducing costs, a major deregulation of the domestic industrial sector was introduced in the Industrial Policy announced on July 24, 1991. The thrust of the new policy is to enable entrepreneurs to take investment decisions based on their own commercial judgement with a greatly reduced regulatory role of Government. These measures are complementary to those taken in the areas of trade policy, exchange rate management, fiscal policy, and financial sector reforms.

The first stage of the reform was announced in July and includes the following key measures:-

(i) Industrial licensing has been abolished for all projects except for a list of 18 industries related to security, strategic, or environmental concerns and certain items of luxury consumption that have a high proportion of imported inputs. The exemption from licensing also applies to the expansion of existing units. Notifications spelling out the new procedures were issued on August 2.

(ii) The Monopolies and Restrictive Trade Practices (MRTP) Act will now be applied in a manner which eliminates the need to seek prior governmental approval for expansion of present undertakings and establishment of new undertakings by large companies. The changes also apply to merger, amalgamation, and takeover. These changes will be introduced with immediate effect through appropriate administrative notifications under the Act.

(iii) The system of phased manufacturing programs, which required the progressive reduction in the import content of certain projects over time, has been discontinued for all new projects.

(iv) Industrial location policies have been streamlined so that only the 23 cities with a population of over 1 million (within a radius of 25 kilometers) will be subject to industrial location rules. Further¬more, these rules will not apply for specified nonpolluting industries or in already designated industrial zones.

(v) The set of activities henceforth reserved for the public sector is now much narrower than before, and there will be no bar to the remaining reserved areas being opened up to the private sector selectively.

Beyond this, it is the Government's intention to review the prior approval requirements that still exist for capital goods imports, with the aim of rapidly reducing their scope. As a first step, all capital goods imports where foreign exchange availability for the imported equipment is assured through foreign equity have now been given automatic clearance. Effective April 1, 1992, imported capital goods that represent less than 25 percent of a project's total plant and equipment costs will also be given automatic approval, up to a value of Rs. 20 million (about $800,000). The Government expects further liberalization during the course of 1992/93.

25. In conjunction with industrial deregulation, the Government intends to provide greatly increased opportunities for foreign investment. Such investment would bring the attendant advantages of technology transfer, marketing expertise, and the introduction of modern managerial technique as well as promoting a much-needed shift in the composition of external private capital inflows toward equity and away from debt-creating flows. In addition, restrictions on technology agreements will be relaxed. With these broad objectives in mind, the following steps have already been announced.

(i) Automatic approval will be given for direct foreign investment up to 51 percent foreign equity ownership in a wide range of approved industries. Previously, all foreign investment was subject to approval, and foreign equity participation was generally limited to 40 percent.

(ii) Other foreign equity proposals will continue to need prior clearance, but procedures will be streamlined and made mare transparent. A special empowered Board will be established to negotiate with large international firms that would provide access to high technology and world markets.

(iii) Automatic permission will be given for foreign technology agreements in the list of industries referred to in item (i) for royalty payments of up to 5 percent of domestic sales or 8 percent of export sales or for lump-sum payments of up to Rs 10 million (about $400,000). Automatic approval for all other royalty payments will also be given if the projects can generate internally the foreign exchange required. All other payments will continue to require approval under existing procedures.

The necessary changes in the application of the Foreign Exchange Regulation Act (FERA) will be introduced by end-October through administrative notifications. It is our intention to explore further options for attracting foreign direct investment and technology.

26. As part of our strategy to promote the international integration of our economy, it is necessary to phase out the excessive and often indiscriminate protection provided to industry which has weakened the incentive to develop a vibrant export sector. An important element of this strategy will be a transition from a regime of quantitative restriction to a price-based system. Our medium-term objective is to progressively eliminate licenses and quantitative restrictions, especially for capital goods and raw materials, so that these items could be increasingly placed on open general license. The shift is proposed to be achieved over a period of three to five years. A high-level committee will work out the modality of achieving this transition, keeping in mind the balance of payments position, in order to provide Indian industry with an appropriate environment to develop international competitiveness. Based on the Committee's recommendations, we will formulate policy proposals by the time of the 1992/93 budget. (See also paragraph 34.)

27. The first step in rationalizing the trade regime was implemented in July. Cash export subsidies

were eliminated at the time of the exchange rate adjustment, and an expanded system of import entitlements, linked to export earnings, has replaced a large part of the administered licensing of imports. The new entitlements, called EXIM scrip, are generally provided at a rate of 30 percent of gross export earnings (with special arrangements for gems, jewelry, and a few other industries), and are freely tradeable; the premium on the scrip, set in the market, represents a further incentive for exporters and a means of allocating imports according to market forces. The arrangement is intended as a transitional one that will serve as a vehicle for further trade liberalization through expansion of import entitlements in the next several years, and it is our intention to administer the system in a manner that prepares Indian industry for a more uniform set of incentives.

28. In addition to the trade reform measures already taken, the Government plans additional action along the following lines:-

(i) Greater transparency will be introduced into the trade regime through the adoption, from September 1, 1991, of a harmonized system of customs classification.

(ii) A high priority will be the earliest possible elimination of the temporary exchange restrictions imposed earlier in the year in response to the foreign exchange crisis--including the limitations on the availability of foreign exchange for capital goods imports, the prior approval by the RBI for certain foreign exchange transactions exceeding specified amounts, and the high cash margin requirements (ranging up to 200 percent) on letters of credit. The first priority will be to eliminate the restrictions that affect exporters. Recently, the RBI has reduced the cash margins on imports by certain exporters and has also relaxed prior approval requirements for exporters. A timetable for eliminating any remaining restrictions will be discussed at the time of the first review.

(iii) Over the years, a number of import and export items had to be exclusively channelled ("canalized") through specified public sector agencies. It has now been decided to reduce sharply the scope of this public sector monopoly, including most export items and a significant number of import items. The Government recognizes that there is a strong case for freeing trade in more items, especially imports of raw materials. Therefore, additional items will be progressively decanalized; for this purpose, a further review of the remaining items will be made in March 1992 and a suitable decision taken with effect from April 1, 1992.

(iv) Actual user requirements, which require that imports be undertaken by the final users, have already been relaxed as a result of the EXIM scrip scheme. Proposals for the removal of the remaining requirements will be formulated.

(v) The 1991/92 Budget began the process of tariff reform, with a reduction in peak tariff rates to a maximum of 150 percent (from as much as 300 percent or more) and a moderate across-the-board reduction in tariffs on capital goods imports. A more broad-based effort to streamline and reduce tariff rates will be proposed in the 1992/93 budget.

29. The public enterprise sector has not generated internal surpluses on a large enough scale and, because of its inadequate exposure to competition, has contributed to a high-cost structure. To address these problems, the Government has decided to adopt a new approach, key elements of which will be: (1) the existing portfolio of public investments will be reviewed with a greater sense of realism to avoid areas where social considerations are not paramount or where the private sector would be more efficient; (2) enterprises in areas where continued public sector involvement is judged appropriate will be provided a much greater degree of managerial autonomy; (3) budgetary transfers to public enterprises will be progressively reduced; (4) to provide further market discipline for public enterprises, competition from the private sector will be encouraged and part of the

equity in selected enterprises will be disinvested; and (5) chronically sick public enterprises will not be allowed to continue incurring heavy losses.

30. Several important measures initiating the new strategy have already been taken. (1) The number of industries reserved for the public sector has been reduced from 17 to 8. Even in these areas, private sector participation will be allowed selectively. Thus, joint ventures with foreign companies in oil exploration and production are now possible. (2) Public enterprises that are chronically sick and unlikely to be turned around will be referred to the Board for Industrial and Financial Reconstruction (BIFR) for rationalization. We expect to have the new procedures in place by end-December 1991. A safety net will be created to protect the interests of workers. (3) The existing system of monitoring enterprises through Memoranda of Understanding (MOU) will be strengthened, with primary emphasis on profitability and the rate of return on capital. (4) Up to 20 percent of government equity in selected public sector enterprises will be disinvested through mutual funds. The objective is that the mutual funds would seek a listing for the shares on the stock market and would have the freedom to dispose of them after a specified time period. Additional sales are expected in 1992/93, by which time proposals for encouraging broader disinvestment options could also be developed.

31. Appropriate exit policies are needed to capture the efficiency gains from policy reform and, at the same time, it is imperative that workers should be protected from the adverse impact of the adjustment process to the maximum extent feasible. Keeping in view the need for a rapid improvement in the efficiency of the economic system and of preserving social cohesion, so vital for ensuring political and social acceptability of the adjustment process, effort is under way to formulate a policy that would facilitate the process of industrial re-structuring, including a suitable framework for reducing barriers to exit. This process will take some time, since it will be essential to build the political consensus

necessary for ensuring durability of policy reform.
We expect that specific policies in this area will
be formulated by the time of the submission of the
1992/93 budget to Parliament. An important component
of these policies is the establishment of a National
Renewal Fund (NRF) introduced in the 1991/92 budget.
The NRF will provide a social safety net to protect
workers from the adverse consequences of adjustment
and technical transformation, most importantly through
the provision of retraining so that they are in a
position to remain productive participants in economic
activit. We visualize the NRF also being supported
by contributions from the States and the private
sector. It is also intended to strengthen the Board
for Industrial and Financial Reconstruction (BIFR),
which was established in 1987 to recommend action--
rehabilitation, merger, or exit--for private sector
firms with negative net worth and meeting certain
eligibility requirements; in addition, its scope will
be widened to include public sector units.

32. Far as the financial system has come in terms
of market widening and deepening, there remain a
number of structural rigidities--notably related
to interest rates and the allocation of credit-
-that have contributed to inefficient financial
intermediation. Important measures have been taken
recently to address these problems, particularly on
the side of liberalizing interest rates. Thus, bank
lending rates on larger loans have been set free, the
short-term money market has been allowed to function
without hindrance, interest ceilings on loans by
term-lending institutions have been abolished, and
all restrictions on private debentures interest
rates have been eliminated. These steps, implying an
elimination of controls at the short and long end of
the maturity spectrum, have made for a considerably
more flexible structure of interest rates. While the
process of interest rate liberalization will be
continued over the next 18 months, the Government
will focus attention on three other key priorities:
promoting a more market-oriented allocation of credit,
implementing policies to further the development of
capital markets, and enhancing the soundness of the

banking system. The recently constituted Committee on the Financial System (Narasimhan Committee) will formulate detailed recommendations in these areas. In addition, the Committee has been requested to make recommendations relating to banks and term-lending financial institutions specifically on (a) their organizational structure, (b) composition and adequacy of the capital structure, and (c) supervisory arrangements. The Committee has been asked to submit its proposals by November 15, and it is the intention of the Government to spell out a timetable for implementation by the time of the first review. Beyond this, as the process of fiscal consolidation takes hold, bank profitability can be expected to improve, thus setting the stage for the extension of interest rate liberalization to bank deposits as well as for a phased reduction, beginning in 1992/93, in the statutory liquidity requirement, under which banks must presently hold selected government and other public sector securities against 38 1/2 per cent of their deposits.

33. To continue the process of developing more competitive capital markets, the Government has decided to promote the development of private sector and joint-venture mutual funds; a comprehensive set of policies and guidelines that will apply equally to both public and private sector mutual funds is being developed. The Government also intends to introduce legislation in the forthcoming winter session of Parliament that would allow the Securities and Exchange Board of India to function as an autonomous body with full statutory powers to regulate equity markets. Two expert committees have also been established to examine the question of trading reforms and institutional improvement of the stock exchanges.

34. In order to make the tax system more elastic, broaden the base of taxation, reduce its dependence on customs revenue, and simplify the existing procedures, the Government intends to implement a major tax reform over the next few years. The major emphasis will be on increasing the share of revenue from direct taxes, so that resources are raised from those most able to

pay; rationalizing domestic indirect taxes including further expansion in the existing MODVAT system; and reducing the level and dispersion of import tariffs. The time available for the new Government before presenting the 1991/92 budget was simply not enough to formulate basic structural changes, but several measures were adopted consistent with our medium-term strategy. Thus, peak import tariffs were reduced and major efforts were made to strengthen tax compliance, including a much increased role for deduction of tax at source. Beyond this, the Government will appoint a committee of experts to prepare a study advising how best our agenda of tax reform can be pursued. The first steps of the tax reform will be introduced in the 1992/93 budget.

Table 1

India: Performance Criteria for Domestic and Financial
Policies in 1991/92 and Indicative Targets for 1992/93

| | Prel. Actual end-July | Performance Criteria, 1991/92 | | | Indicative Targets 1992/93 |
		End-Oct. 1991	End-Dec. 1991	End-Mar. 1992	End-March 1993
		(In billions of rupees)			
Domestic sector (ceilings)					
Overall borrowing requirement of the Union Government 1/	160 2/	275	305	390 3/	325 4/
Net domestic assets (NDA) of the RBI 5/	818.7	865.6	899.1	943.5	1,048
Of which : Net credit to Union Government	973.4	987.6	987.6	955.6	1,018
		(In millions of U.S.dollars)			
External sector (floor)					
Net official international reserves 6/	-1,131	-943	-1,156	-1,195	-703
Memorandum item:		(In billions of rupees)			
Indicative target (ceiling) for bank credit to general Government 7/	1,535	1,546	1,564	1,551	1,675

1/ Cumulative from March 31 of the previous financial year.

2/ End-June figure.

3/ The ceiling for end-March 1992 will be raised (lowered) by the excess(shortfall)of the OCC surplus from Rs.8 billion.

4/ Including projected OCC surplus.

5/ The ceilings will be adjusted for (i) unexpected valuation effects arising from changes in exchange rates and the price of gold; (ii) changes in reserve requirements; and (iii) changes in the net international reserve floor arising from factors described in footnote 6 below.

6/ The floors will be adjusted upward (downward) to the extent that gross commercial borrowing by or guaranteed by the public sector (medium and long¬-term borrowing from commercial banks plus bond issues to foreigners plus any change in the short-term external debt of the State Bank of India) plus exceptional financing exceeds (falls short of) $590 million for the period August 1-October 31, 1991, $840 million for the period August 1-December 31, 1991, and $1,484 million for the period August 1, 1991-March 31, 1992. However, the downward adjustments in the floors will be limited to no more than $300 million by October 31, 1991, $200 million by December 31, 1991, and $400 million by March 31, 1992. The floors will also be adjusted upward (downward) by any increase (decrease) in foreign exchange deposits held by the RBI with the State Bank of India from the level of $600 million.

7/ General Government comprises the Union Government, the States, and Union territories.

Table 2

India: Key Macroeconomic Objectives, 1991/921-1992/93

(In percent unless otherwise indicated)

	1990/91 Est.	1991/9211 Program	1992/93 Program
Real GDP growth	5	3-3 1/2	4
Inflation (end-period)	12.1	9	6
Overall public sector deficit/GDP	12.5	10.0	8.5
Union Government deficit/GDP	9.0	6.5	5.0
Broad money growth	15.3	13.01	11-12
Reserve money growth	13.1	15.5 1/	11-12
External current account/GDP	3.4	2.7	2.6
Gross official reserves (in months of imports) 2/	1.3	1.3 1.7	
Official foreign exchange reserves (in billions of U.S.dollars)	2.2	2.2 3.2	

1/ Excluding the impact of the incremental cash reserve ratio, reserve money growth would be 13 percent.

2/ According to the IMF definition, i.e., including SDR holdings and gold valued at SDR 35 per ounce.

November 11, 1991

Pear Mr. Preston,

1. The Government of India has adopted a package of major policy reforms aimed at macro economic stabilisation and restoration of the growth momentum to the economy. These initiatives are being implemented at a time when the Indian economy faces a serious Balance of Payments crisis. The strategy consists of measures aimed at achieving a sharp reduction in the fiscal deficit, combined with reforms in the key areas of trade policy, industrial policy, the public sector and the financial sector. The effectiveness of these measures in bringing about the desired structural adjustment in the economy while maintaining the momentum of growth depends critically upon the availability of adequate external finance. Accordingly, we are requesting a Structural Adjustment Loan/Credit from the World Bank. We believe that the policies outlined by us are adequate and sufficient to meet the objectives of the programme.

2. It is also our intention to seek IBRD/IDA support for our medium term reforms strategy through a series of Structural/Sectoral Adjustment loans/credits including fast disbursing support for establishing and strengthening the social safety net to mitigate the social burden of the transition process.

3. We have no doubt that with continued support from multilateral financing institutions, particularly the Bank and the Fund, and given the resilience of our economy as well as the support of the international community as a whole, witnessed at a recent meeting of the Aid India Consortium, India would be able to overcome the present economic difficulties and return it to a path of sustained high growth. 1 greatly look forward to your continued support in our endeavour to achieve these objectives.

4. The medium term reform programme of Government is described in the attachment to this letter.

Kind regards,

Yours sincerely,

(Manmonan Singh)

Mr. I.T. Preston,
President,
The World Bank,
Washington D.C.

SUO MOTO STATEMENT BY THE PRIME MINISTER

(made on July 9, 1992 in Parliament)

The events that have unfolded in the last few months in the financial sector of the country have caused grave anxiety to me and the country at large. The ramifications of this matter have to be thoroughly probed and effective measures taken so that the basic integrity of the financial institutions of the country is not jeopardized and the new economic initiatives taken by the Government to strengthen and accelerate the economic growth are in no way inhibited. My Government has been taking concrete and effective steps at every stage in the last few months as required in the circumstances. The inquiry by the CBI and action by the Special Court will be pursued and whatever is required to be done as a consequence thereof, shall be done.

While this aspect is being fully attended to, I feel that there is need for a comprehensive inquiry through the instrument of Parliament which not only fully establishes Parliamentary supremacy but also provides an effective safeguard to protect the country's interests. We have had consultations with all political parties in Parliament and there is consensus on the desirability of setting up a Joint Parliamentary Committee in this regard. I am, therefore, requesting the Hon'ble Speaker to proceed with the formation of a Joint Parliamentary Committee and entrust it with the task I have mentioned which may be completed within a reasonable time.

I would like to assure this august House that my desire and purpose remain, as they have been so far, to unravel the truth, and ensure the smooth transformation to a vibrant economy in the larger interests of the nation.

POLICY ENVIRONMENT

Box 1.1

Supplemental Agreement between the Reserve Bank of India and the Government of India

An Agreement made this ninth day of September 1994 between the President of India acting through the Ministry of Finance, Government of India (hereinafter referred to as "the Government") of the one part and the Reserve Bank of India (hereinafter called "the Bank") of the other part.

2. Whereas the erstwhile Secretary of State for India in Council and the Bank have entered into an agreement dated fifth day of April 1935 (hereinafter referred to as "the principal agreement").

3. Whereas under clause 5 of the principal agreement it is provided that the Bank shall not be entitled to any remuneration for the conduct of ordinary banking business of the Governor General in Council (now Government of India) other than such advantage as may accrue to it from the holding of his cash balance free of obligation to pay interest thereon.

4. Whereas it has been further agreed in November 1937 and January 1955 by enchange of letters that the Government shall maintain with the Bank a cash balance of not less than Rs. 50 crore on Fridays and Rs. 4 crore on other days free of obligation to pay interest thereon and further whenever the balance in the account of the Government falls below the minimum agreed to, the account be replenished by the creation of ad hoc Treasury Bills in favour of the Bank.

5. Whereas it has been announced by the Union Finance Minister in his budget speech for financial year 1994-95 the intention to phase out the Government's access to ad hoc Treasury Bills over a period of three years beginning financial year 1994-95.

6. Whereas it has been agreed between the parties that at the end of the financial year 1994-95, the net issue of ad hoc Treasury Bills should not exceed Rs. 6,000 crore, it has also been agreed that the net issue of ad hoc Treasury Bills should not exceed Rs. 9,000 crore for more than ten continuous working days at any time during the financial year 1994-95. It has further been agreed that, if the net issue of ad hoc Treasury Bills exceeds Rs. 9,000 crore for more than ten continuous working days at any time during the year, the Bank will automatically reduce only the excess beyond the prescribed level of ad hoc Treasury Bills, by auctioning Treasury Bills or flotation of Government of India dated securities. Similar ceilings for the net issue of ad hoc Treasury Bills will be stipulated for 1995-96 and 1996-97. From 1997-98 the

system of *ad hoc* Treasury Bills will be totally discontinued.

7. Whereas it has been agreed between the parties that a suitable monitoring mechanism would be put in place by the Bank so as to furnish the Government up-to-date position about the net issue of *ad hoc* Treasury Bills.

8. Whereas the parties have agreed on certain changes in the matters referred to above, it is now hereby agreed and declared as follows:

(1) This agreement shall be supplemental to the principal agreement and the subsequent letters exchanged and shall come into force with effect from the date of this agreement.

(2) The Bank would monitor, on a daily basis, the position in regard to the net issue of *ad hocs* over the level at the end of the financial year 1993-94; similar monitoring will be provided for each of the financial years 1995-96 and 1996-97. The Bank will advise the Government of the net increase in *ad hocs* on a daily basis; and furthermore, the number of consecutive working days when the net issue of *ad hocs* exceeds the limit prescribed in paragraph 6 hereof. Central Government holidays at New Delhi and bank holidays at Nagpur will be excluded from the computation of the number of consecutive working days. On receipt of the advice, Government could convey to the Bank its views and instructions in regard to regularisation or the extent to which the Bank may raise market borrowing on behalf of Government.

9. In witness whereof Finance Secretary to the Government of India acting for and on behalf of and by the order and direction of the President of India has hereunto set his hand and the common seal of the Reserve Bank of India has been hereunto affixed in the presence of its subscribing officials the day and year first above written.

Signed by the said Shri Montek Singh Ahluwalia, Finance Secretary, Government of India for and on behalf of President of India in the presence of Shri N.P. Bagchee, Additional Secretary (Budget) to the Government of India.	Sd. Montek S. Ahluwalia) Sd. (N.P. Bagchee)
The Common seal of the Reserve Bank of India was affixed hereto in the presence of its Governor Dr. C. Rangarajan who has signed in the presence of Shri S.S. Tarapore, Deputy Governor of Reserve Bank of India.	Sd. (C. Rangarajan) Sd. (S.S. Tarapore)

वित्त सचिव
FINANCE SECRETARY

भारत सरकार
वित्त मंत्रालय
आर्थिक कार्य विभाग
GOVERNMENT OF INDIA
MINISTRY OF FINANCE
Department of Economic Affairs
नई दिल्ली / New Delhi

DO.NO.1855(I)/FS/95   February 24, 1995

Dear Governor,

   I enclose a copy of an Article in TIME magazine about
the crisis of the banking system in Venezuela in the
wake of the privatisation and deregulation of banks in
recent years. The article reveals that many new private
banks which came into existence were merely divisions
of larger financial or industrial groups, which meant
that when the parent companies were strapped for money
they frequently turned to their in-house banks for
loans. Laissez-faire took on a new meaning as bankers
used their institutions as personal "cajas chicas" or
petty cash-drawers. The article provides examples of
banker-extravagance only weeks before their collapse
with very minimal regulatory oversight. According to
later investigations, regulatory officials were paid to
look the other way or lacked the authority or manpower
to intervene.

   2. It is important that we should draw appropriate
lessons from the experience of Venezuela. The Finance
Minister has asked me to convey to you that RBI should
have a separate and strong division to monitor and
supervise the performance of the newly established
banks. In licensing new banks, it must also be ensured
that the new entities are not an extension or a front
for big industrial houses.

   3. I would be grateful if you could give us your
response to these concerns. The Finance Minister has

indicated that he would like to discuss this with you soon after the presentation of the Budget.

   With regards,

                                    Yours sincerely,

                                    (Montek Singh Ahluwalia)

Dr. C. Rangarajan,
Governor,
Reserve Bank of India,
Central Office,
BOMBAY.

भारत सरकार
वित्त मंत्रालय
आर्थिक कार्य विभाग
GOVERNMENT OF INDIA
MINISTRY OF FINANCE
Department of Economic Affairs
नई दिल्ली / New Delhi

वित्त सचिव
FINANCE SECRETARY

DO.NO.2739/FS/96   Friday, April 05, 1996

I am writing to share some thoughts on how we should handle the problem posed by some banks not achieving their capital adequacy norms. The conventional, and possibly unavoidable approach, would be to give the banks a limited relaxation for a specified period. Some discussions have already taken place between RBI and Banking Division along these lines.

2. An alternative would be to insist on capital adequacy norms being met by non complying banks shifting their asset portfolio from risk assets to risk-free assets i.e., government securities. In practice this would mean that banks which do not meet the capital adequacy norms would have to restrict, or even reduce, their commercial lending portfolio in favour of government securities thus achieving compliance with the capital adequacy norms by reducing these risk weighted assets. I recognise that this poses problems especially for the banks and even their clients, but on the other hand it sends the right signal, and it also helps in marketing government securities. To the extent that it reduces the burden on RBI of picking up government securities it extinguishes one source of reserve money expansion and thereby increases the flexibility of the RBI in reducing the CRR. To some extent the reduction in commercial credit by defaulting banks is offset by the enhanced credit made available by other banks because of lower CRRs. It can be argued that this approach would lead to a healthier banking system in the medium term, even if it puts a greater strain on weak banks in the short term.

3. I would like to emphasise that I retain an open mind on this issue and am only making this suggestion with the request that it be given a full examination before a view is taken on how to resolve the problem. I look forward to a discussion of RBI's response on this issue.

4. I am sending a copy of this letter to Deputy Governors, Shri S.S.Tarapore and Shri S.P.Talwar.

    With regards,

                                        Yours sincerely,

                                        (Montek Singh Ahluwalia)

Dr. C. Rangarajan,
Governor,
Reserve Bank of India,
Central Office,
BOMBAY.

Copy to:

1. Shri S.S.Tarapore, Deputy Governor, RBI.
2. Shri S.P.Talwar, Deputy Governor, RBI.

                                        (Montek Singh Ahluwalia)

ECONOMIC REVIEW

Box 1.2
Supplemental Agreement between the Reserve Bank of India and the Government of India

An Agreement made this twenty sixth day of March 1997 between the President of India acting, through the Ministry of Finance, Government of India (hereinafter referred to as "the Government") of the one part and the Reserve Bank of India (hereinafter called "the Bank") of the other part.

A. WHEREAS the erstwhile Secretary of State for India in Council and the Bank have entered into an agreement dated fifth day of April 1935 (hereinafter referred to as "the principal agreement").

B. WHEREAS it has been agreed in November, 1937 and January, 1955 by exchange of letters that the Government shall maintain certain minimum cash balance and further that whenever the balance in the account of the Government falls below the minimum agreed to, the account be replenished by the creation of ad hoc Treasury Bills, in favour of the Bank.

C. WHEREAS the President of India and the Bank have entered, into a Supplemental. Agreement dated ninth day of September 1994 (First Supplemental Agreement) regarding phasing out of ad hoc Treasury Bills, and, in terms of paragraph 6 of First Supplemental Agreement, the system of ad hoc Treasury Bills to replenish the balance of the Government to the agreed minimum level as laid down is to be totally discontinued with effect from 1997-98.

D. WHEREAS the Union Finance Minister in his budget speech for Financial Year 1997-98 has presented concrete propoals setting out modalities for phasing out ad hoc Treasury Bills from April 1, 1997.

E. WHEREAS it has been agreed between the parties that a suitable mechanism would be put in place so as to enable the Government to manage its cash balance position with the Bank.

F. AND WHEREAS the parties have agreed on certain changes in'the matters referred to above.

NOW IT IS HEREBY AGREED AND DECLARE AS FOLLOWS:

(1) This agreement shall be supplemental to the principal agreement. and the First Supplemental Agreement dated September 9, 1994.

(2) The practice of issuing ad hoc Treasury Bills to replenish the cash balance of the Government to the agreed minimum level will be discontinued with effect from April 1, 1997.

(3) The outstanding ad hoc Treasury Bills as on March 31, 1997 would be funded into special securities, without any specified maturity, at an interet rate of 4.6 per cent per annum on April 1,1997. The outstanding Tap Treasury Bills as on March 31, 1997 will be paid off on maturity with an equivalent creation of special securities without any specified maturity, at an interest rate of 4.6 per cent per annum.

(4) From April 1, 1997, the Bank shall make Ways and Means Advances to the Government, if so required, at such rate of interest, as may be mutually agreed from time to time, provided such advances outstanding at any time shall not exceed the limit, as may be mutually agreed upon from time to time. The advances shall be fully paid off within a period not exceeding three months from the date of making such advance. Interest shall be calculated on daily balances and debited to the account of the Government with the Bank at such intervals, as may be decided by the Bank.

(5) In the event of Government's account as at the close of business on any working day emerging and remaining overdrawn beyond the agreed limit for Ways and Means Advances, the Bank may charge interest on the daily balances overdrawn at such rate or rates, as may be mutually agreed upon from time to time, by debit to the account of the Government with the Bank at such intervals, as may be decided by the Bank.

(6) When 75 per cent of the Ways and Means Advances is utilised, the Bank would trigger fresh floatation of Government securities.

(7) Ways and Means Advances and Overdraft would be monitored and regulated on such terms, as may be mutually agreed from time to time.

(8) If the Government runs surplus cash balances beyond an agreed level, the Bank will make investments, as may be mutually agreed from time to time.

(9) Subject to the terms hereinabove, the arrangements for the

fiscal year 1997-98 have been mutually agreed as under:

(i) The limit for Ways and Means Advances will be Rs.12,000 crore for the first half the year (April to September) and Rs.8,000 crore for the second half of the year (October to March).

(ii) The interest rate on Ways and Means Advarices and Overdraft for the Government will be the following:

(a) Up to the Ways and Means Advance Limits : "Calculated Rate" **minus** 3 per cent

(b) For Overdraft beyond the Ways and Means Advances limits. : The rate at (a) **plus** 2 per cent on the Overdraft amount.

NOTE: The "Calculated Rate" for any quarter beginning April ti 1997, will mean the average of the implicit yield at the cut-off price of 91-day Treasury Bill auctions held during the previous quarter.

(10) The arrangement for the fiscal year 1998-99 With regard to limits for Ways and Means Advances, as also interest rate on Ways and Means Advances.

and Overdraft will be through exchange of letters.

(11) (a) The arrangements after fiscal year 1998-99 in respect of limits for Ways and Means Advances and interest rate on Ways and Means Advances and Overdraft will be through exchange:of letters.

(b) Overdraft will not be permissible for periods exceeding ten 'consecutive' working days, after March 31, 1999.

NOTE: For the purpose of computation of the number of 'consecutive' working days, Central Government holidays at New Delhi and bank holidays at Nagpur will be excluded.

12) In witness whereof Finance Secretary to the Government of India acting for and on behalf of and by the order and direction of the President of India has hereunto set his hand and the common seal of the Reserve Bank of India has been hereunto affixed in the presence of its subscribing officials the day and year first above written.

Signed by the said   }
Shri Montek Singh Ahluwalia,   }
Finance Secretary,   }
Government of India for   }
and on behalf of   }   Sd/-
President of India in   }   26.3.97
the presence of Shri J.S. Mathur,   }
Additional Secretary (Budget)   }   Sd/-
to the Government of India   }   26.3.97

The Common seal of   }
the Reserve Bank of India   }
was affixed hereto in the   }
presece of its Governor   }   Sd/-
Dr. C. Rangarajan who has   }
signed in the presence of   }
Dr. Y.V. Reddy,   }   Sd/-
Deputy Governor of   }
Reserve Bank of India   }

This Agreement has far reaching implications for monetary policy and debt management. With the elimination of ad hoc Treasury Bills from April 1, 1997, the 91-day tap Treasury Bills also lost their relevance and were accordingly discontinued simultaneously.

1.9 As regards instruments of monetary policy, the Reserve Bank has been making conscious efforts to reduce the reliance on direct instruments of monetary control, such as administered interest rates with the objective of moving over to indirect methods. Open market operations (OMO), including repo operations, have been emerging as the principal indirect instrument. The interest rate instrument is sought to be developed by reactivating the Bank Rate (BR) as a signalling mechanism to the market, alongside a provision for a general refinance facility. The op it procedures of monetary\pcTc2talta close -c1561-dirration between liquidity management and debt management, as well as institutional developments for widening and deepening securities and money markets along with evolution of risk management strategies for efficient functioning of the financial system.

1.10 The year 1996-97 was significant in many ways in relation to the con uct o monetary policy in India. It was the first-time that the CRR was reduced sharply by 4 percentage points within a financial year. and net sales of Central Government securities under OMO registered the record level of Rs.10,435 crore during a financial year. CRR to be maintained by scheduled commercial banks (excluding RRBs) was gradually reduced during April 1996

V

REFERENCES AND INDEX

Select References

Books

Bose, Sukanya (2005). "Rural Credit in India in Peril", in V.K. Ramachandran and Madhura Swaminathan (eds.), *Financial Liberalization and Rural Credit in India.* International Development Economics Associates & Tulika Books.

Brahmananda, P.R. and V.R. Panchamukhi (eds.) (1987). *Issues in Monetary Policy in the Development Process in the Indian Economy.* Mumbai: Himalaya Publishing House.

Chakravarty, Sukhamoy (1969). *Capital and Development Planning.* Cambridge: MIT Press.

———. (1989). *Development Planning.* New Delhi: Oxford University Press.

———. (1993). *Selected Economic Writings of Sukhamoy Chakravarty.* New Delhi: Oxford University Press.

Goldsmith, R.W. (1983). "FDIC: History of the Eighties—Lessons for the Future, 1997", in *The Financial Development in India: 1860–1977.* New Delhi: Oxford University Press.

International Monetary Fund (1990). *International Financial Statistics.* July.

———. (1988). *World Economic Outlook.*

———. (1998). *World Economic Outlook.*

Boughton, James M. (2012). *Tearing Down Walls: History of the International Monetary Fund 1990-99.*

Jadhav, Narendra (1994). *Monetary Economics for India.* Delhi: Macmillan.

Jalan, Bimal (1993). *Indian Economy: Problems and Prospects.* Delhi: Penguin.

———. (2001). "International Financial Infrastructure: Developing Countries Perspective", in Raj Kapila and Uma Kapila (eds.), *India's Banking and Financial Sector in the New Millennium.* Volume 1. New Delhi: Academic Foundation.

Patel, I.G. (1986). *Essays in Economic Policy and Economic Growth.* New York: St. Martin's Press.

————. (2002). *Glimpses of Indian Economic Policy: An Insider's View.* New Delhi: Oxford University Press.

Rangarajan C. (2000). *Perspectives on Indian Economy: A Collection of Essays.* New Delhi: UBS Publishers and Distributors.

Reddy, Y.V. (2009). *India and Global Financial Crisis, Managing Money and Finance.* New Delhi: Orient Black Swan.

Reserve Bank of India (1941). *Functions and Working of the Reserve Bank of India.*

————. (1958). *The Reserve Bank of India: Functions and Working.*

————. (1970). *Functions and Working.*

————. (1970). *Reserve Bank of India (1935–1951).* Volume 1.

————. (1983). *Functions and Working, Reserve Bank of India.*

————. (1985). *Reserve Bank of India Fifty Years 1935–85.* Da Costa, E.P.W.

————. (1985). *The Reserve Bank and Rural Credit.* Rural Planning and Credit Department.

————. (1997). *50 Years of Central Banking: Governors Speak.*

————. and OUP (1998). *Reserve Bank of India (1951–1967).* Volume 2.

————. (2001). *Reserve Bank of India: Functions and Working.*

————. (2005). *Reserve Bank of India (1967-1981).* Volume 3.

————. (2010). *Mint Road Milestones: RBI at 75.*

Shroff, Manu (2009). "Reform in Indian Banking: Agenda for Action," in Deena Khatkhate (ed.), *Indian Economy: A Retrospective View.* New Delhi: Academic Foundation.

Tharoor, Shashi (2006). *India from the Midnight to the Millennium and Beyond.* New York: Arcade Publishing.

The World Bank (2001). *A Review of Financial Sector Issues.*

www.federalreserveeducation.org. History of the Federal Reserve, 1990s: The Longest Expansion. Federal Reserve Education.

Articles

Aggarwal, K.P., V. Pugazhendhi and K.J.S. Satsai (1997). "Gearing Rural Credit for Twenty First Century", *Economic and Political Weekly*, October 18-24.

Aghevli, Bijan B., Mohsin S. Khan and Peter J. Montiel (1990). "Exchange Rate Policy in Developing Countries: Some Analytical Issues", *Occasional Papers* No.78. IMF.

Blinder, Alan S., Michael Ehrmann, Marcel Fratzsacher, Jackob De Haan, David-Jan Jansen (2008). "Central Bank Communication and Monetary Policy: A Survey of Theory and Evidence," *NBER Working Paper* No.13932.

Burgess, R. and R. Pande (2003, 2005). "Do Rural Banks Matter? Evidence from the Indian Social Banking Experiment", *BREAD Working Paper* No.037/2003 and *American Economic Review* 95(3). June 2005.

Chakrabarty, K.C. (2011). "Technology and the Financial Inclusion Imperative in India", in Sameer Kochhar (ed.), *Growth and Finance: Essays in Honour of C. Rangarajan.* New Delhi: Academic Foundation.

Chalapati Rao, K.S., M.R. Murthy and Biswajit Dhar (n.d.). *Foreign Direct Investment in India since Liberalisation: An Overview.*

Chawla, O.P, K.V. Patil & N.B. Shete (1983). "Impact of Differential Rate of Interests", *NIBM Faculty Occasional Papers* (Book Review).

Chelliah, R.J. (1992). "Growth of India's Public Debt", in Bimal Jalan (ed.), *The Indian Economy: Problems and Prospects.* New Delhi: Viking.

Chona, J.M. (1991). "Role of RBI: Regulatory, Developmental and Constitutional Aspects", *RBI Occasional Papers* 12(3). September/December.

Cline, William R. (1983). "International Debt and the Stability of the World Economy", *Policy Analyses in International Economics* No. 4. Washington: Institute for International Economics. September.

Cole, Shawn A. (2008). "Fixing Market Failures or Fixing Elections? Agricultural Credit in India", *Harvard Business School Working Paper* No.09-001. July.

Devaraja, T.S. (2011). *Rural Credit in India: An Overview of History and Perspectives.* Hassan: Department of Commerce, University of Mysore. May.

Ghosh, Sugata (2011). "Spook on the Bond Market", *The Economic Times,* Golden Jubilee Special Edition. March 24.

Jalan (Bimal) (2002). "International Financial Architecture: Developing Countries' Perspective", in *India's Economy in the New Millennium: Selected Essays.* UBS Publishers.

Itskevich, Jennifer (2002). "What Caused the Stock Market Crash of 1987?", *George Mason University's History News Network.* July 31.

Majumdar, N.A. (1982). "Structural Transformation in the Deployment of Credit: Some Implication", *RBI Occasional Papers* 3(2).

Mihir, Shah, Rangu Rao and P.S. Vijay Shankar (2007). "Rural Credit in 20th Century India: An Overview of History and Perspectives", *Economic and Political Weekly* 42(15). April 14-20.

Panagariya, Arvind (2003). *India in the 1980s and 1990s: A Triumph of Reforms.* November.

Polak, Jacques J. (1995). "Fifty Years of Exchange Rate Research at the IMF," *IMF Staff Papers* 42(4). December.

Rangarajan, C., Anupam Basu and Narendra Jadhav (1989). "Dynamics of Interaction between Government Deficit and Domestic Debt in India", *RBI Occasional Papers* 10(3). September.

Reserve Bank of India (1996). "A Review of Internal Management Policy and Operations for the period ended March 1995", *RBI Bulletin.* November.

————. (1987). "The Burden of Domestic Public Debt in India", *RBI Occasional Papers* 8(1). June.

Satish, P. (2010). "Funds for NABARD", *Economic and Political Weekly.* September 25.

Shirai, Sayuri (2001). "Assessment of India's Banking Sector Reforms from the Perspective of the Governance of the Banking System", Paper presented at the ESCAP-ADB Joint Workshop on *Mobilizing Domestic Finance for Development: Reassessment of Bank Finance and Debt Markets in Asia and the Pacific.* Bangkok. November 22-23.

Schadler, Susan, Maria Carkovic, Adam Bennett and Robert Kahn (1993). "Recent Experiences with Surges in Capital Inflows", *Occasional Papers* 108. IMF.

Shetty S.L. (2002). "Regional, Sectoral and Functional Distribution of Bank Credit: A Critical Review", Paper presented at the workshop on *Financial Liberalisation and Rural Credit in India.* Kolkata: ISI. March.

Tarapore, S.S. (2011). "Episodes from Monetary and Other Financial Policies (1982–1997): An Anecdotal Presentation", in Sameer Kochhar (ed.), *Growth and Finance: Essays in Honour of C. Rangarajan.* New Delhi: Academic Foundation.

Virmani, Arvind (2001). "India's 1990–91 Crisis: Reforms, Myths and Paradoxes", *Working Paper* No.4/2001-PC. New Delhi: Planning Commission. December.

————. (2003). "India's External Reforms: Modest Globalisation Significant Gains", *Economic and Political Weekly* 37(32): 3373-90. August 9-15.

Speeches

Chakravarty, S. (1986). Speech delivered at *Sir Purushotamdas Thakurdas Memorial Lecture.*

Gandhi, Rajiv (1985). Address at the Golden Jubilee Celebrations of the Reserve Bank of India, June 1.

Larosiнre, Jacques De (1992). "The Worldwide Adjustment Process in the 1980s", *C.D. Deshmukh Memorial Lecture.* Mumbai: Reserve Bank of India. March 24.

Macklern, Tiff (2005). "Central Bank Communication and Policy Effectiveness", Commentary at the symposium sponsored by the Federal Reserve Bank of Kansas City. *The Greenspan Era: Lessons for the Future.* August 25-27

Malhotra, R.N. (1985). *Monetary Policy for Dynamic Growth.* Speech at a seminar organised by the Indian Chamber of Commerce. Calcutta. December 12.

————. (1985). Welcome Address at the Golden Jubilee Celebrations of the Reserve Bank of India. June 1.

————. (1986). *Role of Banking in Rural Development.* Fifth Anniversary Lecture. Colombo: Rural Banking and Staff Training College, Central Bank of Sri Lanka. September 19.

————. (1989). Address on the occasion of Annual General Meeting of the Indian Merchants' Chamber. Bombay. February 24.

————. (1989). *H.S. Kamath Memorial Lecture* delivered at the Academy of Administration. Bhopal. September 1.

————. (1989). *Changing Practices of Central Bank Supervision.* Address on the occasion of the 125th Anniversary of Allahabad Bank. Calcutta. December 6.

————. (1989). Address on the occasion of Silver Jubilee of the Reserve Bank Staff College.

————. (1990). *India's Monetary Policy and the Role of Banking System in Economic Development.* Address at the 30th National Defence Course. New Delhi. March 12.

————. (1990). *Service Area Approach.* Valedictory Address at Trainers' Training Programme in Service Area Approach organised by the Bankers' Institute for Rural Development. NABARD: Bombay. August 18.

————. (1990). *Rural Credit: Issues for 1990s.* Inaugural Address at the seminar organised by the Institute of Development Studies. Jaipur. August 27.

————. (1990). "The Evolving Financial System", *The Nineteenth Frank Moraes Memorial Lecture.* Madras. September 3.

————. (1990). Inaugural Address at the inaugural ceremony of the Vysya Bank Housing Finance Ltd. Bangalore. November 28.

Mohan, Rakesh (2004). "Agricultural Credit in India: Status, Issues and Future Agenda", *RBI Bulletin.* November.

————. (2005). "Communications in Central Banks: A Perspective", *SAARCFINANCE Governors' Symposium.* Mumbai. September 9.

————. (2006). "Recent Trends in the Indian Debt Market and Current Initiatives". Based on lectures at the *Fourth India Debt Market Conference.* Organised by Citi Group and Fitch Rating India. January 31 and at the Annual Conference of FIMMDA (jointly organised by FIMMDA and Primary Dealers' Association of India). Mumbai. March 14.

Mohanty, Deepak (2010). *Perspectives on Lending Rates in India.* Speech delivered at Bankers' Club. Kolkata. July.

Ojha, P.D. (1985). *Role of the Urban Banks in the Multi-dimensional Economic Growth of the Country.* Keynote Address delivered at the seminar of Chairmen of Urban Co-operative Banks' Federation. Bombay. August 24.

————. (1988). Address at the *Tenth Lease Financing Seminar.* Asian Leasing. March 10.

Patel, I.G. (1991). Foundation Day Lecture delivered at the Indian Institute of Management (IIM). Bangalore. October 28.

Rangarajan C. (1985). Speech delivered at *20th Junior International Forex Seminar.* New Delhi. December 13.

―――. (1987). *An Analytical Framework of the Chakravarty Committee Report on the Monetary System.* Lecture delivered at the meeting sponsored by the Society of Auditors. Madras. August 29.

―――. (1988). "Central Banking and Economic Development: Indian Experience", Paper presented at the *41st International Banking Summer School.* New Delhi. September 17-30.

―――. (1988). *Issues in Monetary Management.* Presidential Address at the Annual Conference of the Indian Economic Association. Calcutta. December 29.

―――. (1989). *Recent Credit Policy Measures.* Address at the Gujarat Chamber of Commerce and Industry. Ahmedabad. December 9.

―――. (1990). "Domestic Debt Management and Monetary Control", *18th SEANZA Central Banking Course Lectures* (October–December). Mumbai: Reserve Bank of India.

―――. (1991). *Recent Exchange Rate Adjustments: Causes and Consequences.* Bombay Management Association. August.

―――. (1993). "Autonomy of Central Banks", *M.G. Kutty Memorial Lecture.* Calcutta. September 17.

―――. (1994). "Developing the Money and Securities Markets in India", Paper presented at the *Sixth Seminar on Central Banking.* Washington D.C.: International Monetary Fund. March 9.

―――. (1994). Speech delivered at Bankers' Club. Bangalore. May 19.

―――. (1996). Inaugural Address at the *Conference on the Government Securities Market.* Mumbai: STCI. April 6.

―――. (1997). "Dimensions of Monetary Policy", *Anantharamakrishnan Memorial Lecture.* Chennai. February 7.

―――. (1997). Address at the conference organised by the Wharton Economic Forum. Philadelphia. March 21.

―――. (1997). "Activating Debt Markets in India", Keynote Address delivered at the *SBICAP Debt Market Seminar.* Mumbai. September 5.

―――. (1998). "Management of the External Sector", *R.N. Malhotra Memorial Lecture.* New Delhi. December 8.

―――. (2005). "Microfinance: The Road Ahead", Inaugural Address at *The International Conference on Microfinance in India.* New Delhi: CARE. April 12.

Reddy, Y.V. (2008). Remarks, *7th BIS Annual Conference.* Lucerne, Switzerland. June 26.

Robin Leigh-Pemberton (1990). "Economic Liberalism, Central Banking and the Developing World", *L.K Jha Memorial Lecture.* October 16.

Singh, Manmohan (1982). *Credit Policy of the Reserve Bank of India.* Inaugural Address. Mumbai: Maharashtra Economic Development Council. November 18.

_____. (1983). Address at the *First Conference of Officers-in-charge of Regional Offices of NABARD.* April.

_____. (1984). *Indian Banking System in the Seventh Five Year Plan.* Speech delivered at founders' day of Bank of Maharashtra. Pune. September 16.

Singh, V.P. (1985). Presidential Address at the Golden Jubilee Celebrations of the Reserve Bank of India. June 1.

Talwar, S.P. (1997). *Role and Regulations of NBFCs,* Speech delivered at The Associated Chambers of Commerce & Industry of India. New Delhi. August 27.

Tarapore, S.S. (1992). "Towards an Active Internal Debt Management Policy". Speech delivered at the *Seminar on Management of Government Securities.* Mumbai: UTI Institute of Capital Markets. October 10.

_____. (1994). *The Role of an Active Debt Management Policy in the Economic Reform Process.* Speech delivered at the Department of Economics. Mangalore: Mangalore University. September 19.

_____. (1996). *The Liquidity Crunch: Facts and Fiction.* Address at the meeting organised by the Confederation of Indian Industry (Western Region). Mumbai. March 8.

_____. (1996). "The Government Securities Market: The Next Stage of Reform". Valedictory Address at the *Conference on the Government Securities Market.* Mumbai: STCI. April 6.

_____. (2000). "Financial Economics", *T.S. Santhanam Chair in Financial Economics.* Chennai. June 23.

Thorat, Y.S.P. (2005). *Rural Credit in India and Concerns.* Presidential Address at the Indian Society of Agricultural Economics. Ludhiana: NABARD. November 24.

Venkitaramanan, S. (1992). "Gold Mobilisation and its use for External Adjustment". Keynote Address at the *World Gold Conference.* Montreux, Switzerland. June 22.

Official Publications/Internal Records

GoI: Banking Regulation Act, 1949.

GoI: Amendments to Banking Companies Act.

GoI: Banking Laws (Amendment) Act, 1983.

GoI: Banking Laws (Amendment) Act, 1985.

GoI: Budget Documents, various years.

GoI: Budget Speeches of Finance Ministers, various years.

GoI: D.O. Letter No.1 (14)–87, dated October 26, 1987.

GoI: D.O.Dy.No.S-63/TS(ECB)/90, September 04, 1990.

GoI: D.O. Letter of the Finance Secretary's No.47/F3/91-TS, dated March 25, 1991.

GoI: *Draft Mid-term Appraisal of Eighth Five Year Plan (1992-97)*. Planning Commission.

GoI: *Economic Survey*. Ministry of Finance. various issues.

GoI: *Eighth Five Year Plan*. Planning Commission.

GoI: *Finance Commission Reports*, various issues.

GoI: *Foreign Collaborations: A Compilation*. Department of Scientific & Industrial Research, Ministry of Science and Technology.

GoI: *Handbook of Industrial Statistics*. Ministry of Industry. various issues.

GoI: *India's External Debt: A Status Report, 2001*.

GoI: *Induction Material*. Ministry of Finance, Department of Economic Affairs.

GoI: Letter dated July 27, 1957 from Finance Minister to the RBI.

GoI: Letter dated July 13, 1981 from the Ministry of Finance to RBI.

GoI: Letter dated February 14, 1982 to the Governor.

GoI: Letter dated April 5, 1984 to the RBI.

GoI: Letter dated June 6, 1984 from the Ministry of Finance to the RBI.

GoI: Letter dated May 14, 1985 by the Finance Secretary to the RBI.

GoI: Letter dated April 03, 1986 from Shri K.S. Sastry, Joint Secretary (Budget) to the Deputy Governor, Dr. C. Rangarajan.

GoI: Letter dated August 7, 1987 from the Additional Secretary to the Deputy Governor.

GoI: Letter dated January 12, 1988 from Finance Secretary to the RBI.

GoI: Letter from the Ministry of Finance, dated January 27, 1988 to the RBI.

GoI: Letter from District Co-ordinating Office (DCO), Thiruvananathapuram, dated January 07, 1989 to RPCD, C.O., RBI.

GoI: Letter dated June 15, 1989 from Shri C.K. Kuppuswamy, Coimbatore, to the Ministry of Finance.

GoI: Letter No.16 (108)/89-B.O.111, dated March 01, 1990.

GoI: Letter dated April 10, 1991 to the RBI.

GoI: Letter in May 1990 to the RBI.

GoI: Letter dated June 6, 1990 to the RBI.

GoI: Letter dated October 1, 1990 by the Finance Secretary to the Governor.

GoI: Letter dated October 18, 1990 to the RBI.

GoI: Letter dated November 9, 1990 to the RBI.

GoI: Letter dated March 6, 1992 to the RBI.

GoI: Letter from the Finance Secretary, dated March 19, 1991 to the Governor.

GoI: Letter dated June 12, 1991 from the Finance Secretary to the RBI.

GoI: Letter dated July 14, 1992 from the Secretary, Economic Affairs to the Governor, RBI.

GoI: Letter dated November 4, 1992 to the RBI.

GoI: Letter dated May 11, 1993 to the RBI.

GoI: Letter dated May 16, 1994.

GoI: Letter dated December 02, 1994 from the Chief Economic Adviser to the RBI.

GoI: Letter from the Ministry of Finance in February, 1995 to RBI.

GoI: *Mid-term Appraisal of the Ninth Five Year Plan (1997-2002).*

GoI: *National Accounts Statistics,* various issues. Central Statistical Organisation (CSO).

GoI: *National Sample Survey.* NSSO, Central Statistical Organisation.

GoI: Note dated June 30, 1986 by the Ministry of Finance to the Cabinet Committee on Economic Affairs, titled: Proposals for Reduction in the Cost of Money

GoI: Notification on LERMS, dated March 01, 1992.

GoI: Order No.83/90-93, dated February 29, 1992.

GoI: Paper titled "Towards Rupee Convertibility: The Convertible Rupee Account". November 1991. Ministry of Finance.

GoI: Project Report: New Mint–Noida (U.P.) Ministry of Finance. July 23, 1985.

GoI: *Seventh Five Year Plan.* Planning Commission.

GoI: *Sixth Five Year Plan.* Planning Commission.

GoI: Telex message, dated May 13, 1985 from the Finance Secretary to the RBI.

GoI: Telex from the Ministry of Finance to RPCD, February 22, 1989.

GoI: Telex from the Ministry of Finance to RPCD, April, 1989.

GoI: The Principal Agreement dated April 5, 1935 with the RBI.

GoI: The First Supplemental Agreement dated September 9, 1994 with the RBI.

GoI: The Second Supplemental Agreement dated March 26, 1997 with the RBI.

GoI: Paper titled "Towards Rupee Convertibility: A Free Market Exchange Rate Channel". January 21, 1992. Ministry of Finance.

GoI: Trade policy announcement, July 4, 1991, Ministry of Commerce.

NABARD: *Annual Report, 1992–93.*

NABARD: *Review of the Co-operative Movement in India: 1978–82.* Bombay.

RBI: *All India Debt and Investment Survey.*

RBI (DESACS): *Banking Statistics.* (Quarterly Handouts).

RBI (DESACS): *Statistical Tables Relating to Banks in India,* various issues.

RBI: *Annual Report,* various issues.

RBI: Circular no. 20 (AP Series), ECD, June 4, 1980.

RBI: Circular no.PS.BC.4/C.594-83 dated August 22, 1983.

RBI: Circular dated May 25, 1985.

RBI: Circular no. BC Plan 113A22, May 04, 1989.

RBI: Circular dated September 21, 1990.

RBI: Circular dated January 18, 1991.

RBI: Circular dated July 27, 1992 to commercial banks prohibiting discounting of accommodation bills.

RBI: Circular dated June 17, 1994.

RBI: Circular no BP.BC 152 / 21.03.051/94, dated August 29, 1994.

RBI: Credit policy circular dated April 15, 1997.

RBI: Credit policy circular to banks dated April 3, 1996.

RBI: Credit Policy circulars issued by CPC/MPD to banks, dated April 12, 1991; July 3, 1991; October 8, 1991; October 8,1992; April 7, 1993.

RBI: Credit Policy Circular dated April 21, 1992.

RBI: Credit Policy Circular dated April 17, 1995.

RBI: Credit Policy Circular dated April 3, 1996.

RBI: *Database on the Indian Economy.*

RBI: DBOD, Central Office; Office Order No. 223, dated April 20, 1994.

RBI: Deputy Governor's D.O. letter dated November 3, 1992.

RBI: Deputy Governor's letter dated July 24, 1985 to the Government.

RBI: Deputy Governor's letter dated May 03, 1990 to the Finance Secretary.

RBI: Deputy Governor's letter dated March 18, 1997 to the Finance Secretary, Shri Montek Singh Ahluwalia.

RBI: Deputy Governor's office note dated April 16, 1984.

RBI: Deputy Governor's noting dated March 24, 1991.

RBI: Deputy Governor's office note dated October 1, 1992.

RBI: Deputy Governor's office note dated February 16, 1994.

RBI: Deputy Governor's noting dated October 7, 1994.

RBI: Directives to FFSL and its associate companies: DFC (COC) No. 17/169 -91/92, dated July 1, 1992.

RBI: D.O. Letter No.EC.CO. INSP 38/11R – 92/93, dated July 03, 1992.

RBI: ECD Circular No.20, dated June 04, 1980.

RBI: Executive Director's note dated March 22, 1990.

RBI: Executive Director's office note dated March 10, 1990.

RBI: Executive Director's note dated March 29, 1990.

RBI: Executive Director's office note titled: Issues for Discussion, February 1991.

RBI: Executive Director's exploratory note, March 1991.

RBI: Executive Director's note dated September 25, 1991.

RBI: File No.PL.09.02 RPCD, "Guidelines on Advances to Priority Sector".

RBI: *Foreign Collaboration in Indian Industry: Fourth Survey Report, 1985.*

RBI: Governor's letter dated November 6, 1981 to banks.

RBI: Governor's letter dated October 25, 1985 to banks.

RBI: Governor's letter dated January 14, 1986 to GoI.

RBI: Governor's letter dated September 11, 1986 to GoI.

RBI: Governor's letter dated February 07, 1987 to the Prime Minister.

RBI: Governor's letter dated November 06, 1987 to GoI.

RBI: Governor's letter dated July 15, 1988 to GoI.

RBI: Governor's letter dated January 7, 1989 to GoI.

RBI: Governor's letter dated May 24, 1989 to the Finance Minister, Shri S.B. Chavan.

RBI: Governor's letter dated December 18, 1989 to the Finance Minister Prof Madhu Dandavate.

RBI: Governor's letter to the Finance Minister dated April 28, 1990.

RBI: Governor's letter dated May 18, 1990 to GoI.

RBI: Governor's letter dated July 18, 1990 to GoI.

RBI: Governor's letter dated July 18, 1990 to GoI.

RBI: Governor's letter dated October 10, 1990 to GoI.

RBI: Governor's letter dated November 26, 1990 to GoI.

RBI: Governor's letter dated January 08, 1991 to GoI.

RBI: Governor's letter dated May 6, 1991 to GoI.

RBI: Governor's letter dated June 04, 1991 to GoI.

RBI: Governor's letter dated December 10, 1991 to the Finance Minister, Dr Manmohan Singh.

RBI: Governor's letter dated January 2, 1992 to GoI.

RBI: Governor's letter dated February 05, 1992 to GoI.

RBI: Governor's letter dated February 21, 1992 to GoI.

RBI: Governor's letter dated March 25, 1992 to GoI.

RBI: Governor's letter dated April 20, 1992 to GoI.

RBI: Governor's letter dated May 05, 1992 to GoI.

RBI: Governor's letter dated July 28, 1992 to GoI.

RBI: Governor's letter dated February 3, 1993 to GoI.

RBI: Governor's letter dated December 27, 1993 to GoI.

RBI: Governor's letter dated December 31, 1993 to GoI.

RBI: Governor's letter dated May 5, 1994 to GoI.

RBI: Governor's letter dated October 31, 1994 to GoI.

RBI: Governor's letter dated December 20, 1994 to GoI.

RBI: Governor's letter of August 1995 to GoI.

RBI: Governor's letter dated November 04, 1995 to GoI.

RBI: Governor's letter dated June 18, 1996 to GoI.

RBI: Governor's orders dated March 28, 1990.

RBI: *Handbook of Monetary Statistics of India, 2006.*

RBI: *Handbook of Security Instructions.* Central Security Cell. DAPM. January 2006.

RBI: *Handbook of Statistics on the Indian Economy,* various issues.

RBI: Handwritten note dated July 8, 1981.

RBI: Internal note titled "Mintage of Coins: Establishment of New Mint". Department of Currency Management. September 3, 1985.

RBI: Internal note, BP Section, DBOD, December 26, 1985.

RBI: Internal note, Credit Planning Cell, dated January 01, 1986.

RBI: Internal note titled "Follow-up action based on the Finance Minister's Meeting with the Governor". November 03, 1986.

RBI: Internal note dated March 01, 1989.

RBI: Internal note dated March 09, 1989.

RBI: Internal review note, May 1989.

RBI: Internal review, CPC, March 1990.

RBI: Internal note, CPC, October 1994.

RBI: Internal review, December 1996.

RBI: Internal records relating to proceedings of Managers' Conferences.

RBI: Letter dated December 22, 1983 to the Ministry of Finance.

RBI: Letter dated March 15, 1984 to the Government under copy to the Principal Secretary to the Prime Minister.

RBI: Letter dated January 7, 1986 to the Ministry of Finance.

RBI: Letter D.O. DCM. No. 7461/ PN.9-85/86 dated April 4, 1986 from the Chief Officer, RBI to the Ministry of Finance, GoI.

RBI: Letter dated December 23, 1988 to the Ministry of Finance.

RBI: Letter dated January 7, 1989 to GoI.

RBI: Letter dated February 19, 1990 to GoI.

RBI: Letter dated October 22, 1990 to GoI.

RBI Letter dated January 08, 1991 to GoI.

RBI: Letter dated May 11, 1991 to GoI.

RBI: Letter dated August 20, 1991 to GoI.

RBI: Letter dated January 2, 1992 to GoI.

RBI: Letter dated April 20, 1992 to GoI.

RBI: Letter dated December 3, 1992 to GoI.

RBI: Letter dated December 3, 1992 to GoI.

RBI: Letter No. DFC (COC) No.17/169-91/92, dated July 1, 1992.

RBI: Letter dated October 19, 1992 to GoI.

RBI: Letter dated January 7, 1993 to GoI.

RBI: Letter dated March 17, 1993 to GoI.

RBI: Letter tdated March 27, 1993 to GoI.

RBI: Letter dated July 8, 1993 to the GoI.

RBI: Letter dated September 08, 1993 to GoI.

RBI: Letter dated September 18, 1993 to GoI.

RBI: Letter dated October 5, 1993 to GoI.

RBI: Letter dated March 07, 1994 to GoI.

RBI: Letter dated March 29, 1994 to GoI.

RBI: Letter dated October 31, 1994 to GoI.

RBI: Letter dated December 12, 1994 to GoI.

RBI: Letter dated December 20, 1994 to GoI.

RBI: Letter dated July 31, 1996 to GoI.

RBI: Letter dated August 09, 1996 to GoI.

RBI: Letter dated March 18, 1997 to GoI.

RBI: (1986). Fifth meeting of the Standing Advisory Committee for UCBs (Chairman: P.D. Ojha).

RBI: Memoranda to the Central Board of Directors of the Reserve Bank, various dates.

RBI: *RBI Bulletin*, various issues.

RBI: Minutes of the first meeting of the Board for Financial Supervision, December 7, 1994, Bombay.

RBI: Note (CPC), dated May 21, 1981.

RBI: Note (Legal), dated July 8, 1981.

RBI: Note (1986) of CPC titled: Effective Rates of Return on Bank Deposits and Other Selected Instruments of Savings.

RBI: Note of April 1991.

RBI: Note of CPC titled "Interest Rates in the Banking System".

RBI: Notes from the RBI Board Memorandum File F 4159 (30/11/87 to 11/12/87).

RBI: Notification issued by the Reserve Bank on February 27, 1988.

RBI: Office note, CPC, dated May 16, 1985.

RBI: Office note, CPC, dated September 07, 1987.

RBI: Office note, CPC, dated July 4 and 6, 1989.

RBI: Office note, CPC, dated March 22, 1991.

RBI: Office note dated September 28, 1992.

RBI: Office note dated October 1, 1992.

RBI: Office note dated March 17, 1993.

RBI: Office note dated February 16, 1994.

RBI: Paper titled "Liberalised Exchange Rate Arrangements (LERA) (1992)".

RBI: Press Note released on June 04, 1991.

RBI: Press Release: "Write-off of Farm Loans". October 13, 1980.

RBI: *Report on Currency and Finance*, various issues.

RBI: *Report on Trend and Progress of Banking in India*, various issues.

RBI: *Reserve Bank of India (RBI) Act, 1934.*

RBI: *Reserve Bank of India (BFS) Regulations, 1994.*

RBI (DEPR): Report of the Committee to Review and Restructure RBI Bulletin. 2012.

Interviews carried out under the oral history project

Reserve Bank of India

Shri M. Narasimham

Shri Amitabh Ghosh

Shri S. Venkitaramanan

Dr C. Rangarajan

Dr Bimal Jalan

Dr Y.V. Reddy

Shri M. Ramakrishnayya

Dr M.V. Hate

Dr P.D. Ojha

Shri P.R. Nayak

Shri D.R. Mehta

Shri S.P. Talwar

Shri R.V. Gupta

Shri Jagdish Capoor

Dr Rakesh Mohan

Smt K.J. Udeshi

Shri V. Leeladhar

Smt Shyamala Gopinath

Smt Usha Thorat

Shri S.S. Marathe

Dr C.H. Hanumantha Rao

Shri T.N. Anantharam Iyer

Shri C.V. Nair

Ms V. Viswanathan

Shri P.B. Kulkarni

Shri O.P. Sodhani

Shri Hari Kumar

Shri R. Gandhi

Dr C. Batliwala

Shri Sandip Ghose

Shri M.P. Nair

Government of India

Shri Yashwant Sinha

Shri G.K. Arora

Shri S.P. Shukla

Shri Montek Singh Ahluwalia

Dr Ashok Desai

Dr Shankar Acharya

Shri N.K. Singh

Reports of Committees, Working Groups, Study Groups and Expert Groups

Committee of Direction to Examine on an Ongoing Basis the Problem Arising from the Implementation of the Recommendations of the Tandon, Chore and Marathe Committees (1975).

Committee on Regional Rural Banks (1978) (Chairman Shri M.L. Dantwala).

Committee to Review Arrangement for Institutional Credit for Agriculture and Rural Development (CRAFICARD, 1979) (Chairman: Shri B. Sivaraman).

Committee to Examine the Legal and Other Difficulties Faced by Banks and FIs in Rehabilitating Sick Industrial Undertakings (May 14, 1981).

Committee to Review the Working of CAS (November, 1982).

Committee on Mechanisation in Banking Industry (1983) (Chairman: Dr C. Rangarajan).

Committee to Review the Working of Monetary System (1985) (Chairman: Prof Sukhamoy Chakravarty).

Committee to Review the Agricultural Credit System (1986).

Committee on Currency Management (1988) (Chairman: Shri P.R. Nayak).

Committee on Customer Service in Banks (September 15, 1990) (Chairman: Shri M.N. Goiporia).

Committee on the Financial System (1991) (Chairman: Shri M. Narasimham).

Committee to Investigate Irregularities in Funds Management by Commercial Banks and FIs (April 30, 1992) (Chairman: Shri R. Janakiraman).

Committee to Examine the Adequacy of Institutional Credit to SSI Sector and Related Aspects (September, 1992) (Chairman: Shri P.R. Nayak).

Committee on Licensing of New Urban Co-operative Banks (1992).

Committee to Suggest Modalities for Setting-up a Depository along the Lines of SHCIL for Trading in PSU Bonds (1992) (Chairman: Shri S.S. Nadkarni).

Committee on Human Resources Development (1992) (Chairman: Shri S.S. Marathe).

Committee on Technology Issues relating to Payment System, Cheque Clearing and Securities Settlement in the Banking Industry (1994) (Chairman: Shri W.S. Saraf).

Committee on Capital Account Convertibility (1997) (Chairman: Shri S.S. Tarapore).

Committee on Money Supply: Analysis and Methodology of Compilation. (1998) (Chairman: Dr Y.V. Reddy).

Committee Set up to Suggest a System of Preventing Fraud in Banks (Chairman: Shri A. Ghosh).

Committee to Review Matters Relating to Urban Cooperative Banks (Chairman: Shri S.S. Marathe).

Committee to Review the System of Inspection of Banks (Chairman: Shri S. Padmanabhan).

Expert Group for Designing a Supervisory Framework for NBFCs (April 1995) (Chairman: Shri P.R. Khanna).

Group to Prepare a Programme of Reform for the Financial Companies (May 1992) (Chairman: Dr A.C. Shah).

Group to Recommend Measures for the Growth of an Active, Efficient and Orderly Foreign Exchange Market and to Suggest Introduction of Derivative Products (November 1994) (Chairman: Shri O.P. Sodhani).

Group to Examine Major Policy Issues Concerning the Managerial and Financial Restructuring of RRBs (July, 1995) (Chairman: Shri N.K. Thingalaya).

Group to Review the Onsite Supervision of Banks (November 1995) (Chairman: Shri S. Padmanabhan).

Group to Review the Internal Control and Audit System in Banks (Chairman: Shri R. Jilani).

High Level Committee to Review the Flow of Institutional Credit to the Rural Sector (1985) (Chairman: Dr P.D. Ojha).

Internal Group on Bank Rate (March 1997).

Joint Parliamentary Committee (JPC) (August 1992).

Kelkar Committee on Regional Rural Banks (1987).

Rural Credit: Agricultural Review Committee (August 1989) (Chairman: Dr A.M. Khusro).

Report of the IDF Project on NRI Deposits (October, 2000) (Co-ordinator: Shri Deepak Mohanty).

Study Group for the Operational Problems of the State Handloom Development Corporation in Relation to Bank Credit (1984).

Soft Loan Assistance Fund for Rehabilitation of Sick/Small Scale Industrial Units (1985) (Chairman: Dr P.D. Ojha).

Standing Co-ordination Committee to Co-ordinate, Monitor and Guide the Training Arrangements in Bank on an On-going Basis (March 1986).

Standing Advisory Committee to Review the Flow of Bank Credit to SSI Sector (1987) (Chairman: Dr P.D. Ojha).

Study Group on Review, Rationalisation and Redesign of Returns Relating to Core Commercial Banking Areas (January 1995) (Chairman: Shri T.N.A. Iyer).

Standing Committee on Institutional Financial Standards and Codes (2001).

Study Group to Streamline the Arrangements for Flow of Credit and Supply of Inputs and Assets to IRDP Beneficiaries (Chairman: Deputy Governor, RBI).

Working Group to Review the Working of the LBS (1981).

Working Group to Review the Accounting System at Bank Branches (1981) (Chairman: Shri M.N. Goiporia).

Working Group on Bank Deposits (January 1983) (Chairman: Dr C. Rangarajan).

Working Group to Review the Existing System of Inspection of Commercial Banks, RRBs and Urban Cooperative Banks (UCBs) with particular regard to the Objectives of Banking and Credit Policy of the Reserve Bank and the Scope, Coverage, Methodology and Periodicity of the Inspection Mechanisms (October 22, 1983) (Chairman: Shri V.G. Pendharkar).

Working Group on the Money Market (1987) (Chairman: Shri N. Vaghul).

Working Group to Appraise the Operations of Indian Banks Operating Abroad (1988).

Working Group to Review the Audit Systems in the UCBs (December 1995) (Chairman: Shri Uday M. Chitale).

Working Group to Study the Functioning of SHGs and NGOs (1996) (Chairman: Shri S.K. Kalia).

Working Group to Examine the Structure of the RRBs (Chairman: Shri M.C. Bhandari).

Working Group on Funds Management in RRBs (Chairman: Shri K.K. Misra).

Media Reports

The Economic Times dated April 10, 1985.

The Economic Times dated April 29, 1985.

The Economic Times dated May 27, 1985.

The Economic Times dated May 28, 1985.

The Hindu dated July 22, 1985.

The Hindu dated October 16, 1985.

The Economic Times dated December 12, 1985.

The Indian Express, dated February 18, 1987.

The Hindu dated August 17, 1987.

Business Standard, November 26, 1987.

Business Standard dated February 05, 1988.

The Economic Times dated February 18, 1988.

The Economic Times dated October 10, 1989.

The Economic Times dated July 8, 1991.

The Economic Times dated September 10, 1991.

The Economic Times, January 6, 1992.

The Business Standard dated February 22, 1995.

The Economic Times dated May 06, 2010.

Others

IMF: Article IV staff papers.

IMF: Working Papers, various issues.

Letter: D.O. No. F. 10(5)-FIN (TRY)/81 dated February 21, 1986 written by the Chief Minister, Tripura to Shri Janardhana Poojary, Minister of State for Finance, Government of India, New Delhi.

Letter: February 1990 from the Chairman of the Institute of Public Affairs (India) to the Finance Minister with a copy to the Governor.

IMF: Advisory Mission to study the Government, Securities Market in India, headed by Mr. Sergio Pereira Leite, that prepared a note titles "Issues in Developing the Government Securities Market and Open Market Operations in Support of Financial Sector Reforms", July. 1992.

Report of the National Institute of Bank Management (NIBM). Pune. October 1994.

Index